SAP NetWeaver® Application Server Upgrade Guide

 PRESS

SAP PRESS is a joint initiative of SAP and Galileo Press. The know-how offered by SAP specialists combined with the expertise of the publishing house Galileo Press offers the reader expert books in the field. SAP PRESS features first-hand information and expert advice, and provides useful skills for professional decision-making.

SAP PRESS offers a variety of books on technical and business related topics for the SAP user. For further information, please visit our website: *www.sap-press.com*.

Bürckel, Davidenkoff, Werner
Unicode in SAP Systems
2007, 320 pp., hardcover
ISBN 978-1-59229-135-9

Bert Vanstechelman, Mark Mergaerts
The SAP OS/DB Migration Project Guide
SAP PRESS Essentials 5
2005, 88 pp., softcover
ISBN 978-1-59229-056-7

Michael Willinger, Johann Gradl
Migrating Your SAP Data
2008, 2nd., updated and extended edition
approx. 340 pp., hardcover
ISBN 978-1-59229-170-0

Föse, Hagemann, Will
SAP NetWeaver AS ABAP System Administration
2008, 3rd, updated and extended edition
approx. 560 pp., hardcover
ISBN 978-1-59229-174-8

Bert Vanstechelman, Mark Mergaerts, Dirk Matthys

SAP NetWeaver® Application Server Upgrade Guide

Galileo Press

Bonn • Boston

ISBN   978-1-59229-144-1

1st edition 2007

Editor Florian Zimniak
Copy Editor Julie McNamee, Hope, IN
Cover Design Silke Braun
Layout Design Vera Brauner
Production Iris Warkus
Typesetting SatzPro, Krefeld
Printed and bound in Germany

Contents at a Glance

Contents

7   A Guided Tour of the Upgrade Tools 149

1   Introduction

This book is about upgrading SAP systems, which is something of a challenge.

SAP upgrades are challenging from a business perspective because SAP production systems are critical for the functioning of a company and therefore subject to
very strict availability, stability, and consistency requirements. SAP software is
also highly adaptable and customizable. Companies are not clones of one
another, and neither are their SAP systems. Upgrading to a new release must not
interfere with changes or extensions that were designed to meet specific business
needs. The rich functionality of a new release is likely to boost a company's for-
tunes and open previously unattainable opportunities. Like every other opportunity, this comes at a price: human resources are needed for performing and testing the upgrade, employee time must be reserved for attending training sessions,
and, quite possibly, money must be allocated for new and more powerful hardware.

Upgrades are also a technical challenge. Among the uninitiated, they have
acquired a fearsome reputation; many people associate them with exhausted consultants in all-night sessions, peering at arcane screen messages over the cold
remains of last evening's pizza. The consultants do little to dispel this reputation
and often are only too willing to entertain their public with tales of hard-won vic-
tories over the "upgrade from hell." Those stories are of course exaggerated;
there is no magic, black or white, to SAP upgrades. Still, there is a grain of truth.
Upgrading SAP demands advanced knowledge in several fields: knowledge of the
software components that make up the SAP environment, knowledge of the common technical platform (the SAP Basis) on which the SAP product line is built,
and knowledge of the upgrade methods and tools. Upgrades, therefore, belong in
confident hands. By sharing our knowledge and experience, we — battle-scarred
upgrade veterans ourselves — hope to bolster your confidence when you attack
your next upgrade project.

An earlier edition of this book (*mySAP ERP Upgrade Project Guide*, SAP PRESS
Essentials, SAP PRESS 2006) focused on SAP ERP 2004 (ECC 5.0[1]), which was
then the most recent ERP release available and thus the most up-to-date successor
to SAP R/3. Other products in SAP's ever-widening portfolio of solutions, such as

---

1   For a discussion of the term "ECC" — Enterprise Core Component as the core application of
     SAP ERP, see Section 4.2.

SAP Business Intelligence (BI), Supply Chain Management (SCM), and Customer Relationship Management (CRM), were briefly discussed but not covered in detail. While the current book still treats SAP ERP (now ERP 2005 — ECC 6.0) as its centerpiece, upgrades of other SAP solutions are also covered in more detail.

There are two more reasons for widening the scope of our SAP upgrade book: Java and Unicode.

Java

Perhaps the most significant technological change since SAP made the transition from mainframe to distributed computing in the early 1990s was the addition of *Java* as a fully supported application environment beside ABAP. The SAP NetWeaver Application Server Java (AS Java, SAP's implementation of the Java Platform Enterprise Edition) has become an indispensable component for many SAP solutions and its importance is still growing. Depending on the solution and business scenario, a SAP system can now take on three different forms: ABAP only, Java only, or ABAP and Java together (known as a "double-stack" system in the technical community). Like its ABAP companion, the AS Java follows a specific release track, so like ABAP, it must be possible to upgrade it. The upgrade tools for the AS Java display certain similarities with those for ABAP, but they are by no means identical. This book will therefore describe the upgrade of a double-stack system, where the upgrade processes on the ABAP and Java side synchronize their activities.

Unicode

The relentless trend toward globalization means that business processes and user communities are less and less restrained by national and cultural borders. Today a company's customers, suppliers, and employees speak many languages, and the company must speak *their* languages if it is to survive and prosper. For many years, computer software has been capable of operating in multicountry, multilanguage, and possibly multialphabet environments, but the available solutions were technically complex, lacked uniformity between applications, and often suffered from undesirable constraints and side effects. With the advent of *Unicode* it has finally become possible to use multiple languages and writing systems in a simple, transparent, and conflict-free manner.

SAP is a great proponent of Unicode — it is actually part of the select group of Full Members of the Unicode consortium — and is strongly committed to Unicode as the best solution for applications that operate in a global field. Unicode for SAP has been available for several years as the recommended alternative to older and more limited solutions, but with SAP ERP 2005, the process is taken one step further: the most common pre-Unicode method (the codepage-switching approach known as MDMP [*Multi Display — Multi Processing*]) is no longer supported, and users who upgrade their MDMP-based SAP systems to ERP 2005 must therefore also convert to Unicode. To facilitate this process and minimize downtime, SAP has developed a technique to carry out the release upgrade and the transition to Unicode (technically two very different processes) as a single operation. This upgrade method, the *Combined Upgrade and Unicode Conversion* (CU&UC), adds several critical and sometimes complex steps to the upgrade process. No book on SAP upgrades can therefore be complete without in-depth coverage of the CU&UC procedure.

Structure of this Book

The chapters in the book follow a line from the largely nontechnical to the purely technical. In Chapter 2, we start by placing SAP upgrades in a business context and look at the incentives and caveats that surround upgrade projects. Planning aspects are discussed in Chapter 3, where we deal with the critical factors for a successful upgrade in terms of equipment, time, and human resources. With Chapter 4, we move into the technical realm with an overview of the SAP NetWeaver architecture and a discussion of the various components that make up the SAP system and have an impact on the upgrade. Chapter 5 focuses on the upgrade process itself, as we explain the downtime-minimized and resource-minimized upgrade strategies and also present some of the upgrade services that SAP can provide to help you at any stage of the process.

Chapters 6 and 7 lay the groundwork for the detailed upgrade procedures described later in the book. What you learn in these two chapters, you will use in every upgrade, regardless of the SAP component you are dealing with. Chapter 6 describes the preparatory activities such as obtaining the correct documentation and upgrade media, validating and preparing the server infrastructure, and setting up the environment to be used for the upgrade process. Chapter 7 introduces the upgrade tools both for ABAP and Java. You learn how to install and run the tools and how to use them for driving and monitoring the upgrade. You also get some useful tips and tricks for customizing and troubleshooting.

With the foundations laid, it's time to do some real upgrading. The following chapters contain a detailed step-by-step description of a complete SAP upgrade. The information in these chapters is based on upgrading a system to SAP ERP 2005 with both an ABAP and a Java stack. The upgrade information is presented in two groups of four chapters each. Chapters 8 to 11 deal with the ABAP side: preliminary actions (Chapter 8), the ABAP PREPARE process (Chapter 9), the

ABAP upgrade (SAPup) process (Chapter 10), and the postprocessing activities (Chapter 11). The same approach is then used for the Java upgrade: preliminary actions in Chapter 12, the Java PREPARE in Chapter 13, the Java upgrade (SAPJup) in Chapter 14, and finally the postprocessing steps in Chapter 15. The synchronization between the two upgrades is also covered in the two groups of chapters.

While the upgrade tools are the same for all NetWeaver-based components, there are obviously some differences between these components, especially when it comes to the pre-upgrade and post-upgrade actions. Three chapters in the book are devoted to components other than SAP ERP: Chapter 16 talks about upgrading a SAP Business Intelligence (BI, formerly Business Information Warehouse — BW) system. Chapter 17 describes the upgrade of a SAP Supply Chain Management (SCM) system, concentrating specifically on Advanced Planning and Optimization (APO). The subject of Chapter 18 is the upgrade of SAP Customer Relationship Management (CRM) and SAP Supplier Relationship Management (SRM). This chapter is very short because this upgrade differs very little from that of SAP ERP.

For many SAP installations, operating in a global and multilingual environment is an everyday reality. As we pointed out previously, past solutions to allow working with multiple languages and writing systems were far from perfect, and they have all been superseded by Unicode. For SAP R/3 systems that until now used MDMP (Multiple Display Multiple Processing) to combine languages, the transition to Unicode is mandatory when they are upgraded to SAP ERP 2005, which no longer supports MDMP. To facilitate this transition, SAP has developed special methods combining the release upgrade and Unicode conversion. These methods form the subject of Chapters 19 and 20. In Chapter 19, we introduce Unicode, SAP support for Unicode, and the available methods to combine the Unicode migration with the upgrade. Chapter 20 then describes the combined upgrade and Unicode conversion in detail, with emphasis on the Unicode-related activities: the analysis of ABAP code and text data and the migration (using the methodology of heterogeneous system copies) from a non-Unicode to a Unicode platform.

With the last two chapters of the book, we briefly return to the technical upgrade process. Chapter 21 covers what is probably the most critical action during the ABAP upgrade: the Modification Adjustment for SAP dictionary objects with Transaction SPDD. This is the point where your understanding of the SAP system is put to the test and where human error can make the difference between a successful outcome and a dismal restore-and-try-again. Understandably, this is also the step that invariably gives newbie upgraders butterflies in the stomach. We hope that working through this chapter will at least calm down these butterflies, because it's really not as bad as it seems. Finally, the short Chapter 22 contains instructions on how to reset the upgrade when things go wrong and you decide to cut your losses and start over.

The book concludes with a series of Appendices covering documentation references and detailed technical information supporting the other chapters.

Terminology

With SAP, using the right word for the right thing is not always easy. The product structure can be complex; two terms can be synonyms or not quite synonyms; the version numbering sometimes resembles a Sudoku puzzle. Still, like every large organization, SAP wants to achieve a consistent terminology and therefore issues precise branding guidelines. In this book, we do our very best to respect these guidelines, and we sincerely regret any errors. We also make every possible effort to define and explain a term whenever that seems necessary.

During the writing of this book, there were two significant changes in terminology that directly affected our subject; first, SAP dropped the prefix "my" as in mySAP ERP, mySAP SCM, and others. We have immediately adopted this new rule, so all the my's are now gone, and it is simply SAP ERP or SAP SCM. Second, SAP is also abandoning the short-lived practice of identifying product versions by year (such as SAP ERP 2004) or year-cum-suffix (such as SAP NetWeaver 2004s). Although we — and others — find this a great idea, we have not completely banned the old calendar-based naming from these pages. When the book went to press, the two naming methods were still in use and could be found even on the SAP Service Marketplace, where the same release would be called SAP NetWeaver 2004s in one place and SAP NetWeaver 7.0 in another. This is why we still use the year-based names and talk about SAP ERP 2005 or SAP NetWeaver 2004s. Very frequently, we also mention the accompanying component name and version number in parentheses: SAP ERP 2005 (ECC 6.0) or SAP NetWeaver 2004s (Basis 7.00).

Download

On the Web pages for this book on *www.sap-press.com* and *www.sap-press.de/ 1556*, we provide an ABAP program that is useful to examine the start/stop time of every upgrade step. This report reads the upgrade logfile *SAPup.log* and optionally uploads all timings to an Excel file. You can run this program on every SAP system sharing the same transport directory.

Acknowledgements

Dedicating a book to family can hardly be called original but we can testify that anyone who does so, does so with good reason. We put great effort in extending and rewriting the earlier book on SAP upgrades, but we decided quite rightly to change little to the acknowledgements — except to thank even more profusely those who had to put up with our quirks and eccentricities.

Our partners are professional women themselves, although not active in the SAP field. Nevertheless, whatever advice they were able to give was kindly offered, gratefully accepted, and promptly applied. We therefore dedicate this book to our wives Nadine, Ilka, and Ilse, to thank them for their steadfast support, for their enduring patience and — last but not least — for some splendid dinners and lively discussions. Our children Nathalie, Anne, Frederik, Luna, Mauro, and Remo also deserve our gratitude for being kind to their absent-minded and sometimes irritable fathers (and for occasionally letting us use the home PC).

Our most sincere thanks also go to the editors, Florian Zimniak and Julie McNamee of Galileo Press, for their valuable support and advice. Their skill at concentrated reading and unearthing repetitions and contradictions was really quite amazing. Without their efforts this book would not be half as readable as you will hopefully find it to be.

This chapter introduces the SAP upgrade from a project-management point of view. The documentation from SAP regarding release upgrades is enormous (see Appendix E for a detailed list). Unfortunately, most of the SAP documentation is written from the point of view of SAP as solution provider, not as customer. Recognizing your situation in the SAP standard documentation is not easy, as the focus of SAP is on the SAP standard and not on real-life situations.

2 Upgrading SAP: The Project Perspective

This chapter gives you the arguments and the starting points for an upgrade: Why should you embark on this journey? What are the costs? Where will this journey end? And which are the most important steps?

2.1 Why Upgrade?

What makes a company decide to upgrade its SAP systems? The obvious reason is the need for new functionality, dictated by a company's growing business and/or by the need to survive and flourish in a complex and highly competitive environment. Apart from this, there can be direct operational reasons for moving on to a new version.

What are the usual driving forces behind the decision to upgrade SAP? Here are at least some of the more important ones:

▶ **New Features**
The main reason for upgrading has always been additional functionality. Every SAP release brings new features and opportunities. The need for an SAP upgrade is in many cases driven by changing business needs. When new functionality is required, the choice must be made between implementing and developing it yourself or upgrading your SAP system. This is what we call the *solution gap*. Is the solution gap high enough to justify an SAP release upgrade? SAP upgrades are complex and expensive projects. Apart from offering new functionality, you must also be careful not to disrupt existing business processes. Only if there is meaningful value added to the business applications will you get support for upgrading from the user community and business units.

▶ **Out-of-Date Technology**

The SAP system needs to be constantly customized and enhanced to support evolving business needs. The time may, and will, come when the installed release will no longer be able to answer to these needs. In addition, staying on the same SAP release can become unsustainable from an infrastructure point of view. For example, it might no longer be supported on a new server platform, operating system, or RDBMS version.

▶ **Release Support**

Every SAP release has a maintenance limit. When this limit is reached, extended support may be available at extra cost[1], but this will also cease eventually. At that point, the only options are either to upgrade in the short run or to take out an Extended Maintenance contract. The latter is not an attractive choice because it really implies an increased maintenance cost for a reduced service level. (SAP no longer provides support packages for releases that are out of maintenance.)

▶ **Support Packages**

If support packages are not applied on a regular basis, you might consider a release upgrade instead of applying a very large number of support packages. The impact of installing many support packages could be comparable to that of a release upgrade. More or less, the same modification adjustment and integration testing might be in order. In addition, support packages are there in the first place to correct errors in SAP software. There is no added functionality.

▶ **Unicode**

In the world marketplace we live in today, businesses need to be able to interact with customers and partners in many languages. Chances are that many languages need to be supported: Various code pages have enabled the display of national characters, but the Internet has led to the need to support a huge number of languages. Language combinations are only supported as long as they share the same character set[2]. More combinations are possible with Multi Display — Multi Processing (MDMP). Due to the many limitations and difficulties with MDMP, SAP announced that MDMP systems will no longer be

---

1 The release strategy for SAP applications follows the so-called "5–1–2" maintenance concept: five years mainstream maintenance, one year extended maintenance at an additional 2 % fee, and two years of extended maintenance at an additional 4 % fee. After this period, we talk about customer-specific maintenance (SAP delivers no more support packages). Mainstream maintenance begins with the unrestricted shipments of the new release. See *http://service.sap.com/maintenance.*

2 Appendix D lists all languages supported in the Single Code Pages.

supported as of ECC 6.0 (SAP ERP 2005[3]). Even with MDMP, not all language combinations are supported. Full language compliance is only possible through Unicode. A Unicode conversion is possible for all SAP components based on SAP Web Application Server 6.20 or above. The need for Unicode might be a good reason to upgrade to a Unicode-ready SAP version.

2.2   What Is the Effort?

The effort depends on the changes to the SAP standard and business processes, the number of integrations to the outside world, and in-house developed applications. The more closely your system remains to the standard, the less need for extensive testing will be required. Testing and adapting the current business processes into the new SAP system represent a major part of the upgrade effort. This process can take a substantial amount of time; three months or more is not exceptional. During the upgrade, it is possible to implement new features, modules, or applications, but this is not recommended. The primary focus should be on the release upgrade itself (often called a technical upgrade in SAP literature). New features should be implemented afterwards in a separate project to reduce the risk and complexity of the new implementation.

After the upgrade of the development system, you can start to test all SAP applications, custom development, and integrations to other applications (SAP and non-SAP). While issues caused by the release upgrade are being tackled, the production system is still running in the old release. A change-management procedure needs to be set up to support the production system. The best time to do the release upgrade is when few changes to customizing and development objects are needed. This is not always possible.

During the upgrade, not only are changes made to the SAP customizing and the software repository, but changes are also made to the SAP end-user applications. This will require end-user training.

> **Note**
>
> Instead of talking, start doing! To better estimate the workload, execute an upgrade on a sandbox system to get a look and feel of the tools and the new SAP release, and to get a better idea of the impact and the workload.

---

3   The terms ERP and ECC are discussed in more detail in Section 4.2.

2.3   To Which Release?

If the need for an SAP upgrade was driven by business needs, you might be required to go for the latest SAP release. If the target release is not generally available, you have to sign up for a ramp-up project. Although customers receive extensive support and guidance from SAP during their ramp-up projects, it should be clear that this type of project takes much more time and resources, as not many customers are using the target release productively.

If the very latest functionality is not really needed, then go for mainstream releases: versions that are running for at least one year in many companies. The speed at which support packages are being released might suggest something about the maturity of the SAP release.

In other words, you can limit the effort according to your business needs. If Unicode is not a business requirement, you might consider upgrading to ECC 6.0 (*Enterprise Core Component*) first, performing the Unicode conversion at a later stage in a separate project.

2.4   The Technical SAP Upgrade in a Nutshell

Every SAP project member should have a basic understanding of the upgrade methodology. The technical upgrade consists of five major steps:

1. Preparing the environment
2. The PREPARE process
3. The uptime part of the upgrade
4. The downtime part of the upgrade
5. The post-processing activities

As of Application Server 6.20, there are two possible upgrade scenarios:

▶ Downtime minimized
▶ Resource minimized

These are explained in detail in Sections 4.6 and 5.2. Each scenario has its advantages and disadvantages; however, as you will see later, the downtime-minimized scenario is normally preferred. Table 2.1 provides an overview.

Major block	Actions performed	SAP upgrade scenario	
		Downtime minimized	Resource minimized
(1) Preparing the system	Establish a project plan. Identify human resources, technical and functional. Evaluate suitability of current hardware. Examine software compatibility (for example, SAP GUI, other SAP systems in the landscape). Order desired SAP upgrade services. Perform the necessary hardware and software (OS, DB, SAP plug-in) upgrades. Obtain the upgrade media and documentation. Clean up unused objects and solutions in the development environment. Read this book.	Changes can be performed during normal maintenance windows.	
(2) The PREPARE process	Import the tools required for the upgrade and perform extensive checks to see whether the system is ready for upgrading.	Uptime	Uptime
(3) Upgrade part 1 (in uptime or downtime depending on the chosen scenario)	Import all new data dictionary objects, programs, and languages, together with the latest support packages (in a special nonactive state).	Uptime	Downtime
	Compare the new data dictionary objects with those changed by the customer (modifications and notes).	Uptime	Downtime
	Manually resolve data dictionary object conflicts.	Uptime	Downtime
	Activate the data dictionary, still in the special nonactive state.	Uptime	Downtime
	In the Incremental Conversion (ICNV) phase, a mass pre-upgrade conversion of large tables occurs.	Uptime	Downtime

Table 2.1 The Upgrade Scenarios, Downtime Versus Resource Minimized

Major block	Actions performed	SAP upgrade scenario	
		Downtime minimized	Resource minimized
(4) Upgrade part 2 (downtime)	The new repository (dictionary and development objects) becomes the active one.	Downtime	
	Make changes at the database level (for example, creation or conversion of tables).	Downtime	
	Run conversion programs to adapt data in the system to changes in the data model.	Downtime	
	Perform technical activities, such as parameter changes, installation of new add-ons, and so on.	Downtime	
	Import custom modifications to development objects (prepared in the upgraded development system).	Downtime	
	Perform key user testing. (Just after the production upgrade. For development or acceptance, it can be done during uptime)	Downtime	
(5) Post-processing	Perform final checks and release system to end users.	Downtime	
	Start production work in the new release, provide extended helpdesk support.	Uptime	

Table 2.1 The Upgrade Scenarios, Downtime Versus Resource Minimized (cont.)

Legend

▶ Downtime = system is unavailable for the end users.

▶ Uptime = system is generally available.

As a rule of thumb, block (1) could start up to one month before block (2); block (2) could start up to two weeks before block (3). The time between blocks (3) and (4) depends on the chosen scenario but will normally not exceed a few days. More information on this can be found in Chapter 3.

SAP upgrades should be business-driven, given that they impact business applications and processes. The project lead should therefore be left in the hands of the application-services department. An SAP upgrade is not just a technical activity. Generally, less than 25 % of the total workload goes into the pure technical upgrade system level; the majority of the work goes into testing and adapting applications to the new release.

3   The SAP Upgrade Project

An SAP upgrade is a mission-critical task that requires a project approach. This chapter discusses aspects such as project planning, the master project plan, status reporting, and testing.

3.1   Project Planning

An SAP upgrade plan may take several months to draw up. Customer developments, business processes, and authorization schemes should all be tested to verify that they still function as they did before the upgrade. If your company uses a lot of different SAP modules and/or integrations to other applications, many people and teams will need to get involved. So the content of the project plan is also strongly influenced by the current environment and by the chosen upgrade scenario.

3.1.1   Planning Levels

A project plan is needed to follow up the integration testing for the different SAP modules. We identify three different project and step-by-step plans:

▶ **A master project plan describing all actions required to upgrade the current SAP environment**
This contains the different upgrades (development, acceptance, and production) and all necessary steps required on the satellite systems, such as BW (Business Information Warehouse), CRM (Customer Relationship Management), APO (Advanced Planning and Optimization), SCM (Supply Chain Management), Portal, SAP GUI, XI (Exchange Infrastructure)), and so on. These actions should be described at a relatively high level. Microsoft Project is an

excellent tool for revealing the relations between the various steps. The master upgrade project plan is created and maintained by the project leader.

▶ **A detailed plan for each system within the SAP landscape to be upgraded**
This step-by-step plan describes the steps to be carried out before, during, and after the technical upgrade. A spreadsheet is fine, and, if necessary, can include links to any additional documentation. The detailed plan for each system within the SAP landscape is the responsibility of the SAP application services department.

▶ **A detailed step-by-step plan for the technical upgrade at the system level itself**
This is more than just a plan; it is an extensive and detailed description of every action to be taken before, during, and after the technical upgrade. It should be written and maintained by the SAP system administrator or Basis consultant.

> **Tip**
>
> Perform each action as if you are working on the production system, even when you upgrade the development or acceptance system. Be precise and accurate. Take note of the runtime, lessons learned, actions taken (with their proper motivation), intermediate decisions, considerations, contact person(s), and so on.

3.1.2 Critical Success Factors

Testing the different applications and modules is the largest and most difficult task of the upgrade project. Review existing documentation and test scenarios of the business flows. During the test phase, keep track of the progress of all application tests. Their procedure and outcome is crucial to successfully completing the upgrade project.

There should be a comprehensive inventory of all modifications to standard SAP objects. Continuously documenting changes to standard SAP repository objects will save you time during the modification adjustment. This should be a standard practice, even without the future SAP upgrades in mind.

Project members must understand the impact of the upgrade project. Extremely useful in this context are the numerous delta courses provided by SAP for different modules.

Last but not least, involve key users and business analysts in the SAP upgrade project from the outset. Give them continuous feedback on the progress, take note of their concerns, and act on their suggestions. Make sure that you have their support and commitment. Don't forget that the go/no-go decision is theirs.

And don't forget to inform your SAP account manager because he can assist you in escalating SAP support messages.

If you don't have a good understanding of the upgrade process, seek assistance from an experienced Basis consultant.

3.2 Aspects to Consider

Many things need to be taken into consideration when setting up the project plan. In this section, we highlight some of the most important issues.

3.2.1 Ongoing Development and Customizing

Development and customizing projects should be kept to an absolute minimum during the different SAP upgrades (development, acceptance, production). But what about your planned roll-outs of existing modules, new SAP implementations, ongoing changes, and continuous production support? Plan the upgrade period well ahead of time (if possible up to one year) and involve all business units. Try aiming for a period with few implementation changes. In practice, keeping modifications to an absolute minimum during the course of the upgrade project is not much of an issue. The workload generated by the upgrade project is in most cases so large that everyone within the organization will need to focus on the upgrade.

Even if there are only a few changes, you must still set up the transport system in such a way that urgent changes can be transported to production (notes, bug fixes) at any time. In other words, you must guarantee continuous production support. The SAP landscape and transport system during the upgrade is discussed in detail in Section 3.2.8.

3.2.2 Testing

Remember that the changed business processes and programs need to be retested and probably will need to be adapted to customer requirements after the release upgrade of development (and quality assurance, at the latest). Implementing a new SAP module or making significant modifications to an existing one during the course of an SAP upgrade might seriously complicate things because these modifications will have to be included in the integration testing after the release upgrade.

3.2.3 Compatibility of SAP Plug-in Versions

Make sure that the plug-ins on the satellite systems (BW, APO, CRM, and others) are compatible with the target SAP release. A plug-in or support package upgrade on the satellite system might be needed. This should be verified well before the upgrade. For more information on the supported releases, consult the plug-in page on the SAP Service Marketplace (*http://service.sap.com/R3-PLUG-IN*). Decouple the upgrade of the plug-ins from the actual upgrade of the backend SAP system. This makes error analysis easier than when both are upgraded at the same time.

3.2.4 Compatibility of the Operating System and the Database

The SAP upgrade might require an upgrade of the database software or operating system. To make error analysis easier, upgrade the database software and/or operating system before you upgrade the SAP release.

Verify also if the database supports this new release. For example, at the time of writing this chapter, SAP Unicode Systems are not supported on Informix.

3.2.5 Hardware Capacity

Finally, you must consider your hardware. Demands on hardware resources increase with every SAP release. Is enough hardware capacity available (CPU, memory, disk space)? If not, a hardware upgrade or even a hardware replacement might be in order. Moving the SAP environment to new hardware comes with an additional cost. Clearly, this factor will have a significant impact on the duration of the project.

3.2.6 Frontend (SAP GUI)

The frontend software (SAP GUI) needs to be compatible with the new SAP system release. If the frontend software you are using on the source release is not compatible with the target release, it has to be upgraded. The frontend software is always downward compatible, so users will still be able to access systems running a lower SAP release. Distributing the new version can and should be done independently of the SAP release upgrade. The distribution and implementation of a new GUI can be a time-consuming process, requiring close management attention. All frontends for end users must run the new GUI before the production upgrade; those of administrators, developers, and key users must be upgraded well before that time.

Choose a target GUI level at the beginning of the upgrade project, and remain with this version for all systems (development, quality assurance, and production systems).

> **Tip**
>
> You can use the SAP Logon user exit (EXIT_SAPLSUSF_001) to log the current GUI version of the user who is logging on. The standard function modules GUI_GET_ DESKTOP_INFO and GUI_GET_FILE_INFO allow you to determine the GUI level of the user's frontend. This information will help you to manage the GUI distribution project.

> **Tip**
>
> Via function GUI_GET_REGVALUE, you can also read the registry of the PC (user and system parameters, location of the INI file).

3.2.7 SAP Solution Manager

SAP Solution Manager is the gateway to SAP support. SAP Solution Manager is needed for any upgrade or installation of SAP systems running on SAP NetWeaver Application Server 7.00. In addition, Support Package Stacks for Application Server 7.00 released after April 2, 2007 can only be downloaded via the Maintenance Optimizer, available through SAP Solution Manager. The SAP Solution Manager also contains the Upgrade Roadmap, EarlyWatch Alerting, Solution Management and Monitoring capabilities, Change Request Management, Project Management tools, and more. More information on SAP Solution Manager is available in the book *SAP Solution Manager* by Marc O. Schäfer and Matthias Melich (SAP PRESS 2007).

3.2.8 System Landscape During the Upgrade

Various options for configuring and managing the system landscape will be explained in further detail in Section 4.9, but we will highlight some important aspects here:

▶ Until the upgrade of the production system, you may need two development systems: one (often called the "contingency system") still running the old release for providing continuous production support and the other for carrying out activities related to the upgrade, such as adapting custom modifications to programs and screens and functional testing.

▶ In a standard SAP landscape, the satellite development systems, such as BW, CRM, or SCM, are normally connected to the development system of the back-end R/3 system. This is required for continuous production support and new implementations and developments. But as the test activities progress in the upgraded system, at some point, you will have to move the connections between the backend and satellite systems to the upgraded system. Only in this way can you test the integration between the systems. At that time, the configuration is no longer the same as for the production systems. This is rarely a critical issue, but you still have to be aware of it. Put the switchover dates in your master plan, so that everybody is aware of the altered situation. As soon as the connection is changed, the freeze period[1] for the satellite systems kicks in.

3.2.9 Often Overlooked Upgrade Aspects

A few issues in the project preparation may seem so obvious to everybody that no one makes sure they are actually taken care of:

▶ Combining an upgrade with a migration to Unicode can introduce much additional complexity. The transition to Unicode can be done as a part of the upgrade, but in our experience, this is not a recommended practice. However, if your current system uses multiple codepages (MDMP), then you do not have a choice because SAP ERP (Enterprise Resource Planning) no longer supports MDMP. A combined upgrade and Unicode migration is then the only option.

▶ If a significant distance exists between the source and target release, then you might expect considerable changes in the way certain transactions work. End-user training will be required here. The training effort must be included in the project plan because training sessions and maybe also systems and tutors for several modules might be needed (different locations, languages, and so on).

▶ No matter how complete your test scenarios, some things will always slip through. After the release upgrade of the productive system, unforeseen problems might appear. Be ready for the unexpected. Make sure that your help desk is well staffed because it might receive more calls then usual. Your developers should also be on call for rapid assistance. Key users should be well prepared, as they might face many questions from end users. Plan to have fresh people available for the day after because your upgrade team may be exhausted. Spread responsibilities and risks over different people.

▶ Involve the authorization manager in the test phase. The new and modified SAP programs will use new authorization objects and include additional or changed authorization checks. Asking your developers to test these authorizations is normally not an option because they might lack the time or experience to test transaction flows extensively and in line with user practice. Involving end users in authorization tests is probably not a good idea either, as they

---

1 A freeze is a period of time where modifications are limited to the strict minimum.

might get irritated if authorization issues are not solved as quickly as they expect.

► Verify the maintenance weekends of the SAP Support Portal. You find the maintenance dates of the SAP support systems in Note 069345. Do not schedule the upgrade of your production system in such a maintenance weekend.

► Communicate the dates of the upgrade on the production system to all key users as soon as possible to make sure that it does not interfere with other schedules (financial closing, stock counting). Make sure that you have an unambiguous go-ahead regarding the planned downtime.

3.3   Where to Start?

If you are looking for a first foothold, then the SAP ERP Upgrade Portal is a good place to go: *http://service.sap.com/upgrade*. This is the central repository for all upgrade information. It has links to Best Practices documents for SAP upgrades, numerous white papers, and success stories. You will also find the Upgrade Roadmap available for download. The Roadmap is a must for anyone planning to do an SAP upgrade. Many items in the Roadmap refer to "accelerators." These can be Best Practices documents on project management, the functional and technical aspects of upgrading an entire landscape, Word or Excel templates for planning and documentation, PowerPoint presentations, checklists for integration tests, and many more. The Upgrade Roadmap is discussed in detail in Section 3.10.

3.4   The Master Project Plan

The Master Project Plan describes all the actions to be taken to upgrade your SAP landscape to the next release. It contains the main upgrade phases, such as the interactions with other systems, final switchovers for each SAP system to be upgraded, the team members, and an estimation of the duration, business impact, and resource cost of each major upgrade step. The Master Project Plan should be kept at a high level (milestones); it is not intended to serve as detailed documentation. The most important thing here is the time line, as this will drive the process of planning the needed resources.

Figure 3.1 shows an example of a Master Project Plan. One of the first things to decide on is the go-live date for the production system. As soon as the decision is made, Project can be used to calculate the start date of the upgrade project and required resources.

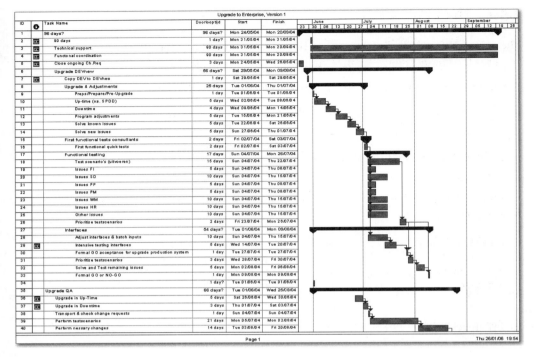

Figure 3.1 Master Project Plan

The following are the main phases:

▶ Upgrade of a separated test system (dry run, we prefer a copy of production because this is the most relevant system and the ultimate goal, the productive upgrade)

▶ Evaluation of the new release (getting the look and feel, to fine-tune the project estimates)

▶ Preparation of the system landscape (hardware and software)

▶ Upgrade of the development system

▶ "Alpha" testing in the development system

▶ Upgrade of the quality assurance system

▶ "Beta" testing in quality assurance

▶ Upgrade of the production system

Depending of the complexity of the system landscape, the project can go from 50 up to 1,000 FTEs[2].

---

2 FTE is Full Time Equivalent (man days).

3.5   The Project Team

The release upgrade is likely to have a big impact on business operations, which requires the commitment, support, and attention of management.

Different teams are needed to bring the release upgrade to a successful end:

▶ A project-management team (meets monthly and after each milestone)

  ▶ Task: Master Plan coordination

  ▶ Reports to the management board

  ▶ Coordinated by the Senior Program manager

Table 3.1 shows the members and their responsibilities on the project-management team

Person	Tasks
Senior program manager	Manage the upgrade project together with all the other ongoing projects within a coherent business plan. Allocate key business users to assist the upgrade team.
Senior IT-project manager	Manage the upgrade project: ▶ Time and budget ▶ Human resources ▶ Project coordination Follow up the upgrade master plan.
IT-change manager	Coordinate the change management before, during, and after the upgrade of each system. Knows the transport system of SAP very well. Make a detailed upgrade plan for the final-upgrade weekend, and create all necessary action lists for each system in each phase.
Functional business information analyst	Manage the test activities for all SAP modules, legacy systems, and interfaces. Create follow-up test scenarios. Be responsible for the cockpit.
Technical upgrade analyst	Run the technical upgrade on a pure SAP Basis (technology) level. Maintain detailed documentation of every action and decision (the upgrade "cookbook").
SAP account manager	If possible, you can also invite your SAP account manager to guarantee SAP's attention. He can provide you valuable input on the Upgrade Services offered by SAP that might be applicable to your situation

Table 3.1 Members of the Project-Management Team and Their Responsibilities

▶ Technical upgrade team (Table 3.2)

　▶ Task: Perform the technical upgrade of the SAP system

　▶ Reports to the Senior IT-Project manager

　▶ Coordinated by the IT-Change manager

Person	Tasks
IT system administrator	Know the whole IT situation and strategy of the company. Manage all the IT aspects of the upgrade for the entire system landscape (hardware, system software, backup, etc.).
Technical upgrade analyst	Focus on the upgrade, system by system, and write the upgrade cookbook.

Table 3.2 Members of the Technical Upgrade Team and Their Responsibilities

▶ Functional workgroups per module (Table 3.3)

　▶ Task: Set up test scenarios and coordinate the integration tests

　▶ Reports to the Senior IT-Project Manager

　▶ Coordinated by the Functional Business Analyst

Person	Tasks
One key business analyst per SAP module	Have in-depth knowledge of the SAP module. Set up, complete, and run all test scenarios within the module.
Developer(s)	Support(s) the business analyst.
Key users	Key business users can greatly contribute to the quality and the realism of the test scenarios (a program is often not smarter than the developer who wrote it).
The authorization manager	Determine the impact of new or changed authorization checks. Ensure that authorizations are adapted so that productive use of the new release is not hampered or disrupted.

Table 3.3 Members of the Workgroups Per Module and Their Responsibilities

3.6　The Testing Phase

After the technical upgrade, the testing phase is next. Testing the new SAP release and adapting it to your business needs is what takes the most resources and time in the upgrade project. A good test strategy and test scenarios should be well defined at the beginning of the upgrade project.

3.6.1 Test Strategy

Even if you have no developments, no modifications, no interfaces, and you run your ERP system in a standalone environment, SAP will still recommend that you set up comprehensive testing scenarios. Even then, testing absolutely everything is simply not possible, and choices will have to be made.

Here are some assumptions that may help you structure your decisions:

► SAP standard applications will do the same as they did before, but with every new release, there are new and added functionalities (consult the release notes).

► Customer developments that generate (compile) successfully may be assumed to work properly, unless the developments are based on a copy of standard SAP software.

► It is not possible to test every single program and transaction, so focus on the most critical business processes.

A good test approach is to work from the bottom up:

► First test all the elementary business blocks. Check the basic business flow within one SAP module. Look at your user exits, modifications, document layout, and so on. All these can, to a large extent, be tested independently of one another (e.g., create customer, material, invoice).

► In the next stage, bring the elementary blocks together. Verify the information flow through the SAP system, based on real-life business scenarios. Make sure that all processes work properly (e.g., create stock, create sales order, create delivery, verify all printed documents, workflows, etc.).

► Next carry out the consolidation tests: How does it all work together in a bigger context (dialog, background jobs, multiple users)?

► Finally, test the integration with other systems (SAP and non-SAP), for example, BI (Business Intelligence), SCM, and CRM. Do not forget to check the integration to external systems such as email, fax, EDI (electronic data interchange), SAP NetWeaver Exchange Infrastructure (XI), and others.

You should use the same SAP GUI version that the end users will have after the production upgrade. This might reveal problems that should be analyzed, solved, and documented.

Many companies already have a lot experience with SAP testing due to former upgrades, installation of support packs, and so on. So don't forget to cross check with earlier lessons learned.

3.6.2 Test Scenarios

As you will probably have to test the business processes several times, it is wise to describe the test procedures in detail. For this, make checklists or write test scenarios. A test scenario is a description of a certain business transaction. It describes the input, the process flow, and the expected output. These test scenarios are not only useful for an upgrade but for every (mass) change of the system, such as support packages. If your test scenarios are well written, they can be run repeatedly by less-experienced users, which allows your business analysts to focus on other issues. Link elementary test scenarios together to test the major business flows. You can reuse the test scenarios for every system (development, quality assurance, and production).

Every test scenario contains the following:

▶ Description of the business process or step

▶ Which transaction, which fields need to be filled in on which screens, and what are the values

▶ Prerequisites for the test scenario

▶ Who can run the scenario

▶ The expected result: print document layout, started workflow items, master data distribution, outbound IDoc, EDI, where to check, and so on

▶ Importance of this business process on a scale of 1 to 10

▶ Time needed to perform the test

▶ Contact person or owner of the scenario

▶ Status (to test, tested, OK, minor problem, error in the tested process flow items, error in the test scenario)

▶ Priority

Testing business scenarios is easily organized as long as they do not span multiple systems. In a network of interrelated systems, testing becomes far more complex or may even be impossible. Not every external system or application can be linked to the upgraded system.

Tip

Use *issue lists* that contain all expected and unexpected problems per module; they describe the problem, the responsible owner of the problem, the priority, and the status. This list will help you assemble the lessons learned or not learned.

3.6.3 Tools

Different tools are available to automate test scenarios. Among those offered by SAP are CATT, eCATT, and SAP Solution Manager. Many other tools are available from third-party software vendors, many of them certified by SAP. However, if you are not already using one of these tools, it does not make sense to implement them just before a release upgrade. Automating test scenarios can be fairly complicated and may take time. It should therefore be seen as a project in its own right.

> **Note**
>
> The service SAP Test Management Optimization makes sure your test scenarios are well managed and that they are repeatable, are comprehensive, and give reliable results. The service SAP Test Management Optimization can be used when implementing support packages during an SAP release upgrade or in preparation for the go-live of an SAP solution. For more information, see *http://service.sap.com/tmo*.

3.7 Status Reporting

Use the output of test scenarios and issue lists per module to follow up the progress of the integration testing.

3.7.1 Global Status Reporting (the Test Cockpit)

As the project progresses, you will end up with many spreadsheets showing the status of various test runs of each team. It is not easy for the project manager to keep a survey of all statuses, so it is useful to summarize all the status information in one graph. This graphic can be used as input for the follow-up meetings (see Figure 3.2).

3.7.2 Make Your Progress Visible

To create and maintain awareness of the project among your IT community, get them involved by informing them of the project planning, status, and progress.

Put the cockpit graph on the bulletin board or at the intranet home page, along with a high-level view of the project. Elements such as the time line, milestones, the testing progress per module or team, and the progress of the open/solved issues should be publicized and kept up to date. This current information will motivate the team members.

Figure 3.2 shows a real-life example of how to present the progress of the test effort in a visually appealing manner. Such a graph is very useful during project management meetings. It is a nice overview of the results per module and makes it easy to follow up the work of the different test teams.

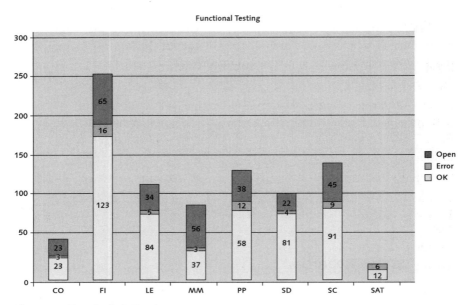

Figure 3.2 Test Cockpit Graph

3.7.3 Estimate the Effort

Estimating the effort needed to upgrade to the next SAP release is not easy. For the project manager, it is probably one of the most difficult challenges. The result of the estimated effort will be a basis for determining the budget, time line, and staffing for the project. The following sections give an overview of the required tasks (for the OLTP [online transaction processing] system).

There are tree big domains where the effort has to be estimated:

1. **The technical upgrade on its own**
   The time needed to do the upgrade depends mainly on the experience of the Basis consultant. As a rule of thumb, you can calculate 14 days for the first upgrade, 1 week for every next upgrade, and 3 to 4 days for production. If your Basis team has to start with reading the books, double the time required.

2. **The development team**
   A major part is the program adjustments; this subject is described in more detail later in this book. The interfaces to the outside world should also not be forgotten.

3. **The functional team**

The number of days and persons required depends on the number of SAP modules in use, their complexity, the availability of former test results, and the experience level of your staff.

3.7.4   The Number of SAP Objects Modified

The Modification Browser (Transaction SE95) gives you a rough idea of how many SAP development objects have been changed in the system (see Figure 3.3). An object can be changed based on a correction supplied via SAP Note. It can also be a customer modification or c³ould even not be changed at all (if it was included in a change request because someone intended to modify it, but they never did).

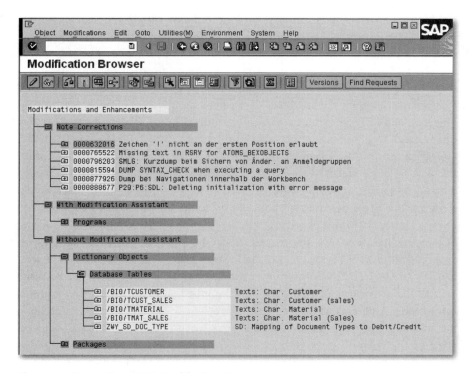

Figure 3.3 Transaction SE95: Modification Browser

The remaining questions are: How many modifications are there? Are they documented? Are they still necessary in the new release or can they be returned to the SAP standard? Was the modification assistant used?[4]

---

3   A modification is a change on a SAP standard program.

Modification Adjustment during the release upgrade (Transaction SPDD) is used to identify and resolve conflicts caused when standard SAP objects overwrite previously modified dictionary objects during an upgrade. These objects include domains, data elements, tables, structure definitions, technical settings, and indexes on transparent tables. Changes to these dictionary objects can result in a loss of data after the upgrade is performed. The technical consultant will compare the changed data-dictionary object with the new version and decide which version needs to be kept. The first time, in the development upgrade, this process may take an entire day. In the quality assurance and production systems, it should take no longer then a few hours. Chapter 21 deals with the process of Modification Adjustment in greater detail.

Modification Adjustment is needed again after the release upgrade for "development" objects (Transaction SPAU), that is, source code, text elements, documentation of program objects, screens, menus, and also certain types of dictionary objects (such as type pools, table types, or search helps) that do not impact data storage. Changes to these objects cannot cause loss of data. In this phase, experienced application developers will compare the changed development objects with the new version that came with the release upgrade. This work may demand a significant number of FTEs (man days), depending on the number of changed objects. The PREPARE process (explained in detail later) lists the number of dictionary and development objects that conflict with the new release and that will appear in Modification Adjustment during and after the upgrade. Try to finish this part within 1 week; however, even with your most experienced developers, depending on the number of objects, it can go from 5 to 25 or more FTEs. Isolate the team in a separate room so they can focus. Modifications can be grouped in a single transport request, or distributed over several transport requests (e.g., per developer). In either case, the requests must be imported into the quality-assurance and production systems after these have been upgraded. In other words, this phase has to be performed once, only for the development system. Some companies perform the SPAU partly on the fourth system, export the requests, refresh the system, and import the request again. This requires a very good understanding of the transport system.

3.7.5 Customer Developments

Look carefully for customer developments that contain SAP standard programs (for example, standard SAP programs that were copied to a customer "Z" program). If during the upgrade, the content of the SAP includes changes (for exam-

---

4 The modification assistant keeps track of all changes to standard SAP programs. Many of these changes can then be reapplied automatically after the upgrade.

ple, SAP introduced a new global field), your custom program might no longer function correctly. A mass compilation of all custom-developed programs and functions can be used to discover such problems.

A similar problem could occur when custom-developed programs call standard SAP function modules. If in the new release, the function input/output parameters or their type has changed, these programs will no longer function. Unfortunately, mass compilation is not sufficient to identify this type of problem; it will be revealed only at runtime (when the now incorrect function call will trigger a short dump).

> **Note**
>
> User exits of the first generation[5] can be overwritten by the upgrade and replaced with new user exits.

One of the first steps after the upgrade of the development system is to carry out a mass syntax check of all custom-developed ABAP (Advanced Business Application Programming) programs. Transaction SAMT can be used to do this: Select the **Syntax Check** option, and then create a program set, for example, based on a range of program names. Start the syntax check in the background. The result will be a list with all programs. Select **Errors** and **Warnings**, and use this report to resolve the coding issues.[6]

To estimate at planning time the effort of reviewing and fixing customer programs, you can use an average of one minute per existing program as a guide.

You can find the number of programs in the system via Transaction SE16 (Table Browser). Specify table TADIR, and fill in the selection fields as follows:

```
PGMID = R3TR
OBJECT = PROG
OBJ_NAME = Y*, Z*, SAPMY*, SAPMZ*
```

(Use the multiple selection mode to enter all the values for field OBJ_NAME.)

Choose **Number of entries**. The value shown will be a precise estimate of the total number of customer programs. Using the 1-minute-per-program rule, divide this value by 480 to obtain FTEs.

---

5 The first-generation user exits were based on "forms" (such as MV45AFZZ). Later versions used the "customer functions" method. More recent techniques are BAPIs (Business API) and BADIs (Business Add-ins).

6 For example, Unicode restrictions, and changed SAP standards includes fieldnames.

For example, if the count in TADIR returns 6,000 customer programs, you can expect to spend around 13 FTEs to review and correct all syntax errors. In previous projects, we learned that there are often also programs that had syntax errors in the old release. Now may be the time to fix (or delete) these.

The next step is a mass syntax check of customer-developed function modules. Here you can use Transaction SE37 (**Utilities • Find**) to count the functions whose names begins with Y or Z. In general, you can take about two minutes per function. There will normally be fewer syntax errors than in programs, but the problem is that changed input/output parameters are not recognized via the syntax check. This is only verified at runtime and results in a dump if the input/output parameters of the function no longer match those passed by the calling program.

Finally, you must also examine customer-developed programs based on batch input[7]. Batch input is based on a transaction-recording[8] mechanism and is therefore sensitive to compatibility issues when the SAP release changes. If the layout of the underlying SAP standard transaction has changed, then the batch input will probably no longer work. If, for example, SAP introduced a new screen in a transaction that changes the flow in all or some situations, then the batch input session will run into an error.

> **Note**
>
> If you use standard batch input programs or BAPI (Business API) functions, then there should be no problem. SAP updates these automatically during the release upgrade. But at the time the report was written, many developers preferred to create their own batch input (because it's easier then using a BAPI or the BAPI didn't exit at that time). You can search for those batch inputs via Transaction SE38, option **Find in source**. Another option is to use the search program RPR_ABAP_SOURCE_SCAN. In both cases, you have to look for the strings CALL TRANSACTION, BDC_INSERT, and BDC_OPEN_GROUP. You can expect to spend one hour per program, depending on the complexity of the transaction and the number of similar batch input programs. Do not forget to also verify your custom developed function modules for batch input calls.

---

7 Batch input is a proven SAP method to upload data into SAP. It simulates normal user input by programmatically emulating the transaction screen flow. The main advantage is that the external data passes through the entire transaction logic and is thus checked for validity and consistency.

8 Via transaction SM35, you run almost all SAP transactions in a recording mode. This means that all screen numbers, field names, and values filled in are kept in a file. This file can be used to generate a batch-input program.

3.7.6 ABAP Unicode Syntax Requirements

If you combine the upgrade with the conversion to Unicode, you must make sure that your programs are compliant with the Unicode syntax. Making your programs Unicode compliant can be a big job depending of the number of your own developments; this activity is not related to the upgrade but to the fact that you go to a Unicode SAP Release. This effort can be performed independent from the upgrade, even months before, and it will make your upgrade project less heavy and shorten up the elapsed time.

ABAP developers must verify that all customer programs are Unicode compliant. Only programs that comply with the Unicode ABAP syntax and semantics will run on a Unicode system. This also applies to all SAP programs modified by the customer. Transaction UCCHECK can be used to scan ABAP code for noncompliant ABAP syntax. This step should not be underestimated, especially in environments in which many customer-written programs are used. As a rule of thumb, take around 30 objects with Unicode errors a day. A detailed description of UCCHECK can be found in Chapter 20.

> **Note**
>
> Some SAP programs are not Unicode-enabled. After the migration, they are automatically regenerated. Do not run UCCHECK for SAP programs, or these programs will also be listed, causing unnecessary confusion.

3.7.7 Custom-Developed Programs No Longer in Use

This is of no concern for the release upgrade, but if you convert to Unicode, you can limit the amount of work required to make in-house development Unicode compliant, if you can exclude no longer used developments (former uploads, test programs, correction programs, interfaces). It is always difficult to decide to delete a program. A saver option is to disable a program and then remove it later, if no one complains.

3.7.8 Estimating the Functional Effort

To estimate the effort of the team at the functional level, you need to know whether this is a purely technical upgrade or whether new functionality is to be introduced at the same time. The recommended practice is to implement new functionality as a separate project after the upgrade. In the first stage, the system should be allowed to stabilize on the new release with just the existing functionality. Only then is it advisable to start work on new functions. Mixing the two increases the likelihood of errors, makes problem resolution more difficult, and risks blurring the focus of developers and key users.

SAP lists the obsolete transactions in the release notes. The impact of obsolete transactions has to be evaluated:

▶ What is the business need?

▶ Who is using the transactions?

▶ What are the alternatives?

▶ Does the obsolete transaction still work in the new release?

▶ Does obsolescence cause an extra customizing effort?

▶ Does replacing the obsolete transaction have an impact on user training?

To reduce the functional effort, perform the following steps:

1. Some transactions are superseded by newly designed versions. The superseding transactions usually have an "N" suffix added to the transaction code, for example ME21/ME21N. Both the look and feel and the functionality of the transaction are likely to have undergone changes. You will have to take this into consideration when planning user training.

2. Existing transactions will normally do the same as before, but minor changes are possible. Again you have to test and evaluate this, and extra training might be needed.

3. Changes to transactions make it necessary to also change test scenarios. Update or actualize your existing test scenarios for the main business processes.

4. Update or actualize your end-user documentation, including training guides for new users.

5. What is the distance (the "delta") between the source and target release? If the source release is R/3 4.6 or R/3 Enterprise (4.70), then functional changes in SAP core modules are relatively minor. However, if you are upgrading from a release lower than 4.6, there will be very significant changes in appearance and functionality, and it will then be wise to consider additional training sessions for the end users. This will also influence the test effort and the scope of your test scenarios.

6. How many user exits and added user exits via a modification are there?. The standard software has been tested and run at a lot of companies. For your own modifications, you are on your own. The more exits, the more tests are required, and this can increase exponentially.

3.7.9 Business Example, Upgrade from 4.6B to ECC[9] 6.0

The two graphs shown in this section are based on the work achieved during an upgrade project of 750 FTEs (see Figure 3.4 and Figure 3.5). The source release was 4.6B. The work done was logged per date and per module. The graphs represent only the efforts done by the application team; the time spent on technical issues by the Basis upgrade team is not mentioned. Figure 3.4 shows the distribution of the FTEs per module.

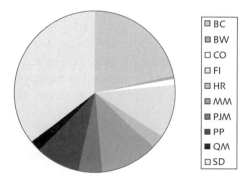

☐ BC
☐ BW
☐ CO
☐ FI
☐ HR
☐ MM
☐ PJM
☐ PP
☐ QM
☐ SD

Figure 3.4 Distribution of the Effort Per SAP Module

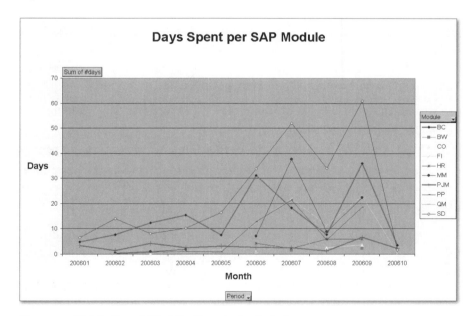

Figure 3.5 Distribution of Effort Per Stage in the Project

---

9 ECC — Enterprise Core Component — as the functional core of SAP ERP is discussed in more detail in Section 4.2

Figure 3.5 shows the upgrade efforts on the project time line. You see that the BC (SAP Basis) effort is highest just after the development upgrade. The more modifications to the SAP standard, the more time is required to test them. There was a dip in August because of the holiday period. If you perform such a project during a holiday period, be aware that not all of your key users, developers, functional staffs, and managers will be available.

3.7.10 Estimating the Technical Upgrade Runtime for the Production System

The duration of the technical upgrade depends mainly on the hardware resources. This makes it very difficult to make an accurate forecast of the production runtimes. The only way to get a fairly accurate idea of the runtime to expect is by doing a test upgrade on a similar hardware configuration with almost the same set of data.

Even without such a close approximation of the production environment, it is essential to keep all the timing data from the other upgrades. At the very end of the technical upgrade process (SAPup), a timing document in HTML format is produced. You can also run the standard SAP report RSUPGSUM, which produces both a printed report and a log file in the upgrade directory.

As an extra to this book, you can also download a report from the catalogue page for this book on *www.sap-press.com* or *www.sap-press.de/1556*, which generates detailed timing information in spreadsheet format, based on the upgrade logs. This program reports four different types of time usage:

▶ The real runtime, that is, the time that the server was busy running the upgrade (upload, conversions, activation, etc)

▶ The think time, that is, the time you needed thinking over what to do next

▶ The lost time, that is, the time the upgrade process waited for your next move, during which you were not active (e.g., the time you slept)

▶ The action time, that is, the time you needed to carry out some activity

The output shows the time of every step. If you export the list to a spreadsheet, then it can be a handy tool for predicting the runtimes and stop times in the next upgrade(s). You can also compare runtimes per phase on different machines to help you determine a speed factor between the different servers and systems. For example, you might determine from the figures that production is 25% faster than acceptance. Figure 3.6 shows an example of such a timing report.

U/D	Nr	Phase	Start	End	Run	Nr.Dia	Dialog	Break	CumRun	CumDialog	CumBreak	CumReelRun	ReelRun	Est.Lost	Est.start
U	10	BEGIN	11/09/2004 16:20	11/09/2004 16:20	00:00:00	0	00:00:00		00:00:00	00:00:00		00:00:00	00:00:00	00:00:00	13/09/2004 19:00
U	20	INITPUT	11/09/2004 16:20	11/09/2004 16:21	00:00:10	1	00:00:10		00:00:10	00:00:10		00:00:00	00:00:00	00:05:00	13/09/2004 19:20
U	30	DBCHK	11/09/2004 16:21	11/09/2004 16:21	00:00:39	1	00:00:34		00:00:49	00:00:44		00:00:05	00:00:05	00:05:00	13/09/2004 19:40
U	40	VERSCHK	11/09/2004 16:21	11/09/2004 16:21	00:00:00	0	00:00:00		00:00:49	00:00:44		00:00:05	00:00:00	00:00:00	13/09/2004 19:40
U	50	UVERS_CHK	11/09/2004 16:21	11/09/2004 16:21	00:00:00	0	00:00:00		00:00:49	00:00:44		00:00:05	00:00:00	00:00:00	13/09/2004 19:40
U	60	BATCHCHK	11/09/2004 16:21	11/09/2004 16:21	00:00:06	0	00:00:00		00:00:55	00:00:44		00:00:11	00:00:06	00:00:00	13/09/2004 19:40
U	70	PATCH_CHK	11/09/2004 16:21	11/09/2004 16:21	00:00:07	0	00:00:00		00:01:02	00:00:44		00:00:18	00:00:07	00:00:00	13/09/2004 19:41
U	80	CLNT_CHK	11/09/2004 16:21	11/09/2004 16:22	00:00:06	0	00:00:00		00:01:08	00:00:44		00:00:24	00:00:06	00:00:00	13/09/2004 19:41
U	90	INTCHK	11/09/2004 16:22	11/09/2004 16:22	00:00:01	0	00:00:00		00:01:09	00:00:44		00:00:25	00:00:01	00:00:00	13/09/2004 19:41
U	100	TOOLVERSION_UPG	11/09/2004 16:22	11/09/2004 16:22	00:00:01	0	00:00:00		00:01:10	00:00:44		00:00:26	00:00:01	00:00:00	13/09/2004 19:41
U	110	KEY_CHK	11/09/2004 16:22	11/09/2004 16:23	00:01:01	2	00:01:01		00:02:11	00:01:45		00:00:26	00:00:00	00:10:00	13/09/2004 20:21
U	120	JDKCHK_UPG	11/09/2004 16:23	11/09/2004 16:23	00:00:01	0	00:00:00		00:02:12	00:01:45		00:00:27	00:00:01	00:00:00	13/09/2004 20:21
U	130	SHDINST_CHK1	11/09/2004 16:23	11/09/2004 16:23	00:00:00	0	00:00:00		00:02:12	00:01:45		00:00:27	00:00:00	00:00:00	13/09/2004 20:21
U	140	DB_ACTION_RUNSTATS	11/09/2004 16:23	11/09/2004 16:23	00:00:00	0	00:00:00		00:02:12	00:01:45		00:00:27	00:00:00	00:00:00	13/09/2004 20:21
U	150	INITSUBST	11/09/2004 16:23	11/09/2004 16:23	00:00:51	4	00:00:51		00:03:03	00:02:36		00:00:27	00:00:00	00:20:00	13/09/2004 21:41
U	160	FRONTREQ	11/09/2004 16:23	11/09/2004 16:24	00:00:07	1	00:00:07		00:03:10	00:02:43		00:00:27	00:00:00	00:05:00	13/09/2004 22:01
U	170	CONFCHK_X	11/09/2004 16:24	11/09/2004 16:25	00:01:21	1	00:01:18		00:04:31	00:04:01		00:00:30	00:00:03	00:05:00	13/09/2004 22:22
U	180	VIEWCHK1	11/09/2004 16:25	11/09/2004 16:25	00:00:02	0	00:00:00		00:04:33	00:04:01		00:00:32	00:00:02	00:00:00	13/09/2004 22:22
U	190	REPACHK1	11/09/2004 16:25	11/09/2004 16:25	00:00:00	0	00:00:00		00:04:33	00:04:01		00:00:32	00:00:00	00:00:00	13/09/2004 22:22
U	200	EXECIC	11/09/2004 16:25	11/09/2004 16:25	00:00:00	0	00:00:00		00:04:33	00:04:01		00:00:32	00:00:00	00:00:00	13/09/2004 22:22
U	210	STOPR3_ICNV	11/09/2004 16:25	11/09/2004 16:25	00:00:00	0	00:00:00		00:04:33	00:04:01		00:00:32	00:00:00	00:00:00	13/09/2004 22:22
U	220	STARTR3_ICNV	11/09/2004 16:25	11/09/2004 16:25	00:00:00	0	00:00:00		00:04:33	00:04:01		00:00:32	00:00:00	00:00:00	13/09/2004 22:22
U	230	JOB_RSVBCHCK2	11/09/2004 16:25	11/09/2004 16:25	00:00:07	0	00:00:00		00:04:40	00:04:01		00:00:39	00:00:07	00:00:00	13/09/2004 22:22
U	240	RUN_RSWBO230	11/09/2004 16:25	11/09/2004 16:25	00:00:04	0	00:00:00		00:04:44	00:04:01		00:00:43	00:00:04	00:00:00	13/09/2004 22:22
U	250	JOB_RXPRECHK	11/09/2004 16:25	11/09/2004 16:25	00:00:00	0	00:00:00		00:04:44	00:04:01		00:00:43	00:00:00	00:00:00	13/09/2004 22:22
U	260	JOB_RDDPURI2	11/09/2004 16:25	11/09/2004 16:25	00:00:10	0	00:00:00		00:04:54	00:04:01		00:00:53	00:00:10	00:00:00	13/09/2004 22:23
U	270	JOB_RS_OLTPSOURCE	11/09/2004 16:25	11/09/2004 16:25	00:00:00	0	00:00:00		00:04:54	00:04:01		00:00:53	00:00:00	00:00:00	13/09/2004 22:23
U	280	JOB_RSAODSACTIVATE	11/09/2004 16:25	11/09/2004 16:25	00:00:00	0	00:00:00		00:04:54	00:04:01		00:00:53	00:00:00	00:00:00	13/09/2004 22:23
U	290	TABSPC_UPG	11/09/2004 16:25	11/09/2004 16:26	00:00:30	0	00:00:00		00:05:24	00:04:01		00:01:23	00:00:30	00:00:00	13/09/2004 22:25
U	300	SPACECHK_ALL	11/09/2004 16:26	11/09/2004 16:26	00:00:07	0	00:00:00		00:05:31	00:04:01		00:01:30	00:00:07	00:00:00	13/09/2004 22:26
U	310	FREECHK_X	11/09/2004 16:26	11/09/2004 16:26	00:00:30	1	00:00:30		00:06:01	00:04:31		00:01:30	00:00:00	00:05:00	13/09/2004 22:46
U	320	DMPSPC_X	11/09/2004 16:26	11/09/2004 16:26	00:00:00	0	00:00:00		00:06:01	00:04:31		00:01:30	00:00:00	00:00:00	13/09/2004 22:46
U	330	JOB_BTCTRNS0	11/09/2004 16:26	11/09/2004 16:26	00:00:00	0	00:00:00		00:06:01	00:04:31		00:01:30	00:00:00	00:00:00	13/09/2004 22:46
U	340	RUN_RSPTBFIL_INIT	11/09/2004 16:26	11/09/2004 16:28	00:01:06	0	00:00:00		00:07:07	00:04:31		00:02:36	00:01:06	00:00:00	13/09/2004 22:50
U	345	<Break>	11/09/2004 16:28	11/09/2004 16:31	00:03:36	0	00:00:00	00:03:36	00:10:43	00:04:31	00:03:36	00:02:36	00:00:00	00:15:00	13/09/2004 23:50

Figure 3.6 Spreadsheet with Upgrade Runtimes

The real runtime, naturally, depends on your hardware. The think time will be long during the first upgrade(s) but can be minimized or even reduced to zero for production, at least if you have maintained high-quality upgrade documentation. The lost time is the time you were not busy with the upgrade, and the system was waiting for you. This is perhaps not a problem for the development or acceptance upgrades, but in production, any lost time must be kept to a minimum. One way to avoid losing time is to have a precise idea of when to expect the upgrade process to stop for input.

The action time is the time needed to do additional steps or manual tasks, for example:

▶ Taking backups

▶ Doing the Modification Adjustment in the dictionary (SPDD)

▶ Importing the transport request with program modification adjustments (SPAU request)

▶ Working on the documentation

▶ Performing final acceptance tests

3.8   Enabling New Customizing and Functionality

In each release, each development object has a certain version, which in SAP terms is called a *program level*. During the upgrade, many SAP objects are replaced:

▶ Objects of the source release that are not replaced by the new release are not touched.

▶ Obsolete objects of the source release are removed.

▶ Common objects that are not changed by the customer are automatically replaced.

▶ Common objects that are changed by the customer require an intervention customer (called *Modification Adjustment,* see Chapter 21 in this book).

Every SAP version comes with new functionality and customizing. Those new customizing settings are imported into the system during the upgrade, but only in client 000 to make sure that standard SAP customizing does not overwrite customer customizing. (This is also why when creating a new client, you perform the copy from 000 instead of 001, the sample client.)

If new functionality is to be implemented, its customizing has to be copied to the customer client manually.

Note

SAP tables are divided into delivery classes. By default, the following table classes exist:

▶ A: Application table (master and transaction data).

▶ C: Customizing table; maintenance only by customer, not SAP import.

▶ L: Table for storing temporary data, delivered empty.

▶ G: Customizing table; protected against SAP Update.

▶ E: Control table; SAP and customer have separate key areas.

▶ S: System table; maintained only by SAP, change equals modification.

▶ W: System table; contents transportable via separate TR objects.

For more information, see OSS Note 2857, "What table delivery classes are there? What is their significance?"

The upgrade process shows different behavior for client-specific and cross-client tables:

▶ **Client-specific tables:**

  ▷ Class A and C: Data is only imported into client 000. Existing data records are overwritten.

  ▷ Class E, S, and W: Data is imported into all clients. Existing data records are overwritten.

  ▷ Class G: In client 000, existing data records are overwritten. In all other clients, new data records are added but data records that already exist are not overwritten.

  ▷ Class L: No data is imported.

▶ **Cross-client tables:**

  ▶ Classes A, L, and C: No import of data is carried out.

  ▶ Classes E, S, and W: Data is imported. Existing data records with the same key are overwritten.

  ▶ Class G: Nonavailable data records are added, but data records that already exist are not overwritten.

After the upgrade, customizing needs to be copied to customer tables manually. SAP offers the following options:

▶ Unpacked customizing can be copied from client 000 with the compare tools, Transaction SCU0 and Transaction SCMP, to compare objects individually.

▶ Packed customizing is collected in a *set*, a kind of bundle (for example, BC sets). These can be activated via Transaction SCPR20.

For more information, the following SAP Notes describe often occurring missing customizing entries after the SAP upgrade:

▶ Note 217012, "Missing pricing Customizing after upgrade"

▶ Note 204693, "Missing countries in Customizing (table T005)"

▶ Note 162594, "Missing customizing entries"

3.9 Capacity Planning When Upgrading to SAP ERP

Resource requirements increase with every SAP release. For an environment that is already operational, this increase is difficult to estimate and depends heavily on the SAP modules and business processes in use, the number of concurrent users, and the amount of business data. Capacity planning is therefore an important matter that should not be neglected or unduly postponed. Capacity bottlenecks can jeopardize the success of your upgrade project because users will not accept deteriorated response times.

Some factors to consider when forecasting the capacity need:

▶ Which SAP modules or business processes are in use?

▶ Does the SAP upgrade imply a database or operating system upgrade?

▶ Is SAP physically moved to a different platform?

▶ Is new functionality going to be implemented after the release upgrade?

▶ Is the number of users going to increase after the release upgrade?

And don't forget if you make the step to Unicode, a lot more resources will be required. The size of the database will grow it will not double in size; but rise up to 30% depending on the UTF format[10]. As one character is represented by two or more bytes, there is an impact on the transfer rates, the CPU power, and the network. SAP provides rough estimates for the extra capacity that will be needed, but you will have to translate these estimates to your own situation. Analyzing the current situation is the first step in estimating the load increase. Performance and tuning is out of the scope of this book, so this chapter merely discusses some general sizing guidelines. Table 3.4 gives a rough estimate of the increase in resource requirements as of SAP release 4.5B. The values are relative to release 4.5B. We emphasize that these are *very general* estimates obtained from a wide range of configurations and not necessarily representative for your specific environment.

Resource	4.5	4.6C	4.70	ECC 5.0	ECC 6.0
CPU DB server (a)	1.00	1.00	1.00	1.00	1.00
DB size (b)	1.00	1.10	1.20	1.25	1.25
CPU app server (c)	1.00	1.10	1.15	1.25	1.25
Memory app server (c)	1.00	1.20	1.25	1.50	1.50
a) Increase in number of DB calls: Additional CPU and memory might be necessary to achieve the same throughput on the database server due to additional indexes, larger table rows, more database users, or different behavior of the cost-based optimizer. CPU and memory requirements of the database server also depend on the database platform and the used database release. An additional impact on the CPU consumption of the application server and the database server was observed when moving from a 32-bit to a 64-bit operating system.					
b) Heavily depends on the database platform and the used R/3 components					
c) Heavily depends on the business processes implemented					

Table 3.4 Resource Increase

Fortunately, there is more to capacity planning then these matrixes. SAP provides the following tools and services.

The *Quick Sizer*, accessible via *http://service.sap.com/quicksizer*, is a Web-based tool that makes the initial design of an SAP system easier and faster. It has been developed by SAP together with several hardware vendors and is used for new SAP implementations. Quick Sizer translates business requirements into techni-

---

10 Unicode Transformation Format. The UTF format defines how many bytes are used to represent a character. See Chapter 19 for details.

cal requirements. The Quick Sizer calculates CPU, disk, and memory resource categories based on throughput numbers and the number of users working with the different SAP components in a hardware- and database-independent format. The purpose of the tool is to give customers an idea about the size of the system necessary to run the proposed workload. Quick Sizer does not support release upgrades by default. You could, however, use the throughput numbers together with the number of users from within the source release and compare this against the target release in Quick Sizer. Your hardware vendor should be able to validate your current hardware environment against the output provided by the tool. If you need more information on the Quick Sizer and on sizing SAP systems in general, refer to *Sizing SAP Systems* by Susanne Janssen and Ulrich Marquard (SAP PRESS Essentials 27, SAP PRESS 2007).

Performance and tuning transactions exist in any SAP system. Performance data is gathered at runtime and can be used for the following:

▶ Disk space analysis via Transaction DB02

▶ CPU analysis via Transaction ST03N and STAD

▶ User analysis with ST03N and STAD

▶ Memory analysis with ST02, ST04, SM04, and STAD

▶ Frontend network load with STAD, ST03N, and ST06 (LAN Check by Ping)

Most of these transactions should be well known by the SAP administrator, as they are used for daily system monitoring tasks and for performance and tuning. With the current performance figures and the initial sizing observations from the other SAP upgrades in the SAP environment, the increase in resource requirements can be estimated and compared with the current productive environment.

The *SAP Functional Upgrade Service* is a service from SAP that helps customers estimates the resource requirements and the system configuration for the new SAP release. The Functional Upgrade Service consists of three sessions. The first session, the Planning Session, should be performed well in advance. It analyzes the target release against the current release, the operating and database system, and all satellite systems in the SAP landscape. The Analysis Session is performed several weeks before the upgrade of the production system. It checks the sizing and resource requirements, resulting in a set of performance recommendations for the target release. The last session, the Verification Session, takes place several weeks after the upgrade and includes a detailed check of performance and the workload distribution of the updated R/3 system.

3.10   SAP Solution Manager and the SAP Upgrade Roadmap

Managing a distributed SAP landscape is not an easy undertaking, as more and more business processes expand beyond system boundaries. SAP Solution Manager is the answer to this ever-growing complexity. It provides central access to project documentation and implementation guidelines and is a platform for Solution Monitoring (based on CCMS) and Change Request Management for the entire SAP landscape. It comes with a Service Desk that allows you to create support messages, send them to SAP, and receive replies from SAP. Finally, SAP Solution Manager comes with some specific components to support customers during their upgrade to ERP or any other SAP Business Suite solution (including CRM, SRM, and SCM). In addition, SAP considers Solution Manager a prerequisite for performing any upgrade or installation of SAP ERP 6.0 and above.

The Upgrade Roadmap is the component within SAP Solution Manager that supports customers during their release upgrades. This content available from SAP provides a methodological guideline to assist you in your upgrade project. It provides a step-by-step activity guide for upgrading SAP components to facilitate any upgrade project. These include analysis of the status of and targets for business processes and underlying IT infrastructure before and after the upgrade, upgrade configuration, and upgraded process testing. Along the way, you will find links to other SAP resources, tools, and services for Best Practices documents and project templates, among other aids for speeding the upgrade process.

The list of available Upgrade Roadmap content is constantly growing. Currently, SAP Upgrade Roadmap has product- and solution-specific information available for every phase and task package, with many upgrade paths that the customer can choose from, such as the following:

▶ From SAP R/3 3.X to SAP R/3 Enterprise 4.7, ECC 5.0, ECC 6.0
▶ From SAP CRM 2.X/3.0 to SAP CRM 4.0, CRM 5.0
▶ From SAP BW 3.X to SAP BW 3.5, BW 7.0

The Upgrade Roadmap is available in a standalone HTML version, shown in Figure 3.7, which can be used even without SAP Solution Manager. The standalone version will provide you with a generic methodology for all the steps in an upgrade project. However, used alone, it won't offer the automated access to content and tools — such as upgrade and implementation content for new solutions, or system landscape analysis linked to your roadmap as project accelerators — that you'll find when using it in conjunction with SAP Solution Manager.

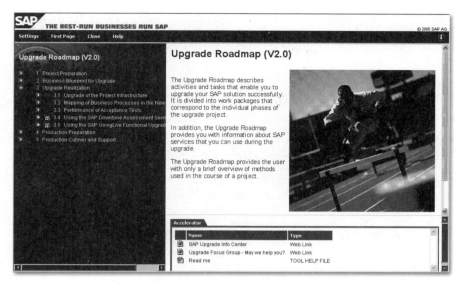

Figure 3.7 The Upgrade Roadmap, HTML Version

Furthermore, at the beginning of the technical upgrade, the upgrade tools will request an upgrade key, which needs to be generated in the Solution Manager System Landscape. If a Solution Manager does not yet exist in your environment, installing one will be one of the first steps in the upgrade project.

3.11 Final Tips and Recommendations

There are a few useful tips that can make life easier during upgrade projects.

3.11.1 Seek Assistance and Information

Inform SAP when you upgrade the production system. They can provide you with a contact person during the upgrade weekend to support you if something unexpected happens.

3.11.2 The Usual Suspects That Need Extra Attention

Following is a short summary of things that frequently cause headaches — or worse — during SAP upgrade projects. All of these items require close scrutiny. Many of these were covered in more detail in the course of this chapter.

▶ Batch input and CALL TRANSACTION programs

▶ SAP standard program modifications

- ▶ The number of installed SAP Notes
- ▶ Obsolete transactions
- ▶ Unnecessary leftovers of previous implementations (one-shot upload programs, unused programs, transactions, or tables)
- ▶ Own developments copied from standard programs
- ▶ Roll out of new GUI version and its impact on PC hardware (memory)
- ▶ Program selection variants (this issue is largely covered by the ASU (Application Specific Upgrade] , discussed later in this book)
- ▶ In-development systems: programs/dictionary structures that were never put into production and might contain errors

Careful planning is needed before you upgrade your SAP system. The following chapter helps you understand the SAP NetWeaver architecture, the upgrade tools, and the upgrade strategy. After reading this chapter, you should be able to plan your upgrade so that downtime is reduced to an absolute minimum and the upgrade runs as efficiently as possible.

4   Technical Background Information

Understanding the backgrounds of a purely technical task like an upgrade is essential — if you don't understand why something is the way it is, how can you treat it properly? In this chapter, we'll discuss the SAP NetWeaver and SAP ERP architecture, certain upgrade-specific technologies and strategies, the SAP system landscape, and other technical aspects.

4.1   The SAP NetWeaver Architecture

The SAP NetWeaver integration and application platform is used across all SAP solutions and selected SAP partner solutions. It aims to integrate people, information, and business processes across a wide range of technologies and sources. SAP NetWeaver offers solutions in each of these three major areas, all built upon a common application platform, the SAP NetWeaver Application Server (SAP NetWeaver AS).

The usual way of graphically presenting the SAP NetWeaver platform (irreverently known as the "fridge") is shown in Figure 4.1.

4.1.1   People Integration

The area of people integration contains all functionality needed to bring information to the right people. Employees work with applications on a daily basis. Access needs to be tailored to their roles within the company. SAP NetWeaver provides the technical solutions to meet these requirements via the following components:

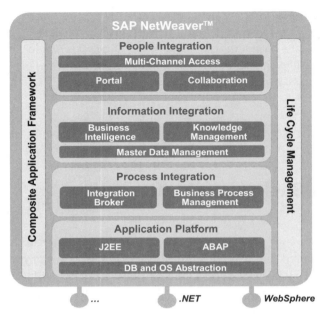

Figure 4.1 The SAP NetWeaver Platform

▶ **Portal Infrastructure**
The SAP NetWeaver Portal provides a company's employees with a central point of access to the applications of various backend systems, tailored to an employee's role within the company. Single Sign-On (SSO) can be used to access applications and information from both the intranet and Internet. SAP NetWeaver Collaboration and Knowledge Management are integrated into SAP NetWeaver Portal and give employees access to structured information.

▶ **SAP NetWeaver Collaboration**
Good internal communication is an important success factor for any company. More and more collaborating teams and even individual team members reside in different buildings, in different countries, or even in different continents. Collaboration provides various tools to support the exchange of information, including collaboration rooms (virtual rooms for exchanging information), real time collaboration with instant messaging and application sharing, and the collaboration launch pad, which displays all online employees.

▶ **Multi-Channel Access or SAP NetWeaver Mobile**
With multi-channel access, you can connect to enterprise systems through voice, mobile, or radio-frequency technology. A service technician, for example, needs access to information regarding spare parts or his next assignment. SAP NetWeaver Mobile is the technical basis for mobile applications of this type.

4.1.2   Information Integration

Information integration makes information available throughout the company. The challenging factor today is filtering what is relevant out of the mountain of information available. SAP NetWeaver meets the requirement by using the following components:

▶ **Knowledge Management**
The Knowledge Management platform enables companies to handle unstructured data. Its main functionality comprises content management of the SAP NetWeaver Portal and Text Retrieval and Classification Engine (TREX). The aim is to bring together information distributed across different servers (for example, file servers, the intranet) in a central repository with tools for searching, classifying, and structuring information. Knowledge Management can be integrated into the SAP NetWeaver Portal.

▶ **Business Intelligence (BI)**
SAP NetWeaver BI holds and retrieves data from SAP and non-SAP systems. This capability enables you to integrate, analyze, and disseminate relevant and timely information.

▶ **Master Data Management**
Many companies have a heterogeneous distributed IT landscape with many different applications. All these applications need to access the same master data, such as business partners, address information, or warehousing. This situation tends to produce difficult data-conversion processes for ensuring data consistency. SAP NetWeaver Master Data Management addresses this problem by providing the same master data across all applications.

4.1.3   Process Integration

Process integration enables business processes to run seamlessly across heterogeneous IT landscapes. The business processes that span systems and organizations have to be well organized to offer high performance. The SAP NetWeaver Exchange Infrastructure (SAP NetWeaver XI) and business-process management form the basis for optimized process management for process chains.

▶ **Exchange Infrastructure**
SAP NetWeaver XI acts as a data hub for SAP and non-SAP systems. It enables XML/SOAP-based (Extensible Markup Language/Simple Object Access Protocol) communication between application components from various sources and vendors.

▶ **Business Process Management**
With business-process management, you can model and drive processes in a dynamic IT environment. This technology allows you to combine underlying applications into adaptive, end-to-end processes spanning the entire value chain.

4.1.4 Application Platform

The SAP NetWeaver Application Server (currently SAP NetWeaver AS Release 7.00) is the basis of all SAP applications. The ABAP (*Advanced Business Application Programming*) stack on which most components are built has been extended with technologies such as the J2EE Engine and the Internet Communication Manager, which handles Internet requests and distributes them to the individual components. The SAP NetWeaver Application Server supports a wide range of technical standards such as HTTP(S), SMTP (*Simple Mail Transfer Protocol*), SOAP (*Simple Object Access Protocol*), Unicode, HTML, and XML.

▶ **Java**
The Java stack of the SAP NetWeaver AS is compliant with the Java 2 Enterprise Edition Platform. The J2EE standard has been defined by SUN Microsystems together with other vendors, including SAP.

▶ **ABAP**
One of the essential application areas of ABAP is the processing of data from the central database. Many of the functions required for this are included in the language content and do not have to be programmed in ABAP itself.

▶ **DB and OS Abstraction**
The SAP NetWeaver platform is supported on most operating systems and databases. There are tools for migrating a running SAP environment from one platform to another. Platform-independence provides a huge business value.

4.2 Introducing SAP ERP

SAP ERP is the current representative in a long and distinguished line of SAP solutions for Enterprise Resource Planning. It is the successor to SAP R/3 and SAP R/3 Enterprise. Users familiar with these will recognize much of the look and feel of those two products. However, SAP ERP, which is powered by the SAP NetWeaver platform, offers a far wider scope of integration into a heterogeneous, standard-based applications environment that is closely linked to the Internet.

From a technical perspective, solutions built on SAP NetWeaver each consist of several software components that can be combined in a variety of ways. For SAP ERP, these components are the following:

▶ The SAP NetWeaver Application Server 7.00 comprises four building blocks: SAP Basis 7.00, SAP ABAP 7.00, SAP BW 7.00, and SAP Basis Plug-in. Several SAP components, such as SAP ERP and SAP SCM, also contain the SAP AP (SAP Application Platform) component.

▶ The SAP ERP Central Component (SAP ECC) version 6.0 contains the core applications (FI, CO, MM, HR, etc.) as well as the SAP plug-in (PI). As of ECC 6.0, the PI is no longer a separate component. It is integrated in the ECC application layer.

▶ The Enterprise Extensions (EA-*) incorporate new functionality that enhances and extends the enterprise core. A SAP ERP system always contains the full set of extensions.

▶ Industry Solutions (IS-*) are specialized solutions directed toward specific industries, for exmaple, utilities, oil, mill products, public transport, and so on. Unlike with ECC 5.0, most of them are part of the standard ERP system.

▶ The Support Tools Plug-In (ST-PI) contains Service Data Control Central, which is used for automatic data collection to provide monitoring and trace tools for service deliveries such as EarlyWatch Alerts. The Support Tools are slightly different for every SAP solution, and different plug-ins exist.

▶ The Application-specific tools for SAP Support Services (ST-A/PI) contain the Application Monitor, the Service Tools Update program, and the ABAP trace for EarlyWatch and Go-live support. As with the Support Tools, a plug-in exists for each SAP solution.

The component layout displayed in Figure 4.2 shows how SAP ERP is built up. To illustrate the modular architecture of SAP solutions, the figure also shows (on the right) the structure of another solution, SAP Supply Chain Management (SCM). As you can see, ERP and SCM share a common technological platform, NetWeaver AS 7.00, which supports the core component of the solution (ECC 6.0 for SAP ERP, SCM 5.00 for SAP SCM). On the SAP ERP side, ECC 6.0 forms the foundation for the Extension Set 6.00 and the Industry Solutions.

Most members of the SAP NetWeaver product group run on the same application server. This common technology base has great advantages from a system-management point of view. Many administrative and technical functions are the same in all solutions, for example, security and output management, performance and tuning, backup and recovery, system and process monitoring, development, and software logistics (change and transport management). This is also true for upgrades; whether you are upgrading an ERP, SCM, CRM (customer relationship management), or BW (Business Information Management) system, the tools and methodology are essentially the same.

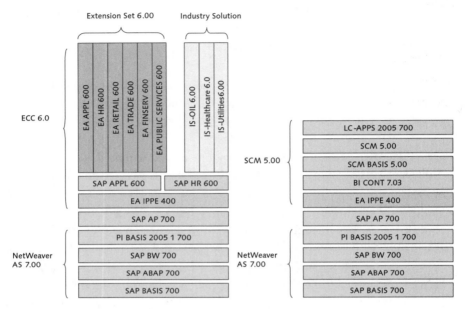

Figure 4.2 The SAP NetWeaver Application Server 7.00 with ECC 6.0 and SCM 5.0

To some extent, components within a solution may also be upgraded independently of one another. For example, the PI_BASIS can be upgraded without also having to upgrade any other component in the system. Extension Sets can be upgraded (as a group, not individually), while leaving the core component unchanged.[1]

4.3   Names and Numbers: An Overview of SAP Releases

There are sound marketing reasons behind the renaming of SAP's ERP software from SAP R/3 to SAP R/3 Enterprise to SAP ERP. As we often experience, however, it has also created a good deal of confusion among the user community. This is exacerbated by the shift from a "monolithic" architecture toward one with multiple components, each with its own name and release track.

---

1   This possibility was used in SAP R/3 Enterprise, where SAP released two versions of the extension set (1.10 and 2.00) while retaining the same 4.70 core. At present SAP, ERP does not provide separate upgrade paths for the Extensions, but the possibility is of course still there.

Table 4.1 should make things clearer. For each major release (intermediate releases such as 4.5A and 4.6B are left out), the table shows the version number of the Basis (technology) layer, the core applications, and the application extensions.

Release	SAP Basis	Core Applications	Extensions
SAP R/3 3.1I	3.1I	–	–
SAP R/3 4.0B	4.0B	–	–
SAP R/3 4.5B	4.5B	–	–
SAP R/3 4.6C	4.6C	–	–
SAP R/3 Enterprise 470x110	6.20	4.70	1.10
SAP R/3 Enterprise 470x200	6.20	4.70	2.00
SAP ERP 5.0	6.40	5.00	5.00
SAP ERP 6.0	7.00	6.00	6.00

Table 4.1 SAP ERP Releases and Components

Until SAP R/3 4.6C, the Basis and core applications formed a single component with a single release number. Extensions did not exist (Industry Solutions — not shown in the table — did). With the advent of the SAP Web AS (today known as SAP NetWeaver AS), SAP Basis became an independent component,[2] and SAP R/3 Enterprise introduced both the concept of extensions and that of a separate SAP Basis release. This structure persists in SAP ERP; here the extensions have the same release code as the core, but this is a matter of choice and not of necessity.

4.4   Support Packages and Add-ons

As of SAP Basis Release 3.0D, SAP delivers support packages to remove any errors that appear in important transactions. A *support package* is a bundle of corrections that fixes errors in the ABAP repository. They are available for download through the Software Distribution Center at the SAP Service Marketplace (*http://service.sap.com/PATCHES*).

Like the R/3 software, support packages started off as "monolithic" entities. Each support package contained corrections for all components in the system, the technological areas, the development environment, and the business applica-

---

2   Actually, the first independent SAP Basis release was 4.6D, but there was never an R/3 product that was based on this release. 4.6D was followed by 6.10, which was also not used for R/3.

tions. This remained so until SAP R/3 4.5B. In Release 4.6, separate support package queues were created for the Basis component (SAP_BASIS), the development environment (SAP_ABA), and the applications (SAP_APPL). There was also a fourth type for Human Resources (SAP_HR).

In SAP R/3 Enterprise and SAP ERP, each component has its own support package queue. For a standard SAP ERP installation, this results in no less than 20 types: 5 for the SAP NetWeaver AS (SAP_BASIS, SAP_ABA, SAP_BW, SAP_AP, and PI_BASIS), 2 for the SAP ECC (SAP_APPL and SAP_HR), 1 for each of the 12 extensions, and not to forget, the plug-ins for the Support Tools and Application Specific Tools for SAP Support. This approach is consistent with the modular architecture of NetWeaver-based solutions, but it raises issues of compatibility: Can you freely decide to install SAP_BASIS patch X along with SAP_BW patch Y, SAP_APPL patch Z, and so on?

To address this looming problem, SAP introduced the concept of *Support Package Stacks* (SP Stacks). SP Stacks are fully tested combinations of patches for a diverse set of components. Installing an SP stack rather than a self-determined set of patches will guarantee that no compatibility issues between patches of different components arise.

Deciding on a target patch level is an important preparatory task, driven both by business and technical requirements. Determining a proper patch strategy is a trade-off between the need for reliability and the need for stability. Upgrade projects will often go for the highest SP stack available at the time of the first upgrade in the landscape. For all following upgrades, up to the production system, they will then stay with this same SP stack unless there are very compelling reasons to go higher.

We return to the subject of support packages and SP Stacks in Section 6.6.

4.5   The System Switch Upgrade

In the past, an SAP system was upgraded using the *repository switch upgrade* mechanism. Although the new repository was first imported into shadow tables, which already reduced downtime significantly compared to the 3.x upgrades, long-running phases such as data dictionary activation, binding support packages, and table conversions had to be done in the downtime phases of the upgrade.

As of Web Application Server 6.10, SAP introduced the so-called *system switch upgrade*. With this method, the majority of the upgrade work — including customer development, modifications, activation, and distribution — is done in a protected area of the database during uptime. During the upgrade, a second "shadow" instance is installed in the same database as the source system to be upgraded (see Figure 4.3). The shadow instance uses the same kernel as the target release but only offers functions needed by the upgrade mechanism. No access to application data is possible. The shadow instance is used to adjust the delivered target release according to the customer requirements and to integrate support packages, add-ons, and customer modifications into the target release while the system is still being used productively.

In the production database, the new repository is created in shadow tables under an alternative name. The shadow system enables you to access these tables. If you choose an upgrade strategy that is downtime-minimized, you can perform upgrade actions that previously had to be performed during downtime before downtime starts. Several phases may run during uptime, such as activation and distribution. As a consequence of the modification adjustment, activation, and distribution during uptime, the new table layout is already known in an early stage of the upgrade. This increases the number of tables in which data can be loaded in the shadow import and the number of tables that can the take part in the Incremental Table Conversion (ICNV).

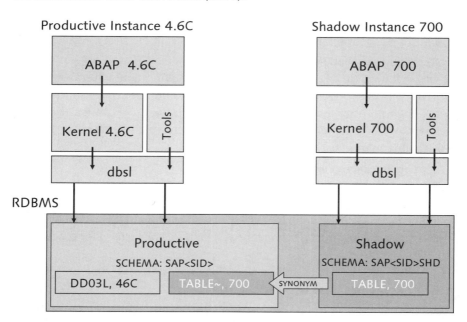

Figure 4.3 The System Switch Upgrade with the Shadow Instance

All DDIC (*Data Dictionary*) objects are adjusted and activated in the shadow instance. Afterwards, a distribution program calculates how to achieve the transition from an object in the source release to the target. This phase can take up to several hours. As both DDIC modification and activation run during uptime, downtime is no longer dependent on the number of support packages or add-ons included in the upgrade. During the downtime phases, the switch is made to the new system, and any remaining data is imported. Any parts of the source release system that are no longer needed are deleted.

The System Switch Upgrade, in contrast to the Repository Switch Upgrade, has the following consequences on the methodology of the technical upgrade:

▶ **Increased resource and space requirements**
Operating the shadow instance in parallel with the production instance increases demands on system resources. The shadow instance can be installed on a separate server, if the available system resources on the productive instance are too limited.

▶ **The shadow instance**
The Installation module of the PREPARE program is used to install the shadow instance. PREPARE first creates profiles, directories, as well as an extra database user, and copies programs and files needed by the shadow instance. All tables needed for the SAP Web Application Server are imported into the database. Additional table contents are copied into the shadow system to enable adjustment, activation, and distribution functions in the shadow system.

▶ **Operating the shadow system**
The shadow system is used to perform the modification adjustment of the ABAP Dictionary objects and activate and distribute the requests included in the upgrade. After the modification adjustment, there is a consistent inactive repository with the descriptions of the table structures of the target release, including support packages and add-ons.

▶ **Support packages and add-ons**
The total runtime of the upgrade increases with the number of support packages integrated into the upgrade, especially the import phase into the shadow tables and the activation phase, which expand enormously. Fortunately, these run in the shadow instance while the system is still being used for production.

4.6   Upgrade Strategy Planning

The System Switch Upgrade strategy can be either resource-minimized or downtime-minimized. Choose the strategy that is best suited to your SAP system and to your requirements concerning system availability. The decision depends on two factors: maximum permitted downtime and available system resources. The two strategies are compared in Table 4.2.

Strategy	Advantages	Disadvantages
Downtime-minimized	Shorter downtime	Increased demand on system resources due to parallel operation of production and shadow system
Resource-minimized	No additional system resources during upgrade	Longer downtime

Table 4.2 Comparison of Upgrade Strategies

The resource-minimized strategy provides the following features:

▶ Operation of the production and shadow system are only possible independently of each other, and therefore no additional resources are needed.

▶ Production operation stops before the import of the substitution set into the shadow tables or, at the least, before the shadow instance is started for the first time.

▶ The Incremental Table Conversion (ICNV, see also Section 10.13) is not used. All tables are converted during downtime, which begins in an early stage of the upgrade.

The downtime-minimized strategy has the following features:

▶ Higher demand on system resources. The shadow system is running next to the production system. If needed, the shadow instance can be installed on a separate server.

▶ The modification adjustment of the ABAP Dictionary objects is performed before downtime. This is possible because the complete version management is available in the shadow system.

▶ Activation and distribution of all ABAP Dictionary objects that the SAP upgrade and the support packages included with the upgrade modify in the delivered release, as well as objects that are modified or created by the customer. Where many included support packages or add-ons are involved or where systems have been modified greatly, this procedure may take several hours. Fortunately, the duration of the activation is not an issue in the downtime-minimized method because it runs in the shadow system while the system is still being used in production.

▶ The number of candidates for the incremental table conversion is increased, given that the target structure of the tables can be calculated at the customer site. Transaction ICNV can therefore be used for tables modified by customers, add-ons, and support packages. This is particularly noticeable in the shorter downtime for upgrades that include one or more add-ons.

▶ The shadow system is used to calculate the target release state of a table before downtime starts. Because the shadow tables are created in their final structure during production operation, the number of tables into which data can be imported in advance can be increased. Until now, this was only possible for new tables and substituted tables.

▶ Because these processes occur during production operation, downtime is reduced considerably, and some phases of downtime are much shorter. In contrast to the Repository Switch Upgrade procedure, downtime is independent of the number of languages, support packages, and add-ons included in the upgrade.

The upgrade strategy determines how much downtime is involved. Figure 4.4 shows the course of the upgrade for both strategies. The upgrade is divided into phases. In terms of downtime, EU_IMPORT1, REQSTOPPROD, and MODPROF_TRANS are important phases because they mark the start of downtime (depending on the chosen upgrade and archiving strategy). The course of the upgrade is identical in all strategies up to the EU_IMPORT1 phase. For the resource-minimized strategy, the downtime either begins in the EU_IMPORT1 phase or the REQSTOPPROD phase. For the downtime-minimized strategy, downtime begins in the MODPROF_TRANS phase.

The following factors influence the total runtime of the upgrade:

▶ **Available hardware resources**
Many upgrade phases can run in parallel. Increasing the number of parallel processes will reduce the overall runtime of the upgrade but might have a performance impact on the SAP system.

▶ **Size of tables**
The duration of table conversions and data conversions depends on the size of the tables and the amount of data to convert. There is no direct correlation between the size of the database and the duration of the upgrade.

▶ **Modifications to standard SAP objects**
The duration of the activation phase is affected by how many of these modifications are made.

▶ **The number of clients**
This has a direct impact on the duration of the data conversions, as they cascade in every client.

▶ **Languages**
The more languages installed, the more data that needs to be imported.

The upgrade runtime and downtime depend on the upgrade strategy you choose, the hardware, and the amount of time required to create the database backups.

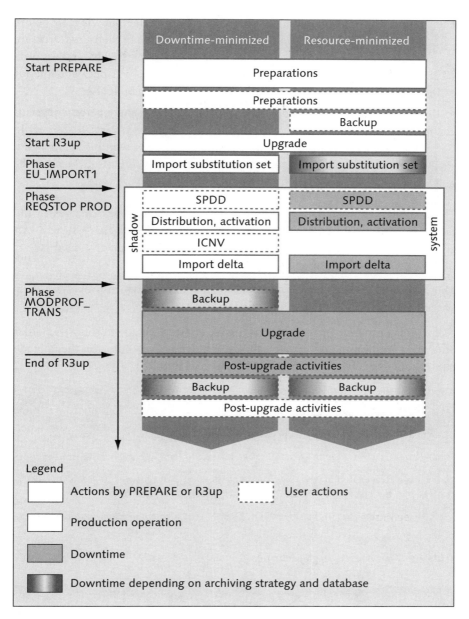

Figure 4.4 Course of the Upgrade

With the downtime-minimized strategy, the shadow system runs in parallel with the production system. This increases the overall runtime but shortens downtime. The size of your database only has a secondary role in determining the runtime of the upgrade.

The runtime of the upgrade can be minimized by doing the following:

► Deleting unnecessary clients

► Archiving unnecessary business data

► Using the downtime-minimized upgrade strategy with the ICNV

► Decoupling the SAP R/3 upgrade from the database and operating system upgrades

4.7 Database-Specific Aspects

The archiving strategy defines how the database system saves changes to the database. This in turn determines to which extent the database system can recover lost data. Archiving must always be activated for productive databases. It may be deactivated during the downtime phases of the upgrade.

This subject is discussed in more detail in Appendix C, which provides a database-specific overview of archiving modes.

The upgrade program prompts you at the start of the upgrade to choose whether and when you want to deactivate database archiving. Depending on the upgrade strategy, the options shown in Table 4.3 are available.

Archiving Strategy	Downtime-Minimized	Resource-Minimized
Archiving is activated during the entire upgrade.	Possible	Possible
Archiving is deactivated in the EU_IMPORT1 phase.	Not applicable	Recommended
Archiving is deactivated before you start the shadow instance for the first time in the REQSTOPPROD phase.	Not recommended	Recommended
Archiving is deactivated in the MODPROF_TRANS phase.	Recommended	Not applicable

Table 4.3 Archiving and Upgrade Strategy Options

Caution

After you have deactivated archiving, you must no longer use the SAP system in production operation.

The archiving strategies that are marked as "recommended" ensure that you can run your SAP system in production mode as long as possible. The archiving strategies that are marked as "possible" are only useful in certain cases.

> **Caution**
>
> If you specified during PREPARE that you are performing the upgrade in a Multiple Components in One Database System (MCOD—see Section 4.8 later in this chapter), meaning that multiple SAP systems are installed in your database, then the upgrade will not prompt you about archiving. The reason is that SAP systems that are not being upgraded remain in normal use and therefore should be able to log data changes.

The upgrade strategy defines the downtime and resource usage. The archiving mode is dependent on the upgrade strategy chosen and is specified separately. The archiving strategy, however, defines when production operation ceases and downtime begins.

As displayed in Figure 4.5, for the downtime-minimized strategy, archiving can be switched off when the shadow instance is started for the first time. This is not recommended because the system is still being used in production. In addition, on most database systems, downtime is needed to switch the archiving mode. Archiving can also be deactivated at the beginning of the downtime or left on during the entire course of the upgrade.

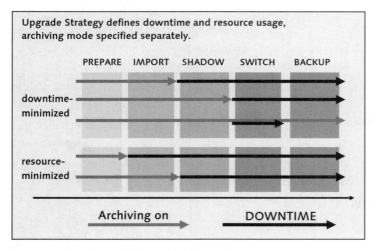

Figure 4.5 The Upgrade Strategy and Downtime

For the resource-minimized strategy, archiving can be switched off at the beginning of the import or at the start of the shadow instance. Archiving should be deactivated when productive operation ceases.

If archiving is deactivated at some stage during the upgrade, you have to make a full backup of the database before you switch archiving back on. The archiving strategy that you choose also determines when you will need to make a full backup of the database.

If you choose the downtime-minimized upgrade strategy, the full backup is made at the beginning of downtime, that is, before the MODPROF_TRANS phase. If you choose the resource-minimized upgrade strategy, the full backup is made before the substitution set (the new repository) is imported, either during production operation or during downtime.

As a general recommendation, you should always take a full backup after the upgrade and before the system is released to the end users.

4.8 Upgrades in an MCOD System Landscape

With Multiple Components in one Database (MCOD), several independent SAP components can be installed in one database. Every component uses a different database user schema. Different table spaces are used if the database system uses the table- space concept. We do not recommend deploying an R/3 system, which is an OLTP (online transaction processing) application, with BW or SCM, which are OLAP (online analytical processing) applications. Installing CRM and EBP (Enterprise Buyer Professional) with R/3 might be an option to consider, for the following reasons:

▶ CRM and SRM read and write data from and to the backend system (R/3). They need the backend system to function correctly.

▶ CRM, SRM, and R/3 are OLTP applications. All of them are running on the Application Server ABAP.

▶ CRM and SRM systems are most often not very large. In most installations, they do not represent more than 10 % of the total size of the R/3 system.

▶ CRM and SRM should always be in sync with the backend system. If they share the same database, they remain in sync even after a point-in-time recovery. A consistent backup/restore/point-in-time-recovery of the complete landscape is possible.

The following should be taken into account when upgrading in an MCOD environment:

▶ The database user, tablespaces (DB2 UDB and Oracle), dbspaces (Informix), or devspaces (MaxDB) of an MCOD system always contain the SID (SAP system ID). Table 4.4 shows an example of an MCOD system with CRM, EBP, and R/3. All SAP instances share the same database. Each SAP instance, however, has its own set of table spaces and database schema.

	CRM	EBP	R3
SID	CRP	EBP	PRD
DBSID	DB1	DB1	DB1
DB SCHEMA	SAPCRP	SAPEBP	SAPPRD
TABLESPACE	PSAPCRP	PSAPEBP	PSAPPRD
	PSAPCRPUSR	PSAPEBPUSR	PSAPPRDUSR

Table 4.4 Layout of an MCOD System with CRM, EBP, and R/3

▶ Do not switch off archiving when upgrading in an MCOD system landscape. All SAP systems in the database are affected if you need to reset the upgrade.

▶ PREPARE[3] asks you at the start of the upgrade whether more than one SAP system is installed in the database. If more than one SAP system is installed in the database, do not switch off archiving during the upgrade. The upgrade tools will no longer prompt you to deactivate archiving.

▶ Using parallel processes during the upgrade might affect the performance of the other MCOD components.

▶ Downtime is needed on all components during the downtime phases of the component being upgraded. If the upgrade fails during these phases, a database restore up to the beginning of the downtime is the only option. This affects all components in the database (see Figure 4.6).

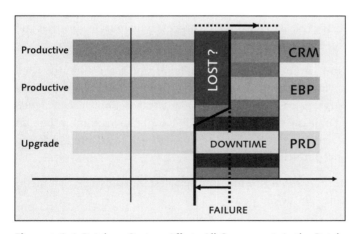

Figure 4.6 A Database Restore Affects All Components in the Database

---

3 PREPARE is one of the most important phases of the upgrade. It prepares the upgrade tools and verifies whether the system is ready to be upgraded. It is discussed in detail in Chapter 9.

4.9 The SAP Landscape During the Upgrade

Upgrading to the next release of SAP has an impact on the SAP landscape. Your SAP systems will be at a different release level during several stages of the upgrade project. During this time, support for the production system must be guaranteed. In this section, we discuss the impact of the upgrade on the SAP landscape and the different options to deal with the issues involved.

4.9.1 The Impact of the Upgrade on the Landscape

In a standard three-system SAP environment, you upgrade your development system, quality assurance, and the production system. However, there is much more to do than just upgrading: The impact of the new SAP release on the existing environment can be enormous. Ideally, every business process should be retested for its functionality in the new release. In addition, the customer development objects (e.g., reports), the interfaces to the outside world, and the authorization schemes must be tested to ensure that they still function as expected.

While the new SAP release is being tested and adapted to meet expectations, ongoing changes to the production system must be kept up. An upgrade project might extend over several months. Prohibiting every single change to the production system during all that time is unrealistic, as maintenance and support of the production environment simply cannot be suspended. Instead, these changes must be taken into consideration as part of the upgrade project; your mission is to find a solution for maintaining two release tracks without conflict or disruption. Because change management is so critical to the upgrade process, you must ensure that you have a system landscape that makes change management as easy as possible.

Another important aspect influencing the system landscape is the potential need for a training system. This is especially important if there is a sizeable difference between source and target release. For example, many transactions have changed considerably between release 4.0B and SAP ERP. To obtain maximum benefit from the new release, end users will need training to get acquainted with the new layout and enhanced functionality.

The following prerequisites should be met before a system landscape that meets the project requirements can be defined:

▶ A project plan for the upgrade has been created and approved by all parties involved.

▶ Key parameters have been identified, such as the acceptable duration of development freeze and maximum permitted downtime for the upgrade on the production system.

▶ Dependencies on current and planned projects have been identified.

▶ The hardware requirements and the availability of additional hardware for the temporary systems have been defined.

These prerequisites determine which of the strategies are applicable to a particular landscape.

4.9.2 Scenarios for the Landscape Setup

There are three options for setting up the landscape:

▶ **With a sandbox system**
Rehearsal of the upgrade process on a separate, standalone R/3 sandbox system, with the intent of rolling out the upgrade to the production landscape at a later point in time.

▶ **With extra development and quality assurance systems**
Upgrade is done on a copy of development and after a period of time on a copy of acceptance. The old development and acceptance systems are used for contingencies during the upgrade project and disappear after the release upgrade of production. This strategy is often used if the hardware needs to be replaced before the release upgrade because of insufficient resources. In this strategy, production is copied to new hardware before it is upgraded to the new release. The move of the new hardware can be done independently from the upgrade project.

▶ **With a contingency system**
Upgrade of the development system happens right away, followed after a certain period of time by the upgrade of the acceptance and production system. A temporary development system is installed to support the production system in the old release.

4.9.3 Scenario 1: The Sandbox System

The sandbox system is, in most cases, a copy of the production system. After the technical upgrade, functional consultants, ABAP programmers, and key users can start with the adaptation of the new SAP functionality to the customer requirements and vice versa. This *adaptation phase* can take from several weeks to six months. The upgrade is only started on the productive SAP landscape when functional consultants, ABAP developers, key users, and the Basis administrator feel comfortable with the process. The advantage of the sandbox method is that it can be rehearsed as many times as needed. The sandbox system can easily be destroyed and re-created as another copy of one of the existing systems.

Before you create the sandbox system, you have to decide which of the existing R/3 systems should be used as the source. In a standard three-system landscape, the development system, quality-assurance system, and production system each has characteristics that make it more or less ideal than the others for this purpose.

The best choice is the production system because it contains real-world application data. A roadblock might be the volume of the production system. If it is a large database, it might exceed the available disk storage space, in which case you would need to purchase additional space.

If the production system is too large, the quality-assurance system is a good second choice. If managed correctly, the quality-assurance and production systems should be functionally identical. They differ only in the volume of application data present in the system. If this is the case, the quality-assurance system is a perfect choice because it allows for valid functional tests without requiring duplication of enormous amounts of application data. However, in many SAP environments, the quality-assurance system is refreshed with production data regularly. The same disk-storage problem is likely to occur.

A development system is the least ideal system. Its repository is most "out of sync" with the other systems. It probably contains a lot of try-outs that might cause problems during the release upgrade, which will never occur during the upgrade of the production system. In addition, it is unlikely to contain any valid master or transaction data.

The current TMS (Transport Management System) configuration does not need to be changed if the upgrade is rehearsed on a sandbox system. A transport route needs to be created for the upgrade system (here called "UPG") if you want to export changes from the sandbox to then import them again between two upgrade rehearsals. As shown in Figure 4.7, this can be accomplished by defining a virtual system (here called "VIR") as a consolidation system for the sandbox system UPG.

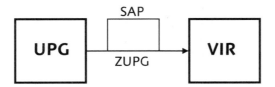

Figure 4.7 TMS Configuration for the Sandbox System

In addition, you must also define a transport route for customer objects. In Figure 4.7 this is the route ZUPG between UPG and the virtual system. Without this route, change requests created in UPG are not transportable and cannot be exported out of the system. If your policy is to allow modifications of SAP objects during the upgrade process, then you also need to establish the SAP transport route between these two systems. The VIR transport buffer contains a sequential list of the changes exported from UPG. If you need to import these changes into another system or back into UPG after a refresh, you can copy the transport buffer at the operating system level and use it to perform the import.

During the upgrade project, the production-system landscape is constantly being changed. There are two methods of integrating these changes into the sandbox:

▶ **Manually reenter all changes in the sandbox**
This might be difficult to maintain if there is a high volume of production changes. Business processes might change between SAP releases making the manual reentry of the modification impossible.

▶ **Introduce changes at the next refresh**
Instead of bringing production-support changes directly into the sandbox, wait with for the next refresh and upgrade rehearsal. The higher the volume of production changes, the higher the frequency with which the sandbox system needs to be refreshed. The number of refreshes should be decided upon in an early stage of the project.

4.9.4 Scenario 2: Extra Development and Quality-Assurance Systems

The development and acceptance instance are copied to new hardware and upgraded to the target release. The old development and acceptance systems are used for ongoing support of the production system only. The advantage of this setup is that both development and acceptance are upgraded, and the old development and acceptance remain for contingency. This scenario is often used to replace the current hardware environment because it has insufficient resources to support the target SAP release.

The existing TMS configuration needs to be changed after copying the development and acceptance to the new systems. If you keep the system names (DEV and ACC) and rename the original systems, the ownership of the customer objects moves with the copied systems. Modifications to those in the original systems will be treated as repairs.

Because you no longer want automatic transports from the old DEV (DV2) or QAS (QA2) to PRD, the delivery route between those systems needs to be deleted. A new delivery route needs to be created between the new development and acceptance systems, which is identical to the one that previously existed.

A virtual system (shown as VIR in Figure 4.8) needs to be created as a delivery system from the new quality assurance system. The transport buffer for this non-existent system represents the transport requests that should be applied to the production system after the upgrade, in their proper import sequence. Keep in mind that these changes should include all the changes made to support the production environment, as those changes should have been manually entered in DEV and transported to QAS along with upgrade-related changes. With proper testing and quality control, applying these changes after PRD has been upgraded should not be harmful.

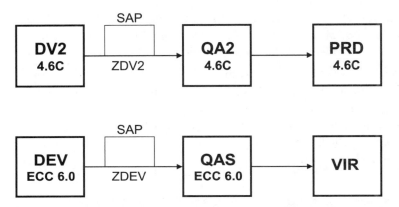

Figure 4.8 TMS Configuration with Extra Development and Quality-Assurance Systems

Again, you need to decide whether modifications to SAP objects are allowed in DV2 and add the "SAP" transport routes to the configuration accordingly. In addition, you need to determine whether to permit changes to customer-owned objects in DV2. These objects would be treated as repairs in DV2 because they would still reflect that the originating system was DEV. If your policy is to allow these changes to be made and transported to PRD, set up the ZDV2 transport route accordingly.

The advantage of the second method is that it reduces the overall time required to upgrade by minimizing the actual number of upgrades necessary to move the entire landscape to the new release. The reason for this is that only three upgrades are ultimately required to get the entire landscape to the new release. In addition, the upgrade can be rehearsed on the new acceptance system as many times as needed.

4.9.5   Scenario 3: Contingency System

The development system is upgraded right away, without prior testing on a separate sandbox system. After a period of time, the quality-assurance system is upgraded, followed by the upgrade of the production system. For ongoing support of the productive system, a secondary development system is built. The advantage of this method is that it reduces the overall time needed to upgrade by minimizing the actual number of upgrades necessary to move the entire landscape to the new release. Ultimately, only three upgrades are needed to get the entire landscape to the new release.

The existing TMS configuration needs to be changed, as you no longer want automatic transports from DEV or QAS to PRD. The delivery route between those systems needs to be deleted. Between the temporary development system and production, a new delivery route needs to be created that is nearly identical to the one that previously existed.

A virtual system (shown as VIR in Figure 4.9) needs to be created as the delivery system from the acceptance system. The transport buffer for this nonexistent system represents the transport requests that should be applied to the production system after the upgrade, in their proper import sequence.

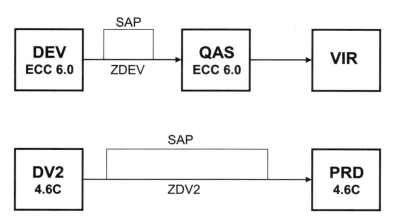

Figure 4.9 TMS Configuration for the Temporary Method

Again, you need to decide whether modifications to SAP objects are allowed in DV2 and add the SAP transport routes to the configuration accordingly. In addition, you need to determine whether to permit changes to customer-owned objects in DV2. These objects would be treated as repairs in DV2 because they would still reflect that the originating system was DEV. If your policy is to allow these changes to be made and transported to PRD, set up the ZDV2 transport route accordingly.

The advantage of this method is that it reduces the overall time required to upgrade by minimizing the actual number of upgrades necessary to move the entire landscape to the new release. The reason for this is that only three upgrades are ultimately required.

Incorporating production support changes remains an issue with this method. However, the upgraded systems will never be rebuilt or refreshed. Therefore, you must re-enter all production support changes in DEV manually. This method is suitable for more stable production systems (e.g., those with relatively few changes being introduced) or those upgrade projects that are relatively simple in their scope and complexity.

4.10   Upgrading the Frontend Software

The frontend software (SAP GUI) needs to be compatible with the new SAP system release. If the frontend software you are using on the source release is not compatible with the target release, the latest possible time for upgrading the frontend software is before you start the shadow system for the first time. If you need or want to use different frontend software, you can import it as soon as you receive the software package; the newer frontend releases are always backward compatible with older SAP versions.

> **Note**
>
> You can use the SAP frontend installation software, SAPSetup, to optimize the deployment of SAP GUI to thousands of clients. You can tailor installation packages to match your requirements, distribute patches, and set up automatic update processes for your clients. For more information on installing the frontend software and using SAPSetup, see the *SAP Front End Installation Guide*. The guide is available, together with all installations and upgrade guides, at *http://service.sap.com*.

4.11   The Customer-Based Upgrade

The Customer-Based Upgrade (CBU) is a special upgrade procedure designed to significantly reduce the overall downtime when you upgrade the SAP production system. Downtime is already reduced thanks to the downtime-minimized upgrade strategy. CBU attempts to reduce the downtime even further by including all customer-specific adjustments, which are normally done after the upgrade.

During CBU, a customer-specific repository is imported into the productive system as opposed to the standard repository released by SAP.

CBU consists of the following steps, also shown in Figure 4.10:

▶ **Step 1:** A copy of the production system is created and installed on a sandbox system. At this point, changes to the repository in the production system are no longer allowed.

▶ **Step 2:** The copy is upgraded to the new release using the standard procedure. Modifications are taken over from development and quality assurance, which were upgraded earlier. After the upgrade, all customer-specific transports are imported into the system. ABAP loads can be generated as well (SGEN), and these generated objects will be integrated into the customer repository. After this phase, an exact target customer-specific repository exists.

▶ **Step 3:** The target repository is exported. The directory structure looks like the standard export CD set.

▶ **Step 4:** To ensure that the CD set is created correctly, it has to be validated. Production is copied again to the sandbox.

▶ **Step 5:** Production is upgraded using the CBU CD set.

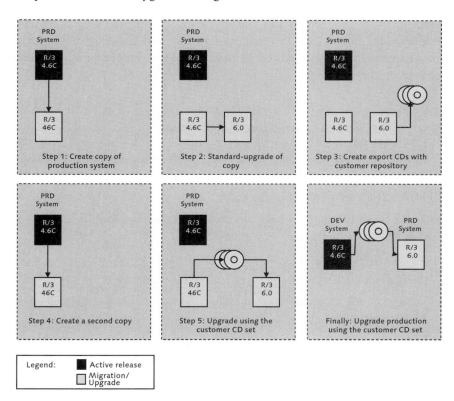

Figure 4.10 The Customer-Based Upgrade

The following requirements must be met before CBU can be performed:

▶ Transports from development must be available for the modification adjustment and adjustments for your own development objects.

▶ Changes to the repository of production are no longer allowed. Any fix transport may cause unexpected problems as the change in the repository was not foreseen in the target repository.

The benefits of CBU include the following:

▶ No modification adjustments needed.

▶ No transports after upgrade. All modifications are included in the customer-upgrade CD set.

▶ Report loads pregenerated and part of export data.

▶ Reductions in application adjustment.

▶ Accurate timing for production upgrade.

The System Switch Upgrade with the shadow instances has greatly reduced the need for CBU. CBU complicates and lengthens the upgrade project. CBUs are only intended for use in SAP environments with many customer-developed systems that need to be adapted for the new SAP release before the system can be used again in production.

4.12   The Application Specific Upgrade

The Application Specific Upgrade (ASU) is a toolbox that assists developers and customizing consultants with the resolution of "known" problems during and after the release upgrade.

After the technical upgrade has been finished, numerous problems are discovered during the initial testing. For example:

▶ Transactions no longer function as expected or in different ways than before the upgrade. Other transactions generate short dumps or error messages

▶ Variants of ABAP programs can no longer be used because the corresponding ABAP program has changed.

▶ Customer user exits no longer work because the structure of tables has changed.

The ASU toolbox is a collection of reports, conversions programs, and documentation. It is the entry point of all upgrade information and problem resolution:

▶ The *Application Specific Upgrade* guide is a collection of known application problems before, during, and after the upgrade. Documentation exists for the most-used SAP modules. The documentation contains detailed descriptions of upgrade-related problems or changes occurring during the upgrade and is based on problems reported by customers. The guides are constantly being revised and updated.

▶ The Application Specific Repair toolbox is a collection of reports that do necessary conversions in the system after the upgrade. Most of these reports are attached to SAP Notes. The ASU Repair toolbox is an easy to use central entry point for all correction programs. The conversion programs are explained in detail in the ASU upgrade guides.

▶ The Variant Save tool is used for the conversion of variants; programs change during the release upgrade, and data supplied in the variants might no longer be valid. SAP developed a tool that stores the content of variants in transparent tables. These tables are preserved during the upgrade. Variants can easily be adjusted to the new report in the new release after the upgrade.[4]

The ASU toolbox is used by developers and customizing consultants. The Basis administrator is responsible for its installation. It consists of several transports, some should be imported before, and others should be imported after the release upgrade. The ASU toolbox is delivered through SAP Note 623723. The ASU upgrade guides and the transports for the ASU Repair and Variant Save tool are attached to this note.

4.13 Synchronized Upgrade of Double-Stacked Systems

To minimize overall downtime, the upgrade of the SAP AS Java is synchronized with the upgrade of the SAP AS ABAP. If you run a Web application server with ABAP and Java in the same instance, you have to upgrade them in parallel. The look and feel of the ABAP upgrade tools has been changed to that of the Java Web AS to make this process easier to comprehend. The two upgrade processes require synchronization that affects the upgrade process, user management, profile changes and kernel switch, beginning of downtime, and upgrade reset.

As of AS 7.00, the J2EE engine is part of any standard SAP AS. The new upgrade tools for the AS Java are comparable to those of the AS ABAP: Java Upgrade Man-

---

4 When you upgrade to SAP ERP 2005, you must not import a transport prior to the upgrade. The ASU variant restorer is part of the tool import in PREPARE. When you select JOB_RASUVAR1(2) in the SAVE_VAR_CHECK phase, you can activate the variant restorer without restricting the source release of the upgrade.

agement Program (the upgrade assistant); PREPARE with the modules Initialization, Extraction, Configuration, General Checks, and Finalization (see Figure 4.11); and upgrade with uptime and downtime phases.

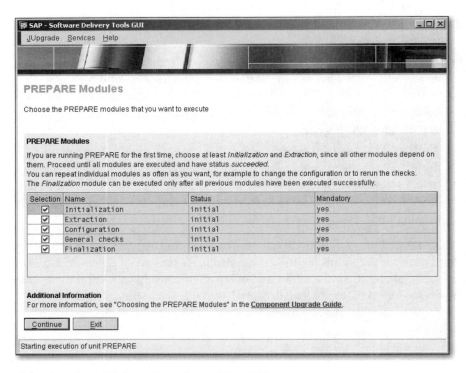

Figure 4.11 PREPARE for an Upgrade to AS Java 7.00

4.13.1 Upgrade Process

The ABAP and Java upgrade need to be synchronized. When you start the upgrade of the ABAP instance, the upgrade tools detect the Java instance and prompt you to start the upgrade of the Java stack as well. In the same way, the upgrade of the Java instance prompt and wait for the upgrade of the ABAP instance.

The upgrade tools synchronize themselves at three points during the upgrade. If one upgrade has already reached a synchronization point, but the other has not, the first one waits. After both have reached the synchronization point, they proceed automatically.

The following synchronization points exist (see Figure 4.12):

▶ **Beginning and end of downtime**
The ABAP upgrade program changes the profile parameters for starting and stopping the SAP system so that the Java instance is not started automatically together with the SAP Web AS ABAP. The Java upgrade program starts and stops the J2EE Engine using internal commands if required.

In addition, if the J2EE User Management Engine (UME) uses ABAP user management, it cannot access this during the downtime phases of the ABAP upgrade. SAPJup therefore switches the UME configuration to data source "local." This is reset automatically at the end of the upgrade.

▶ **Profile changes and Kernel Switch**
If ABAP and Java both run Unicode, only one kernel is used during the productive operation. Some synchronization is therefore needed during the upgrade.

No dependencies exist if the ABAP runs non-Unicode and the Java Unicode because separate kernel directories are used.

▶ **Reset of the upgrade in case of disaster**
If one upgrade fails, both must be rolled back.

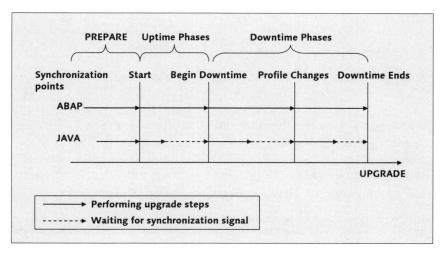

Figure 4.12 Integrated AS ABAP and Java Upgrade, Synchronization Points

4.13.2 Technical Implementation

The upgrade tool SAPup for the ABAP instance and SAPJup for the J2EE instance synchronize automatically via the *SYNC.DAT* file, which resides in the `mig` directory in the `upgrade` directory of the ABAP system (for example, `/usr/sap/put/mig`). A clear message is displayed in the upgrade assistant when an upgrade (SAPup or SAPJup) is waiting for the other to catch up (see Figure 4.13).

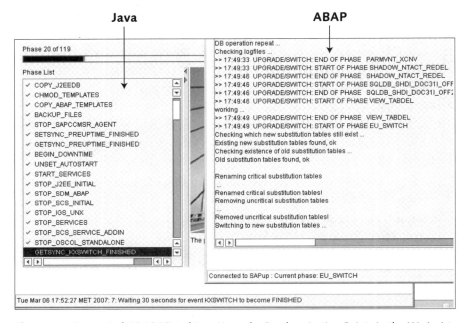

Figure 4.13 Integrated AS ABAP and Java Upgrade, Synchronization Points in the UA Assistant

The naming convention of the synchronization phases is SETSYNC_<PHASE> (for example, SETSYNC_PROFILES_CHANGED, which is set by SAPup when the instance profiles have been changed). Phases waiting for synchronization are called GETSYNC_<PHASE> (for example, GETSYNC_KXXSWITCH_FINISHED, in which SAPJup waits for SAPup to put the new kernel in place).

> **Note**
>
> The upgrade directory for the AS Java is `/usr/sap/jupgrade`. To use an upgrade directory other then the default one, you have to specify the directory when you start PREPARE for the first time.

Chapter 4 gave you an overview of the upgrade process and presented the different upgrade strategies. In this and the following chapters, we shall examine each step in the upgrade process in greater detail. As a starting point before getting into the nuts-and-bolts of the process, let's again look at the major phases of an SAP upgrade.

5 Planning the Upgrade

Before starting to technically prepare the upgrade, a few decisions have to be made: What is the project's time line? Which upgrade strategy do we choose? Will we work in database archiving mode or not?

5.1 Top-Level View

Figure 5.1 provides a top-level view of the upgrade depicted on a time axis. Times are relative to a point X, which denotes the start of downtime. The SAP system is production-capable in the old release up to X, and becomes productive in the new release at the start of the post-upgrade phase (shaded rectangles at bottom).

The pre-upgrade phase encompasses various preparatory activities, both long term and short term. It is difficult to give a precise starting point for this phase, hence the "X − ??" on the time axis. However, the work will start as soon as a release upgrade is being realistically considered. This does not mean that a firm decision to upgrade has been made by then. The functional analysis, capacity-planning exercise, calculation of the financial impact, and other factors can still lead to the upgrade project being delayed or even cancelled. Assuming that the upgrade does take place, the activities in the pre-upgrade phase will become more and more specific as the start of the technical upgrade approaches.

The technical upgrade process is the actual transition of the SAP system from the old to the new release. This transition is carried out by means of SAP utilities, which run under control of the SAP-supplied upgrade control program SAPup. SAPup runs twice, the first time in PREPARE mode and the second time — under its real name — in *upgrade* mode. During this second run, production activity ceases, and the actual switch to the new release happens.

93

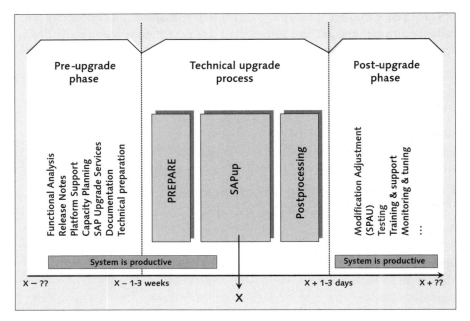

Figure 5.1 Upgrade Phases — the Big Picture

When SAPup is finished, the system is operational in the new release but is not yet ready for normal business use: Customer modifications have not yet been reintegrated, code has not been regenerated, authorizations have not yet been adjusted, and so on. Various postprocessing actions are required to bring the system to a state where it can be released for production use. While these actions take place, the system is inaccessible to all but a few key users, so this postprocessing phase must be considered as downtime (although technically the system is up and running). This is the reason we include the postprocessing in the technical upgrade process.

The release of the system to its end users marks the beginning of the post-upgrade phase. Both the contents and duration of this phase depend on the type of system being upgraded. For development systems, the modification adjustment (bringing custom-made changes to SAP programs, screens, etc. back in line with the new release) will often be the most important task, possibly taking several weeks. In test systems, comprehensive testing of business processes on current or quasi-current production data will dominate the post-upgrade activity. Like the modification adjustment in the development system, these tests may take weeks and involve significant human resources. In production systems, post-upgrade work should be limited mostly to end-user support, monitoring and tuning, and minor problem resolution. Ideally, the duration of the post-upgrade phase in the production system should be near zero, although realistically even a well-prepared and well-performed upgrade will require a few days of "baby-sitting" after the system goes live again.

5.2   Downtime-Minimized Versus Resource-Minimized

With the introduction of the *system switch upgrade* method in SAP Basis 6.10, two upgrade strategies are available: downtime-minimized and resource-minimized. As the names indicate, the downtime-minimized strategy is geared toward reducing downtime (at the expense of using additional server resources), whereas the resource-minimized strategy uses fewer resources but results in longer downtime.

An important technical innovation that emerged with the system switch upgrade is the shadow instance. This *shadow instance* is used for executing part of the upgrade phases that formerly had to run in downtime. The shadow instance already runs on the new release, while the central instance (CI) and dialog instances (application servers) remain on the old release.

Both the downtime-minimized and resource-minimized strategies use the shadow instance but with an important difference. In downtime-minimized mode, the shadow instance runs parallel with the "normal" instance or instances of the system. Because these are not stopped, the system remains productive. In resource-minimized mode, on the other hand, the CI and the application servers must be stopped before the shadow instance becomes active. As a result, no two instances (normal and shadow) are ever active at the same time, a situation that results in less use of resources but longer downtime.

Figure 5.2 illustrates the difference between the two strategies and the effect on upgrade downtime. Major sections of the SAPup process are shown along with the names of the principal upgrade phases. Note that the figure only concerns the SAPup part of the technical upgrade process. The choice of strategy has no influence on PREPARE (which is always uptime) nor on the postprocessing steps (which are always downtime).

In resource-minimized mode, system downtime begins at the start of the data import or, alternatively, when the shadow instance is first started after the data import. Which of these two marks the beginning of downtime depends on the choice of database archiving mode (see Section 4.7). The system then remains in downtime until the end of the technical upgrade process.

In downtime-minimized mode, the data import is always part of uptime, and also the shadow instance runs while the system is still in normal use. After the shadow system shuts down and is discarded, the technical upgrade continues for several more hours in the central instance before it reaches the point (phase MODPROF_TRANS) where downtime must begin.

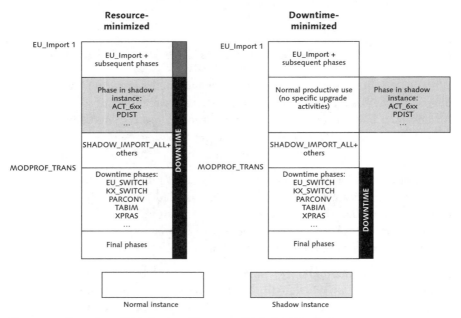

Figure 5.2 Downtime-Minimized and Resource-Minimized Strategies

5.3 Database Archiving Mode

All relational databases have a mechanism, known generically as *transaction logging*, to actively keep track of all changes made to the data. In addition, database systems let you choose between two types of transaction logging:

▶ An *archiving mode* in which all changes are saved in a persistent manner, for example, an external file or a backup tape.

▶ A *nonarchiving mode* in which changes are only preserved until the physical space allocated to the transaction log fills up. When this happens, the transaction log rolls over, and old logs are overwritten.

> **Note**
>
> We are not concerned here with the technical aspects of transaction logging, so we simply use the generic terms *archiving mode* and *nonarchiving mode*. For the correct DBMS-specific terms, see Appendix C.

Recovering from physical or logical damage to the database without data loss is only possible if you have a backup of the database and a backup of all the changes between the time of the backup and the time of the disaster. In other words, your database must be in *archiving* mode if you want to be able to recover all data. This is why most SAP systems will always have their database operate in archiving mode; for production systems, this is mandatory.[1]

During upgrades, the situation is somewhat different. The technical upgrade process imports a massive amount of data into the database, which means that an enormous number of transaction logs will be created. The actual figures vary, but log volumes of 30GB and more (with 10GB or more created in the course of a few hours) are quite possible. As long as the system is productive, this can't be helped: Running in archiving mode is necessary because the database is modified not only by the upgrade programs but also by normal business transactions.

During downtime, however, there is little or no point in archiving all the logs. The downtime part of the upgrade is really an "all-or-nothing" operation. If a serious problem occurs, such as a disk crash or a major upgrade error, then you want to return to the state the system was in at the beginning of downtime, discarding all changes made since that time. Therefore, it makes good sense to switch the database to nonarchiving mode at the beginning of downtime and to return to archiving mode only at the end of SAPup. You can postpone the return to archiving mode even further, to a point in time after the heaviest postprocessing (but of course always *before* releasing the system for production use).

If you decide to perform the downtime part of the upgrade with database log archiving switched off, then you must back up the database before changing the logging mode. A backup after the end of SAPup is always necessary, regardless of the archiving mode; even if your log archiving stayed on during downtime, a roll-forward recovery using a backup made before downtime would have to reapply a very large number of logs and might run for an unacceptably long time.

Looking again at Figure 5.2, you can see that in the downtime-minimized strategy, log archiving must remain enabled up to the MODPROF_TRANS phase because the system is productive until that moment. In resource-minimized mode, you can choose between two different times:

---

1 This does not mean that running in non-archiving mode is useless. Most database systems need the transaction log to roll back incorrect transactions. It is also possible to recover from a crash as long as the database on disk is not physically damaged; that is, you can recover from a software or server failure. Very few databases therefore allow disabling the transaction log entirely, and running without transaction log is never supported for an active SAP system.

▶ **Before the start of the data import (phase EU_IMPORT1)**
This increases the downtime by several hours but improves performance because the overhead of log archiving is eliminated. Furthermore there is no risk of the upgrade getting stuck on an "archive full" situation. As a result, the overall runtime of the upgrade will decrease.

▶ **Before starting the shadow instance for the first time (phase REQSTOP-PROD)**
This reduces downtime at the expense of more overhead during the import.

If we combine the upgrade strategy with the log-archiving mode, then three scenarios are possible, each representing a different trade-off between resource usage and duration of downtime. These are shown in Figure 5.3.

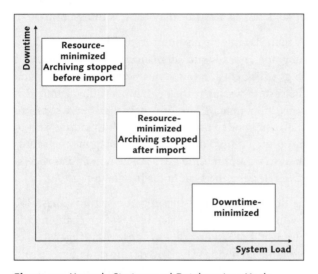

Figure 5.3 Upgrade Strategy and Database Log Mode

5.4 Which Strategy Is the Best?

The answer to this kind of question is usually a more-or-less elaborate version of "it depends." Not so, however, in the case of upgrade strategies — at least in our view. Here we can without hesitation offer clear-cut advice: Use the downtime-minimized strategy.

Why so emphatic an opinion? Except in the unlikely case that you run a very small production system on a hugely powerful server and/or production downtime is of no concern, downtime-minimized will normally be the only acceptable method for your production upgrade. One of the main aims of the upgrades of the test and development systems is to prepare a correct and efficient procedure for the production upgrade. That really means that whatever you will do in production, you must already have done before. Of course, you can never eliminate the risk that a problem will occur for the first time during the production upgrade, but you should not amplify that risk by venturing into uncharted territory!

The argument of lower resource use and thus better performance with the resource-minimized strategy does not hold water either. In our experience, the shadow instance does not create excessive load on the system. A server with a reasonable amount of spare capacity should be able to handle the extra activity without trouble. If the server is loaded to such an extent that it cannot bear the extra load of the shadow instance, then how can you expect it to cope with the new release and its increased resource requirements?

Finally, the downtime-minimized strategy truly delivers on its promise: It drastically reduces downtime. For the system switch-based upgrade, we have carried out so far, the downtime part of SAPup mostly ran between five and eight hours. Longer runtimes are possible, for instance, due to large offline table conversions or long-running data conversion (XPRA) programs, but these will become apparent during the test upgrades. The shortened downtime makes it possible to plan the production upgrade during a normal two-day weekend. In a typical scenario, the upgrade would enter downtime late on Friday evening. The SAPup would be ready by Saturday morning (even allowing time for a backup), at which time postprocessing would start. This should be ready by late afternoon, leaving Saturday night free for another backup, an update of the database statistics, and other tasks. Key users then have all Sunday to do their testing. If they give the green light, the end users then find the system ready for business on Monday morning.

5.5   Time Schedule for Technical Upgrade

To assist you in setting up a workable schedule for the production upgrade, we will give a practical timing example of the technical upgrade process. The example, described in Table 5.1, assumes that the downtime-minimized strategy is used and that a database backup takes four hours. The schedule is comfortable in that there is a large safety margin for the completion of the uptime part of SAPup (36 hours, from Thursday 6 a.m. to Friday 6 p.m.), and there is even slack time during the upgrade weekend.

Time	Uptime/ Downtime	Activity
Saturday (week 1)	DOWN	Upgrade DBMS (if necessary). Set database and SAP profile parameters (e.g., DIR_PUT) to values required for upgrade (if necessary).
Monday 9 a.m.	UP	Start PREPARE.
Monday 5 p.m.	UP	PREPARE ends. Review and correct PREPARE errors. Restart PREPARE.
Tuesday 9 a.m.	UP	Start SAPup. Slow down import (e.g., allow 24 hours).
Wednesday 9 a.m.	UP	Import ends.
Wednesday 12 noon	UP	Dictionary modification adjustment (SPDD). Start activation.
Wednesday 6 a.m.	UP	First activation run ends (with errors). Process activation errors. Restart activation.
Wednesday 9 p.m.	UP	Activation ends. SAPup starts remaining predowntime phases.
Thursday 6 a.m.	UP	SAPup reaches downtime switch point (MODPROF_TRANS). Let the process wait.
Friday 6 p.m.	DOWN	Stop user activity. Suspend background jobs. Isolate system.
Friday 6:30 p.m.	DOWN	BACKUP.
Friday 10:30 p.m.	DOWN	Start SAPup downtime part.
Saturday 5:30 p.m.	DOWN	SAPup downtime ends. Switch database log mode. BACKUP.
Saturday 9:30 a.m.	DOWN	Postprocessing (technical).
Saturday 2:30 p.m.	DOWN	Import transport queue.
Saturday 5:30 p.m.	DOWN	Development and functional postprocessing.
Saturday 10 p.m.	DOWN	BACKUP.

Table 5.1 Example Schedule for Technical Upgrade

Time	Uptime/ Downtime	Activity
Sunday 2 a.m.	DOWN	Update database statistics.
Sunday 8 a.m.	DOWN	Key users start testing.
Sunday 6 p.m.	DOWN	End testing — give final go/ no-go.
Sunday 7 p.m.	DOWN	BACKUP (Restore in case of no-go).
Monday 7 a.m.	UP	Unlock users. Reschedule background jobs.

Table 5.1 Example Schedule for Technical Upgrade (cont.)

5.6 Pre-Upgrade Downtime

You will need to obtain and organize planned downtime before the upgrade in the following cases:

► Hardware change or operating-system upgrade

► Database software upgrade

► SAP kernel upgrade

► Support package upgrade

► Parameter changes for the upgrade

If a change of hardware, operating system, or database version is necessary, then you will know this from the hardware/software prerequisite check (see Section 6.2). A too-low kernel or support package level of the source release will be reported early in the PREPARE run.

<table>
<tr><td>

Note

Even if you choose not to upgrade the entire source kernel before the upgrade, it is still a good idea to replace R3trans and tp with the latest versions.

</td></tr>
</table>

Sometimes it is also necessary to change operating system, database, or SAP profile parameters in preparation of the upgrade. For example, if the path of the upgrade directory is different from the standard, then you must set the profile parameter DIR_PUT explicitly. This is not the best of examples because DIR_PUT is dynamically changeable in many source versions; however, other static SAP parameters might also have to be changed. Parameter changes also may be needed to improve the performance of the upgrade. For example, if your DBMS is Oracle, then during the upgrade, the shared pool should be bigger than 400MB. The shared pool size can be altered dynamically up to an upper limit set by SGA_MAX_SIZE. SGA_MAX_SIZE, however, cannot be increased without bouncing the instance. For this, a stop and restart is needed.

5.7 Upgrade Services

Upgrading your system is not an easy endeavor. Fortunately, you are not on your own. SAP provides upgrade services for the planning, implementing, and running of your next release.

5.7.1 SAP GoingLive Functional Upgrade Check

The SAP GoingLive Functional Upgrade Check is part of the standard maintenance. The service consists of two to three service sessions delivered via remote connection by certified consultants. There is a planning session, an analysis session, and a verification session. The service will identify potential hardware capacity and software compatibility issues early in the project. Recently, the analysis session has been extended so that it also checks Unicode compliance of the current system.

5.7.2 SAP Safeguarding for Upgrade

The SAP GoingLive Functional Upgrade Check can form the basis of a further SAP engagement in the upgrade project, namely the SAP Safeguarding for Upgrade program. The program uses the result of the first GoingLive session (the planning session) to identify potential pain points when the upgrade project is still in its planning stage. This results in a service plan specifically aimed at addressing these critical issues. Under the Safeguarding for Upgrade program, you will also be assigned an *upgrade coach*. This is an upgrade expert who will act as your single point of contact within SAP for all matters relating to the upgrade project. The upgrade coach also performs an on-site assessment of the project (this includes a knowledge-transfer session) and conducts on-site reviews at key project milestones.

5.7.3 Other Upgrade Services

Apart from the GoingLive Functional Upgrade Check and the Safeguarding for Upgrade services, SAP has created an extensive range of upgrade services covering a wide range of topics and aimed at different audiences. The service portfolio is constantly being extended and enhanced, so we do not list all these services here. However, we do want to point out that these services go well beyond project assistance or technical advice for the upgrade. Following are just a few of the areas for which SAP also has a service offering:

▶ Help in determining the business case for an upgrade and the added value of SAP ERP (via the SAP Value Assessment and SAP Accelerated Value Assessment)

▶ Cover temporary extra hardware requirements (SAP Upgrade Hosting)

▶ Provide a named contact person for weekend/holiday support during the production upgrade (SAP Upgrade Weekend Support)

▶ Provide training on the features and functionality of the new release to key users, end users, and/or support personnel (SAP End-User Delta Training)

5.7.4   Information Links for SAP Upgrade Services

Table 5.2 lists useful links for information about SAP upgrade services and information.

http://service.sap.com/GOINGLIVE-FU	SAP GoingLive Functional Upgrade Check
http://service.sap.com/UPGRADESERVICES	SAP Safeguarding for Upgrade SAP Upgrade Coach All other SAP upgrade services that are not part of standard maintenance
http://service.sap.com/SERVICECATALOG	Information and ordering for all SAP Support Services
http://service.sap.com/UPGRADE-ERP	SAP ERP upgrades with links to many useful information areas

Table 5.2 SAP Service Marketplace Resources for Upgrades

With the business case for the release upgrade made, the go-ahead given, the resources allocated, and the project plan ready, it is now time to turn to the technical upgrade process. The two chapters that follow, "Preparing the Technical Upgrade" and "A Guided Tour of the Upgrade Tools," lay the foundation for the different upgrade scenarios we describe later in this book. What you learn here, you will practice everywhere.

6 Preparing the Technical Upgrade

By *technical upgrade*, we mean the process of upgrading the SAP system from the current to the new release by means of software specifically designed for this purpose: the "upgrade tools."

For a successful technical upgrade, various preparations are required. Without these, the upgrade tools will not be able to run, let alone succeed. The first step is to gather all the documentation you need about the release upgrade. Using the SAP-supplied information as a starting point, you should also build your own detailed process documentation, which will be of tremendous help when you come to the production upgrade.

With the documentation in hand, you can then start planning and preparing the upgrade. Some of these preparatory steps are purely technical, such as creating file systems or downloading support packages. Others, however, might have a far more profound impact on the environment. For instance, an upgrade of the database or operating system might be required; downtime for this must be planned well in advance. Even worse, it might turn out that the capacity of the present servers is insufficient to support the new release and all that it entails, such as Unicode or the addition of a Java stack. Getting the necessary approvals, allocating the budget, placing the orders, making the deliveries, and completing the installation and testing of the new equipment can be a long and tedious process. Therefore, the analysis of the present system environment must start long before the upgrade; otherwise, you run the risk of nasty last-minute surprises and possibly severe delays.

6.1 The Upgrade Documentation

Even with years of upgrade experience, starting a SAP release upgrade without proper documentation would be something of a death leap. SAP publishes detailed *upgrade guides* for every product version and every Support Release. It also keeps the upgrade information meticulously up to date by means of *upgrade notes*. Even if you develop your own documentation for the upgrade — which we recommend and will expand on later — then it is still of primordial importance that you obtain and read(!) the SAP documentation.

6.1.1 The Upgrade Guides

Upgrade guides are located in the *Installation and Upgrade Guides* area on the SAP Service Marketplace, *http://service.sap.com/INSTGUIDES*. They are published in PDF format, so you need the Adobe Reader.

Upgrade Guides for SAP NetWeaver

For NetWeaver-based components (BW/BI, XI/PI, Portal), expand *SAP NetWeaver • SAP NetWeaver 7.0 (2004s)*.

On the page that opens, you will see hyperlinks to the different guides; at the bottom of the screen, you find a structured list of the available materials (see Figure 6.1).

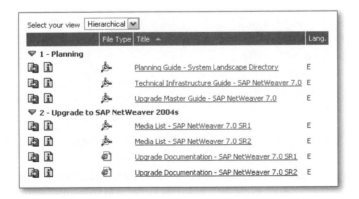

Figure 6.1 Upgrade Guides for SAP NetWeaver 2004s

From here, you can already download the *Upgrade Master Guide* for SAP NetWeaver and the Media List for SR2. The link *Upgrade Documentation – SAP NetWeaver 7.0 SR2* will take you further to the actual upgrade guides. For SR2, the guides are divided into three major categories:

- AS ABAP

- AS Java

- Business Intelligence ABAP; these are specialized guides for upgrading SAP Business Information Warehouse to BI (Business Intelligence) 7.0

In the two ABAP categories, there are separate upgrade guides per operating system (UNIX, Windows, iSeries) and per database system supported on this OS platform.

The upgrade guides for AS Java are only divided by operating system. Each guide covers all the supported database systems.

There is also a separate link to the document called *Installation Guide – SAP Software on UNIX: OS Dependencies*. This document applies only to UNIX platforms (including Linux) and gives specific information for each UNIX-based SAP platform. This document exists mainly because system administration and configuration tasks are not standardized between the different UNIX "flavors." No similar document exists — nor is one needed — for iSeries and Windows.

Finally, there is a link to information in the SAP Help Portal (*http://help.sap.com*) about upgrading SAP NetWeaver Mobile (MI). For MI, special upgrade scenarios and procedures exist depending on the start release, and the help page gives you all the necessary information.

Upgrade Guides for SAP Business Suite

You find the upgrade guides for the Business Suite products SAP ERP, SAP CRM, SAP SCM, and SAP SRM via the link *SAP Business Suite Applications • (choose product) • (choose version)*, for example, *SAP ERP • SAP ERP 2005*.

From here, you can download the Upgrade Master Guide for the selected component, which is SAP ERP 2005 in the example of Figure 6.2. The link to the upgrade documentation then takes you to a page with the technical upgrade guides. As with NetWeaver, there are dedicated ABAP upgrade guides per OS/DB combination and Java upgrade guides per OS.

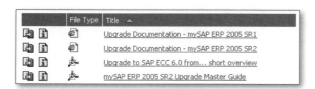

Figure 6.2 Upgrade Guides for SAP ERP 2005

There is no link here to the *Software on UNIX: OS Dependencies* document, although you will still find this document useful if the server platform is UNIX/Linux. Therefore, you should go to the NetWeaver upgrade guide page and download the Software Dependencies document from there.

The Upgrade Master Guide

The Upgrade Master Guide, which exists for SAP NetWeaver 2004s and for the individual Business Suite products, contains extensive information about the new release, including a description of its components, supported business scenarios with their requirements, technological data, and more. The guide is intended for both a business and a technical audience.

Although the Upgrade Master Guide is not the primary source of information for the technical upgrade, you should at least give it a quick read so that you know what's in it and which questions it will be able to answer. For example, an often-asked question is "do we need to install a Java stack after the upgrade?"; you are likely to need the Upgrade Master Guide for the correct answer.

The Technical Upgrade Guide

The upgrade guide for the specific OS/DB combination (ABAP upgrades) or the specific OS (Java upgrades) describes the necessary preparations, upgrade actions, and postprocessing steps for the entire technical upgrade. This guide is the centerpiece of the technical documentation and should also be the starting point for your own documentation.

The most efficient way to use the upgrade guide is to start from the chapter *Upgrade – Step by Step*. Here you find a brief summary of every step in the upgrade process with a link to a more elaborate explanation in chapters about the PREPARE, upgrade, and follow-up activities.

Another important section of the upgrade guide is the list of SAP Notes, which you find in the introduction (Chapter 1 of the guide). This section first lists the core upgrade notes (we'll refer to these as the "core notes" from now on), followed by a longer list of supporting notes containing additional information. As you will see later in this chapter, the key notes are absolutely essential reading — and should actually be reread before every upgrade — while the supporting notes can be used on an as-needed basis.

The Media List

This upgrade guide contains the list of all DVD media provided for the upgrade. A separate media list exists only for SAP NetWeaver 2004s. For Business Suite components, you find media information in the Upgrade Master Guide for the component.

You may find the large number of upgrade DVD's bewildering and therefore put your hopes into the media list to tell you exactly which media you need and which you can forget about. Although the guide is useful, don't expect too much. A traditional problem that everyone doing upgrades (and installations) has to deal with is the vague description of the required media in the documentation and even in the tools themselves (messages like "Please mount the Java DVD," which may refer to any number of Java-related media and requires trial and error to find out which one is meant). The media list does nothing to clarify this confusion, so in this respect, it isn't of much help.

6.1.2 The Upgrade Notes

The Upgrade Guide contains a long list of SAP Notes. Some of these — the "core notes" — contain information that is crucial for a successful upgrade. Others concern specific components or platforms or cover subjects related to the upgrade in a more general way. The core notes are indispensable reading; for the other notes, you must make a sensible selection of what you deem to be useful.

The core upgrade notes for the components based on SAP NetWeaver 2004s are listed in Appendix E. The notes referenced there are for Support Release 2.

Every component has one or usually two main upgrade notes: one for the AS ABAP and the other for the AS Java. These upgrade notes are platform-independent, that is, they are relevant for all operating systems and databases. Apart from these main upgrade notes, there is also a platform-specific note for each database system. The platform-specific notes normally apply to the complete SAP NetWeaver 2004s platform, not just to one component. Most of these notes concern only the ABAP stack, although SAP may also release a platform-specific note for the Java stack as well.

You must use the main upgrade note for the component, which you find in the table "General Notes for Components" in Appendix E with the platform-specific note from the tables "Platform-Specific: ABAP" and/or "Platform-Specific: Java."

Examples
You want to upgrade a SAP R/3 system to SAP ERP 2005 with database system Oracle. In that case, the core notes for the upgrade are Note 961410 (component upgrade ERP 2005 SR2) and Note 819655 (NetWeaver 2004s SR2 ABAP, Oracle).

> You want to upgrade a double-stack CRM system with database DB2 UDB. Here you need Core Notes 961511 (CRM 5.0 ABAP), 995764 (CRM 5.0 Java), and 819876 (NetWeaver 2004s SR2 ABAP, DB2/UDB).

In the main upgrade note and the platform-specific notes, each information item bears a timestamp. Thanks to this, you only have to work through the entire note before the first time. For subsequent upgrades, you need only check the items that were added since. The chapter "Chronological Summary" at the end of the note lists all items in chronological order, with the most recent first. Figure 6.3 shows this section in the main upgrade note for SAP NetWeaver 2004s ABAP.

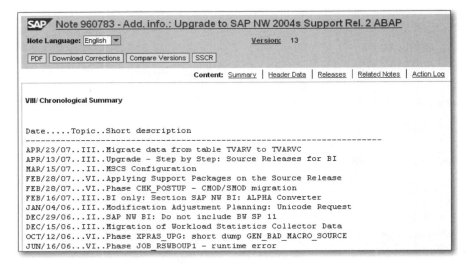

Figure 6.3 Chronological Summary Section in SAP Upgrade Notes

---

Tip

You can also save work by checking only the changes made to a note since the last time you consulted it. For this, you can use the version comparison function in the Web frontend (*http://service.sap.com/NOTES*):

▶ Display the note.

▶ On the right-hand side of the header, click on the small arrow next to **Display Versions**.

▶ In the pop-up window with the list of versions, mark the current version and the version at the time of the previous upgrade (make sure you write down this version number in your documentation).

▶ Scroll to the bottom of the window, and choose **Compare**.

This method works for all notes, not just for the ones with a chronological list.

> **Tip**
>
> Do not print notes. Instead, download them to your PC, and install one of the new desktop search engines (most of which are freeware and come from reliable sources). This will greatly facilitate note lookups during the upgrade. Thick binders full of printed notes are difficult to use and tedious to keep updated.

6.1.3 Creating Your Own Documentation

The SAP upgrade documentation, which has to cover every possible upgrade scenario on every supported platform, is essential reading, but it is not really suitable as a detailed handbook for your specific upgrade. Using the Upgrade Guides and notes as a start, you will have to create your own documentation. As the upgrade progresses, you can add new information to this document, such as errors encountered and corrective actions taken, timing data, and so on. SAP does not lay down any rules about the format or the contents of this user documentation, leaving you complete freedom. In the next section, we describe our own standard, the Upgrade Control Document, which we have been using successfully for several years.

The Upgrade Control Document

The SAP upgrade guides and notes are indispensable for a successful upgrade, but we think that something more is needed: a detailed and tailor-made documentation for your current landscape and upgrade project. For all upgrades that we do, we systematically create such documentation (which we call the "Upgrade Control Document"). This document is very elaborate — the final version typically runs up to 80–120 pages — but it is also extremely helpful. By describing clearly and systematically every step of the process, from the first preparation to the last cleanup step, the upgrade becomes much easier and the risk of mistakes and oversights is almost completely eliminated. Our aim is that by the time we do the production upgrade, we just open the document and simply do what the book says. We very much prefer to concentrate our mental energy on any unexpected issues that may arise, not on frantically trying to remember how we solved something that happened several times before but somehow did not get properly written down.

Creating such documentation requires a good deal of time and effort. Especially during the first (test) upgrade, you will spend many hours typing, copying, and pasting. There are several long phases in an upgrade during which you can work on your document, but if you have to spend time writing while the upgrade is waiting and thus prolong the duration of this test upgrade, then so be it. The time "wasted" now will pay dividends later while upgrading more critical systems.

Also, later changes to the document will probably be very limited. In our experience, the Upgrade Control Document is about 90% complete after the first upgrade and only needs little maintenance in the course of the subsequent upgrades. By the time you reach production, the document should have become virtually read-only.

Structure of the Control Document

SAP does not provide formal guidelines about structuring your own upgrade documentation. We will explain how we do things and hope that you find this helpful. The important thing is that the documentation is set up in such a way that it does the job for you and that you feel comfortable working with it.

For the document format, we use Microsoft Word. That is just a matter of choice, but we do advise you to create the documentation in a word-processing format and not, for instance, as a spreadsheet. After you have established your own documentation standard, it is useful to create a template for this, for example, a DOT file (document template) in Word.

Also keep a copy on your own PC of every upgrade control document you have ever created, and install a desktop search engine that indexes the contents of your files and allows advanced search operations.

If the upgrade is a team effort, you will have to set some rules about the ownership of the document so that only one person changes it at a time. Keep these rules light and easy to follow; try not to get caught in top-heavy bureaucratic document maintenance standards, which actually frighten people away from keeping their documents up to date.

When inserting parts of the upgrade process — for example, an input screen of PREPARE and SAPup — into your documentation, then copy/paste text rather than graphical screenshots. Screenshots look nice, but they don't allow text searches. Content and usability are more important than fancy looks.

Here is an overview of the chapters of a typical Upgrade Control Document along with a brief description:

- ▶ **System and version data**
  Contains information about the servers and the source and target software versions.

- ▶ **Information sources**
  References to upgrade guides, upgrade notes (with version numbers and date when last checked so that you can use the chronological summary and the version compare function; see Section 6.1.2) and any other documentation needed.

▶ **Pre-upgrade planning**
All actions to be undertaken before the technical upgrade, with emphasis on those actions that will require downtime (e.g., database upgrade).

▶ **Infrastructure and logistics**
Details on Upgrade Directories and Media Directory; space requirements in other file systems; users in SAP system; development class for upgrade in SAP.

▶ **Upgrade preparations**
All preparatory actions for the technical upgrade (fix buffers, support packages, review open repairs, etc.).

▶ **PREPARE**
Extraction of the upgrade tools and complete description of the PREPARE process, including all user interaction and all actions undertaken to fix the errors reported by PREPARE (e.g., database extensions).

▶ **Actions between PREPARE and SAPup**
All activities between the end of PREPARE and the beginning of the upgrade. In a combined upgrade and Unicode conversion, this includes a description of the SPUM4/SPUMG data analysis process, although this is such an extensive action that we normally create a separate document

▶ **Upgrade Part 1 — Uptime**
Describes the complete uptime part of the technical upgrade; this includes all the activities in the shadow instance (SPDD and activation), although the SPDD details are placed in a separate appendix.

▶ **Downtime preparations**
All actions to prepare the system for the upgrade downtime.

▶ **Upgrade Part 2 — Downtime**
Describes the technical upgrade from the beginning of downtime until the end of SAPup.

▶ **Postprocessing Part 1**
The postprocessing activities are distributed over three chapters, depending on the level of access that can be allowed to other users. The activities in Part 1 require exclusive access by the technical upgrade team, mainly because they require the system to be stopped and restarted. Examples are kernel upgrades or post-upgrade changes to database or SAP profile parameters.

▶ **Postprocessing Part 2**
Part 2 groups the activities that do not require stopping and starting the system and therefore allow limited access by other users, for example, designated functional testers. This is normally the largest of the three postprocessing chapters, covering everything from importing the transport queue to language supplementation and reviewing the nonfatal upgrade errors (more on all this

in Chapters 11 and 15 on postprocessing activities for ABAP and Java). The final action in Part 2 is normally the release of the system for productive use.

▶ **Postprocessing Part 3**
Activities in Part 3 are noncritical, mainly cleanup activities, which can be deferred until the system is back in production. Examples are saving the upgrade logs, filling out the upgrade evaluation form, removing temporary backups made during the upgrade, and so on.

▶ **Appendix: SPDD**
Dictionary adjustment with SPDD happens during the first (uptime) part of the upgrade, but the amount of documentation needed for this step is so substantial that we keep it in a separate chapter. We return later to the subject of SPDD and how to document it properly.

▶ **Appendix: Database upgrades**
If the upgrade requires a database upgrade, then we put the detailed procedure in an appendix. In the case of an SCM upgrade, there may be two such appendixes: one for the relational database of the SAP SCM system and one for the liveCache.

▶ **Appendix: Other software upgrades**
If there are other components to upgrade, then we document these procedures as well. An example is the upgrade of the Optimizers for SAP SCM systems.

▶ **Appendix: SAP support messages**
Here we keep track of all support messages sent to SAP regarding the upgrade.

▶ **Appendix: Contacts**
Contact information (names, mobile phones, email) of the upgrade team and everyone else involved in the upgrade project.

6.2 Hardware and Software Requirements

Well in advance of the upgrade, you must make sure that the SAP servers meet the hardware and software requirements for the new release:

▶ Is the hardware platform still supported?

▶ Is the current operating system version supported?

▶ Is the current database version supported?

▶ Is the capacity of the hardware sufficient to maintain satisfactory performance?

Platform support issues must be identified long before the upgrade because it may be necessary to order and install new equipment and to move the SAP systems to this new platform. Even in the "simplest" case, an upgrade of the operating system or database software version, downtime, and a test period must be planned.

The capacity of the hardware must also be verified well before the upgrade takes place. The new SAP release by itself already puts an extra load on the system; other elements such as Unicode or the addition of a Java stack will need even more horsepower under the hood.

6.2.1 SAP Platform Availability Matrix (PAM)

The central source of information about supported software and platform combinations is the Platform Availability Matrix (PAM). You can access the matrix in the SAP Service Marketplace at *http://service.sap.com/PAM*. After logging in with your Support User ID (S-user), the PAM opens in a separate browser window. Expand the list on the right-hand side until you see the component you are interested in.

The opening **General Data** tab lists the product releases from which you can upgrade to this release, as well as the releases you can upgrade to from this release. The screen also shows the release date, the planned end date of mainstream maintenance, and a list of useful links about the product release (including a link to the Upgrade Guides).

The **Database Platforms** tab lists the supported platforms and operating systems for every database type. Caution: There is a list per SAP kernel family (32/64-bit, Unicode/non-Unicode). Make sure that you select the correct type of kernel.

The **Operating Systems** tab does not concern the server but only the frontend platforms. Once more, be cautious because this area of the PAM is again divided into tabs, one for each frontend type. The frontend you are most likely interested in — the SAP GUI — is to the right (look for the tab marker **SAP Frontend GUIs**).

The other tabs in the PAM, which we will not describe in detail, deal with support Web browsers, servers, and platforms, as well as with the J2EE Engine, the Java release, and the JDBC (Java Database Connectivity). Again, most of these sections are further subdivided, so you must take care to choose the correct component.

6.2.2 Informix No Longer Supported

Perhaps the most significant change in terms of database support, and therefore well worth a separate mention, is that SAP NetWeaver 2004s no longer supports the Informix database management system. If the SAP system is currently running on Informix, then it must be migrated to another supported database system before the upgrade. This requires an OS/DB Migration, that is, a heterogeneous system copy whereby the SAP system changes over to a different database system, a different operating system, or both. An OS/DB Migration is a significant project in its own right. Sufficient time must be allowed for migrating to the new landscape, and the release upgrade should not follow the platform too closely. For an OS/DB migration, it is mandatory to submit a project plan to SAP, and you are not likely to get a green light if your timing for the migration and upgrade appears unrealistically tight.

You can find more information on the OS/DB Migration process on the SAP Service Marketplace at *http://service.sap.com/OSDBMIGRATION*. Note that this type of migration requires the assistance of a specially certified consultant. Another good source of information is *The SAP OS/DB Migration Project Guide* by Bert Vanstechelman and Mark Mergaerts (SAP PRESS Essentials 5, SAP PRESS 2005).

SAP does not support Unicode with any Informix release. If the system is running on Informix and you are planning a Unicode conversion, then you cannot convert the system to Unicode before migrating to another database platform. However, you can perform the preconversion activities for Unicode (Transactions SPUMG/SPUM4) while still on Informix. More details follow later in Chapters 19 and 20 on the Combined Upgrade and Unicode Conversion (CU&UC).

6.2.3 Capacity Requirements

As software becomes more sophisticated and richer in functionality with every new release, more demand is placed upon computer resources, both on the server and on the client side. Conversely, existing processes will often be optimized, alleviating or removing known bottlenecks. These two opposite effects partly, but never wholly, offset each other. The impact of new functionality almost always outweighs the optimization effort so that the new release will need more resources than the old one. Between versions that are neighbors or near-neighbors, the difference is likely to be small. However, if you are making a longer leap, say from 4.0B to SAP ERP 2005, then the impact will be significant.

Requirements for the New Release

A new SAP release typically demands more resources in three areas:

▶ CPU (on the database server and on the application servers)

▶ Main memory (also on database and application servers)

▶ Space in the database

In the case of R/3, you can make a first estimate of the load increase in each area by consulting a set of SAP Notes that gives a (rough) comparison of the resource usage between a release and its immediate predecessor. If the upgrade skips over one or more releases, you must combine all the intermediate notes to arrive at your estimate. For example, for an upgrade with 4.0B as the start release, you should look at the resource usage notes for 4.5B, 4.6C, SAP R/3 Enterprise, SAP ERP 2004, and SAP ERP 2005, and calculate a cumulative figure.

Table 6.1 lists the numbers of the resource comparison notes starting with release 4.0B.

Note No.	Release Covered
089305	Resource requirements R/3 4.0
113795	Resource requirements R/3 4.5
151508	Resource requirements R/3 4.6A
178616	Resource requirements R/3 4.6B
323263	Resource requirements R/3 4.6C SR1
517085	Resource requirements R/3 Enterprise 47x110
752532	Resource requirements R/3 Enterprise 47x200
778774	Resource requirements ECC 5.00 (SAP ERP 2004)
901070	Resource requirements ECC 6.00 (SAP ERP 2005)

Table 6.1 Resource Comparison Notes

Requirements for Unicode

Unicode also makes extra demands upon the capacity of the hardware, so if you plan a Unicode conversion, you must combine the estimated extra requirement for the new release with that for Unicode. How much extra machine power is needed depends on several factors, but the increase is always significant. More information on this can be found in Chapter 19.

Requirements for Java

For certain products or business scenarios, upgrading to a SAP NetWeaver 2004s-based release may also mean that you will have to add Application Server Java (AS Java) to the system after the upgrade. This would happen, for example, when you upgrade from SAP Business Information Warehouse (BW) 3.5 or lower to SAP Business Intelligence (BI) 7.0. The Master Guides for the target product and release will make clear whether AS Java is needed or not.

How much processing capacity AS Java needs depends to a large extent on its specific purpose (BI, Portal, PI [Process Integration], etc.). Here are some useful information sources that can assist with this process:

▶ Sizing documentation for many components and usage types can be found on *http://service.sap.com/SIZING* • *Sizing Guidelines* • *Solutions & Platforms*.

▶ For SAP BI, also see SAP Note 927530 and *http://service.sap.com/BI* • *Media Library* • *Performance*.

▶ A formal sizing exercise can be done with the SAP Quick Sizer tool (*http://service.sap.com/QUICKSIZER*).

▶ A search on the SAP Developer Network (SDN, *http://sdn.sap.com*) is often very helpful as well. Open the **Advanced Search** window, and search for "sizing" combined with the name of the component.

Disk Space Requirements

SAP upgrades need a significant amount of disk space. A good part of this is used only temporarily, for instance, by the upgrade directory and media directory, but another part is permanent.

Although it is not possible to give exact requirements covering all possible scenarios, we can at least explain where the space will be needed and provide an order of magnitude.

Space in the Database

The ABAP upgrade imports a completely new version of the SAP repository. After the upgrade, the old repository can be dropped, but as the repository becomes bigger with each release, the net result is always an increase in used database space. Furthermore, during the upgrade, the two repositories will exist side by side, creating an even larger demand for space. Changes to the structure of tables and the creation of extra indexes will also lead to a permanent increase in space.

Table 6.2 lists estimated extra space requirements on behalf of the *ABAP* upgrade for different database systems. The figures come from the Support Release 2 Upgrade Guides for SAP NetWeaver 2004s and the Business Suite components based on SAP NetWeaver 2004s. They should be seen as a minimum.

DBMS	CRM, SRM, NW, BI	SCM	ERP
DB2 UDB	26GB	26GB	50GB
DB2 z/OS	20GB	20GB	50GB
DB2 iSeries	40GB	40GB	80GB (1)
MaxDB	24GB	24GB	50GB
Oracle	28GB	35GB (2)	50GB
SQL Server (3)	autogrow	autogrow	autogrow

(1) May grow to 120GB during the upgrade.

(2) The Oracle guide for Windows quotes both 28GB (same amount as for the other DBMS) and 35GB without commenting. The guide for UNIX only quotes the higher figure.

(3) The Upgrade Guides for SQL Server simply state that the database files have automatic growth enabled during the upgrade but do not give a figure for the additional space used. For SQL Server, the database growth during upgrades is typically comparable to or slightly lower than that for MaxDB. Database space requirements for the *Java* upgrade are not given in the SAP Upgrade Guides but in Note 970039. We do not reproduce the figures here because the note also specifies the distribution over database storage areas (tablespaces) or data/logging areas. The space requirement varies with the database system and the usage type (pure application server, BI, Enterprise Portal (EP), or Development Infrastructure [DI]). For most databases and usage types, it lies between 2GB and 4GB, except for BI/Oracle and EP/Oracle, where around 13GB are needed.

Table 6.2 Database Space Requirements for ABAP Upgrade

For the Java components of Business Suite products, refer to Notes 995764 (CRM), 995762 (ERP), 995761 (SCM), and 995763 (SRM).

Space for the Upgrade Directory
This is discussed in detail in Section 6.3.1, subsection *Disc Space*. The upgrade directory exists for every upgraded system, but it is temporary.

Space for the Media Directory
The media directory exists for the duration of the upgrade project. Normally it is present only once and is shared among the SAP servers. (Section 6.4 provides more information about the media directory.)

Extra Space in the Transport Directory (/usr/sap/trans)

You must unpack the extra support packages that are to be bound into the upgrade. The unpacked patch files are stored in the normal location, that is the "EPS Inbox" (see Section 6.6.3, subsection *Extract ABAP packages to "EPS Inbox"*). The space required there is roughly the same as what you need for the downloaded archive files (CAR files). The data files and cofiles, which are generated from the extracted patch files, are placed in the upgrade directory and not in the transport directory. Add-On packages to be bound into the upgrade are also extracted to the EPS Inbox.

Extra space must also be available in the transport directory to save the upgrade logs at the end of the upgrade. It is strongly recommended to save a permanent copy of all the logs (which could take 800MB or more per upgrade), and, as you will see later, it is a good idea to compress the logs. If you use compression, then 100MB per upgrade should be amply sufficient. In this book, we will give you a convenient procedure to save the logs in compressed form.

The transport directory is normally shared by all SAP systems in the landscape, so the space for add-on and support packages is needed only once. The packages are no longer needed after they have been applied in all the systems, so the space can be recovered. However, many SAP installations that we see do not have proper procedures in place to regularly clean out the EPS Inbox, which then keeps growing ever bigger. In landscapes with several SAP components and especially if Java is involved, the EPS Inbox can become very large and very messy. Ideally, try preparing a cleanup procedure for after the last upgrade.

Extra Space in the SAP Instance Directory

The instance directory is normally called */usr/sap/SID/DVEBMGSxx* for ABAP and double-stack systems, and */usr/sap/SID/JCxx* for Java-only systems, with "xx" denoting the instance number. In a pure ABAP system, this directory contains mostly logs, traces, and intermediate data files. This does not change with SAP NetWeaver 2004s, so there is normally no need to plan for extra space here. Java, however, uses the instance directory for installing software modules, property files, and so on. These are located under the *j2ee* and *SDM* subdirectories and use a substantial amount of space. The SAP Upgrade Guides for Java only and double-stack systems quote an extra space requirement in the instance directory of at least 5GB.

The Java Support Package Manager (JSPM) also needs space in the instance directory. The space required for the support package installation is approximately three times the total size of the SCA files to be deployed. Details are in Note 891895. The JSPM stops with an error when it runs out of space, but this error will not necessarily say that lack of disk space is the cause of the problem. The JSPM also cleans up its temporary space before stopping or aborting, so it will not be immediately obvious that lack of free space caused the problem.

6.2.4   SAP Solution Manager System

As amply explained in the SAP Service Marketplace, you can use the SAP Solution Manager as a source of information about the entire upgrade process. Apart from these obvious benefits, having an installed SAP Solution Manager system is *mandatory* for a technical reason. The PREPARE will ask you for an upgrade key, which you can only generate in SAP Solution Manager. The procedure to create the key is described in Section 8.1, but at this point, you should make sure that a SAP Solution Manager system is available that meets the minimum release requirement (version 4.0, version 3.2 with minimum SP 4, or version 3.1 with minimum SP 20).

If it is impossible to meet this requirement, you can obtain an upgrade key from SAP, although only when absolutely necessary. SAP consultants or support engineers cannot provide this key themselves, so a certain delay is likely.

6.3   The Upgrade Directory

All programs, scripts, parameter files, scripts, logs, traces, and so on used in or created during the upgrade reside in an *upgrade directory*. You must create this directory before the first run of PREPARE. If you decide to restart PREPARE from scratch, then you must empty the upgrade directory first.

The ABAP and Java upgrades each have their own upgrade directory with a different name and structure. If you perform a double-stack (ABAP plus Java) upgrade, then you need both directories.

6.3.1 ABAP Upgrade Directory: Path, Location, and Subdirectories

The ABAP upgrade directory must reside on the central instance server. The default path name is */usr/sap/put*[1]. For Windows, you must use backslashes and also include a drive letter. Because the *\usr\sap* subdirectory in SAP installations on Windows is shared under the name SAPLOC, the path for the ABAP upgrade directory can also be written in UNC notation as *\\<CIHOST>\SAPLOC\PUT*, where CIHOST denotes the host name of the central instance computer.

The upgrade directory contains several subdirectories. Because a significant part of the technical upgrade consists of transports, you will find many of the subdirectories that also exist below the transport directory */usr/sap/trans* such as *bin, buffer, cofiles, data, log, tmp,* and others. These subdirectories have the same function for the upgrade as their counterparts for normal transports.

There are also subdirectories for the kernel of the target release (*exe*), the kernel upgrade (*exenew*), the Upgrade Assistant (*ua*), executables for the source release (*preexe*), and upgrade tools for source and target (*pretools, tools*). There is also a subdirectory with upgrade documentation (*htdoc*). The documentation is in HTML format and can be called up from a browser.

The directory */usr/sap/put/SID* (where SID denotes the system ID) is used for the shadow instance. This directory has the same structure as the standard SAP system directory */usr/sap/SID*.

> **Caution**
>
> You must not create any subdirectories of your own below */usr/sap/put*. The directory must be for the exclusive use of the upgrade and must initially be empty.

Changing the Path Name

It is possible to use a path name for the ABAP upgrade directory that is different from the default. This can be useful, for example, if the server contains several SAP systems, and you do not want to discard the files of a previous upgrade before setting out on the next one, or if you have to run more than one upgrade simultaneously.

---

1 Throughout the technical chapters, we always use forward slashes " /" in path names, which is valid for UNIX and iSeries. On Windows platforms, the actual path name will of course contain backslashes "\" and may also be preceded by a drive letter or a share name. For instance, the default path on Windows for the ABAP upgrade directory is *<drive>:\usr\sap\ put*. File and directory names are also shown case-sensitive in line with UNIX requirements; for Windows, the case does not matter.

Whenever it is necessary to mention UNIX and Windows separately, we will use the naming conventions pertaining to that platform

If you want to use a different path name, then you must do two things:

▶ Set the SAP profile parameter DIR_PUT to the path name you will use. Add the parameter to the instance profile, and restart the SAP system to activate the new value.

▶ Depending on the source release, DIR_PUT can also be a dynamically changeable parameter. In that case, you can change the value online using Transaction RZ11. Even then, you should also add the parameter to the instance profile, so that it will remain in effect if for some reason the SAP system is restarted.

Always specify the extra argument upgdir=<PUTDIR> when running PREPARE or SAPup.

Symbolic Link (UNIX)

Instead of giving the upgrade directory a different name, on UNIX you can also use a symbolic link with the name */usr/sap/put*. The actual upgrade directory can then have any path name. This is the easiest option if you plan to do several upgrades on the same server but never two at the same time. You can then create all the upgrade directories or file systems anywhere on the system and just let the symbolic link point to the one you are currently using. Example:

```
mkdir /mydir/sapupg/DEV   # upgrade directory for system DEV
mkdir /mydir/sapupg/QAS   # for system QAS
### Before the DEV upgrade:
ln -s /mydir/sapupg/DEV /usr/sap/put
### Before the QAS upgrade:
ln -s /mydir/sapupg/QAS /usr/sap/put
```

Disk Space

How much space you need in the ABAP upgrade directory depends on the product you are upgrading, on the number of additional languages in the system (on top of the default English and German), and, to a lesser extent, on the number of support packages bound into the upgrade. For ABAP (not for Java), the space requirement is higher for iSeries than for the other operating systems.

Table 6.3 shows the minimum size required for the ABAP and Java upgrade directories according to the SAP Upgrade Guides (you find this information in the *Upgrade – Step by Step* chapter of the Upgrade Guide). For iSeries, the guides also quote a value per extra language in addition to DE/EN (German and English). No such value is given for the other platforms, but obviously the language files need space there too. In our experience, the figures given in the upgrade guide are very low. For SAP ERP, for example, 500–600MB per additional language is more realistic.

Platform	CRM	ERP	SCM	SRM	NetWeaver 2004s	NetWeaver 2004s for SAP BI
ABAP on UNIX, Windows, zOS	3000	7000	3800	3800	1800	3500
ABAP on iSeries	4000 + 120/lang	7000 + 350/lang	4000 + 120/lang	4000 + 120/lang	4000 + 120/lang	4000 + 120/lang
Java on All O/Ses	3500	3500	3500	3500	3500	3500

Table 6.3 Minimum Sizes of the Upgrade Directory

ABAP Support Packages bound into the upgrade also occupy space in the upgrade directory. You extract the support package archives to the EPS Inbox (we cover the exact procedure for this in section 6.6.3), but the data files, cofiles, and logs are placed in the upgrade directory. As a rule of thumb, take the sum of the downloaded ABAP support package archives (CAR files) and multiply this by 2 to get an estimate of the extra space you will need.

On top of all this, allow for a reasonable safety margin. The usual SAP advice is to plan for 25% of extra space.

Let's summarize all this in a formula:

$$S = 1.25 \times (G + 2 \times SPC + (NL - 2) \times LS)$$

- ▶ S = Overall space for ABAP upgrade directory
- ▶ G = Minimum space from SAP Upgrade Guide for this component/platform
- ▶ SPC = Total size of CAR files of ABAP support packages
- ▶ NL = Number of languages in the system, including DE and EN
- ▶ LS = Estimated extra space per language

> **Example**
>
> Upgrade of a SAP BI system, support package CAR files occupy 320MB, five languages installed, assuming 300MB per language (except DE/EN):
>
> $S = 1.25 \times (3500 + 2 \times 320 + (5–2) \times 300) = 1.25 \times 5040 = 6300MB$

A formula puts a scientific gloss on the space calculation, but as with many other aspects of the upgrade, only the first test upgrade in the current landscape will give you a precise indication of how much space the ABAP upgrade directory will really need. As long as you do not have an exact idea, you should be liberal with disk space because running out of space in the middle of the upgrade can be awkward.

Technically, the upgrade directory is temporary in nature. You will eventually be able to reclaim the space, but be aware that the directory will probably remain in existence for several months.

6.3.2 Java Upgrade Directory: Path, Location, and Subdirectories

The Java upgrade directory resides on the host running the Java central instance. The default path name is */usr/sap/jupgrade*. The default path on Windows (in UNC notation) is \\<CIHOST>\SAPLOC\JUPGRADE, with CIHOST denoting the host name of the computer with the Java central instance. This UNC path maps to the physical directory *<drive>:\usr\sap\jupgrade*, that is, the same path as on UNIX and iSeries with only the addition of the drive letter.

As with the ABAP upgrade directory, an entire subdirectory tree exists within the Java directory; some of these exist in both, and others are specific to Java. You must leave the management of the directory to the Java upgrade tools and not create or delete any subdirectories yourself, except when you reset the upgrade (in which case, you empty the directory completely before starting over).

For you, the most important subdirectory is */usr/sap/jupgrade/log*, which contains all the Java upgrade logs.

Changing the Path Name

You can use a path name for the Java upgrade directory that is different from the default. For this, create the directory with the chosen name, and then specify its path on the command line when you execute the JPREPARE script for the first time (see Chapter 7 for instructions on running the Java upgrade tools). Example:

```
JPREPARE /usr/sap/jupgr700DEV
```

Notice that here you do not use the prefix upgdir= as you do when specifying an alternative path for the ABAP upgrade directory.

There is also no equivalent for the DIR_PUT parameter, so you do not need to adapt any parameter profiles if you use a different path.

Symbolic Link (UNIX)

The upgrade directory path can be a symbolic link instead of a real directory. The technique is the same as for the ABAP directory (see Section 6.3.1 earlier).

Disk Space

The recommended size given in the upgrade guides for the Application Server Java is 3500MB, but the guides also advise to observe a 25 % safety margin, so starting off with 4500MB in the first upgrade in the landscape is reasonable. This first upgrade will then allow you to make a fairly precise estimate.

6.4   The Media Directory

The upgrade directories for ABAP and Java are standard SAP requirements; the upgrade procedure needs them, so it is impossible to perform an upgrade without them. In contrast, what we call here the "media directory" is entirely our own invention. SAP does not know about this directory and you can carry out the upgrade without it — although not comfortably. We find it convenient, efficient, and useful with every upgrade. Therefore, the following is our Best Practice advice.

6.4.1   Purpose of the Media Directory

We use the Media Directory in the first place to store a copy on disk of all the media needed for the upgrade. These media are explained in Section 6.5. By "needed for the upgrade" we do not just mean those media that the upgrade tools will explicitly request, but also those that we have to use before or after the upgrade (e.g., the DVDs for a DBMS software upgrade).

Moreover, we also keep in the Media Directory everything else that is of use for the upgrade and that does not have its place in the upgrade directory itself. This includes the following:

▶ The downloaded archive files for all the support packages (ABAP, Java, and kernel).

▶ Other downloads for the upgrade project, for example, database patches. We also keep the download files for the fix buffers and SAPup patches here.

▶ Fixes for the source release, such as the archive with the latest SPAM/SAINT version for the source release or the archives with the latest source kernel (if a kernel upgrade of the source system before the SAP upgrade is necessary).

▶ All shell scripts, SQL scripts, and any other procedure or information file that you need at any time during the upgrade.

6.4.2 Location and Path Name

Because the Media Directory is of your own making, you are free to place it wherever and call it whatever you like. However, there are a few guidelines that you should observe.

First set up your Media Directory in a location with enough disk space. A copy on disk of every DVD needed in the upgrade will already set you back at least 10GB and, depending on the component and database system, could run up to 30GB. You can save on this, for example, by not keeping the DBMS upgrade media online if these are not requested during the upgrade. As far as the key upgrade media themselves are concerned (upgrade export, kernel, upgrade master, DE/EN language DVD), it's very much TINA — There Is No Alternative. You don't want to play disk jockey with the server's DVD drive in the middle of the night — even if you have access to the computer room, which is by no means guaranteed.

Secondly, place the Media Directory in a location that can be shared across servers on the network, so that you do not have to copy it with every new upgrade. There is no problem mounting the Media Directory from another server on the (local) network via NFS (Network File System) (UNIX) or via network shares (Windows). However, network mounts might be subject to security rules, so you must sort this out with the system and network administrators first (after persuading them to give you the gigabytes).

Finally — and this is not as trivial as it seems — choose path names that are easy to type. You will have to enter the directory names quite a few times in the course of the upgrade; apart from inflicting self-torture on all but the most competent typists, monstrous directory paths are also error-prone. There is also a technical reason for keeping the names as short as possible: if the path name for the Language CD's is longer than 50 characters, PREPARE is unable to find the media and stops with the error CANNOT_GET_COMPONENTS "Language Disk".

If network paths or other naming rules prevent you from assigning short path names, then use symbolic links or shortcuts.

6.4.3 Directory Structure

In this section, you will see an example of a typical Media Directory as we set it up during our upgrades. The example is for a system running Oracle, but that only means there are a few Oracle-specific subdirectories and does not affect the basic organization.

Again, this is just the way *we* do things. You are perfectly free to use a different setup if you are more comfortable with that. The only purpose is to have everything at hand without having to chase around for stuff that the upgrade needs but that you can't find anywhere.

The following example is an extract from one of our upgrade control documents. Notice that we define a placeholder $DIRMEDIA to refer to the Media Directory path throughout the documentation; as a matter of fact, we also declare an environment variable DIRMEDIA to the login environment of the SAP administrator user at O/S level, hence the leading "$" sign[2].

Upgrade Media
Upgrade media used: SAP ERP 2005 (ECC 6.00) SR 2
To enable the environment variables, change the login profiles of the *sidadm* and *orasid* users.
Path (referred to as $DIRMEDIA in the remainder of this document):
/nfs001/install/software/SAP/UPGRADE_ECC600_SR2
Caution! Long path names cause trouble in PREPARE ("could not identify language CD"). Action: create symbolic link /var/sapupgrade on the upgrade host pointing to $DIRMEDIA. Use this symbolic link when entering path names in PREPARE.
The following table shows a list of subdirectories:

Path below $DIRMEDIA	Content
UPGMASTER	ECC 600 Upgrade Master (non-Unicode)
KERNEL_NUC	Kernel SR2 (non-Unicode)
UPGRADE1	Upgrade #1
UPGRADE2	Upgrade #2
UPGRADE3	Upgrade #3
SPS08	Support Package Stack ERP 2005 SP08
SPS08/ABAP	ABAP support packages SPS08
SPS08/KERNEL	Kernel upgrade 700/95
ORACLE102	Oracle 10.2.0 RDBMS
ORACLE10202	Oracle 10.2.0.2 Patch Set
ORACLIENT102	Oracle Instant Client 10.2.0.2
ORACLIENT9207	Oracle Client 9.2.0.7
ORAPATCHES	Interim patches + latest OPATCH version

---

2 In Windows, you do not use a $ sign to refer to environment variables; instead you enclose the variable name in percentage signs, for example, %DIRMEDIA%.

Path below $DIRMEDIA	Content
LANGUAGES/LANG1	Language CD #1
LANGUAGES/LANG2	Language CD #2
LANGUAGES/LANG3	Language CD #3
LANGUAGES/LANG4	Language CD #4
LANGUAGES/LANG5	Language CD #5
LANGUAGES/LANG6	Language CD #6
WPPI	Enterprise Portal Plug-in (WPPI) 600_46C
CEE_100_600	Core CEE 110_600 add-on (installation + upgrade)
fixes	Correction transports from SAP ("fix buffer") Latest SAPup version SPAM/SAINT for 4.6C Other fixes
bin	Shell scripts, SQL scripts, and so on

Note

When you make changes to $DIRMEDIA, always adapt ownership and access afterward, so that both sidadm and orasid have full access:

```
cd $DIRMEDIA
chown -R <sid>adm:dba *
chmod -R ug+rwx *
```

6.5   The Upgrade Media

SAP delivers all the data, procedures, transports, and other software needed for the release upgrade via the *upgrade media*. The upgrade media are made up of an impressive set of DVD discs (with the growing volume of data that comes with every new release, the old CD-ROM has long been abandoned).

6.5.1   Packages and Downloads

The normal procedure is that once you have decided on upgrading, you order an upgrade package for your platform through the Software Catalog on the SAP Service Marketplace (*http://service.sap.com/SOFTWARECATALOG*). For products covered by your license, you are entitled to receive upgrade packages for new releases free of charge.

Alternatively, you can also download the upgrade media from the SAP Software Distribution Center (*http://service.sap.com/SWDC*). Here you can find the upgrade media under *Download • Installations and Upgrades • Entry by Application Group* (see Figure 6.4).

Figure 6.4 Installations and Upgrades Page in SWDC

From here open one of the following nodes:

▶ **SAP Application Components**
Under this node, you find links to the installation and upgrade for SAP ERP, SAP CRM, SAP SCM, and SAP SRM. Under the product node, you must choose a release (e.g., SAP ERP 2005).

▶ **SAP NetWeaver**
Under the SAP NetWeaver link, select the release (for all the components discussed in this book, that release is SAP NetWeaver 2004s). There is a single download area for the installation and upgrade media of NetWeaver 2004s. This covers all the components that are defined as usage types for the NetWeaver system, such as BI (successor of BW), PI (successor of XI), or SAP NetWeaver Portal.

In the download area for the selected product and release, you will see a long — possibly a *very* long — list of DVD media. Downloading all of them would keep you busy for a few weeks, but fortunately that is not necessary. Next you will see how to identify the media that you really need.

Table 6.4 gives the location of the upgrade media for SAP NetWeaver 2004s and the SAP Business Suite 2005 products.

Component	Path to Upgrade Media
SAP NetWeaver 2004s (SAP Basis)	*SAP NetWeaver • SAP NETWEAVER • SAP NETWEAVER 2004S • Installation and Upgrade • [choose O/S platform] (see below) • [choose database]* (see below) To locate the Upgrade Master media, you may select any operating system or database. All download folders contain links to the Upgrade Masters for all platforms.
SAP ERP 2005	*SAP Application Components • SAP ERP • SAP ERP 2005 • Installation and Upgrade* This download folder also contains the media for SAP SRM 5.0 (SRM Server 5.5).
SAP SRM (EBP)	*SAP Application Components • SAP SRM (with SAP EBP) • SAP SRM 5.0 or SAP SRM 6.0 • Installation and Upgrade* The download folder contains the media for SAP SRM 5.0 (SRM Server 5.5). These media can also be found in the download folder for SAP ERP 2005.
SAP CRM	*SAP Application Components • SAP SRM (with SAP EBP) • SAP CRM 5.0 • Installation and Upgrade*
SAP SCM (APO)	*SAP Application Components • SAP SCM • SAP SCM 5.0 • Installation and Upgrade • [choose O/S platform] (see below) • [choose database]* (see below) To locate the Upgrade Master media, you may select any operating system or database. All download folders contain links to the Upgrade Masters for all platforms.
SAP BW	*SAP NetWeaver • SAP NETWEAVER • SAP NETWEAVER 2004S • Installation and Upgrade* Since SAP_BW is now a standard component of all NetWeaver systems, there are no separate upgrade media for BW. Use the upgrade media of NetWeaver 2004s plus the media for the BI Content (BI_CONT) add-on, which you find under *SAP NetWeaver • SAP NETWEAVER • SAP NETWEAVER 2004S • Installation and Upgrade • BI Content for SAP NetWeaver*.

Table 6.4 Paths of Upgrade Media in the Software Distribution Center

6.5.2 Selecting the Media Needed for the Upgrade

Determining which media the upgrade will require without actually carrying out the upgrade is not an easy task. Only the first test upgrade in a landscape will allow you to select the correct set of DVDs that you will need.

However, there are some media that you will *always* use. Table 6.5 lists this minimum set of media for ABAP and for Java. For a double-stack upgrade, you must simply add up the two lists. The Kernel DVD is common to both stacks.

ABAP	Java
Upgrade Master ABAP	Upgrade Master Java
Upgrade Export ABAP	Java Components NW2004s
Language DVD for every installed language	Java Components BS 2005 (for Business Suite products with Java stack)
Kernel for Upgrade	

Table 6.5 Mandatory Upgrade Media

6.5.3 The Upgrade Master Media

SAP delivers the upgrade tools for both ABAP and Java on the *Upgrade Master* DVD set. You'll find the DVD for your component and target version in the upgrade package you receive from SAP; alternatively, you can download the DVD from the Software Download Center (see Table 6.4 for the paths).

Upgrade Master ABAP

For the same component and release, there are specific ABAP Upgrade Master media depending on the following:

▶ The application component: SAP ERP or SAP SRM.

▶ The hardware platform and operating system. Table 6.6 lists supported platforms and operating systems. There is no distinction by database type: The upgrade media for a specific operating system contain the upgrade files for all databases supported on that operating system. The fact that the download path for some components (NetWeaver and SCM) differs depending on the operating system and database has no bearing on this.

▶ Unicode or non-Unicode systems. In the Software Download Center, you can recognize the Unicode media because they have the acronym "UC" in their title.

Figure 6.5 shows part of the download list for the SAP ERP 2005 installation and upgrade media (not all platforms are shown; Upgrade Master media for SAP SRM is also not shown). The last two items in the screenshot are for Unicode, and the others are for non-Unicode. Also notice that the Upgrade Master is fairly small (the rightmost column shows the media size in kilobytes), so downloading it is relatively painless.

SAP uses some specific conventions to identify operating systems and hardware platforms. To avoid mistakes, we briefly summarize the typical SAP notation along with the hardware or processor family they refer to (see Table 6.6).

☐	ⓘ	ZIP	51032294_10	ERP 2005 SR2 Upgrade Master OS/400	Info	117979
☐	ⓘ	ZIP	51032294_11	ERP 2005 SR2 Upgrade Master Solaris on SPARC 64bit	Info	56228
☐	ⓘ	ZIP	51032294_12	ERP 2005 SR2 Upgrade Master Windows Server on IA32 32bit	Info	63924
☐	ⓘ	ZIP	51032294_13	ERP 2005 SR2 Upgrade Master Windows Server on IA64 64bit	Info	47335
☐	ⓘ	ZIP	51032294_14	ERP 2005 SR2 Upgrade Master Windows Server on x64 64bit	Info	64710
☐	ⓘ	ZIP	51032294_15	ERP 2005 SR2 UC-Upgrade Master AIX 64bit	Info	58515
☐	ⓘ	ZIP	51032294_16	ERP 2005 SR2 UC-Upgrade Master HP-UX on IA64 64bit	Info	75481

Figure 6.5 Upgrade Master Media for ABAP

SAP Notation	Operating System	Platform
OS/400	OS/400 (IBM)	IBM iSeries (former AS/400)
Solaris on SPARC	Solaris (Sun)	SPARC
Windows Server on IA32	Microsoft Windows	Intel 32-bit (e.g., Pentium, Xeon)
Windows Server on IA64	Microsoft Windows	Itanium 64-bit
Windows Server on x64	Microsoft Windows	AMD and Intel 64-bit (AMD Opteron, Intel EM64T)
AIX	AIX (IBM)	POWER (IBM)
HP-UX on IA64	HP-UX (Hewlett Packard)	Itanium 64-bit
HP-UX on PA-RISC	HP-UX (Hewlett Packard)	PA-RISC (HP)
Linux on IA32	Linux	Intel 32-bit (e.g., Pentium, Xeon)
Linux on IA64	Linux	Itanium 64-bit
Linux on x86_64	Linux	AMD and Intel 64-bit (AMD Opteron, Intel EM64T)
Linux on Power	Linux	POWER (IBM)
Linux on zSeries	Linux	IBM zSeries (former S/390)

Table 6.6 Supported Platforms for SAP Upgrade Media

Upgrade Master Java

If you are going to upgrade AS Java, then you also need the Java Upgrade Master medium. Like the ABAP Upgrade Master, you receive this DVD as part of the upgrade package, or you can download it from the SAP Software Download Center.

In Figure 6.6, you see again a part of the installation and upgrade media list for SAP ERP 2005. There are separate Upgrade Masters for SAP ERP and SAP SRM (like for ABAP); however, the Java Upgrade Master combines all operating systems on a single medium. Since Java is always Unicode, there are also no separate Unicode and non-Unicode media.

☐ ⓘ ZIP	51032237	SAP SRM 5.0 SR2 Components	Info	201513
☐ ⓘ ZIP	51032238_1	SAP SRM 5.5 SR2 Java Upgrade for all OS	Info	132387
☐ ⓘ ZIP	51032238_10	SAP SRM 5.5 SR2 Upgrade Master OS/400	Info	116914
☐ ⓘ ZIP	51032285	SAP ERP 2005 SR2 Components	Info	1171153
☐ ⓘ ZIP	51032294_1	ERP 2005 SR2 Java Upgrade for all OS	Info	132394
☐ ⓘ ZIP	51032294_10	ERP 2005 SR2 Upgrade Master OS/400	Info	117979
☐ ⓘ ZIP	51032294_11	ERP 2005 SR2 Upgrade Master Solaris on SPARC 64bit	Info	56228

Figure 6.6 Upgrade Master Media for Java

6.5.4 Kernel Media

The Kernel DVD contains the SAP kernel for the new release. You always need this DVD, although in most cases you will upgrade the system to a higher kernel release, namely the one that goes with the target Support Package stack, than the one delivered on the upgrade media.

The kernel media are in the download area of SAP NetWeaver 2004s, not in the download area of individual products like SAP ERP 2005. For each platform, there are four versions of the kernel media:

▶ Non-Unicode

▶ Non-Unicode Upgrade

▶ Unicode

▶ Unicode Upgrade

Figure 6.7 shows an example for OS/400.

☐ ⓘ ZIP	51032264_3	NW 2004s SR2 Kernel 7.00 OS/400
☐ ⓘ ZIP	51032264_4	NW 2004s SR2 Kernel 7.00 OS/400 Upgrade
☐ ⓘ ZIP	51032264_7	NW 2004s SR2 UC-Kernel 7.00 OS/400
☐ ⓘ ZIP	51032264_8	NW 2004s SR2 UC-Kernel 7.00 OS/400 Upgrade

Figure 6.7 Kernel Media

For upgrades, you use the "Upgrade" flavor of the kernel DVD. The DVD contains both the database-independent and the database-dependent kernel files for the selected OS and DBMS. If you are planning to perform CU&UC, then you need the "Upgrade" version of the non-Unicode kernel DVD plus the normal (Non-upgrade) Unicode kernel DVD.

6.5.5 ABAP Upgrade Export

The Upgrade Export media for ABAP contain all the data, including the new Repository, which will be imported for the new release. The Upgrade Export media are located in the download area of their respective components, for example, SAP ERP 2005. The number of media differs depending on the component. For products such as SAP ERP, try to avoid having to download the media because there are no less than 16 media with an overall size of more than 10GB.

6.5.6 Java Components

For the Java upgrade, you need the Java Components media. You need the media set "NetWeaver 2004s SR2 Java-based SW Components", which contains the common part of the new AS Java version.

If you are upgrading a SAP Business Suite product (ERP, CRM, SCM, SRM) with a Java stack, then you also need the DVD "BS 2005 SR2 Java Components".

6.5.7 The Language Media (ABAP)

For the ABAP upgrade, you also need at least one and possibly more language media. There is a separate set of language media for each product (ERP, etc.). Even if your system only contains the default languages DE and EN, you must still have the language medium containing these two languages.

6.5.8 The RDBMS Upgrade Media

SAP delivers the media to upgrade the database software to the release required by SAP NetWeaver 2004s. You can also download the upgrade media for your RDBMS from the Installation/Upgrade area for SAP NetWeaver 2004s on the SAP Service Marketplace[3]. Depending on the database, there may be one or several DVDs for the upgrade.

6.5.9 Other Media

For most upgrades, the media listed in the previous paragraphs will be sufficient. The upgrade files for add-ons are usually delivered in the form of upgrade packages that you install in the EPS Inbox (*/usr/sap/trans/EPS/in* directory). If

---

3 Except for SQL Server.

additional media are required, you will find this out at the time of the first upgrade. If these media are not immediately available, then obtaining them could take some time. Make sure that you include this in your contingency plan for this first upgrade. If a CD or DVD is requested for an add-on and you haven't got the media, do not make the mistake of not upgrading the add-on in question because this may lead to data loss or inconsistencies in the system later.

6.5.10 File Formats for Downloads

Most files in the download areas on *http://service.sap.com/SWDC* are compressed in ZIP or RAR format. To extract these compressed archives, you must have the uncompress tool (unzip or unrar) for the target platform. If the utility is not present on the server, then you can download it for a wide range of platforms from the following sites:

▶ unzip: *www.info-zip.org/UnZip.html*

▶ unrar: *www.rarlab.com/rar_add.htm*

6.6 Support Packages and Other Fixes

As of SAP Basis R/3.0D, SAP delivers support packages to remove any error that appears in important transactions. A support package is a bundle of corrections that fix errors in the ABAP repository. For releases up to Basis 6.40, the patches are available for download through the Software Distribution Center at the SAP Service Marketplace (*http://service.sap.com/PATCHES*). For all products based on SAP NetWeaver 2004s/Basis 7.00, you must use the Maintenance Optimizer in the Solution Manager system[4] to select the patches and add them to the download basket, after which you can download them using the SAP Download Manager. At the time of writing, it was also still possible to select patches for download (using the SAP Download Manager) directly in the SAP Service Marketplace.

Like the R/3 software itself, support packages started off as "monolithic" entities. Each support package contained corrections for all components in the system, the technological areas, the development environment, and the business applications. This remained so until SAP R/3 4.5B. In 4.6, separate support package queues were created for the Basis component (SAP_BASIS), the development environment (SAP_ABA), and the applications (SAP_APPL). There was also a fourth type for Human Resources (SAP_HR).

---

4 For more information on installing, configuring, and using the Maintenance Optimizer, see *http://service.sap.com/SOLMAN-MOPZ* and SAP Note 1024932.

6.6.1   Support Package Stacks (SP Stacks)

In SAP R/3 Enterprise and SAP ERP, all components, including the extensions and industry solutions delivered with the standard product, have their own support package queue. For a standard SAP ERP installation, this results in a considerable number of different support package types. This approach is consistent with the modular architecture of NetWeaver-based solutions, but it raises issues of compatibility: Can you freely decide to install SAP_BASIS patch X along with SAP_BW patch Y, SAP_APPL patch Z, and so on? The situation becomes even more challenging when you also consider AS Java, for which SAP also provides support packages.

To address this looming problem, SAP introduced the concept of *support package stacks* (SP stacks). SP Stacks are fully tested combinations of patches for a diverse set of components; installing an SP stack rather than a self-determined set of patches will guarantee that no compatibility issues between patches of different components arise.

Deciding on a target patch level is an important preparatory task, driven both by business and technical requirements. Determining a proper patch strategy is a trade-off between the need for reliability and the need for stability. Upgrade projects will often go for the highest SP stack available at the time of the first upgrade in the landscape. For all following upgrades, up to the production system, they will then stay with this same SP stack unless there are critical reasons to go higher.

6.6.2   Support Releases (SR)

Besides releasing new SP stacks, SAP will also regularly (roughly once or twice a year) prepare a Support Release (SR) of its products. For SR, SAP incorporates the latest SP stack available at that moment into the standard delivery and prepares a new set of upgrade media. SRs are numbered sequentially: SR1, SR2, and so on. Using the latest available SR for the upgrade (or for a new installation, for that matter) has the advantage that many corrections are already included in the standard software and that you need to apply fewer additional support packages in the upgrade or installation.

Before starting the first upgrade in the landscape, determine the latest available SR for the product you are upgrading. SAP always delivers upgrade packages for the most recent SR, and you can also easily find this information by looking at the download area for the upgrade media on the SAP Service Marketplace.

The next step is a bit trickier. To avoid downloading loads of support packages that you won't need because they are already in the upgrade delivery, you must find out which SP stack is included in SR. This is tricky because SAP does not clearly advertise where this information is to be found; the obvious place, the Upgrade Master Guide for the product and SR, is silent on the subject. The key is SAP Note 357442, "Support Releases and corresponding Support Package status." This note contains pointers to all product-specific notes. Table 6.7 gives the reference note, SR, and included SP stack for SAP NetWeaver 2004s-based products at the time of writing (July 2007).

Product	Note	SR	SP Stack
NetWeaver	789220	NetWeaver 2004s SR 2	SPS 09
SAP ERP and R/3 Enterprise	774615	ERP 2005 SR 2	SPS 06
SAP CRM	837413	CRM 5.0 SR 2	SPS 06
SAP SCM	850038	SCM 5.0 SR 2	SPS 06
SAP SRM	819722	SRM 5.0 SR 2	SPS 06
Solution Manager	781448	Solution Manager 4.0 SR 2	SPS 09
R/3 <= 4.6C	357442	–	–

Table 6.7 Correspondence Between SR and SP Stack

Note that SPS 06, which is used for the SAP Business Suite products (ERP, CRM, SCM, and SRM), is itself based on SAP NetWeaver 2004s SPS 09; therefore, SR 2 represents a consistent patch level for all SAP components.

6.6.3 Selecting and Downloading the SP Stack with the Maintenance Optimizer

In the Solution Manager system, start Transaction SOLUTION_MANAGER, and open the solution of which the system to be upgraded is part. Click on the tab **Change Management,** and then click on **Support Package Stacks**. Click on the **Maintenance Optimizer** button. Assign a priority to the maintenance project, and enter a short amount of text. In the **Product Version** list, select the target release (if this release is not available, assign it to the system via Transaction SMSY first).

Select the system again, and click on **Continue**. In the next window, click on **Select Files for <product>**. A browser session now opens on the patch download page of the selected component. Click on **Support Package Stacks**.

Select the patches as explained in the next Section, *Patch Selection in SAP Service Marketplace*. After selecting the files, return to the Maintenance Optimizer, and click on **Continue**. Click **Confirm Files in Download Basket**. Mark all the files in the list, and choose **Confirm Download** at the bottom of the screen.

Patch Selection in the SAP Service Marketplace

In this section, we explain how to determine the support package stack and how to select the support packages, download them, and extract the downloaded files to the upgrade server.

Source and Target Stack Selection

You reach the Support Package Stack page via the Maintenance Optimizer or by going to *http://service.sap.com/SP-STACKS*. All products for which SP Stacks exist are listed here; click on the product that you are going to upgrade, for example, **SAP ERP 2005**. The Support Package Stack download application is started in a new window; you are now at the same point as when you started the browser via the Maintenance Optimizer.

First choose the target stack; by default, the highest available stack is shown, and, in most cases, this is the one you will use.

By default, the source stack is empty, which means that you will select all patches since the initial product release. This is normally not necessary because the SR delivered on the upgrade media already incorporates a certain SP stack already. Use Table 6.7 shown earlier to determine the SP stack included in the release you are using for the upgrade.

Figure 6.8 shows the selection for ERP 2005 SP Stack 09 with an SR 2 installation or upgrade as the starting point.

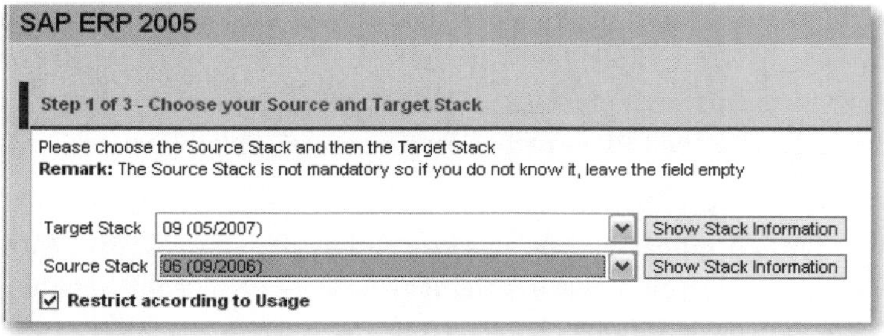

Figure 6.8 SP Stack Selection

Release Information Note (RIN)

For every SP stack, SAP publishes a note with detailed information. This note is known as the Release Information Note (RIN). You must always consult the RIN for the target stack. To do this, click on **Show Stack Information** button to the right of the Target Stack. A window opens that lists the exact support package level of every component. This window also contains a link to the RIN (see Figure 6.9).

SAP ERP 2005 Support Package Stack 09 (05/2007)

This is the summary of the content of SAP ERP 2005 Support Package Stack 09 (05/2007) .
The summary should help to identify the defined Support Packages of a Support Package Stack.

General information about SAP Support Package Stacks can be found under Quick Link /sp-stacks
For more FAQs concerning the Support Package Stack Download, refer to the FAQ document.

Product version :	SAP ERP 2005		
Release- & Information Note (RIN) :	SAP Note 0001046863		
	Defined Level	Recommended Level	Minimum Level
SAP ECC Server			
EA-APPL 600	SAPKGPAD09		
EA-DFPS 600	SAPKGPDD09		
EA-FINSERV 600	SAPKGPFD09		
EA-GLTRADE 600	SAPKGPGD09		
EA-HR 600	SAPKGPHD16		
EA-IPPE 400	SAPKGPID09		
EA-PS 600	SAPKGPPD09		
EA-RETAIL 600	SAPKGPRD09		

Figure 6.9 SP Stack Detail and Link to RIN

Usage Type Selection

Below the **Target Stack** and **Source Stack** drop-down lists, you can specify the usage types configured for the system. The usage types determine for which components support packages will be presented for download. If you are a technical person, you might need advice from someone with functional knowledge of the system to know exactly which usage types are needed; this is especially true for Business Suite products. For an upgrade to SAP ERP 2005, it is quite possible that you will only have to mark the **ERP Central Component (ECC)** (see Figure 6.10).

For upgrades of NetWeaver 2004s systems, the choice is often easier, first because the usage types **Application Server ABAP** and **Application Server JAVA** are perfectly obvious; and second because the other usage types really denote a high-level component, which fully characterizes the system. There is little chance, for example, of confusing a BW system with an XI system. Nonetheless, it is still advisable to check the Master Guide for SAP NetWeaver 2004s to make sure that you do not overlook any dependencies.

Figure 6.11 shows the usage type selection for a double-stack PI (formerly known as XI) system.

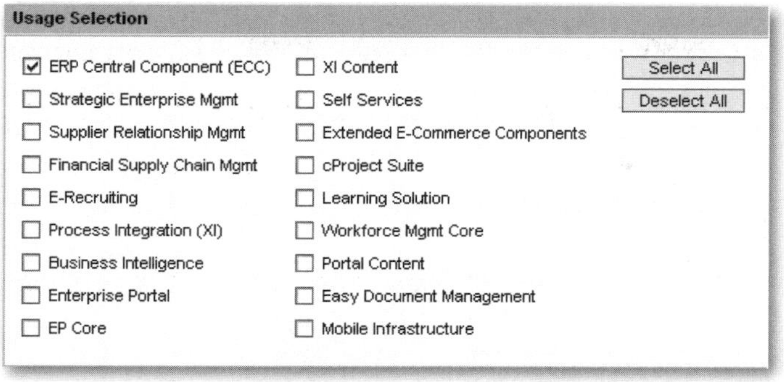

Figure 6.10 Usage Types for SAP ERP 2005

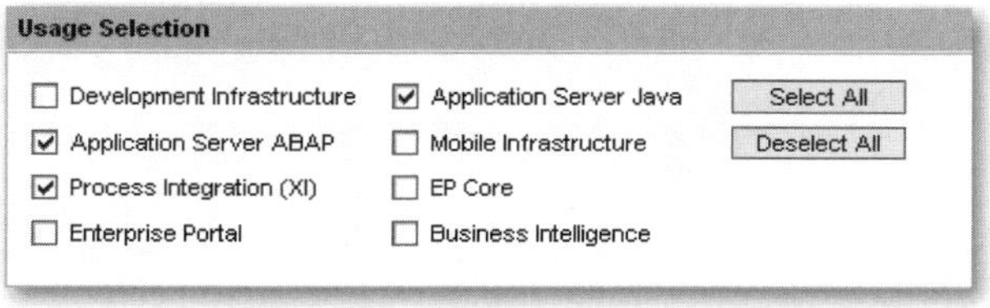

Figure 6.11 Usage types for NetWeaver 2004s

Kernel Module Selection

After selecting the target and source stack and marking the appropriate usage types, click on **Next step**. On the second screen, you must select the kernel upgrade.

First open the IGS item (Internet Graphics Server), and mark the check box for your O/S platform.

Next, open the item for the kernel type matching your installation (32-bit or 64-bit, Unicode or non-Unicode). Select the correct database system. The check box **#Database independent** is automatically enabled at the same time as shown in Figure 6.12.

Support Package Selection

Choose **Next step again**. The complete list of patches matching your selection now appears. By default, all packages are selected for the download basket as shown in Figure 6.13. In the case of SAP ERP, it is very unlikely that you will need all these packages because the list covers every possible extension and industry solution. Again, some assistance from a functional specialist might be welcome, although industry-specific components can often be eliminated quite easily — an insurance company is not very likely to use IS-OIL. If in doubt, try the Master Guide. If still in doubt, err on the side of safety and select the packages anyway.

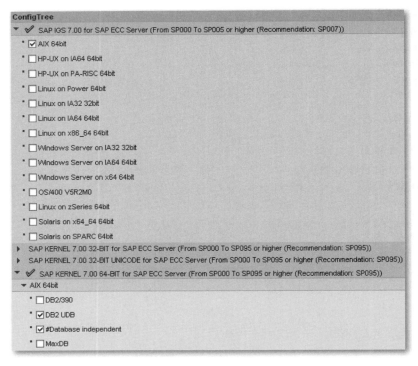

Figure 6.12 Kernel Module Selection

Regardless of what the system is used for, do *not* deselect the support packages for components SAP_BASIS, SAP_APPL, SAP_BW, SAP_APPL (in ERP systems), SAP_AP (when present), and PI_BASIS. Also leave the packages for ST-PI (Solution Tools) in the selection.

If Java packages are included, you can recognize these by the extension .sca (Software Component Archive).

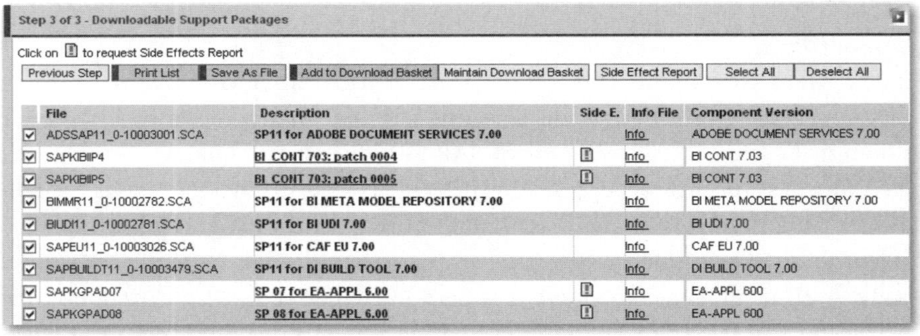

Figure 6.13 Support Package List (ABAP and Java)

XML and CSV Files

When you click on **Save as File**, a pop-up window appears where you can choose to save the patch list in Comma Separated Value (CSV) format and/or in XML format. The CSV format is helpful if you want to keep the patch list in spreadsheet format. The XML file is more important, at least if Java packages are selected. In that case, it is mandatory that you download the XML file and later on place it in the EPS Inbox before applying the support packages. The file is used by the Java Support Package Manager (JSPM). More information is available in SAP Note 884537. Make it a matter of habit always to generate the XML and the CSV files.

Side Effect Report

Support packages can have certain side effects, and it is best to be aware of these potential issues before you apply the packages. The button **Side Effect Report** opens a window where you can request an automatic analysis of the possible side effects based on the support packages in your selection. To request the report, scroll to the bottom of the window, verify your email address, and choose **Submit**. After at most a few hours, you will receive a message in your mailbox with a hyperlink to the report.

Add Selected Packages to the Download Basket

Choose **Add to Download Basket** to place the selected packages in the download basket of the S-user under whose ID you are logged on in the SAP Service Marketplace. If you are using the Maintenance Optimizer, then this S-user was set in the customizing actions.

Start the SAP Download Manager to download the packages.

> **Caution**
>
> Only the support packages created before April 2, 2007 will immediately be visible in the download list. Any support package created after this date can only be downloaded under control of the Maintenance Optimizer. In the Download Manager, these packages are displayed under the tab **Approval list**.

After downloading the packages, transfer them to the upgrade server using binary FTP.

Support Package for SPAM/SAINT

For the upgrade, you should use the latest version of the ABAP Support Package Manager (SPAM) and Add-on Installation Tool (SAINT), and this for both the source and the target release. For unclear reasons, the SPAM/SAINT update is not included in the SP stack, so you must select it separately.

You find the packages under *http://service.sap.com/PATCHES • Entry by Application group • Additional Components • SAP SPAM/SAINT Update*. The package for the target release is 700. Usually several versions of SPAM/SAINT are available for download; always download the latest one.

The SPAM/SAINT update for the source version can be found at the same location given in the previous paragraph, at least for release 4.0B and higher. If the source release is 3.1I, go to *http://service.sap.com/PATCHES • Archive for Support Packages and Patches • Entry by Application group • Additional Components • SAP SPAM/SAINT Update*.

Extract ABAP Packages to EPS Inbox

To bind the support packages into the upgrade, which is the recommended method, they must be visible to PREPARE. For this, you must place the packages in the EPS Inbox. To find the path of the EPS, Inbox do the following:

1. Start transaction SPAM in the ABAP system.

2. Choose **Extras → Settings**.

3. Click on the tab **Load packages**. The path to the EPS Inbox is shown in the field **Directory on Application Server**.

Support packages for ABAP are delivered in CAR (Compressed Archive) format. The files are stored in the CAR archive with a path relative to the main transport directory (the path name begins with *EPS/in*), so you must make that the current working directory when extracting. For the extraction, you use SAPCAR.

Extract all the ABAP packages that you downloaded, not forgetting the SPAM/SAINT update package for the source and target release.

► UNIX (assuming default location for EPS Inbox):

Log on as <sid>adm and enter:

```
cd /usr/sap/trans
SAPCAR -xvf <package>.CAR
```

► Windows (assuming default location for EPS Inbox):

Log on as <sid>adm and enter:

```
cmd
rem - <transhost> is the host name of the server where the
rem - transport directory resides
pushd \\<transhost>\sapmnt\trans
SAPCAR -xvf <package>.CAR
```

Copy Java Packages to EPS Inbox

If Java support packages are included, then simply copy the SCA files[5] to the EPS Inbox. Do not extract[6] the files; the JSPM will do this.

6.6.4 Corrections for the Upgrade Tools: The Fix Buffers

SAP will continuously correct problems in the upgrade programs and control files that were discovered after the initial release of the upgrade media. These corrections are made available in the form of a *fix buffer*, both for ABAP and for Java.

You must place the appropriate fix buffer in the upgrade directory before starting the PREPARE phase. If PREPARE cannot find the fix buffer for its components, it will stop and request that you install the fix buffer.

For ABAP upgrades, you must also download the latest version of the SAPup program. After the initial extraction of the upgrade tools from the Upgrade Master medium, you replace the version of SAPup that came from the DVD with this newer version. For information regarding the SAPup version, see Note 821032.

> **Important**
>
> Always download and install the latest version of the fix buffer and SAPup with *every* upgrade. This is an exception to the rule that you should keep the versions of software components (e.g., target kernel, target support package level) constant throughout the upgrade of the landscape.

Selecting the Correct Fix Buffer

The fix buffers for all components based on SAP NetWeaver 2004s (including SAP ERP 2005) are listed in SAP Note 813658. For each component, the note shows the name of the ABAP package and, where applicable, the Java package that contains the fixes.

Figure 6.14 shows the relevant section from Note 813658. Of course, this screenshot shows the list at the time of writing. Use the actual note and not the figure to determine which fix buffers you need.

---

5 Some Java patches have a different format, for example, ZIP, but most have the SCA (Software Component Archive) format.
6 Technically, however, this is possible because SCA files are compatible with the ZIP format.

Product	ABAP package name	Java package name
NW AS 7.0	FIX_NWAS700.UPG	FIX_J_NW04S.UPG
ERP 2005	FIX_ERP2005.UPG	FIX_J_BS05.UPG
SRM 5.0	FIX_SRM50.UPG	FIX_J_BS05.UPG
(SRM Server 5.5)		
CRM 5.0	FIX_CRM50.UPG	FIX_J_BS05.UPG
SCM 5.0	FIX_SCM50.UPG	FIX_J_BS05.UPG
NW AS 7.0 SR1	FIX_NWAS700SR1.UPG	FIX_J_NW04SSR1.UPG
ERP 2005 SR1	FIX_ERP2005SR1.UPG	
SRM 5.0 SR1	FIX_SRM50SR1.UPG	
(SRM Server 5.5)		
CRM 5.0 SR1	FIX_CRM50SR1.UPG	
SCM 5.0 SR1	FIX_SCM50SR1.UPG	
NW AS 7.0 SR2	FIX_NWAS700SR2.UPG	FIX_J_NW04SSR2.UPG
ERP 2005 SR2	FIX_ERP2005SR2.UPG	
SRM 5.0 SR2	FIX_SRM50SR2.UPG	
(SRM Server 5.5)		
CRM 5.0 SR2	FIX_CRM50SR2.UPG	
SCM 5.0 SR2	FIX_SCM50SR2.UPG	
SRM 6.0	FIX_SRM60.UPG	FIX_J_SRM60.UPG

Figure 6.14 List of Fix Buffers (Note 813658)

Notice the following:

▶ The fix buffer package differs not only according to the component but also according to SR. For example, you can see from the list that there are three fix buffers for SAP ERP 2005: one for the initial release, one for SR1, and one for SR2. Make sure you download and install the correct one (PREPARE will check this and will refuse to work with a nonmatching package).

▶ On the Java side, there are fewer packages, and some of these are shared between components; for example, there is a common package FIX_J_ BS05.UPG for ERP, SRM, SCM, and CRM (BS05 is Business Suite 2005).

Download and Install Fix Buffers

We now explain how to locate and download the fix buffer and how to extract the contents of the downloaded file into the upgrade directory. The extraction step really belongs in Chapter 7, but we prefer to keep the technical instructions together in one place. We'll make a reference back to this paragraph in Chapter 7.

Proceed as follows to download and install the fix buffers for ABAP and Java:

1. Find the correct name of the ABAP and Java fix buffers in Note 813658.

2. Go to *http://service.sap.com/PATCHES*.

3. Expand the entry by choosing *Application Group • Additional Components • Upgrade Tools • Corrections for Upgrade • Corrections for Upgrade 7.00 • OS Independent*.

4. Click on the tab **Downloads**. You now see the list of fix packages for ABAP and Java, each contained in a SAR (service application archive) file. A package also has a patch level. For most fix buffers, only one patch level will be listed; if there are more, choose the most recent one.

5. Add the packages you need to your download basket, download them, and transfer them to the upgrade directory on the server. Note 813658 instructs you to place the SAR file directly in the upgrade directory (e.g., */usr/sap/put*, */usr/sap/jupgrade*), but this is not necessary. Only the extracted files have to be placed there, but this is something you will do when you extract the package.

6. Extract the ABAP fix buffer to the ABAP upgrade directory.

   In the following example, we assume that you have placed the SAP upgrade media in a directory */sapcd* and that you also created a subdirectory */sapcd/fixes* to hold various corrections (fix buffers and others). The fix buffer used in the example is the one with patch level 12 for SAP ERP 2005 SR2.

   The extracted files must be placed in the top directory (not in a subdirectory — logged on as ⟨sid⟩adm):

   ```
   cd /usr/sap/put
   SAPCAR -xvf /sapcd/fixes/ERP2005SR2_12-20000914.SAR
   ```

   This will extract two files, one with extension .upg and an information file. Do not attempt to extract or process the UPG file; PREPARE will take care of this.

7. Extract the Java fix buffer to the Java upgrade directory. In the example, we extract the fix buffer with patch level 11 for SAP Business Suite 2005 (logged on as ⟨sid⟩adm):

   ```
   cd /usr/sap/jupgrade
   SAPCAR -xvf /sapcd/fixes/JNW04SSR2_8-20000914.SAR.SAR
   ```

   Again two files are extracted to the top directory, a UPG file and an info file.

SAPup Patch (ABAP)

Before starting the ABAP upgrade, you should replace the version of the SAPup executable delivered on the ABAP Upgrade Master DVD with the latest available patch. As with the fix buffer, always use the latest available version of SAPup with every upgrade rather than using the same version throughout the upgrade project.

It is possible for SAP to provide different "flavors" of SAPup depending on the component. These are denoted 7.00/1, 7.00/2, and so on. At the time of writing, only one flavor, 7.00/2, was in use, and this may remain so in the future. SAP Note 821032 describes which SAPup variant is needed for each component, so make sure you consult this note before downloading the patch.

Unlike the fix buffer, you can only install the SAPup patch after the initial extraction of the upgrade tools and not during the preparatory activities. Therefore, in this case, we do split up the instructions for locating and downloading the patch, which follow right after this, and the instructions for installing the SAPup patch, which you will find in Chapter 7.

Proceed as follows to select and download the SAPup patch:

1. Read the latest version of SAP Note 821032 to determine which SAPup variant you need for the component you will upgrade.
2. Go to *http://service.sap.com/PATCHES*.
3. Expand the entry by choosing *Application group • Additional Components • Upgrade Tools • SAPUP or SAPUP UNICODE • SAPUP 7.00 • [your operating system]*.
4. Add the SAR file with the correct SAPup patch to your download basket.
5. Start the Download Manager to download the file to your PC, and then transfer it to the server using FTP in binary mode.

Just as a reminder: Do not extract the SAR file with the SAPup patch into the upgrade directory yet because the script that will do the initial extraction of the upgrade tools installs the SAPup version from the Upgrade Master DVD. This would overwrite any other version of SAPup you had already placed in the upgrade directory. You must wait until after this initial extraction and then replace SAPup.

In the previous chapter, you learned about the organizational measures, system checks, research, and other actions that are necessary to prepare for the technical upgrade. Now the time has come to actually start the upgrade. This chapter will explain which upgrade tools exist, how they work, and how you use them to control and monitor the upgrade.

7 A Guided Tour of the Upgrade Tools

The purpose of this chapter is to introduce you to the SAP upgrade tools. You will learn how they work, where to find them, how to install them and get them going, and how to use their management and monitoring features so that you stay in control of the upgrade and know at all times what is happening.

The information presented in this chapter lays the common foundation for everything that is to follow. By "common," we mean those functions, mostly in the area of monitoring and managing the upgrade, that you can use in any upgrade scenario regardless of the component and release you are upgrading. Viewing the upgrade logs, changing the passwords of upgrade users, or asking the upgrade process to trigger an alert when it stops are useful functions in every upgrade.

When we describe the upgrade procedure for various components in the coming chapters, features of the upgrade tools will be shown as and when they are needed. However, those chapters concentrate on the task at hand rather than on the mechanics of the tools themselves. When dealing with a complex process such as an SAP upgrade — especially when things go awry — knowledge is power. That knowledge begins with becoming familiar with the upgrade programs and user interfaces. Being comfortable with these will greatly improve your effectiveness; you will do the right thing at the right moment, and you will be able to correctly identify and solve problems if and when they arise.

Compared with earlier versions, the current generation of SAP upgrade tools is either brand-new or at least comes equipped with a new look and feel. However, the tools are built upon operational concepts and methods of user interaction that have been around since early versions of SAP R/3 and have had plenty of time to stabilize and mature. The tools have been thoroughly tested and tweaked, and when the going gets tough, they will serve you reliably. They won't tie themselves into knots, spew gibberish at you (or go incommunicado), or vanish into thin air altogether.

7.1 Introducing the Tools

Since Basis release 6.20, SAP delivers and supports both the SAP NetWeaver Application Server ABAP and the SAP NetWeaver Application Server Java.

Whichever component you upgrade, if it is based on the SAP NetWeaver 2004s platform, you will always use the same upgrade programs:

▶ SAPup for the upgrade of ABAP

▶ SAPJup for the upgrade of Java

SAPup is the successor to the *R3up* program, which was used in all previous versions of SAP. SAPJup is new because SAP NetWeaver 2004s with AS 7.00 is the first release that provides an upgrade procedure for the AS Java.

To control the upgrade process and to interface with the user running the upgrade, the ABAP and Java components also provide applications of their own:

▶ The Upgrade Assistant Server and Upgrade Assistant GUI for the ABAP upgrade

▶ The SDT Server and SDT GUI for the Java upgrade (SDT stands for Software Delivery Tools)

If the system to be upgraded only runs one stack, then you only use the upgrade tools for that stack. For a pure ABAP system, you use the ABAP tools SAPup and the Upgrade Assistant. For a pure Java system, you use the Java tools SAPJup and the SDT Server and GUI. With double-stack systems (ABAP + Java), you use the two combined.

7.1.1 Synchronized Upgrades

If the system runs both an ABAP and a Java stack, then you will need both sets of upgrade tools. The tools are designed in such a way that each knows of the other's existence; more than that, at several points during the upgrade, they will synchronize their activity, allowing the other upgrade to catch up or waiting until the other side has completed a critical task. For example, just before the ABAP upgrade hits the point where it shuts down the SAP central instance, marking the beginning of downtime, it will verify how far the concurrently running Java upgrade has progressed. If SAPJup has not yet reached its beginning of downtime, then ABAP will wait. The inverse is also true.

By running in a synchronized manner, the ABAP and Java upgrades can be executed simultaneously without the risk of conflicts (e.g., one side stopping the SAP system at a time when the other side is working in it). There is one precondition, however, you must always *start the ABAP upgrade (SAPup) first*. The ABAP side determines that the SAP system is double-stack and takes the necessary measures to make sure that the ABAP and Java upgrades will be able to run together.

The requirement to start the ABAP upgrade first has little or no effect on the overall time needed to upgrade the system. Unless it runs into some serious trouble, the runtime of the Java upgrade is much shorter than that of the ABAP upgrade. This is true both for the uptime part of the upgrade (especially if you artificially slow down the ABAP import phases) and for the downtime part (where the Java side mostly does software deployment, whereas the ABAP side also has to deal with things like table conversions and data conversion programs).

7.1.2 Upgrade Program and Control Program

The general architecture of the ABAP and Java upgrade tools is very similar. Both are made up of the actual upgrade program (SAPup, SAPJup) and a control program (Upgrade Assistant, SDT). The upgrade program drives the actual upgrade activities, such as data imports, structure conversions of objects in the database, Java deployment and ABAP transports, and so on. The control program does not do any technical upgrade work. Its main responsibility is to handle communication with the users (who are connected via their GUI) and to control and monitor the upgrade processes. Via the control program, you will instruct the upgrade program to start (and sometimes to stop). If errors occur, you will be notified of these through the control program; after investigating and fixing the error, you will, once more via the control program, order the upgrade process to retry the failed step.

7.1.3 The Upgrade Programs: SAPup and SAPJup

SAPup (for ABAP) and SAPJup (for Java) are responsible for running the entire upgrade process from start to — hopefully successful — finish. However, they do not do any of the dirty work themselves; this they leave to the appropriate utility, such as *tp* (to import transport requests into the AS ABAP) or *JSPM* (Java Support Package Manager, to deploy software on the AS Java). The main task of the upgrade programs is to start these worker utilities when needed, to monitor them and examine their result, to interrupt or slow down the upgrade when needed, to obtain input and instructions (not directly but via the control program) from the user who administers the upgrade, and to report the progress of the upgrade and alert the user in case of problems (again through the control program).

An upgrade is really a serial process made up of a long series of activity steps or *phases*. The total number of phases depends on the SAP release and the nature of the upgraded component, but in an ABAP upgrade, there are well over 200 phases and in a Java upgrade over 150. Each phase in the upgrade deals with one specific task. What the phase has to do can range from the simple and almost trivial, such as checking or modifying a flag in a database table, to the very complex and elaborate, such as activating the new dictionary or deploying the new versions of business applications. With such vast differences in the amount of work a phase must do, it is easy to understand that the runtime of the upgrade phases will also vary widely. Many phases will take just fractions of a second (which does not make them any less important!), but others may run for several hours. One group of phases, the ABAP database import, can even be slowed done artificially to minimize its impact on the server load (more on this later).

The fact that the upgrade process is *serial* in nature does not mean that it is also *single-threaded*. Some heavy-duty phases, such as dictionary activation, table conversion, or the huge data imports and data conversion runs during downtime, use parallel processing to benefit as much as possible from the capacity of the server and thus reduce the upgrade time.

7.1.4   PREPARE versus Upgrade

Both the ABAP and Java upgrade processes are divided into two major parts: one is called PREPARE, and the other is the actual upgrade. Both the PREPARE and the upgrade are subdivided into phases, as explained previously.

PREPARE

As you can guess from the name, PREPARE deals with all the preparatory activities in the system to be upgraded. The first thing PREPARE will do is prompt you for the parameters of the upgrade, such as the location of the upgrade media, host names, passwords, and so on. These parameters will be used throughout the upgrade, and you will not have to enter them again (not that anything you enter is irreversible; you have the opportunity to change parameters later on if necessary).

After asking for the upgrade parameters, PREPARE copies data and programs into the upgrade directory, imports the upgrade tools into the database, and installs the shadow instance (for ABAP). Add-ons, support packages, and languages are integrated into the upgrade. After the initial configuration of the upgrade, PREPARE verifies that the source system meets the requirements of the upgrade process and of the target release. This produces an action list, which must be taken care of before the actual upgrade can start. If the first pass of PREPARE detects errors (i.e., preconditions for the upgrade that are not met), then you must repeat the corresponding parts of PREPARE until no more problems are reported.

PREPARE is executed with the system up and running. End users are not affected. As explained elsewhere in this book, you normally run PREPARE several days before the actual upgrade. Runtimes vary, but for a "typical" ABAP PREPARE, you should expect a runtime between four and eight hours, mostly depending on factors such as the number of support packages to bind into the upgrade, the number of languages, and quite a few more.

Java PREPARE also runs during uptime. Like ABAP PREPARE, its first action is to prompt for the upgrade parameters. Its other tasks are also similar to those of ABAP PREPARE, but it normally has less work to do and therefore has a shorter runtime (typically between 1.5 and 3 hours, but again this is just an estimate based on our own upgrade experience).

Upgrade (ABAP)

When PREPARE has done its work and is satisfied with the condition of the system, you can start the actual upgrade. Way back yonder, this was the moment when you asked users of the SAP system to kindly log off and find some other occupation for the next few days. Today, that will happen only if you unwisely decided to run the upgrade in resource-minimized mode. You find more information about the downtime-minimized and resource-minimized upgrade modes in Chapter 4.

If you opted for the downtime-minimized method — as you ought to do — then the first (and longer) part of the upgrade happens while the SAP system is still in normal use. During this time, the upgrade performs all the necessary actions to build the shadow repository containing not only the new release but also a copy of all your own development. Early on in the process, the upgrade imports the data from the Upgrade Export media into the database. Because of the performance impact this data import may have and because of the number of database logs it will generate, you have the option of artificially slowing down the import. In this way, the upgrade takes as few resources as possible away from the production system. A slowed-down import also enables the backup procedures to keep up with the volume of database logs.

Not very long after the database import finishes, the upgrade starts up the shadow instance. After some preparatory work to make this instance fully usable, the upgrade will stop and ask you to carry out the dictionary modification adjustment using Transaction SPDD. When this is finished, the activation of the new dictionary begins (still in the shadow instance and shadow repository). After the activation and some other phases, the upgrade shuts down the shadow instance, which will not be needed again. Next, the main upgrade transports and the support packages that were bound into the upgrade are imported into the shadow repository. All the while, the main system remains productive.

Finally, with the shadow repository fully built up, the upgrade will inform you that all its uptime processing is done, and that it now waits for your permission to shut down the system and enter downtime. With correct planning and without accidents, this should happen some time before the start of the planned downtime window. For instance, the upgrade might reach the downtime point on Thursday afternoon while planned downtime begins at 7 p.m. Friday evening. In that case, you simply leave the upgrade waiting.

After the downtime window begins, you inform the upgrade via the upgrade GUI that it may stop the SAP system. Between then and a time quite close to the end of the upgrade, the upgrade process takes full control of the system, stopping and starting it as and when required. During this downtime phase, the system is placed in "upgrade lock" mode, which means that you can only log on as SAP* or DDIC. Except for problem solving, there is normally no need to log on to the system (and you are bound to be kicked out without warning anyway when the upgrade reaches a phase in which it has to stop the SAP system).

Near the end of its run, the upgrade process unlocks the system, which by now is fully on the new version, and restarts it for the last time. The upgrade has only a few more phases to run (although some of these, e.g., the variant restore, can still be quite lengthy), but during this time, you can already log on to the system and start on the postprocessing tasks. After some final interaction, the upgrade kindly informs you that the upgrade is complete (somewhat optimistically because there is still a load of post-upgrade work waiting), produces a timing document and an evaluation form, and then stops.

Upgrade (Java)

The Java upgrade process (SAPJup) is on the whole a simpler affair than its ABAP counterpart and is likely to take less time. By far the most important task for the Java upgrade is the deployment of the new release on the AS Java.

After you start SAPJup, the process will soon stop to announce the beginning of downtime. Once you confirm this, SAPJup takes control of the AS Java, stopping and restarting it whenever necessary.

When it reaches the end of downtime, the upgrade will again stop, prompt you to back up the database and Java upgrade directory, and restart the AS Java. After producing an evaluation form, the upgrade process ends.

The Java upgrade does not use a shadow instance.

Synchronized Upgrade (ABAP and Java)

With a double-stack system, you run two PREPAREs and also two upgrade programs. The ABAP upgrade must *always* be started first, before the Java upgrade. Each side is aware of the other's existence. During much of the time, the two upgrades work independently, each on its own stack, but at some critical points, it is necessary that they synchronize with each other. For example, the ABAP upgrade will not enter downtime unless the Java upgrade is ready to do so as well (and vice versa). The one who reaches the downtime point first will wait for the other to catch up. Another example is that in a double-stack upgrade, the ABAP side is responsible for installing the new kernel. If the Java upgrade reaches the point where it needs the new kernel and sees that the ABAP side still has to carry out the kernel switch, it will wait for ABAP.

This superficial description of the double-stack upgrade process only serves as an introduction. Chapters 8 to 15 describe a complete ABAP-cum-Java upgrade, including the two PREPARE processes.

7.1.5 The Control Programs: Upgrade Assistant and SDT Server/GUI

Both control programs are designed as two-tier client-server applications, with a server program running on the upgrade (SAP central instance) host, and a GUI running on the user's workstation.

Despite this similarity in design, the ABAP and Java upgrade control programs are not completely identical. Their look-and-feel is not quite the same, nor are they used in exactly the same manner. In part, this goes back to their origins. The ancestor of the current ABAP upgrade tools was a program called *R3up*, which back in the old days was used for upgrades to SAP R/3 releases 2.x and 3.x. The old R3up was both upgrade and control program. It had no GUI client; you simply started it from the OS command line and interacted with it via this same OS session window. In a less than perfect world, this had obvious drawbacks: even the briefest network failure between server and PC could kill the active upgrade process, not to mention a hanging PC, a Windows error, or user mistakes such as a badly aimed mouse click or Ctrl+C.

With the advent of release 4.0, SAP redesigned the upgrade program, separating the server activity (upgrading) from the user interaction (monitoring, parameter input, starting and stopping). The former was still handled by R3up[1], which had now become a strictly server-based program running in the background and thus invulnerable to whatever went wrong at the frontend. The interaction and com-

---

1 The program continued to be called *R3*up until SAP NetWeaver 2004 (Basis release 6.40). With SAP NetWeaver 2004s/Basis 7.00, the name changed to SAPup.

munication part was confided to a new Upgrade Assistant (UA), which itself consisted of a server process running on the upgrade host — and like R3up shielded against frontend trouble — and a GUI, which could be used to connect to and disconnect from the upgrade at will.

> **Note**
>
> Even today, it is possible to run SAPup (the successor to R3up) in the so-called "scroll mode", where you run it in an OS session window like a DOS shell for Windows or a Telnet session for UNIX and interact with it directly. This can help if for some reason using the UA GUI is impossible, but it should only be used as a last resort.

SDT for Java is a very close relative of the installation utility SAPINST (the picture of the cable-stayed bridge on the progress screen will be familiar to you if you have ever done SAP installations for Basis 6.40 or higher). Like UA, SDT consists of a server and a GUI client. However, as you'll see next, its features are more limited and it does not provide the same flexibility as UA for ABAP.

7.1.6 The ABAP Upgrade Assistant (UA)

Chances are that you will be doing far more ABAP upgrades than Java upgrades. Therefore, let's look at the Upgrade Assistant (UA) for ABAP first.

UA is the "driver" program of the entire upgrade process. The UA itself does not do any technical upgrade work. Its main responsibility is to handle communication with the users (who are connected via their UA GUI) and to control and monitor the upgrade processes.

The UA is designed as a two-tier client-server application with an Upgrade Assistant Server (UA Server) running on the upgrade host and one or more UA GUI sessions on users' workstations.

An important characteristic of the ABAP UA (which it does not share with its Java counterpart) is its capability to have multiple users logged on via GUI to the running upgrade, and the distinction that it makes between two user roles: the "administrator" and the "observer." We'll discuss these upgrade roles first before taking a closer look at the UA Server and GUI.

Users: admin and observer

When you use the UA GUI for the ABAP PREPARE and upgrade, you must *log on* to the GUI as a valid user; this is one of the main differences between the ABAP UA and the Java SDT. UA knows two users: the Upgrade administrator (user ID: *admin*) and the Upgrade observer (user ID: *observer*).

▶ The *administrator* has active control over the upgrade process. This user has the ability to start and stop upgrade processes and to interact with the upgrade via input screens in GUI.

▶ An *observer* has only a passive role. Observers can monitor the progress of the upgrade via GUI, but they cannot actively influence it. Their GUI screens are not enabled for input.

At any time during the upgrade, at most one administrator session can be logged on, but there can be any number of observers. While they are connected to UA, GUI users can dynamically change roles: administrators can demote themselves to observers, and an observer can promote himself to administrator (thereby automatically demoting the current administrator if one is logged on).

Administrators and observers are roles defined by the UA GUI. It is not necessary for an UA GUI to be active at any time; the upgrade can run nicely even without any user session connected. For instance, if a lengthy upgrade phase starts late in the evening and is likely to run through the best part of the night, the administrator and the present observers may decide to log off from their UA GUI and go home. At that moment, there is neither an administrator nor an observer, but that does not bother the running upgrade in any way. If the upgrade stops, for example because of an error, then it will simply wait until an administrator comes online and communicates with the upgrade via the error screen in the UA GUI. If the alert service is enabled (discussed later), then UA will also invoke the alert script so that someone is notified of the stop.

Both user roles are protected by a password. You set the administrator password the first time you start the UA Server (discussed next). You do not create named users for UA; to log on with a certain role, you simply enter the password of that role. The logon screen of the UA GUI does give you the option to enter a name, but this is optional and purely informative; you may choose to enter your real name there or anything that helps others to identify you. You can also enter a contact telephone number on the logon screen.

The UA Server

The server side of UA is the Upgrade Assistant Server (UA Server). This process runs on the same host as the actual upgrade, that is, the host where the central instance of the SAP system resides. You do not interact directly with the UA Server except once: When you start the server for the first time, it will prompt you for the password of the administrator. After that, the server will never interact directly with you again, so you may then let it run as a background process (on OSs supporting this). You'll see the commands to run the UA Server later in this chapter. All further communication between the administrator and the UA Server are via the UA GUI.

The PREPARE and the ABAP upgrade program (SAPup) run under the control of the UA Server. The server will start these processes when instructed to do so from the administrator's UA GUI session. From then on, it monitors the processes, forwarding their console output to all open UA GUI windows. When an upgrade stops for interaction, either because it needs parameter input or because an error has occurred, the server will handle the user interaction via the administrator's UA GUI session (if an administrator is currently logged on), and pass on this input to the upgrade process.

The server is started from the OS command line. It is stopped from inside the UA GUI, or you can also terminate it at the OS level when it is no longer needed. All this will be covered in detail next.

The UA GUI

The client is the UA GUI. Client and server communicate with each other via a TCP/IP port (port 4241). On a second port (4239), the UA Server is capable of receiving HTTP requests, allowing it to interact with a browser running on a user's PC. Access via a browser can be used to launch the UA GUI or to request information related to the upgrade, such as the phase list or the evaluation form. We'll take a closer look at the browser interface later.

Although the UA GUI runs on the user's PC, it is not necessary to perform a separate installation of the upgrade tools on the PC. The UA GUI (like the UA Server) is a Java application that is uploaded to the server during the initial run of the PREPARE script (described later in this chapter). Both the UA Server and UA GUI are Java applications residing in Java Archive (JAR) files. When the user starts the UA GUI from the browser, the Java code for the UA GUI is loaded onto the PC under control of Java Web Start.

Java Web Start is a Java application used to deploy and run *client-side* Java applications. The traditional method for client-side code is the use of applets, but applets face two major limitations that make them very difficult to use in many environments:

▶ Applets work under serious security restrictions; for example, they normally cannot access local files or external network addresses.

▶ Applets depend on the Java VM (virtual machine) built into the browser, which may cause version problems and incompatibilities.

Java Web Start deploys and starts applications to the client and is also capable of uploading and installing the correct version of the Java Runtime Environment (JRE) at the same time.

Figure 7.1 shows a simple diagram of the architecture of the UA. Here an administrator and several observers are logged on to the UA GUI; there are also active browser sessions communicating with the server via its HTTP interface.

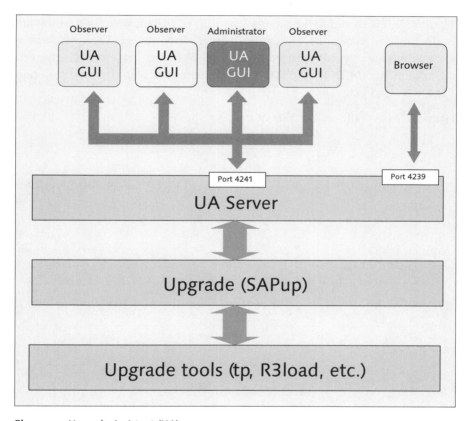

Figure 7.1 Upgrade Assistant (UA)

7.1.7   SDT for Java

Like UA for ABAP, the upgrade tool for Java has a client-server design, consisting of the SDT Server and SDT GUI. SDT is the underlying framework that the Java upgrade tool has in common with the SAP installation utility SAPINST. Being built on the same platform, SAPINST and the Java upgrade GUI have much the same look and feel as we mentioned earlier.

The Java upgrade behaves in a way that is very similar to its ABAP counterpart. The server runs on the upgrade host and does not interact directly with the user. It controls the two major phases of the upgrade, the Java PREPARE and the Java upgrade (SAPJup). The server also handles all communication between the user and the upgrade process. Messages from the upgrade process, including requests for user input and error reports, are sent on to the SDT GUI. User commands and user input are transmitted from the GUI via the server to the upgrade process.

The SDT GUI is started in the same way as the UA GUI, namely from a browser. In the browser, you connect to the SDT Server via port 6239. The application is loaded from the server and started via the Java Web Start framework (see the earlier section *The UA GUI*). The SDT GUI communicates with the server via port 6241.

Figure 7.2 shows the architecture of the Java upgrade.

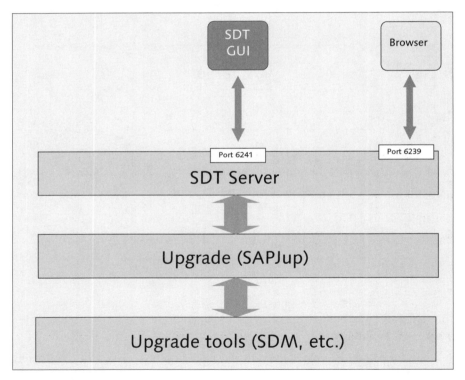

Figure 7.2 Java Upgrade

The similarity with the ABAP upgrade is clear, but you may be struck by a major difference too. In Figure 7.1, several users were connected to the ABAP upgrade via their UA GUI; only one of them, the administrator, could be in control, but there could be any number of observers simultaneously logged on. In Figure 7.2 for Java, you only see one SDT GUI connected. This is because the Java upgrade has no notion of different users. It does not make a distinction between active administrators and passive observers, and only allows one user to be logged on to the SDT GUI at any one time. Any attempt to open a second SDT GUI on a running Java upgrade will simply produce a rather terse error message (see Figure 7.3) and leave you no other choice but to close this GUI.

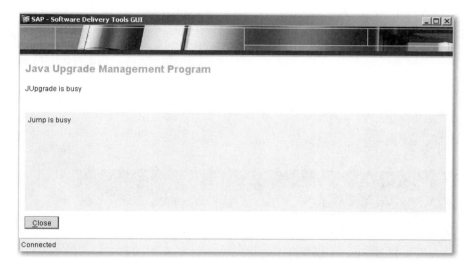

Figure 7.3 Error When Starting a Second SDT GUI

7.1.8 Prerequisites for the Upgrade Tools

The upgrade tools for both ABAP and Java need a Java installation on the server and on the workstation where you run the GUI.

Java SDK or JRE for ABAP Upgrade Assistant

The ABAP UA is a Java application, which means that a JVM must be installed on the upgrade host (where the UA Server runs) and also on every workstation where you intend to run the UA GUI.

The Java requirement is strictest on the server side. The UA *Server* requires the Java Software Development Kit (SDK) version 1.4 or higher. An installation of the JRE is not sufficient.

The UA GUI is less demanding. Here the Java version must be 1.1 or higher, and both the Java SDK and JRE will do.

> **Important**
>
> If the SAP system to be upgraded contains a Java stack, then the host must also meet the requirements for AS Java. These will normally be stricter than those for the UA Server. With AS 7.0, the Java SDK version must be 1.4, not lower (1.3), nor higher (1.5). More precise restrictions, for example, a specific minimum version of the 1.4 Java SDK, may apply. Full details are in SAP Note 723909 and in a set of platform-dependent notes, which are all listed in Note 723909. In practice, you should always use the latest available Java SDK within the range of supported versions (which is actually what Note 723909 tells you to do).

To check the currently installed Java version, both on the server and on the GUI workstations, open a command shell, log in as the SAP administrator (user `<sid>adm`), and type the command:

```
java -version
```

Figure 7.4 shows an example on a Windows PC.

```
C:\users\dx1adm>java -version
java version "1.5.0_06"
Java(TM) 2 Runtime Environment, Standard Edition (build 1.5.0_06-b05)
Java HotSpot(TM) Client VM (build 1.5.0_06-b05, mixed mode)
```

Figure 7.4 Checking the Java Version

This workstation runs a Java 1.5 version. For UA (Server or GUI), this is all right. For AS 7.0 Java, this would *not* be all right (only 1.4 supported).

Java SDK or JRE for SDT

SDT is also a Java application. Because SDT is used to upgrade AS Java systems, a Java SDK must obviously be installed on the server. As explained previously, version 1.4 SDK is required. At the time of writing, 1.5 SDK was not supported. 1.4 SDK also meets the requirements for the Java upgrade tools on the server side.

On the client side, the workstation must meet the requirements of the SAPINST tool, that is, a Java JRE must be present. We recommend that you use 1.4 JRE or SDK on the workstation like on the server, although 1.5 should also be okay.

7.2   Installation of the Upgrade Tools: ABAP

Making the upgrade tools ready for use is easy: all you need to do is run a script and, in the case of ABAP, replace the extracted version of the SAPup utility with the latest patch.

7.2.1 Initial Run of PREPARE

The script for the initial extraction is located on the ABAP Upgrade Master DVD. This script is called PREPARE, which is a little confusing because the first major phase of the upgrade is also called PREPARE. Keep in mind that the two are not related.

The following section describes how to use the PREPARE script on UNIX/Linux and on Windows. For IBM iSeries, the procedure is different; refer to the section *Starting PREPARE for the First Time* in the Upgrade Guide for IBM iSeries for the exact commands.

7.2.2 Initial PREPARE Run: UNIX and Linux

In this example, we assume that you have placed disk copies of the upgrade media in a server directory */sapcd*. You have placed the ABAP Upgrade Master CD in a subdirectory named */sapcd/UPGMSTR_ABAP*.

To run PREPARE initially, proceed as follows:

1. Log on as user `<sid>adm`.
2. Switch to the upgrade directory:

   `cd /usr/sap/put`

3. Type the command:

   `/sapcd/UPGMSTR_ABAP/PREPARE`

   If the name of the ABAP upgrade directory is not */usr/sap/put,* then you must specify the path via a command-line argument, for example:

   `/sapcd/UPGMSTR_ABAP/PREPARE upgdir=/usr/sap/putPRD`

   Keep in mind that to use an upgrade directory with a name different from the default, you must also adapt the SAP profile parameter DIR_PUT.

4. The PREPARE script creates the required subdirectories in the upgrade directory, installs the initial set of upgrade tools (including the SAPup executable), and performs some basic tests, for example, checking the availability of the C++ runtime library.

5. Finally, PREPARE prompts you for an action:

   ```
   Select operation mode:
                - "EXIT"
                - "SERVER"
                - "SCROLL"
   Enter one of these options [EXIT] :=
   ```

Possible choices at this point are:

▶ EXIT

End the script. This is the default choice and also the one we recommend you use.

▶ SERVER

This starts the UA Server. It is preferable to start the UA Server manually later.

▶ SCROLL

Starts SAPup in scroll mode (see Section 7.1.5). Except in very special circumstances, you will never use this option.

7.2.3 Initial PREPARE run: Windows

The command file *PREPARE.BAT* does nothing other than invoke the JavaScript file *PREPARE.JS*. For this method to work, Windows Script Host (WSH) must be available. WSH is a facility that provides powerful scripting capabilities. WSH is installed by default, so normally it will always be available. However, it is possible for system administrators to disable or uninstall WSH for security reasons (scripts have been abused as virus carriers). The WSH version on the SAP server might also be too low. The SAP upgrade requires at least WSH version 5.6.

You don't need to check anything related to WSH before starting the PREPARE script. If WSH is missing or its version is too low, then PREPARE will report this. If you do want to check the WSH version upfront, then do the following:

1. Open a DOS shell (CMD).

2. Type the command

   cscript

3. The output shows the version banner followed by the command-line options.

4. If necessary, you can download WSH free of charge from the Microsoft Download Center at *http://www.microsoft.com/downloads*.

5. To run the PREPARE script, you must log on as the <sid>adm user.

6. To start the script, open Explorer, and browse to the directory of the Upgrade Master DVD (see Figure 7.5).

7. Start *PREPARE.BAT*.

8. A file selection box opens (see Figure 7.6). Browse to the ABAP upgrade directory.

9. Click **OK**. After a few seconds, a DOS box opens prompting you for an action (see Figure 7.7).

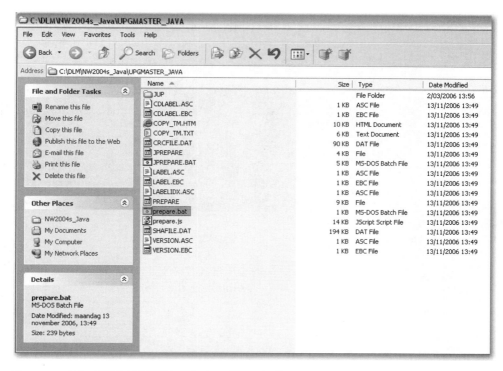

Figure 7.5 Select PREPARE.BAT in Windows Upgrade Master

Figure 7.6 Select Upgrade Directory

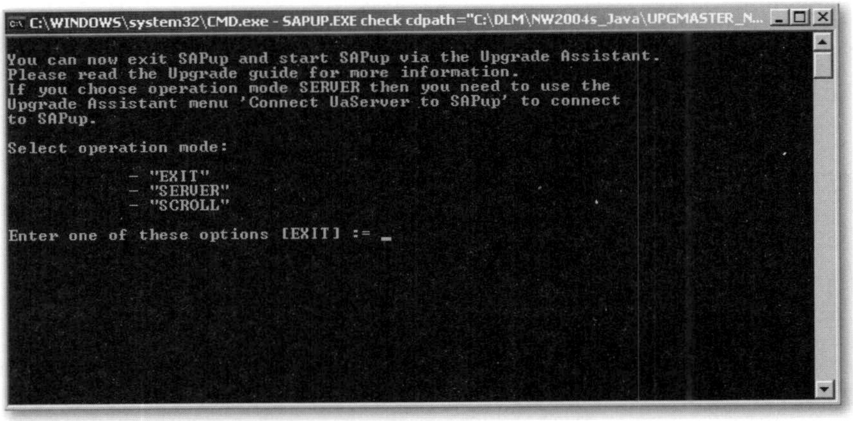

Figure 7.7 Action Prompt After Initial Extraction

The available choices are the same as with UNIX: EXIT (the default), SERVER, and SCROLL. See Section 7.2.2 for a description of the choices.

7.2.4 Replace SAPup

The script has installed the SAPup executable (*SAPUP.EXE* in the case of Windows) in the subdirectory *bin* of your upgrade directory. Before starting the upgrade, you must now replace this version of SAPup with the latest patch, which you downloaded earlier from the SAP Service Marketplace. Instructions for identifying and downloading the required SAPup patch were given in Chapter 6.

Use the following instructions to install the SAPup patch *after* you have run the initial PREPARE extraction script:

1. Open a command shell on the server and log on as <sid>adm.

2. Determine the current version of SAPup:

Unix/Linux

`./SAPup -V`

Windows

`.\SAPup -V`

This will also show the flavor. Example:

`This is SAPup version 7.00/2, build 24.067`

3. Optionally, save a copy of the current SAPup:

   Unix/Linux:

   ```
   cd /usr/sap/put/bin
   mv SAPup SAPup.orig
   ```

   Windows:

   ```
   cd \usr\sap\put\bin
   rename sapup.exe sapup_orig.exe
   ```

4. Extract the patch archive. The actual name changes with the patch level. <...> denotes the variable part of the name:

   ```
   SAPCAR -xvf SAPup7002_<...>.SAR
   ```

5. Repeat the version check. The version will be higher, but the flavor must be the same.

   Unix/Linux:

   ```
   ./SAPup -V
   ```

   Windows:

   ```
   .\SAPup -V
   ```

> **Caution!**
>
> Exchange the version of SAPup only *before* you start the upgrade. Never change SAPup during the *upgrade* unless SAP instructs you to do so!

7.3   Using the ABAP Upgrade Assistant

In this section you will learn how to start the ABAP UA and how to use the functions of the UA GUI.

7.3.1   Starting the UA Server

If possible, you should let the UA Server run as a background process to prevent unwanted terminations, for example, because you accidentally close the window it is running in, or because the network connection server and PC is interrupted. Windows does not give you this possibility, so you will have to run the UA Server in a DOS shell that normally remains open throughout the upgrade. On UNIX/Linux, you can start the UA Server as a background process; there you can also use the nohup[2] facility to make sure the server process keeps running even after the session from where it was started logs off.

The very first time you run the UA Server, it will prompt you for the administrator password. User interaction is only possible with a process running in the foreground, so the first start of the server should always be in the foreground, even on UNIX and Linux.

For the first run, follow these steps:

1. Open a command shell on the upgrade host (DOS box, Telnet session), and log in as <sid>adm.

2. Type the command:

   ```
   java -cp /usr/sap/put/ua/ua.jar UaServer
   ```

   For Windows, use the same command with the slashes reversed.

   The name of the Java class (UaServer) is case-sensitive, also on Windows.

3. The server prompts for the password of the *administrator* user. Enter and confirm the password.

   ```
   Please enter administrator password
   Enter password:*********
   Confirm password:*********
   ```

4. On Windows, you can leave this server process running. The following steps are for UNIX/Linux only.

5. On UNIX/Linux, wait until you see the message

   ```
   UaServer> Ready
   ```

6. At that point, terminate the running server with Ctrl + C.

7. Restart the UA Server as a background and no-hangup process:

   ```
   nohup java -cp /usr/sap/put/ua/ua.jar UaServer &
   ```

7.3.2 Starting the UA GUI

To start the UA GUI, you first connect to the UA Server using an Internet browser. The Java Web Start framework will then launch the GUI on your workstation.

---

2 nohup (no-hangup) is a feature of UNIX that allows you to start a background process inside a command session and keeps this process alive when your session ends (normal background processes terminate along with the shell from where they were started). For example, to run a command comm. in this way, type "nohup comm. &" (the ampersand specifies that comm. must run in the background, and the nohup prefix ensures the command does not get terminated when the session ends).

Connect to UA Server via a Browser

1. To connect to the UA server, open a browser on your PC.

2. Type the URL *http://<server>:4239* where *<server>* is the host name (or possibly the full domain name, depending on how networking is set up) of the host where the UA Server is running. Example:

   http://sapdev.mycomp.com:4239

   If you decide to start the browser on the upgrade host itself rather than on a local PC, you may also use the URL *http://localhost:4239.*

3. The main page of the ABAP UA now opens (see Figure 7.8).

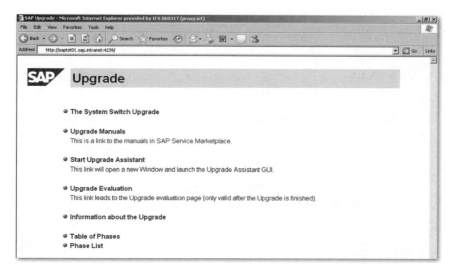

Figure 7.8 ABAP UA Main Page

4. If you do not see this window, check the following:

   ▶ Is the host name you specified correct and can it be resolved to an IP address from your PC? Use `ping` to check this.

   ▶ Is the UA Server running and ready to receive browser requests? Open the command window where you started the UA server and make sure the server has displayed the messages:

   ```
   UaServer> Starting HTTP server
   UaServer> HTTP server started
   UaServer> Ready
   ```

   ▶ If you started the server as a `nohup` background process (UNIX and Linux), then you might not see these messages in the command window. In that case, look at the standard output file (typically *nohup.out* in the directory from where you started the server).

If the server encounters an error, it writes a Java stack trace and terminates. This trace can be quite long, but the first few messages will usually reveal what the problem was.

In some cases, the port 4239, which is used for communication between the browser and the UA Server, may be unusable, for instance, because it is blocked by a firewall or because it is already in use by another application (which could even be another SAP upgrade running on the same host). In that case, ask the network administrator either to open the ports for the UA (if blocking by the firewall is the problem) or to determine alternative port numbers you can use. See Section 7.3.4 for information about the port numbers used by the UA.

Start the UA GUI

1. On the main upgrade page, click on **Start Upgrade Assistant**.

2. The Java Web Start window pops up, and the loading of the application begins (seee Figure 7.9).

Figure 7.9 Java Web Start Loading the UA GUI

Sometimes Java Web Start encounters an error while it loads the UA GUI to the workstation; see the section *Java Web Start errors while loading the UA GUI*.

3. When the loading is complete, the logon screen of the UA GUI appears (see Figure 7.10).

4. Log on as administrator. The user name and password fields are mandatory. What you enter for the user name is entirely up to you; anything that identifies you is acceptable. The UA GUI only demands that the user name be at least two characters long.

If you expect that several users will access the UA GUI during the upgrade, then it is convenient that you also specify your telephone number.

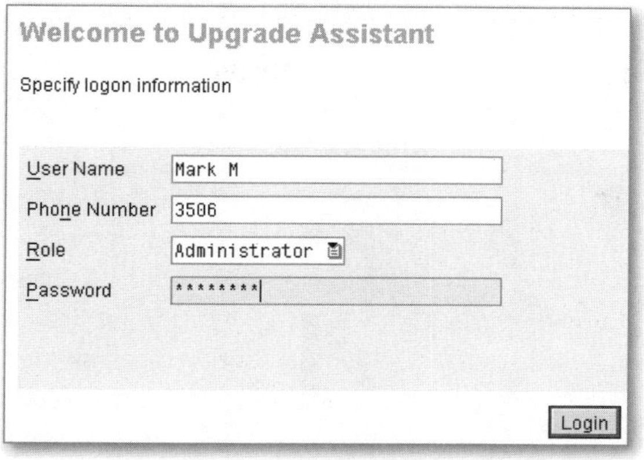

Figure 7.10 Logon Screen of UA GUI

5. Click on **Login**.

6. On the next screen, you can choose functions from the menu. In the next section, we describe the available functions in more detail. These functions are common to all ABAP upgrades (the UA GUI menu is always the same regardless of the product you are upgrading).

Java Web Start Errors While Loading the UA GUI

If Java Web Start is unable to upload and start the UA GUI to your workstation, an error Unable to launch Upgrade Assistant appears (see Figure 7.11). Click on the **Details** button to see more information about the problem. The most useful information is probably in the upper parts of the Java stack trace, which you find under the **Exceptions** tab.

Java stack traces are not gems of readability, but most of the time you will be able to find at least one interesting term pointing to the cause of the error. In this case UnknownHostException followed by a server name indicates that Java Web Start was unable to resolve the host name of the server. In our experience, this is the most common problem you can encounter with the Java Web Start mechanism. The usual cause is that the host name of the SAP server is not known in the network configuration (DNS). Adding an entry in the local HOSTS file on the PC often — but not always — helps; otherwise, you must report the problem to the network administrator.

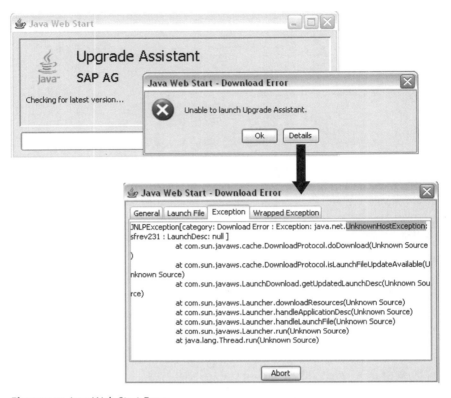

Figure 7.11 Java Web Start Error

7.3.3 Features of the UA GUI

Let's begin with a brief tour of the menu functions, and then we'll turn our attention to the different services UA provides for controlling the upgrade and, whenever necessary, changing its behavior.

The **File** menu:

▶ **File → Change Role**
Switches the UA GUI session between administrator and observer roles. If you switch from observer to administrator, the current administrator (if there is one) is automatically demoted to observer.

In Figure 7.12, user *Mark* changes his current role from administrator to observer.

▶ **File → List of users**
Lists all users currently logged on to UA. A pop-up window opens showing the name, telephone number, and current role of all connected users (see Figure 7.13).

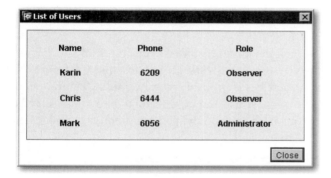

Figure 7.12 Change Role in UA GUI

List of Users

Name	Phone	Role
Karin	6209	Observer
Chris	6444	Observer
Mark	6056	Administrator

Close

Figure 7.13 Users Logged on to UA

► **File → Exit**
Ends your UA GUI session. Leaving the UA GUI has no effect at all on the UA Server (and thus the upgrade), which simply continue running.

The **Administrator** menu:

► **Administrator → Start PREPARE**
Starts SAPup in PREPARE mode.

► **Administrator → Start SAPup**
Starts SAPup in upgrade mode. PREPARE must be complete for this.

► **Administrator → Start SAPup with options**
Starts SAPup with a command option. You can run SAPup interactively to perform some special operations. You can do this directly on the host (via the command line) or via the function **Start SAPup with options** inside the UA GUI. The default command option here is set stdpar, which is the option you need if for some reason you want to change the upgrade parameters. See Section 7.3.4 for more information about SAPup command options.

▶ **Administrator → Stop SAPup after current phase**

This instructs a running SAPup process (in PREPARE or upgrade mode) to halt after it finishes the current upgrade phase. This option is useful if for some reason you need to interrupt the upgrade, for example, to reboot the server, to change database or SAP profile parameters, and so on.

▶ **Administrator → Terminate SAPup**

Terminates a running SAPup process immediately. This is the emergency brake, which you should only use in exceptional circumstances.

▶ **Administrator → Connect UaServer to SAPup**

With this function, which is rarely used, you can instruct a newly started UA Server to connect to an already running SAPup process. You could use this, for instance, when the UA Server stopped abnormally and had to be restarted. The new UA Server would then connect to SAPup (which was not affected by the abnormal stop of the server).

This is, to put it mildly, not the most reliable of UA features; in fact, our experience is that this rarely — if ever — works. If you lose the UA Server while SAPup is running, your best bet is probably to wait until a "natural" stop of SAPup, for example, to request user input, and then stop and restart both SAPup and the UA Server. In the meantime, you can monitor the upgrade via the logs in the upgrade directory.

▶ **Administrator → Disconnect UaServer from SAPup**

This breaks the connection between the UA Server and SAPup. SAPup will continue until it needs to interact with the user and will then stop. We have never used this function and, given the quirky behavior of its **Connect** counterpart, we're not likely to try.

▶ **Administrator → Set Alert**

Use this function to make the UA GUI invoke a script or command of your choice when it stops for interaction. This is a very useful feature if you want to let the upgrade run unattended, but you want to be informed when your intervention is needed. The alert function is described in section *The Alert Service*.

▶ **Administrator → Change Passwords**

This function lets you change the administrator and observer passwords. If you forget the administrator password, then you need a special procedure because you cannot log on to the UA GUI; see *Setting a New Administrator Password* in Section 7.3.5 for the solution.

▶ **Administrator → Terminate Upgrade Assistant Server**

This function stops the UA Server. It is a clean alternative to killing the server from the OS.

The **Services** menu:

▶ **Services → File Service**
Lets you select and display files on the upgrade host. This is normally used to display upgrade logs. See the upcoming section *The File Service* for details

▶ **Services → Upgrade Monitor**
Brings up a progress window showing the upgrade phases. See the upcoming section *The Upgrade Monitor*.

▶ **Services → Console Window**
Displays the main upgrade log. See the upcoming section *The Console Service*.

▶ **Services → SAP Notes Search**
Opens a browser session in the SAP Service Marketplace to search notes. See the upcoming section *The Notes Service*.

The Help menu:

▶ **Help → Introduction**
Opens a browser session with information about the upgrade tools. Interesting reading but unfortunately not always up to date. At the time of writing, the information provided here was for the upgrade tools of Basis 6.40 and not of Basis 7.00, which could be confusing.

▶ **Help → About**
Shows the version of the UA and the copyright notice.

The Alert Service

Unless you work in a round-the-clock team and an administrator is constantly watching, chances are that the upgrade will at certain times run unattended. Although this may give you a welcome opportunity to get some sleep or to do some other important task, you don't want to come back to the upgrade to find out that it has stopped for user input or because of an error and has been in that idle state for many hours. To prevent these nasty surprises and the resulting loss of time, you can instruct the UA Server to trigger an alert whenever it stops. When the alert goes off, the UA Server invokes a command of your choice. This could be a shell script to send an email to the members of the technical upgrade team or a script that sends an SMS (Short Message Service) message to your mobile phone, for instance.

To enable alerts, do the following:

1. Choose **Administrator** → **Set Alert** in the UA GUI menu.

2. In **Alert Command,** type the full path name of the command or script you want the UA Server to call.

3. In **Alert Text File,** you can specify the name of a file on the host where the UA Server will write the same information that it sent to the UA GUI when the upgrade stopped.

4. In **Alert Delay,** enter a delay the UA Server must observe between the moment the upgrade stops and the moment the alert is triggered. The default is 500 seconds. You might want to reduce this somewhat, for example, to 2 or 3 minutes, but do not set the delay to 0 because this will cause many unnecessary alerts.

5. With the **Set active** flag, you can enable and disable the alert configuration at will.

If alerts are active, then the following happens when the upgrade stops for user interaction (this may be normal interaction, i.e., prompting for user input, or an error stop):

1. The UA Server waits for the amount of time set in the **Alert Delay**.

2. If the user does not restart the upgrade before this delay expires, the UA Server writes the text of the upgrade message to the alert text file.

3. The UA Server then invokes the alert command.

In the example given in Figure 7.14, the UA Server is instructed to call a script `upgrade_sms` whenever the upgrade stops for more than 2 minutes. Judging by the name, the script creates an SMS message, which it sends to some administrator's cell phone. More sophisticated scripts are, of course, possible; you could, for instance, design a shell script that "noisily" alerts the administrator by sending a brief SMS and at the same time also sends an email with the contents of the alert text file.

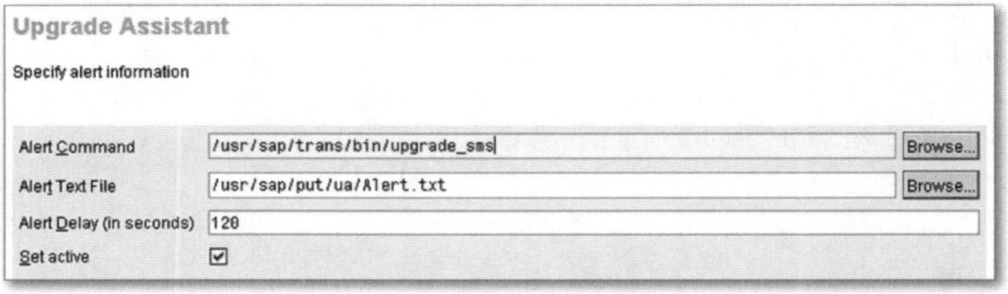

Figure 7.14 Defining an Alert

Figure 7.15 shows an example of an alert text file. Here the upgrade stopped not because of an error but to notify the user that action is needed, which, in this case, is upgrading the liveCache during an APO (Advanced Planning and Optimization) upgrade.

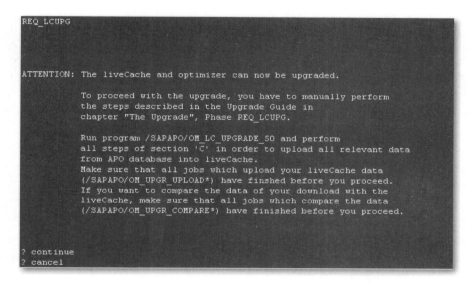

```
REQ_LCUPG




ATTENTION: The liveCache and optimizer can now be upgraded.

           To proceed with the upgrade, you have to manually perform
           the steps described in the Upgrade Guide in
           chapter "The Upgrade", Phase REQ_LCUPG.

           Run program /SAPAPO/OM_LC_UPGRADE_50 and perform
           all steps of section 'C' in order to upload all relevant data
           from APO database into liveCache.
           Make sure that all jobs which upload your liveCache data
           (/SAPAPO/OM_UPGR_UPLOAD*) have finshed before you proceed.
           If you want to compare the data of your download with the
           liveCache, make sure that all jobs which compare the data
           (/SAPAPO/OM_UPGR_COMPARE*) have finished before you proceed.




? continue
? cancel
```

Figure 7.15 Alert Text File

The File Service

The File Service in the UA GUI lets you select and display files on the upgrade host. A file selection window opens, showing the directory structure of the host. You can use this window to navigate through the directory tree. Alternatively, if you know the full path name of the file you want to display, you can type this into the **File** input field at the bottom (Figure 7.16, left). The file is displayed directly. Unfortunately, you can only enter file names and not directory names into this field.

If the directory contains files, the file chooser window lists them (Figure 7.16, right).

Double-clicking on a file opens a new window with the contents of that file (see Figure 7.17). With long files, use the **More** and **End of File** buttons to navigate.

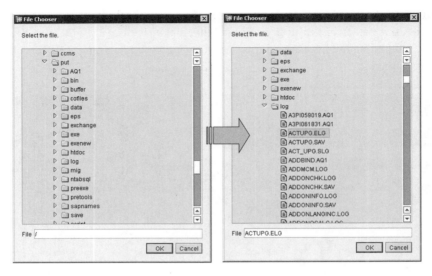

Figure 7.16 UA File Service — File Chooser

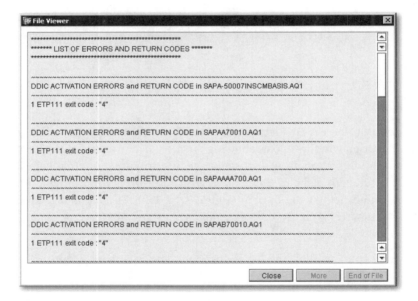

Figure 7.17 UA File Service — Display File

The Upgrade Monitor

Via **Services** → **Upgrade Monitor,** you can see how far the upgrade has progressed. Click on **Close** to leave the monitor screen and return to the main UA GUI window.

Figure 7.18 shows the Upgrade Monitor during the actual upgrade. Here the progress screen shows all the upgrade phases.

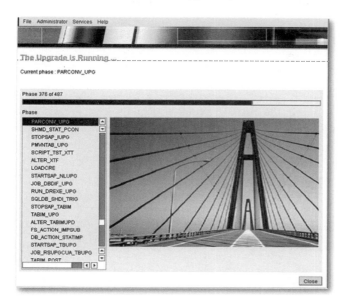

Figure 7.18 Upgrade Monitor in UA GUI

During PREPARE, which is subdivided into modules, you only see the phases of the currently executing module. You see an example of this in Figure 7.19.

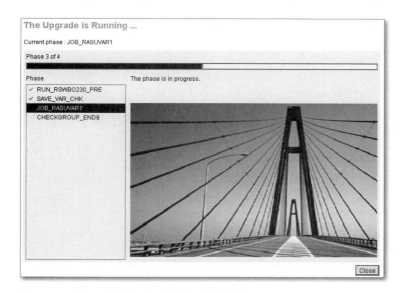

Figure 7.19 Upgrade Monitor During PREPARE

The Console Service

While the upgrade is running, the UA GUI window displays a progress screen that contains messages for the beginning and end of each phase, other messages shown to the user (e.g., to signal errors), and all interaction with the upgrade administrator (prompts and replies). You can scroll back inside this window to see all the messages and user input since the beginning of the upgrade.

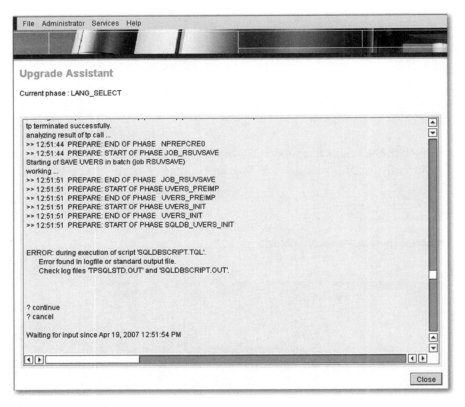

Figure 7.20 Console Service

When the upgrade stops to interact with the user, this progress screen is temporarily replaced with an input window. If you want to look at the progress screen at this point, for example, because you want to check some input you entered in an earlier phase, then choose **Services → Console window**. The progress screen will then reappear (see Figure 7.20).

Another advantage of the console window is that copying text is enabled here. This is useful if you want to copy/paste parts of the upgrade dialog into your documentation.

Click on the **Close** button to return to the input screen.

The Notes Service

The Notes Service function starts a browser on your PC and brings up a page for searching SAP Notes in the SAP Service Marketplace (see Figure 7.21). As you can see, this is not the usual page for searching notes (*http://service.sap.com/NOTES*).

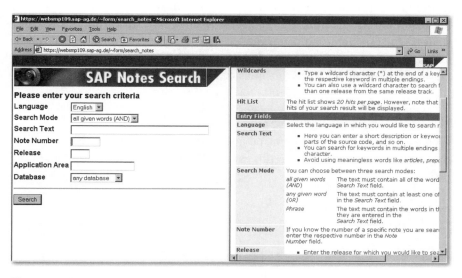

Figure 7.21 Notes Service

Providing the ability to search SAP Notes directly from the GUI is a nice idea, but, in practice, there is just one tiny problem: It doesn't work. No matter what you enter in the search fields, the search result is always "no notes found." This is a bit silly but can hardly be called a major irritant. Just open a separate browser and go to the normal notes search page.

7.3.4 SAPup Command Options

The principal function of SAPup is to run in the background and to control the ABAP PREPARE and the ABAP upgrade. In addition, SAPup also offers a command interface, which you can use to perform certain special operations.

You can invoke the command mode of SAPup in two ways:

▶ On the upgrade host via the command line
▶ From inside the UA GUI

To see the available functions and command options, type the following command:

```
/usr/sap/put/bin/SAPup -h
```

SAPup will prompt you for the path to the upgrade directory (press **Enter** if the default path shown is correct).

Most of the functions are not intended for your direct use. They are either called internally during the upgrade process or needed only in exceptional circumstances. The functions that you will need most often are the ones that allow you to change parameters of the upgrade and those that control the shadow instance. These and some other useful functions of SAPup are described next.

Specifying the Upgrade Directory

If you run SAPup from the command line, SAPup will prompt you for the path to the upgrade directory. To avoid this extra prompt, use the upgdir option. Example:

```
SAPup -h upgdir=/usr/sap/put
```

Show SAPup Version

This command displays the version. Example:

```
> ./SAPup -V upgdir=/usr/sap/put
This is SAPup version 7.00/2, build 24.081
```

Start and Stop Shadow Instance

Use the startshd and stopshd functions to start and stop the shadow instance. This is normally not necessary because SAPup takes care of starting and stopping the shadow instance at the right moment. However, it is sometimes necessary to do a manual stop/start, for instance, if you have to change profile parameters of the shadow instance.

Commands:

```
SAPup [upgdir=<upgrade_dir>] startshd
SAPup [upgdir=<upgrade_dir>] stopshd
```

Unlock and Lock the Shadow Instance

Like the main instance during downtime, the shadow instance normally runs in upgrade lock mode, meaning that logging on to the instance is only possible for the users SAP* and DDIC, and that workbench objects cannot be changed. At the beginning of the modification adjustment (Transaction SPDD), SAPup will unlock the shadow instance automatically. When activation begins after you have finished SPDD, SAPup also locks the shadow instance again.

If, however, as is often the case, the activation phase reports errors for some dictionary objects, then you must manually unlock the shadow instance to be able to log on as a user with development authority and to modify objects in the ABAP workbench. When you are finished with correcting the activation errors, lock the shadow instance manually before resuming the upgrade.

Commands:

```
SAPup [upgdir=<upgrade_dir>] unlockshd
SAPup [upgdir=<upgrade_dir>] lockshd
```

Change Parameters of the Upgrade

Early on in the PREPARE process, you will be prompted for all the parameters that the upgrade process needs, such as host names, locations of the upgrade media, and so on. These parameters are then used throughout the entire upgrade, and normally you will not change them again. If you do need to change a parameter later in the upgrade (for example, because you had to move the upgrade DVDs to a different disk or file system), then use the following function:

```
SAPup [upgdir=<upgrade_dir>] set stdpar
```

As always, you can execute this command from inside the UA GUI or directly via the command line of the OS. In this case, calling the command in the UA GUI is more convenient because you are presented with the same graphical input windows as during PREPARE.

Change Parameters of the Shadow Instance

PREPARE also prompts you for the shadow instance parameters (instance number, port numbers, etc.). Again, you can change these parameters later if necessary by using the function

```
SAPup [upgdir=<upgrade_dir>] set shdpar
```

Change Parameters for Upgrade Strategy and Parallel Processing

SAPup (not PREPARE) prompts you for the upgrade strategy you want to use (downtime-minimized or resource-minimized) as well as for some other parameters that affect the resource usage by the upgrade:

- Allotted time for the database import
- Upgrade phase from where database archiving is to be disabled
- Number of parallel batch processes

If you need to change these parameters, you can do so with the function

```
./SAPup upgdir=/usr/sap/put set rswpar
```

Change DDIC Password

During the initial parameter input, PREPARE prompts for the password of user DDIC in client 000. DDIC in 000 is used throughout the entire upgrade for all phases that need a connection to the SAP system. It is good practice to set the DDIC password at the beginning of the upgrade and leave it unchanged until the end, but this is not always possible. The password might expire during the upgrade, or you might need to change it for any other unexpected reason.

If you alter the DDIC password, then you must inform the upgrade process of this with following SAPup function:

```
./SAPup upgdir=/usr/sap/put set ddicpwd
```

Note that this command by itself does not *change* the password (you need Transaction SU01 for that); it simply informs SAPup of the password change.

Change the DDIC Password in the Shadow Instance

In the shadow instance, which has its own user configuration, user DDIC in client 000 is created with the same password as in the source system. If you change the DDIC password in the shadow instance for whatever reason, then you must again make SAPup aware of this:

```
./SAPup upgdir=/usr/sap/put set shdddicpwd
```

(Be careful: It's three d's in a row!)

Resetting PREPARE

Situations may arise — hopefully not too often — in which you decide that you want to abandon the active PREPARE altogether and start over. What could also happen is that you run PREPARE in a system but then decide not to upgrade that system after all. Leaving traces of this unfinished business in the system is not a good idea because it would prevent upgrading the system in the future. To reset PREPARE and thus erase any trace of the attempted upgrade, use the command

```
./SAPup upgdir=/usr/sap/put reset prepare
```

At this point, we only mention the command because resetting PREPARE is covered in Section 9.30.

Other Functions

SAPup -h will list numerous other functions than the ones described in the previous paragraphs. You normally do not need these functions and unless SAP instructs you to use one of them, it is best to keep to the straight and narrow. Don't start experimenting with them in a live upgrade!

7.3.5   Tips and Tricks

We end this section with two useful tips:

▶ How to make the UA use different network ports
▶ How to change the administrator password

Change the Port Numbers for the Upgrade Assistant

The UA uses a total of four ports for all its communication. By default, these ports are 4238, 4239, 4240, and 4241. These numbers are defined in the configuration file */usr/sap/put/ua/UaServer.properties*:

```
UA_R3UP_PORT     = 4240
UA_GUI_PORT      = 4241
UA_MONITOR_PORT  = 4238
(...)
UA_HTTP_PORT     = 4239
```

The first three entries are grouped together near the beginning of the file. The UA_HTTP_PORT entry can be found further down in the section for the HTTP server settings.

Normally there is no reason to change the port numbers, but there are situations where this becomes necessary. One or more of the ports might be in use by another application or access to these ports might be blocked by a firewall. If you run several ABAP upgrades simultaneously on the same host, then you will have to change the port numbers for all but one of these upgrades; otherwise, the respective UA Servers will attempt to open the same ports, which results in an error stop.

Before you assign new port numbers, make sure that these new numbers will be usable:

▶ The ports must not be blocked by the firewall.

▶ They must not be used by other applications. To check whether a port is currently in use, type the following command:

netstat -an | grep <portnr> (Unix/Linux)

netstat -an | findstr <portnr> (Windows)

In the following example, you want to use the port 4339, but this port turns out to be in use. The entry *.4339 indicates that some local program is listening on the port (see Figure 7.22). The other entries show the IP address and port of the host in the first column, and the IP address and connected port of all the clients currently using this port.

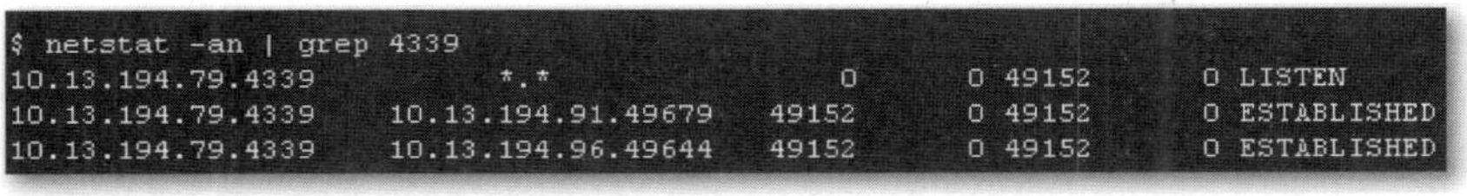

```
$ netstat -an | grep 4339
10.13.194.79.4339          *.*                    0      0 49152      0 LISTEN
10.13.194.79.4339     10.13.194.91.49679      49152      0 49152      0 ESTABLISHED
10.13.194.79.4339     10.13.194.96.49644      49152      0 49152      0 ESTABLISHED
```

Figure 7.22 Network Port in Use

You must also check whether the ports have not been assigned for use by other applications, even if those applications are not active at present. You do this by looking for an entry with this port number in the *services* file on the host. The name of this file is */etc/services* (Unix/Linux) or *C:\WINDOWS\SYSTEM32\DRIV-ERS\ETC\SERVICES* (Windows).

> **Note**
>
> Depending on the version of Windows, the top directory might be called WINDOWS or WINNT.

The entry in the services file in Figure 7.23 indicates that port 4339 is destined for use by another (in this case non-SAP) application.

Figure 7.23 Port Reserved in Services File

After choosing a new set of port numbers and ascertaining that these ports can be used for the UA, you can configure the new ports:

1. Stop the UA Server if it is still running

2. Make a backup of the current properties file, for example:
   ```
   cd /usr/sap/put/ua
   mv UaServer.properties UaServer.properties.default
   ```

3. Use a text editor to change the four port entries in the *UaServer.properties* file. Let's suppose that you chose to use ports 8238 to 8241:
   ```
   UA_R3UP_PORT     = 8240
   UA_GUI_PORT      = 8241
   UA_MONITOR_PORT  = 8238
   (...)
   UA_HTTP_PORT     = 8239
   ```

4. Restart the UA Server, and wait for the "Ready" message.

5. Call the main upgrade page, using the new port number 8239: *http://host-name:8239*.

6. Start the UA GUI, and specify the new port number on the logon screen.

Setting a New Administrator Password

As explained earlier, you specify the password for the administrator role in the UA when you first start the UA Server. If you intend to use the observer role, then you set its password in the UA GUI.

To change the administrator and observer passwords, you also use the UA GUI, and you must obviously be logged on as administrator.

But what if you forgot the administrator password, and you do *not* have an open UA GUI administrator session? Stopping and restarting the UA Server won't help you; the UA Server will not prompt for the password again. Looking up the answer in the Upgrade Guides or in the SAP Notes won't do you any good either; both are silent on the subject. Fortunately, the solution is not difficult:

1. If the UA Server is currently running, then terminate it with OS means, such as the `kill` command in UNIX or the `End Process` function in the Windows Task Manager, at the first convenient moment (preferably not in the middle of a critical or long-running upgrade phase):

2. Remove the file `/usr/sap/put/UaState`.

3. Remove the file `/usr/sap/put/ua/ks` (the "keystore").

4. Start the UA Server, which will now prompt for the administrator password like it did the first time you ran it.

> **Note**
>
> Depending on the UA release, you might also need to delete the following files in the *ua* subdirectory:
>
> *.sdt_storage*
> *.sdt_keystore*

The UA Server prompts for the password if it does not find the file *ua/UaState*. If you only remove this file but leave the keystore untouched, then the next start of the UA Server will prompt for the password but will then abort with an exception stack trace that includes the message:

```
java.io.IOException
Keystore was tampered with, or password was incorrect
```

7.4   Installation of the Upgrade Tools: Java

Compared with the ABAP side, installing and operating the upgrade tools for Java is a pretty simple affair. This is not necessarily an advantage because the interface for Java also offers fewer facilities than its ABAP counterpart, the UA. As we mentioned earlier, the Java SDT has no notion of different user roles (administrator/observer) and does not allow more than one GUI to be connected at any one time. These are characteristics the upgrade GUI for Java shares with its very close relative, the SAPINST installation utility.

Before you start, you must have downloaded the Java fix buffer and extracted the fix to the Java upgrade directory, as described in Section 6.3.2. The next step is to extract the tools to the upgrade directory. Like on the ABAP side, this is done with a script located on the Java Upgrade Master DVD (for UNIX/Linux and Windows; for IBM iSeries, see the instructions in the SAP Upgrade Guide for that platform).

7.4.1 Initial PREPARE Run: UNIX and Linux

In this example, we assume that you have placed disk copies of the upgrade media in a server directory */sapmedia*. You have placed the Java Upgrade Master CD in a subdirectory named */sapmedia/UPGMSTR_JAVA*. The Java Upgrade Master contains the installation script for the Java upgrade tools.

For the Java upgrade directory, we assume that you use the default path name */usr/sap/jupgrade*.

Follow these steps:

1. Log on as user `<sid>adm`.
2. Switch to the upgrade directory:

   `cd /usr/sap/jupgrade`

3. Type the command

   `/sapmedia/UPGMSTR_JAVA/JPREPARE`

   If the name of the Java upgrade directory is not `/usr/sap/jupgrade`, then you must specify the path via a command-line argument, for example:

   `/sapmedia/UPGMSTR_JAVA/JPREPARE /usr/sap/jupgPRD`

   Note that here you simply specify the directory path as the command argument; you do not add the `upgdir=` keyword as with ABAP.

   If the upgrade directory does not exist, then JPREPARE will create it.

4. If the fix buffer was already placed in the upgrade directory as described in the Section 6.6.4, subsection *Download and install fix buffers*, then JPREPARE will also unpack the UPG file. This is a minor difference with ABAP, where the buffer is extracted during PREPARE and not by the initial script. If JPREPARE creates the upgrade directory, or the fix buffer is not yet present, then the PREPARE process will take care of the fix buffer later; appropriate screens will appear in the SDT GUI.

5. JPREPARE then unpacks the upgrade files to `/usr/sap/jupgrade` and finally displays the message:

```
Waiting for SDTServer to connect on hostname <host>/<address> socket
6240 ...
```

6. At this point, you can start the GUI, but it is a good idea not to let the process run in the foreground. To free up the terminal window and start a background process, break with `Ctrl` + `C` and then restart as follows (as <sid>adm):

```
cd /usr/sap/jupgrade/exe
nohup ./PREPARE &
```

Note that now the name is just PREPARE, not JPREPARE.

7.4.2 Initial PREPARE Run: Windows

For the Windows example, we assume that the upgrade media are in the folder *D:\SAPMEDIA*, with the Upgrade Master in the subfolder *UPGMSTR_JAVA*.

1. Go to the Upgrade Master folder, and start the script PREPARE.BAT:

```
cd /D D:\SAPMEDIA\UPGMSTR_JAVA
jprepare
```

This assumes that you use the default path for the Java upgrade directory. This default path is *\usr\sap\jupgrade* on the drive pointed at by the SAPLOC share. If you want to use a different path name and/or a different drive for the upgrade directory, then you must specify the path on the command line, for example:

```
jprepare F:\sapadmin\jupgrade
```

Caution
You cannot specify a path in UNC format (*host\share\path*).

2. If the upgrade directory does not exist, JPREPARE creates it. It then creates the subfolders (see Figure 7.24) and unpacks the upgrade tools.

3. Finally, JPREPARE launches the PREPARE process. At this point, you will see the following message:

```
call exe\jump -cddir=D:\sapmedia\UPGMSTR_JAVA\\JUP run prepare
Waiting for SDTServer to connect on hostname <server>/<ip> socket 6240
```

4. If you already placed the fix buffer into the upgrade directory (see Section 6.6.4, subsection *Download and install fix buffers*), then PREPARE will immediately unpack the UPG file:

```
Unpacking fix archive 'FIX_J_NW04SSR2.UPG'...
```

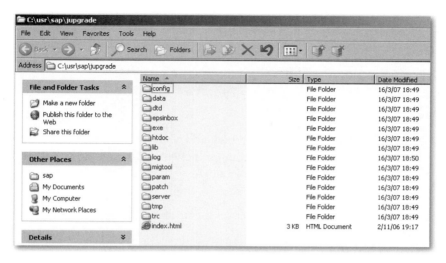

Figure 7.24 Java Upgrade Directory After Initial JPREPARE Run

5. If JPREPARE creates the upgrade directory, or the fix buffer is not yet present, then the PREPARE process will take care of the fix buffer later; appropriate screens will appear in the SDT GUI.

6. Minimize but do not close the command window where PREPARE is waiting. You are now ready to start the GUI.

7. If you have to restart the PREPARE process later, then proceed as follows:

```
cd \usr\sap\jupgrade\exe
prepare
```

There is no need to specify a path here even if you are not using the default path name for the upgrade directory.

7.5 Using the Java SDT GUI

Starting the Java upgrade involves an Internet browser and the Java Web Start, but that is where the similarity with the ABAP UA ends. Let's see how it works.

7.5.1 Starting the SDT Server

You do not start the SDT Server explicitly. When you start the SDT GUI as described next, the server process also starts and connects to the waiting PRE-PARE process. At this point, the command window of PREPARE displays a "connected" message:

```
Waiting for SDTServer to connect on hostname <server>/<ip> socket 6240
... connected.
```

7.5.2   Starting the SDT GUI

To start the SDT GUI, follow these steps:

1. Open a browser on your PC.

2. Type the URL *http://<server>:6239* where *<server>* is the host name (or possibly the full domain name, depending on how networking is set up) of the host where the UA Server is running. Example:

   http://sapdev.mycomp.com:6239

3. If you decide to start the browser on the upgrade host itself rather than on a local PC, you may also use the URL

   http://localhost:6239

4. The main Java Upgrade page now opens (see Figure 7.25).

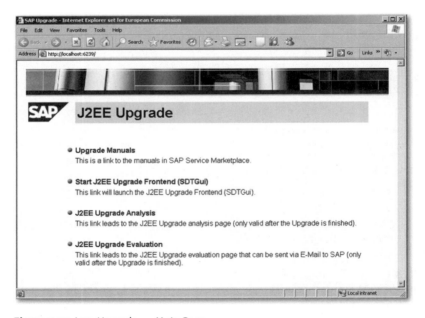

Figure 7.25 Java Upgrade — Main Page

5. The Java Web Start window pops up, and the application begins to load (see Figure 7.26).

Figure 7.26 Java Web Start Loading the SDT GUI

6. See Section 7.3.2, subsection *Java Web Start Errors While Loading the UA GUI,* if Java Web Start fails to load and start the application.

7. The Welcome screen of the SDT GUI appears (see Figure 7.27). Remember that the Java upgrade does not have the concept of administrator and observer users, so there is no logon screen.

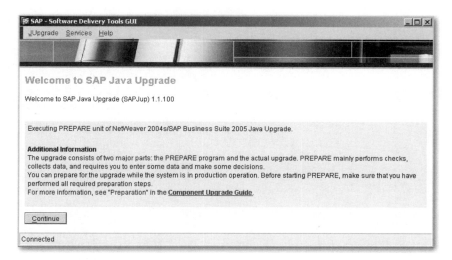

Figure 7.27 SDT GUI Welcome Screen

7.5.3 Features of the SDT GUI

As we did for the ABAP UA GUI, let's again make a brief tour of the menu functions, of which there are only a few.

The **JUpgrade** menu:

▶ **JUpgrade → Exit**
Ends the SDT GUI session. Leaving the SDT GUI does not end the active PRE-PARE or upgrade process, so you can safely do this.

The **Services** menu:

▶ **Services → File Service**
Lets you select and display files on the upgrade host. This is normally used to display upgrade logs. This function is identical to the File Service in the UA GUI. See Section 7.3.3, subsection *The File Service* for a description.

▶ **Services → Log Service**
This service provides immediate access to the Java upgrade logs. The left pane lists the existing log and error files in */usr/sap/jupgrade/log*. By clicking on a file, its contents are displayed in the right-hand pane. Figure 7.28 shows the log service for a normal text log, which is displayed in free-format fashion.

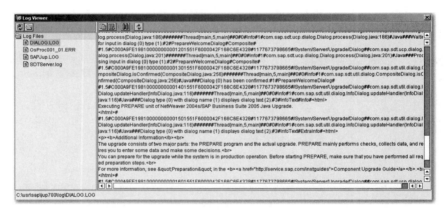

Figure 7.28 SDT GUI Log Service (Free-Format Display)

Many of the upgrade logs, including the main *SAPJup.LOG*, are displayed in a more structured, tabular form showing the severity, date and time, message text, and call location. You can use the arrows in the toolbar at the top of the screen to move through the file. You can also filter messages by choosing the minimum severity level, as shown in Figure 7.29.

Figure 7.29 SDT GUI Log Service (Structured Display)

The **Help** menu:

▶ **Help** → **About**
Shows the version of the Java Upgrade GUI and the copyright notice.

7.5.4 Tips and Tricks

Like on the ABAP side (see the earlier Section 7.3.5), you can change the network ports used for the Java upgrade if necessary. The default ports used by the Java upgrade are 6239 (for HTTP connections from the browser) and 6241 (for the SDT GUI). You find these port numbers in the file

/usr/sap/jupgrade/server/sdtserver.xml

Note that here we are not dealing with a simple text file but with an XML file. To edit the file, you could use a specialized XML editor, but a standard text editor such as Notepad or *vi* will do just as well. Simply search for the strings "6239" and "6241"; each appears only once in the file, with the respective tags ⟨HTTP-Port⟩ and ⟨GuiPort⟩.

The same warnings and restrictions apply as for the ABAP UA:

▶ Don't change the port numbers unless you have to.

▶ Make sure the new port numbers are not already used by another application.

▶ Also make sure the server ports are accessible (not blocked by a firewall) from the workstation you intend to use during the upgrade.

See Section 7.3.5, subsection *Change the Port Numbers for the Upgrade Assistant*, for instructions on how to check these requirements.

7.6   Ready to Go

In the preceding chapters, you have learned how to make all the necessary preparations and set up the infrastructure to carry out the technical upgrade. You also know which upgrade tools exist; how to start, stop, and control them; and how to monitor their activities. With this knowledge, you are now ready to attack the upgrade at hand.

Proper preparation of the upgrade is essential. Without it, you run an inordinate risk of encountering known and preventable problems. Your main preparation tasks are to perform several verification and preparation activities in the SAP system.

8 Preparing the Upgrade for SAP ECC

In this chapter, we'll briefly discuss the necessary preparatory steps in the SAP Solution Manager and the SAP system, as well as the final reviews of your transport requests.

8.1 SAP Solution Manager System

As amply explained at the SAP Service Marketplace, you can use the SAP Solution Manager as a source of information about the entire upgrade process. Apart from these obvious benefits, having an installed Solution Manager system is *mandatory* for a technical reason: PREPARE will ask you for an upgrade key, which you can only generate in SAP Solution Manager. The Solution Manager system that is available should meet the minimum release requirement[1].

> **Note**
>
> If for any reason it is impossible to meet this requirement, you can obtain an upgrade key from SAP. This procedure should only be used in exceptional situations. SAP consultants or support engineers cannot provide this key themselves, so a certain delay may be involved.

Here is the procedure to generate the key in the Solution Manager system:

1. Log on to the Solution Manager system.
2. Call Transaction SMSY (see Figure 8.1).
3. Open **Landscape Components**.
4. If the system has not been defined yet, right-click on the **Systems** entry.
5. Enter the System ID, and select the SAP product and product version. Click **Save** when finished.

---

1 See Note 811923. For SAP ERP 2005, you require Version 3.2 with SP 8 or higher.

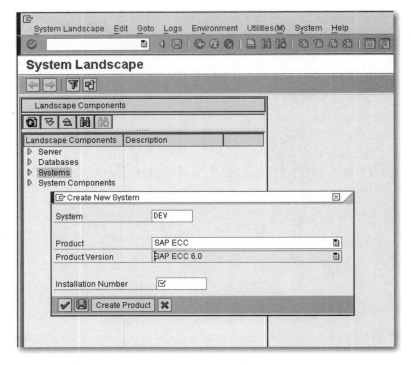

Figure 8.1 Create an ECC 6.0 System in SAP Solution Manager

6. To generate the key, choose **System · Other object.**

7. Mark **System,** and enter the SID.

8. Click **Generate Installation/Upgrade Key** (key-shaped icon).

9. Enter the system number and message server host (without domain). Note that in some versions, the system changes the host name to uppercase, but this is of no importance.

10. Click **Generate Key**. The 10-character key value is displayed (see Figure 8.2).

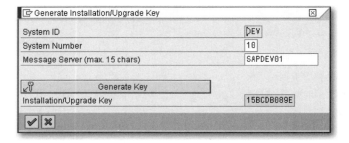

Figure 8.2 Generate Upgrade Key in Solution Manager

8.2　　Review of Transport Requests

Starting with the upgrade of the development system, the developers will create numerous transport requests for the new release. These include transports for the Modification Adjustment to programs, screens, and so on (Transaction SPAU), and probably also other changes and enhancements. As you saw in Section 4.9, the preferred approach is to accumulate these requests in a virtual import buffer, which you then import into every newly upgraded system. By the time you reach production, importing the transport buffer will have become one of the most critical — and possibly one of the most time-consuming — post-upgrade actions.

Except for the upgrade of the development system itself, it is technically possible to continue development work on the new release while the upgrade is in progress. However, when it comes to importing these transports, you will have to draw a line somewhere; you probably do not want to import every request up to the very last one (which might still be wholly or partly untested). There are various solutions to this: You can activate approval of requests with the TMS Quality Assurance procedure or with the Transport Workflow[2]; another very easy solution is to place a *stopmark* in the virtual transport buffer[3].

Apart from controlling new requests added to the import buffer, you should also have developers double-check the requests that are already there. Unless there is a sound approval procedure in place, there is always a risk of faulty or undesirable transport requests that have been released into the buffer. Ask developers to review all their requests, so that they can remove the bad ones in time. An easy approach here is to download the transport queue list in Transaction STMS to a spreadsheet and to distribute this to the entire development team. Don't adopt a "no news is good news" attitude here. Instead, demand that each developer who has transports in the buffer give you an explicit go-ahead.

8.3　　Activities in the SAP System

Before the upgrade, activities are needed in the SAP system. Some of these activities are mentioned in the Component Upgrade guide. However, we prefer to list

---

2　Both methods prevent the release and/or import of a request before they have been formally approved. For a full explanation, go to *http://help.sap.com* • *ERP 6.0 Central Component* • *SAP NetWeaver* • *Solution Life Cycle Management* • *Software Change Management* • *Transport Management System* (BC-CTS-TMS).

3　A stopmark is a special entry in a transport buffer. When you import a complete queue (import all), then only requests before the stopmark are actually imported. You set a stopmark in the queue display via **Queue** • **Close** or using the command `tp setstopmark <SID>`.

them here as well and explain them in somewhat more detail. Other activities come from our personal experience with previous upgrades.

8.3.1 Create a User for the Upgrade

Although this step is optional, and the SAP upgrade guide does not mention it, we find it a good idea to create a user in SAP for all upgrade-related activities. This makes it easier later on to relate a transport request, a change to a program or table, and so on to the upgrade (by looking at the ownership).

Make sure you create this user in every production client and in client 000. The user should be fully privileged (SAP_ALL) and preferably have a developer key. The name can be chosen freely but should make clear that this is a user created for a specific release upgrade, for example, UPGRADE. For security reasons, you should restrict this user in time by setting the "Valid to" date in Transaction SU01.

8.3.2 Create a Development Class (Package) for the Upgrade

Another optional step is to create a package (formerly known as *development class*). You can then use this package for all objects created during the upgrade, such as append structures in SPDD (covered in Chapter 21), special ABAP programs for the upgrade, and so on.

Choose again a meaningful name, for example, ZUPG.

8.3.3 Repairs — Updates — Pending DB Conversions

The Upgrade Guide instructs you to release all open repairs, to delete all pending update requests, and to either carry out or cancel all pending database conversions. Technically speaking, you may do this shortly before the upgrade (in the case of pending updates, you may even wait until the beginning of upgrade downtime). However, practice shows that this often requires investigation and sometimes incurs a good deal of hesitation and resistance. Therefore, it is best to tackle these touchy points well beforehand. Review all open repairs and database conversions with the responsible developers. Check failed update requests with the user listed in Transaction SM13. Release and delete as much as you can so that come upgrade time, you only have to look at the most recent activities.

8.3.4 Substitution Tables in Wrong Database Space

This topic is only relevant if the following are true:

▶ Your source release is SAP R/3 Enterprise 4.70 Extension Set 1.10 (including Service Release 1).

▶ You use a database system with explicit storage areas (tablespaces or dbspaces). Although we cannot cover every platform-specific upgrade issue in these chapters, we make a point of explaining things here because many SAP installations fulfill these conditions, which guarantees that the problem will occur. You can find background information in SAP Note 674070.

Owing to a bug in the installation and upgrade software for Enterprise 470x110, some database tables were mistakenly placed in the tablespaces/dbspaces of the 6.20 repository rather than in *permanent* areas of the database. During the ERP upgrade, after the switch to the new release, all the tables of the old repository are deleted. As a result, the containers of the old repository should be empty at the end of the upgrade so that they can be dropped (see Section 11.2.4). However, because the upgrade obviously does not delete any tables that do not belong to the old repository, the effect of the bug is that the tablespaces/dbspaces are not empty after the upgrade.

The majority of the tables affected are very small or empty, but one table, E071K (which contains the key values stored in all customizing change requests), is often quite large.

Using the instructions from Note 674070, you can solve the problem before or after the upgrade. Solving it before the upgrade is safer. Here is the procedure you can use:

1. Download the SAR archive with the transport request that you find in the attachment of Note 674070. Unpack the archive and import the transport request into the system.

2. Run program RSCHECKEXC with an empty selection screen. The program does not produce report output, but it writes a log /usr/sap/trans/tmp/ RSCHKEXC.<SID>.

3. If near the end of this log you find the message <n> empty tables could be recreated, re-execute this report with mode=DRCR; then run the program again with MODE = DRCR, preferably at a time of minimal activity in the system. In this mode, the program moves empty tables from the 6.20 repository area to a safe location.

4. Run the program once more, this time with MODE = ICNV. The program now creates a work list for incremental conversion (ICNV) with all the nonempty tables.

5. Wait for a time of low system activity (or keep users off the system for a few minutes if possible). Start Transaction ICNV. The work list is displayed (see Figure 8.3).

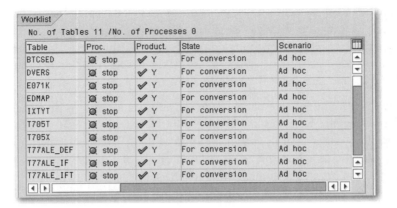

Figure 8.3 Work List for Incremental Conversion

6. Choose **Control · Initialization**. Mark all tables, and press **Enter**. In the next window, change the **Start Condition** to **Now**.

7. Refresh the screen until the state has changed from **For conversion** to **Convers.** for all the tables and **Productive** changes back to **Yes**. This will go quickly for most tables, but E071K might take a few minutes.

8. Normal user activity may now resume.

9. Choose **Control · Data Transfer · Start.**

10. After a few seconds, switch to the **Performance Analysis** view. Most tables are small and will show as 100 % converted after just a few refreshes. E071K is again the exception.

11. Monitor the conversion of E071K by regularly refreshing the **Performance Analysis** display or choosing **Goto · Statistical data**. Avoid using the **Compute Progress** function. If the process status changes to **Stop**, which may happen intermittently, then restart it with **Control · Data Transfer · Start.**

12. Note that the conversion of E071K may take several hours. In the meantime, users can work normally, and you may continue with all other pre-upgrade tasks, including running PREPARE.

13. When all tables are 100 % converted, wait again for a time of low activity, and then choose **Control · Switch**. Select all the listed tables, and press **Enter**. Choose **Start now** in the next window.

14. Change back from the **Performance Analysis** view to the **State display** view. Refresh the screen until the state becomes **Completed** for all (this does not take long).

15. Finally, choose **Control · Delete entry**, select all tables, and refresh until all entries have disappeared from the list.

8.3.5 Migration of Workload Statistics Data to SAP NetWeaver 2004s

As of SAP NetWeaver 2004s (Basis Release 7.00), the workload statistics collector has been redeveloped. The new statistics collector is incompatible with the earlier workload statistics data. To be able to read the workload statistics data from older releases after the upgrade with Transaction ST03, you must save the data before the upgrade and convert it after the upgrade and import it into the new data store. Follow these steps:

1. Create table ZWNCMOMIGR. This table is used to import converted workload data. This table must be created manually.

2. Call Transaction SE11, and create table ZWNCMOMIGR with the following attributes and technical settings:

   ▶ Short text: Upgrade Basis 7.00: Migration of workload statistics

   ▶ Delivery class: L

   ▶ Fields:

Field	Key	Data Type	Length
RELID	X	CHAR	2
COMPONENT	X	CHAR	40
COMPTYPE	X	CHAR	20
ASSIGNDSYS	X	CHAR	32
PERIODTYPE	X	CHAR	1
PERIODSTRT	X	DATS	8
SRTF2	X	INT4	10
PROFILVERS		INT4	10
CLUSTR		INT2	5
CLUSTD		LRAW	2886

   ▶ Data class: APPL1

   ▶ Size category: largest available

   ▶ No buffering/logging

3. Execute report RSMIGR12 using the default parameters. If report RSMIGR12 does not exist in your system, implement SAP Note 1005238. Report RSMIGR12 can be started as many times as needed. During each execution, the system examines which workload statistics data has changed since the last execution. Only the delta is processed.

The SAP Upgrade Component Guide covers some additional preparation steps. Carry out the instructions for your operating system, database, and SAP components before starting PREPARE. Different activities need to be executed depending on the SAP source release, the components in use, and the system being a non-Unicode or Unicode system.

8.3.6 Ready to Go!

Assuming that you have done all of the preceding, you now have a sufficiently powerful machine with an OS and DBMS that the new SAP release will support. You have found enough disk space to expand the database and to hold the upgrade directory, the upgrade media, and the extra downloads. You have a Solution Manager system up and running. You have adapted all necessary parameters. You have sorted out repairs, updates, and old database conversions.

That means you are ready to go ... let's PREPARE!

PREPARE is the first major part of the upgrade. Data and programs are copied to the upgrade directory, tools are imported into the database, and the shadow instance is installed. Add-ons, support packages, and languages are integrated into the upgrade. After the initial configuration of the upgrade, PREPARE verifies that the source system meets the requirements of the upgrade process and of the target release. This produces an action list that must be taken care of before the actual upgrade can start.

PREPARE is executed with the system running. End users are not affected.

9 PREPARE Process for SAP ECC

During PREPARE, the system is made ready for the upgrade. Data and programs are copied to the upgrade directory, tools are imported into the database, and the shadow instance is installed. Add-ons, support packages, user modifications (transports) and the languages installed on the source release to be upgraded are integrated into the upgrade. After the initial configuration of the upgrade tools, the source system is verified against the requirements of the upgrade process and the target release.

9.1 PREPARE

Careful preparation of the upgrade is the best guarantee that it will run without errors. Extensive checks are required for the upgrade. The PREPARE program uses a series of checks to support the preparation of the upgrade without affecting productive operation. PREPARE can be used entirely on its own and at a completely different time from the upgrade.

PREPARE has numerous advantages:

▶ It uses the same upgrade tools as used during the upgrade (technically, PREPARE is a special-run mode of the upgrade program SAPup).

▶ It is completely integrated into the upgrade process.

▶ It can be executed while the system is being used for production. You should note that it does have an impact on performance. The number of parallel processes PREPARE is allowed to use should be chosen carefully. Section 9.14 deals with this subject in more detail.

▶ It checks the requirements for the upgrade and provides further information where needed.

▶ It displays the objects that will appear during Modification Adjustment.

▶ It forecasts the number of database conversions, calculates the space requirement in the database, and requests allocation of additional space if necessary.

▶ It can be undone and re-started at any time.

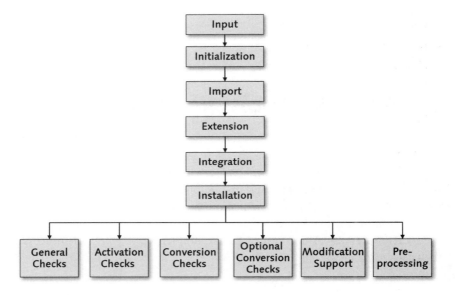

Figure 9.1 Diagram of the PREPARE Modules

PREPARE is divided in modules as shown schematically in Figure 9.1. Let us look at the modules in more detail:

▶ **Input**
Requests information on the system to be upgraded (instance id, instance number, hostname, etc.) and the key generated by the Solution Manager, and performs some basic consistency checks.

▶ **Initialization**
No interaction is needed during the initialization phase. Some basic checks are performed to see if the upgrade on the source system is possible anyway. The source release of SAP and the database are verified. The phase checks if there are unconfirmed support packages or clients that are locked for SAP system

upgrade. PREPARE also verifies that the needed space for the upgrade tools is available on the file system and database.

▶ **Import**
The tools needed for the upgrade are imported into the database and installed in the upgrade directory.

▶ **Extension**
The add-ons, support packages, user modifications (transports), and languages installed on the source release to be upgraded are integrated into the upgrade. The extension phase is one of the most important modules of PREPARE, as the target version of every SAP component and add-on in the SAP system is decided upon (you might consider it one of the most important phases of the upgrade).

▶ **Integration**
No input is needed in the integration phase. It is an addition to extension. The support packages, add-ons, and additional transports (customer modifications) are prepared and integrated into the upgrade. The extra space they will take up and the space needed for the languages to be upgraded in the database is calculated as well. The integration and extension phases are closely linked together. If the wrong target level for one of the SAP components or add-ons was entered in the extension phase, and the integration phase has already run, PREPARE should be reset and restarted from the beginning.

▶ **Installation**
The shadow instance is installed in the installation phase. The shadow schema is created inside the database and the instance profiles are set up. Instead of installing the shadow instance next to the central instance, you can choose to install it on an additional application server in the SAP landscape. Although this complicates things, it might be an option if you're having performance problems on the server running the central instance.

▶ **Verification Modules**
At this point, all the tools needed for the upgrade are installed. The remaining modules verify that the source environment meets all requirements for the upgrade. The general checks module identifies among many things, the version of both the source and target kernel. It verifies that all executables in the kernel directory can be replaced, looks for locked objects that might interfere with the upgrade, and determines if there's enough free space in the database. The other verification modules verify the data dictionary, list the tables to be converted, and list the number of DDIC and repository objects that conflict with the new release and will appear in Modification Adjustment during and after the upgrade.

To make sure that all requirements are met, run PREPARE as soon as possible. PREPARE can be reset and rerun as often as needed before the actual upgrade. The successful execution of PREPARE, including the regular checks, is a prerequisite for starting the upgrade. Although PREPARE makes a distinction between mandatory and optional verification modules, you should always run all of them and act on all warnings reported by the modules before starting the upgrade.

9.2 The Upgrade Assistant (UA)

The application that manages the upgrade process is the Upgrade Assistant (UA). The UA is delivered on the Upgrade Master DVD, and it is installed into the *ua* subdirectory of the upgrade directory.

The UA has two components: the *server* and the *client*:

▶ The UA Server runs on the upgrade host. It drives and controls the technical upgrade program (SAPup) and interacts with the UA Clients.

▶ The UA GUI is the graphical user interface (GUI) used to control and monitor the upgrade.

The GUI can run on the same host as the server but also on a different host (typically an administrator's PC). The UA GUI communicates with the UA Server via TCP/IP ports. It can run as a standalone application or as an applet started from a Web browser.

You'll find screenshots of the Upgrade Assistant and Upgrade Monitor in Section 7.3.

Tip

The UA for SAP ERP 2005 has few differences with that of previous releases. If you already used the UA for past upgrades, then you will be immediately familiar with it.

9.2.1 Administrator and Observer Modes

Any number of UA GUI sessions can connect to the UA Server simultaneously. Only one session, however, can be in control of the upgrade at any one time. This session is the upgrade administrator. Whenever the UA Server needs user input, a data entry window will automatically open in the administrator session.

All other UA GUI sessions are observers. They show the current phase of the upgrade and will also show (but in read-only) the user interaction that takes place with the administrator session.

When you start the UA server, the UA prompts you to enter a password for the administrator and observer. You can change the password or assign different passwords to the roles in the Upgrade Assistant menu (choose **Administrator** → **Change passwords**).

When you log on to the UA GUI, you specify the role you want your session to take on by entering a password (see Figure 9.2).

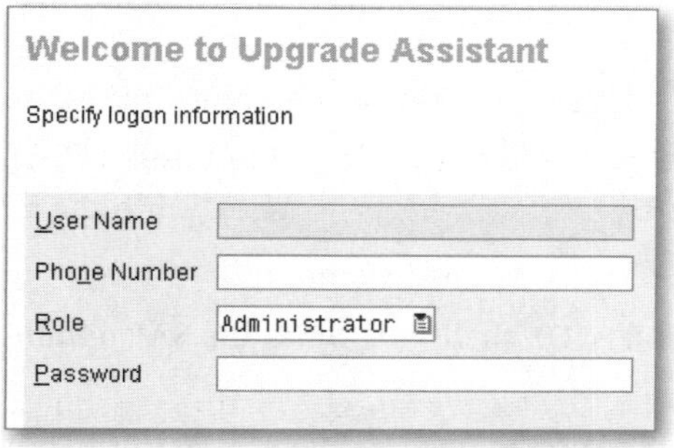

Welcome to Upgrade Assistant

Specify logon information

User Name	
Phone Number	
Role	Administrator
Password	

Figure 9.2 The Upgrade Assistant GUI Login Screen

Provided he knows the administrator password, it is possible for an observer to take over the administrator role. The current administrator is then automatically demoted to observer. This happens without interaction; that is, the UA GUI will not ask the current administrator to allow or acknowledge the take-over and his own demotion. This may seem a bit drastic, but it is actually smart. Imagine that during a long-running upgrade, the workstation currently running the UA GUI in administrator mode at some point becomes out of reach (you have gone home and want to continue the upgrade from your home PC via a VPN [Virtual Private Network] connection). In such a case, it makes perfect sense not to interact with the current administrator when switching roles.

9.2.2 Scroll Mode

You can also run the upgrade and interact with it from a plain command window, such as a Telnet session or a DOS shell. In this case, you do not use the UA GUI. This method is called *scroll mode* and is similar to the old method used up to SAP release 3.x, when SAPup was a terminal-based process.

There is really no reason to run in scroll mode because the disadvantages are significant. Apart from the fact that user interaction is much less user-friendly, the upgrade process is also far more vulnerable because it depends on the network connection of the terminal session. If this connection fails or you accidentally close the session window, the upgrade stops, and specific recovery actions are necessary before you can safely restart it.[1]

9.3 The Initial Extraction Script

The very first step in the technical upgrade process is to run a script that extracts a minimum set of files (including the UA) to the upgrade directory and also performs some basic checks of the server. This script is located on the Upgrade Master CD and is — somewhat confusingly — called PREPARE (it is not the same as the PREPARE process, which is the first major step of the upgrade and is not run via this script).

1. As a starting condition, the upgrade directory must be empty.

2. In a command window (Telnet session, DOS shell), log on as the SAP administrator account (<sid>adm).

3. Locate the PREPARE script for your OS platform on the Upgrade Master CD.

4. Execute the script. Example (user input is shown in **bold**):

    Select operation mode • **EXIT**

9.4 SAPup and Correction Transports

Before you continue with the technical upgrade, now is the time to replace the SAPup from the upgrade kit with the fixed version (see Section 7.2.4, under the heading *SAPup Fix and Correction Transports*) and also to copy the SAR archive with the correction transports (see the same section) to its proper location.

9.4.1 Replace SAPup

> **Caution**
>
> You should only replace SAPup before the first run of PREPARE. Never replace SAPup *during* the upgrade unless instructed to do so by SAP!

1. Go to directory *<PUTDIR>/bin*.

2. Rename SAPup, for example to SAPup.orig.

3. Copy the fixed SAPup you downloaded earlier to *<PUTDIR>/bin*. Make sure that ownership and file access are the same as for the original SAPup file.

---

1 For details, see the *Restarting the Upgrade in Scroll Mode* section in the SAP Upgrade Guide.

9.4.2 Correction Transports (Fix Buffer)

Unpack the *ERP2005SR2_9.SAR* archive that contains the correction transports to the top level of the upgrade directory (logged on as <sid>adm):

```
cd <PUTDIR>
SAPCAR -xvf <path>/ERP2005SR2_9.SAR
```

Two files will be extracted. One has extension *.info*, and the other is again an SAR archive named *FIX_ERP2005SR2_9.UPG*.

9.5   Copy Phase List Files to PC (Optional)

The list of upgrade phases is no longer in the upgrade manual; instead it comes as a set of HTML files, which you can transfer to the PC.

Copy the following files to your PC:

▶ *<PUTDIR>/htdoc/phaselist.htm*

▶ *<PUTDIR>/htdoc/phase_toc.htm*

PHASE_TOC.HTM lists all upgrade phases as hyperlinks to the detailed phase list. *PHASELIST.HTM* contains the actual phase list for PREPARE and SAPup, divided into major sections. This corresponds to the phase list that used to be part of the upgrade manual in earlier releases.

9.6   Install UA GUI on Workstation (Optional)

This step is only necessary if you want to run the UA GUI as a standalone application from your workstation. If you choose to run the UA GUI as an applet from a browser, then you may skip this step.

1. Create a folder on the PC to hold the UA GUI files (e.g., *C:\UAGUI*).

2. Transfer (in binary mode) the following file from the server to the folder you have just created: *<PUTDIR>/ua/uagui.jar*.

3. Open a DOS shell, and try starting the UA GUI:

   ```
   cd C:\UAGUI
   java -cp uagui.jar UaGui
   ```

4. The UA GUI logon screen must appear. Exit for now because you haven't got the server running yet.

9.7 Start the UA Server

Follow these instructions to start the UA Server.

UNIX (see upcoming note):

(logged on as <sid>adm)

```
java -cp <PUTDIR>/ua/ua.jar UaServer
```

Windows:

(logged on as <sid>adm)

```
java -cp <PUTDIR>\ua\ua.jar UaServer
```

iSeries:

```
ADDLIBLE SAPUP
ADDENVVAR ENVVAR(PASE_LIBPATH) VALUE('<PUTDIR>/bin')
JAVA CLASS(UaServer) CLASSPATH('<PUTDIR>/ua/ua.jar')
PROP((os400.file.io.mode TEXT)(os400.verify.checks.disable 3))
```

The first time the UA server starts, it asks you to provide a password (see the following listing). The password you set applies to both the administrator and observer. You can change the password or assign different passwords to the roles in the Upgrade Assistant menu later (choose **Administrator → Change passwords**).

```
# java -cp /usr/sap/put/ua/ua.jar UaServer
UaServer> Stable storage file '/usr/sap/put/ua/UaState' read
Please enter administrator password
Enter password:********
Confirm password:********
UaServer> Temporary directory is '/usr/sap/put/ua'
UaServer> Property file '/usr/sap/put/ua/UaServer.properties' read
UaServer> Configuring HTTP server
UaServer> Using HTTP index file name: index.html
UaServer> Signing JAR file uagui.jar
```

Note for UNIX

It is not a good idea to run the UA Server in a dedicated terminal window, because the server then would abort if the terminal window was closed or if the network connection to the PC failed. Use Ctrl+C to terminate the UA Server after providing the administrator password, and restart it in background:

```
# nohup java -cp <PUTDIR>/ua/ua.jar UaServer &
```

9.8   Start UA GUI and Log In

The procedure to run the UA GUI and log on to the UA Server is slightly different depending on whether you run the UA GUI as a standalone application or via a browser.

9.8.1   Starting from a Browser

1. Open a Web browser, and enter the URL:

    http://<upghost>:4239

    <upghost> is the host name or IP address of the host where the UA Server runs. The HTTP port of the UA Server is 4239. The SAP Upgrade main page is displayed (see Figure 9.3).

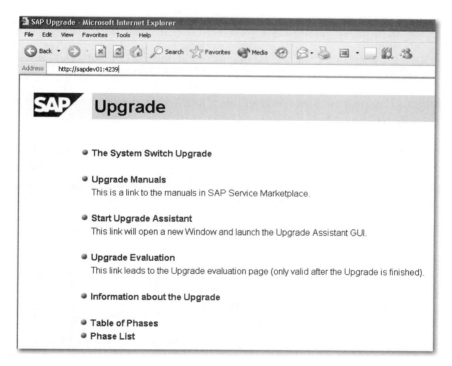

Figure 9.3 Initial Browser Screen for Upgrade

2. To start the UA GUI, click on **Start Upgrade Assistant**. A login screen appears. On this screen enter the following:

    ▶ A freely chosen user name (this can be your real name, as the only purpose is to identify who is currently connected to the UAGUI)

▶ Your telephone number (optional)

▶ The password for the *administrator* role which you specified earlier

3. Choose **Login,** and continue with the instructions in Section 7.3.

> **Note**
>
> To call the UA GUI directly, use the URL *http://<server>:4239/ua/UaGui.html*.

9.8.2 Starting as a Standalone Application

Open a command shell on the PC, and type the command to start the UA GUI as shown earlier in Section 9.6. Because at this point you have not yet identified the upgrade host, a window opens asking for the upgrade host and port:

▶ **Host name**
Name or IP address of the host where the UA Server runs.

▶ **Port number**
Accept the default 4241 (notice that different ports, 4239 and 4241, are used depending on how you run the UA GUI).

You can also pass the host name and port number on the command line in the form of a SAP route string, for example:

```
java -cp C:\UAGUI\uagui.jar -host /H/sapdev01/S/4241
```

This will skip the first screen; that is, the UA GUI will now behave as it does when you run it from a browser.

9.9 Runtime of PREPARE

Many factors influence the total runtime of PREPARE, and it is difficult to make a prediction. You should typically expect a runtime of between four and eight hours. Although there are some lengthy phases during which PREPARE runs unattended, the program will request user input at many different points. This means that PREPARE is not suitable to run overnight without human monitoring.

9.10 Input Up to Phase Selection

> **Note**
>
> For better readability, the PREPARE dialogs in this section are shown as text (not as actual screenshots) on a shaded background. User input appears in bold. Whenever an input screen requires further explanation, this information is presented in plain text. Actual screenshots are shown when beneficial to the discussion.

1. In the UA GUI window, choose **Administrator** → **Start PREPARE**.

```
Enter at least the mount point for the CD titled "Upgrade Master
CD/DVD."
```

2. Type the path of the Upgrade Master CD, and press **Enter**. The archives are unpacked:

```
Welcome to the SAP upgrade control program.
Important information for this upgrade is included in the upgrade
note and further notes mentioned therein.
Refer to the upgrade manual for the number of this note.
It is advisable to obtain this note before starting any process since
 it also contains important information about preparing the upgrade.
It is essential that you get a current version of this note before
starting the upgrade with SAPup. It contains a keyword which is
necessary to start the upgrade procedure.
Please look into the SAP Service Marketplace or, if not available,
use the form in your packet to request the upgrade note.
```

3. Click **Continue**.

```
SAP  UPGRADE  CONTROL  PROGRAM
Target SAP system is <SID>, ORACLE database
SAPup started in PREPARE mode.
```

4. Click **Continue**.

```
The following options are available:
select: Display screen for selecting PREPARE modules
status: Display the statuses of the PREPARE modules
exit:   Exit PREPARE
help:   Getting help about PREPARE
```

5. Choose **Select**.

6. Next, all Prepare Modules are displayed (see Figure 9.4) Mark all phases, and then click **OK**.

Selection	Name	Status	Mandatory
☐	Parameter input	initial	yes
☐	Initialization	initial	yes
☐	Import	initial	yes
☐	Extension	initial	yes
☐	Integration	initial	yes
☐	Installation	initial	yes
☐	General checks	initial	yes
☐	Activation checks	initial	yes
☐	Necessary checks for...	initial	yes
☐	Optional checks for ...	initial	no
☐	Modification support	initial	no
☐	Pre-processing	initial	no

Figure 9.4 ABAP Prepare Modules

> **Note**
>
> Ignore the fact that some phases are marked as mandatory and others are not. Always execute *all* phases.

```
You selected the following PREPARE modules:
(The phase list follows — scroll down to see the radio buttons)
```

7. Choose **Execute**, and then click **OK**.

8. Enter the SAPup keyword(s).

```
Enter the SAPup keyword of Note 961410
? SAPup keyword =
```

The SAPup keyword for ECC 6.0 is "29781129".

The keyword is a numeric "password" needed to do the upgrade. There is nothing secret about it; you find it in the first section of the core upgrade note referenced in the message (here 961410). The keyword is simply there to check that at least you took the trouble to access the note.

9.11   Entering the CD/DVD Mount Points

```
Mount points for DVDs
```

Enter the paths of the online copies of the upgrade media.

The path of the Upgrade Master medium is already filled in. You must still enter the paths for the kernel medium, the language media, and the different upgrade media. Fortunately, you only have to do this once! Unlike earlier versions of the UA GUI, this one lets you copy/paste path names.

9.12   Kernel Extraction and Optional Replacement

The extraction of the kernel now begins. If you plan to upgrade the SAP kernel to a higher level than the one delivered on the upgrade media, then you can already bind the new kernel into the upgrade when PREPARE next stops for further input.

```
SAP System ID
SAP System Host
Instance number
```

The values shown should be okay. At this point, you can upload the new kernel (described next).

To bind the new kernel into the upgrade, do the following:

1. Log on as <sid>adm.

2. Unpack the *SAPEXE*.SAR* and *SAPEXEDB.** packages you downloaded from the SAP Service Marketplace (see Section 6.6.3, heading *Support Package Selection*):

```
cd <PUTDIR>/exe
SAPCAR -xvf <downloadpath>/SAPEXE*.SAR
SAPCAR -xvf <downloadpath>/SAPEXEDB*.SAR
```

As of target release 7.00, there are two executable directories, directory *exe* and *exenew*. As such, the kernel that came with the support package stack can be used during the upgrade (*exe* directory), and the latest kernel can be deployed for the target release at the end of the upgrade during postprocessing to make sure that your system runs the latest available kernel (*exenew* directory). We recommend, however, that you use the latest kernel during the upgrade as well.

```
cd <PUTDIR>/exenew
SAPCAR -xvf <downloadpath>/SAPEXE*.SAR
SAPCAR -xvf <downloadpath>/SAPEXEDB*.SAR
```

If the extraction was successful for both archives, reply **OK** in the PREPARE window.

9.13 Input for Server and Path Names

PREPARE now requests information about the server environment and various directory paths needed for the upgrade.

```
Kernel path
```

Click **OK**.

```
Database ID, Database host
```

Values shown should be okay.

```
The password for ORACLE user "SYSTEM":
  (may be MANAGER)
? SYSTEM PASSWORD =

Verification of the password for ORACLE user "SYSTEM":
? SYSTEM PASSWORD =
```

Enter and confirm the password of user SYSTEM (Oracle only).

```
DDIC password
```

Enter and confirm the password of user DDIC in client 000.

```
Batch host
```

Set to host of central instance (default).

9.14 Input for Parallel Processing

```
Maximum uptime processes
```

1. See the following.

```
R3trans processes
```

2. See the following.

```
Maximum SYNC time
```

3. Enter "120".

The value for **Maximum uptime processes** determines the number of parallel tasks that will run in the shadow instance during the dictionary activation phase. With the downtime-minimized strategy, these tasks will run together with normal use of the system. Values of 3 to 5 are reasonable.

R3trans processes sets the number of parallel import processes (R3trans) during the upgrade. The phases most affected by this are SHADOW_UPGRADE (an uptime phase in the downtime-minimized mode) and TABIM (table data import; always in downtime). Too high a number may overload the server and also lead to contention between the different imports. Too low a value needlessly lengthens the duration of the upgrade. A suitable value in most cases is 4.

The **SYNC time** controls internal buffer synchronization. Do not change this value.

9.15 Further Input for Path Names

```
EPS root Local SYSLOG path
```

The values shown should be okay.

```
STARTSAP path
```

The path (kernel directory) should be okay.

9.16 Input for MCOD

```
Is there more than one system running in this database?
(MCOD: Multiple components in one database)
```

Enter "No" unless you are upgrading an MCOD system.

The dialog box shown here is for a non-MCOD configuration. This covers most situations.

9.17 Upgrade Key (from SAP Solution Manager)

```
The SAP Solution Manager Key is required for the upgrade. Further
information can be found in the upgrade guide, the SAP Service
Marketplace and SAP note 805390!
```

1. Continue.
2. The vague reference to the SAP Service Marketplace in this prompt is not of much use. Note 805390 is more informative.

```
SAP Solution Manager Key =
```

3. Enter the upgrade key. See Section 8.1 for instructions.

9.18 J2EE Instance (Double-Stacked System)

```
The upgrade procedure detected an ABAP and a J2EE server running.
The ABAP/J2EE upgrade procedures are synchronized and must run in
parallel.
Check the upgrade manual for a detailed description.
```

If a J2EE instance is running, the upgrade tool prompts you to start the PREPARE of the J2EE instance. In the same way, the upgrade of the J2EE instance will prompt for PREPARE of the ABAP instance (see Chapter 13 for more information).

9.19   Tool Import

```
     The PREPARE module Import will be started now.
During this module programs, structures, and table entries required
by PREPARE are imported (the so-called "tool import").
Note: This can cause a loss of performance in R/3.
In rare cases, a concurrent transport via the transport directory
may disturb the tool import. Please avoid any concurrent import
during this PREPARE module.
```

Click **Continue**.

PREPARE will duly warn you that the import may cause some pressure on the server. Although in practice this is rarely problematic, you may choose to wait for a quieter period before confirming this prompt. Also pay heed to the warning about concurrent transports.

9.20   Input for Language Selection

The following input screen concerns additional languages found in the system. If the system only contains the standard languages English and German, then PRE-PARE does not stop here.

```
Confirm that all selected languages have to be updated. Remove the
flag to exclude a language from import, but be aware that it will
not be possible to work in this language after the upgrade is
finished.
[x] DUTCH
[x] FRENCH
[x] SPANISH
[x] ITALIAN
[X] DANISH
[X] FINISH
[X] SWEDISH
```

Confirm the languages to be upgraded. Note that a language that is not integrated into the upgrade will become unusable and will have to be reinstalled in the target release. Only deselect a language if it no longer will be used in the new release. English and German are updated automatically, and there is no way of removing either of these languages.

9.21   Add-on and Patch Binding

The Add-on and Patch Binding module (module extension) is probably the most important module in the PREPARE. Some consider it the most important step in the upgrade. During add-on and patch binding, you instruct PREPARE to look for add-on components and additional support packages to be bound into the upgrade. During the add-on and patch binding, the target release level of every SAP component is decided upon.

9.21.1   Add-on Components

The PREPARE window asks you:

```
If you intend to include Add-on Upgrades or Support Packages into
the upgrade, you can now make available the needed CDs and packages.
All fitting CDs and packages will then be chosen as default
selection in the phase IS_SELECT for the Add-on Packages and CDs
and in the phase BIND_PATCH for the Support Packages
Do you want to add (further) Add-on CDs?
? Yes
? No
```

1. Click **Yes** if you need to provide an additional mount point to an add-on CD or DVD.

```
Do you want to search for new packages in directory
"/usr/sap/trans/EPS/in"?
```

2. Click **Search**.

Here you instruct PREPARE to look for all add-on and support packages to be bound into the upgrade. Including add-ons is mandatory because every ERP system contains at least the full set of application extensions (EA-*), the Plug-in (PI), and the Basis Plug-in (PI_BASIS). Including support packages is always recommended, and in some situations, is mandatory (PREPARE will notify you of this).

The first step is to specify the add-ons. PREPARE finds out which add-ons are installed in the current system and then looks for an appropriate upgrade medium or file. The HR system we are upgrading has two add-ons, C-EE and HR-CEE. As they are not included in the standard ECC bundle, PREPARE needs your input on what to do (see Figure 9.5).

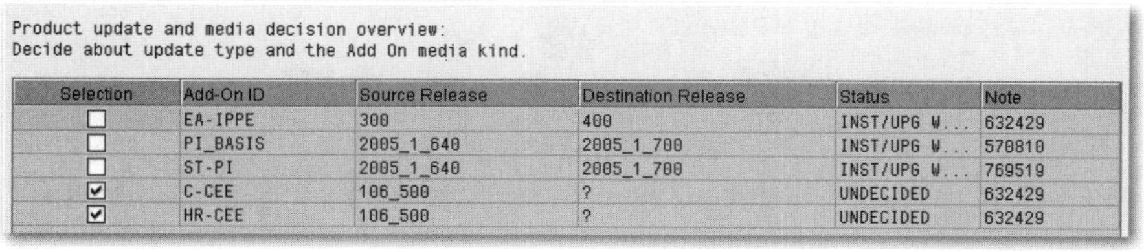

Product update and media decision overview:
Decide about update type and the Add On media kind.

Selection	Add-On ID	Source Release	Destination Release	Status	Note
☐	EA-IPPE	300	400	INST/UPG W...	632429
☐	PI_BASIS	2005_1_640	2005_1_700	INST/UPG W...	570810
☐	ST-PI	2005_1_640	2005_1_700	INST/UPG W...	769519
☑	C-CEE	106_500	?	UNDECIDED	632429
☑	HR-CEE	106_500	?	UNDECIDED	632429

Figure 9.5 Extension Module — Integrate Add-ons

PREPARE discovered two add-ons in our system (C-CEE and HR-CEE). For each add-on, you need to decide if it should be upgraded, deleted, or kept as is. In most cases, you will upgrade the component to a target release compatible to the target SAP release. Keeping the add-on can only be done in special cases. Keeping or deleting the add-ons requires a password from SAP.

Mark the components with status **UNDECIDED,** and click **OK.** For each selected component, PREPARE asks you what to do (see Figure 9.6)

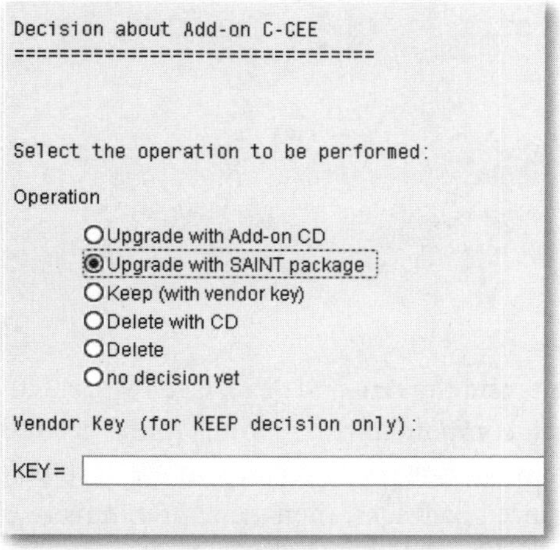

```
Decision about Add-on C-CEE
===================================



Select the operation to be performed:

Operation

        ○ Upgrade with Add-on CD
        ◉ Upgrade with SAINT package
        ○ Keep (with vendor key)
        ○ Delete with CD
        ○ Delete
        ○ no decision yet

Vendor Key (for KEEP decision only):

KEY = [                              ]
```

Figure 9.6 Extension Module — Integrate Add-on with SAINT Package

Select **Upgrade with Add-on CD** if the component is to be upgraded using an add-on CD. Select **Upgrade with SAINT package** if it is to be upgraded using a SAINT packages. SAINT packages should reside in the EPS Inbox of the transport directory from which they will be picked-up by SAPup.

After selecting the operation to be performed, PREPARE lists all components found in the system together with their upgrade path (see Figure 9.7).

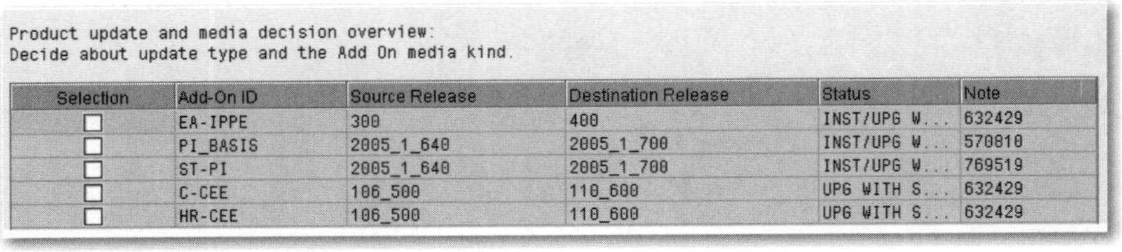

```
Product update and media decision overview:
Decide about update type and the Add On media kind.
```

Selection	Add-On ID	Source Release	Destination Release	Status	Note
☐	EA-IPPE	300	400	INST/UPG W...	632429
☐	PI_BASIS	2005_1_640	2005_1_700	INST/UPG W...	570810
☐	ST-PI	2005_1_640	2005_1_700	INST/UPG W...	769519
☐	C-CEE	106_500	110_600	UPG WITH S...	632429
☐	HR-CEE	106_500	110_600	UPG WITH S...	632429

Figure 9.7 Extension Module — Bind Patches

Click **OK** to confirm the selection.

9.21.2 Patch Binding

The next step is to choose the support packages to be bound into the upgrade:

```
Do you want to search for new packages in directory "/usr/sap/trans/
EPS/in" first?
This scan may run for some minutes. You can skip the inbox scan, if
the package descriptions have been uploaded already to this system.
```

1. Choose **Search**.

```
According to the uploaded packages the queue calculator could
generate a valid support package queue. Do you want to take over
the calculated package levels as default selection?
```

2. Choose **Yes**.

Screens now appear with the components and the target SP level (see Figure 9.8). Check that the highest SP shown for each component corresponds to the desired target level. If you see a *lower* target than what you need, and you are sure that you have correctly unpacked all the required packages, then some prerequisite is not being met. For example, if you want to bind SAP_APPL SP 6 into the upgrade, but you did not unpack BW SP 9, then the patch queue calculator will not bind SAP_APPL 6. If you are unsure what the problem is, then enter the desired SP level (6 in our example). PREPARE will return with an error, explaining which prerequisite patches it is missing. If your target level corresponds to a SAP SP Stack, then this situation should not occur.

Please select the Support Packages to include:

Component	Minimum Level	Equivalent Level	Current Level	Selection
SAP_BASIS	0007	0007	0006	9
SAP_ABA	0007	0007	0006	9
PI_BASIS	0007	0007	0006	9
ST-PI	<none>	<none>	0001	2
SAP_BW	0007	0007	0006	9
SAP_AP	0004	0004	0003	6
SAP_APPL	0004	0004	0003	6
SAP_HR	<none>	0004	0003	8
EA-IPPE	<none>	<none>	0003	6
EA-FINSERV	<none>	<none>	0003	
EA-GLTRADE	<none>	<none>	0003	
FINBASIS	<none>	0004	0003	5
EA-HR	<none>	0004	0003	8
EA-APPL	<none>	<none>	0003	6
EA-DFPS	<none>	<none>	0003	
EA-RETAIL	<none>	<none>	0003	
EA-PS	<none>	<none>	0003	
C-CEE	<none>	<none>	<none>	3
HR-CEE	<none>	<none>	<none>	4
ERECRUIT	<none>	0004	0003	6
LSOFE	<none>	0004	0003	6
SEM-BW	<none>	<none>	0003	

Figure 9.8 Extension Module — Bind Patches Overview

Click **OK** to confirm the target package level.

> **Note**
>
> If you have to unpack additional patches to the EPS area, PREPARE will *not* notice this until you restart the phase When you restart the phase, PREPARE will offer you the option to search the EPS area again. To do this, click the **Search button**.

```
Do you want to include a SPAM Update for release 700?
(We recommend to include the newest available SPAM Update.)
```

Click **Yes**.

```
The following SPAM Update package has been found:
Request: SAPKD70021    Version: 0021
Text:    SPAM/SAINT Update — Version 700/0021
```

Choose **Include**.

```
Do you want to include a Single Change Request?
```

Click **No**.

This prompt is meant for Customer-Based Upgrades (CBU), where at this point, you specify the transport requests prepared in the initial upgrade.

```
The following packages will be included:

  Component SAP_BASIS Support Package (SAP_BASIS) 7 - 9
  Component SAP_ABA Support Package (SAP_ABA) 7 - 9
  Component PI_BASIS Support Package (PI_BASIS) 7 - 9
  Component ST-PI Support Package (ST-PI) 2
  Component SAP_BW Support Package (SAP_BW) 7 - 9
  Component SAP_AP Support Package (SAP_AP) 4 - 6
  Component SAP_APPL Support Package (SAP_APPL) 4 - 6
  Component SAP_HR Support Package (SAP_HR) 4 - 8
  Component EA-IPPE Support Package (EA-IPPE) 4 - 6
  Component FINBASIS Support Package (FINBASIS) 4 - 5
  Component EA-HR Support Package (EA-HR) 4 - 8
  Component EA-APPL Support Package (EA-APPL) 4 - 6
  Component C-CEE Support Package (C-CEE) 1 - 3
  Component HR-CEE Support Package (HR-CEE) 1 - 4
  Component ERECRUIT Support Package (ERECRUIT) 4 - 6
  Component LSOFE Support Package (LSOFE) 4 - 6

The following SPAM Update for release 700 will be included:
  SAPKD70021

The total size of all data files is 905269 KBytes.
```

Do a final check that the target levels are correct, and choose **Confirm** if it is okay. Parameter input for add-on and patch binding is now done.

9.22   Input for Modification Adjustment

The next stop concerns Modification Adjustment. In Transactions SPDD and SPAU, you have the option to register the transport request containing all the modifications on behalf of later upgrades. During the next upgrade in the same landscape, you can then have the upgrade process import this request rather than having to make the modifications manually. However, as you will see later, we recommend that you *do* repeat the manual modification in all systems that you upgrade (at least for the dictionary adjustment with Transaction SPDD).

You are now at the point where PREPARE looks for registered Modification Adjustment transports and asks you—if it finds one—whether to use it during the upgrade. The transport request is registered in a flat file called *umodauto.lst* in the transport directory */usr/sap/trans/bin*.

The input window of PREPARE depends on the situation. There are three possibilities:

1. The file *umodauto.lst* does not exist, either because this is the first upgrade or because you did not bother to register the Modification Adjustment transport during the preceding upgrades:

```
For automatically maintaining your modifications in your system
during the upgrade transport requests from earlier upgrades
are searched in file umodauto.lst in directory /usr/sap/trans/bin.
The file could not be read. There are several reasons why this may
be correct, e.g. "this is your first upgrade" or "your system is not
modified". Did you expect a list of transports being found?
```

Click **No**.

2. The file *umodauto.lst* exists and contains a single reference to a transport request:

```
The following transport request(s) may be used to automatically
maintain your modifications in your system during the upgrade.
<details about transport request> Do you want to use these transport
requests?
```

Click **No**.

3. The file *umodauto.lst* exists and contains more than one transport request. This would happen if you carried out the Modification Adjustment manually in several systems, and each time registered the transport request created in the process. If you did, PREPARE will offer you the transport of each system created in each system already upgraded.

```
For automatically maintaining your modifications in your system
during the upgrade transport requests from different source systems
have been found. Please decide which source system should be used.
When you are sure that you do not want to use one of these source systems
choose 'NONE'. Otherwise the upgrade procedure will ask for further
details at a later stage. Please choose a source system on the
next screen.
? continue
? cancel
```

4. Choose **Continue.** On the next screen (list of systems), choose **None** and **OK**.

If you do the SPDD adjustment manually, then naturally you always reply in the negative.

9.23   Input for the Shadow Instance

PREPARE will request information necessary to configure the shadow instance. The instance is not started up yet; this only happens during the upgrade itself.

```
INFO: During the upgrade a temporary instance is installed to perform
the modification adjustment and activation. For the installation of
the shadow system instance, you have to supply an unused instance
number and free port numbers.
```

Click **Continue**.

```
Enter an unused instance number for the shadow system:
```

Assign a two-digit instance number.

As with any other SAP instance, the shadow instance must be identified by a two-digit instance number. This number must be unique on the application server where the shadow instance will run (normally the central instance host). Check the number of all other SAP instances running on the same host, and then assign a number that is not yet in use.

```
Port numbers
```

Normally **OK** but must be checked (see below)!

After prompting for the instance number, PREPARE asks you to enter four port numbers, all used by the SAP system log facility: the send-daemon talk port (13xx), the send-daemon listen port (37xx), the collect-daemon talk port (39xx), and the collect- daemon listen port (40xx), where xx denotes the instance number you chose for the shadow instance.

> **Caution**
>
> There seems to be a bug in SAPup that sometimes causes the default service numbers to have just the two leading digits, e.g., "13" instead of "13xx". Never accept these two-digit port numbers because they collide with other network services and will cause problems in the shadow instance.

For the shadow instance to work, an additional entry must be configured in the services file on the upgrade host. This entry defines the service name and port for the message server of the shadow instance, and must look as follows (with xx again, the number chosen for the shadow instance):

```
sapmsshdSID 36xx/tcp
```

Changing the services file requires super user access, so you may need to involve the system administrator here.

> For the upgrade strategy — Downtime-minimized — there is the option to run the so called shadow instance on an additional application server of your system landscape. Are you planning to apply this possibility?

Choose **No**.

If you answer **No**, the shadow instance will run on the same host as the SAP central instance. You have the option here of running the shadow instance on another application server.[2]

> **Note**
>
> If you answer **Yes** here, several extra actions are necessary on the designated application server. Follow the instructions in the SAP Upgrade Guide; section *Making Entries for the Installation Module*.

> You have the alternative to use the profiles from a test upgrade with identical environment for the so-called shadow instance. If you choose this alternative the profiles will be taken from the subdirectory <save>. Please also refer to the upgrade manual for more details! Do you want to take the profiles?

Choose **No**.

This (rarely used) option allows you to use the parameter profiles of the shadow instance of a previous upgrade. This could be useful if you made changes to the shadow instance parameters, and the current server is identical or nearly identical in terms of capacity. Manually changing the shadow instance parameters is normally not necessary and should only be done with care.

9.24   Application-Specific Upgrade (ASU)

After the input for the shadow instance, PREPARE runs without interaction for a considerable length of time. The next input screen appears when PREPARE is about to start the pre-upgrade part of the ASU:

---

2   This option is not available for DB2 on z/OS.

```
The next phase runs a report which saves and restores variants from
your system. Please read note 712297 carefully. Do you want to run
the phases JOB_RASUVAR1(2)?
```

RASUVAR1 starts a background job, which soon starts several tasks running in parallel in dialog work processes. This process may take several hours.

> **Note**
>
> While the ASU process is running, keep an eye on short dumps in the system (Transaction ST22). In certain circumstances, the job might generate hundreds of dumps. This does not mean, however, that the process is faulty, and you must let the job continue. If necessary, periodically clean up short dumps using report RSSNAPDL. See Note 712297 for more information.

9.25 Result of PREPARE

Saving the variants is the last PREPARE phase. The global result window then appears. For each major process phase, the outcome is either *succeeded* or *failed*. It is very likely that the first run of PREPARE will discover at least a few problems, in which case the status of the corresponding phase is *failed*.

```
Execution of the selected PREPARE modules finished with the statuses
as follows:
'Parameter input' status: succeeded
'Initialization' status: succeeded
'Import' status: succeeded
'Extension' status: succeeded
'Integration' status: succeeded
'Installation' status: succeeded
'General checks' status: failed

'Activation checks' status: succeeded
'Necessary checks for conversions' status: succeeded
'Optional checks for conversions' status: failed
'Modification support' status: succeeded
'Pre-processing' status: succeeded
```

9.26 Correcting Errors Reported by PREPARE

The Verification Modules of PREPARE have almost always something to complain about. The errors and warnings reported do not necessarily mean that there is something wrong with the running system. They do mean that, if they are not taken care of before the upgrade, the upgrade might fail. All errors and warnings should be dealt with and the Verification Modules that failed repeated until they end successfully.

9.26.1 The CHECKS.LOG File

Together with the result window, PREPARE also opens a GUI window that shows the contents of the log, which contains the detail of all errors and warnings. You can also view this log on the server. Its path is *<PUTDIR>/log/CHECKS.LOG*.

9.26.2 PREPARE Errors

Many factors could cause PREPARE to complain. Because the SAPup process will refuse to run unless PREPARE has given the system a clean bill of health, you must investigate and solve all these errors before the upgrade can begin.

You should understand that a PREPARE "error" does not mean that your system is somehow inconsistent or corrupt. PREPARE reports an error when it discovers anything that might cause conflicts or problems during or after the upgrade.

You find instructions for dealing with most errors in the SAP Upgrade Guide, section *Evaluating the Results of PREPARE*. It is not possible to discuss every possible PREPARE error in this book, but a few common or especially interesting problems should be mentioned.

9.26.3 Database Extensions

For databases that use explicit storage assignment (tablespaces in Oracle and DB2), PREPARE lists the storage spaces that need to be created or extended. For the SAP repository of the target release, you have to create new storage spaces: one (or two[3]) to hold the source versions of programs, dictionary objects, and so on, and another one (or two) for the compiled versions (loads). The names of these storage areas contain the SAP Basis release code ("700" for Basis 700) and a letter indicating the contents: "S" for source and "L" for load.

> **Tip**
>
> Create the load (L) space significantly larger than what PREPARE tells you. ABAP load generation (Transaction SGEN) after the upgrade greatly improves performance, but the generated loads take up a good deal of space. Add 1.5GB — 2GB to the space requested by PREPARE.

---

3 Databases that use separate storage areas for tables and indexes (Oracle with pre-6.20 database structure, DB2 UDB) use two spaces for the sources and two for the loads. Databases that do not make this separation (Oracle with new database structure) only use one.

On top of this, the upgrade may also need extra space in the existing database files. PREPARE will calculate the space requirement and will request an extension if not enough free space is left. Databases that do not use an explicit storage assignment (such as Microsoft SQL Server and MaxDB) obviously do not require specific storage areas, but they might still need extra space.

Although most databases support an *auto-extend* mode — meaning that database files will grow automatically when they become full — it is best not to rely on this feature during the upgrade. If the database is filled close to capacity, incessant extensions will occur while new data is being written. This causes significant overhead and can seriously slow down the database-intensive upgrade phases.

> **Tip**
>
> To save time you can already start creating the new tablespaces/dbspaces while PRE-PARE is still running. When PREPARE reaches the point where it asks for the shadow instance parameters (see Section 9.26.1), you can take a "sneak peek" at the *CHECKS.LOG* file. The request to create the new tablespaces is already in the log at that moment.

9.26.4 Change the Permissions of Executables

All kernel executables are replaced during the upgrade. PREPARE will report all kernel files for which the SAP administrator account `<sid>adm` lacks the necessary access rights. This is a common occurrence on UNIX platforms because some parts of the kernel run with the identity of the database administrator account or even the super user (`root`).

> **Caution (UNIX)**
>
> To grant the required permissions to the SAP administrator, follow the instructions in the Upgrade Guide, that is, set group ownership of the affected files to `sapsys` and grant write access on the file to that group. Do not, as we have sometimes seen, grant unlimited access (777) to the files because this would create a severe security issue.

9.26.5 Target Kernel Too Low

The PREPARE log contains the following error:

```
CAUTION: There are dependencies between Basis Support Packages
included in phase BIND_PATCH and the patch level of the target release
kernel in directory /usr/sap/put<SID>/exe. The disp+work needs at
least patch level <nnn>or higher. Please proceed as described in Note
211077.
```

It is possible for a Basis support package (SAP_BASIS component) to require a minimum kernel version. If you bind Basis SP into the upgrade, and one of these packages requires a kernel level higher than the one you will install with the upgrade, PREPARE will report this conflict. The solution is to use a higher level of the target kernel in the upgrade, a procedure explained in Note 211077. This problem cannot occur if your target support package and kernel-patch level correspond to a SAP SP stack. On this topic, see Section 6.6.

9.26.6 SAP Objects Locked in Repairs

The following error is reported:

```
WARNING: Locked SAP-objects were found in open repairs and/or trans-
port requests. If these requests are not released, you will not be
able to adjust these objects. Release these repairs and transport
requests to ensurethat the objects can be adjusted!!! For a list of
the transport orders and repairs see below:  <list follows>
```

All repairs of SAP objects must be released prior to the upgrade. Locked objects cannot be modified or replaced by the release upgrade. The message includes a list of all transport requests and their owners. This is not the responsibility of the Basis administrator. Instead, forward the transport requests to their owners, and ask them to release them.

Note that at this time, locked SAP objects only result in a warning. This is because the system is still operational, and it is possible to continue working on the open repairs and only to release them later, before the actual upgrade.

9.26.7 Doomed Dictionary Objects

The new release not only introduces new dictionary objects into the system but also deletes objects that have become obsolete. If a customer object refers to one of these "doomed" objects (e.g., a customer table refers to a SAP data element or a customer data element to an SAP domain[4] that is bound to disappear with the new release), then that customer object would become inconsistent after the upgrade. PREPARE notices this and warns you that the reference to the SAP object will no longer be valid.

---

4 Data elements and domains together set the characteristics of table fields in the SAP dictionary. The domain defines the field's technical characteristics like the data type and length. Data elements define semantic attributes of the field.

The solution is to have a developer create a custom copy of the SAP object and to have the affected customer object refer to this custom copy rather than to the original SAP object.

9.26.8 Pending Update Records

Update records with error status must be cleaned up before the downtime phase of the upgrade. PREPARE will report their existence but only as a warning. The update records will be checked two more times, once in the uptime part of SAPup (where you will get another warning) and finally in the downtime part (where you *must* clean them up).

9.26.9 Address Conversion

If your start release is 3.1 or 4.0, address data is converted to the Central Address Management during the downtime phase of the upgrade. Depending on the amount of data involved, the conversion process could take a very long time. PREPARE will look at the size of the affected tables and report a warning if they are larger than a critical threshold. In that case, you must apply SAP Note 097032 before you start the upgrade. If the current release is 4.5 or higher, then the data is already in the expected format and no conversion occurs.

9.26.10 Overlap in Address Number Range

The PREPARE log shows the following error:

```
2EEF2777 OSS 379769: Client "000"—
current no. level of ADRNR 01 must be increased to "<value>"
```

The long text that accompanies this error message, which occurs fairly often, will give background information. You solve the problem as follows:

1. Log on as to the client mentioned in the message (the error does not necessarily appear for every client in the system).

2. Call Transaction SA01.

3. Click **Change Status**.

4. In the range indicated in the message ("01" in the example), change the **Current number** field. Set the value to that shown in the error text.

5. Save the change.

6. Confirm the warning about transporting number range intervals.

9.26.11 Number of Objects for Modification Adjustment

CHECKS.LOG also lists the number of objects that will need to be processed in the Modification Adjustment. Separate counts are shown for dictionary objects (Transaction SPDD — to be executed by you in the shadow instance during the upgrade) and for ABAP development objects (Transaction SPAU — to be executed by the developers after the upgrade). Example:

```
CAUTION: During the upgrade 93 ABAP Dictionary objects will be
imported in your SID system that have been modified there. You can
have a look at these modifications in detail by running Transaction
SPDD in your <SID> system now.
CAUTION: During the upgrade, 1,862 ABAP development objects will be
imported in your SID system, which have been modified there. You can
have a look at these modifications in detail by running Transaction
SPAU in your <SID> system now.
```

9.27 Repeating PREPARE

After you have corrected the PREPARE errors, you must repeat PREPARE until it is error free. In the UA GUI, proceed as follows:

1. Choose **Continue** on the PREPARE screen showing the result of each phase.

2. Choose **Select**.

3. Mark only the phases that have status **Failed,** and choose **OK**.

4. Choose **execute**.

> **Note**
>
> If the repeated phase contains parameter input, you will have to re-enter the same data as before. If you have to repeat the phase "Installation," then this will happen for the shadow instance parameters (the default instance number and port numbers are already correct).

5. Repeat this process until *all* phases have the status **Succeeded**. You cannot start the actual upgrade (SAPup) as long as PREPARE reports errors.

6. When all phases have the status **Succeeded**, choose **Exit** to stop PREPARE.

9.28 After the End of PREPARE

PREPARE does not verify everything. Some checks and actions must be done manually. Most of them are listed in the SAP component Upgrade Guides. We consider those discussed in the next section too important to be neglected.

9.28.1 Post-PREPARE Activities

Between the end of PREPARE and the start of SAPup, some additional steps must be carried out. Which actions are necessary depends on your OS database system, the source release, and the applications you use. In the SAP ERP 6.0 Upgrade Guides, all the post-PREPARE activities are described in the *Making Preparations at the Operating System Level* section, continuing up to the end of the chapter.

9.28.2 Back Up Database and Upgrade Directory

Always back up the database between the end of PREPARE and the beginning of SAPup. Together with the database, you should also back up the entire upgrade directory. You can make an online database backup, but no upgrade activity should be taking place; that is, neither PREPARE nor SAPup may be running.

9.28.3 Clean Up Database Archives

If you run in downtime-minimized mode (or in resource-minimized mode with downtime starting after the import), the system will be in normal production use during the SAPup data import. This implies that during the import, database archiving will still be enabled. Because of the sheer volume of database logs the SAPup import produces, your archive-backup procedure could come under pressure and might even break down, which could lead to a system standstill. You therefore must make sure that your procedures for storing and backing up database archive logs are ready to handle the surge in logging activity by doing the following:

▶ Back up and delete all existing database logs so that the storage area for the logs is as empty as possible.

▶ Increase the storage area if possible.

▶ Increase the frequency of database log backups.

On no account should you switch *off* database logging because this would expose you to serious loss of business data in case of a database failure.

You must pay proper attention to database-log backups in the production upgrade because this is one of the few things that is difficult to prepare for.

Although you do the development and test upgrades with the system technically up and running, the level of activity in these systems is usually so much lower than in production that bottlenecks in the database-log backups remain unnoticed.

9.29 SAP Start and Stop Scripts (UNIX)

On UNIX platforms, including Linux, the procedure for starting and stopping SAP is implemented in the form of shell scripts. If your start release is 3.1I or 4.6C, then an important change happens. Up to SAP 4.6, the two scripts reside in the home directory of the SAP administrator user sidadm. The names of these scripts are:

```
startsap_<host>_<nr>
stopsap_<host>_<nr>
```

where <host> is the host name of the server, and <nr> is the 2-digit instance number.

With SAP ERP (and more generally with all SAP systems running on Basis 6.20 or higher), these scripts are no longer used. They are replaced with two new shell scripts, simply called startsap and stopsap, which are installed in the SAP kernel directory /sapmnt/SID/exe.

If you made changes to the start and stop scripts, something that is occasionally done, for example, to start or stop other applications along with SAP, then you must carry over these changes to the new scripts after the upgrade. Future upgrades may replace the scripts again, so you should always back them up before you start the upgrade. This is particularly important if your start release is SAP R/3 Enterprise (4.70). This release is based on Basis 6.20 and thus already uses the new scripts.

9.30 Resetting PREPARE

If for some reason you decide not to proceed with PREPARE, or to begin again from zero, then it is easy to reset PREPARE. Chapter 22 explains how to do this.

The SAPup process performs the actual upgrade of the system. SAPup imports all the data and repository objects belonging to the new release. It installs the new kernel, adapts existing objects like tables and structures, and performs all the necessary data conversions. When SAPup is done, the system is up and running with the new SAP release, and — after a series of additional postprocessing steps described in Chapter 11 — is ready to be returned to normal production.

10 The Upgrade Process for SAP ECC

The upgrade process needs some input on how to perform the upgrade (the upgrade strategy, the number of background processes, when to close the development workbench). Afterwards, it runs normally error-free up to the activation phase in which conflicts between the new standard and customer-modified DDIC objects need to be resolved. Then, it runs up to the beginning of the downtime in which the switch to the new release is made.

10.1 Uptime or Downtime?

Regardless of the upgrade strategy that you choose, SAPup always runs partly in system uptime and partly in downtime. The upgrade strategies — downtime-minimized and resource-minimized — were already discussed in Chapters 4 and 5. As a reminder, Table 10.1 shows a brief summary for the three possible scenarios. The second column gives the name of the SAPup phase where the system will enter downtime. The last column gives the duration of downtime as a percentage of the overall runtime of the SAPup process. These percentages are approximations and in reality may vary strongly depending on the actual circumstances of the upgrade (e.g., whether you slow down the data import).

Scenario	Phase Marking Start of Downtime	Duration of Downtime Relative to Duration of Entire SAPup
Resource-minimized Data import in DOWNTIME	EU_IMPORT1	100 %
Resource-minimized Data import in UPTIME	REQSTOPPROD	± 70 %
Downtime-minimized	MODPROF_TRANS	± 35 %

Table 10.1 Upgrade Scenarios Versus Downtime

When SAPup reaches the indicated phase, it will open an input window in the UA GUI. When the upgrade administrator confirms this window, the downtime effectively begins. SAPup then shuts down the central instance, replaces the parameter profiles, restarts the central instance, and locks the system against all user access (except by SAP* and DDIC).

10.2 Starting SAPup Without an Error-Free PREPARE

One of the first things SAPup does is to check whether PREPARE ended without errors. If it is found that errors remained when you last ran PREPARE, then SAPup will display an error. This error window has an **Ignore** option, which would allow you to start the upgrade regardless of the outcome of PREPARE. However, to use **Ignore,** you need a password from SAP, and the company will provide one only if there are legitimate reasons to proceed in this way.

> **Warning for SAP Personnel**
>
> If you are an employee of SAP, then you have access to the internal note listing the passwords needed to ignore upgrade errors. This does not grant you a license to use this feature! In the majority of cases, doing a password-protected **Ignore** to jump over errors is a straight road to disaster. Never ignore upgrade errors by using a password unless expressly instructed to do so by SAP support.

10.3 Upgrade Assistant (UA)

Like PREPARE, SAPup uses the Upgrade Assistant (UA). You start the UA Server on the upgrade host as explained in Section 7.1.6, and you communicate with the upgrade process through the UA GUI. The administrator/observer concept remains the same (see Section 7.1.6, heading *Administrator and Observer Modes*).

10.4　Starting the Upgrade

Open an UA GUI (via a browser or as a standalone application — see Section 7.3).
In the UA GUI window, choose **Administrator · Start SAPup**.

The interaction shown in the next section is for an upgrade in downtime-minimized mode. For the other strategies, appropriate input windows will open at the beginning of downtime, either in phase EU_IMPORT1 or in phase REQSTOP-PROD.

10.5　Interaction Until Start of Import

At startup, SAPup shows its version, the SAP components contained in the upgrade package and the target SAP system and database.

```
SAP  UPGRADE  CONTROL  PROGRAM
===================================


This is SAPup version 7.00/2 upgrade to release
        600 of EA-APPL
        600 of EA-DFPS
        600 of EA-FINSERV
        600 of EA-GLTRADE
        600 of EA-HR
        400 of EA-IPPE
        600 of EA-PS
        600 of EA-RETAIL
        600 of ECC-DIMP
        600 of ERECRUIT
        600 of FI-CA
        600 of FI-CAX
        600 of FINBASIS
        600 of INSURANCE
        600 of IS-CWM
        600 of IS-H
        600 of IS-M
        600 of IS-OIL
        600 of IS-PS-CA
        600 of IS-UT
        600 of LSOFE
        2005_1_700 of PI_BASIS
        700 of SAP_ABA
        700 of SAP_AP
        600 of SAP_APPL
        700 of SAP_BASIS
```

```
      700 of SAP_BW
      600 of SAP_HR
      600 of SEM-BW
      2005_1_700 of ST-PI
Target SAP system is <SID>, ORACLE database
```

Click **Continue**.

```
Do you have to change any parameter of the upgrade?
```

Click **No**.

If you answer **Yes** here, then the same parameter-input dialog will happen as it did at the start of PREPARE. Normally, there is no need for this, but exceptions are always possible (e.g., if you have changed the directory path for the CD/DVD media).

```
Enter the IS keyword of note 86985 (IS "C-CEE", version "110_600")
? IS keyword =
```

Enter "4571044".

```
Enter the IS keyword of note 86985 (IS "HR-CEE", version "110_600")
? IS keyword =
```

Enter "5145477".

Some add-on modules (but not the ones that are part of the standard SAP ERP) require keywords of their own. In that case, SAPup will issue additional keyword requests. The prompts for the C-CEE and HR-CEE keywords in the two preceding data entry screens are just examples. The text in the window will always point you to the note where you can find the keyword. As with the upgrade keyword, the keywords are only a wake up call that you should read the note before continuing.

```
Select an upgrade strategy (read the upgrade manual !!!):
- Downtime-minimized: Parallel to the production instance, an
instance on the target system will be established to minimize
downtime
- Resource-minimized: There is only one system alive, either the
instance on the start or on the target release to minimize the
resources needed
Select the upgrade strategy (current selection is Downtime-
minimized):
```

Select **Downtime-minimized**.

For the resource-minimized strategy, a further prompt appears to ask you at which point to enter downtime, before or after the import.

```
You selected upgrade strategy Downtime-minimized, where the import of
the mass data in the EU_IMPORT phases should be slowed down to avoid
performance drawbacks during production operation.
Please enter the time that this import shall take minus 20% as
security distance.
The time for mass-import (EU_IMPORT-phases) in hours:
IMPORT TIME =
```

Enter "0" if you do not want to slow down the import; otherwise, specify a time in hours.

The data import, which happens very early in the upgrade process, has a significant impact on the server and also fills a tremendous number of database logs, as we mentioned earlier. If you let the import run full blast in parallel with normal system use, then there is a risk that performance might suffer or that the procedure to back up and drain off database logs might be unable to cope. If the system is open to end users during the data import, then SAPup offers the possibility of artificially slowing down the import phases.

If you do not want to reduce the speed of the data import, then enter "0". Otherwise, enter a reasonable amount of time for the import to complete. To determine this, we do the following. After the data import, the system will have quite a lot of work to do before it reaches the downtime phase. By the time you reach production, you should have a fair idea of the upgrade phase runtimes. In that case, you should calculate the distance between the current time and the time when you want the upgrade to reach the end of uptime processing. Subtract from this the time needed to do the post-import phases, allowing a reasonable safety margin.

As an example, assume that you start SAPup on Tuesday afternoon at 2 p.m. Upgrade downtime is due to begin on Friday at 6 p.m., which is 76 hours away. However, as a safety precaution, you want SAPup to finish its uptime processing by Thursday evening 6 p.m., which is 52 hours away. From the previous upgrades, you know that the upgrade process needs about 12 hours to run the phases required after the data import (time mostly spent on the Modification Adjustment, dictionary activation, and shadow import). This leaves 40 hours for the import, so you enter "40" or a number close to 40.

It is useful to do at least one of your test upgrades with the data import running at full speed. This will give you an idea of the speed-reduction factor. If, for instance, the import at normal speed takes 15 hours and you grant 24 hours in production, then you only slow it down by a factor of roughly 1.5. Conversely, if the import at normal speed only takes 3 hours, then there is not really a need to grant it 24 hours in production. You might grant it 15 — 18 hours, giving you some slack in the upgrade timing.

```
Select an upgrade phase for disabling the archive mode (read the
upgrade manual!): If the archive mode is disabled, all productive
operations have to be stopped. Current selection is:
- No disabling of the archive mode during the whole upgrade
? Archiving on
? MODPROF_TRANS
```

In downtime-minimized mode, choose **MODPROF_TRANS**.

At the specified phase, SAPup will stop and inform you that now is the time to switch off database log archiving. For the resource-minimized mode, you can also choose between phase EU_IMPORT1 (start of the database import) and phase REQSTOPPROD (after the import and before running SPDD in the shadow instance). For the downtime-minimized mode, phase MODPROF_TRANS is the last possible time for the system to remain up. Another choice is to leave archiving on throughout the entire upgrade, including the downtime part. We do not recommend this as it creates extra overhead and increases the runtime. The advantage you gain by running entirely with archiving enabled is that after the upgrade, you do not need to back up the database straight away. This is a dubious benefit though, as you would have to recover your database starting from a pre-upgrade backup, potentially forcing you to apply hundreds of archives.

```
Enter maximum number of batch processes during the upgrade [3]
? BATCH PROCESSES =
```

Choose a number.

For upgrade phases that start background jobs in SAP (for example, the PCON conversion phase), this number indicates how many jobs may run in parallel. A rule of thumb that has always worked quite well for us is to take three for one-CPU and two-CPU servers, four for three-CPU and four-CPU servers, and five for servers with more than four processors. Going above five is probably not wise because the jobs then tend to become I/O-bound.

```
Note:
    The front end software could be updated at any time
    before or during the upgrade. It must be updated
    before the start of the shadow instance
    in phase START_SHDI_FIRST.
    Refer to the upgrade manual if you do not
    know how to perform the update procedure.
```

Choose **Continue**.

This screen warns you that to log on to the shadow instance (which already runs SAP ERP), you must have a compatible SAP GUI. See Section 3.2.6 for details.

The following screens appear if there are still failed update requests in Transaction SM13.

```
        BATCHJOB RSVBCHCK FAILED
ERROR: errors found in logfile (accumulated in file PSVBCHCK.ELG)
```

Choose **Continue**.

```
CHECKS AFTER UPGRADE PHASE JOB_RSVBCHCK2 WERE NEGATIVE !!!
```

Choose **Ignore**.

This is the last time you will get away with a warning. The next and final check happens shortly after entering downtime, and by then, there must be no update requests left in the system. Pending update requests must have been processed and failed updates deleted.

Note that this is a case where you may choose **Ignore** without SAPup requesting a password.

```
Note:
    Directory /usr/sap/<SID>/SYS/exe/run will be cleaned
    during the upgrade. You should be able to restore
    the contents of this directory.

    Files and subdirectories can be protected from
    deletion if they appear in a file "protect.lst" in
    the same directory (each protected name in a separate
    line).
```

Choose **Continue**.

Some backup agents have their configuration files stored in the SAP kernel directory. To protect them from deletion during the upgrade, you should list them in the *protect.lst* file in the same directory.

```
The development has to be locked in phase REPACHK2 at the latest.
Alternatively you can lock it now, so the upgrade will not stop again
in phase REPACHK2.
The cost is, that no one can change any development object from now
on, if you lock on the next page.
Lock development environment now or in REPACHK2?
? lock NOW
? lock later
```

Lock **NOW**.

With the downtime-minimized strategy, the workbench is locked either before the start of the import in phase LOCKEU_PRE or after the import in phase REPACHK2. Once the workbench is locked, it is no longer possible to make any kind of modification to development objects, which means:

▶ No development transactions

▶ No transports into or out of the system

A "late" lock (in REPACHK2) has the disadvantage of causing an extra stop after the data import. However, this stop happens relatively close (one to two hours) before the first start of the shadow instance (phase START_SHDI_FIRST), when you might want to be around anyway.

The following approach is one sensible way to decide on the development stop time. Plan a late stop (REPACHK2) if the following are true:

▶ The data import is carried out long before the downtime, for example, during the previous weekend.

▶ You are upgrading the development system, and developers need more time to finish off their pre-upgrade work. Note, however, that by this time, development activity should be reduced to the strict minimum.

▶ You are upgrading a BW (Business Information Warehouse) or APO (Advanced Planning and Optimization) system (it is important to mention this, even though it has nothing to do with SAP ERP. When development is locked, it is no longer possible to save queries in the Business Explorer).

Plan an early stop if the following are true:

▸ Development activity on the source release has ceased anyway, and you want the system to remain stable and unaltered from now until the end of the upgrade.

▸ You do not artificially slow down the import, and you cannot afford the upgrade standing idle for several hours.

10.6 Data Import

The upgrade process now starts the data import. The import phases are named EU_IMPORT1, 2, and so on, and unless you decided not to slow them down, they will take the amount of time you entered earlier.

This part of the process imports the new repository. In databases with explicit storage areas, such as Oracle and DB2 UDB, you will see that space usage in the new tablespaces gradually increases. The live repository at this time is naturally still one of the source releases. Therefore, the new repository being imported now is called the *shadow repository* (not to be confused with the shadow instance).

10.7 The Shadow Instance

The shadow instance was installed during the installation module of the PRE-PARE program. All tables needed for the SAP Web Application Server were imported into the database. Additional table contents were copied into the shadow system to enable modification adjustment, activation, and distribution functions in the shadow system.

10.7.1 First Start (Phase START_SHDI_FIRST)

After the end of the data import, the upgrade typically runs for another hour to two hours until it reaches the START_SHDI_FIRST phase. This is where the shadow instance starts up. Unless you chose this as the point to disable database-archive logging, SAPup does not stop for user interaction here. Instead, it starts the shadow instance and, if successful, goes on with the next phase.

Although in our experience, the shadow instance startup is a reliable process that rarely gives trouble, you might want to be around just in case.

10.7.2 Manually Starting and Stopping the Shadow Instance

Normally, the upgrade process takes care of starting and stopping the shadow instance. However, if for some reason you must stop and restart it manually, you can do so with the following commands:

To *stop* the shadow instance, log in as <sid>adm, and use the following command:

```
cd <PUTDIR>/bin
./SAPup stopshd <SID>
```

Then, confirm the path to the upgrade directory.

To *start* the shadow instance, log in as <sid>adm and use the command line as follows:

```
cd <PUTDIR>/bin
./SAPup startshd <SID>
```

Confirm the path to the upgrade directory.

10.7.3 Service for Shadow Instance on Windows

On Windows systems, the upgrade process creates and starts a service SAPSID_ ## for the shadow instance (## = shadow instance number). When the shadow instance is no longer needed, the service is stopped but remains in existence until the very end of the upgrade. You will continue to see the (stopped) shadow instance in the SAP Management Console. Only at the very end, in phase EXIT, will the service be deleted (the UA GUI displays a message when this happens).

10.8 Stop for Modification Adjustment

Normally, the next time the upgrade process stops is at the start of the dictionary activation phase (ACT_700). Except in the unlikely case that not a single SAP dictionary object was changed in your system, you will have to reconcile these changes with the version of the objects in the new repository. You find more information on this process in Chapter 21.

The stop for Modification Adjustment (which we'll simply call the *SPDD stop*) usually occurs within 1 hour after the start of the shadow instance. This timing is something to take into account. Using SPDD, especially in the first upgrade in the landscape, can be quite time-consuming. Also, you will need to be very focused, and it is possible that you will have to call on other people for assistance. Ideally, you should plan for the SPDD stop to happen during working hours and preferably early in the day when your mind and body are still fresh. Remember that you can influence the timing by tweaking the data import. In our example in Section 10.5, where we allowed 40 hours for the import starting at 2 p.m. on Tuesday, the SPDD stop would occur at a very good time. Assuming the upgrade goes on for 2 – 4 hours after the end of the import and until it hits the activation phase, the SPDD stop would happen on Thursday between 8 a.m. and 10 a.m.

This is the dialog at the SPDD stop (beginning of phase ACT_700):

```
You must now include your repository modifications in the new SAP
import.
93 modified objects are found to be adjusted and 0 objects are
automatically maintained by import of an adjustment transport bound
to this upgrade.
CAUTION: It is impossible to keep these modifications
         after you have confirmed this query.
Do you want to make adjustments to ABAP dictionary objects ?
```

Choose **Make Adjustments**.

```
Repository adjustment processed ?
[ ] Repository ok
[ ] exit
```

Do not reply yet! You must first do the SPDD. (Alternatively, you may choose **exit** and restart the UA GUI when SPDD is finished.)

Proceed as follows:

1. Log on to the shadow instance as user DDIC in client 000. You will need to create an entry in your SAP Logon menu for this. Remember that the shadow instance runs on the same host as the central instance (unless you decided otherwise during PREPARE) and that it has its own instance number (also assigned in the PREPARE).

2. Set the **System Change** option with Transaction SE06. Change the **Global Setting** to **Modifiable**, and save. Confirm the pop-ups that state that some components cannot be set to **Modifiable**. Keep saving until no pop-ups appear and the system reports that the changes were saved.

3. Start Transaction SCC4, and open client 000 for repository changes.

4. Start Transaction SU01, and create a user to do the modification adjustment. Create this user as a copy of DDIC. Preferably use the same name you assigned

to the upgrade user. This user initially does not exist in the shadow instance, so you must create it again here.

5. Log on to the shadow instance in client 000 as the upgrade user. Call Transaction SPDD. Follow the instructions in Chapter 21.

> **Note**
>
> If the logon fails with the message `Upgrade still running—logon not possible`, then you must unlock the shadow instance manually as follows (as `<sid>adm`):
>
> ```
> cd <PUTDIR>/bin
> ./SAPup unlockshd <SID>
> ```

10.9 The Activation Phase

After you are finished with SPDD, you resume the upgrade by confirming the open input window in the UA GUI:

```
Repository adjustment processed ?
[ ] Repository ok
[ ] exit
```

Now choose **Repository OK**.

The activation begins. This is often the longest phase of the upgrade and also one of the most complex. In many cases, it will report errors for certain dictionary objects, and you will need to take action.

If you want you can stay logged on to the shadow instance and monitor the activation processes with Transaction SM50; this is what you will see:

► At first, only a single batch process will be active, mostly accessing dictionary tables (table names starting with "DD"). This can go on for quite a while, sometimes even for up to an hour.

► After this initial phase, parallel activation processes will become active in dialog processes. Usually after a few minutes, the number of active processes begins to fall until they are all gone. Soon, however, a new batch will appear, and the same process repeats. Each "burst" of parallel tasks corresponds to an activation level. As the activation progresses, these bursts will take less and less time.

► Still later, the parallel tasks disappear entirely, and the background job itself (which was asleep for most of the time while there were parallel tasks) becomes active again. This corresponds to the lowest activation levels, where there are too few objects left to warrant the scheduling of parallel tasks.

▶ If there are errors (as there almost always are), the activation phase is programmed to auto-repeat once. This is useful because an activation error may result from cross-dependency between objects, which would disappear when the activation is repeated. As a result, you will see in SM50 that the whole scenario starts all over again without the UA stopping for interaction.

▶ If you want to monitor the activation process even more closely, then look at the phase logs. During the activation, the logs are in *<PUTDIR>/tmp*. They have names starting with "SAPA." Several logs will be present, but only one gets updated because the parallel activation method concentrates all messages in a single file. This log gets updated at the beginning and end of every level. Figure 10.1 shows an example.

The log records written at the beginning of a level show the number of objects to activate at this level and the estimated cost. The cost is not expressed in a particular unit. It merely indicates how "heavy" the activation at this level is likely to be. The cost is a function of the number of objects and also the type of object. For example, the activation cost of a table or view is much higher than that of a domain or data element.

The log records from the end of the level show the elapsed time. In the example shown in Figure 10.1, activating 8,285 objects took about 34 minutes (2,033 seconds).

```
→ Information at start of activation level
1 EDO533X*** Activate objects at level "3"
3 EDO631 * Parallel execution with maximal "3" concurrent tasks *
3 EDO677 Total of "8.285" objects with &3"8.714.280" costs in &2"62" tasks

→ Information at end of activation level
2 EDO348XServer Usage ***********************************************************
2 EDO313 Server..............|Workp|Tasks|Error|.Timesum|Objcount|ms/Obj|..KCosts|ms/KCs
2 EDO313 ----------------------------------------------------------------------------
2 EDO313 obelix_ON1_14.......|....3|...62|.....|...6.098|...8.285|...736|...8.714|...700
2 EDO678 Parallel execution: "2.033" sec., Phase out time: "0" sec., Load: "99,98" percent
```

Figure 10.1 Extract from the Activation Log

At the beginning of the activation log (not shown here) is a list of all levels and the number of objects to activate at each level. With this information, it is possible to know how far the activation has advanced. Keep in mind, however, that there is likely to be an auto-repeat to try and fix errors from the first run, so the phase will work through the activation levels twice (although, normally much faster the second time around).

If errors remain after the one auto-repeat (and again, this is usually the case), then the UA GUI stops, reports the errors[1], and opens a window showing the summary log of the activation run. Scroll down through this window until you come to the list of objects that caused errors. The name of this log on the server is *<PUTDIR>/log/ACTUPG.ELG* (see Figure 10.2).

```
~~~~~~~~~~~~~~~~~~~~~~~~~~~~~~~~~~~~~~~~~~~~~~~~~~~~~~~~~~~~~~~~~~~~~~~~~~~
DDIC ACTIVATION ERRORS and RETURN CODE in SAPAAAA640.D05
~~~~~~~~~~~~~~~~~~~~~~~~~~~~~~~~~~~~~~~~~~~~~~~~~~~~~~~~~~~~~~~~~~~~~~~~~~~
1EED0519X"Table" "T256Z" could not be activated
1EED0519 "Table" "BPBT" could not be activated
1EED0519 "Table" "BPBY" could not be activated
1EED0519 "Table" "BPDY" could not be activated
1EED0519 "Table" "FMCCFD" could not be activated
1EED0519 "Table" "FMCHA1" could not be activated
1EED0519 "Table" "MDSFEEDBACK_REQUEST1" could not be activated
1EED0519 "Table" "MDSFEEDBACK_REQ_DATA1" could not be activated
1 ETP111 exit code          : "8"
```

Figure 10.2 Extract from the Activation Errors Reported by SAPup

10.10 Handling Activation Errors

Rarely does the activation phase finish without errors. The errors are in most cases related to conflicts between SAP and customer data dictionary objects. As we will discuss later on, some activation errors may be ignored. It is good practice, however, to solve as many as possible.

10.10.1 Open the System and Call Transaction SE11

To check — and possibly solve — the activation errors, you must run dictionary transactions in the shadow instance. First unlock the instance (as <sid>adm):

```
cd <PUTDIR>/bin
./SAPup unlockshd <SID>
```

Check and confirm the upgrade directory path, and choose **Continue**.

Log on to the shadow instance in client 000 and with the upgrade user you created for the SPDD. Do not log on as DDIC or SAP* because these users are barred from changing repository objects.

---

1 This window also mentions the number of errors, but this number is often preposterous. It is apparently obtained by counting lines containing error codes in the detailed activation log and bears absolutely no relation to the number of objects in error. You might see frightening messages like 89 activation errors occurred when, in reality, only four or five objects were affected.

Open the system for modification in Transaction SE06 (toggle **Modifiable • Non-modifiable • Modifiable**).

Start the dictionary maintenance Transaction SE11. If you are not comfortable with SAP development (which means you probably didn't do the SPDD yourself, either), then get help from a developer.

> **Tip**
>
> Also log on in the source release because some functions, for example, the Where-Used List, do not work correctly in the shadow instance. To avoid mistakes, don't run Transaction SE11 in the source system but use the display-only Transaction SE12.

10.10.2 Identifying the Problem

The message in the activation log is sometimes not sufficient to determine exactly why the object does not activate. Therefore, your first action must always be to call the **Check** function in Transaction SE11.

There are many different reasons why a dictionary object may fail to activate, and we cannot possibly discuss them all. Nevertheless, some errors occur more often than others, and in the following paragraphs, we take a closer look at five problems that together account for a large percentage of all activation errors.

10.10.3 Field Defined Twice

This error is reported when the new release adds one or more extra fields to a table or structure, but the table or structure already has a field of the same name in the current release.

The usual cause of this error is that the field was added in the source release based on an advance correction given in a SAP Note. The field is then normally placed in an *append structure*. Append structures are the proper means of adding customer fields to standard SAP tables and structures. In the new release, the field becomes part of the standard. However, the append structure is still there, and thus the field name is found twice.

If the append structure contains only the duplicate field, then you can delete the entire append structure. If it also contains other fields, remove just the offending one (unless those other fields are duplicates too).

Save the main table/structure, but do not activate it. Repeat the object check until it is error-free.

10.10.4 Identical Indexes

In the source release, you created an index on a table, usually based on a performance note from SAP. SAP has integrated this index in the new release, so its dictionary definition comes in during the upgrade. Because two indexes cannot have exactly the same list of fields — no database system allows this — the new index causes an activation error.

The clear solution is to delete one of the conflicting indexes from the dictionary. You are not supposed to delete standard SAP objects, so your original index has to go. Delete it in Transaction SE11. Note that this will cause another activation error when you repeat the phase, but you may ignore that error.[2]

10.10.5 Object Incorrect in Source Release

If a dictionary object was already incorrect before the upgrade, then obviously it will still be incorrect in the new release. This error is quite common during upgrades of development systems. Half-finished objects or objects someone started working on but then abandoned are left lying around. These objects then cause errors during the activation phase. Using the **Check** function in Transaction SE12 in the source system will reveal the problem.

The solution is to ignore the error. After the upgrade, have a developer either fix the object or get rid of it for good.

10.10.6 References to an Object Deleted in the Upgrade

An object (typically a view, lock object, or search help) contains references to another dictionary object (a table or field), which is deleted in the new release. The activation fails because of these references to nonexistent objects.

We already touched on the subject of "doomed" data elements and domains in Section 9.26.7 because those will be reported as errors in PREPARE. However, the same situation can occur for other dictionary relationships, and PREPARE does not report these. For example, if you created a view on one or more SAP tables, and this customer view includes a deleted field in one of those tables, an activation error will occur.

---

2 Some people use a different method: They change the field list of the customer index so that it no longer overlaps. This avoids the extra activation error, but it will cause the creation of a useless and possibly large index during the conversion phase. This index then has to be dropped after the upgrade. Deleting the customer index upfront is therefore the cleaner approach despite the extra activation error.

These problems are fairly easy to fix; simply delete the invalid reference, for example, the view field. You must follow this up after the upgrade because it might lead to knock-on errors (for example, if custom ABAP code refers to that same field).

10.10.7 Objects Listed in SAP Notes

If the upgrade itself contains erroneous objects, then the SAP upgrade notes will probably mention these. If the problem is not obvious, and the object is in the SAP name range, then search through the notes, using as search keys the name of the object plus a term like "upgrade" or "activate." Examples for the SAP ERP upgrade are the PI_BASIS structures MDSFEEDBACK_REQUEST1, and MDSFEEDBACK_REQ_DATA1.

10.11 Repeat the Activation

Correct as many activation errors as possible. Keep a list of those objects you are unable to fix but for which you choose to ignore the error.

To repeat the activation, confirm the error windows in the UA GUI, and choose **Repeat**. The activation restarts.

If you did not fix all objects, then inevitably another error stop will occur at the end of the second activation run. Look at the erroneous objects listed in the activation log. If only objects remain that are on your "okay-to-ignore" list, then confirm the error windows and next, instead of **Repeat**, choose **Ignore**. SAPup will not ask for a password in this case.[3]

10.12 Shadow Instance Stopped

After the ACT_700 phase, the upgrade continues unattended for a good while. The shadow instance is shut down during this time, and it will not be needed again.

---

3 This is acceptable unless there was a hard error, for example, a process that aborted in one of the activations. In this case, you will see an exit code 12 or higher in the activation logs. **Ignore** then does need a password. You must never ignore an exit code above 8.

10.13 Incremental Conversion (ICNV)

The structure of some tables changes during the release upgrade, with the conversion occurring in the downtime phase of the upgrade. An incremental conversion can be started during uptime. This reduces downtime enormously if big tables are involved. The candidates for conversion are determined after Modification Adjustment, and thus after their target structure is defined. These include tables that contain large volumes of data and, therefore, would increase the downtime significantly. The System Switch Upgrade also enables you to use Transaction ICNV for tables that have been modified by support packages, add-ons, or customer development. Use of the incremental conversion function is optional. If you do not want to use incremental conversion, the tables are converted during downtime.

During the incremental table conversion, a copy of the original table is created, which already applies to the new data dictionary layout. While the system is still being used in production, data is copied to the new table. In the downtime phase of the upgrade, only the remaining entries are copied from the old to the new table. Upon completion, the old table is deleted, and the shadow table is renamed.

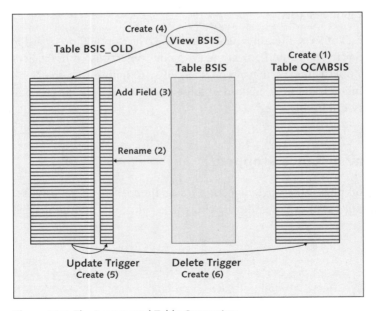

Figure 10.3 The Incremental Table Conversion

Here is the sequence of steps during the incremental table conversion (see Figure 10.3):

1. The conversion table candidates are selected.

2. A table with the new structure is created. This table has the name of the base with the prefix "QCM."

3. The table BSIS is renamed to BSIS_OLD (or QCM1BSIS depending on the release).

4. An additional status field is added to the table. The status field is used to keep track of already copied entries.

5. A view of the old table structure is created. The applications access the view from now on. To log these changes, the update (5) and the delete (6) trigger is needed.

The table content is copied with low priority to the shadow table QCMBSIS. QCMBSIS is filled by periodic runs.

The data is copied from the original table using a background process. BSIS is still accessible by the applications. Therefore, the changes during the data transfer must be logged. The status field indicates if an entry was already copied to the corresponding fields in QCMBSIS. The applications still access and modify the original table. Changes are logged as follows:

▶ The update trigger erases the already-copied flag, if an already converted entry is updated.

▶ The delete trigger deletes the entry in the new table immediately if the converted entry is deleted.

▶ If a new record is inserted, the flag field remains empty.

> **Note**
>
> If you expect large tables to be converted with the ICNV, you should start the upgrade much earlier to have enough time for all operations that need to be executed before the downtime begins. Report RSUPGSUM lists all tables converted during the upgrade. Use the report from the upgrade of the quality assurance to estimate the time needed for the conversion on production.

The data conversion is controlled through Transaction ICNV. The upgrade tools prompt you to start Transaction ICNV in phase ICNVREQ.

By calling of Transaction ICNV, all potential candidates are displayed with their current selection status. You can decide which of the preselected tables should be processed by ICNV. Tables can be excluded from being processed by ICNV with **Do not perform ICNV**. This should be used for tables with many updates and/or deletes because, in this case, the ICNV can be inefficient. The delete operations are especially critical. The load on the database is doubled by performing a delete on a table processed by ICNV. Remember that the delete trigger, explained previously, deletes the entry in the new table immediately.

Transaction ICNV offers several features with which to configure the conversion process:

▶ Batch hosts can be specified.

▶ The number of running batch processes in parallel is adjustable.

▶ Exclusion times can be defined. These are periods in which the copying of data should not run, for example, during the night when other applications modify a lot of entries in the tables to be converted.

▶ Estimates can be made for the runtime of the conversion.

▶ The logfiles of the conversion processes for each table can be accessed.

The progress of the data conversion can be monitored by ICNV (see Figure 10.4).

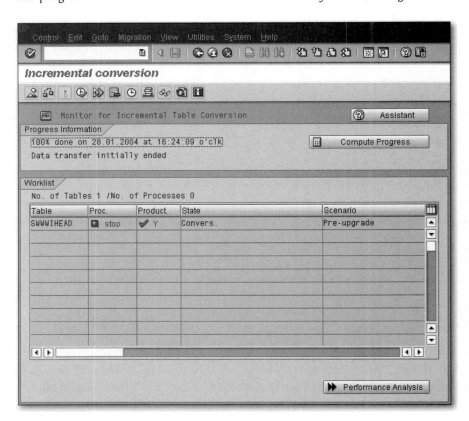

Figure 10.4 The Incremental Table Conversion (ICNV)

The monitor displays the following information:

▶ Table name

▶ Number of runs

▶ Number of processes working on the table (up to AS 6.40, this is restricted to one)

▶ Number of data records that were transferred by the current/previous/first run

After deciding what to do with all tables, the user can choose to be guided through the necessary steps by an ICNV Assistant. For the upgrade scenario, only two steps have to be started manually:

▶ The initialization, which creates the database objects (intermediate table, views, triggers) to support the conversion

▶ The data transfer

The switch and delete in ICNV are performed by SAPup during the downtime phases of the upgrade (PCON). For up-to-date information, see SAP Note 490788. For more information, call Transaction ICNV, and press F1 or choose **Information**.

Note the following carefully:

▶ Tables with frequent updates should, if possible, be excluded from the Incremental Table Conversion. The upgrade tools do not verify this and present all candidates by default. Carefully choose which tables are to be included in the Incremental Table Conversion and which are to be converted entirely during the downtime phases of the upgrade.

▶ You can use Incremental Table Conversion only if you use the upgrade downtime-minimized strategy.

▶ If you use the Incremental Table Conversion, do not start SAP archiving for these tables, as this can lead to performance bottlenecks. You should archive as much as possible before the upgrade.

▶ The incremental conversions require double the space for each table being converted. The continuous transfer of data results in more transactions being performed. Database free space and archiving should be monitored.

▶ The downtime should not begin before at least 95 % of the total data has been converted. Remaining data is transferred entirely during downtime. This would increase the downtime, depending on the remaining data to be converted.

The incremental conversion runs in the background. A sufficient number of background processes should be available. Ideally, there should be one process for each table to be converted. If you cannot have one process for each table because you are dealing with a large number of tables, you can still convert the tables: Transaction ICNV distributes the tables by itself to the available background processes. However, completing the incremental conversion takes longer, and therefore more time is needed before beginning the upgrade downtime.

The upgrade process looks at the size of the tables to be converted and builds a list of candidates for ICNV. If there are large tables that qualify for incremental conversion, then SAPup will stop in the phase ICNVREQ_GO:

```
INCREMENTAL CONVERSION NOT STARTED YET! You can start ICNV now by
calling Transaction ICNV in the R/3 system and follow the
instructions given there. If you do not go to Transaction ICNV and
start the conversion, the tables will be converted during system
down time.
```

As the preceding text makes clear, ICNV is voluntary. You may decide not to schedule an incremental conversion and leave the full conversion until downtime, although this probably defeats the purpose of running in downtime-minimized mode.

Because the ICNV must be finished before you enter upgrade downtime, large-table conversions can have great impact on the upgrade planning. You will possibly have to bring the start of the upgrade forward to allow sufficient conversion time. The upgrade of your acceptance system, which is in most cases a copy of production, will reveal how long it takes to convert the big tables.

The next sets of numbered instructions describe the procedure for ICNV.

> **Note**
>
> These instructions are largely the same as those you may have used to solve the table application problem of Section 8.3.4. The main difference is that for the ICNV during the upgrade, you do not perform the final switch yourself.

1. Log on to the main instance (remember that the shadow instance no longer exists!) with the special upgrade user.

2. Call ICNV. You will see a screen with the candidate tables in status **Perform ICNV** (see Figure 10.5).

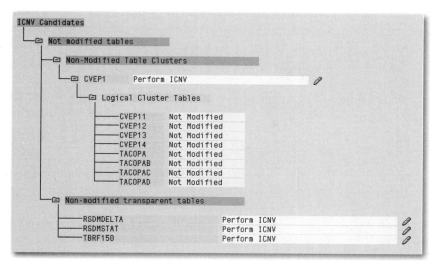

Figure 10.5 ICNV: Select Candidates

3. Click the **Change** icon next to the table to modify the default decision. Tables that are heavily modified should probably not be converted during the uptime phases of the upgrade because of the high performance impact the conversion may have. Those tables need to be converted intirely in the downtime phases. SAPup is unable to detect this and offers all tables to be converted by default.

4. **Choose Save decision** in the mainscreen if you are satisfied with the decisions.

5. Click the green arrow. The conversion screen appears listing all the tables selected for incremental conversion (see 6).

Worklist					
No. of Tables 5 /No. of Processes 0					
Table	Proc.	Product.	State	Scenario	
/BIC/PGPGBLE	Hold	Y	For conversion	Pre-upgrade	
CVEP1	Hold	Y	For conversion	Pre-upgrade	
RSDMDELTA	Hold	Y	For conversion	Pre-upgrade	
RSDMSTAT	Hold	Y	For conversion	Pre-upgrade	
TBRF150	Hold	Y	For conversion	Pre-upgrade	

Figure 10.6 ICNV: Tables Selected for Conversion

6. Choose **Control · Initialization**. Mark all the tables in the list as shown in Figure 10.6.

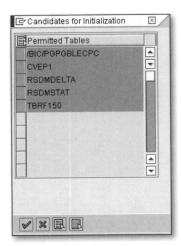

Figure 10.7 ICNV: Initialize Candidates for Conversion

7. Choose **Start Now** on the pop-up. A message appears that initialization is triggered; confirm this.

8. Refresh the status. Wait until the **Proc.** column again shows **Stop,** and the **State** column has changed from **For conversion** to **Convers.** (see Figure 10.8). During the initialization, the **Product.** column briefly changes from **Yes** to **No** but then returns to **Yes**.

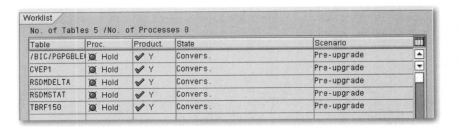

Figure 10.8 ICNV: Tables Are Ready for Conversion

9. If any table appears with status **Error**, double-click on the entry. On the pop-up, click **Display log**.

10. Choose **Edit • Options • Number of processes**. Press **Enter** on the pop-up. Set the desired number of processes. There is only one conversion job per table (no parallel processing of the same table), so it is pointless to configure more processes than there are tables to convert. Press **Enter** to confirm the number. Leave the pop-ups by clicking on the **Cancel** icon.

11. Choose **Control • Data transfer • Start** to start the conversion.

12. Verify in Transaction SM50 that the conversion jobs run. After a period of read activity in the beginning, you will see inserts into the target tables ("QCM1 %").

13. There is a function **Compute progress** in ICNV, but you should *avoid* using that because it will suspend the conversion for several minutes. A better method is to monitor the operation using the function **Goto · Statistical data** in ICNV.

14. When the conversions are running, proceed with the upgrade (click **Continue** on the ICNV information screen).

15. The ICNV documentation explains that after the conversion you must carry out the **Switch** function, which replaces the original table with the converted one. In the context of an upgrade, however, the switch is carried out by the upgrade process. Therefore, when the conversion is finished, just leave things as they are. ICNV will not allow you to carry out the **Switch** function. The upgrade will take care of this during the standalone phase. Occasionally, an ICNV job will start to check for further updates to the table data; these records are then copied to the new table. Whenever this happens, the status in ICNV changes from **Stop** to **Runs**.

If an error occurs (usually running out of disk space), do the following:

1. Determine from the short dump which tablespace is affected.

2. Correct the problem, for example, extend the database.

3. In ICNV, choose **Control · Data transfer · Optimize** (not **Start!**).

4. The new jobs will first determine the number of converted rows for all three tables, which may take several minutes. For tables not yet completely processed, the conversion will then resume.

10.14 Import Language Data and Support Packages

During the upgrade, entries to several thousand tables are imported. Because the source release is still being used in production, these entries are loaded into the tables of the new (shadow) repository. This is handled by the upgrade phase SHADOW_IMPORT_ALL. This phase imports all the new data entries of the new release, including language data and data for the support packages that were bound into the upgrade.

This phase takes several hours and creates a large number of database logs. Unlike the EU_IMPORT* phase, the shadow import cannot be slowed down, so keep an eye on your database archives while it is running.

Unless errors occur, there is no user interaction during the phase. The best way of monitoring it is to look at the appearance and growth of the logs in *<PUTDIR>/tmp*.

10.15 Upgrade Waits for the J2EE Upgrade

When upgrading double-stacked systems, SAPup waits in phase GETSYNC_ PREUP_FINI_D for the J2EE upgrade.

```
The parallel running J2EE upgrade needs some more time...
Please be patient...
```

Start the uptime phases of the J2EE upgrade (proceed as described in Chapter 14 The Upgrade Process for the AS Java). Note that SAPJup has no "reset upgrade" functionality. The term *uptime phases* of the J2EE instance are therefore somewhat misleading. Wait until the beginning of the planned downtime and perform all steps described in Section 10.17.

SAPup waits for SAPJup to set the sync mark in phase SETSYNC_PREUPTIME_ FINISHED and continues automatically if it does. SAPup continues up to phase MODPROF_TRANS while SAPJup continues up to phase BEGIN_DOWNTIME, at which downtime for both is about to begin.

10.16 Upgrade Reaches Downtime Point

Not long after the end of the shadow import, the upgrade reaches the phase MODPROF_TRANS, which marks the beginning of downtime for the downtime-minimized strategy.

A window in the UA GUI states the following:

```
CAUTION: When the next query is confirmed,
         all productive activities have to be closed,
         and all users have to be logged out, because
         the central application server is shutdown.
         Refer to the upgrade manual
         how to isolate the central SAP instance.
Do you want to continue ?
```

Do not answer yet, even if it is okay for the system to be shut down now! You must first isolate the central instance. When upgrading a double-stacked system, the central instance should already have been isolated, and you can just continue with the upgrade.

There is nothing left to do except wait until the beginning of planned downtime. You can leave the UA GUI open, or exit now and restart it later.

10.17 Isolating the Central Instance

When the downtime has arrived, don't resume the upgrade right away. You must first carry out a series of actions to isolate the system. These actions are intended to make sure that no concurrent system activity can take place during the upgrade, to allow existing kernel files to be replaced, and in general to prevent problems during the subsequent critical phases.

10.17.1 Final Checks

Check that the system meets these requirements:

▶ ICNV is complete.

▶ All update requests must be deleted; the SM13 list must be empty (and this time it *is* a must).

▶ There are no more open repairs. For checking this proceed as follows:

1. Transaction SE09: Click the **Tools** icon, open **Requests/Tasks,** and choose **Find Requests**.

2. Empty the selection fields.

3. Click the green arrow next to **Request type**. In the pop-up list, clear all check boxes; mark **Repair,** and press **Enter**.

4. Mark the check boxes **Modifiable** and **Release Started,** and then click **Execute**.

5. The list should be empty. If any open repairs are shown, have their owners release them now (or take ownership and release them yourself).

10.17.2 Lock the Users

You should preferably lock all users, except SAP*, DDIC, and your upgrade user, by using Transaction SU10.

10.17.3 Disable Background Jobs (Release 3.1I – 4.0B)

This action is required only if your start release is 3.1 or 4.0. In Release 4.5 and higher, the upgrade process does this automatically using the report BTCTRNS1.

You must disable all batch jobs *except* the transport control job RDDIMPDP:

- ▶ Call Transaction SM37, and enter the following values:
  - ▷ **Job name**: User name = *
  - ▷ **Start date**: a date in the distant past
  - ▷ **End date**: "31.12.9999"
  - ▷ **Start after event**: *
  - ▷ **Job status**: *only* **Released**
- ▶ Print the list of jobs, and save it to a local text file.
- ▶ Select all jobs *except* RDDIMPDP, and choose **Job ∙ Schedule job ∙ Cancel**. The status of all affected jobs must change from **Released** to **Scheduled**.

> **Note**
>
> As we have just mentioned, starting Releases 4.5 and higher automatically disables background jobs. The systems do this by running the ABAP program BTCTRNS1. When this method is used, you will see the jobs in SM37 with the status *Released/Suspended*. Jobs in this state cannot be changed in any way in SM37.

10.17.4 Operation Modes

Call Transaction RZ04, and choose **Instances/Operation Modes**. Verify that all the operation modes refer only to instances that are part of your current system. This is probably not an issue in systems that are never refreshed using a homogeneous system copy (production, development), but the old instances might still exist in test systems copied from production. Delete all instances that are not part of this system; otherwise, background job scheduling problems can arise during the downtime phases. If a DUMMY operation mode exists, then you must also check and, if necessary, adapt that.

No operation mode switches must happen during the upgrade. A good approach here is to create an operation mode in RZ04, which you might call "Upgrade," for example, and then to create an exception timetable (Transaction SM63, or RZ04; choose **Operation Mode ∙ Timetable**). Assign the **Upgrade** operation mode to the expected upgrade period.

10.17.5 Back Up Database, Upgrade Directory, and Source Kernel

Should a major problem occur during the downtime part of the upgrade, then you must be able to restore the database to its current state. As you were productive up to this point and had database-log archiving enabled, you could of course restore an older backup and perform a roll-forward recovery. However, because of the intense database log activity generated by the upgrade, such a recovery could be quite heavy. Consequently, it is a good idea to back up the database after all productive activity has ceased and before entering the upgrade downtime.

As we stated earlier, you must always back up the entire upgrade directory *<PUTDIR>* along with the database at a time when there is no upgrade activity. You can only repeat the upgrade after a database restore if the upgrade directory is perfectly in sync with the contents of the database.

It is also advisable to upgrade the SAP kernel of the source release. Make a full backup of the directory */usr/sap/<SID>/SYS/exe/run*. It is recommended that you stop the SAP system for this (restart it after the backup so that the upgrade process will find the system up and running as expected). You can skip this backup if you already have a backup of the kernel or if you can copy it from another SAP system that is still on the source release.

10.17.6 Open Client 000 for Development

Allow workbench maintenance in client 000 by using Transaction SCC4 (Client Administration) to set the status of the client to **Changes to Repository and cross-client Customizing allowed**. You do not have to change the global system-change options.

This setting is useful in case you have to make a program change during the downtime phases. In some phases, Transaction SCC4 is not yet operational, so it is best to open the client beforehand.

10.17.7 Other Activities

Several isolating activities are specific to the OS or database. You find these in the respective Upgrade Guides, in the *Isolating the Central Instance* section. Carry out all the actions as described there.

10.18 Entering Downtime

In the UA GUI, you may now confirm that the system can be shut down.

1. Choose **Administrator • Start SAPup** from the Upgrade Assistant main screen.

2. The upgrade resumes at phase MODPROF_TRANS, and a window opens, informing you of the beginning of downtime.

```
CAUTION: When the next query is confirmed,
         all productive activities have to be closed,
         and all users have to be logged out, because
         the central application server is shutdown.
         Refer to the upgrade manual
         how to isolate the central R/3 instance.
Do you want to continue ?
```

3. Choose **Next**.

```
Note: All secondary application servers of R/3 system <SID>
      must be shutdown now.
      Did you backup the upgrade directory?
This is essential in the case of a hardware failure.
```

4. Choose **Continue**.

```
Note: "Database log mode" should be set to
      "No Archive Mode" now. Make sure that
      database can be restored. Check your database
      log mode with
            sqlplus '/ as sysdba'
      and "archive log list".
      Do not mix up "Database log mode" with
                    "Automatic archival".
Database log mode disabled?
```

5. Switch off the archive log mode, and continue.

```
IMPORTANT: Backup the upgrade root directory
           "/usr/sap/put" now.
           If you later on have to recover the database
           back to the current status, this directory
           must be restored also, to be able to restart
           the upgrade from this point.
```

6. Choose **Backup done**.

10.19 Logging on to SAP During Downtime

During the downtime phase of the upgrade, the system is locked. If you want to log on to the system, you can only do so as 000/DDIC or 000/SAP*. Other users will receive the error Logon not possible: upgrade still running.

While the upgrade is running, there is no real reason to log on. If you do so, restrict yourself to using simple monitoring transactions such as SM50. Keep in mind that the SAPup process is in full control and can shut down the system at any moment, so you might find yourself kicked out without warning.

Notice also that, during downtime, the default logon client is always 000.

10.20 Unlock the System to Correct Errors

Although the system is locked during downtime phases, in some circumstances, it may be necessary for you to log on to the system to fix an error. Users SAP* or DDIC can always log on, but if you have to change development objects, then you must log on as another user.

To unlock the system, use the following commands:

▶ UNIX:

```
cd <PUTDIR>/bin
<PUTDIR>/exe/tp unlocksys pf=<TRANSPROFILE>
<PUTDIR>/exe/tp unlock_eu pf=<TRANSPROFILE>
```

▶ Windows:

```
cd <PUTDIR>\exe
tp.exe unlocksys pf=<TRANSPROFILE>
tp.exe unlock_eu pf=<TRANSPROFILE>
```

▶ iSeries:

```
cd '<PUTDIR>/bin'
tp 'unlocksys pf=<TRANSPROFILE>'
tp 'unlock_eu pf=<TRANSPROFILE>'
```

<TRANSPROFILE> denotes the transport profile of the domain to which the system belongs. This is normally a file called */usr/sap/trans/TP_DOMAIN_<SID>.PFL* (where *SID* is the system ID of the transport domain controller, not necessarily that of the current system).

The unlocksys argument of the first TP command enables logging on for users other than SAP* or DDIC. The unlock_eu argument unlocks the development workbench to allow repository changes.

10.21 User Interaction and Monitoring During Downtime

If no errors occur, the upgrade process will run without user interaction nearly to the end. This does not mean that you can switch off the lights and go home. Remember that you are in downtime, so time is precious. If anything goes wrong, someone must be at hand to take action right away.

10.22 The Switch Phases: EU_SWITCH and KX_SWITCH_1

During two downtime phases (which run without interaction), the system makes the effective transition to the new release:

▶ The EU_SWITCH phase performs the repository switch. The newly imported repository becomes the active one.

▶ The KX_SWITCH_1 phase copies the kernel used during the upgrade, from the executable directory in the upgrade directory to the executable directory of the current system.

10.23 Table-Conversion Phase: PARCONV_UPG

The PARCONV_UPG phase completes the conversion of all application tables. This includes the following:

▶ Performing the switch for tables that were converted in ICNV

▶ Running all table conversions that were not part of the ICNV

▶ Creating or converting indexes

▶ Activating the dictionary runtime object of the converted tables

Again, the best method to follow this phase is to look at the logfiles in *<PUTDIR>/tmp*. Objects are processed in alphabetical order. During PARCONV_UPG, there is again no user interaction.

10.24 Import Control Data: TABIM_UPG

The TABIM_UPG phase imports additional control and language data into the several database tables. This can take several hours.

10.25 Conversion Programs: XPRAS_UPG

The XPRAS_UPG phase consists of automatic conversion reports that perform all kinds of data conversions. This phase can take a long time. Although some reports need to run sequentially, several reports run in parallel. The XPRAS phase is therefore repeated once, if errors occurred, because it assumes that the sequence might not have been respected.

10.25.1 XPRAs: Purpose and Behavior

XPRA (**ex**ecute **pr**ogram **a**fter import) is a program scheduled to run after the import step of a transport request. It exists not only for upgrades but also for support packages and even for normal transports. The usual purpose of an XPRA is to perform application data conversions based on changes in the functional data model. An example cited earlier is the conversion of the pre-Release 4.5 method of storing address data to the Central Address Management.

Many XPRA programs will run during upgrades. Some have very little work to do, but others sometimes have to deal with vast amounts of data and may run for several hours. Knowing what to expect for the XPRA runtime is one of the important reasons why you should do at least one test upgrade on a full copy of the production data.

The impact of the XPRA phase also depends on the distance between the source and target release. A peculiar characteristic of this phase is that it is subdivided into "rounds," with one round (batch of XPRAs) per release in the upgrade path. For example, if you upgrade from 4.0B to SAP ERP 2005, then the phase will first run the Release 4.5 XPRAs, then those of 4.6, then those of R/3 Enterprise (4.70), and finally those of SAP ERP (5.00 and 6.00). If errors occur, the upgrade will not wait till the end of the entire phase before stopping; it will stop and show an error screen at the end of the "round" in which the error occurred.

10.25.2 Dealing with XPRA Errors

If you are a technical person — as you are likely to be if you do SAP upgrades — then analyzing and correcting XPRA errors can be awkward because most XPRAs belong to business applications. The problems they encounter often have no "physical" cause, such as lack of space in the database or shortage of process memory, but rather a "logical" cause related to the application's data model. Error messages such as `unable to extend database table` may hold no secrets, but a message such as `control structure inconsistent with business area` probably sounds as intelligible as random beeps from outer space.

If you run into this kind of mysterious error, always consult the SAP Notes first, using the name of the XPRA as the principal search term. Many XPRA errors, especially the really weird ones, are known and documented. If the SAP Notes don't help, and you feel like doing some sleuthing yourself, you can run the XPRA under control of the debugger. Note that by the time the upgrade reaches the XPRA stage, the system is technically completely functional, so all development transactions should work. If you skip the detective work, or if the trail of clues goes cold, call upon an application specialist to investigate — if there is time — or open a customer message in the SAP Support Portal.

In the unlikely event of an XPRA error in the production upgrade not encountered during any of the test upgrades, don't delay, and open a message in the SAP Support Portal immediately. For production-upgrade stops (and *only* then), you are entitled to open a message with "Very High" priority.

10.25.3 Action After an Error

In case of errors in an XPRA round, the UA GUI will show the usual error window. In this situation, however, there is an extra option you can choose. In some cases (always to be authorized by SAP support), it is admissible to ignore errors, at least those that result in an exit code 8; that is, the program ran correctly but discovered an error in the data it processed. To ignore such errors, first choose **Ignore,** and on the next screen, choose **Repair severe errors**. This arcane formulation really means "ignore errors resulting in exit code 8."

We stress again that you must never do this on your own initiative, or even on the advice of your functional specialists. Only SAP can give you the green light to skip over failed XPRAs.

Exit codes higher than 8, indicating a malfunction of the program itself, cannot be skipped in this way. Choosing **Ignore** in this case will require a password and will almost certainly lead to a massive failure of the upgrade, unless SAP allows it.

SAP Note 122597 has more information about ignoring XPRA errors and also about postponing them as described next.

10.25.4 Postponing an XPRA

It is also possible to postpone the execution of an XPRA until after the upgrade. This can be done to overcome errors but also to shorten downtime in case of very long runtimes. Running the heavy XPRA can then be postponed until the postprocessing time, where it can then execute in parallel with other activities.

Once again, postponing an XPRA is not something you can freely decide. The reason is that some XPRAs perform tasks that can *only* be done during the upgrade, not after. If you try running these after the upgrade, they will immediately stop with an error.

The procedure for taking an XPRA out of the upgrade schedule is explained in Note 122597. It uses the ABAP program RSXPRAUP. All this program actually does is comment out the XPRA entry in the object list of the relevant upgrade transport.

10.26 The Kernel Switch KX_SWITCH_2

In the KX_SWITCH_2 phase, SAPup installs and enables the new kernel. The target kernel is copied from the *exenew* directory in the upgrade directory to the executable directory of the current system.

At the end of KX_SWITCH_2, you have a SAP ERP system!

10.27 The Final Phases

At the end of the XPRA phase, the upgrade is nearly complete; only a few relatively short phases remain.

The first "normal" interaction with the UA GUI since downtime began occurs in phase MODPROFP_UPG:

```
Note: For upgrade strategy Downtime-minimized the database log
      mode should be enabled now. Make a full backup
      of your database after archiving is enabled again.
      Check your database log mode with
      "sqlplus '/ as sysdba'" and "archive log list".
      Do not mix up "Database log mode" with
                    "Automatic archival".
```

Answer **Yes**, even if you do not really enable archive logging at this time.

```
Note: All secondary application servers of SAP system <SID>
      can be restarted now.
```

Choose **Continue** (but do not start up the application servers if there are any).

From a purely technical point of view, MODPROFP_UPG marks the end of downtime. The upgrade process unlocks the system and reinstates the normal parameter profiles. This is mostly theoretical, however. For actual business, the system is not in a usable state until you have carried out the postprocessing actions. This is also why you must leave the secondary application servers down (if any exist).

```
The upgrade descheduled all batch jobs when your upgrade began
downtime. The right time to reschedule these batch jobs depends on
your requirements. For this reason, the jobs are not automatically
rescheduled by SAPup.
You can now reschedule the system's periodic batch jobs for the first
time. To do this, start the report
            ************
            * BTCTRNS2 *
            ************
as user DDIC in Transaction SE38.
```

Choose **Continue**.

This is a purely informative message, telling you which ABAP report to use to release the background jobs. We deal with this later in the postprocessing chapter. This message does not appear if your start release was 3.1 or 4.0 because in those versions, you had to block background jobs manually, and you will have to unblock them manually also.

The upgrade now starts the phase JOB_RASUVAR2, which restores the variants saved during the later stages of PREPARE by the program RASUVAR1. This is about the only phase in the final post-XPRA part of the upgrade, which can have a relatively long runtime.

```
INFO: Please refer to OSS note 823941 on how to use installsapinit.
sh to setup automatic start of the SAP start service (sapstartsrv)
during Operating system startup.
```

Choose **Continue**.

This is an information screen telling you where to find information on how to integrate the start and stop of the SAP system in the startup and shutdown of the OS.

```
Your SAP system contains only a few ABAP/4 loads at this time.
It is recommended that you generate the most relevant ABAP/4 loads
now.
Start Transaction SGEN and select the load generation after an
upgrade. Generation of the ABAP/4 loads is being done with help of
a background job (for details press the INFO buttons in Transaction
SGEN).
```

```
Depending on the number of objects to be generated, the background
job might run several hours. For this reason, it is very helpful to
restrict the generation list to the components majorly used in your
system. This select option of SGEN is activated by default.
If you plan to generate the ABAP/4 loads of all components, you have
to consider the additional DB free space required to hold the loads.
On database type ORACLE, the load tables are located in tablespace
PSAPEL<rel>D and PSAPEL<rel>I.
On database type INFORMIX, the equivalent DBspace is psapel<rel>.
Typical space requirements are values of several 100 MBytes, an
entire system generation needs approximately 2 GBytes free space.
```

This is again an information screen telling you about the generation of ABAP loads with Transaction SGEN. See Chapter 11 for details. Choose **Continue**.

```
With the new release it is possible to use special security options
for the message server.
Details can be found in note 821875!
```

Again an information screen appears informing you where to find information on the new high-availability option for the message server. Choose **Continue**

```
Errors occurred during the upgrade that require revision:
It is strongly recommended to solve those problems before starting
the productive operation of your SAP system!!
Please consult the following file for detailed information:
/usr/sap/put/log/LONGPOST.LOG
You might find it helpful to use the message class and the message
number as a search index for obtaining relevant notes from the SAP
Service Marketplace (e.g. search for keyword 'TG123').
Phase names and number of problems that occurred in this phase:
            RUN_RSUPGDEC_UPG        6
            JOB_RDDNTPUR       13
```

Choose **Continue**.

This screen tells you about so-called *P errors*, which are nonfatal errors detected and logged by various upgrade phases. A type P error is not serious enough to stop the upgrade, but it should still be dealt with during postprocessing. P errors take their name from the letter used to indicate their severity in the upgrade logs (similarly to E = error, W = warning, A = abort). As the text explains, all P error messages are gathered into a single logfile called *LONGPOST.LOG*.

```
Please choose 'exit' to leave SAPup in order to analyze the problems
that are reported in file /usr/sap/put/log/LONGPOST.LOG
Or choose 'revision completed' to confirm that you already finished
your checks and eliminated all problems.
NOTE: The upgrade can't be finished completely before you confirm
the solution of the problems with the first option.
```

Choose **Revision completed**.

Here you tell the upgrade that you have looked at the P errors and have fixed them. Of course you haven't (yet), but in this case it's all right to be economical with the truth.

```
INFO concerning SPAU
There are 1,862 development objects that have been imported by the
upgrade, that you have also modified previously in your system <SID>.
Please continue with <CR> for further instruction.
```

Choose **Continue**.

Transaction SPAU is the counterpart of SPDD. Where SPDD works with dictionary objects, SPAU is meant for programs, functions, screens, and the like. These two transactions together make up the Modification Adjustment, which is so crucial in every upgrade. SPDD was done earlier on in the shadow instance. SPAU can wait until after the upgrade and is usually not handled by a single person but by the entire development team. The message from SAPup here informs you of how many objects will appear in SPAU. This can range from just a few in systems that have stayed very close to the standard, up to many thousands if there were extensive modifications to SAP development objects.

```
Besides the adjustments in Transaction SPAU your upgrade is completed
now and productive operation is possible.
All SPAU activities can be performed without SSCR for a period of 14
days after you first entered this phase.
Do  n o t  continue with SAPup if you plan to use the result of the
adjustments for any subsequent SAP system.
Exit now and restart SAPup, after SPAU has been finished.
```

Choose **Continue**.

This screen tells you two important things:

▶ There is a "grace period" of two weeks during which you can change SAP objects in Transaction SPAU without being prompted for an object key.

▶ As in SPDD, you have the option to concentrate all SPAU modifications in a single transport request and then to register this transport for use in the following upgrades. If you decide to use this function, then you must leave the upgrade pending at this point, and developers must process the SPAU. This method is not often used. In most cases, developers will collect their SPAU work in a set of transport requests to be imported after the upgrade.

```
Please decide which log files will be saved now!
There are three possibilities each needing a different amount of disk
space where the logs will be written
  MODE | description                          | space requirement
-------+--------------------------------------+-------------------
   all | all logs (recommended)               |      877750
normal | important logs only                  |       99478
  none | no logs                              |           0
Free space:                                         1421944
Archive Directory: /usr/sap/trans/upgrade/<SID>/700
```

SAPup will save the upgrade logs in a backup directory in the transport area. The full path for upgrades to SAP ERP or to any other product based on SAP NetWeaver AS 7.00 is */usr/sap/trans/upgrade/<SID>/700*.

The screen lets you choose between three possibilities for saving the upgrade logs. **All** saves the entire contents of *<putdir>/log*. **Normal** saves only the most important logs, for example, the global upgrade logs, but leaves out the logs of individual transport. **None** does not save any logs at all.

Choose **All** or **None** (logs are saved in compressed form later).

As a rule, you should always save *all* upgrade logs. Especially during the upgrade project, it is important that you — and SAP support — have access to all the logs of previous upgrades. If you choose **All**, SAPup will copy the logs to the backup directory here and now. Another option, and the one we prefer, is to answer **None** here and then to copy (and compress) the logs manually at the end of the postprocessing. The reason for this advice is that copying the logs sometimes takes surprisingly long (we have seen copy times of 30 – 45 minutes) and there is no point in waiting that long for the completion of a noncritical activity that can just as well be done later.

Avoid using the **Normal** option because this will not save detailed information that might be needed later for problem analysis.

```
Note: Post-upgrade activities have to be performed. Please refer to
the upgrade manual for the subsequent processing. Examples for these
activities are:
- Script saproot.sh
- Distributing the new kernel
- Report generation
- Checking the database mode
- Database backup
```

Choose **Continue**.

This window just reminds you of the postprocessing activities to be done after the end of the upgrade process. We describe these activities in Chapter 11.

```
              ************
       *******            *******
    ***                        ***
   *     YOUR UPGRADE IS COMPLETE   *
    ***                        ***
       *******            *******
              ************
```

Choose **Continue**.

This window (the "balloon") will be a welcome sight — but your work is not done yet!

10.28 Upgrade Information Files

After you confirm the "balloon" window, the process computes statistical data about the upgrade and generates an evaluation form. A pop-up window then appears giving you the URL to view this form (shown next). Fill out this form inside the Web browser, and transmit it to SAP.

Another very interesting file is the *Upgrade Information* file. This file contains a complete summary of the upgrade, including the server information, the list of installed components, and the run times of all upgrade phases.

You can access the files via the following URL:

▶ Evaluation form: *http://<server>:4239/htdoc/eval/index.htm*

▶ Upgrade information: *http://<server>:4239/htdoc/eval/upana.htm*

The HTML files are physically located in *<PUTDIR>/htdoc/eval*.

> **Note**
>
> The upgrade information file replaces the ABAP report RSUPGSUM, which you were asked to run in older releases. The report is still there, however, and it is useful still to execute it because it creates a text file (named *RUNTIMES*) with the upgrade information in the log directory. If you empty the upgrade directory in preparation for a new upgrade, and you accidentally forget to save the HTML files in *htdoc*, then at least you still have the information.

10.29 Closing the Upgrade Assistant

Finally, the message Connection to Upgrade was closed appears in the UA GUI window. Choose **Administrator • Terminate Upgrade Assistant Server**. This will also close the UA GUI. The upgrade process is finished and you can start of the postprocessing work — but take a break first.

10.29.1 Resetting the Upgrade

If you find yourself compelled to cancel the upgrade and undo all the changes it has made to the SAP system (Chapter 22 gives some possible reasons why you might take this unusual step), then you must reset the upgrade. Various procedures apply, depending on whether the update has only affected the shadow system (before phase MODPROF_TRANS) or has made changes in the real system (MODPROF_TRANS and after). Use the instructions in Chapter 22.

You made it! The upgrade has been completed. Although it is not ready for production, the hard part has been done. The best course of action might be to make a backup before continuing the post-upgrade activities and to use the backup time to take a break.

11 Upgrade Postprocessing for SAP ECC

The SAP ERP Upgrade Guides cover the postprocessing actions in the *Follow-up Activities* section. Carry out the instructions for your OS. The activities follow the same three-phase order as described here.

This chapter does not try to replicate or improve on the SAP Upgrade Guides by describing every action for every platform. Instead, we concentrate on specific actions that merit special attention or require extra explanation.

Upgrade postprocessing is manual work. It is not driven by a process like PRE-PARE and SAPup, and thus it has no fixed sequence. The following approach is a good way to organize the postprocessing to save time and avoid collisions with other users:

1. Carry out all activities that may require the system or the database to be shut down. No other users should be allowed on the system.

2. Do the other technical work that is necessary before you can release the system back to production but that does not require the system to be stopped and restarted. During this time, you can allow limited access to key users, developers, and so on.

3. Put off noncritical tasks, such as compressing the upgrade logs, generating the timing report, and so on, until the system is back in normal use.

11.1 Actions at Operating System Level

Some activities are to be done on Operating System level such as the upgrade of the application servers, which at this point still run the old release.

11.1.1 The saproot.sh Script (UNIX)

On UNIX hosts (including Linux), the ownership of some kernel executables needs to be changed; for these executables, the SUID bit[1] is set. This is necessary for the `saposcol` collector, which must run with super user (`root`) privileges. For several RDBMSs (Relational Database Management Systems), Oracle, for example, the SAP kernel contains specific tools for database administration. These programs must often also run with the identity of the DBA user or even the super user.

The procedure for changing ownership and privileges of the affected kernel programs is delivered as a shell script `saproot.sh`, which is located in the kernel directory used by the upgrade (*/usr/sap/put/exe*). You must be `root` to run this script. This is the *only* activity in the entire upgrade requiring `root` access. Many sites do not allow SAP administrators to log in as `root`. If this is the case, you must ensure that a system administrator is at hand to run the script for you.

11.1.2 Upgrade the Kernel on the Application Servers

If your system has application servers, and you have not enabled the SAPCPE mechanism to automatically distribute kernel updates from the central instance to the application servers, then you now must copy the kernel installed on the central instance to the kernel directory of the application servers.

11.2 Actions at Database Level

For each DBMS, the component Upgrade Guide contains a section with database-specific postprocessing activities such as backing up the database and running the optimizer statistics. Some database parameters might need to be changed due to the increased system requirements of the new release. And last but not least, the old repository tablespaces can be deleted after the upgrade to gain some free space.

11.2.1 Back Up the Database

One of the first tasks here is to perform a full backup of the database. You should do this whether the backup ran with archive logging enabled or disabled during the downtime part of the upgrade. Even if archive logging was enabled throughout the process, recovering from a pre-downtime backup would probably be very time-consuming.

---

1 The SUID (Set User ID) bit is an indicator in the program's directory entry that causes that program to run with the identity (and thus the privileges) of its owner, rather than with the identity of the user running the program. This bit is also (incorrectly) known as the "sticky bit."

11.2.2 Update Statistics

Another important action here is to update the database statistics. The upgrade has made massive changes in the database, and many statistics are likely to be outdated. While the new statistics are being calculated — which may take several hours — you can carry out other unrelated tasks, provided these do not require the database to be stopped. The statistics should be up to date by the time functional testing begins; otherwise, the test users might experience unsatisfactory performance.

11.2.3 Parameter Changes

If database parameters were changed specifically for the upgrade, then return them to their normal operational values now. An example of this is the SGA_MAX_SIZE in Oracle, which had to be enlarged to avoid performance problems during the activation phase.

11.2.4 Dropping the Old Repository

In database systems with explicit storage allocation (Oracle and DB2 UDB), the storage areas that used to contain the old repository are emptied during the upgrade and should be dropped afterwards to reclaim the disk space. The exact names of these areas are DBMS-dependent, and you find them in the upgrade guide. The names always contain the old release, for example, *PSAPES40BD* would be the name of a 4.0B repository tablespace in Oracle. The storage spaces for SAP ERP always have the release code "700" as part of their names.

You must use database-specific methods or SAP database tools to drop the old repository. The procedure is simple, but you should not do this before you have a good backup.

11.3 Activities in the SAP System

Finally, some activities are needed in the SAP system to make it ready for production. Among the most important ones, we have the import of the correction transports created during Modification Adjustment of the development system (see Chapter 21 on Modification Adjustment), the ABAP generation, and the language supplementation.

11.3.1 Parameter Changes

After the upgrade, use Transaction RZ10 to reimport the parameter profiles with **Utilities • Import profiles • Of active servers**. The upgrade sometimes adds or changes certain parameter settings in the parameter text files, so you must make sure to save these settings in the database.

SAP notes might also recommend certain changes to parameters or your own monitoring of upgraded systems might show that changes are needed (e.g., increasing certain memory buffers). Apply these parameter changes now, and save the modified profiles. To activate these changes, either stop and restart the system immediately, or wait for the (optional, but recommended) restart after the ABAP load generation in Transaction SGEN.

> **Note**
>
> A parameter you will need to add in many cases is `zcsa/second_language`. See the section on language supplementation later in this chapter.

11.3.2 ABAP Load Generation (SGEN)

After the upgrade, ABAP code exists only in source form in the new repository. This is the reason for the numerous "Compiling" messages and the resulting long wait times when you start using the newly upgraded system. As you probably do not want production users to wait this long when they run their transactions, you must generate the ABAP loads beforehand. For this, you use Transaction SGEN.

Transaction SGEN starts a background job, which in its turn launches a series of parallel generation tasks. Each of these tasks occupies a dialog process. This parallel execution speeds up processing but also places a significant load on the server. The best solution to this, if time is available, is to schedule the SGEN job to run during the night. For example, if you complete your postprocessing work on Saturday evening, and system testing is only to start on Sunday morning, you can schedule SGEN for Saturday night when there is no other activity.

If there is no period of inactivity you can use, then you can start SGEN immediately and do your other work at the same time. In this case, however, it is best to restrict the number of work processes SGEN can use. You do this by restricting the quota for the RFC server group parallel generators in Transaction RZ12:

1. Call Transaction RZ12 (RFC Server Group Maintenance).

2. Select the group **parallel_generators**. If no such group exists, then create it.

3. In the window showing the RFC quota for the group, reduce the value of **Max. no. of WP used**. This value is a percentage of the total number of dialog work

processes, with a default of 75. You may want to keep SGEN down to two or three parallel tasks if you plan to keep working. Check the number of DIA work processes (dialog work processes), and restrict the percentage accordingly. For example, if there are 15 DIA processes, and you want to restrict SGEN to three parallel tasks, set **Max. no. of WP used** to 20.

4. Optionally, you can also increase the value of **Min. no. of free WP**. This sets the minimum number of DIA work processes that must be kept free regardless of the percentage quota. The default is 1 (this is a number of processes, not a percentage).

5. Do not forget to save your changes before leaving RZ12.

After the SGEN run, it is a good idea to stop and restart the SAP central instance (the database does not have to be restarted) because SGEN causes serious pressure on the memory buffers. You can see this when you start Transaction ST02 when SGEN is finished, as many buffers will show an extremely high number of swaps. A quick restart of the instance will clean this up.

11.3.3 Configure the Transport Management System (TMS)

Until the last upgrade is finished, the SAP system landscape contains both systems on the old and on the new release. The two groups of systems should be kept apart transport-wise and should not be on the same transport route.

Various scenarios for organizing transports are possible, depending on the complexity of the landscape, the duration of the upgrade project, the available server infrastructure, the development needs, and other factors. One of the more common methods is to first create a "contingency" development system as a copy of the live development system. This contingency system remains on the old release and is used to support the production system for as long as this has not been upgraded. The live development is upgraded first (apart from earlier test upgrades outside the live landscape). At the same time, a virtual system is defined in TMS to act as receiver of all transports released in the upgraded development system (such as SPAU requests).

For a detailed discussion of the landscape configuration scenarios during the upgrade, see Section 4.9. At this point, you must run Transaction STMS (from client 000 in the domain controller) and adapt the configuration, and specifically the transport routes. Distribute the changes to the entire landscape. Next, create and release a dummy transport request in the upgraded development system, and make sure that it follows the correct route all the way down to the virtual upgrade buffer (see Section 4.9).

11.3.4   Nonfatal (Type P) Upgrade Errors

One of the last UA GUI screens of the upgrade informed you that there were errors that require revision. These are the so-called *type P* errors, which are not serious enough to justify an error stop during the upgrade but are too serious to simply be reported as warnings.

The upgrade process finds all type P errors in the detail logs and collects them into a single logfile *<PUTDIR>/log/LONGPOST.LOG*. The messages are grouped by their error number and text; for each error, the log contains an accompanying explanatory text, which is sometimes useful but more often obscure. Many type P errors come from functional areas, so if you can't make sense out of them, maybe a functional specialist on your upgrade team can. Most errors are related to known upgrade issues, and there is often a SAP Note that tells you how to fix them. Use the error number (everything that follows the "2PE" prefix on the message line) and the error text as search keys.

The following is a type P error that is frequently seen:

```
3PETG447 Table and runtime object "<tab>" exist without DDIC
reference ("Transp. table")
```

This error means that a table exists in the SAP database without being defined in the dictionary. Many of these cases are documented in SAP Notes (use TG447 and ETG447 as search keys), and most are harmless.

If you see this error for a table for which there is no SAP Note, then do *not* ignore this. Open a customer message with SAP Support. Use the SQL utility of your database system to verify whether the table contains data. For safety, make a backup copy of the table in the database, for example, using CREATE TABLE <tab_save> AS (SELECT * from <tab>).

11.3.5   Glossary and Terminology Data

After the upgrade, you must run a program to complete the import language-specific *glossary and terminology data*. During the upgrade, this data was imported into intermediate container tables but — to save time — was not imported into the actual language tables.

This action is necessary even if you only have the default languages English (EN) and German (DE). The job only needs to run once for the whole system, not in every client.

To start the program, call the transaction for managing languages, SMLT. Any fully authorized user, such as the upgrade user, can start SMLT.

SMLT will recognize that the glossary/terminology import is incomplete and will automatically start a background job RSTLAN_AFTER_UPGRADE. In the SMLT status window, you see the message Follow-up actions for glossary/termi-nology started (see long text).

The runtime varies but is often in the 30 – 60 minute range (less if only DE and EN are present).

11.3.6 Language Supplementation

Not every text item in the SAP system (including menu titles, buttons, etc.) has necessarily been translated into every language. After importing a language, these gaps in the translation will be filled by using texts from a "supplementing" language, which can be English or German, the two languages that are guaranteed to be complete. This process, known as *language supplementation*, ensures that users will at least see descriptive text, even if not in their own language, rather than an empty menu or featureless button.

Supplementation is necessary for all languages in your system except English and German. The guide *SAP Web Application Server 7.00 Language Transport* clearly states: "After the upgrade, you must use Transaction SMLT to supplement the imported languages."

If it hasn't already been done, you must first set the SAP parameter zsca/second_language to the language you intend to use for supplementation. Set this parameter in all the instance profiles of the SAP system. Assign the value "E" for English or "D" for German. Stop and restart the instance(s) to activate the parameter.

Now log on in client 000 as the upgrade user. Call Transaction SMLT. First choose **Language · Classify**. Select the language you want to supplement, and choose the supplementation language. Click **Save**. If you get the error that the language key already exists, then classification was already done earlier, and you may proceed.

Now place the cursor on the language to supplement and choose **Language · Supplement Language**. The Supplement Language window opens (see Figure 11.1).

In client 000, the supplementation will include both cross-client (client-independent) and client-dependent tables.

Enter a description of this supplementation run. In the right-hand pane, set the start time for the supplementation job (immediate or at a later date/time) and click **Execute**.

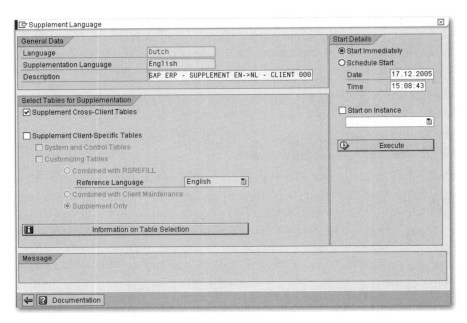

Figure 11.1 Configure Language Supplementation

You must carry out a supplementation per language (other than German and English) and per client, which means client 000 as well as all other clients in actual use. You do not need to run supplementation in client 001 if it exists or in client 066. In clients other than 000, only the client-specific tables will be supplemented (the check box **Supplement Cross-Client Tables** is empty).

To save time, try running more than one supplementation in parallel. For this, you must bear in mind the following:

▶ You can supplement different languages in parallel (also for the same client), but you cannot supplement the same language in parallel in different clients.

▶ To reduce competition for resources between jobs writing to the same database tables, we recommend not starting the parallel supplementation jobs at exactly the same moment but rather using a "staggered" approach, for instance by leaving 5–10 minutes between the start of consecutive jobs.

When the language postprocessing is finished, log on in all languages and run a few important transactions to see whether the texts, menus, buttons, and so on appear as expected.

11.3.7 Reschedule Background Jobs

All released background jobs were disabled at the start of upgrade downtime. If your start release was 3.1I or 4.0B, then you had to manually change the jobs from "Released" to "Scheduled" state in SM37. You must now do the inverse operation and release the jobs again. For time-dependent jobs whose start time has passed, you will have to change the start date and time.

For start Release 4.5 and higher, the system automatically set all released jobs to the "Released/Suspended" state. You cannot change these jobs with SM37. To release them again, start Transaction SE38, and execute the report `BTCTRNS2`. You do not need to change the start date/time of any job.

`BTCTRNS2` releases all suspended jobs at once, without possibility of selection. This is unfortunate because it often makes sense to release some system jobs at an early stage (such as the hourly performance collector), but to leave jobs that affect business processes suspended until the very end, just before going back into production.

To avoid unleashing all jobs at the same time, do the following:

1. Restart the SAP instance without background processes (`rdisp/wp_no_btc=0`). Alternatively, you can create an operation mode without any batch, create an exception timetable with this operation mode, and force an immediate switch using Transaction RZ03. This is a bit more work, but you avoid the extra system stop.

2. As an extra safety precaution, set the parameter `rdisp/btctime` to 0. This parameter is dynamically changeable without having to restart the instance; use Transaction RZ11 for this.

3. Run `BTCTRNS2`.

4. Call SM37, and select all released jobs. Jobs that you do not want to start can be reset to "Scheduled" state (choose **Jobs • Released • Scheduled**), or you can move forward their planned start time.

> **Caution**
>
> Do not change the status of the job `RDDIMPDP`.

5. Reconfigure the background processes either by starting the system with `rdisp/wp_no_btc > 0`, or by switching back to the standard operation mode.

6. Restore `rdisp/btctime` to its original value.

11.3.8 Import the Transport Queue

Before starting the import, a few precautions might be useful. Some of these we already discussed in Section 8.2. Requests added to the buffer after the agreed "cut-off" point must not be imported unless justified; developers must have reviewed and signed off on their transports.

If possible, also back up the database before the import. In the — admittedly rare — case that the import causes irreversible damage, you can choose to restore the database and start again. If you have not made too many changes to the system since the end of the upgrade and/or you have reenabled the archiving of database logs, then you can skip this extra backup.

Always use the **Import All** function; do not import request by request. With **Import All**, dependencies between transports are handled much better, and the process will also take less time. Objects found to be in error cause their requests to end with an exit code 8 (= error). This will propagate to the overall exit code of the entire import process. However, getting an exit code 8 for your **Import All** does not mean the system is compromised. Developers should review the affected objects and take appropriate action.

An exit code 12 or higher means that an import process broke down or that an import job running in the SAP system ended in error, probably with an accompanying short dump. In this case, the import stops and must be restarted after the problem has been identified and corrected.

11.3.9 Cleanup

Release the change requests that you opened during the upgrade (SPDD, activation errors) and possibly during the postprocessing.

If you opened client 000 for repository changes during the upgrade, but this client is normally not open for development activities, then use Transaction SCC4 to close the client again. Also verify the global setting via SE06, **System Change** option.

11.3.10 Migration of Workload Statistics Data to SAP NetWeaver 2004s

As of SAP NetWeaver 2004s (Basis Release 7.00), the workload statistics collector has been redeveloped. The new statistics collector is incompatible with the earlier workload statistics data. The data were saved before the upgrade. Now it's time to restore and convert the statistics data to the new layout.

Follow these steps:

1. Deactivate the SWNCREORG report in the TCOLL table.

2. Call Transaction ST03, and choose **Collector and Performance DB · Performance Monitor Collector · Execution Times · Table maintenance**.

3. Remove the "X" in the hourly schedule for program SWNCREORG (or remove all the Xs in the list of weekdays). Then, save the changes.

4. Implement program SWNCMIGRATION1, which is contained in SAP Note 1006116.

5. Execute program SWNCMIGRATION1. The ZWNCMOMIGR table is converted and saved in the SWNCMONI table.

6. Check the data in Transaction ST03N. The instance names in the workload statistics data get a prefix consisting of the release identification before the upgrade. As such, data is cleary separated.

7. Check the retention times of the workload statistics. Call Transaction ST03, and choose **Collector and Performance DB · Performance Database · Monitoring Database · Reorganization**.

8. Activate the SWNCREORG report in the TCOLL table again.

9. After you have completed the data migration successfully, you can delete the data that is contained in the ZWNCMOMIGR database table.

11.3.11 Additional Postprocessing Steps

The SAP Upgrade Component Guide covers some additional postprocessing steps. Carry out the instructions for your OS, database, and SAP components before resuming productive operation. Different activities need to be executed depending on the SAP source release, the components in use, and whether the system is non-Unicode or Unicode.

11.4 Save the Upgrade Logs

One of the last input windows during the upgrade asked you which upgrade logs you wanted to save. You were offered the choice between saving all logs, saving just the more important ones (not something we recommend!), or saving none at all. At the time, we advised you to choose **All** or **None**. You wouldn't choose the latter because the logs are unimportant, but because choosing it saves valuable time and you can always save the logs later.

As you know, the upgrade logs are in *<PUTDIR>/log*. Because the *<PUTDIR>* does not exist indefinitely and may actually have quite a short lifetime, the upgrade logs are saved to the directory */usr/sap/trans/upgrade/<SID>/700*. If you chose **All** during the upgrade, a complete copy of the logs now exists there; if you chose **None**, the directory exists but does not contain any upgrade logs.

For further action, don't waste valuable time while the system is still unavailable to end users; wait until business is back to normal. Our normal approach is to save the logs in compressed format. A complete backup of all logs takes well over a gigabyte, and space in */usr/sap/trans* is often at a premium. The logs are text files, so they compress very well, and compression can save you 90 % or more. For quick reference, however, we keep some important logs in uncompressed form. Our normal choice is to leave the following logs uncompressed:

- *SAPup.log*: The main upgrade log.
- *SAPupchk.log*: The main log of the PREPARE run.
- *CHECKS.LOG*: The final diagnosis of PREPARE.
- *CHECKS.SAV*: Previous PREPARE logs, showing the errors and the database space requests.
- *UpgDialog.log*: The log containing the entire dialog (messages and user input) of PREPARE and SAPup.
- *RUNTIMES*: The analysis file created by the RSUPGSUM report.

Here are sample commands (logged on as user <sid>adm) to save the upgrade logs (shown for UNIX but easily ported to other OSs). We assume the backup directory is still empty.

```
cd /usr/sap/put/log
SAVEDIR="/usr/sap/trans/upgrade/PRD/700"
SAPCAR -cvf $SAVEDIR/UPLOGS.SAR *²
# Uncompressed backup of critical logs:
cp SAPup.log $SAVEDIR
cp SAPupchk.log $SAVEDIR
```

---

2 With UNIX and the C-shell (default for the <sid>adm user), specifying * here may cause the error Too many arguments. You can normally work around this by switching your session to the Korn (ksh) or Bash shell (bash).

In the preceding chapters, you learned about the upgrade of the ABAP system and the synchronization between the ABAP and Java upgrades in a double-stack system. We now turn our attention to the Java side.

12 Prepare the Upgrade for the AS Java

Proper preparation of the upgrade is essential. Without it, you run an inordinate risk of encountering known and preventable problems. Your main preparation tasks are to perform several verification and preparation activities in the SAP system.

12.1 Activities in the SAP System

In this chapter, we'll briefly discuss the necessary preparatory steps in the Application Server Java and the upgrade prerequisites for the Software Deployment Manager.

12.1.1 Checking the Java Development Kit Version

SAP NetWeaver Application Server Java requires a specific version of the Java Software Development Kit (Java SDK), which might be different from the one currently installed on your system. Check the Java SDK versions that are released for SAP systems on SAP Service Marketplace in the Product Availability Matrix (*https://service.sap.com/platforms* • *SAP NetWeaver* • *SAP NetWeaver '04S* • *JSE Platforms*). Check the installed Java SDK version on the server by using the command `java -version`.

If necessary, download and install the required Java SDK version. Note that neither the Java SDK nor the Java Runtime Environment (JRE) is part of the SAP upgrade kit. You must download Java from a public repository, for example, *java.sun.com*, or from the site of the OS vendor. The installation of the Java SDK/JRE is not in the scope of this book.

For systems using strong encryption, if you have installed a new Java SDK version, update the JCE (Java Cryptography Extension) jurisdiction policy files. The JCE jurisdiction policy files are not copied automatically to the new Java SDK directory. This has to be done manually:

1. Download the JCE jurisdiction policy files from your Java SDK provider. For more information, see your Java SDK provider's documentation.

2. Copy the JCE jurisdiction policy files into the Java SDK directory.

3. Unpack the zip or tar file to the *<Java SDK_dir>/jre/lib/security* directory. For additional steps, see your Java SDK provider's documentation.

The configuration of the J2EE instance has to be changed:

1. Edit the instance profile in */usr/sap/<SID>/SYS/profile/<SID>_JC<num>_<host>*, and add the following line:

```
jstartup/vm/home = <location of the new Java SDK>.
```

> **Note**
>
> Because this setting has precedence over individual Java SDK settings in the J2EE Engine configuration database and the *sdm_jstartup.properties* file, the new JVM (Java virtual machine) will be picked up by all processes that are started through the startup framework — including the SDM (Software Deployment Manager). Manually changing the *sdm_jstartup.properties* file is not necessary.

2. Delete the following files (they will be recreated on the next restart of the engine):

   ▶ */usr/sap/<SID>/<INSTANCE>/j2ee/cluster/instance.properties.vmprop*

   ▶ */usr/sap/<SID>/<INSTANCE>/SDM/program/config/sdm_jstartup.properties.vmprop*

3. Restart the J2EE Engine.

The Visual Administrator, Config Tool, and SDM GUI have their Java SDK configured in the startup batch files. Modify these scripts for the new Java SDK manually.

Make sure that the JAVA_HOME environment variable of the user who wants to run the administration tools (for example, the Visual Administrator, Config Tool, SDM, JSPM) contains the path to the new Java Development Kit (Java SDK) of the J2EE Engine.

12.1.2 Checking the Memory and JVM Settings

SAP NetWeaver 2004s may require different memory and JVM settings for your Java SDK than those currently set. You have to adjust these settings before the upgrade. For information about required memory and JVM settings, see SAP Note 723909 and the SAP Notes for each supported Java SDK referenced within this SAP Note.

12.1.3 Checking the Software Deployment Manager[1] Version

The upgrade requires Software Deployment Manager (SDM) version 6.40 Support Package 13. If you have a lower SDM version, you need to update the SDM before you start PREPARE.

Download the SDM support package from SAP Service Marketplace:

1. Enter the SAP Service Marketplace at *https://service.sap.com/patches*.
2. In the left-hand pane, choose **Entry by application group**.
3. In the right-hand pane, choose **SAP NetWeaver · SAP NETWEAVER SAP NETWEAVER04 · Entry by Component Application Server Java SAP J2EE Engine 6.40 · OS independent**. The appropriate files are displayed on the **Download** tab.
4. Select the required file named *J2EERT<SP_Number>_<Patch_level>-<Counter>.SAR*, and download it to your server.
5. To extract *SDMKIT.jar*, enter:

   ```
   SAPCAR.exe -xvf J2EERT<SP_Number>_<Patch_level>-<Counter>.SAR J2EE-
   RUNT-CD/SDM/SDMKIT.JAR
   ```

Update SDM before starting PREPARE by following these steps:

1. Go to the SDM installation directory (default directory is */usr/sap/<SAP-SID>/<Instance>/SDM/program*).
2. Stop SDM by entering the command `./StopServer.sh`.
3. Set SDM to operate in standalone mode by entering the command `./sdm.sh jstartup mode=standalone`.
4. Copy *sdmkit.jar* to the temporary folder *<sdm_temp>*.
5. In *<sdm_temp>*, extract *sdmkit.jar* with the command `jar -xvf SDMKIT.JAR`.
6. Execute the script `./update.sh`.
7. You are asked for the SDM installation directory. In a standard installation, this is */usr/sap/<SAPSID>/<INSTANCE>/SDM/program*.
8. Switch to the SDM installation directory.
9. Set SDM to operate in the integrated mode by entering `/sdm.sh jstartup mode=integrated`.
10. Start SDM: `./StartServer.sh`.

---

1 The official SAP terminology allows both Software Deployment Manager and Software Delivery Manager. We prefer the former term because it is the one most fequently used in the SAP documentation and because it gives a better idea of its function (installation of application software in the Java world is generally known as "deployment").

12.1.4 Undeploying the Software Component NWMADMIN

If your source release system has support package level 6.40 SP15 or higher, you have to undeploy the software component NWMADMIN before the upgrade:

1. Start the SDM GUI.

2. Open the **Undeployment tab**.

3. Scroll down to the components starting with tc/mobile (there are six, see Figure 12.1).

4. Mark all six components (use Shift – left mouse button to mark a group).

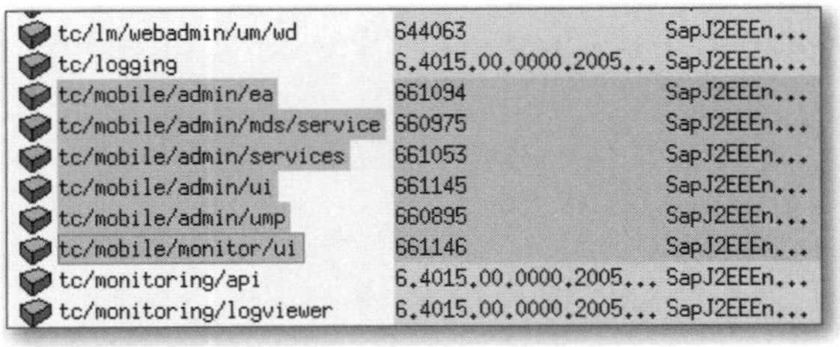

```
tc/lm/webadmin/um/wd        644063              SapJ2EEEn...
tc/logging                  6.4015.00.0000.2005... SapJ2EEEn...
tc/mobile/admin/ea          661094              SapJ2EEEn...
tc/mobile/admin/mds/service 660975              SapJ2EEEn...
tc/mobile/admin/services    661053              SapJ2EEEn...
tc/mobile/admin/ui          661145              SapJ2EEEn...
tc/mobile/admin/ump         660895              SapJ2EEEn...
tc/mobile/monitor/ui        661146              SapJ2EEEn...
tc/monitoring/api           6.4015.00.0000.2005... SapJ2EEEn...
tc/monitoring/logviewer     6.4015.00.0000.2005... SapJ2EEEn...
```

Figure 12.1 Undeploying the Software Component NWMADMIN

5. Click on **Select** to add the components to the **Undeployment** list.

6. Click **Start Undeployment**.

12.1.5 Additional Preparation Steps

The SAP NetWeaver Upgrade Guide covers some additional preparation steps. Carry out the instructions for the SAP components deployed in the source release before starting PREPARE. Different activities need to be executed depending on the SAP source release and the J2EE components in use.

12.2 Ready to Go!

With the preparatory actions completed, you are now ready to run the Java PREPARE, which is covered in the next chapter.

As with ABAP, the technical upgrade process for Java consists of a PRE-PARE run, followed by the actual upgrade. In this chapter, we look at the Java PREPARE.

13 The PREPARE Process for the AS Java

Like its ABAP counterpart, PREPARE collects all needed data and programs and verifies that the source system is ready to be upgraded. PREPARE makes sure that the source system meets the requirements of the upgrade process as well as those of the target release. Handling the issues reported by PREPARE is a prerequisite to a successful upgrade.

13.1 Functions of PREPARE

Java PREPARE has several important tasks, all of which are crucial for the upgrade:

- **Verifying the source system**
  PREPARE verifies whether all prerequisites have been met and determines the system settings for the upgrade automatically (SAP system profiles, SDM [Software Deployment Manager] settings, source release components, etc.).

- **Gathering needed software**
  DVD content is extracted to the upgrade directory.

- **Target release configuration**
  PREPARE maps the source release components to the target release software units. In this way, it determines which components need to be upgraded and which new components have to be installed during the upgrade. The upgrade program always deploys complete software units. For example, if the SAP NetWeaver Portal installation is detected by PREPARE, PREPARE automatically integrates the Portal, Knowledge Management Collaboration (KMC), KMC content management, Universal Work list, and the Collaboration Process Engine into the upgrade.

- **Support packages**
  Support packages can also be included in the upgrade process. The Support packages are then imported during the upgrade, and your system has the most up-to-date state after the upgrade.

▸ **Other software components (SCs)**
PREPARE also enables you to include software components (SCs) that are not part of the shipment, such as customer developments or third-party software. Customers can also specify that components should not be upgraded but remain unchanged. If SAP components have been modified, these components are detected by the PREPARE program. You can then decide whether you want to keep the old version or provide a new one.

13.2 Modification Adjustment

Special steps are needed for the upgrade of SAP systems in which customer developments or third-party software have been installed or in which SAP software was modified. This section limits to modifications done without the SAP NetWeaver Development Infrastructure (NWDI, see Section 13.3 for modifications done using the NWDI).

SAPJup, the upgrade program for AS Java (see Chapter 7), detects modifications automatically for modified SCs where the name of the component vendor was modified. In the **Configuration** module of PREPARE, the operation **Scan inbox** is available for these components. This enables you to provide adjusted SCA (Software Component Archive) files, which are then deployed during the upgrade.

Follow these steps:

1. Compare your modified SCs with the new SAP versions of the SCs.
2. Redo the modifications where necessary, and create your own SCA files.
3. Copy the SCA files to the EPS Inbox of your transport directory (see Chapter 6). Java uses the same EPS Inbox directory as ABAP.
4. In the PREPARE module **Configuration**, specify that SAPJup deploys these SCA files.

SAPJup is unable to detect modifications if you have modified SC without modifying the name of the component vendor. The new SAP component will be deployed, and all your modifications will be lost. In the PREPARE module **Configuration**, the operation **Scan inbox** is not offered for these components.

Follow these steps:

1. Run PREPARE until the EXTRACT_ROMS phase.
2. Get the new SAP version for these components from *<upgrade directory>\data\ archives*.
3. Adapt/transport your modifications to the new version, and build a new component (SCA).

4. Put the SCA in the EPS Inbox directory, and continue with PREPARE.

5. In the BIND_SUPPORT_PACKAGES phase, select your archive to be deployed from the drop-down list, and continue. This way, SAPJup believes that it is installing the latest version of the SAP component while it is actually deploying your modified version.

If third-party components were installed in your system or you have installed custom developments that have been developed without using the NWDI, SAP-Jup offers the operation **Scan inbox** for these components during PREPARE. You have to provide new versions of these components, that is, versions that are valid for the target release. Put them into the EPS Inbox, and specify during PREPARE that SAPJup deploys these new versions.

13.3   Upgrade in a NWDI Landscape

The SAP NWDI keeps track of all SCs in the SAP landscape and knows the upgrade sequence of software applications in a system landscape. Several extra actions are needed if the system to be upgraded is part of a system landscape controlled by NWDI.

The upgrade process for development and consolidation systems differs from the upgrade of quality assurance and production systems. In the development and consolidation system, you can adjust the new SAP component versions to your modifications and build SC archives (SCAs). The adjusted SCAs are then deployed during the upgrade of the quality assurance and production system.

During PREPARE, SAPJup asks whether the system to be upgraded is configured as a runtime system in an NWDI track. If it is, you have to specify whether the system is a development system (DEV), consolidation system (CONS), quality assurance system (QA), or production system (PROD).

For the upgrade of development and consolidation systems, perform the following steps:

1. After you have entered the path to the NWDI transport directory, SAPJup copies all SAP components included in the shipment to this directory.

2. Any components that you modified in the source release, have the status **Managed by NWDI** on the selection screen for the target release components (PREPARE module **Configuration**). These components are not deployed during the upgrade.

3. After the upgrade, you can take the components from the NWDI transport directory and perform the Modification Adjustment by using the NWDI. Then, deploy the adjusted SCs to the upgraded development or consolidation system.

4. In the consolidation system, you assemble the modified SCs as SCAs.

During the upgrade of quality assurance and production systems, SAPJup deploys the modified components that you have built in the consolidation system. In the PREPARE module **Configuration**, all modified components have the status **Scan inbox** on the selection screen for the target release components. You have to select the new versions from the inbox to rebuild the component list. The modified components are then included in the deployment.

13.4 Starting PREPARE for the First Time

The initial run of the JPREPARE script was already discussed in Chapter 7. The following brief instructions serve only as a reminder.

> **Note**
>
> If you are upgrading a double-stacked system (ABAP and Java), you should first start PREPARE for the ABAP stack. This is essential for proper synchronization of both upgrades. Start PREPARE of the Java stack after PREPARE of the ABAP stack prompts you to do so.

When you start PREPARE for the very first time, the script extracts a minimum set of files (including the SDT server and GUI, the Java counterparts of the ABAP Upgrade Assistant [UA]) to the upgrade directory and performs some basic checks of the server. This script is located on the Upgrade Master CD and is called JPREPARE.

1. As a starting condition, the upgrade directory must be empty.

2. Mount the Upgrade Master DVD.

3. As user <sid>adm, go to the mount directory and execute the command JPRE-PARE. The script copies the required programs to the upgrade directory and waits for a connection of the Upgrade GUI, as you can see in the following system output:

```
# <CDDIR>/JPREPARE
SAPCAR: processing archive JUP/CONFIG/COMMON/CONTROL.SAR (version 2.01)
SAPCAR: 255 file(s) extracted
SAPCAR: processing archive JUP/CONFIG/OS/UNX/CONTROL_
UNX.SAR (version 2.01)
SAPCAR: 13 file(s) extracted
SAPCAR: processing archive JUP/JARS/COMMON/SDT.SAR (version 2.01)
SAPCAR: 14 file(s) extracted
SAPCAR: processing archive JUP/JARS/COMMON/EXTLIB.SAR (version 2.01)
SAPCAR: 71 file(s) extracted
SAPCAR: processing archive JUP/JARS/OS/UNX/SDT_UNX.SAR (version 2.01)
SAPCAR: 4 file(s) extracted
Waiting for SDTServer to connect on hostname hgvb14/193.202.68.111
socket 6240 ...
```

If you want to use a different upgrade directory, start PREPARE from the command line, and specify the upgrade directory path; for example, enter "# JPREPARE <your_upgrade_directory>".

To restart PREPARE from the upgrade directory, proceed as follows:

1. Go to *<upgrade directory>\exe*.
2. To start PREPARE, execute the command PREPARE (not JPREPARE).

If something went wrong, and you need to repeat PREPARE completely from the beginning, remove the upgrade directory and start PREPARE from the DVD as described previously.

Before you continue with the technical upgrade, now is the time to copy the SAR archive with the SAPJup correction transports (the "fix buffer", see Section 6.6.4, under the heading *SAPJup Correction Transports*) to its proper location.

Unpack the archive that contains the correction transports to the top level of the upgrade directory. In the following example, we are using thre archive *JNW04SSR2_9.SAR*; in an actual upgrade you will have to determine the fix buffer to use from SAP Note 813658:

```
# cd /usr/sap/jupgrade
# SAPCAR -xvf <path>/JNW04SSR2_9.SAR
```

The archive contains two files: the correction itself (a file with extension UPG), which will be processed by SAPJup, and an info file showing the version of the correction.

Note

Do not unpack the *.UPG* file yourself! This will be done automatically by the upgrade tool. Do not rename any archive or use a different archive as the one requested by SAPJup! During the initialization phase, SAPJup searches the upgrade directory for the correct correction package. If SAPJup is successful, the package is automatically integrated into the upgrade. If SAPJup does not find a valid package, the system displays a user dialog requesting that you place the correction package in the upgrade directory. The dialog gives you the correct name of the correction package required.

13.5   Starting the SDTGui

You can control the upgrade on the host where you started the upgrade, as well as from a remote host. To control it from a remote host, you must start the SDT-Gui in a Web browser, which requires Java Web Start technology.

Starting the SDTGui in a Web browser:

1. Start a Web browser, and enter "http://<hostname>:6239" in the **Address** field.

2. Choose **Start J2EE Upgrade Front-end (SDTGui)**.

For starting the SDTGui locally, do as follows:

1. Change to *<upgrade directory>/exe*.

2. Execute the command startgui.

On the next screen (see Figure 13.1), make the following entries:

1. In the **Host** field, enter the host where the central instance is running.

2. In the **Port** field, do not change the default value 6241.

3. Choose **Log on**.

4. The **Welcome to the SAP Jave Upgrade** screen appears. Click **Continue** to continue.

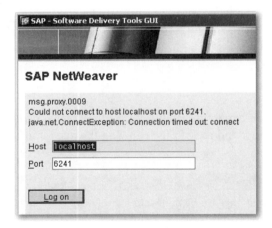

Figure 13.1 Starting the SDTGui Locally

13.6   Start PREPARE

PREPARE consists of the following five modules (see Figure 13.2): **Initialization**, **Extraction**, **Configuration**, **General Checks**, and **Finalization**. Each module has a status (initial, succeeded, or error). All modules are mandatory and have to be executed one after the other because they depend on their predecessors. You can repeat individual modules as often as you want.

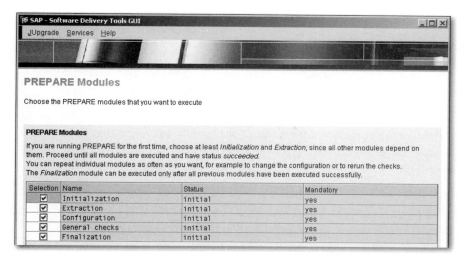

Figure 13.2 The PREPARE Modules

Select all modules, and choose **Continue**.

When an error occurs or a PREPARE or UPGRADE phase terminates, the SAPJup program stops and offers five options on how to proceed:

1. **Repeat phase from point of failure**
   After you have corrected the error, you repeat the phase from exactly the point where the error occurred.

2. **Repeat phase**
   After you have corrected the error, you may want to repeat the whole phase.

3. **Ignore error and go to next phase**
   This option requires a very deep understanding of the upgrade procedure. To avoid followup problems with the upgrade, you have to consult SAP Support. SAP Support will provide you with a password, if it is safe to continue the upgrade like this, or will solve the problem and allow you to continue the upgrade without the need for a password. In our experience, this option should never be used in the upgrade of production systems.

4. **Jump to another phase**
   This option allows you to jump to another phase. As with **Ignore error and go to next phase**, a password from SAP Support is needed. This option should never be used in the upgrade of production systems.

5. **Exit program**
   The upgrade stops and you exit the upgrade program. In case of PREPARE, you can reset it by deleting the upgrade directory and restarting PREPARE in which it will restart from the beginning.

13.6.1 Logfiles

All actions are logged in upgrade logs, which you can use as your starting point for troubleshooting. There is a logfile for each PREPARE and upgrade phase. Additional programs, which are called from the upgrade program, also write logfiles. The logfiles are stored in the log directory of the upgrade directory.

Logfiles have the following naming convention: *<phase name><three-character-id><nn>.log* where *<nn>* is the number of phase iterations you have already performed. For example, the log for the DEPLOY_ONLINE phase when run for the second time would be *DEPLOY_ONLINE_DON_02.LOG*.

Logs that end with the extensions *.out and *.err belong to service programs (programs called by SAPJup). The one in the preceding example is the logfile of SDM.

SAPJup logs the overall status information about the upgrade process in *SAPJup.log*.

> **Note**
>
> You can easily view the logfiles using the log viewer, which is integrated into the SDT GUI. To access it, choose **Services • Log Viewer** from within the Upgrade GUI. The advantage of the log viewer (see Figure 13.3) is that it formats messages in a readable format, which is not the case if you access the logfiles directly.

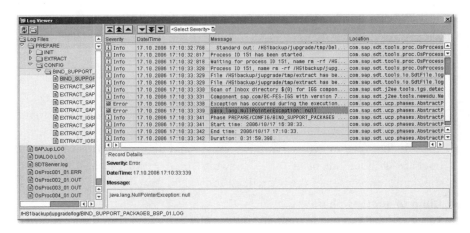

Figure 13.3 The Log Viewer

13.6.2 Trouble Tickets

SAPJup creates a *trouble ticket* every time a phase fails. Trouble tickets are stored under *<upgrade directory>/log* and use the following naming convention: *Trouble_*

Ticket_<xx>.log, where *<xx>* is the number of the error (not related to the phase number). The trouble ticket contains general information about the system and the error. It references the names of the logfiles for the phase and the external processes. You can use the terms at the end of the ticket to search for SAP Notes related to the error. If you open an error message, attach the trouble ticket and all logfiles referenced by the error to provide SAP Support with the information.

13.6.3 Trace Files

During the upgrade, a *trace file* is written and saved under *<upgrade directory>/trc*. As a default, the trace level is set to **ERROR**. If you encounter any upgrade problems, you can raise the trace level to gather more information.

1. To raise the trace level, open the file *<upgrade directory>/param/logging.properties*.
2. Set the parameter *com.sap.sdt.severity* to **DEBUG**.
3. In the STD GUI, choose **Repeat phase from point of failure**.

13.7 PREPARE Modules: Initialization and Extraction

In the **Initialization** and **Extraction** phase, SAPJup asks for the characteristics of the system to be upgraded and prepares the upgrade directory by installing the needed programs, scripts, and tools.

1. The first prompt is for the correction package (see Figure 13.4). The correction package provides the latest corrections for the upgrade program. The correction package was already extracted in Section 13.6.

Figure 13.4 SAPJup Requests the Correction Package

2. Choose **Continue**.

3. A second screen appears showing the package about to be integrated. Choose **Continue** again. SAPJup extracts and integrates the package. To do this, it exits and restarts itself, at which time, you will lose the connection to SAPJup. After the restart of the upgrade, you must restart the SDTGui and reconnect to the upgrade (see Section 13.5).

4. As soon as you are reconnected, SAPJup asks for the upgrade keyword applicable to this upgrade (see Figure 13.5). The keyword is a numeric "password" needed to do the upgrade. There is nothing secret about it; you find it in the first section of the core upgrade note referenced in the message (here, 913972). The keyword is simply there as a wake up call that you should at least read the core upgrade note. Supply the keyword, and choose **Continue**.

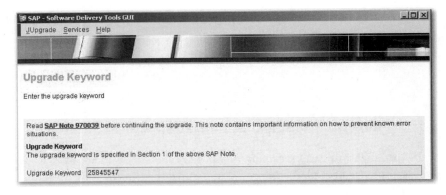

Figure 13.5 SAPJup Prompts for the Upgrade Keyword

5. If you are doing an upgrade of a standalone Java system, a second pop-up appears for the Solution Manager key, You must generate and enter a key in the SAP Solution Manager to proceed with the upgrade (see Section 8.1). If you are performing an upgrade of a double-stack system, you only have to enter the Solution Manager key during the upgrade of the ABAP system, and this interruption does not occur. Click on **Continue**.

6. SAPJup prompts you from the SAP System ID (SAP SID); enter the SAP SID, and click on **Continue**.

7. If you are upgrading a high-availability system, enter the path to the central file share and an instance number for the temporary Central Service Instance (SCS) instance. This pop-up appears if SAPJup detects that the central instance share is located on another server. SAPJup assumes that the upgrade is running in a high-available environment if it is. As SAPJup cannot access or control the processes on the remote (cluster) SCS server, it will install a temporary SCS server on the central instance host. You will have to stop the remote SCS

instance at the begining of downtime and start it again after the upgrade manually. The temporary SCS server is removed by SAPJup at the end of the upgrade automatically. Click on **Continue**.

8. SAPjup displays the ID of the system to be upgraded. Check that the SAP system ID from the system that you want to upgrade is displayed. If it is correct, choose **Confirm**. It's highly unlikely that you would start the upgrade using the wrong <sid>adm user, but if that happens, cancel the phase, exit SAPJup, and restart it using the correct user.

9. In you are upgrading a double-stacked system (ABAP and Java), SAPJup warns that the upgrade of both systems should be synchronized (see Figure 13.6). Note that the PREPARE of the ABAP stack should be started before the PREPARE of the Java stack to avoid synchronization issues. Click on **Continue**.

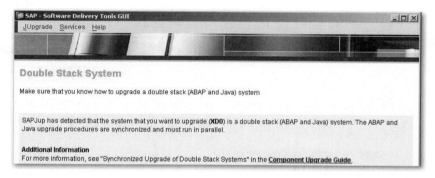

Figure 13.6 SAPJup Prompts You to Start the Upgrade of the ABAP System

10. Set a password for the J2EE super admin user (SAP*, see Figure 13.7). During the upgrade, the User Management Engine (UME) is reconfigured, so that only the SAP* user can access the system during the upgrade downtime. The upgrade procedure initializes the account, and you have to provide a password.

11. Provide the password, and click on **Continue**.

> **Note**
>
> The SAP* user is only active during the upgrade downtime. SAPJup deactivates it after the downtime has finished and restores the original UME configuration. Remember the password in case you have to access the J2EE engine during downtime.

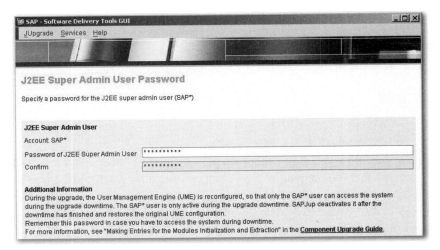

Figure 13.7 SAPJup Prompts for the J2EE Super Admin User Password

---

Caution

Do not change the SAP* password manually once it is set. This would lead to a failure later in the upgrade process.

Proceed as follows if the password was modified to manually set the SAP* user password in the UME service properties using the Config Tool, to the value specified during PREPARE:

▶ Open the J2EE engine Config Tool.

▶ Go to **Cluster-data • Global server configuration • services • com.sap.security.core.ume.service**.

▶ Scroll down to the **ume.superadmin.password** field.

▶ Enter the SAP* user password that you have entered in PREPARE in the **Value** field, and click on **Set**.

▶ In the **Please retype the new secured value** dialog, retype the password one more time.

▶ Click the **Apply changes** button in the toolbar, and exit the Config Tool.

You need to restart the engine for the changes to take effect. The easiest way to do this is to restart the server0 process via the Microsoft Management Console MMC on Windows or jcmon on UNIX. If you are upgrading a double-stack system, you have to start jcmon from the *<jupgrade_dir>/exe* directory using the following command line:

./jcmon pf=<central_instance_profile>.

After you have successfully restarted the engine, repeat the failed phase from the point of failure. Don't forget to close MMC if you have started it before continuing with the upgrade.

12. On the next screen (see Figure 13.8), select **System is under NWDI control**
if it is (see Section 13.3 for more information). Select or leave the checkbox
unselected depending on your configuration, and click on **Continue**. In most
cases, you will leave the checkbox unselected.

Figure 13.8 SAPJup Asks If the System Is Under NDWI Control

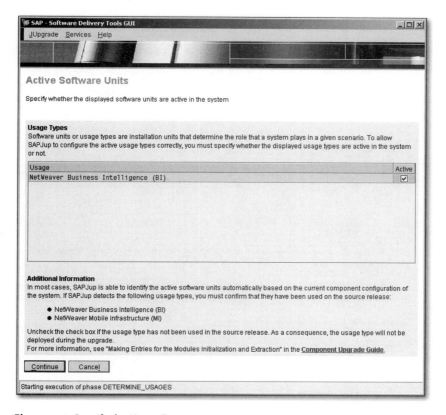

Figure 13.9 Specify the Usage Types

13. Confirm the usage of Business Intelligence (BI) and Mobile Infrastructure (MI), if required (see Figure 13.9). If SAPJup detects BI or MI, you are asked to confirm that they have been used in the source release. If they haven't been used in the source release, they will not be deployed during the upgrade. The safest approach is to leave them as is. Click on **Continue**.

14. A summary of all system parameters that have been detected is displayed. Click on **Continue**.

15. SAPJup asks for the upgrade DVDs. Enter the paths to all required upgrade DVDs (see Figure 13.10).

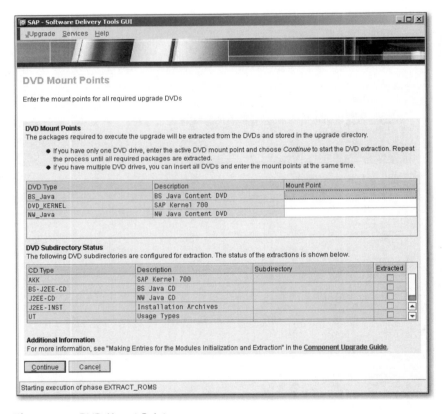

Figure 13.10 DVD Mount Points

If you have access to only one DVD drive, you have to insert the DVDs one after the other:

1. Insert the first DVD.

2. Enter the mount point.

3. Choose **Continue** to start the DVD extraction.

Repeat this process until the lower table on the dialog screen displays the status **Extracted**.

If you copied the DVDs to a file system before starting PREPARE, you can just enter the mount point for each of them. Choose **Continue**. The upgrade program extracts the contents into *<upgrade directory>/data/archives*.

13.8   PREPARE Module: Configuration

In the **Configuration** module, you decide which support packages you want to include in the upgrade. Support packages that are in the EPS Inbox of your transport directory are displayed on the dialog screen. Specify the support package level for each target release component. You can put further support packages in the EPS Inbox and then display them, by choosing **Rescan**. Including support packages in the upgrade assures that the system is at the latest release after the upgrade (see Figure 13.11).

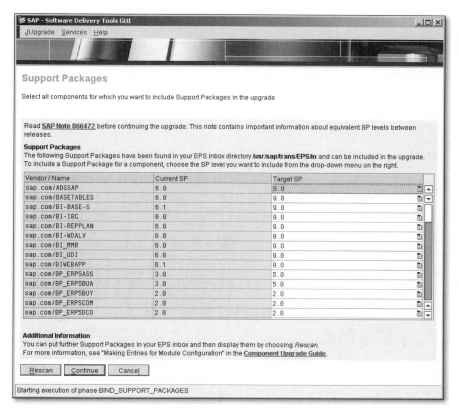

Figure 13.11 Bind Support Packages into the Upgrade

Note the following if SAPJup is not displaying some support packages although you stored them in the EPS Inbox:

▶ SAPJup only displays support packages applicable to the source release.

▶ For components already installed on the source release, the support packages in the EPS Inbox must be newer than those currently installed For components that will be installed as part of the upgrade procedure, the support packages in the EPS Inbox must be newer than those that are included on the upgrade DVDs.

Verify the target level of each component, and click on **Continue**.

Proceed as follows to include more support packages in the upgrade:

1. Log on as user <SID>adm.

2. Move all the SCAs downloaded previously to the \usr\sap\trans\EPS\in directory.

3. To integrate a newer SAP Kernel and Internet Graphics Server into the upgrade, copy the appropriate downloaded files to the EPS Inbox directory as <sid>adm. The copy commands (here for UNIX) are shown here:

```
# cp SAPEXE_<SP_Number>_<Patch_level>-
<Counter>.SAR /usr/sap/trans/EPS/in/SAPEXE.SAR
# cp SAPEXEDB_<SP_Number>_<Patch_level>-
<Counter>.SAR /usr/sap/trans/EPS/in/SAPEXEDB.SAR
# cp  IGSEXE_<SP_Number>_<Patch_level>-
<Counter>.SAR /usr/sap/trans/EPS/in/IGSEXE.SAR
```

4. In the SDTGui, click on **Rescan**.

> **Note**
>
> All support packages uploaded during the upgrade are to be stored in the TRANS-PORT directory (/usr/sap/trans/EPS/in). At least 5GB of free space are needed (EPS files, data files, logs).

> **Note**
>
> If you want to integrate additional kernel patches into the upgrade, you can extract them to directory /usr/sap/jupgrade/data/kernel after PREPARE and before starting the upgrade.

> **Note: Upgrade of a Double-Stacked System**
>
> During the sequence of upgrade steps, at the end of downtime, the kernel used by the Java server is copied to the executable directory. If you want to include the latest available kernel in such an upgrade, it needs to be extracted in the /usr/sap/jupgrade/data/kernel directory after the PREPARE of the Java system.

If you agree with the target support package level displayed, click on **Continue**.

The next screen (see Figure 13.12) lists all components involved in the upgrade because they exist in the source release or because they come with the target release and will be deployed. For each component, the following information is displayed:

▶ Vendor

▶ Component

▶ Release

▶ Support Package level

▶ Patch level

▶ Provider

▶ Operation

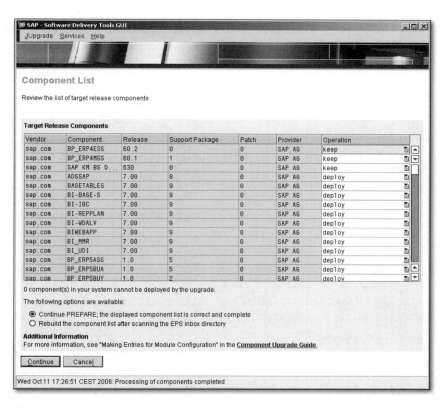

Figure 13.12 Build the Target Component List

In the **Operation** column, you can find the action that will be performed for each component. The operation types are set automatically. You only have to decide what to do for the components that have **Scan inbox** specified as the operation. The following four operation types exist:

▶ **Action Scan inbox** is assigned to components for which the upgrade program cannot find any successor, such as customer developments or third-party software. You can either update the components or keep them unchanged.

To update these components:

▷ Provide a deployment archive (for example, SCAs) with the target release version of the component in your EPS Inbox.

▷ Select the **Rebuild component list after scanning inbox** radio button at the bottom of the dialog screen.

▷ Choose **Continue**. SAPJup rescans the EPS Inbox and adapts the operation of the component that can be deployed.

▶ Action **Keep** is set to components for which no successor exists. Make sure that they are compatible to the new release. The component will remain unchanged during the upgrade. If you do not have a successor for the components, and you are sure that the components are compatible with the new release, you can change the operation to **Keep**.

▶ Action **Deploy** is the normal upgrade operation. The component will be installed.

▶ Action **Undeploy** applies to those components that no longer exist in the new release or that have been renamed. They will be removed (undeployed) during the upgrade.

Confirm the list of components to proceed with the PREPARE program.

13.9 PREPARE Modules: General Checks and Finalization

The upgrade program checks the OS and database versions and the Java SDK version. It will display a message if it detects a version that is not supported for the target release software.

Enter the patch to the directory containing a Java SDK version supported by the target release (see Figure 13.13), and click on **Continue**.

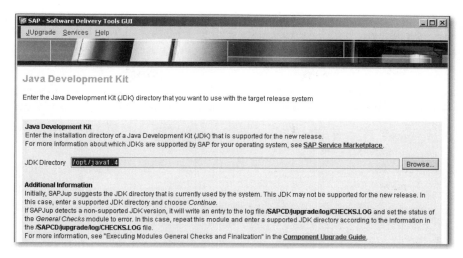

Figure 13.13 Enter the Java Development Kit to Be Used by the Target Release

Finally, the status of all PREPARE modules is displayed (see Figure 13.14). The **General Checks** and **Finalization** modules need to finish successfully. If SAPJup has detected any errors, for example, an OS or database version that is not supported for the target release, it displays a message telling you to check entries in the logfile *CHECKS.LOG*. Both the **General Checks** and **Finalization** modules can be repeated as needed. Choose **Exit Prepare** and **Continue** to close PREPARE.

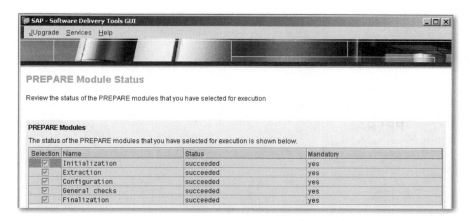

Figure 13.14 PREPARE Module Status — Finished Successfully

After PREPARE, the actual upgrade of the Java system can begin. In this chapter, we look at the entire upgrade process with the SAPJup program.

14 The Upgrade Process for the AS Java

SAPJup upgrades the system to the new version. SAPJup imports the data and deploys the components belonging to the target release. When SAPJup is done, the system is up and running with the new SAP release, and — after a series of additional postprocessing steps described in Chapter 15 — is again ready for productive use.

14.1 Starting the Upgrade

The upgrade upgrades the system and deploys the new components. It consists of the following major steps:

1. Start of downtime.

2. Update of the SAP Kernel, SDM, and the SAP Management Console (Windows).

3. Deployment of the core engine modules, database, and file system components.

4. Offline deployment: The Java Migration Tool (JMT) converts and migrates structures and the core data of the J2EE engine.

5. Online deployment: The J2EE engine is started in safe mode and application-specific components are deployed.

6. Deployment of the additional software components specified during PREPARE.

7. Restart of the J2EE engine in normal mode.

8. Ready the system for productive operation.

> **Note**
>
> Additional dialog instances in the cluster need to be manually shut down before the upgrade. They are not included in the upgrade procedure and need to be reinstalled manually after the upgrade

> **Note**
>
> On Windows, don't forget to stop SAP Management Console (MMC).

Do not start the upgrade until the following are true:

- ► All user activity has ceased. Downtime has arrived.
- ► A database backup was made, or you are sure that you can recover the database to the present point in time.
- ► A backup of the upgrade directory was made.
- ► If a double-stacked system is being upgraded, the ABAP system has been isolated (see Section 10.17).

For starting the J2EE upgrade, perform the following steps:

1. Stop all J2EE dialog instances before continuing. On Windows, close the SAP MMC.

   Login as `<sid>adm`, and go to the upgrade directory:

   ```
   # su - <sid>adm
   # cd /usr/sap/jupgrade/exe
   ```

2. Start the upgrade:

   ```
   # nohup ./UPGRADE &
   ```

The upgrade program starts and waits for the SDTGui to connect.

Now, it's time to start the SDTGui in a Web browser:

1. Start a Web browser, and enter "http://<hostname>:6239" in the address field.

2. Choose **Start J2EE Upgrade Front-end (SDTGui)**.

   The **SAP Java Upgrade** screen appears. Click on **Continue** to start the upgrade. The Java upgrade continues up to phase BEGIN_DOWNTIME, in which the system is about to be stopped (see Figure 14.1).

3. Click on **Continue** to start the upgrade.

> **Note: Double-Stacked System Upgrade (ABAP and Java)**
>
> The Java upgrade sets a sync point at SETSYNC_PREUPTIME_FINISHED. The ABAP upgrade is waiting for this and continues immediately after it has been received. The ABAP upgrade continues up to phase MODPROF_TRANS, in which it waits for further instructions (see Section 10.16). At this point, both the ABAP and Java upgrades are waiting for the downtime to begin.

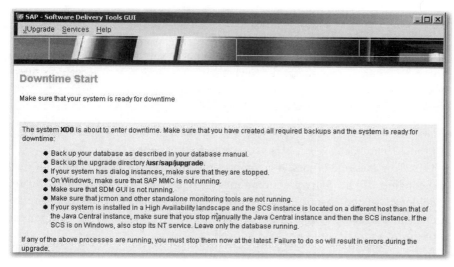

Figure 14.1 SAPJup Downtime Start

14.2   UPGRADE Phases: DEPLOY_<name>

The Software Deployment Manager (SDM) deploys the components. The deployment of the target release components takes place in different phases:

▶ **DEPLOY_FS**

Deployment of the file system content. The J2EE engine is stopped during the deployment.

▶ **DEPLOY_JDD**

Deployment of database content. The J2EE engine is stopped during the deployment.

▶ **DEPLOY_OFFLINE**

Deployment of core engine components. The J2EE engine is stopped during the deployment.

▶ **DEPLOY_ONLINE**

Deployment of all other software components (SCs). The J2EE engine is running during the deployment.

14.2.1   Error Handling

Most upgrade problems occur in the deployment phases, the online deployment more specifically. If an error occurs, SAPJup creates a trouble ticket. The ticket contains the exact name of the SDM logfile, which adheres to the following naming convention: *DEPLOY_SLOT_<x>__<three character ID>_<nn>.LOG*. In the SDM logfile, search for the string `Error`.

There are many different reasons why a component cannot be deployed, and we cannot possibly discuss them all. Nevertheless, some errors occur more often than others, and in the following paragraphs, we take a closer look at several problems that together account for a large percentage of all deployment errors.

▶ `Not deployed. Deploy Service returned ERROR: java.rmi.RemoteException: Cannot deploy application <application name>.`
This error message occurs, if a component cannot be deployed. You can find the name of the Software Component Archive (SCA) which failed to be deployed, at the end of the logfile. If you detect such a problem, create an error message and assign it to component BC-CTS-SDM or to the component of the SCA which could not be deployed.

▶ `java.rmi.RemoteException: The application start is forbidden, because of the server mode and action.`
You can ignore this error message.

▶ `An error occurred in the JStartup Framework. The instance with instance name <instance name> did not respond within 300 seconds.`
Try to find the reason for the J2EE engine startup failure. If the startup process was faultless but simply slow, increase the timeout as follows:

  ▶ Launch the Config Tool. Use *\usr\sap\<SID>\JCxx\j2ee\configtool\configtool.bat* on Windows or */usr/sap/<SID>/JCxx/j2ee/configtool/configtool.sh* on UNIX.

  ▶ In the tree on the left, under the top-level node **cluster-data**, open the node `instance_ID<xxx>` where `<xxx>` is a seven-digit number (this is the number internally assigned to the Java instance).

  ▶ Open the **Message Server & Bootstrap** tab on the right, and go to the input field **Java Parameters** under **Bootstrap Java Settings**.

  ▶ Add `-Dstartup.defaultTimeout=900000`.

  ▶ Save the settings.

  ▶ Open the node `dispatcher_ID<xxx>` for the instance, and open the **Bootstrap** tab. Add again the same parameter in the **Java Parameters** field: `-Dstartup.defaultTimeout=900000`.

  ▶ Save the settings.

  ▶ Open the node `server_ID<xxx>` for the instance, and open the **Bootstrap** tab. Add again the same parameter into the **Java Parameters** field: `-Dstartup.defaultTimeout=900000`.

▶ Save the settings.

▶ Restart the J2EE engine.

▶ Repeat the DEPLOY_ONLINE phase.

If there is no error message, but the DEPLOY_ONLINE phase runs very long, then check the *DEPLOY_SLOT_** logfile for activity. If there is no activity in the logfile, and the timestamp is not changing, check if there is a problem with the database.

The failure of DEPLOY_* phases can be related to a wrong system state of the J2EE engine. During the runtime of the DEPLOY_* phases, the system has to be in a defined state; that is, the J2EE engine must either be stopped or must be running (see Section 14.2.2). If the system is not in this defined state because of errors in the start or stop procedures, the phases fail. Proceed as follows:

1. Open the *phaselist.xml* file located in *<DRIVE>:\<upgrade directory>\param*, and search for the failed phase.

2. Check the previous phase (START_*, STOP_*) to find out in which state the J2EE engine should be.

3. Check the state of your J2EE engine. If it isn't in the expected state, then start or stop the J2EE engine, as required.

4. Repeat the phase.

14.2.2 Starting and Stopping the J2EE Engine Manually

If a problem with the upgrade occurs, you might need to start and stop the J2EE engine manually. The procedure for starting and stopping the J2EE engine during the upgrade downtime differs, depending on whether you have an ABAP and Java double stack or a standalone J2EE engine. During an ABAP and Java double-stack upgrade, the J2EE engine is uncoupled from the ABAP server with regard to starting or stopping the J2EE engine. That is, the J2EE engine is not started and stopped together with the ABAP server using SAP MMC but by internal commands.

Double-Stack Upgrade

1. To start the J2EE engine, execute the command

```
<upgrade directory>\data\kernel\jcontrol -DSAPSTART=1 pf=<Drive>\usr\
sap\<SID>\SYS\profile\<instance profile>.
```

2. To stop the J2EE engine, execute the command

```
<upgrade directory>\data\kernel\sapntkill -KILL <jcontrol-pid>
```

where `<jcontrol-pid>` is the process ID (PID) of the `Jcontrol` process. You can get the PID by using command `ps -ef | grep jcontrol` (UNIX) from the Windows Task Manager (Windows).

Starting and Stopping a Standalone J2EE Engine During the Upgrade

1. To start the J2EE engine, execute the command

   ```
   startsap.exe name=<SID> nr=<instance number> SAPDIAHOST=<hostname>
   ```

2. To stop the J2EE engine, execute the command

   ```
   stopsap.exe name=<SID> nr=<instance number> SAPDIAHOST=<hostname>
   ```

14.3   Upgrade Phase: DOWNTIME_END

At the end of the downtime, SAPJup prompts you to create a backup of the database and a backup of the upgrade directory (see Figure 14.2).

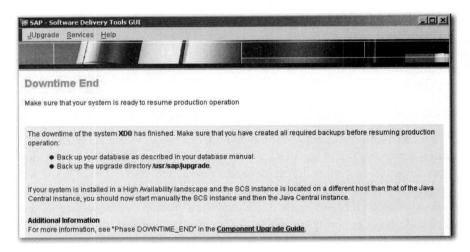

Figure 14.2 SAPJup Downtime End

Click on **Continue**.

Next, SAPJup prompts you that an upgrade evaluation document was generated and stored in the *htdoc* directory of the upgrade directory (see Figure 14.3). It contains valuable information for the planning of the next, probably productive, upgrade. This file contains a complete summary of the upgrade, including the server information, the list of installed components, and the runtimes of all upgrade phases.

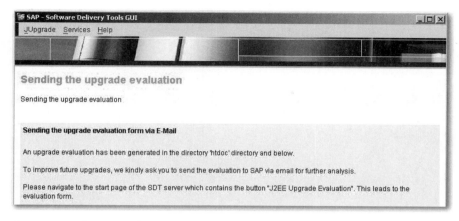

Figure 14.3 Information About the Upgrade Evaluation

You can access the files via the following URLs:

▶ Evaluation form: *http://<server>:6239/htdoc/eval/EvalForm.html*

▶ Upgrade information: *http://<server>:6239/htdoc/UpgAnalysis.html*

The HTML files are physically located in *<PUTDIR>/htdoc.*

SAP requests that customers send the evaluation document to SAP to improve future upgrades. Click on **Continue**.

Finally, SAPJup tells you that the Java upgrade has finished (see Figure 14.4). Click on **Exit** to exit and close the Upgrade.

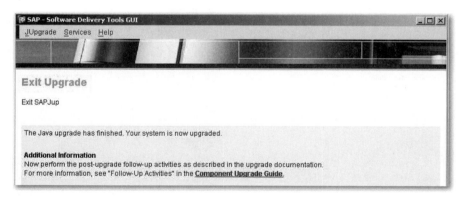

Figure 14.4 Exit SAPJup

The Java upgrade is finished, but don't let those champagne corks pop just yet. There is still some postprocessing work — albeit less than on the ABAP side — before users can get back to work, and you can get some rest.

15 Upgrade Postprocessing for the AS Java

The Upgrade Guide for Application Server (AS) Java covers the postprocessing actions in the *Followup Activities* section. Carry out the instructions for your OS, database, and deployed SAP components. This chapter deals with postprocessing steps applicable to all usage types of the AS Java and those we feel need special attention or require extra explanation.

15.1 The saproot.sh Script (UNIX)

As with the ABAP stack, some kernel executables needs their ownerships changed; for these executables, the SUID bit[1] is set. This is necessary for the saposcol collector, which must run with super user (root) privileges. For several RDBMSs, Oracle for example, the SAP kernel contains specific tools for database administration. These programs must often also run with the identity of the DBA user or even the super user. See Section 11.1 for a detailed description.

> **Note**
>
> The script saproot.sh is applicable to both ABAP and J2EE systems. In double-stack systems (ABAP and J2EE), it only needs to be executed once.

15.2 Upgrading the Dialog Instances

After the upgrade of the central instance, you need to upgrade the dialog instance to the new release. To do this, you uninstall the old dialog instances and then

---

1 The SUID (Set User ID) bit is an indicator in the program's directory entry that causes that program to run with the identity (and thus the privileges) of its owner, rather than with the identity of the user running the program. This bit is widely (but incorrectly) known as the "sticky bit."

install the new dialog instance using the tool SAP Installation Tools (SAPINST). See the Installation Guide applicable to your OS and database for more information. When reinstalling dialog instances, make sure to use the same instance number as on the source release.

15.3 Changing Passwords

As of SAP NetWeaver 2004s Support Package 03, new security policies apply. You have to change the J2EE administrator password, if the following are true:

- ▶ Your password is older than 90 days.
- ▶ Your password does not contain between 6 and 12 characters and does not consist of both letters and numerals.
- ▶ Your password equals a user name.

If you change the J2EE engine administrator password, you have to make sure that external tools (for example, SDM [Software Deployment Manager) and JSPM [Java Support Package Manager]) can read the password. These tools read the J2EE engine administrator password from the secure store. The secure store is not automatically updated, so you have to do this manually.

Proceed as follows:

1. Start the Config Tool by executing the `configtool` script in */usr/sap/<SID>/ <Instance name>/j2ee/configtool/*.
2. Select **Secure store**.
3. Select the `admin/password/<SID>` entry.
4. Enter the new password for the J2EE engine administrator in the **Value** field, and choose **Add**.
5. To save the data, choose **File Apply**.
6. Restart the J2EE engine.

15.4 Updating the SLD Content

The SLD (System Landscape Directory) contains a software catalog of all installable SAP products and software components. The software catalog includes information about support packages and dependencies between the products and software components. You have to make sure that this content is always up-to-date. On the SLD, you need to update the SLD content and data model. Download the latest SLD content from the SAP Service Marketplace, and import it into the SLD. Updates of the Software Catalog can be found at *http://service.sap.com/SWDC •* *SAP Software Distribution Center • Download • Support Packages and Patches • Entry by Application Group • SAP Technology Components • SAP Master Data for SLD.* The updates of the software catalog are provided as deltas to the previous version. Therefore, you do not need to download and install the complete software catalog every time.

Proceed as follows to upload the new SLD content:

1. Copy the file (in binary mode) to your PC. Do not unzip it.
2. In your Web browser, enter the URL of the SLD: "http://<host>:<port>/sld".
3. Log on as a user with the SAP_SLD_ADMINISTRATOR role.
4. Choose **Administration • Import** from the SLD home page.
5. Choose **Browse,** and browse to the ZIP file you want to import (see Figure 15.1).

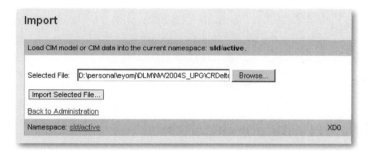

Figure 15.1 Import the Latest Available Component Information Model CIM Model or CIM Data into the SLD

6. Choose **Import Selected File**.
7. The preconditions are checked. If the file is okay, the window shown in Figure 15.2 appears.
8. Click on **Continue Import**.
9. The SLD Administration page reappears, with a progress bar at the top. The status automatically refreshes every five seconds. The import can take several hours. The status at the end of the update is shown in Figure 15.3.

Figure 15.2 The SLD Has Verified the CIM Model or CIM Data to be Imported and Is Ready to Start

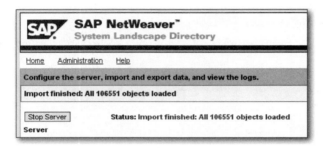

Figure 15.3 Status at the End of the Update

15.5 Additional Postprocessing Steps

The SAP NetWeaver Upgrade Guide covers some additional postprocessing steps. Carry out the instructions for your OS, database, and SAP components before resuming productive operation. Different activities are needed for the Adobe Document Services, Business Intelligence (BI), the SAP NetWeaver Portal and Knowledge Warehouse, and the Exchange Infrastructure. Be aware that some components depend on others. BI depends on functionality delivered by the Portal. In such a system, postprocessing actions are needed for both BI and Portal.

The technical upgrade procedure of a Business Intelligence (BI) system is equal to the procedure used for any R/3 system. Modification Adjustment is minimal, as there is almost no development in these types of systems. There are some specific BI actions to be performed before, during, and after the upgrade, most of which should be done by customizing consultants.

16 Upgrade of SAP NetWeaver Business Intelligence

SAP NetWeaver Business Intelligence (BI) is the NetWeaver component used for data warehousing tasks. It is the successor of the SAP Business Information Warehouse (BW). Although SAP no longer uses the name Business Information Warehouse, the technical upgrade documentation still refers to this term. We, therefore, use the old BW name throughout this chapter.

BW is included as base component as of Application Server (AS) 6.40. AS 6.40 consists of the following building blocks: the SAP Basis, ABAP, BW, and SAP Basis Plug-in (PI Basis).

Most BW systems have several add-ons installed. All of them must be accounted for during the upgrade. It is not possible to remove an add-on during a SAP BW upgrade (even though the option may be available in the upgrade tools).

Examples of such add-ons are Business Content, the SAP Basis Plug-in, SAP Strategic Enterprise Management (SEM), and the SAP NetWeaver Portal or Workplace Plug-in (WP-PI).

Some add-ons are automatically managed by the upgrade:

▶ **Business Content**
Business Content is a standard component as of BW Release 3.1. It is released independently of SAP BW. Instead of the Business Content that came with the upgrade kit, include in the upgrade the latest Business Content release with its support packages.

▶ **Basis Plug-in**
If you start with release SAP BW 3.x or higher, PI Basis is already installed in your system. PI Basis is tied to the underlying SAP NetWeaver AS release. The

upgrade will automatically upgrade PI Basis to the version for SAP NetWeaver AS 7.00. A new release of the SAP PI Basis is released about every year. We recommend including the current SAP Basis PI instead of the one that came with the upgrade kit.

▶ **SAP NetWeaver Portal Plug-in or Workplace Plug-in**
The SAP NetWeaver Portal or Workplace Plug-in (WP-PI) may have been installed in your SAP BW system. Before the upgrade starts, ensure that the version is the 6.00 version (version 5.00 is no longer supported). During the upgrade, the WP-PI is automatically deleted. In the future, all the WP-PI features/functions will be delivered in the PI_BASIS component.

▶ **Others**
If you are upgrading a SAP BW system where major non-SAP BW add-ons have been installed (e.g., SEM-BW and FINBASIS), you should consider the SAP Notes and Upgrade Guides specific to add-ons as the primary guides and the SAP BW actions as secondary. A newer version of each add-on installed in the system will have to be included in the upgrade.

16.1 BW-Specific Tasks

In addition to the standard release upgrade tasks, an upgrade of a BW system up to Release 7 contains the steps described in this section. Only the most important ones are listed. A detailed list of all tasks before, during, and after the upgrade is provided in the Upgrade Guide for SAP NetWeaver 2004s BI ABAP.

16.1.1 Checking Number Ranges

The elementary test of number ranges checks whether a number range object exists for the SID of the characteristic with the maximum SID. If this is the case, it checks whether the largest SID used is smaller than, or if it has the same status as, the number range object. If this is not the case, an error has occurred. The status of the number range object can be corrected in repair mode. A number range object is also created here if it is missing.

To make sure that the number ranges have the right level, proceed as follows:

1. Call Transaction RSRV. All available consistency checks are displayed on the left-hand side. The right hand-side is initially empty. Open **All Elementary Test • Master Data**.

2. Select **Comparison of Number Range and Max. SID (all Characteristics)**, right-click, and select **Select Test**. The selected test is displayed on the right-hand side.

3. Choose **Execute**.

4. If a red bullet is displayed in the Result column, inconsistencies exist. Choose **Correct error**.

16.1.2 Checking the Logical System

To prevent errors in the XPRAs phase, you must have a logical system name defined for your production client. Proceed as follows:

1. Log on to the SAP system.

2. Call Transaction SCC4 (client maintenance).

3. Select your production client.

4. Display the details.

5. Check that a logical system name is defined.

If a logical system is not defined, create and assign one prior to starting the upgrade. For information on problems with logical system names, see SAP Note 210919.

16.1.3 Checking the Consistency of the Web Templates

Before you upgrade your BW system, make the consistency check for the BW Web templates as described in SAP Note 484519. This consistency check informs you of inconsistencies in Web objects that already exist in your BW 2.x system. It also ensures that any inconsistencies in the Web objects are removed from your BW system before the upgrade. You can also ensure that only those errors are displayed that were caused by the conversion of Web objects. This makes error analysis easier when you convert the Web objects.

The check program is available as of SAP BW 2.0 (SP 21), or SAP BW 2.1 (SP 13). You can execute it in Transaction RSRV (select the **Miscellaneous** tab).

> **Note**
>
> The Reporting Agent settings for precalculating BW Web templates are not converted. For more information, refer to SAP Note 597050.

16.1.4 Checking Inconsistent InfoObjects

Before the upgrade, you have to check the InfoObjects and repair them if necessary. Inconsistencies can be repaired via Transaction RSD1. After they have been corrected, check them again, and manually correct any remaining inconsistencies.

Proceed as follows:

1. Log on to the production client.

2. Execute Transaction RSD1 and choose **Extras • Repair InfoObjects**.

3. Choose **Mode = only display,** and click on **Execute**.

4. Click on **Object selection** to set additional options.

5. Clear all check boxes, and only mark the ones shown in Figure 16.1.

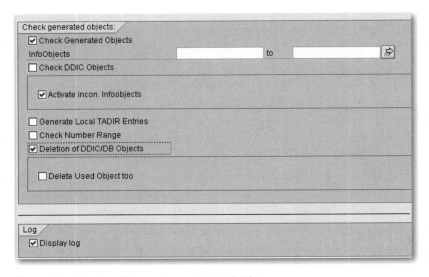

Figure 16.1 Check and Repair Inconsistent InfoObjects

6. Choose **Execute** in the pop-up window.

7. On the main selection screen, choose **Program • Execute in background** (you will get a timeout otherwise).

8. Monitor the background job via Transaction SM37.

9. When the job is finished, return to Transaction RSD1, and choose **Extras • Repair InfoObjects.** Choose **Display Logs** on the selection screen.

Before the upgrade, all InfoCubes should be activated by following these steps:

1. Activate the InfoCubes via the Administrator Workbench (Transaction RSA1) or Edit InfoCubes (Transaction RSDCUBE). Alternatively, you can use the program RSDG_CUBE_ACTIVATE.

2. All InfoCubes should be actived before the upgrade. PREPARE will complain otherwise.

In addition, all transfer structures and rules must be activated. Activate them in the Administrator Workbench (Transaction RSA1).

Report RSUPGRCHECK can be used to check the consistency of generated DDIC (data dictionary) objects for BI metadata as InfoObjects, InfoCubes, and transfer rules. It determines whether the DDIC tables required for the BI meta object are active. While the report itself does not eliminate any inconsistencies, it does enter the incorrect objects in a log. The inconsistent BI objects must be reactivated before the upgrade. The report is called automatically (prepare phase) in the upgrade. The user or system administrator must use BW transactions to edit (postactivate) the inconsistent BW objects found because this may otherwise cause errors and terminations due to nonactivated DDIC tables during the upgrade. See SAP Note 449160 for more information.

16.1.5 Converting Data Classes of InfoCubes

In many BW systems, InfoCubes are isolated in dedicated tablespaces to improve performance, data growth, and manageability. The InfoCubes are assigned to those tablespaces via the delivery class in the data dictionary. Problems might arise during the upgrade if these delivery classes or DDART table data classes do not correspond with the naming convention required by SAP (see SAP Note 46272). Data classes that do not comply with the naming convention are lost during the upgrade. This implies that tables generated for the InfoCube can no longer be activated (error message unknown data class occurs).

Go to Transaction SE16, and display the contents of tables TAORA (for data tablespaces) and IAORA (index tablespaces).

> **Note**
>
> For Informix, verify tables TAINF and IAINF; for DB2, verify tables TADB6 and IADB6.

Proceed as follows:

1. Make sure that all the data classes (TABART) comply with the SAP naming convention.
2. If not, set up new data classes as described here.
3. Define the new data class.

   Data classes are maintained via table DDART. Data classes are used to group together tables whose contents have matching logical attributes. For example, the data class APPL1 is assigned to transparent tables with transaction data. Add a new data class or classes to the table DDART. Use the following name range: USER1, USER2 ... USER9. Table entries that comply with this name range are retained during the upgrade.

For example:

```
DDART-DDCLASS = 'USER5'
```

Furthermore, enter

```
DDART-DDCLASS = 'USR'
```

where you declare the data class as customer-specific.

The DDART entries are also used in the **Possible Entries** button in the transaction to maintain/display technical settings. It is therefore necessary to describe the new data classes in the corresponding text table DARTT.

Enter the data class in the field DARTT-TABART, the language indicator for your logon language in the field DARTT-DDLANGU, and a short description of the data class in the field DARTT-DARTTEXT. This short description must be translated into all languages in which you use the maintenance/display of technical settings.

4. Define the link data class and the area in the database. You do this with entries in the following tables:

DB2 UDB for UNIX and Windows: TADB6 and IADB6

```
TADB6-TABART = <Name of data class>
TADB6-TABSPACE = <Name of table memory area>
IADB6-TABART = <Name data class>
IADB6-TABSPACE = <Name of index memory area>
```

Informix: TAINF and IAINF

```
TAINF-TABART = <Name of data class>
TAINF-DBSPACES = <Name of table memory area>
TAINF-LOCKMODE = 'ROW'
IAINF-TABART = <Name of data class>
IAINF-DBSPACES = <Name of index memory area>
```

Oracle: TAORA

```
TAORA-TABART = <Name of data class>
TAORA-TABSPACE = <Name of table memory area>
TAORA-PCTINC = '0000'
TAORA-OFREELIST = '001'
TAORA-OFREEGROUP = '01'
TAORA-OPCTFREE = '10'
TAORA-OPCTUSED = '40'
```

IAORA

```
IAORA-TABART = <Name of data class>
IAORA-TABSPACE = <Name of index memory area>
```

```
IAORA-PCTINC = '0000'
IAORA-OFREELIST = '01'
IAORA-OPCTFREE = '10'
```

5. Execute report RSDG_DATCLS_ASSIGN to assign the InfoCube (see Figure 16.2).

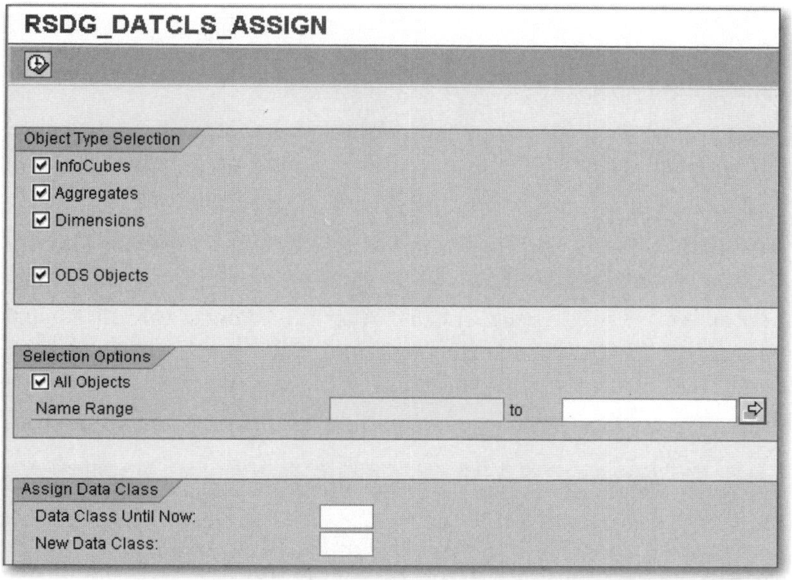

Figure 16.2 Report RSDG_DATCLS_ASSIGN

16.1.6 Converting Inconsistent Characteristics Values/Alpha Conversion

The alpha conversion is not part of the SAP BW upgrade itself but is a prerequisite for the upgrade. The runtime of the alpha conversion should not be underestimated because it has to scan and, if necessary, modify all InfoObjects. It should be executed the weekend before the upgrade, at the latest.

Alpha conversion essentially converts all ALPHA, NUMCV, and GJAHR fields by adding leading zeros to them as shown in Table 16.1.

Before the Alpha Conversion	After the Alpha Conversion
12345	0000012345

Table 16.1 Before and After Alpha Conversion

> **Note**
>
> The alpha conversion must be executed on all SAP BW 2.0B, 2.1C, and all "new installed" SAP BW 3.0B systems (i.e., those not previously upgraded to SAP BW 3.0B).

Proceed as follows:

1. Call Transaction RSMDCNVEXIT.
2. The system status is displayed:
   - ▶ All Characteristics Have Correct Internal Values: The Alpha converter has been successful executed. The upgrade preparation can continue.
   - ▶ No Check yet/Inconsistent Internal Vales exist: The Alpha converter check has not been executed.
   - ▶ Characteristics have Inconsistent Internal Values: The Alpha converter tool check has been executed, and data problems have been detected. The InfoObject and data must be processed before the upgrade can be started.

> **Note**
>
> The system is locked during conversion, so that data (master data, hierarchies, and transaction data in InfoCubes and Data Store objects) cannot be loaded or processed. Nor can you start conversion as long as data are being loaded or meta objects are being processed. End all load processes before you start the conversion. We recommend that you close the system during the whole conversion and that you only allow administrators to log on. The lock remains until all data have been converted.

The alpha conversion consists of the following steps:

1. Preliminary Check/Estimating Workload
2. Check Internal Values and Determine Conversion Characteristics
3. Processing Inconsistent Characteristics
4. Converting Characteristics

Step 1: Preliminary Check/Estimating Workload

Click on **Evaluate pre-check/expense**. This starts a job RSMD_CHECK. The status field will still read No check yet / Inconsistent values present.

Step 2: Check Internal Values and Determine Conversion Characteristics

You must first check the characteristics. Do this by selecting the **Check Internal Value, Determine Character to be converted** button. A background job is started that searches for inconsistent values in the SID table of all characteristics with conversion routines.

Step 3: Processing Inconsistent Characteristics

After the job for step 2 completes, click on **Refresh Status** again. If the status remains Not checked yet/Inconsistent values present, then an alpha conversion is required.

Click on **Edit Characteristics**. For each characteristic listed (with a green or red status), there are two choices: **Remove Conversion Routine** or **Convert Characteristic**. These actions are described in Note 447341. Characteristics with a green status have default action **Convert**, whereas for those with a red status, there is no default. Because both choices affect the BW data, a BW specialist should evaluate this.

Step 4: Converting Characteristics

Click on **Convert Internal Values** to start the conversion. When the job is finished, click on **Refresh** again in RSMDCNVEXIT. The status should now become All characteristics only have correct internal values (see Figure 16.3). To refresh the **System is locked** checkbox, you must restart the transaction.

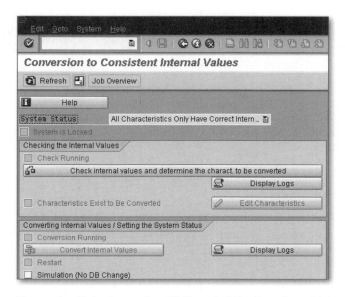

Figure 16.3 Alpha Conversion, All Characteristics Have Correct Internal Values

The alpha conversion and Transaction RSMDCNTEXIT are explained in detail in SAP Note 447341 and in the online documentation that comes with the transaction. As the alpha conversions touch the BW data, it should be a joint venture of the SAP Basis Administrator and the BW consultant.

Usually, the alpha conversion requires between 3 and 20 hours for production systems. For very big systems (greater than 1TB), it could also take up to several days. From our experience, the most decisive factor for the duration is the size of the ODS (Operational Data Source) objects. As a rough rule of thumb, approximately 2.5 million records per hour can be converted within ODS objects (status SAP BW 2.0B SP 27 respective SAP BW 2.1C SP 19). To improve the conversion for ODS objects, keep the change log small (i.e., delete old entries) because all change log records will be converted, too. Furthermore, the size of the master data tables (which include characters with one of the ALPHA, NUMCV, or GJAHR conversions) has impact on the runtime of the upgrade. Parallel processing is available as of Support Package 29 for BW 2.0B or Support Package 21 for BW 2.1C. As of this support package level, the conversion of the ODS tables can be processed in parallel. This can considerably improve performance. Refer to Note 559524.

16.1.7   Migrating InfoPackage Groups to Process Chains

InfoPackage group functions are no longer supported in BI 7.0, so they should be converted to process chains.

Proceed as follows:

1. Execute Transaction RSA1.
2. Go to **Monitoring**.
3. Go to **InfoPackages**, and double click on the InfoPackage.

To migrate the InfoPackage group, choose **Process Chain Management**.

It is still possible to work with InfoPackage groups after the upgrade (with Transaction RSA1OLD), however, we recommend that you migrate them to process chains before the upgrade.

16.1.8   Changing Read Modes

For SAP NetWeaver 2004s, some read modes you are using in SAP BW 2.x are no longer valid on the target release. To avoid errors when running queries, you must change the read mode before the upgrade.

Proceed as follows:

1. Call Transaction RSRT.

2. From the menu, choose **Environment All Queries Readmode**.

3. Change the read mode to **Queries Read Upon Each Navigation/Hierarchy Expand**.

16.1.9 Connections to the Backend Systems

Determine whether the plug-ins on the backend systems still support the target BW release. A plug-in upgrade on the backend R/3 system might be needed. This should be verified before the upgrade. For more information on the supported releases, consult the plug-in page at the SAP Service Marketplace (*http://service.sap.com/R3-PLUG-IN*). Decouple the upgrade of the backend plug-ins from the upgrade of BW to make error analysis of data extractions easier than if they were upgraded at the same time.

16.2 The PREPARE and Upgrade Process for SAP BW

The PREPARE process for SAP BW is comparable to the PREPARE process of SAP ECC (see Chapters 5 and 9). This chapter only outlines the differences.

16.2.1 During PREPARE

As with the upgrade for ECC, during PREPARE, the system is made ready for the upgrade. Data and programs are copied to the upgrade directory, tools are imported into the database, and the shadow instance is installed. Add-ons, support packages, user modifications (transports), and the languages installed on the source release to be upgraded are integrated into the upgrade. After the initial configuration of the upgrade tools, the source system is verified against the requirements of the upgrade process and the target release. This produces an action list that needs to be taken care of before the actual upgrade can start.

Actions for Add-On Packages

As with the PREPARE process for SAP ECC, the list of current add-ons is displayed in the Extension phase (see Figure 16.4). For each add-on, a new version needs to be supplied.

Selection	Add-On ID	Source Release	Destination Release	Status	Note
☐	PI_BASIS	2005_1_640	2005_1_700	INST/UPG ...	570810
☑	BI_CONT	353	?	UNDECIDED	632429
☑	FINBASIS	300	?	UNDECIDED	632429
☑	SEM-BW	400	?	UNDECIDED	632429
☑	ST-A/PI	01H_BCO640	?	UNDECIDED	69455
☑	ST-PI	2005_1_640	?	UNDECIDED	769519

Figure 16.4 PREPARE: Actions for Add-On Packages

Choose **OK**; for each undecided add-on you must now supply a package.

The add-ons for BW are supplied via so-called SAINT packages. They need to be extracted in the transport directory from which they will be picked up by SAPup.

First extract the packages. Every component consists of two archives: an archive containing the component and an archive containing the language for the component.

```
# cd /usr/sap/trans
```

For BI Content 7.03:

```
# SAPCAR -xvf <CDDIR>/UPGR/DATA/KIBIIUH.SAR
# SAPCAR -xvf <CDDIR>/LANGUAGE/KIBIIIL.SAR
```

For FINBASIS:

```
# SAPCAR -xvf <CDDIR>/FINBASIS/UPGR/DATA/KIEQ07U.SAR
# SAPCAR -xvf <CDDIR>/FINBASIS/LANGUAGE/FIB600L0.SAR
```

For SEM-BW:

```
# SAPCAR -xvf <CDDIR>/SEMBW/UPGR/DATA/KIEN11U.SAR
# SAPCAR -xvf <CDDIR>/SEMBW/LANGUAGE/SEM600L0.SAR
```

For the Solution Tools Plug-in (ST-PI):

```
# SAPCAR -xvf <CDDIR>/addons/KITLQIG.CAR
```

Decision Process

PREPARE discovered the BI add-ons BI_CONT, FIN_BASIS, and SEM_BW. For each add-on, you need to decide if it should be upgraded, deleted, or kept as is. In most cases, you will upgrade the component to a target release compatible to the target SAP release. Keeping the add-on can only be done in special cases. Keeping or deleting the add-ons requires a password from SAP.

Mark the components with status **UNDECIDED** and click on **OK**. For each selected component, PREPARE asks you what to do:

1. BI_CONT: Choose **Upgrade with SAINT package**. Initially, PREPARE reports that no package was found and asks whether you want to use an add-on CD. Reply **No**. On the next screen, choose **Search**. The package should now be found and uploaded.

2. FINBASIS: Choose **Upgrade with SAINT package**.

3. SEM-BW: Choose **Upgrade with SAINT package**.

4. ST-A/PI: The plug-in for the Service Tools for Applications (see SAP Note 069455) cannot be upgraded. It is deleted in the upgrade and reinstalled afterwards. Therefore, choose **Delete**.

5. ST-PI: Choose **Upgrade with SAINT package**.

The final status is shown in Figure 16.5.

Selection	Add-On ID	Source Release	Destination Release	Status	Note
☐	PI_BASIS	2005_1_640	2005_1_700	INST/UPG WITH...	570810
☐	BI_CONT	353	703	UPG WITH SAIN...	632429
☐	FINBASIS	300	600	UPG WITH SAIN...	632429
☐	SEM-BW	400	600	UPG WITH SAIN...	632429
☐	ST-A/PI	01H_BC0640	-	DELETE	69455
☐	ST-PI	2005_1_640	2005_1_700	UPG WITH SAIN...	769519

Figure 16.5 PREPARE: Binding Support Packages for BW

Results of PREPARE Applicable to BW Systems

PREPARE complains if it finds inconsistent or inactive InfoObjects:

```
"InfoObject XXXX is not" "consistent - activate it"
```

Before running PREPARE, all InfoObjects need to be consistent. PREPARE will complain if some of them are not.

Proceed as follows:

1. Call Transaction RSD1.

2. Choose **Extras • Repair InfoObjects**.

3. Enable **Execute Repair**.

4. Choose **Object Selection**.

5. On the next screen, activate the following checkboxes:

▸ **Check Generated Objects**

▸ **Activate Inconsistent InfoObjects**

▸ **Delete DDIC Objects**

▸ **Display log**

6. Execute the program.

Inconsistent InfoObjects are repaired automatically. After the program has run, verify them, and correct remaining InfoObjects manually.

Proceed as follows to activate inactive InfoObjects:

1. Call Transaction RSD1.

2. Enter the object name.

3. Select **Maintain · Activate**.

All requests in ODS objects should be activated. PREPARE complains if inactive data in ODS objects are found:

```
Activate all requests in ODS object "OSD_OO6" ("RTSCHAUD")
Activate all requests in ODS object "GBAPSDO1" ("DPANKOV2")
Activate all requests in ODS object "STLIO3UM" ("RTSCHAUD")
Activate all requests in ODS object "STSD_OO6" ("JAINSW")
```

Proceed as follows:

1. Execute Transaction RSA1.

2. Select **InfoProviders**. Use **Find** to look up the ODS object by its technical name.

3. Position the cursor on the object, right-click, and select **Delete data** (not **Delete!**).

4. On the pop-up, choose **Delete entries**.

5. In the logfile, the following output is displayed: `Database table <x> deleted and recreated`.

16.2.2 During the Upgrade

There is not much difference between the upgrade of a BW system and any other SAP system. Data is imported, data dictionary modifications need to be dealt with in the shadow instance, and the final switch to the new release is made during the downtime phases of the upgrade

Downtime-Minimized versus Resource-Minimized: A BW Perspective

With System Switch Upgrade and the downtime-minimized upgrade strategy, the BW system (as with the other SAP systems) can be used up to the beginning of downtime. From a BW perspective, this refers to the capability to execute queries against the BW system. BW operations such as data loading, data and BW administration, and query building should cease at the start of the upgrade. These activities create objects in the data dictionary and database. The development workbench will be locked during the upgrade, making such operations no longer possible (see the *Changeability of SAP BW Objects During the Upgrade* section below). If this is unacceptable, you should choose the resource-minimized upgrade strategy as it has the fastest overall runtime.

Changeability of SAP BW Objects During the Upgrade

The system is locked (set to **nonchangeable**) in the LOCKEU_PRE phase or at the latest in the REPACHK2 phase of the upgrade. This is of no concern in R/3 systems because repository objects should no longer be changed when started. This is different for BW systems because changes to InfoPackages or groups of InfoPackages are also no longer allowed. In some situations, it might make sense to make changes up to the beginning of downtime. Depending on the support package level of your source release, you are able to change some objects, InfoPackage groups, and InfoPackages until the beginning of downtime. For more information, see SAP Note 851449.

Keywords for the Add-On Upgrade

As with the ECC upgrade, the upgrade keyword (see Figure 16.6) and the Solution Manager Key is requested in the PREPARE process. The keywords of the add-ons are requested at the beginning of the upgrade. (The browser opens at the same time, showing Note 086985.)

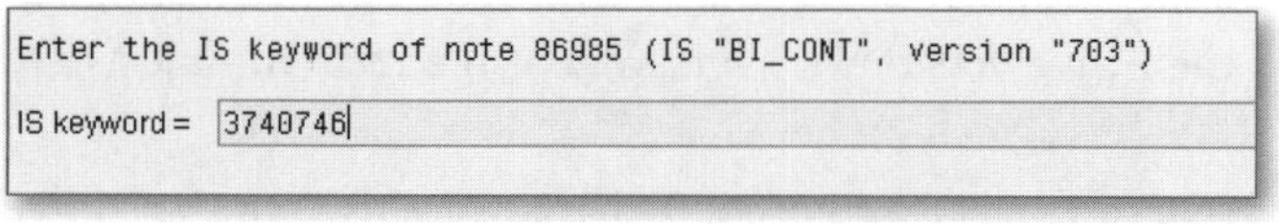

```
Enter the IS keyword of note 86985 (IS "BI_CONT", version "703")

IS keyword =  3740746
```

Figure 16.6 SAPup: Keyword for the Add-on BI_CONT

The passwords are given in Table 16.2. Note 86985 is just a reference note.

Add-On	Note	Keyword
BI_CONT 7.03	916834	3740746
FINBASIS 600	852448	4735387
SEM-BW 600	852448	No keyword requested

Table 16.2 Upgrade Keywords

16.3 Upgrade Postprocessing for SAP BW

Most of the postprocessing actions applicable to SAP ECC also apply to SAP BW (see Chapter 11 for more information on the postprocessing activities for SAP ECC).

In addition, the following postprocessing actions are BW-specific and should probably be left in the hands of an experienced BW administrator or BW consultant. These activities are discussed in detail in the Upgrade Component Guide for SAP NetWeaver 2004s Business Intelligence.

16.3.1 BW Post-processing Actions

1. As of BW 3.5, BW is a component of SAP NetWeaver, and the area menu is no longer set automatically in the NetWeaver components. You can use Transaction SSM2 to set it manually. Set area menu **RSG00** for BI or **UG00** for SEM (Strategic Enterprise Management).

2. If you want to use the BEx Web in SAP BW 3.x, you have to convert the Web objects (Web templates,query views, Web items, and Web reports [URLs]) from BW2.x to 3.x immediately after the upgrade. The Web objects that are delivered for SAP BW 3.x with the BW Business Content are already delivered in the new structures. The new Business Content objects (Web templates, Web items, query views) are installed during the normal content installation. In your system, only the active versions (A versions) of the content objects are converted.

3. The conversion of chart settings is required, if charts were used in the source release.

4. The design of Web items and templates have changed considerably. If you have used them, they must be converted to the new format.

5. Switching to the new template for ad-hoc analysis.

6. Followup activities for the enterprise data warehousing scenarios.

7. For SAP NetWeaver 2004s, fixed values for hierarchy versions have changed. To avoid problems when working with hierarchy nodes, you must activate all hierarchy versions again with the program `RRINCLTAB_REBUILD`.

When performing the BI-specific postprocessing actions, keep in mind that with SAP NetWeaver 7.0, the following terminology changes have been made in the area of data warehousing:

1. The Administrator Workbench is now called *Data Warehousing Workbench*.
2. The ODS object is now called the *DataStore object*.
3. The transactional ODS object is now called *DataStore object for direct update*.
4. The transactional InfoCube is now called *real time InfoCube*.
5. The RemoteCube, SAP RemoteCube, and virtual InfoCube with services are now referred to as *virtualProviders*.
6. The monitor is now called the *extraction monitor*, to distinguish it from the other monitors.
7. OLAP statistics are now called *BI Runtime Statistics*.
8. The reporting authorizations are now called *analysis authorizations*. We use the term *standard authorizations* to distinguish authorizations from the standard authorization concept for SAP NetWeaver from the analysis authorizations in BI.

You may still come across instances of the old terminology in the documentation.

16.3.2 Installing the Java Components

The J2EE engine is an integral part of SAP BI. Whether it is used largely depends on the business scenario you are upgrading to. When upgrading, two different cases exist, depending on your system landscape in the source release:

▶ A J2EE Engine 6.40 existed in the source release. A double-stacked upgrade was done. The J2EE engine has been upgraded to 7.00. No further actions are needed.

▶ The J2EE engine does not exist, or there is an installation of a 6.20 J2EE engine on the source release. In both cases, install the J2EE engine as described in the installation guide for your platform. If a J2EE Engine 6.20 exists, it will be replaced with the J2EE Engine 7.00 during the installation.

With the multitude of components attached to SAP's SCM solution, the upgrade procedure is a little more demanding than for some other solutions. In this chapter, we explain the ins and outs of upgrading APO and the other SCM components.

17 Upgrade of SAP SCM

SAP Supply Chain Management (SAP SCM) is part of the SAP Business Suite group of products. The current version, SCM 5.0, is built on the SAP NetWeaver 2004s platform (SAP NetWeaver Application Server 7.00).

SAP SCM comprises the following applications:

▶ APO (Advanced Planning and Optimization)

▶ ICH (Inventory Collaboration Hub)

▶ EM (Event Management)

▶ F&R (Forecasting and Replenishment)

▶ EWM (Extended Warehouse Management)

Describing these components and the business process scenarios that can be implemented using them falls outside the scope of this book. There is a good presentation about the architecture of SAP SCM on the SAP Service Marketplace at *http://service.sap.com/SCM • SAP SCM Technology • Architecture Overview*. You can also consult the Master Guide for SCM 5.0, which you find at *http://service.sap.com/INSTGUIDES*.

In practice, most SCM systems you are likely to encounter use the APO component. This chapter will concentrate on upgrading APO systems, not just because they are so widespread but mainly because upgrading APO poses some specific challenges.

17.1 Upgrading SCM APO

We begin by providing some background information on the components of APO and on the approach to an APO upgrade.

17.1.1 Components of APO

From a technical perspective, an SCM APO system contains several software components that have an impact on the technical upgrade process:

1. APO systems have a built-in BI (Business Intelligence) component. Several, though not all, APO modules — for example, Demand Planning — actively use BI functionality.

2. In addition to the standard relational database, APO systems also require a second database, the liveCache. liveCache is an *In-Memory Database Management System*, which means that in normal operation, all data is loaded into the main memory of the server (with persistent storage of the data on disk volumes). When data is loaded into the liveCache, its representation is also changed. Instead of the normal relational format, which would require complex traversals of many tables via key relations, an object-based representation is used. This is known as the *Object Management Store* (OMS). Only a small fraction of the data in the liveCache is stored in relational tables.

   Technologically the liveCache is built on the MaxDB (former SAP DB) database platform, with which it shares many architectural features (although not its memory-centric and object-based nature). liveCache also uses the database administration tools as MaxDB.

3. Many APO systems also use an Optimizer. The Optimizer is a set of programs and libraries designed to run complex, processing-intensive algorithms, such as linear programming. Because of its "number cruncher" nature, the Optimizer is normally installed on a separate server, typically a workstation with very fast CPUs. The Optimizer software exists only for Windows platforms. If the main APO system runs on a different OS such as iSeries or UNIX, then a separate Windows-based computer is needed for the Optimizer.

When you upgrade an SCM APO system, you must take all three special characteristics (BI, liveCache, Optimizer) into account. How to deal with BI-specific upgrade issues is the subject of Chapter 16 of this book, but the upgrades of the liveCache and Optimizer will be described later in this chapter.

17.1.2 Upgrade of liveCache and Optimizer

As part of the upgrade to SCM 5.0, the liveCache will be upgraded to release 7.6. The liveCache upgrade happens during the downtime phase. At the start of downtime, the contents of the liveCache are unloaded to temporary tables in the relational database. After the liveCache upgrade, the data is reloaded and verified. We'll return to these activities in more detail later.

The Optimizer consists only of executable programs and libraries. Technically speaking, you do not actually upgrade it but simply replace the old version with the new one (or install the new version next to the old one). Communication between the APO system and the Optimizer occurs via a standalone SAP gateway installed on the Optimizer server. You may choose to upgrade this gateway as well, although this is not a requirement. The gateway installation files are on the Presentation DVD (the DVD that also includes the SAP GUI).

17.1.3   Integration with R/3

Another important aspect is the tight integration of a company's APO systems with its R/3 and ERP systems. There is an intense exchange of data in both directions between R/3 and APO via the *CIF (Core Interface)*, which is itself built on the SAP Plug-In (PI) technology. Data consistency is very critical in the context of APO and must be maintained at two levels:

▶ Internally within the system, that is, between the relational database and the liveCache

▶ Externally between APO and the connected R/3 system.

Before, during, and after the upgrade, several actions are required to check and preserve the consistency of the system.

17.1.4   Functional Aspects During the Technical Upgrade

Every upgrade of a SAP system involves certain "functional" — as opposed to purely technical — activities. The members of the technical upgrade team normally do not have the knowledge and skills to carry out these activities and therefore have to call upon other resources (application specialists, developers, key users) to assist them.

This is a general rule, but in our experience it applies even more strongly to APO systems. APO is a complex field that demands extensive and specialized knowledge. People with such knowledge must be available to advise and assist, especially during the preparatory phase and of course also during post-upgrade evaluation and testing. We can assure you that without such people, you will be lost; you will be unable to judge whether a certain activity is necessary, unable to carry it out, unable to evaluate its result, and definitely unable to correct any resulting errors or exception conditions.

In practice, we have never had any problem with this. APO users and administrators are pretty high-level, and we have never run into a lack of good in-house knowledge of the application. In most cases, a functional APO consultant is also on site, or at least reachable, during the first upgrade and normally also for the production upgrade. Make sure that you identify these people in time and that you have them on board, not full time but available at short notice. Also request (well, ask politely) that they keep up the same documentation standards as those used for the technical upgrade. Either merge their documentation into your own, or at least use hyperlinks in the upgrade control document so that the functional documentation can be retrieved easily, and nothing gets lost. Note in the control document *who* does *what when*, so that the availability of the functional specialists during later upgrades can be well planned in advance.

17.2   Preparatory Actions

The basic upgrade method for SCM APO systems is the same as for the other SAP NetWeaver and SAP Business Suite products, so the instructions in Chapters 6 and 7 are applicable. However, there are a few specific factors that you must be aware of.

17.2.1   Additional Documents and Notes

In addition to the Upgrade Guides for SCM 5.0 and the upgrade notes for SCM 5.0 and SAP NetWeaver 2004s, you will also need the following:

▶ The Upgrade Guide for the liveCache. You find the guide at *http://service.sap.com/INSTGUIDES • SAP Business Suite Applications • SAP SCM • Using SAP SCM Server 5.0 • Upgrade – SAP liveCache Technology on <platform> – SR 2*. There are separate guides for UNIX and Windows. Make sure that you download the *upgrade* and not the *installation* guide.

▶ SAP Note 832561 (upgrade note for liveCache 7.6).

▶ SAP Note 857475 (upgrade note for SCM 5.0 Optimizer); there is no Upgrade Guide for the optimizer because the upgrade procedure is almost trivial.

17.2.2   Additional Upgrade Media

To upgrade the liveCache, you need the NetWeaver 2004s SR2 liveCache 7.6.0 DVD for the OS platform of the liveCache server. You find the DVD in the download area for the SCM 5.0 installation and upgrade media: *http://service.sap.com/SWDC • Installations and Upgrades • SAP Application Components • SAP SCM • SAP SCM 5.0 • Installation and Upgrade • <O/S platform> • Database*.

Make sure that you select the medium for the OS of the liveCache server, if the liveCache is running on a different platform than the APO system itself.

17.2.3 SAP Plug-In (PI) Version in R/3 Backend Systems

On backend systems, the version of the SAP Plug-In (PI) must be PI 2004_1 with Support Package >= 10. This applies to R/3, R/3 Enterprise, and SAP ERP 2004 (ECC 5.0) systems where the PI is still a separate component. In SAP ERP 2005 (ECC 6.0), the PI is part of the basis system and therefore no restriction applies.

If the PI in the backend systems currently has a lower version, it must be upgraded before the SCM 5.0 upgrade. It is crucial that you determine as early as possible whether this PI upgrade will be needed because many companies see it as a critical component (it is used for all types of integration between SAP systems, not just for the APO CIF). Planning and performing the PI upgrade is not a routine task that you can get organized in the short run.

> **Caution**
>
> Don't confuse the SAP Plug-in (PI) with the Basis Plug-In (PI_BASIS). In R/3 Enterprise and SAP ERP 2004 systems, both are installed. There is no minimum version requirement for the PI_BASIS.

17.2.4 liveCache No Longer Supported on 32-Bit

You find the list of supported platforms and OS versions in the Platform Availability Matrix at *http://service.sap.com/PAM* • *SAP Application Components* • *SAP SCM* • *SAP SCM 5.0*. Go to the **Operating systems** tab, and then the **SAP live-Cache** tab.

If the current APO release is 3.0A, 3.10, or 4.0, then you should note that 32-bit platforms are no longer supported for the liveCache. For example, if you must upgrade an APO 3.0A system with the liveCache on a Windows 32-bit server, then the liveCache must be migrated to a 64-bit platform.

The following scenarios are possible for the transition to 64-bit liveCache:

▶ **APO release is 3.10 or 4.0**
  You can migrate the current liveCache to 64-bit before the upgrade. Both UNIX and Windows IA64 (Itanium) platforms are supported. Windows x_64 (AMD64) platforms are not supported, however. If this is the target platform for the liveCache, then you must install the target liveCache on the 64-bit platform during the upgrade (in downtime, at phase REQ_LCUPG).

▶ **APO release is 3.0**
  Only UNIX is supported as a 64-bit platform for the liveCache. If you want to migrate to 64-bit Windows, then you install the target liveCache on the 64-bit platform during the upgrade (in downtime, at phase REQ_LCUPG).

17.2.5 Support Package Stacks

Like for any other upgrade, you will normally include the latest support package stack (that is, latest at the time of the first upgrade). The upgrade media for SCM 5.0 Support Release 2 already contain Support Package Stack 06. Therefore, you must only download and extract the difference between the latest stack and Stack 06.

Some specific remarks for the SCM stack are in order here.

Include liveCache and Optimizer Patch

On the screen where you select the kernel and IGS (Internet Graphics Server), you will see additional nodes for the liveCache and liveCache Applications (LCA)[1] (node SAP LC/LCAPPS) and for the Optimizer (see Figure 17.1).

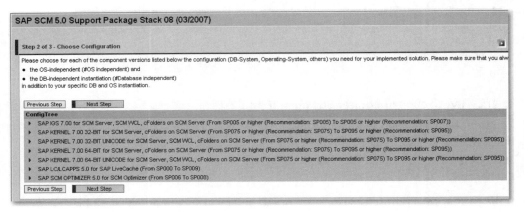

Figure 17.1 liveCache and Optimizer in SP Stack Selection

Don't forget to select these two components. Also make sure that the LC/LCAPPS component is listed. We have known cases where this component did not appear (SAP Note 1004491 describes a similar issue, but we experienced it with target Stack 07 as well), forcing us to download the liveCache package separately. Should this be necessary for some reason, you can find this package at *http://service.sap.com/PATCHES • SAP Application Components • SAP SCM • SAP SCM 5.0 • Entry by Component • SAP liveCache • SAP LC/LCAPPS 5.0.*

When you do this, be aware that the liveCache Support Package number is normally *one higher* than the number of the corresponding SCM SP Stack; for example, SCM stack 08 contains liveCache Support Package 09. Check the Release Information Note (RIN) for the SCM SP Stack to make sure that you download the

---

1 The liveCache Applications (LCA) are stored procedures running inside the liveCache. Until APO 3.x, they were generally known as *COM routines*.

correct package. If you use the liveCache package with the same number as that of the SCM Stack, the system will be in an unsupported state!

The download path for the Optimizer packages is *http://service.sap.com/PATCHES • SAP Application Components • SAP SCM • SAP SCM 5.0 • Entry by Component • SCM Optimizer • SAP SCM Optimizer 5.0 • (Windows platform).*

Java Packages Included

When selecting a support package stack for SCM, you cannot restrict the selection to specific components or usage types like you can with SAP NetWeaver or SAP ERP. As a result, the selected package list always includes Java packages (extension .sca, sometimes .jar) as well. If the APO system does not have a Java stack, you do not need to download these.

Minimum Set of Components

The components for which you should apply support packages in a pure APO system (no other SCM applications in use) are the following:

- SAP_ABA
- SAP_BASIS
- SAP_BW
- SAP_AP
- PI_BASIS
- LCAPPS
- EA-IPPE
- SCM
- SCM_BASIS
- QIE
- BI_CONT
- ST-PI

Some components may have no patches listed because there is no difference between the SR 2 delivery (SPS 06) and the target support package stack that you have selected.

> **Caution**
>
> Do not bind SAP_BW Support Packages 11, 12, or 13 as the highest SP into the upgrade because this will cause an error in phase SHADOW_IMPORT_UPG2 (see SAP Note 1013807). If you accidentally do bind one of these packages for SAP_BW as the highest support package into the upgrade and the error consequently occurs, open a support

message with SAP to ask for a remedy. Don't accept the answer that the problem is irre-coverable and that you must restart the upgrade; there *is* a workaround (to be applied by SAP support only!).

17.2.6 BW-Specific Preparations

Chapter 4 of the Upgrade Guide describes some preparatory activities for the BW objects in the system. The most important of these is "Converting Inconsistent Characteristic Values," also known as the *alpha conversion*. This is a critical activity not just because of its impact on the data, but also because it requires pre-upgrade downtime (logical downtime, i.e., the system is technically up and running, but no end user access is allowed). The alpha conversion applies only to APO start Releases 3.0 and 3.1 (i.e., releases with a built-in BW 2.x).

17.2.7 SCM-Specific Preparations

Chapters 3 and 4 of the Upgrade Guide also list several preparations specifically for SCM. There aren't very many of these, but you will need the input of a functional specialist to know whether they are applicable and to take corrective actions if errors occur.

An activity that you must carry out at any rate if you use the APO modules concerned is "Planning the Upgrade of DP/SNP Macro Books." Detailed instructions are in the SCM Upgrade Guide (Chapter 3). The program to analyze the macro books, /SAPAPO/ADV_UPGRADE_50, does not come with the upgrade tools but with a support package for the source release. You can find the required support package level as well as extensive information on the checks performed by the program in Note 865333; you can also use this note to create the program if you do not have the required support package in the source system yet.

17.2.8 Other Preparations

The other preparations are mostly the same as for other upgrades; simply follow Chapter 4 of the SCM Upgrade Guide.

17.3 Program /SAPAPO/OM_LC_UPGRADE_50

For every SCM release since 4.0, SAP provides an ABAP program to assist with the upgrade of the data in the liveCache. For the upgrade to SCM 5.0 this program is called /SAPAPO/OM_LC_UPGRADE_50. PREPARE and SAPup will stop at the appropriate moments and prompt you to carry out the relevant part of the program.

17.3.1 Program sections

/SAPAPO/OM_LC_UPGRADE_50 is divided into four Sections: A, B, C, and D. These sections are further subdivided into individual action steps. The actions in phase A are executed during the PREPARE. Phase B actions are carried out at the beginning of the upgrade downtime. Phase C occurs near the end of the upgrade downtime; at this point, you will also upgrade the liveCache. Phase D cleans up the temporary storage tables used during the upgrade; the only action in this phase (empty the tables) can be performed weeks or months after the upgrade.

Calling the program is simple. PREPARE or SAPup will stop and request that you carry out all the steps for a specific section (A-B-C). Figure 17.2 shows the PREPARE screen that prompts for the execution of phase A. Do not reply in this screen until you have performed all the steps in the phase. When done, you may click on **Continue**.

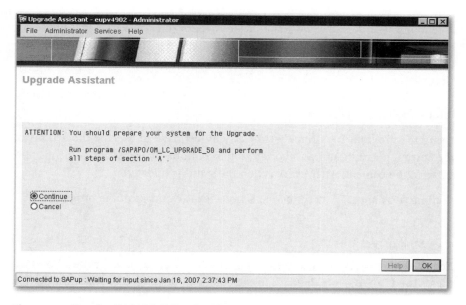

Figure 17.2 Stop for /SAPAPO/OM_LC_UPGRADE_50

When prompted to do so by PREPARE or SAPup, log on to the SAP system (fully authorization user in the *production* client, not in client 000). Call Transaction SE38, and execute /SAPAPO/OM_LC_UPGRADE_50. The selection screen (see Figure 17.3) shows the phases and the individual actions.

You start an action step by clicking its button. Actions that are not allowed in the present situation are grayed out, and you cannot invoke the underlying action. On the right of each button, there is a traffic light icon and a status message.

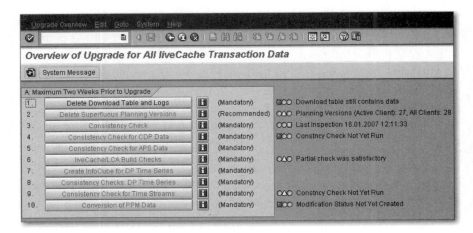

Figure 17.3 Selection Screen of /SAPAPO/OM_LC_UPGRADE_50

A red light indicates that the action has not yet been executed or that the status of the action is not correct in function of the upgrade. A yellow light indicates that the action has been executed, but that some condition exists that needs closer attention. Finally, a green light means that the action was completely successful. The **I** (information) icon opens a concise help window that gives more information about an action.

Using the program is extremely simple; you just have to execute the actions of the current phase in numerical order, top to bottom. The selection screen is sensitive to the context: After every action the status is updated.

Sections 17.4 and 17.7 describe the actions for each phase of the program.

17.3.2 Corrections

Before using the program, you must apply a series of corrective notes. You find these listed in SAP Note 932837. In the course of the upgrade, you must do this twice:

▶ The first time in the source release before executing Section A

▶ The second time in the target release before executing Section C (which restores the data to the upgraded liveCache)

You can apply the corrections for the source release when PREPARE stops for Section A (described next) and before running the program. Some of the corrections are supplied in the fix buffer; no further action is needed because you must always use the latest fix buffer in every upgrade. The notes not included in the fix buffer can be applied using the SAP Note Assistant (Transaction SNOTE).

Implementing the corrections for the target release is trickier. At the stop for Section C, the upgrade is still in downtime, and the system is locked for modifications and transports. In those circumstances, you cannot use SNOTE. Note 809504 has the solution, which is to slightly delay executing Section C until the upgrade has unlocked the system. We return to this later when we describe the activities for Section C.

17.4   PREPARE and Uptime Part of Upgrade

This section deals with the APO-specific steps to follow while the system is still productive in the old release.

17.4.1   /SAPAPO/OM_LC_UPGRADE_50 — Section A

In phase REQ_APOUPG0, PREPARE stops and requests that you execute the actions in Section A. The stop occurs at the beginning of the PREPARE module *Necessary checks for conversion*. According to the Upgrade Guide, Section A should be carried out at most two weeks before the upgrade.

Apply Correction Notes

As mentioned previously, start by applying the corrections for Section A listed in SAP Note 932837 (except the ones already integrated into the fix buffer).

Start /SAPAPO/OM_LC_UPGRADE_50

Log on to the APO production client, run the program via Transaction SE38, and carry out all activities listed under **Section A** in the order shown.

We give a brief description of the steps in the following paragraphs. The paragraph header corresponds to the name of the activity on the control screen of the program, followed by its sequence number (A1, A2, etc.).

The information we provide here concentrates on how to run the activity and on the way it behaves. For functional background, use the step descriptions in Chapter 4 of the SCM Upgrade Guide; for several actions, you also get useful information by clicking on the **I** (Information) icon to the right of the action button.

Delete Download Table and Logs (Action A1)

This step deletes data and logs left over from previous upgrades (the technique of saving the liveCache data in temporary tables in the relational database existed also for upgrades to SCM 4.0 and 4.1).

Confirm the pop-up window. The operation usually takes only a few seconds. Another pop-up appears at the end.

Delete Superfluous Planning Versions (A2)

This step is optional but strongly recommended because it can save significant time. During the upgrade downtime, the liveCache data of all planning versions is first saved and later reloaded and verified. If planning versions exist that are no longer needed, then you should delete these beforehand. Obviously, it is not up to the technical team to decide which planning versions can be discarded; you must ask the functional APO team to look into this and to do the deletions.

If the amount of data in the liveCache is small, which is often true in development systems, then you need not bother. However, in the QA and certainly in the production system, a proactive cleanup of the planning versions is almost always a good idea.

Consistency Check (A3)

This step invokes the standard Transaction /SAPAPO/OM17 for the internal consistency check (database versus liveCache) but without the options to suspend activity in APO (e.g., locking the users). The step is mandatory but may be skipped if the status is already green, which means that a consistency check was already run sometime in the past 24 hours. Most APO installations have a procedure in place to run /SAPAPO/OM17 regularly.

Background information on the consistency check is in SAP Note 425825.

Proceed as follows to run the check:

1. Mark all the check boxes.
2. Select the planning versions.
3. Execute in the foreground or in the background.

If you choose background execution, jobs named SYNC_LC_DB_<area> run in parallel. You can further divide the work, for instance, by scheduling one background run for planning version 000 and another for all other planning versions.

To analyze the result, choose **Evaluate Last Background Job** or **Evaluate Any Background Job**. All errors reported by the consistency check must be reviewed and, if necessary, corrected by the APO specialists. Correction options (**Correct Selected Inconsistencies** and **Correct All Inconsistencies**) are available on the transaction screen, but refrain from clicking on these buttons if you don't know what the effect will be.

Note that some errors may occur because the consistency check runs together with ongoing activity in the system. This might lead to errors like the following:

```
Product Allocations    92 errors    Surplus of incoming orders quantity
```

The consistency check will be repeated at the beginning of the upgrade downtime after productive activity in APO has ceased.

Consistency Check for CDP Data (A4)

The check of the CDP (*Characteristics Dependent Planning*) data is mandatory.

A frequent event with this step is that you get a red status with the message `Number range object IB_SYM_ID missing`. In this case, proceed as follows (instructions based on SAP Note 203446):

1. Log on to the client mentioned in the error message; if the error is reported for multiple clients, you will have to perform the action in each of them.
2. Call Transaction SNRO, specify the object `IB_SYM_ID`, and click on **Number ranges**.
3. Choose **Change Intervals · Insert Interval** (button with green "+" sign).
4. Fill in the **Insert Interval** pop-up window:
   ▸ Number range number = 01
   ▸ Interval: from number = 000000000001
   ▸ to number = 999999999999
5. Click on the **Insert** icon in the lower-left corner of the window, and save. Confirm the message about number range intervals not being saved in transport requests.
6. Repeat the consistency check; the error should no longer occur.

Consistency Check for Activities Data (A5)

The check of the APS (*Advanced Planning and Scheduling*) data is mandatory.

You must execute the check for each planning version separately. Refer to the instructions in the SCM Upgrade Guide if errors are reported. Note that there is no traffic light in the main window to indicate the check status.

liveCache/LCA Build Checks (A6)

This calls /SAPAPO/OM13, the standard verification transaction for the liveCache and liveCache Applications (LCA). Verify the status indicators under the **Checks** tab. Red and yellow conditions must be checked and corrected, especially if they concern RFC connections. Because the check is only partial, the status in the /SAPAPO/OM_LC_UPGRADE_50 menu always remains yellow.

Create InfoCube for DP Time Series (A7)

Source Release 3.0 or 3.1

When upgrading from APO 3.0 or 3.1 to 4.0, DP (Demand Planning) or SNP (Supply Network Planning) time series data must be saved to an InfoCube in the APO system. To do this, it is possible to either use an existing InfoCube or create a new one specifically for the purpose. If the APO team decides to use a new InfoCube, then it must be created now at the latest (it is also acceptable to create it earlier).

You need the cooperation of the functional team for this action; they must decide what data to save and how. Many APO sites already have a procedure in place to save time series data into an InfoCube so the functional experts will probably be on familiar ground here.

Source Release 4.0 or 4.1

This function only brings up an information pop-up.

As of release SCM 4.0, DP and SNP time series data is saved automatically during the upgrade with the liveCache transaction data (step B1) and is then reloaded again (step C7). This means the runtime-intensive method using InfoCubes is no longer required, and you no longer have to execute steps A7, B2, or C10.

As the message makes clear, no action is needed.

Consistency check DP Time Series (A8)

Starting this activity brings up a window with three subfunctions (see Figure 17.4):

▶ **Consistency Check: DP Time Series**
Select the planning version. You may want to disable the fields **Lock planning version** and **Repair**, especially in production systems. If errors are reported, invoke the help of the APO specialists and let them decide whether you can run the check again with the **Repair** flag switched on.

▶ **Consistency Check: DP Time Series SNP**

You must specify a planning area and planning version. Proceed as in the previous case, that is, the first time run with the **Lock** and **Repair** options disabled. In case of errors, repeat under control of the APO functional team with **Repair** enabled.

▶ **Consistency Check: Time Series Networks**

This action performs a full check without bringing up a selection screen. The program is likely to run for several minutes. At the end, a result screen appears with the status of all checks for all areas (see Figure 17.5). Any error (red) conditions must be tackled by the APO functional team. Some of these errors are harmless, but that is for the APO specialists to decide.

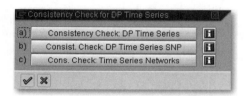

Figure 17.4 Functions for DP Time Series Consistency Check

If an error is reported for the **Storage buckets profile check** (see Figure 17.5), then SAP Note 892482 must be applied.

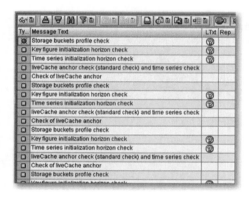

Figure 17.5 Result Screen for Time Series Networks Consistency Check

Consistency Check for Time Streams (A9)

There is no selection screen for this activity; you will simply see the message Jobs were scheduled. A background job OM_UPGR_TSTR_CHECK_<client>_ <plvers> is created per planning version. Wait until all jobs complete. At that point, refresh the screen in /SAPAPO/OM_LC_UPGRADE_50; the status of the action will become green.

To display the application logs of the consistency check, call Transaction SLG1, and specify object APO and subobject UPGRADE (see Figure 17.6).

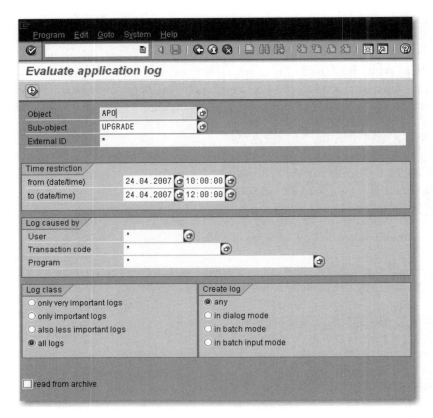

Figure 17.6 Display Application Logs of Consistency Check

Conversion of PPM Data (A10)

A pop-up opens asking "Do you now want to start the report for the final UTC conversion status determination?"; answer **Yes**.

If you receive the message Evaluation of all clients not yet executed -> see log, proceed as follows (after obtaining the consent of the APO team):

1. In the production client, call Transaction SE38.

2. Execute the report /SAPAPO/PPM_UTC_PREPARE_DATA02.

3. Choose **Convert all PPMS**.

4. The pop-up **All PPMs converted into UTC time format during upgrade** appears.

5. Repeat this in the other clients, including client 000.

6. Refresh the window: The status must now change from red to yellow (`Modi-fication status created for the individual clients`).

Run /SAPAPO/OM_TS_LCCONS (Extra Step)

According to the main SCM upgrade note (961512) you must also run an extra consistency check for time series data. For this, follow the instructions in SAP Note 1007367.

17.4.2   Resume PREPARE

After completing all steps of Section A, resume PREPARE by choosing **Continue**. Proceed as with the other upgrade scenarios, repeating the failed PREPARE modules until no more errors remain.

17.5   Actions Between PREPARE and the Start of the Upgrade

No specific SCM-related activities occur between the end of PREPARE and the beginning of the upgrade, although you may choose to carry out certain actions, such as the analysis of the macro books (see Section 17.2.7) at this time rather than before starting PREPARE.

A BW-related activity that you must execute before starting the upgrade is activating all objects in the ODS (Operational Data Source) in the APO system. For this, proceed as follows:

1. Call Transaction SE38, and run program `RSDG_ODSO_ACTIVATE`.

2. Enter "*" for the ODS object selection; do not leave the field empty.

3. Mark **Only Check — No Activation**.

4. All objects must be reported as consistent. If not, run the program again with the check box unmarked.

Perform all other activities as described in the SCM Upgrade Guide and upgrade notes.

17.6 Uptime Part of Upgrade

There are no specific activities or user dialogs for SCM in the uptime part of the upgrade, so the procedure for this part of the process is not different from that of other upgrades.

17.7 Downtime Part of Upgrade

In downtime-minimized mode, the upgrade downtime for SCM starts in the phase REQSTOP_APO3. This is different from other upgrades, where the transition from uptime to downtime happens in phase MODPROF_TRANS. In practice, REQSTOP_APO3 and MODPROF_TRANS lie very close to one another.

When SAPup reaches the phase REQSTOP_APO3, it stops with the following prompt:

```
ATTENTION: After locking the system during the next phase,
           the SAP system will be restarted.
           All productive operations have to be stopped then.
```

You must then let the upgrade wait until the beginning of the planned downtime period. When the downtime has arrived, proceed as explained in the following sections.

17.7.1 Enter Downtime

When entering the downtime, perform the following steps:

1. Stop all user activity. The upgrade process automatically suspends background jobs when downtime starts. However it can be useful to review the list of planned jobs and to manually change from **Released** to **Scheduled** those jobs that must be released after the upgrade in controlled fashion rather than via the mass release with BTCTRNS2.

2. Have the system administrator or the APO team stop the CIF queues in the APO system and in the backend systems. The instructions for this are in the SCM Upgrade Guide, but the local administrators will probably have their own guidelines for this.

3. When all activity has stopped, and the queues are closed, choose **Continue** in the UA GUI window.

4. On the next screen, confirm that the system may be locked.

5. SAPup reports that the SAP system will now be shut down; confirm this.

The system is stopped and restarted. Very shortly after this, SAPup stops and informs you that you must now carry out Section B of the upgrade program /SAPAPO/OM_LC_UPGRADE_50.

17.7.2 /SAPAPO/OM_LC_UPGRADE_50 — Section B

Section B of program /SAPAPO/OM_LC_UPGRADE_50 is executed at the beginning of downtime; the system is no longer available for productive use in the old release. The most important activity in Section B is saving the contents of the liveCache to backup tables in the APO database.

Repeat Consistency Checks

Carry out the different consistency checks that you already ran (but with concurrent activity in the system) during Section A. The functional APO team is best placed to do this.

Check Space in the Database

The download table for the liveCache data is called /SAPAPO/OM_UPGR. In databases with tablespaces (DB2, Oracle) this table resides in the BTABD space (the name can vary, e.g., PSAPBTABD or PSAP<SID> in Oracle, and <SID>#BTABD in DB2). The data is compressed so it will occupy less space than the data volume in the liveCache. For the first upgrade in a system with a production-size liveCache, make a note of the data volume in the liveCache and of the physical size of the /SAPAPO/OM_UPGR table after you have saved the liveCache data. You can then use this information to make sure sufficient free space will exist in the production database.

Start /SAPAPO/OM_LC_UPGRADE_50

1. Log on to the APO production client as user DDIC or SAP*. You cannot log on with another user ID, including that of the upgrade user, because the system is now locked.

2. Run the program via Transaction SE38, and carry out all activities listed under Section B in the order shown.

3. A brief description of the steps follows. As we did for Section A in Section 17.4.1, the paragraph header shows the name and sequence number of the activity.

Download liveCache Data (B1)

The download runs in the background with one dedicated job per planning version. If there are multiple planning versions, then make sure sufficient background work processes are available to provide efficient parallel processing.

1. Click the action button, and a selection screen appears:

   ▶ **Planning version**: enter "*"

   ▶ **Client-specific**: leave blank

   ▶ Choose **Execute**.

2. A job definition screen appears; specify **Immediate** start.

3. A job named /SAPAPO/OM_UPGR_DOWNLOAD starts running; this job acts as dispatcher and launches jobs named /SAPAPO/OM_UPGR_DOWNLOAD_<CLI>_<PV> (CLI = client, PV = planning version). Wait until the jobs finish, and verify their spool list. All the messages in the list should have a green status. Always look at the output; the fact that the job finishes normally and does not cancel does not mean that there are no errors or warnings.

   The download job for the active planning version 000 is likely to take the longest. The runtime of the jobs will obviously depend on the amount of data in the planning version and the performance of the server. Normally we are not talking in terms of hours here; based on our experience with SCM production upgrades, the runtime for planning version 000 is most often less than one hour.

> **Tip**
>
> ▶ Create a table in your upgrade control document with the runtime of each download job. It is very useful to have this information when you upgrade the production system.
>
> ▶ The liveCache download is a good time to already upgrade the DBM GUI; see upcoming Section 17.7.3, subsection *Upgrade the Database Manager GUI* for instructions.

When all the jobs are finished and you have verified the logs, return to the main screen of /SAPAPO/OM_LC_UPGRADE_50; the activity status must now be green.

Extract Time Series (B2)

Source Release 3.0 or 3.1

When upgrading from APO 3.0 or 3.1 to 4.0, DP or SNP time series data must be saved to an InfoCube in the APO system. During PREPARE, you were prompted in action A7 to create an InfoCube for this purpose; it is also possible to use an existing cube. You are now at the point when the time series data must be extracted and saved. General instructions for this are in the SCM Upgrade Guide, but this action should really be placed in the hands of the functional APO team. Note that the extractions may potentially run for several hours; this is an important timing factor that you must consider when planning the downtime.

Source Release 4.0 or 4.1

This function is no longer used (the button is disabled); see earlier Section 17.4.1, subsection *Create InfoCube for DP Time Series (A7)*.

Stop liveCache (B3)

This brings up the liveCache administration Transaction LC10.

Enter "LCA" for the **Connection Name,** and choose **Administration • Operating • Stop liveCache**.

Complete Backup (B4)

This button may be disabled; however, a backup of the liveCache is still strongly recommended. Back up the liveCache in **ADMIN (cold)** mode with the DBM GUI.

Resume the Upgrade and Begin Downtime Processing

You may now resume the upgrade by choosing **Continue** in the SAPup screen. The upgrade immediately stops at the "general" downtime phase MODPROF_TRANS.

1. Carry out the general steps for isolating the system just as you have for other upgrades (disable operation modes, final check on update requests in SM13, etc.).
2. Back up the APO database (you have already backed up the liveCache).
3. Back up the ABAP upgrade directory so that you can return to this point in the upgrade if a major error occurs.
4. Disable the archive logging mode of the database if necessary.
5. The liveCache is already in **ADMIN (cold)** mode. You can leave it like this or stop it altogether.
6. When you are ready with these actions, resume the upgrade, and reply to the various prompts that will appear in the UA GUI. These are the same prompts as for other upgrades; nothing here is special for SCM.

7. The downtime phases begin; as always, these will probably run for several hours. Again, the process is the same as for other upgrades. There is nothing special to do on your part on behalf of SCM.

8. A few minutes after the end of the XPRA phase, the upgrade reaches the phase REQ_LCUPG and stops with following message:

```
ATTENTION: The liveCache and optimizer can now be upgraded.
To proceed with the upgrade, you have to manually perform the steps
described in the Upgrade Guide in chapter "The Upgrade", Phase REQ_
LCUPG.
Run program /SAPAPO/OM_LC_UPGRADE_50 and perform all steps of
section 'C' in order to upload all relevant data from APO database
into liveCache.
Make sure that all jobs which upload your liveCache data (/SAPAPO/OM_
UPGR_UPLOAD*) have finshed before you proceed.
If you want to compare the data of your download with the liveCache,
make sure that all jobs which compare the data (/SAPAPO/OM_UPGR_
COMPARE*) have finished before you proceed.
```

The next few hours will bring some hard and concentrated work because next you will have to do the following:

► Upgrade the liveCache software.

► Execute Section C of /SAPAPO/SAPAPO/OM_LC_UPGRADE_50, which includes reloading and verifying the liveCache data.

► Install the new Optimizer.

17.7.3   liveCache Upgrade

For this activity, you will need the Upgrade Guide and upgrade note for live-Cache version 7.6; see Section 17.2.1 earlier for information on where to find these documents.

Upgrade Methods

In general, there are two methods for upgrading the liveCache:

► With an *inplace upgrade,* only the liveCache software is replaced. The live-Cache database itself remains intact.

► With an *extract/load upgrade,* the liveCache data is first saved in the relational APO database. The liveCache software is upgraded, and the existing liveCache database structures are overwritten and reinitialized. After the upgrade, the data is reloaded from the backup tables into the liveCache.

When upgrading to SCM 5.0, you always use the extract/load method. In fact, you already carried out the first step — saving the liveCache data in the APO database — when you did Section B of the upgrade utility at the beginning of the downtime. The second step, the actual liveCache upgrade, is what you are about to do now. The final step, reloading the data, is part of the Section C process that will be covered later.

Upgrade the Database Manager GUI

To manage the new version of the liveCache, you need version 7.6 of the Database Manager GUI (DBM GUI), the graphical administration tool for MaxDB and liveCache. The DBM GUI does not reside on the liveCache server but on the workstation(s) of the administrators; hence, it does not get upgraded along with the liveCache software on the server.

DBM GUI 7.6 is downward compatible, so check first that it has not already been installed.

You can download DBM GUI 7.6 from the SAP Service Marketplace at *http://service.sap.com/PATCHES • Entry by Application Group • Additional Components • MaxDB • MAXDB GUI Components/Tools* (caution: the correct item is "MaxDB" and not its neighbor "SAP DB").

You only need the MaxDB DBM GUI package to administer the liveCache. SQL Studio can also be quite useful, so we normally download and install that as well. SQL Studio is a graphical utility to look at relational tables in the database and to execute SQL statements interactively.

Both packages are self-extracting *.exe* files. Simply double-click on the package to start the installation. Make sure that you have local administrator rights on the PC where you do the installation; otherwise, the installation seemingly succeeds but is in fact incomplete. Reboot the PC if you are asked to do so.

After the installation, start the DBM GUI, and register the connection to the liveCache:

1. Start the DBM GUI.
2. Choose **Register**.
3. Enter the host name of the liveCache server, and click on the exclamation mark.
4. Select the liveCache from the list of MaxDB/liveCache instances on the server, and click on **Register**.

5. Enter the user name and password of the DBM user. The APO system administrator can provide this. Chances are that the user name and password are both "control".

6. Close the registration window, and check that the newly registered liveCache now appears in the top pane.

Obtain User Access on the liveCache Server

For the liveCache upgrade, you must log in on the server as a user with local administration rights (Windows) or as `root` (UNIX)[2]. Access with the liveCache administrator account (user `<lcsid>adm`) is *not* enough.

Stop Other liveCache and MaxDB Instances on the Server

If the liveCache server of the upgrade system also runs other instances of live-Cache or MaxDB, then all these instances must be stopped. This is relevant for servers with more than one liveCache (e.g., APO development and APO QA sharing the same host) or servers with at least one MaxDB installation (SAP systems using MaxDB but also the SAP Content Server, for example). Make sure that this is foreseen in the planning, especially if production systems or other systems with strict uptime requirements are affected.

Changes to Users and Groups (UNIX)

The instructions here apply only to UNIX (including Linux) servers. Starting with MaxDB release 7.5, critical database resources are better protected from unauthorized access by assigning the ownership of these resources to a special OS user (named `sdb`) and an OS group (`sdba`). The user `sdb` must then be locked so that this user ID cannot log on to the server.

If users and groups are managed directly on the server (i.e., no central management system such a NIS [Network Information Service] or LDAP [Lightweight Directory Access Protocol] is in use), then the liveCache upgrade script will create the user and group with the proper settings. If users and groups are managed centrally, or if (as happened to us a few times) the upgrade script runs into an error when it tries creating the user and group, then you must do this manually before the liveCache upgrade:

---

2 If you are an external consultant or contractor, then it is possible that you will be denied `root` access on legal grounds, for example, because of provisions under the Sarbanes-Oxley Act. In that case, your only choice is to ask an authorized user to carry out the liveCache upgrade under your guidance. It is *not* possible to do the upgrade without `root` privileges.

1. Create the user `sdb`.

2. Create the group `sdba`.

3. Make `sdb` and the liveCache administration user `<lcsid>adm` members of the `sdba` group.

4. Owners of other liveCache or MaxDB instances with release below 7.5 must also be made members of the `sdba` group.

5. Lock the user `sdb`.

The commands and utilities for managing UNIX users and groups vary between platforms. Ask the system administrator of the UNIX server to do this or to assist you. If you have to do the job yourself without help, then you can use the following information sources:

▶ The *Installation Guide* (not the Upgrade Guide) for SAP NetWeaver 2004s and your UNIX platform describes the commands to manage users and groups in the OS.

▶ The platform-dependent instructions to lock a user are listed in the liveCache Upgrade Guide.

Stop the Remote SQL Process (X Server)

Log on to the OS as the liveCache administration user (`<lcsid>adm`). Open an OS session (Telnet session for UNIX; command [CMD] shell for Windows), and enter the command

```
x_server stop
```

Execute the Upgrade Script

A shell script is used to start and control the liveCache upgrade. The script runs entirely inside a character-based terminal session; you do not need any graphical tools. The shell script is located on the liveCache upgrade medium, which should be available in your Media Directory.

Instructions for UNIX:

1. Log in as `root`.

2. Locate the script `LCUPDATE.SH` (in uppercase) in the directory where you downloaded the liveCache upgrade DVD. The script is normally in a subdirectory referring to the hardware platform.

3. Start the script (without any command-line parameters):
   ```
   LCUPDATE.SH
   ```

4. Reply to the prompts issued by the script:

   ▶ liveCache name

   ▶ DBM user and password (possibly "control" and "control"; otherwise, check with the APO administrator)

5. The upgrade files are unpacked, and the liveCache software is upgraded. At the end of the upgrade, the liveCache is in offline state.

Instructions for Windows:

1. Open a CMD window.

2. Locate the script LCUPDATE.BAT in the directory where you downloaded the liveCache upgrade DVD. The script is normally in a subdirectory referring to the hardware platform.

3. Change to this directory.

4. Start the script (with command-line parameters):

   ```
   LCUPDATE.BAT -d <LCSID> -u <DBMuser,DBMpasswd>
   [-d <tempdir>]
   ```

   LCSID is the name of the liveCache; DBMuser and DBMpasswd are the user name and password of the DBM user (possibly "control" and "control"; otherwise, check with the APO administrator).

   The optional argument -d <tempdir> is only required if you want the script to use a temporary directory other than C:\TEMP.

5. The upgrade files are unpacked, and the liveCache software is upgraded. At the end of the upgrade, the liveCache is in offline state.

Install the liveCache Client Software

The liveCache client software is necessary to allow connecting to the liveCache from other servers in the network. If the APO system is on a different server from the liveCache, then you must install the liveCache client on the APO host. If they are on the same server, then the client installation is not needed.

Proceed as follows:

1. Stop the APO system.

2. Stop any other MaxDB or liveCache instance on the same server as the APO system; if any exist, then also stop the remote SQL service (x_server stop).

3. Make sure that you can access the directory with the liveCache Upgrade DVD.

4. Run the upgrade script with the extra argument -client on the APO system:

   ▶ UNIX: LCUPDATE.SH -client

   ▶ Windows: LCUPDATE.BAT -client

Install the liveCache Patch

After upgrading the liveCache to the version delivered on the DVD, you must now apply the latest support package. Note that you cannot use the procedure described here to perform the actual liveCache upgrade to 7.6; you must first carry out the upgrade procedure as described in the previous paragraph and then apply the patch.

The patch installation does not use a shell script but instead uses the utility SDBUPD. The detailed instructions for applying the liveCache patch (both for UNIX and Windows) are in SAP Note 875662.

Start/Stop Test

At this point, it is a good idea to do a simple start/stop test for the liveCache using OS commands. In the following example, we assume that the liveCache is called "LCP" and that the DBM user and password are "control"; adapt these commands as needed. You must log on as lcpadm first:

```
dbmcli db_enum
dbmcli -d LCP -u control,control db_state
dbmcli -d LCP -u control,control db_online
dbmcli -d LCP -u control,control db_state
dbmcli -d LCP -u control,control db_offline
```

Adapt liveCache Parameters

Like for other database systems, SAP publishes recommendations for liveCache parameter settings. For version 7.6 these are in SAP Notes 719652 and 833216. After the liveCache upgrade, you must review and, where necessary, adapt the parameter settings.

To change and modify liveCache parameters, use either the DBM GUI or the OS command-line utility dbmcli.

With DBM GUI:

1. Connect to the liveCache instance.
2. Click on the **Configuration** button in the lower-left corner.
3. Open **Parameters**.
4. To change a parameter, double-click on its value.
5. Stop and restart the liveCache.

With dbmcli (we again assume liveCache is named "LCP" and DBM user and password are "control"; adapt the commands as necessary, and log in as lcpadm first):

```
dbmcli -d LCP -u control,control
> param_directgetall
> param_directput <parameter> <newvalue>
> param_checkall
> exit
```

Then stop and restart the liveCache:

```
dbmcli -d LCP -u control,control db_offline
dbmcli -d LCP -u control,control db_online
```

Final Actions

If you had to shut down other liveCache or MaxDB instances, then restart them now. If the SAP APO system was shut down for the upgrade of the liveCache client, then also restart it.

At this point, the liveCache is upgraded but still empty. You are now ready to start Section C of the /SAPAO/OM_LC_UPGRADE_50 program. Before that, you should also upgrade the Optimizer.

17.7.4 Optimizer Upgrade

The Optimizer resides on a separate Windows server, so you must log on to that server for the upgrade, for instance, via a Windows Terminal Server connection. Your user must have write access to the Optimizer directory and should preferable have local administration rights.

As mentioned earlier, there is not much to an Optimizer upgrade because it consists only of executables and libraries. In fact, all you do is replace the old version with the new or install a new version alongside the old one, if the latter is still needed.

The installation file you need is the SAR archive with the Optimizer version, which you downloaded from the SAP Service Marketplace, either as part of the support package stack or separately (see Section 17.2.5, subsection *Include live-Cache and Optimizer patch*). Transfer this file to the Optimizer server, or open a share to the Media Directory if that is possible.

The upgrade instructions are in Note 857475. They amount to little more than unpacking the SAR archive into a temporary working directory and then copying these files to a designated subdirectory of the Optimizer installation.

If you apply the note literally, then the old version of the Optimizer is overwritten by the new one. This is because the note refers to the default path *<drive>:\ APOOPT*. If you want the old and new Optimizer versions to coexist, then simply create a different path for the new version, such as *\APOOPT\SCM50* and then place the executables below that new path in subdirectories like *\APOOPT\ SCM50\DPS\BIN*, *\APOOPT\SCM50\SNP\BIN*, and so on. In that case, you must adapt the RFC destinations for the Optimizer in the SCM 5.0 system (TCP/IP destinations starting with "OPT") with Transaction SM59 so that they refer to this new path.

Other setups are also possible — in fact, with the Optimizer you are pretty much free to organize things the way you want. Another possibility is to have the development and QA system share the same 5.0 Optimizer. In that scenario, you upgrade the Optimizer at the time of the SCM development upgrade; when you upgrade the SCM QA system, all you need to do there is change the RFC destinations so that they now point to the Optimizer of the development system.

After the upgrade, do a version check from the APO system; this will also test the connection to the Optimizer server. Run Transaction /SAPAPO/OPT09 for this check. Figure 17.7 shows a system with SP04 (this screenshot does not come from an upgraded system because the support package level in SR 2 is already SP06). In addition to /SAPAPO/OPT09, also perform an Optimizer test with Transaction /SAPAPO/OPT_INST.

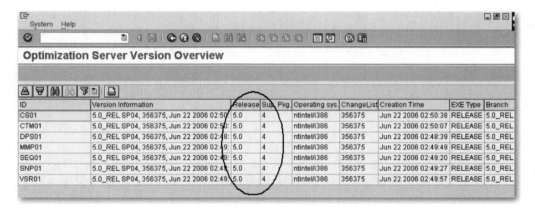

Figure 17.7 Optimizer Connection and Version Check

17.7.5 /SAPAPO/OM_LC_UPGRADE_50 — Section C

Section C is the last section whose actions you must execute during the upgrade (Section D only contains a cleanup activity and is normally not run until several weeks after the upgrade). In this section, you will reload and verify the liveCache data and in general bring the liveCache into a fit state to be used with the new SCM APO release.

Timing

In the standard procedure, you would start work in Section C immediately after you finish the liveCache upgrade. The SCM upgrade itself keeps waiting in phase REQ_LCUPG. However, if you follow the advice in SAP Note 932837, you must implement a series of note-based corrections before you start Section C; to apply these you need the SAP Note Assistant (Transaction SNOTE).

At phase REQ_LCUPG, the system is still locked, which means that no development is possible, and you cannot use SNOTE here. To work around this, you could manually unlock the system and the development workbench, but since the upgrade is very close to doing that itself, you can just as well let SAPup continue for a few phases. This is the approach described in Note 809504.

Proceed as follows if you want to defer running Section C until after the system is unlocked:

1. Choose **Continue** in the waiting UA GUI window.
2. The upgrade performs several phases that are not specific for SCM. The APO system may be stopped and restarted during this time.
3. After a few minutes, the upgrade reaches phase MODPROFP_UPG (switch from downtime back to uptime). On the first prompt, which asks you whether you have enabled database log mode, answer **Yes** (regardless of whether you enabled it or not).
4. The system is now unlocked and the following prompt is shown in the UA GUI:

   ```
   Note: All secondary application servers of SAP system <SID> can be
   restarted now.
   ```

5. Do not reply to this prompt yet; at this point, you can apply the corrections from Note 932837 with the Note Assistant and start working on Section C.

6. It is absolutely essential that no APO data arrives in the system before Section C is complete. Since logging on to the system is technically possible again, you must take precautions to prevent any unwanted activity (keep CIF files closed and users locked).

Applying Corrections

The second section of Note 932837 gives a list of all the notes that you must apply before starting Section C. Next to the number of the note to implement, you find the SCM support package into which the note is integrated. You only have to manually apply those notes whose support package level is higher than that of the support package stack bound into the upgrade.

Start /SAPAPO/OM_LC_UPGRADE_50

Log on to the APO production client If the upgrade is in phase REQ_LCUPG, the system is still locked, and you must log on as SAP* or DDIC. If you let the upgrade continue to MODPROFP_UPG, then you can use other authorized users as well, including your upgrade user.

Run the program via Transaction SE38, and carry out all activities listed under Section C in the order shown.

A brief description of the steps follows next. As for Sections A and B, the paragraph header shows the name and sequence number of the activity.

Maintain Logical Database Connection (C1)

In this step, you must maintain the database connection data for the liveCache in Transaction LC10. You must specify the liveCache name (LCSID), the host name of the liveCache server, the user name and password for the DBM user (often "CONTROL"), and the name and password of the SAP user in liveCache (named either "SAPR3" or "SAP<LCSID>"). You must do this for both logical connection names, LCA and LDA (see Figure 17.8 for an example).

If the status light for activity C1 is already green, the connection data is already correct. Verify this in Transaction LC10 anyway.

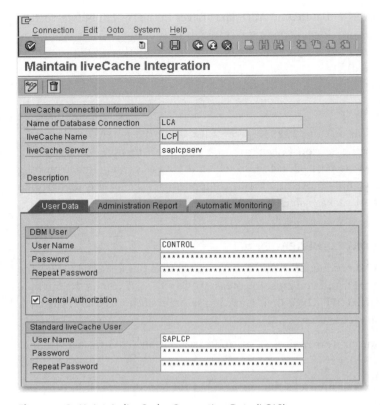

Figure 17.8 Maintain liveCache Connection Data (LC10)

Convert CDP Data (C2)

This activity can be skipped if the source version was SCM 4.0 or 4.1. For upgrades from APO 3.x, however, it is a necessary step.

1. You first see an overview of all clients where CDP data qualifying for conversion exists. You can then start the conversion in all qualifying clients by clicking on the **Execute** (**CDP Data Conversion**) icon. The conversion will run in the background with parallel jobs named MC01_3X_40_<client>.

2. Wait until the jobs finish and the action status becomes green.

3. Alternatively, you can run the conversion report /SAPAPO/MC01_3X_40 manually in each client with CDP data.

4. You can see the conversion results via the application log viewer (Transaction SLG1). The Object ID is /SAPAPO/MC013X40, and the External ID (not the subobject) is CDP_3X40 (see Figure 17.9).

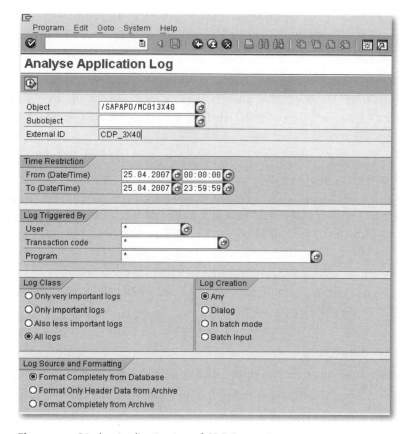

Figure 17.9 Display Application Log of CDP Conversion

Customizing for Clients with Active Time Series (C3)

1. Start the activity, and accept the parameters as shown on the selection screen.

2. Choose **Execute**. This brings up a screen like the one in Figure 17.10 (list of clients).

Client	Day Limit	Shift Receipts	Buckets/Day	Local Buckets	Equal Distribution	ATP Ti...	Fcst Ti...
000	00:00:00	12:00:00	1	☑	☑	☐	☐
001	00:00:00	12:00:00	1	☑	☑	☑	☑

Figure 17.10 Clients with Active Time Series

3. Check with the functional APO team concerning which checkboxes to enable. For more information, click the **I** (information) icon next to the button in the Section C list.

4. Save your changes, and return to main program screen; the status of the activity must now be green.

Logging Off, Start liveCache (C4)

This activity stops the liveCache, disables logging, and restarts the liveCache. There is no user interaction. The final status should be a green light with message `liveCache WARM`.

Refresh Database Statistics (C5)

When you start this action, a pop-up message appears: `Database statistics for CDP tables being refreshed`. This pop-up remains on the screen while the system is busy. Note that this is an activity in the APO database and not in the live-Cache.

At the end, a new pop-up appears: `Database statistics for CDP tables were refreshed successfully`. Confirm this message. An application log is displayed; check that it contains only green messages.

Load Master Data (C6)

1. When asked **Do you want to import master data**, answer **Yes**.

2. Numerous compile messages appear while a pop-up is displayed.

3. The next screen displays the message:

```
Create Master Data in Initial liveCache
Initialization in Client <client> started
```

You may exit from this screen; the status on the main Section C screen is still red but with the message `Jobs for creating master data still running`.

4. Start SM37 in another session, and wait until the following jobs have the status **Completed**:

   ▶ `PEGAREA_LC_CLIENT_<client>`
   ▶ `RESOURCE_LC_CLIENT_<client>`

The activity status in Section C will then become green.

Upload liveCache Data (C7)

The same selection screen appears as when you saved the data in Section B (see Section 17.7.2, subsection *Download liveCache Data [B1]*). All planning versions that were saved are displayed.

1. Enter the following parameters:
   - ▶ **Planning version**: enter "*"
   - ▶ **Client-specific**: leave blank
   - ▶ Choose **Execute**.

2. A job definition screen appears; specify an **immediate** start.

3. Monitor the background jobs with SM37, and wait until all jobs named `/SAPAPO/OM_UPGR_UPLOAD_<CLI>_<PV>` (`CLI` = client, `PV` = planning version) are completed. Verify the spool list of every finished job. All the messages in the list should have a green status. Always look at the output; the fact that the job finishes normally instead of cancelling does not mean that there are no errors or warnings.

4. Create a table in your upgrade control document with the runtime of each upload job, just like you did for the download jobs in Section B. The upload will normally take longer than the download; it takes on average twice as long, but the actual figures vary widely.

Compare liveCache with Download (C8)

The selection screen and parameters are the same as for the upload in C7.

Schedule the jobs for immediate execution, and monitor them in SM37. The jobs are named `/SAPAPO/OM_UPGR_COMPARE_<CLI>_<PV>` (`CLI` = client, `PV` = planning version).

As with the download and upload, the results of the comparison are written to the spool list of the job. If warnings or errors occur, then the job will send a pop-up to the screen of the scheduling user (see Figure 17.11).

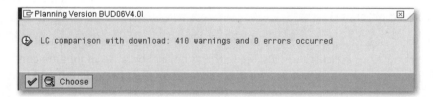

Figure 17.11 Comparison Warning/Error After liveCache Upload

If this happens, then have the APO team examine the yellow and red messages in the spool list in detail. If the difference occurs in a noncritical planning version, then you can let it go and continue with the other activities. In other cases, however, you will need specialist intervention and perhaps assistance from SAP support.

Make another table with the runtimes in your upgrade documentation. In our experience, the runtime of the compare is usually comparable with that of the upload, but deviations are always possible.

Convert Shipments (C9)

This starts two background jobs:

▶ VS_OM_UPGRADE_SCM_50_<client>
▶ /SAPAPO/VS_SEL_INDEX_UPDATE

For the first job, look at the spool list; for the second job, check the job log.

Reload Time Series (C10)

Source Release 3.0 or 3.1
At this point, the time series data, which was retrieved from the liveCache and saved in an InfoCube at the beginning of downtime (action B2), must be reloaded. General instructions are in the SCM Upgrade Guide, but you should again call upon the functional team to carry out this activity. Make sure that you test this at least once with a data volume comparable to that of the production system and that you have a reliable estimate of the time needed for this reload.

Source Release 4.0 or 4.1
This function is no longer used (the button is disabled); see activities A7 and B2 earlier.

17.7.6 liveCache/LCA Build Checks (C11)

This again brings up Transaction /SAPAPO/OM13 (verification of liveCache and liveCache Applications).

Under the **Checks** tab, the status of the /SAPAPO/OM* reorganization jobs will be red or yellow (jobs are currently disabled); this is normal because all jobs are currently suspended for the upgrade. The other statuses on the **Checks** tab should be green.

Also open the **Versions** tab, and check the value in the **Build** column (see Figure 17.12). This must correspond with the liveCache/LCA support package that you installed (in the screenshot this is SP11).

Return to the main program screen; the status of the activity remains yellow.

Current LCA Version									
Mod.	Rele...	Build	Pat...	Opsys	Change ...	Last Changed on	Size (Bytes)	Branch	D..
libCOMBase	50	11	1	Solaris Sp...	368.043	Thu Apr 05 17:10:07 2007	4.839.128	5.0_REL	0
libSAPAPO	50	11	1	Solaris Sp...	368.043	Thu Apr 05 20:54:49 2007	5.507.584	5.0_REL	0
libSAPATP	50	11	1	Solaris Sp...	368.043	Thu Apr 05 18:14:57 2007	35.800.144	5.0_REL	0
libSAPTS	50	11	1	Solaris Sp...	368.043	Thu Apr 05 17:31:11 2007	3.126.424	5.0_REL	0

No. of LCA Routines   424

dbsdbslib   700.08 Patch 95

Figure 17.12 LCA Build Number

Activate Logging (C12)

This step reenables the liveCache logging. There is no user interaction.

The status becomes green with **Logging activated**. As a result, the preceding activity **Logging off, start liveCache** return to a red status; this is perfectly normal.

Complete Backup (C13)

At this point, carry out a complete backup of the liveCache.

Start CIF Queues (C14)

Verify whether starting the CIF is desirable at this point or is better postponed until after the upgrade. The latter is more likely because the system is still logically in downtime and has not yet been released for productive use.

Resume the Upgrade

Confirm the input window in the UA GUI to continue with the upgrade. The remaining phases are not specific for SCM.

17.8 Postprocessing Activities for SCM

On top of the standard postprocessing actions, extra steps are needed before the new SCM version is ready for end users.

17.8.1 Review and Adapt Macro Books

This is a followup action for the pre-upgrade activity "Planning the Upgrade of DP/SNP Macro Books" of Section 17.2.7. Before the upgrade, you (or rather an APO functional specialist) used the tool /SAPAPO/ADV_UPGRADE_50 to determine which macro books would automatically be switched to compatibility mode in the upgrade (yellow) and which macros required manual intervention because they were incorrect or used unsupported functionality (red). After the upgrade, macro books for which compatibility mode is still enabled are displayed in yellow. Those for which you have switched off compatibility mode, possibly after adjusting them to the new release, are shown in green.

The instructions for disabling the compatibility mode are in Chapter 6 of the SCM Upgrade Guide, section *SAP SCM: Deactivating the Compatibility Mode for DP/SNP Macro Books*.

17.8.2 liveCache Connection "LEA"

When connecting to the liveCache, the APO system addresses the liveCache not by its physical name but by a logical connection name. In fact, there have always been two logical connections, both pointing to the same physical liveCache: LCA and LDA. These two connections basically exist because there are circumstances in which an APO transaction must simultaneously maintain two mutually independent transactions on the liveCache. In SCM 5.0, a third logical connection called LEA is added. This new connection is used by the *lock server* mechanism, which provides a locking service similar to the enqueue service in a SAP system. The lock server functionality is used by APO and also by BI[3]. More details about this are given in Note 829963.

The connection LEA is created during the Section C activities. In some cases, however, the automatic creation does not work. This was a known problem up to SP 05 (see Note 945617), but we have encountered situations in which LEA did not get created even at higher SP stacks. Therefore, you should always check the existence and correct definition of LEA via Transaction LC10 after the upgrade.

If the connection does not exist, then create it via Transaction LC10, **Integration**, using the same characteristics as for LDA.

---

3 Contrary to what most people think, the liveCache is not and has never been an APO-only component. The intention was to use the object-based, in-memory technology of the live-Cache in other suitable contexts as well. The optional lock server in SAP BI systems is an example of this wider scope.

17.8.3 SCM-Related Activities from the Upgrade Guide

Chapter 6 of the Upgrade Guide, which lists the postprocessing activities, mentions various actions for SCM. The description in the section title is always preceded by "SAP SCM:". We do not go into detail about these activities here; most of them are of a purely functional nature, so you will have to confide these tasks to the APO specialist team.

17.8.4 Prepare for Return to Production

The final activities before releasing the upgraded system back to productive use are also explained in the SCM Upgrade Guide. In summary, they are the following:

▶ Reactivate the Alert Monitor (Transaction LC10, **liveCache: Monitoring**, double-click on **Alert Monitor** in the left-hand list; confirm that the monitor must start).

▶ Make a full backup of the liveCache.

▶ Perform a final check with /SAPAPO/OM13.

▶ Inform the APO administrator that the CIF queues can be opened; follow the procedure "Reactivating Interrupted CIF Activities" in the Upgrade Guide for this.

17.8.5 /SAPAPO/OM_LC_UPGRADE_50 — Section D

This will probably be the very last upgrade task; it can (and should) wait until several weeks after the upgrade. SAP recommends waiting four weeks.

The sole activity in Section D is to delete the data from the intermediate tables that were used to hold the liveCache data during the upgrade. If you are an external consultant, you'll probably be long gone by this time, so ask the system administrator to take care of this small chore when the time comes.

The upgrade of CRM and SRM is comparable to the upgrade of R/3 with these differences: The duration is much smaller because these systems are much smaller than the traditional R/3 systems. In addition, modification adjustment is limited because there is almost no development in these types of systems. CRM and SRM have many connections to the outside world. This is what makes these upgrades complicated.

18 Upgrade of SAP CRM and SRM

The procedure to upgrade a Customer Relationship Management (CRM) or Supplier Relationship Management (SRM) system is comparable to the procedure used for any R/3 system. The difficulty in these types of upgrades lies not in the upgrade itself, but in the fact that these systems have many connections and make use of other SAP and non-SAP applications.

Depending on the business scenario implemented, the CRM or SRM architecture consists of the following applications:

▶ The CRM server is the central system within the CRM system landscape. Most business scenarios run on this system.

▶ The Internet Pricing and Configurator.

▶ Backend systems such as SAP R/3, BI (Business Intelligence), and SCM (Supply Chain Management).

▶ Text Retrieval & Information Extraction (TREX) tools support flexible document searching, structuring of extensive document collections by using automatic document classification, and extraction of interesting information. In CRM environments, the Index Management Service and the TREX Search Engine are used.

▶ CRM Mobile Clients are usually laptops running the Mobile Sales or Mobile Service application client.

The SAP Component Upgrade Guides for CRM and SRM contain chapters and guidelines for each of the components communicating with either CRM or SRM. Most of the actions listed are to be performed by customizing consultants. The Component Upgrade Guide, unfortunately, does not contain a list of minimal release requirements for every middleware application. This information should be verified at an early stage of the upgrade project. If needed, extra time should be allotted in the project plan for the PREPARE or even the upgrade of these middleware applications.

The SAP landscape shown in Figure 18.1 is a standard e-procurement landscape. All the connecting applications to and from the SRM system will need to be verified after the upgrade of the SRM system. Extra time should be accounted for in the project plan for comprehensive interface setup and verification.

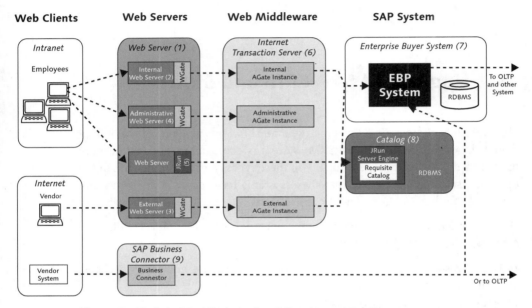

Figure 18.1 Technical Architecture of an E-Procurement Solution

In this and the next chapter, we bring up a new and important topic: Unicode. The upgrade to a new SAP release and the conversion to Unicode both represent major transitions requiring computer capacity, planning, downtime, testing, and a great deal of technical work. In certain cases, they must be done simultaneously because non-Unicode operation is no longer supported in the new version. To help with this double transition, SAP provides two methods for integrating the upgrade and Unicode conversion processes: the Combined Upgrade and Unicode Conversion and the Twin Upgrade and Unicode Conversion. Before looking at these methods, we first introduce Unicode and SAP support for Unicode.

19 Unicode and the Combined Upgrade and Unicode Conversion

Operating in a global environment implies coming into contact with a rich variety of cultures, attitudes, expectations, and taboos. On a practical level, it also means having to deal with a multitude of languages and writing systems with sometimes vastly different characteristics. The question of how computers can support multiple languages and scripts is almost as old as computing itself, but as you will see in the next section, the technical solutions that were available in the past provided only partial answers; they also tended to be complex and hard to implement and manage. The pressures of increasing internationalization and the possibilities opened up by technological advance went hand in hand to provide the ultimate answer: Unicode.

For an application such as SAP, which often operates at the very heart of a company's business, the capability to work anywhere and to communicate with anyone is a critical success factor. SAP R/3 has supported multilanguage environments almost since its inception in the early 1990s. However, as in the computing world at large, the technical solutions were subject to restrictions, which, if ignored, could compromise the operation of the system and even the integrity of the data itself. It is hardly surprising therefore that SAP has taken such a firm commitment to Unicode. Newly installed ABAP[1] systems should[2] be

---

1 The distinction Unicode/non-Unicode only applies to ABAP. Java is always Unicode.
2 Today it is still "should" and not "must." Technically, the option to install a new non-Unicode system is still open (as long as it is single-codepage). However, doing so would be unwise.

installed with Unicode from the start. Existing non-Unicode systems can — and sometimes must, as will become clear in this chapter — be converted to Unicode.

The transition to Unicode is a step toward smooth global operation of the SAP applications, but more prosaically, it is also a conversion of data from one format to another. All the text data that is currently in an "old" non-Unicode format must be read, analyzed, unloaded, changed to Unicode, and reloaded into the database. This is no small thing: In large systems with many languages, that is, the ones most in need of Unicode, it can become a significant challenge. Fortunately, to support its drive toward Unicode, SAP provides a powerful and sophisticated set of tools to help with the conversion. The most complex and time-consuming part of the process, the analysis of existing text data and assignment to a language, can even be done in uptime.

In many cases, SAP customers can choose when to carry out the Unicode conversion, either in the short run or in the near or more distant future. However, in some situations, that choice is not available because they are upgrading to a new SAP release that no longer supports the pre-Unicode solution for multilingual operation. This is specifically true for the numerous R/3 systems (including R/3 Enterprise and SAP ERP 5.0) that use Multiple Display Multiple Codepage (MDMP). When these systems upgrade to SAP ERP 6.0, which no longer supports MDMP, a conversion to Unicode becomes mandatory. Without special assistance, this would mean first doing an upgrade and then a Unicode conversion, resulting in two downtime periods, two testing cycles, and many other costly inconveniences. Fortunately, SAP has again come to the rescue. Although the upgrade and Unicode conversion are two separate processes, SAP has adapted its upgrade methodology to support the double transition upgrade/Unicode so that the entire process can be handled in one go. The system is first upgraded, but immediately afterwards, it is also converted to Unicode using the results of the preconversion analysis (which was done during uptime). As a result, end users go from the old system to the new ERP-plus-Unicode system in one seamless move.

The existence of these methods explains why Unicode is prominently present in this book. In this chapter, we first look at multilanguage support and Unicode in general; next, we concentrate on SAP, explaining the pre-Unicode solutions and then looking at SAP support for Unicode, the requirements to run a Unicode system, and the different conversion strategies. After this, we introduce the two methods for integrating the release upgrade and the migration to Unicode: the Combined Upgrade and Unicode Conversion (CU&UC) and the Twin Upgrade & Unicode Conversion (TU&UC). The CU&UC method receives more attention because this is the method that will occur more often in real upgrade scenarios; it is also the method that has the greater impact on the upgrade tools.

19.1 The Case for Unicode

In any business-oriented computer application, the processing and storage of text data[3] has always been of crucial importance. Textual elements make the data meaningful and usable for reporting and analysis. A customer number is fairly useless without a corresponding company name and address. A product code makes little sense to a prospective buyer without a product description.

Text data also dominates the way in which humans interact with the computers. Employees would have a hard time doing their work if their computer screens displayed meaningless field names and function codes rather than labels and menus in their own language. If the product catalogue on your Portal only showed codes and internal references, Web users would not give your site a second glance, let alone make a purchase.

Conventions about the representation of text data were one of the first aspects of electronic data processing to be standardized. From your schooldays or the early days of your professional life you undoubtedly remember the table of ASCII codes, usually found in the back of any respectable book about computing. ASCII (*American Standard Code for Information Interchange*) and its IBM counterpart EBCDIC (*Extended Binary Coded Decimal Interchange Code*) defined — and still define — the way computers will translate bit sequences into characters. For example, the ASCII standard states that the bit sequence 01000001 (decimal 65, hex 41) denotes uppercase A, at least if the byte containing this bit sequence is part of a text field. In EBCDIC, the bit sequence 11000001 (decimal 193, hex C1) would denote this same uppercase A. ASCII and EBCDIC not only define values for letters but also for digits, punctuation marks, various symbols used in text (e.g., the dollar sign or the percentage sign), and last but not least a range of non-printable "control" characters. Such a character-encoding scheme is known as a *codepage*, a term originally coined by IBM but used throughout the computer industry.

If you dig up your dog-eared ASCII table (or look one up on the Internet), you will see that ASCII is strictly 26-letter-Latin-alphabet-only (EBCDIC is somewhat more advanced in that respect). The only letters having a value assigned to them are uppercase A to Z and lowercase a to z.

In reality, very few languages (one of them English) can make do with just these basic letters. Most languages can cover their pronunciation and spelling needs only by extending the alphabet. They do this by adding diacritical marks to exist-

---

3 We use the term "text data" to refer to all computer data represented in the form of strings of characters and intended to reproduce elements of a human language, such as words or proper names.

ing letters (accents, umlauts, cedillas, tildes, etc.), or sometimes by creating new letters altogether, such as the German sharp s "ß."

The question of representing text data is even more challenging because not every language uses the Latin alphabet. If American, French, and German users are entitled to talk to their computers in their own language, then how could that same privilege be denied to Chinese, Japanese, Russian, or Greek users? Unless early computer users all over the globe had been willing (which they weren't) to use computers exclusively in English, some solution had to be found to accommodate the needs of this immense variety of languages.

EBCDIC already includes a range of "special" letters, for example, vowels with accents or umlauts. ASCII does not, but then ASCII only defines an encoding scheme for half of the possible byte values (0 to 127). Extending ASCII with encodings for the values 128 to 255 thus provided a relatively straightforward way to cover a set of special characters. Yet, for several reasons, this was not nearly enough to solve the question of universal language support:

Even with 128 extra positions available, not all extensions to the Latin alphabet can be covered. This made it necessary to design several codepages, each suitable to a group of languages. For example, there is an ISO codepage for "Western" languages, another for Eastern and Central European languages, another for Turkish, and so on. Non-Latin alphabets, such as Cyrillic and Greek, also have their own codepage.

Single-byte codepages offering 256 possible encodings are sufficient for alphabets such as Latin, Greek, or Cyrillic, where each letter represents a sound and consequently the number of characters is limited. However, there are other types of scripts in which one character represents a syllable (syllabic scripts, e.g., Japanese Katakana) or even an entire semantic unit (logographic scripts, e.g., Chinese or Japanese Kanji). Such scripts typically have hundreds (syllabic) to many thousands (logographic) of different characters, which obviously do not fit into the confined space of a single byte. To support these scripts, *multibyte* codepages had to be designed, in which one character occupied 2 or more bytes rather than just 1 byte.

With a wide choice of codepages available, computer applications were now able to support every language or group of languages. If you wanted your computer program to understand and speak Russian, you implemented the Cyrillic codepage. To make it fluent in Japanese, you chose a Japanese codepage.

But what if your application needed Russian *and* Japanese? No single codepage is able to cover the two languages and scripts. In the past, this question often did not arise. Computer applications were accessed by small, local groups of users all speaking the same language (IT staff often preferred to use English, but English did not present a problem because it needed no more than the ASCII character set common to all codepages). Even software manufacturers that operated on a worldwide scale only had to supply properly localized versions, for example, Russian (with English) in Russia, and Japanese (with English) in Japan.

With business processes becoming increasingly global and companies reaching out to a community of users spanning continents or even the entire planet, the picture has changed dramatically. A central application or database now has to support users and store data in any number of languages, many of which are incompatible from a codepage perspective. Within the traditional framework of distinct codepages, there was really no satisfactory solution to this. Methods to provide multilingual support were not standardized and thus difficult to implement and support. Furthermore, these methods often imposed restrictions, which — if not properly observed — could lead to data being incorrectly displayed or even corrupted in the database. This situation was (and is) clearly not satisfactory.

Along came Unicode. Unicode is an industry standard that provides a single consistent encoding scheme for all writing systems in the world. Going too deeply into the technical characteristics of Unicode is outside the scope of this book. If you are interested in the subject (and it *is* quite fascinating), then you should read *Unicode in SAP Systems* by N. Bürckel, A. Davidenkoff, and D. Werner (SAP PRESS 2007). Other useful sources of information are the Web site of the Unicode consortium (*www.unicode.org*) and the Unicode areas on the SAP Service Marketplace, *http://service.sap.com/UNICODE* and *http://service.sap.com/UNICODE@SAP* (the latter is more technically oriented and is the place where you find the Unicode conversion and Upgrade Guides).

In Unicode, every possible character in every possible script (both living and defunct — Unicode was developed not just for business but also for the research community and others) has a unique value assigned to it. By convention, this value is denoted as "U+" followed by the hexadecimal representation of the character value. For example, Cyrillic capital Ya (Я) encodes as U+042F. Incidentally, the first 128 positions of Unicode are the same as in ASCII, so uppercase A still encodes as U+0041.

The relation between character and encoding value is strictly one-to-one: every character has just one value, and every value corresponds to just one character. This is a formidable improvement over non-Unicode codepages. With standard codepages, the Russian Я could only be represented by using the Cyrillic codepage (where the character encodes as hex CF). However, users with a different codepage looking at this Russian data would not see the Я but whatever character encoded as hex CF in *their* codepage. For example, in the Western codepage, the character would show up as Ï. Valid data would turn into gobbledygook and, in the worst case, could even get damaged in the database. Not so with Unicode. As long as the user's display is able to display the character, Я always remains Я.

So is Unicode the panacea to all the linguistic woes computer programs used to suffer from? It is, but Unicode's universality comes at a price. Because Unicode includes every possible character and symbol, the 256 possible values of a single byte are way too little to cover all of them. In Unicode, a character uses (or can use) more than 1 byte. One common misconception is that Unicode characters are always 2 bytes (16 bits) long. This was true in the very early design, but 2 bytes still only offer 65,536 (2^{16}) encodings, which is not enough to include all the world's scripts. Today several different Unicode encoding methods (known as UTF [Unicode Transformation Format]) exist:

▶ **UTF-8 (and a variant known as CESU-8)**
Here a character occupies 1, 2, 3, or 4 bytes. In UTF-8, the standard ASCII characters still only use 1 byte.

▶ **UTF-16**
Characters occupy 2 or 4 bytes. Because UTF-16 characters are processed in groups of 2 bytes, a distinction is made between different byte orders: "big-endian" (most significant byte first) and "little-endian" (most significant byte last).

▶ **UTF-32**
Characters always occupy 4 bytes. This encoding method is not widely used because of its high memory requirements. It is of no importance in the SAP context.

Different components of a system may use different Unicode formats. For example, the SAP application server always works in UTF-16. The underlying database might use UTF-8 or UTF-16. Data transmitted via Remote Function Call (RFC) uses UTF-8. At first sight, this might seem alarming because it conjures up the image of character data going through an elaborate translation from one standard to another or, in other words, multiple codepages all over again. However, the conversion between UTF formats is algorithmic (one encoding can be derived from another through bit manipulation; no lookup in a conversion table is needed) and is thus very fast.

The fact that characters may occupy more than 1 byte and may even be variable in length also imposes an extra burden on computer resources. More space is needed in the database to store text data. More space is needed in main memory to process text data in a running program. Some extra CPU cycles need to be spent on decoding characters. All this means that capacity requirements for a

Unicode application are higher than for one using the more limited codepages. In the next section, where we discuss Unicode support in SAP, you will find an estimate of extra space and CPU power that your SAP systems will need when converted to Unicode.

19.2 SAP and Multilanguage Support

Like other global software suppliers, SAP had to face the question of how to support multiple languages, belonging to different codepages, in the context of a single centralized application. Over the years, several methods were developed:

- ▶ **Multi National Language Support (MNLS)**
  MNLS was introduced in SAP release 2.2 back in 1995. In MNLS, each codepage to be supported in the system needed a dedicated application server. This method is obsolete and no longer supported.

- ▶ **Multi Display Single Processing Codepage (MDSP)**
  In an MDSP system, the user interface (menus, screen texts, etc.) can be displayed in languages from different codepages, but data entered and stored in the system must always belong to just one codepage. For example, MDSP could be used to let Chinese users access a SAP system configured with the Western (Latin-1) codepage. These users would then see a user interface in Chinese, but they would only be able to display and enter data in characters common to their display codepage (Chinese) and the system codepage (Latin-1). This would mean in practice that Chinese users could only handle data in 7-bit ASCII. MDSP is therefore very restrictive and its use is no longer recommended (see SAP Note 493913).

- ▶ **Multi Display Multi Processing (MDMP)**
  Introduced in R/3 Release 3.1, MDMP enables the application server to adapt dynamically to the logon language of a user. In the previous example, the SAP system would no longer be configured to use only the Western Latin-1 codepage but also the appropriate Chinese codepage. When a Chinese user logs on in his language, then that user's session will dynamically switch to the Chinese system codepage. This enables the user to not only see a user interface in his own language but also to display and enter data in that language. The restriction is that in an MDMP system, users can only view and process data that is compatible with their codepage. For example, German users could not display or enter Chinese data, and vice versa, because German and Chinese do not have a common codepage. Data entered in English, using only standard Latin characters, would be accessible to both Chinese and German users because these characters are part of 7-bit ASCII and therefore shared by all codepages.

MDMP is definitely the most popular solution for multilingual support in SAP. However it is not supported for some SAP solutions, notably SAP NetWeaver BI and SAP APO.

▶ **Blended codepages**
These are "custom" codepages designed by SAP to allow language combinations not normally available in the standard codepages (since R/3 Release 3.0D). There are two types of blended code pages: unambiguous and ambiguous. In an unambiguous codepage, each encoding value corresponds to one and exactly one character. In an ambiguous codepage, some positions map to more than one character, typically to characters that are only used in one specific language. Take, for example, the French character "û" and the Hungarian character "ű". French and Hungarian are both supported under the ambiguous blended codepage SAP Unification. The French character is not used in Hungarian and vice versa, so language-specific data should not cause a problem. However, collisions would arise when, for instance, a French user views an international list of customers with Hungarian names that contain the colliding character. Obviously, this type of codepage is problematic when migrating to Unicode because it is not possible to automatically determine which character the byte value represents. This is why SAP recommends against using ambiguous blended codepages. Unambiguous codepages do not present this problem, but they only give a solution for specific combinations of languages, whereas MDMP allows any combination.

▶ **Unicode**
This is the subject of the next section.

19.3   SAP and Unicode

SAP's commitment to Unicode is very clear: The company is 1 of the 13 full members of the Unicode consortium. Support for Unicode in SAP began with Basis Release 6.20. Starting with that release, customers installing a new SAP system have been given the choice between creating a Unicode or non-Unicode system (with a strong preference for Unicode[4]). Existing non-Unicode systems can be converted to Unicode, but for this they must first be upgraded to a version that uses SAP Basis 6.20 or higher. In the R/3 context this means: SAP R/3 Enterprise (4.70), SAP ERP 2004 (ECC 5.0), or SAP ERP 2005 (ECC 6.0).

For products released in or after 2007, SAP will no longer let you choose between Unicode and non-Unicode at the time of installation; new systems will

---

4 For all SAP products released in 2007 and later, you will only be allowed to install a new system in Unicode.

always be Unicode. However, in many cases, it is still possible to upgrade a non-Unicode system to the latest SAP release and continue to run it in non-Unicode mode.

19.3.1 Impact of Unicode on SAP Systems

The transition to Unicode affects a SAP system in two major areas:

▶ Text data, that is, text fields in database tables

▶ ABAP code

Impact on Data

All textual data containing non-USASCII characters must be assigned to the correct codepage so that during the conversion, these characters are correctly translated to Unicode. In our earlier example, we saw that the characters Ï (from the Latin-1 codepage) and Я (from the Cyrillic codepage) have the same hexadecimal representation in their respective non-Unicode codepages. In Unicode, however, these two characters each have their own unique representation. Therefore, it is crucial that any text string containing either of these characters be assigned to a specific language (and thus to a specific codepage); otherwise, during the conversion, Я might end up as Ï and vice versa.

The conversion consists of three steps:

▶ Preconversion analysis in the non-Unicode source system using Transaction SPUMG (SPUM4 in R/3 4.6C systems). In this phase, all texts that require conversion are identified and assigned to a codepage.

▶ Unicode conversion through a database export/import with the SAP tool R3load.

▶ Conversion completion. In the new Unicode system, Transaction SUMG is used to correct text data that was not converted, for example, because no language assignment was made in the preconversion step.

In the *preconversion* phase, SAP analysis tools scan the entire database and look at all textual data. In a system running Basis 6.20 or higher, the transaction that drives the analysis process is SPUMG. This transaction is already present in the system because these Basis releases support Unicode. In R/3 4.6C, which does not support Unicode, the equivalent transaction, here called SPUM4, is imported during the PREPARE step of the upgrade if you choose the CU&UC strategy.

As a result of the SPUMG/SPUM4 scans, every word found anywhere in a text field that contains codepage-dependent characters, that is, anything that is not

USASCII, is added to a "vocabulary." Through the use of various automatic, semi-automatic, and, in last resort, manual methods, each word in this vocabulary must then be assigned to the proper codepage. The first time you carry out this analysis in a SAP landscape, the process is likely to take weeks. The scanning of the tables alone, especially the large cluster tables, may run for several days. After that, the task of assigning text strings to a codepage is likely to take even longer, especially in an MDMP system supporting a wide range of codepages.

Fortunately, you can save the results of the vocabulary analysis and import it into subsequent systems in the landscape. By the time you reach the production system, it should be possible to limit the preconversion analysis to a small number of recently added or modified texts.

For the actual *conversion* to Unicode, all data is exported from the existing non-Unicode database, converted, and imported into a new Unicode database. The conversion is done with the SAP utility R3load, which uses a DBMS-independent format, unlike the native export/import tools supplied by the database vendors. R3load is also used for homogeneous and heterogeneous system copies (the latter are better known as OS/DB migrations), but here it is used in a special way to convert data on a codepage-dependent basis.

In the *conversion completion* step, data that could not be converted by R3load, typically because no information was supplied about the codepage during SPUMG/SPUM4, is presented for repair. R3load records a reference to all unconverted data in special logs; these logs then form the basis for the correction process in the Unicode system. The correction is partly automatic, and partly manual.

Impact on ABAP Code

Support for Unicode also has repercussions on ABAP program development. For an in-depth discussion of the changes to the language, refer to the aforementioned SAP PRESS book *Unicode in SAP Systems* and to the SAP documentation. Suffice it to say here that under Unicode, the syntax check has become stricter, especially in the following areas:

▶ ABAP statements that used to assume that one character equals 1 byte must now make explicit whether they operate in "character" or "byte" mode.

▶ Statements that apply character-type operations to structured variables containing both character and noncharacter data fields are no longer allowed. Such statements were often a sign of inattentive or sloppy coding, but the syntax check silently tolerated them because no alignment trouble could arise at runtime. With Unicode, this is no longer true, and the syntax check will no longer let these statements pass.

▶ Access to external files (OPEN DATASET) must now specify the encoding method for the data in the file.

To identify programs whose code does not comply with the Unicode rules, SAP supplies a transaction, UCCHECK, which carries out a mass syntax check and reports all programs containing noncompliant statements (or other syntax errors).

SAP now also supports a *Unicode flag*, which is part of the program attributes. In a Unicode system, only programs that have the Unicode flag set can be executed. In a non-Unicode system, programs without the Unicode flag will still run, unless you set a profile parameter, which makes the system behave as if it were Unicode and therefore reject these programs.

You must be aware that using Transaction UCCHECK and adapting ABAP code to Unicode can *only* be done in a system running a release that supports Unicode, that is, with Basis 6.20 or higher (the system does not actually have to be converted to Unicode for UCCHECK; it must simply be on a Unicode-compliant version). This is especially important in the context of a CU&UC (discussed in an upcoming section) where the start release is SAP R/3 4.6C. In a CU&UC scenario, the preconversion data analysis (SPUM4) takes place in the 4.6C source release, but the ABAP syntax revision requires a system (typically the development system or a copy of the development system) already upgraded to a Unicode-compliant version, for example, SAP ERP 2005.

19.3.2 Upgrading Single Codepage Systems

If the SAP system uses a single codepage, then a conversion to Unicode is not mandatory before the upgrade (if the source release already supports Unicode) or after. Nevertheless, you may still opt for a Unicode conversion in combination with your release upgrade. Therefore, the information in this chapter about the different strategies for converting to Unicode and upgrading at the same time also apply to single codepage systems. The only difference is that with a single-codepage system, you are free to choose, whereas with MDMP, you are not.

19.3.3 Upgrading MDMP Systems

Beginning with SAP ERP 2005, MDMP systems are no longer supported. If you intend to upgrade an R/3 system from a lower release to ERP 2005, then you *must* also convert it to Unicode. Technically, you can achieve this in three ways:

▶ First migrate the system to Unicode, and then upgrade it to ERP 2005. This option is only available if the start release is already compatible with Unicode, for example, R/3 Enterprise 4.70.

▶ Upgrade the MDMP system to ERP 2005, and then migrate the system to Unicode. Choosing this option implies that for some time (between the release upgrade and the Unicode conversion), the system will run on ERP 2005 in an MDMP configuration. SAP will only support this for a limited time (typically around four weeks) and under the condition that no functionality must be used in ERP 2005 that was not already available in R/3 4.6C. Implementing new functionality must be postponed until after the system is converted to Unicode. A disclaimer to this effect must be signed; see SAP Note 896144 for details.

▶ Carry out the release upgrade and the Unicode conversion together. You can use this option for any start release. SAP provides two methods to combine the upgrade and Unicode conversion:

▶ **Combined Upgrade and Unicode Conversion (CU&UC).**
This method is available for start releases R/3 4.6C, Basis 4.6D (not relevant for R/3), R/3 Enterprise 4.70, and SAP ERP 2004 (ECC 5.0). With CU&UC, the Unicode preconversion steps (including the lengthy and complex analysis of all text data in the database) are done while the system is still productive in the source version. The tools needed for this analysis are imported during the PREPARE step of the upgrade.

▶ **Twin Upgrade and Unicode Conversion (TU&UC).**
This method must be used if the start release does not support the CU&UC approach. TU&UC must be used if the start release is lower than 4.6C and also for Basis 6.10 (the latter is not relevant for R/3 systems because there has never been an R/3 release based on 6.10). With TU&UC, the Unicode preconversion analysis is done in a copy of the production system (the "twin"), which is first upgraded to ERP 2005. The results of the analysis are then applied in the production system after that system has also been upgraded.

19.3.4 Hardware Capacity

Before you embark upon a Unicode conversion, you must make sure that the hardware will be able to support the additional capacity requirements. Note that these Unicode-specific demands come on top of the extra capacity needed for the new SAP release.

The figures quoted in Table 19.1 are based on benchmarks of otherwise identical Unicode and non-Unicode systems. They were taken from the SAP presentation *Hardware Requirements in Unicode Systems*, available at *http://service.sap.com/UNICODE@SAP • Unicode Overview Library • Presentations* (version of November 2006).

Hardware Item	Additional Demand
CPU	+ 30 %
RAM memory	+ 50 % (SAP application server uses UTF-16)
Database size	Data stored in UTF-8: +10 % Data stored in UTF-16: +30–60 %
SAP GUI Network load	Almost no change due to efficient compression
SAP APO liveCache	+5–10 % (source version < 7.4.3) 0 % (source version >= 7.4.3)

Table 19.1 Additional Hardware Demands of Unicode Systems Compared to Non-Unicode

For the database, the expected growth depends on the type of encoding used. UTF-8 is more efficient in this respect because ASCII characters (which account for the greater part of text data in many systems) remain 1 byte in length. The following databases use UTF-8: Oracle, DB2/UDB for UNIX, and DB2/UDB for Windows. Databases using UTF-16 are DB2 for iSeries, DB2 for z/OS, MaxDB, and SQL Server?

19.3.5 Documentation Sources

To successfully carry through the Unicode conversion — whether in the context of a CU&UC, a TU&UC, or as a standalone operation — you need the conversion documentation that SAP supplies. The following documents should be on hand:

► **Unicode Conversion Guides**

(Source: *http://service.sap.com/UNICODE@SAP • Unicode Conversion Guides*)

Documents required:

▹ **Unicode Conversion Checklist**

Under this node, you find a release-dependent checklist document for MDMP systems and a generic checklist for single codepage systems.

▹ **Unicode Conversion Guide 7.00**

Here you find the detailed guides for the Unicode conversion under NetWeaver 2004s. There is a separate conversion guide per support package stack level. Although the guides follow the usual SAP format, they are in DOC (Word) format rather than in PDF format, which means that you can annotate or modify the documentation after you download it.

▹ **Unicode Conversion Tips & Tricks**

Apart from the Tips & Tricks document itself, this node also contains a link to a page describing various optimization techniques for the system copy process. This information will come in useful during the actual Unicode conversion (database export/import).

▶ **Combined Upgrade and Unicode Migration (CU&UC) Guides**
(Source: *http://service.sap.com/UNICODE@SAP* • *Combined Upgrade & Unicode Conversion Library*)

Under the node *CU&UC Guides,* you find the guide for your current release (note that here you need the guide for the *source* release, whereas for the Upgrade Guide, you use the one for the *target* release). CU&UC Guides are available for 4.6C, Basis 6.20 (including R/3 Enterprise), and Basis 6.40 (SAP ERP 2004 – ECC 5.0).

Like the Conversion Guides, the CU&UC guides are delivered in DOC format.

▶ **Twin Upgrade and Unicode Migration (TU&UC) Guide**
(Source: *http://service.sap.com/UNICODE@SAP* • *Unicode Conversion Guides*)

Under the node *TU&UC Guide,* you find the documentation for the TU&UC process. This guide covers releases 3.1I to 4.6B.

▶ **ABAP modifications for Unicode**
(Source: *http://service.sap.com/UNICODE@SAP* • *ABAP and Unicode Library*)

Here you find detailed technical documentation about the impact of Unicode on ABAP programming, as well as various sessions from SAP TechEd. This documentation is very useful for making the ABAP code Unicode-compliant using Transaction UCCHECK (see Section 20.1).

▶ **SAP Notes**
The most important notes for the Unicode conversion and the CU&UC and TU&UC processes are listed in Appendix E.2. For the actual database export/import, you will need the notes that apply to your OS and database from section E.3 of the Appendix.

For the Unicode conversion, the best starting Notes are 548016 and 541344 (the latter contains the Unicode Conversion Guides and other documentation as attachments). The core notes for the two upgrade scenarios are 928729 (for CU&UC) and 959698 (for TU&UC).

▶ **Codepage Charts**
Especially during the analysis phases (SPUM4/SPUMG, SUMG), we have often found the codepage charts for the non-Unicode codepages very useful. These charts show you the byte position and the corresponding character for all codepages. This can be helpful if you want to examine a character string that does not display correctly in your SAP GUI window because you do not have the correct codepage installed to view the data in the proper format.

There is a complete list of codepage charts (both ISO 8859 and Microsoft) in an appendix of the SAP PRESS book *Unicode in SAP Systems.* Another good source on the Internet is *http://czyborra.com/charsets/iso8859.html.*

19.4 Combined Upgrade and Unicode Conversion (CU&UC): The Procedure

Let us now go deeper into the CU&UC procedure. The CU&UC procedure affects both the execution and the timing of the upgrade in very significant ways, which justifies this detailed coverage.

With CU&UC, the SAP system makes the transition from the old to the new release *and* the transition from non-Unicode to Unicode in one step. Both major changes happen within a single downtime window. This will yield important benefits such as increased system availability, simplified planning, or avoidance of two full testing cycles.

The fact that the upgrade and the conversion to Unicode happen together must not lead you to think that they are actually one and the same. Upgrading and converting are two clearly distinct technical operations; they are based on different methods and tools and affect the data in the system in very different ways. In a CU&UC scenario, the upgrade happens first and the Unicode conversion second. Only to the outside world, that is, to anyone not involved in the technical process, do they appear as a single entity.

19.4.1 Supported Source Versions

At the time of writing (June 2007), CU&UC is available for the following R/3 source releases:

▶ SAP R/3 4.6C

▶ SAP R/3 Enterprise (4.70) Extension Set 1.10 and 2.00

▶ SAP ERP 2004 (ECC 5.0)

For other products than R/3 and ERP, CU&UC is available as a pilot project as long as their SAP Basis release is 4.6C, 4.6D, 6.20, or 6.40. However, we stress once more that this is the situation at one specific time. Things may change and may indeed have changed by the time you read this. You find the latest information on the availability of CU&UC in SAP Note 928729.

Two of the three supported R/3 source releases are already Unicode-enabled: R/3 Enterprise (which runs on Basis 6.20) and SAP ERP 2004 (on Basis 6.40). In these two cases, it is possible to convert to Unicode before the upgrade if desired. R/3 4.6C is the odd one out here. This release does not yet support Unicode, so you cannot convert the system to Unicode before the release upgrade. However, SAP has back-ported the preconversion analysis tool SPUMG to 4.6C (where it is called SPUM4) so that you can perform this potentially complex and time-consuming task while the system is still productive in the old release.

19.4.2 Supported Codepage Configurations in the Source System

CU&UC is meant in the first place for the conversion to Unicode of MDMP systems. This covers two types of configuration:

▶ MDMP systems using only ISO codepages

▶ MDMP systems using also (or exclusively) SAP unambiguous blended codepages

As mentioned previously, CU&UC is also available for single-codepage systems (ISO or SAP unambiguous blended), but here it is not mandatory. For systems with SAP *ambiguous* blended codepages, CU&UC is released for start versions 6.20 and 6.40. It is not supported for start version 4.6C.

> **Note**
>
> Again, keep in mind that this reflects the status in July 2007. Consult SAP Note 928729 for an up-to-date status.

19.4.3 Restrictions for Unicode Conversion

Some restrictions on Unicode conversion that you need to be aware of are the following:

▶ Unicode and non-Unicode systems cannot coexist inside one database (Multiple Components One Database [MCOD]).

▶ Unicode is not released for database system Informix.

▶ You cannot convert back from Unicode to non-Unicode.

▶ Special rules apply for customers using codepage 8340, *Hong Kong Supplementary Character Set* (HKSCS). See the SAP Unicode Conversion Guides for details.

19.4.4 Source Database Informix

SAP does not support Unicode on systems running Informix. Also, Informix is no longer a supported database platform with SAP NetWeaver 2004s and all products based on AS 7.0 (including SAP ERP 2005). This means that the system must be migrated from Informix to another database system *before* the release upgrade.

In combination with the Unicode conversion, the following scenarios exist:

▶ Systems with Basis 6.20 and 6.40 can be migrated to the new database system and converted to Unicode at the same time. This is possible and supported because the OS/DB Migration and the Unicode conversion use the same tools. The preconversion analysis with SPUMG can be done in the Informix system.

▶ Systems with Basis 4.6D or lower (e.g., R/3 4.6C) must be migrated to the new database system while still on the source release. Afterwards, they can be upgraded and converted to Unicode, either simultaneously (CU&UC, TU&UC) or in the case of single-codepage systems separately (upgrade first, convert to Unicode later).

19.4.5 Steps in a CU&UC Project

So what happens when you go for CU&UC? Every Unicode conversion, regardless of whether a release upgrade is also involved or not, basically consists of the three major steps described in Section 19.3.1 earlier:

▶ Preconversion (SPUM4/SPUMG)
▶ Conversion (R3load)
▶ Conversion completion (SUMG)

In the CU&UC context, these exact same steps are carried out, but the upgrade process is aware of the fact that a Unicode conversion is also to take place:

▶ The tools for the preconversion analysis are imported by PREPARE.
▶ The preconversion happens in the source release, after PREPARE but before the upgrade.
▶ During the upgrade, the ABAP programs that were made Unicode-compliant (UCCHECK) are imported.
▶ At the end of the upgrade downtime, the upgrade will request that you carry out the database export/import for the actual migration of the data to Unicode.

Figure 19.1 shows the major operations in a CU&UC scenario on a time line.

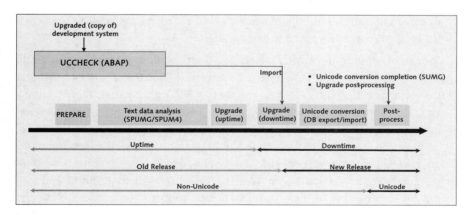

Figure 19.1 Time Line of CU&UC

19.4.6 Planning Aspects

The preparation of the CU&UC (or of any Unicode conversion for that matter) should start several weeks before the actual upgrade and migration. "Several weeks" might even be too optimistic. The preparations should probably begin several months before the conversion if the system has many languages or if a large quantity of ABAP code must be adapted to the Unicode syntax.

The ABAP Preparation System

The first step in a specific R/3 landscape will normally be to create a copy of a system that contains all the custom development and to upgrade this copy to SAP ERP 6.0. The system can then be used to carry out the review and adaptation of the ABAP programs (UCCHECK). In the SAP conversion guides, this system is called the *ABAP Preparation System*. Various scenarios can be imagined for setting up the ABAP Preparation System:

▶ If the source release supports Unicode (Basis 6.20/6.40), then no upgrade is needed. You can use UCCHECK in the existing system to make your ABAP programs Unicode-compatible.

▶ If the source release does not support Unicode (Basis 4.6C/4.6D), then you must upgrade the ABAP Preparation System before you can use UCCHECK. You do not have to convert the data in this system to Unicode. This is true even for MDMP systems; even though ERP 6.0 does not support MDMP, you will never use the ABAP Preparation System productively. As long as the system is used only for UCCHECK and code modification, there is no problem in the system remaining MDMP. The only way to avoid this "unsupported" state would be to upgrade the system to an intermediate version (R/3 Enterprise or ECC 5.0) and do the ABAP preparations there. However, this would force you to carry out a different upgrade, which is of no relevance at all to the actual landscape. Such a procedure is best avoided.

▶ Instead of copying an existing system and then upgrading that copy, you could also create a new sandbox system directly in ERP 6.0, import all customer developments into this sandbox, and do the ABAP preparation there. In practice, this approach is often problematic. Transplanting an entire customer development environment to a new system is rarely an easy task. This is not because the transport tools cannot handle it, but because the developments are embedded into a very specific setup defined by the configuration, customizing, user rights, interfaces, and so on of the source system. Running and testing ABAP programs in their familiar surroundings rather than in a new and alien environment will save trouble and allow the development team to concentrate on the task at hand, that is, to make the programs ready for Unicode.

The Unicode conversion guides recommend that you use a copy of the production system as the ABAP Preparation System. This is sound advice because only productive ABAP code will then be examined and adapted. Another advantage is that the release upgrade of the ABAP Preparation System will serve as a first test of the actual production upgrade. If copying the production system is not possible, for instance, because no sufficient spare storage capacity is available, then you can also use a copy of the development system for UCCHECK. In that case, however, developers must make sure that they concentrate their effort on production code and do not spend too much time and effort on short-lived test programs and the other ballast usually found in development systems.

The fact that a program exists in the production system does not necessarily mean that it is still useful. One characteristic almost all SAP systems share is that many development objects are created or imported, but nothing ever gets deleted. The result is that even in production systems, there are murky corners with cobweb-covered programs that no one uses anymore and most people have forgotten about. The trouble is that it is often very hard to tell which code is dead and which is alive. If customer development is substantial, then it may be useful to leave the dead in peace and concentrate on code that is still in active use.

One helpful tool here is the *SAP Coverage Analyzer* (Transaction SCOV). The Coverage Analyzer provides facilities to monitor and record the execution of programs on a systemwide basis. You can also use SCOV to follow up the testing process because you can keep track of code usage down to the level of individual executable units such as functions or subroutines. The SAP Coverage Analyzer is fully documented in the SAP NetWeaver 2004s section on the on the SAP Help Portal (*http://help.sap.com*) in the guide *ABAP Analysis Tools*.

A detailed description of UCCHECK and the ABAP code adjustment process is outside the scope of this book. The SAP PRESS book *Unicode in SAP Systems* (N. Bürckel, A. Davidenkoff, D. Werner, 2007) extensively describes the process as well as all the ABAP constructs that have been changed for Unicode.

How much time the ABAP preparation will need depends on the number of customer programs and users, the number of Unicode-related syntax errors reported in UCCHECK, and the availability of ABAP developers to correct and test the code. To avoid unpleasant surprises, especially if ABAP development resources are scarce, you should start with the ABAP preparation several months before the first "live" upgrade.

The end result of the ABAP preparation must be a set of transport requests containing the Unicode-compliant programs. The PREPARE step of the upgrade will prompt you for the list of transport requests, which will then be imported during the upgrade.

The ABAP preparation is really a maintenance activity; no new functionality is introduced. Nevertheless, it does have an impact on ongoing development projects. If a program is adapted for Unicode in the ABAP Preparation System and later on functional enhancements or modifications not related to Unicode are made to that same program in the live development system, then the version of the program in the ABAP Preparation System becomes useless and must certainly not be imported into production after the upgrade. In that case, the program in the original development system should be made Unicode-compliant (if possible — not all Unicode-compliant constructs are available in pre-Unicode SAP releases); alternatively, the new version can be transported into the ABAP Preparation System and reprocessed there. Either way, you'll have to be extremely careful with development changes.

Preparation System for Data Conversion

The analysis of the text data in preparation of the Unicode conversion (Transaction SPUMG/SPUM4) is another process that will demand time and resources. Unlike the ABAP preparation, the data analysis takes place *before* the system is upgraded. As already mentioned, the tools for the analysis are imported into the system during PREPARE.

For the ABAP preparation, it is recommended to use a copy of the production system, but if necessary a copy of the development system can be used as well. For the text data analysis, however, you definitely need a system that contains all or almost all the production data. A copy of development won't do here because development systems usually contain only a small amount of none-too-recent business data.

Because the preconversion analysis does not require the system to be upgraded, it can also be carried out in an original system in the landscape rather than a copy. The QA system of the R/3 landscape could be a valid candidate for this because it is often a fairly recent (and complete) copy of the production environment. Theoretically, the production system itself could be used as well, but most SAP customers will not feel comfortable with this; there would not be much benefit in using the production system anyway because data will of course change between the initial analysis and the production upgrade. This "delta" must be processed anyhow, so not much is lost by using a recent copy of the production data instead of the current production data.

How long the first SPUMG/SPUM4 data analysis will take again depends on several factors:

▶ The amount of data without explicit language indicator (language flag) in the system

▶ The number of codepages and languages used

▶ The number of people available to inspect the data and assign it to the proper language (or at least to the proper codepage)

The volume of text data without language indicator is likely to be substantial. Many SAP tables contain a language field — often named SPRAS or LANGU, and always of data type LANG — to make clear in which language the text field(s) in a row have been entered. However, language flags mainly occur in the context of customizing and documentation data. Master and transaction data normally contain no such indicator. This means in practice that many of the largest or most critical tables in the system contain text data without any form of language identification. Common examples are the tables KNA1 (customers), LFA1 (suppliers)[5], BSEG (financial documents), and the "index" tables constructed around the BSEG cluster, such as BSIS, BSAD, and so on.

As mentioned earlier, the preconversion analysis scans all the tables in the database and records every single string containing a codepage-dependent (i.e., non-ASCII) character in a vocabulary. Unless users consistently limited themselves to English or another of the very few languages that are ASCII-only, that vocabulary is likely to be large. In our experience, a vocabulary with 20,000 to 50,000 terms is modest in size. More "difficult" cases may well go over 500,000 entries. Of course, not all these words must be examined and assigned manually. Various methods for mass assignment, described in Chapter 20, will in most cases solve a large majority of the words in the vocabulary. Still, a residue of unassigned terms will inevitably be left for manual resolution. In an MDMP system, especially one that supports different writing systems, assigning the remaining unsolved terms is an elaborate task for which you will need to engage the help of native speakers who have the knowledge — and the computer equipment — to display and evaluate the vocabulary entries in each language and script. This shared effort is likely to stretch across continents and time zones, so it should be planned and organized well in advance.

Even then, some unassigned texts are likely to be left over. Not every text string in the system corresponds to human language. There can be encrypted strings, codes, company-specific terms and abbreviations, or just plain garbage. Most of the time, achieving a 100 % resolution rate in the preconversion analysis phase is an illusion. However, unresolved entries can still be handled after the conversion (in Transaction SUMG).

---

5 KNA1 and LFA1 actually do contain a language field of type LANG, but this field does not indicate the language/codepage of the text data in the corresponding row. Starting with Basis 6.20, a Text Language flag is used for this purpose; see Section 20.3.2, subsection *Text language field*, for more information.

Although the SPUMG/SPUM4 analysis process has to be repeated in every system in the landscape, the overall time needed for the analysis will become progressively shorter. This is because at the end of the analysis, with almost all text entries assigned to a codepage, the processed vocabulary is exported. This export can then be reused in subsequent systems, so that only a small delta must be evaluated again. The initial table scans to build the vocabulary still remain necessary, however, so you must always plan sufficient time for these (normally several days).

Total Downtime

In a CU&UC process, the downtime window must be sufficiently long to cover the downtime phases of the upgrade, the Unicode migration using database export/import, the Unicode postprocessing, and the upgrade postprocessing. It is indispensable to test, optimize, and time the main downtime processes — repeatedly if needed — so that on the day of the production upgrade, you will be able to stay within the available downtime window.

SAP Note 857081 contains information that may help with an initial estimate of the downtime you will need for the Unicode conversion. This note points to other notes dealing with methods and tools that speed up the migration, optimal database parameter settings, and the like. Make sure you implement the advice given in these notes from the beginning. Only by testing will you then be able to establish whether the CU&UC is possible given the allowed downtime. If the downtime is too short (including a reasonable safety margin!), then CU&UC is not the appropriate method for this system, and you should separate the upgrade and Unicode conversion.

Time now to have a close look at the technical procedure for a Combined Upgrade and Unicode Conversion (CU&UC). As you will soon find out, this chapter will have little upgrade and much conversion in it. The upgrade procedure differs little from a standard upgrade; the main difference lies in the analysis steps, both before and after the conversion, and in the conversion (migration) itself. Take care that your mental batteries are fully charged before reading on: This is a big chapter!

20 Combined Upgrade and Unicode Conversion (CU&UC) in Detail

In the following sections, we describe the Combined Upgrade and Unicode Conversion (CU&UC) in detail. Much of the information is not specific to the CU&UC scenario but applies to any Unicode conversion. We adopt a strict "how-to" approach, showing you what to do, when, and how; for instance, when we talk about UCCHECK, we show how to identify problematic code; explaining *why* that code is problematic in Unicode falls outside the scope of this book. For extensive background information, refer to the SAP PRESS book *Unicode in SAP Systems* (N. Bürckel, A. Davidenkoff, D. Werner, 2007).

The sections covering the CU&UC process are organized by main procedure step as follows:

- ▶ Section 20.1: UCCHECK and ABAP Preparation
- ▶ Section 20.2: PREPARE activities
- ▶ Section 20.3: SPUM4/SPUMG Preconversion Analysis, including vocabulary processing
- ▶ Section 20.4: Upgrade and post-upgrade preparations for the Unicode conversion
- ▶ Section 20.5: Unicode conversion
- ▶ Section 20.6: CU&UC Postprocessing

You will see a table like the one in the next section in every section that describes a major CU&UC activity. It gives a high-level description of the activity and situates it inside the overall upgrade and conversion process.

20.1   UCCHECK and ABAP Preparation

Why?	In Unicode, a more rigorous ABAP syntax check is applicable. Existing code that does not meet these requirements must be identified and corrected.
When?	At least several weeks, and possibly a few months, before the first upgrade and Unicode conversion in the landscape.
Where?	In a non-Unicode system upgraded to a release that supports Unicode (SAP Basis 6.20 or higher); not possible in a lower release.
	Ideally in a copy of the production system; otherwise, in a copy of the development system.
	During the live upgrades, the transport requests containing the corrected ABAP code are imported, so the preparation only has to be done once.
How?	Transaction UCCHECK to perform a mass syntax check and list offending programs. ABAP Workbench (SE80, SE38, SE37) to correct the code.

20.1.1   Determine the Programs to Check

Only programs that comply with the stricter ABAP syntax and semantics intro-duced in Basis 6.x will run in a Unicode system, so you must ensure that all your programs are compliant before you can convert a system to Unicode. This also applies for any SAP programs you modified, including customer exits that you use (see SAP Note 549143 for more information). You can use the Modification Browser (Transaction SE95) to determine which programs you modified. Select the programs from the sections "With Modification Assistant" and "Without Modification Assistant." Code changes that you implemented using the Note Assistant (Transaction SNOTE) do not have to be checked because these changes only comprise SAP code.

You must check all objects in the customer namespace, all objects of type FUGS[1], and the SAP programs you modified.

20.1.2   Object Types Checked

The following object types can be checked:

- PROG: ABAP Report
- CLAS: Object Class
- FUGR: Function groups
- FUGX: Function group (with customer include, customer area)

---

1   The object type R3TR FUGS is used for function groups containing customer includes (i.e. customer exits)

▶ FUGS: Function group (with customer include, SAP area)

▶ LDBA: Logical Database

▶ CNTX: Context

▶ TYPE: Type pool

▶ INTF: Interface

20.1.3 Using UCCHECK

Let's make a quick tour of the UCCHECK selection screen to clarify the options that are available.

Documentation Links

Two buttons in the menu bar of UCCHECK give you access to valuable documentation:

▶ **Docu for ABAP + Unicode**
Opens an extensive ABAP help topic about the features and rules of ABAP with Unicode.

▶ **UCCHECK Documentation**
Displays the program documentation for UCCHECK. This includes a description of all the selection screen fields.

Program Selections

UCCHECK has an extensive selection screen, divided into four groups of parameters, which we describe later in this section.

In the part of the selection screen contained in Figure 20.1, you specify which objects must be analyzed. By default, no selections are made.

You can select objects based on the following:

▶ The names of the objects.

▶ Object types; this is the object type used throughout the SAP repository and the transport system, for example, PROG for programs, FUGR for function groups, and so on.

▶ Author (owner) of the object. This is a useful option to subdivide the UCCHECK workload over a team of developers.

▶ Package (also called the development class).

▶ Original system. This is the SAP system where the object was originally developed (field SRCSYSTEM of table TADIR).

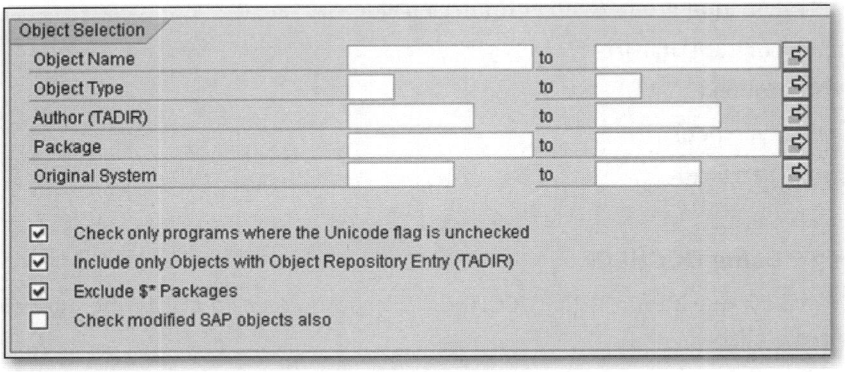

Object Selection				
Object Name		to		⇨
Object Type		to		⇨
Author (TADIR)		to		⇨
Package		to		⇨
Original System		to		⇨

☑ Check only programs where the Unicode flag is unchecked
☑ Include only Objects with Object Repository Entry (TADIR)
☑ Exclude $* Packages
☐ Check modified SAP objects also

Figure 20.1 UCCHECK Selection Screen (Part 1)

Further selections parameters in this section include the following:

▶ **Check only programs where the Unicode flag is unchecked**
By default UCCHECK only looks at programs that do not yet have the Unicode check flag set. This behavior is correct most of the time because you would expect only such unchecked programs to still contain non-Unicode compliant code. Sometimes, however, it makes sense to have UCCHECK also examine programs that do have the Unicode flag set. This is true, for example, when you examine local modifications made to SAP function groups. In this case, the object to specify for analysis is the SAP function group (R3TR FUGR), but because this function group was imported with the release upgrade, it has the Unicode flag enabled. To root out potential Unicode syntax errors inside these objects, you must disable this flag when analyzing them.

▶ **Include only Objects with Object Repository Entry (TADIR)**
Some programs in the system are not created using workbench transactions but are generated internally by certain transactions. These programs are not recorded in the repository directory (TADIR). By default, UCCHECK does not consider these generated programs. By disabling this flag, you can have UCCHECK look at generated code as well. Any such program found to contain Unicode-related errors should then be regenerated.

▶ **Exclude $* Packages**
With this option, you choose whether local, nontransportable objects must be checked. These are often quick test programs, created at some time in the past and very often not used any longer. By default, UCCHECK will not check these programs. Since these programs are nontransportable, they cannot be placed in a change request that you will import during the upgrade, so they play no further role in the CU&UC process. Still, it might be useful to run UCCHECK once for these local programs. When you do this, uncheck the **Exclude $***

packages option and also enter "$*" into the **Package** field so that only local objects are considered.

▶ **Check modified SAP objects also**

By default, this option is disabled, meaning that only customer objects are checked. If SAP objects were modified in the system (which is likely), then you must run UCCHECK for these modified objects. In that case, specify only the changed SAP objects listed in SE95 (you can also query the table SMODILOG directly), *enable* the check box **Check modified SAP objects also,** and *disable* the check box **Check only programs where the Unicode flag is unchecked**.

To prevent timeouts due to long runtimes, UCCHECK will, by default, only process a maximum of 50 objects at a time. You can set this parameter on the selection screen (see Figure 20.2).

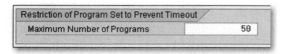

Figure 20.2 UCCHECK Selection Screen (Part 2)

If the number of objects selected exceeds the threshold set in the **Maximum number of programs** parameter, then UCCHECK reports this "overflow" and invites you to refine your selection criteria, raise the number of objects, or use an alternative method (the ABAP mass processing Transaction SAMT) for analyzing large groups of objects.

You can run the program in the background for larger sets. With a background run, the results are written to the spool (see Figure 20.3). The disadvantage is that you cannot drill down into the program source by double-clicking.

To have UCCHECK process all the objects meeting the selection criteria, enter an arbitrary high value, for example, 999999. Do not leave the field empty because UCCHECK interprets this as 0.

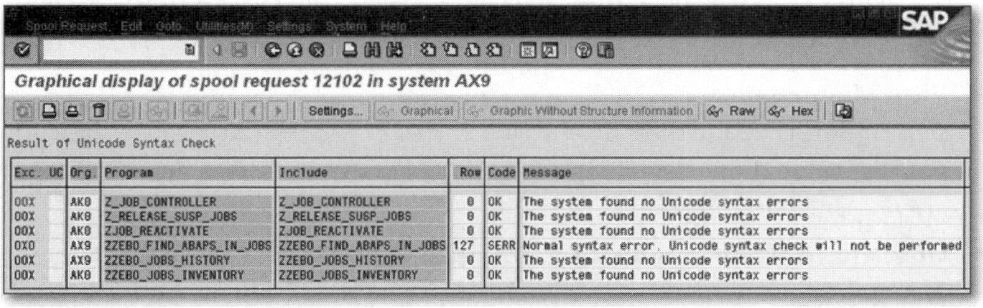

Figure 20.3 Output of UCCHECK in the Background

The following method is a good compromise:

- Perform a mass run on a large set of objects in the background.
- From the spool file of the job, select the programs that have errors.
- Process these programs in the foreground.

Part 3 of the selection screen contains the following select options (see Figure 20.4):

- **Display lines that cannot be analyzed statically**
  Turned off by default, you can use this option to also list program lines where Unicode compliance cannot be derived from the source code, for example, because a program variable only receives a type at runtime.

- **Show also Locations Hidden with "#EC *"**
  The string # EC * is a pseudo-comment that can be added to ABAP code to exclude a line of code from the ABAP Extended Syntax Check (Transaction SLIN). You find this pseudo-comment very often in SAP program corrections. In customer code, it occurs much more rarely. Enable this option if for some reason you also want these lines analyzed.

- **Includes to Be Displayed**
  Here you can specify a list of INCLUDE modules to be left out of the check. By default, UCCHECK excludes all include files whose name begins with LSVIM; these are include modules used for viewing maintenance dialogs and are excluded because they may create numerous irrelevant warning messages in UCCHECK.

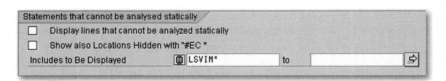

Figure 20.4 UCCHECK Selection Screen (Part 3)

Part 4 allows you to activate or deactivate the following checkboxes (see Figure 20.5):

- **View Maintenance**
  This option is enabled by default and instructs UCCHECK to verify function pools generated for view maintenance dialogs and to display an error if they are not Unicode-compliant.

- **Obsolete Function Modules: UPLOAD/DOWNLOAD**
  The traditional method to have an ABAP program upload files from the user's workstation or download files to the workstation, was to call the function

modules DOWNLOAD, UPLOAD, WS_DOWNLOAD, or WS_UPLOAD. These function modules can no longer be used in a Unicode system. Instead you must use the new function modules GUI_DOWNLOAD and GUI_UPLOAD. See the function module documentation in the ABAP Function Builder (Transaction SE37) for details on these new functions. By default, this option is enabled in the UCCHECK selection screen so that you will be informed of every program where the old function modules are still used.

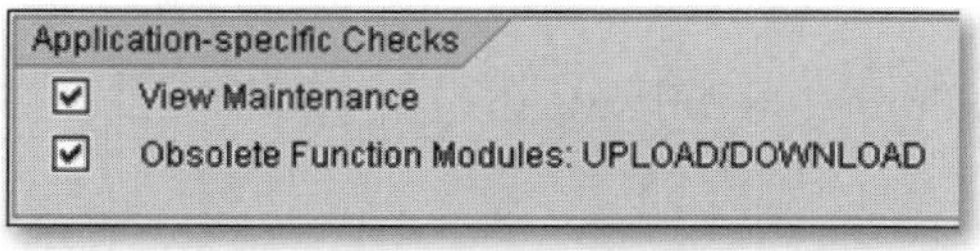

Figure 20.5 UCCHECK Selection Screen (Part 4)

Useful Selection Variants for UCCHECK

You are free to run UCCHECK with whatever selections you like as long as you achieve complete coverage of all the custom-changed code. We usually start by creating three selection variants: one for customer code, one for customer exit function groups, and one for modified SAP code.

Variant 1

This step processes all objects starting with Y or Z. This does not include the function groups of customer exists (R3TR FUGS), which are checked in the next step.

Input on the selection screen:

▶ **Object name**: Y*, Z*.

▶ **Object type**: Leave empty (selects all types).

▶ **Maximum number of programs**: Set to a high value, for example, 999999. Do not leave the value blank because this is treated as 0.

▶ **Other parameters**: Leave at default setting.

▶ Save as variant for later reuse

▶ Execute in background

Variant 2

This step processes function groups of customer exits (R3TR FUGS, R3TR FUGX).

Input on the selection screen:

▶ **Object name**: Leave blank.

▶ **Object type**: Specify FUGS and FUGX.

▶ *Disable* the option **Check only programs where the Unicode flag is unchecked**.

▶ **Maximum number of programs**: Set to a high value, for example, 999999. Do not leave the value blank because this is treated as 0.

▶ **Other parameters:** Leave at default setting.

▶ Save as variant for later reuse

▶ Execute in background

Variant 3

This step processes SAP objects modified in this system.

Input on the selection screen:

▶ **Object name**: Enter all the names of modified SAP objects as reported in the Modification Browser (SE95). If the list is too long for manual entry, you can try and capture the object names in a text file on your PC (by copy/paste or possibly by a direct selection in table SMODILOG) and then use the **Import from text file** option in the **Multiple Selection** box (see Figure 20.6)

▶ **Object type**: Leave blank

▶ *Disable* the option **Check only programs where the Unicode flag is unchecked**.

▶ *Enable* the check box **Check modified SAP objects also**.

▶ **Maximum number of programs**: Set to a high value, for example, 999999. Do not leave the value blank because this is treated as 0.

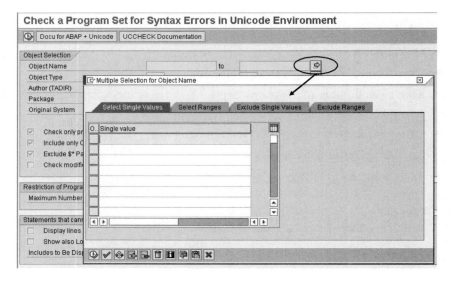

Figure 20.6 UCCHECK — Multiple Selection Box for Object Name

▶ **Other parameters:** Leave at default setting.

▶ Save as variant for later reuse.

▶ Execute in background.

These variants will produce three large lists in the spoolfile of their respective background jobs. You can then use these lists to run UCCHECK online for smaller sets of objects. When used online, the result list of UCCHECK appears in ALV format and can be used actively, for example, to call the editor for the program directly or to set the Unicode flag.

20.1.4 Making Programs Unicode-Compatible

The process of making the code objects reported by UCCHECK Unicode-compliant consists of the following steps:

▶ Correct the code in the ABAP Workbench (Transaction SE80). All modified programs are recorded in one or more change requests. During the CU&UC, PREPARE will prompt you for these change requests, which will be imported during the upgrade downtime.

▶ Test the modified programs. This is necessary since some violations of the Unicode rules can only be detected at runtime. To follow up the testing process and ensure its completeness, you can use the Coverage Analyzer (Transaction SCOV).

▶ If the programs compile and run without Unicode violation, then you can set their Unicode flag via UCCHECK. In the result list of UCCHECK, mark the error-free programs (click on the small square to the left of each line or on the **Select all** icon in the top-left corner), and choose **Set Unicode Attribute**. A pop-up will appears asking whether you want to set the Unicode flag only for error-free programs. All programs for which the Unicode flag is set are added to a transport request.

▶ Switch on the profile parameter to enforce Unicode syntax checks. By setting the profile parameter `abap/unicode_check` = on in the non-Unicode system where you have carried out the UCCHECK, the system will always perform Unicode checks, regardless of whether the program has the **Unicode checks active** attribute set or not.

20.2 PREPARE

Why?	PREPARE is always the first part of the release upgrade. In a CU&UC, extra actions are performed.
When?	In the first system, where you will have to do the complete Unicode preconversion analysis with SPUM4/SPUMG, execute PREPARE at least several weeks before the planned upgrade. In later upgrades, where the SPUM4/SPUMG takes less time, you can run PREPARE closer to the planned upgrade date but not as close as with standard (non CU&UC) upgrades; two weeks or longer before the upgrade downtime is still advisable.
Where?	In the source release of the system to be upgraded.
How?	Using the standard upgrade tools. No "special" version of PREPARE or SAPup is required for CU&UC upgrades.

20.2.1 Activities in PREPARE

Several PREPARE phases deal with the CU&UC process. Some of these phases expect user input.

Phase UCMIG_DECISION

In this phase, PREPARE determines the codepage configuration of the system. In single-codepage systems, you are given the option to carry out a CU&UC or not. The screen shown in Figure 20.7 appears.

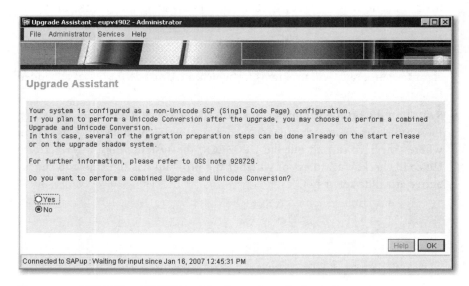

Figure 20.7 PREPARE — CU&UC Decision Screen for a Single-Codepage System

In MDMP (Multiple Display Multiple Codepage) systems, there is no choice, and PREPARE informs you that a CU&UC is mandatory (see Figure 20.8).

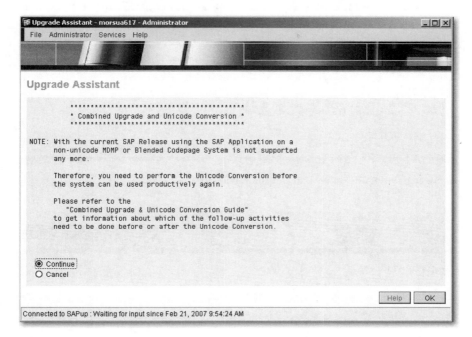

Figure 20.8 PREPARE — CU&UC Decision Screen for an MDMP System

Phase TOOLIMP4_UCMIG

In this phase, PREPARE imports the tools for the CU&UC. No user interaction occurs.

After the end of this phase and before you use any of the preconversion tools, you must import the latest fix transport from Note 867193; see Section 20.3.2, subsection *SPUM4 Corrections* for instructions.

Phase UCMIG_REQINC

In this phase, PREPARE prompts for the numbers of the transport requests with the ABAP corrections made with UCCHECK (see Figure 20.9). If you answer yes, PREPARE prompts for the number of the request (see Figure 20.10).

Next, PREPARE asks you again whether you want to include further requests. If there are more requests, answer **Yes**. Continue entering any additional requests; when you are done, answer **No**.

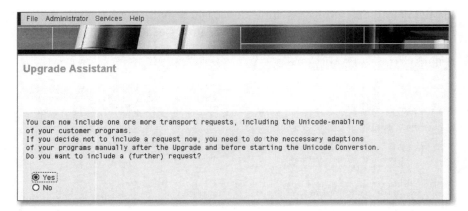

Figure 20.9 PREPARE Prompts for UCCHECK Requests

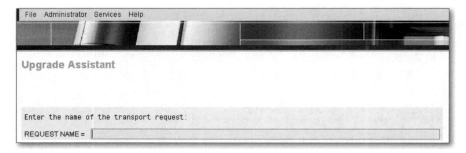

Figure 20.10 Enter Request Number

20.3 Preconversion Data Analysis with SPUMG/SPUM4

Why?	Text data containing codepage-dependent strings (strings with at least one non-ASCII character) must be assigned to the proper codepage before conversion.
When?	The first time at least one month before the first upgrade and Unicode conversion in the landscape. In subsequent systems, still at least two weeks before the CU&UC downtime to allow sufficient time for the table scans and the codepage assignment of new data.
Where?	The first time in a copy of the production system or in the live QA system; *not* in a development system because little business data exists there. Subsequently in every system that you upgrade with the CU&UC method. In these systems, you import the result of the previous analysis, so that only the delta (new transaction data) has to be processed.
How?	Transaction SPUMG (Source Release Basis 6.20/6.40) or SPUM4 (Source Release 4.6C/4.6D).

20.3.1 Procedure Steps

The SPUMG/SPUM4 analysis is a sequential series of steps:

- ▶ Build work list and configure SPUMG/SPUM4 settings.
- ▶ Scan all text data and build up the vocabulary.
    - ▶ **Scan 1**: Consistency Check
    - ▶ **Scan 2**: tables without language information
    - ▶ **Scan 3**: tables with ambiguous language information
    - ▶ **Scan 4**: INDX-like tables (binary part)
- ▶ Process the vocabulary.
    - ▶ Import vocabularies
    - ▶ **Scan 5**: tables with language information
    - ▶ Technical and statistical methods
    - ▶ Vocabulary patterns
    - ▶ Hints
    - ▶ Manual processing
- ▶ Perform final activities to prepare the Unicode conversion.
    - ▶ **Scan 6**: reprocessing scan
    - ▶ Process reprocessing log
    - ▶ **Scan 7**: INDX repair scan
    - ▶ Process INDX logs

As you can see, the preconversion process involves several table scans, each of which covers a subset of the tables in the database. After a Consistency Check (scan 1), three scan processes — each working on a subset of the tables in the database — collect all text data containing non-USASCII characters in a vocabulary. The fifth scan resolves part of the vocabulary based on the texts found in language-dependent tables. The sixth and seventh scan finalize the analysis; after this, the system is ready for the conversion to Unicode.

In the following sections, we describe the different phases of the SPUMG/SPUM4 process. An in-depth discussion of each analysis step would be out of place here — for that we refer as always to the Unicode conversion documentation and literature — and we concentrate instead on how to use the transaction, so that you can carry out and monitor the analysis efficiently. For one subject, the creation of vocabulary hints, we do go into more detail because this is an important feature, which is explained only very superficially in the available documentation.

20.3.2 Preparations

Before you can start the analysis process in SPUMG/SPUM4, various preparatory activities are necessary. Which preparations are needed depends on factors such as the source release and the applications being used in the system. Therefore, it does not make much sense to describe every possible activity here; instead, we choose to provide you with references to the information sources where the actions are described. Some preparations, which are always required and merit closer attention, are described in more detail.

Information Sources

The documentation that you need for the Unicode conversion was described in Chapter 19. As a starting point for the preparations, use the following documents:

▶ The Unicode Conversion Checklist document. This contains links to all other relevant documents and SAP Notes, but it does not deal with the CU&UC or TU&UC scenarios.

▶ The CU&UC Guide for your start release.

Minimum Kernel Version in Source System

For 4.6C/4.6D, the minimum kernel version required for SPUM4 is 46D patch 2108 (SAP Note 867193). However, if during the SPUM4 analysis, you run into the problem described in Note 696379, you will have to upgrade the kernel to at least patch level 2297.

For a CU&UC with start release Basis 6.20 or 6.40, no specific minimum kernel version is given. However, to avoid the problem of Note 696379, kernel patch 6.40/135[2] or higher is required.

SPUM4 Corrections

Just as it did for the upgrade, SAP supplies a fix transport for SPUM4. You must import this transport after PREPARE has imported the SPUM4 toolset from the upgrade media (phase TOOLIMP4_UCMIG). The fix transport is delivered in ZIP format as an attachment to Note 867193. Always download and import the latest version of the transport.

---

2 The CU&UC guides for 6.20 and 6.40 mention a patch level 1700, but this is for the 6.20 kernel, which is no longer delivered.

Parts of the CU&UC process takes place during upgrade downtime, when the SAP system is already on the new release. Corrections for these phases are not delivered in the form of a transport but are integrated into Basis support packages. Therefore, Note 867193 recommends integrating the highest possible target support package into the upgrade. Setting the latest available support package stack as the target is always advisable for the first upgrade in a landscape anyway.

Preparations for HR

If HR is used in the system, then various additional preparations for Unicode are required. These are described in detail in SAP Notes 573044 and 543680.

Preparation for Country Add-On for RU/UA/KZ

If the country add-on for Russia/Ukraine/Kazakhstan is installed (the exact versions are mentioned in the CU&UC Guide), then an extra preparation is necessary *before* starting SPUM4/SPUMG. The details are in Note 947544. If these steps are omitted, data loss will occur!

Restrictions for SAP Office

SAP Note 691407 lists various functions of SAP office that do not and will not support Unicode (and will actually no longer be enhanced in any way). This includes, among others, the interfaces to edit messages in Microsoft Outlook (SAP MAPI provider) and to synchronize the appointment calendar in SAP Office with the calendar in Outlook. If these functions are important, then consult Note 691407 for possible solutions (which might include implementing third-party groupware).

In the context of SAP Office, also check Note 690074, which describes a possible problem with displaying sent spool lists in Unicode systems.

Preparations in Translation Systems

If the system is used for translations using the SAP translation environment (Transaction SE63), then various preparatory actions are needed. General information is given in the CU&UC Guide for your start release; in addition, you must use the instructions from SAP Note 585116, including the documentation files attached to that note.

SAP GUI Requirements

Check the CU&UC Guide for requirements regarding the SAP GUI frontend software.

Database-Specific Requirements

Some database systems, for example, MaxDB, may also demand special preparations; if applicable, the CU&UC Guide will describe them.

Table-Specific Preparations

Quite a few tables in the database demand special actions to prepare them for the Unicode conversion.

Actions in the CU&UC Guide

Specific actions may be required or recommended for individual tables; the CU&UC guide for your start release will describe these. An example is the mandatory action for the address management table ADRP, which is described in SAP Note 712619.

Preparation Report UMG_ADD_PREP_STEP

In 6.20 and higher, many of the table-specific programs are executed as a group under control of the report UMG_ADD_PREP_STEP. If the start release for the CU&UC is 6.20 or 6.40, then UMG_ADD_PREP_STEP is already available in the source release, and you can execute it before starting the SPUMG analysis.

With start release 4.6C or 4.6D, the report does not exist in the source release. Here you must carry out manually some of the preparations (especially the cleanup actions that avoid large numbers of entries being added to the vocabulary). UMG_ADD_PREP_STEP will come in with the new release. If the target support package level is Basis 7.00 SP 11 or higher, then UMG_ADD_PREP_STEP is started automatically when you run the postprocessing report UM4_FINISH_PREPARATION after the upgrade. If the target patch level is Basis 7.00 SP 10 or lower, then you must execute the report manually after the upgrade and before the database export.

Proceed as follows:

1. Call Transaction SE38.
2. Start report UMG_ADD_PREP_STEP (see Figure 20.11).
3. On the next screen, the included reports are displayed. Choose **Background** to start them all at once.

4. Click on the **Refresh** button to monitor progress. Reports switch to green if they were successfully executed or yellow if problems occurred. For each report executed, the SAP note number relative to the report is displayed.

Figure 20.11 Report UMG_ADD_PREP_STEP

INDX Entries for Application SM

An action that we recommend you carry out, although not mentioned in the CU&UC guides, is to clean up the Schedule Manager entries in the INDX table. See SAP Note 977726 for details. The note contains an ABAP report to clean up the entries. This action might not be relevant in all circumstances but we have seen cases where these unneeded records were responsible for more than 30,000 entries in the SPUM4 vocabulary.

Clean Up Table OCSCMPLOBJ

This table should be emptied before you start the Unicode preparation. Instructions are in Note 889596. For start release 6.20/6.20, use the report RSSPAM_ PREPARE_UC. In 4.6C/D systems, run report RSSPAM17, and specify "*" in the **Object List** selection field. Execute the report in the background because the runtime might cause a timeout if you run the program online.

Printing Old Spool Requests

Spool lists created in the non-Unicode system may cause various errors when you try to display or print them after the conversion to Unicode. These errors and the possible solutions are described in SAP Note 842767. The safest approach is to print the lists or to save them in a different format; the note gives various methods to do this. You can also convert a spool request to Unicode after the Unicode conversion of the system; for this, see SAP Note 901004.

Archiving or Removing Old Data

To minimize the amount of data that must be analyzed and later converted to Unicode, archive and/or clean up as much data as possible. To help you with this, consult the *Data Management Guide*, which you can download from *http://service.sap.com/ILM*[3] • *Data Archiving* • *Media Library* • *Literature and Brochures*. This guide describes many possible strategies to archive or delete unneeded data from the system.

> **Note**
>
> If you are archiving in an MDMP system with release <= 4.6D, make sure that you read SAP Note 449918. An additional configuration action, described in the note, may be required after the Unicode conversion to ensure that the archive data is still readable. Reloading non-Unicode archived data into a Unicode system is never allowed.

Text Language Field

As mentioned earlier, the SAP database contains numerous language-dependent tables. The rows of these tables contain a field of data type LANG (Language key), which indicates the language (and thus the codepage) of the text data in that row.

Every language-dependent table has a field of type LANG, but the inverse is not true: a table that contains a field of type LANG is not necessarily a language-dependent table. LANG fields can also serve different purposes; for example, in tables like KNA1 (customers) and LFA1 (vendors), the language field indicates the language to be used for correspondence with the party involved. This does by no means reveal the language used to create the text elements in that customer's or vendor's master record.

There are various situations in which the system will make assumptions about the codepage of the data based on the language key. In MDMP systems, the Unicode conversion uses the language key to decide the codepage to convert from. In all systems, both MDMP and single codepage, RFC (Remote Function Call) uses the language key when communicating with remote systems. To do this correctly, the system must clearly be able to distinguish "true" language keys (which convey information about the codepage of the text data) from "false" ones (which have a business-specific meaning but do not carry codepage information). For this purpose, a new attribute, the Text Language flag, was introduced in Basis 6.20. This attribute only applies to table fields with data type LANG and indicates whether the LANG field does indeed identify the language of the text fields. You can display this attribute in the dictionary Transactions SE11/SE12: display the

---

3 The */ILM* (Information Lifecycle Management) link replaces the */DATA-ARCHIVING* link, which the Unicode Conversion Guides still refer to.

table and double-click on the name of the field of data type LANG. Figure 20.12 shows an example (field SPRAS of table TSTCT, which contains the descriptive text of transactions).

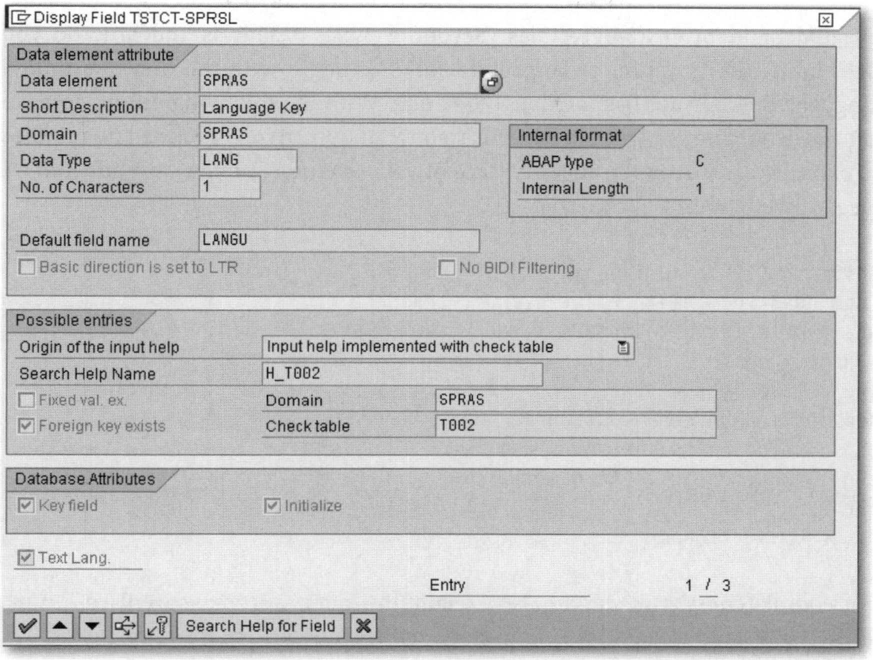

Figure 20.12 Text Language Indicator for LANGU Fields (>=6.20)

When upgrading to a release based on SAP NetWeaver 2004s (Basis 7.0), the Text Language flag is set for SAP tables during the upgrade. However, this still leaves two open issues:

▶ Customer tables might also contain a language key field.

▶ In 4.6C/4.6D, the Text Language flag is not yet available.

As part of the import of the preconversion tools for 4.6, PREPARE also imports the table UM4TXFLAG. This table holds information about all the Text Language flags for SAP tables. Before you start the SPUM4 analysis, you must manually add information about customer tables to UM4TXFLAG. This is what the CU&UC Guide for Start Release 4.6C has to say:

> *If you have created your own objects, you must enter the Text Lang. flag information for them manually in table UM4TXFLAG:*
> *Open Transaction SE16, enter UM4TXFLAG and choose Create entries. Enter:*
> *TABNAME = name of the table for which the Text lang. flag should be set*

429

LANGFLDNM = *name of language field (e.g., SPRAS or LANG)*
LANGFLDPOS = *Position of language field (numbering starts with 1)*
STATUS = *K*

Quite correct... but perhaps a little superficial. First of all, how do you find all language-dependent customer tables? Secondly, what exactly is and how do you determine this "position of language field"? To begin with the first question, a language field always has the data type LANG. With the following query, you can get the list in one go. You can run this statement (which might take a few minutes to execute) directly in the SQL interface of your database, or you can code it more elegantly in ABAP:

```
select distinct dd.tabname
from dd031 dd, tadir ta, tdevc tc, trnspace tn
where dd.datatype = 'LANG'
and    ta.pgmid = 'R3TR'
and    ta.object = 'TABL'
and    ta.obj_name = dd.tabname
and    tc.devclass = ta.devclass
and    tn.namespace = tc.namespace
and    tn.role = 'P'
order by dd.tabname;
```

For completeness, you should also execute this query for views: replace 'TABL' with 'VIEW' and also add the condition where dd.tabclass = 'VIEW'.

As to the second question, the field position is the position of the LANG-type field in the *nametab* (i.e., the compiled version of the dictionary object) of the table. To display this nametab, call up the table or view in Transaction SE12, and choose **Utilities · Runtime Object · Display**. In the field list in the lower part of the window, you find the fields with their name, type, and position (see Figure 20.13).

Field Name	Fiel...	De...	Data ...	ABA...	DB len...	De...	Field...
LAND1	5	0	CHAR	3	3	0	57
WAERS	6	0	CUKY	5	5	0	60
SPRAS	7	0	LANG	1	1	0	65
KTOPL	8	0	CHAR	4	4	0	66
WAABW	9	0	NUMC	2	2	0	70

Figure 20.13 Field Position in Runtime Object (Nametab)

You now have all the information to insert the entry for the customer table into table UM4TXFLAG.

The program that will actually set the Text Language attribute in the customer tables is called RADNTLANG. You only execute this program after the upgrade in the new release. However, adding the entries to UM4TXFLAG must be done before the upgrade, which is why we discuss it here at length.

Check Consistency of Clusters

The CU&UC Guide recommends that you check the cluster tables in the database with the R3check utility before starting SPUM4. This action only has recommended and not mandatory status; also it takes some effort and usually a lot of time to carry out. Nevertheless, we strongly advise you to perform this check. Integrity problems with cluster records are best detected and solved in time; otherwise, they could cause trouble during the database export when you will be more pressed for time than you are now.

Instructions for running R3check are in SAP Note 089384, but we give a brief overview here. R3check uses a command file (similar to R3trans for those familiar with that program). One tricky thing is that the command file to process a cluster must not refer to the physical cluster itself but to one of the logical tables in that cluster. For example, to perform a Consistency Check of physical cluster RFBLG, you could use the following command file, which refers to the member table BSEG and not to RFBLG itself:

```
export
file='/dev/null'     (Windows: specify 'NUL')
dumping=yes
client=200
select * from BSEG
```

To check the complete cluster, you only need to specify one of its members. The following ABAP code snippet will do this for you:

```
types: begin of ty_clusters,
   sqltab      like dd021-sqltab,
   tabname     like dd021-tabname,
end of ty_clusters.

data: gt_clu      type standard table of ty_clusters,
      gw_clu      like line of gt_clu,
      gw_clu_detl like line of gt_clu.
```

```
select tabname sqltab from dd021
      into corresponding fields of table gt_clu
      where as4local = 'A'
      and    tabclass = 'CLUSTER'.
sort gt_clu by sqltab tabname.
loop at gt_clu into gw_clu.
  at new sqltab.
    read table gt_clu index sy-tabix into gw_clu_detl.
    write: / gw_clu_detl-sqltab, gw_clu_detl-tabname.
  endat.
endloop.
```

This code will list each physical cluster along with just one of its member tables. You can use the output to build the command files for R3check. An example is shown in the preceding code. Make sure that you specify the production client number and that you use the correct file name to refer to the null device (/dev/null or NUL); the file name must be enclosed in single quotes.

For large clusters like RFBLG or CDCLS, the R3check analysis will probably run for several hours.

You start the R3check analysis from the OS command line; log in as the SAP administration user. Assume, for example, that you have called the command file to analyze the CDCLS cluster checkCDCLS.ctl. The command could then look as follows:

```
R3check -w checkCDCLS.log checkCDCLS.ctl >checkCDCLS.out
```

The redirection of standard output (with ">") is crucial. For every record R3check decides to report, the primary key together with the status/error message is written to this output file. Example:

```
REGUC     : 20050010905KNTSE Z1203      NE034434    (I007)
            20050020110KN201 Z1203      NE045520    (I007)
```

Here two records from the REGUC cluster are reported with error code I007. Incidentally, codes starting with "I" are only informational and may be ignored. Error codes starting with "D" indicate that the SQL statement to read the data encountered an error; the detailed error message is in the R3check output file and R3check itself ends with exit code 12. If a D-error occurs, try correcting the condition that led to the error and run R3check again.

```
CDCLS    :       (D010)
2EETW125 SQL error "1652" during "CDPOS" access: "ORA-01652:
unable to extend temp segment by 128 in tablespace "PSAPTEMP"
R3check finished (0012).
```

All other error codes, however (normally these start with E, P, M, or N), must be reported to SAP for analysis.

20.3.3 Initialization and Language List Configuration

To run SPUMG or SPUM4, log on in a language that will allow you to see the texts you are interested in. The menus, field labels, and other texts of SPUMG/SPUM4 are always in English.

1. Call the Transaction SPUMG in 6.20/6.40, and call SPUM4 in 4.6C/4.6D.

2. First choose **Scanner · Reset all scans** (confirm pop-up). This deletes all existing scan results. This only takes a few seconds when you do it for the first time.

3. Next choose **Scanner · Initialize · Language List**.

4. The Status message Languages were inserted successfully appears almost immediately. Use **Edit · Language List** to view and if necessary adapt the language list. You might, for instance, want to exclude languages that are installed in the system but not used. To exclude a language, select its entry, and click on the **Delete Language** icon. You must then add these languages manually to the Ambiguous Language List (see the next paragraph).

5. You must then check and if necessary edit the ambiguous language list. This list contains languages for which no codepage assignment can be determined, and also languages that you deleted from the language list. Choose **Edit · Ambiguous Language List**. In MDMP systems, an entry with language = SPACE is mandatory and is automatically added. In systems with Ambiguous Blended Codepages, an entry will also exist for English (EN).

6. Check the invalid language list with **Edit · Invalid Language List**. This list should be empty.

20.3.4 Configure Settings

After the language list, you must also configure the SPUMG/SPUM4 parameters. For this, choose **Scanner · Settings** (see Figure 20.14).

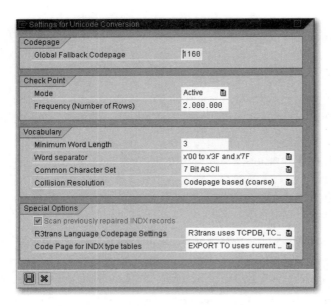

Figure 20.14 SPUM4 Scanner Settings

This screen provides the following options:

▶ **Global Fallback Codepage**
This is the default codepage that R3load will use during the conversion if no specific codepage information is available. By default, the value of this field is "1100" (Latin-1), but you must change this to "1160" (Microsoft Codepage CP1252, Western languages). This change has to do with the conversion of some characters (for example, the Euro currency sign €), which are not present in the ISO Latin-1 codepage.

▶ **Checkpoint mode**
With checkpoint mode enabled, it is possible to restart an aborted scan at the point of failure, which is especially useful with very large tables. Although there is a slight overhead, we recommend setting this to **Active**.

▶ **Checkpoint frequency (number of rows)**
This value determines after how many rows the scan process will record a checkpoint. The default value is 2 million; there is no obvious reason to change this.

▶ **Minimum word length**
Sets the minimum length in bytes of what the table scans will consider a "word." Strings shorter than this length are not added to the vocabulary but appear in the Reprocess log. The default is 3, and in our experience is best left alone.

The maximum word length for the scans is hard-coded at 30 and cannot be changed.

▶ **Word separator**

Determines which byte values are treated not as part of a word but as separators between words. The default behavior is to treat byte values in the range hex 00–3F and hex 7F as separators, which is normally correct.

▶ **Common character set**

This sets the range of characters that are common to all codepages. The default value is that only 7-bit ASCII characters are common. The alternative setting, **Intersection of active languages** applies only to MDMP systems with codepages Latin-1 and Latin-2. These codepages have several byte positions for special characters in common (notably the special characters of German). With the setting **Intersection of active languages,** words containing only these special characters will not be added to the vocabulary because they will convert correctly with either codepage.

▶ **Collision Resolution**

If the same data row contains words assigned to incompatible languages in the vocabulary, then these rows will be reported in the Reprocess log. With the setting **Character-based (fine)**, the entry will not be presented for reprocessing if the words contain special characters with the same codepoint in the codepages involved (German characters in Latin-1 and Latin-2). With the setting **Codepage based (coarse),** all rows with colliding codepages end up in the Reprocess log. The coarse setting is mandatory in MDMP systems that use double-byte (Asian) languages.

▶ **R3trans language codepage setting**

This determines the codepage R3trans will use for transport requests between systems. With the default settings, R3trans derives the codepage mappings from the standard codepage configuration tables in the system. With the alternative setting **R3trans uses SPUMG language list,** R3trans derives the codepage mapping from the language list in SPUM4/SPUMG. This setting can only be changed after the Consistency Check.

> **Note**
>
> For information on transports between Unicode and non-Unicode systems, see SAP Note 638357.

▶ **Codepage for INDX type tables**

This setting is only relevant for systems with Ambiguous Blended Codepages. The default value is set depending on whether such codepages are present or not and should normally not be changed. Press F1 (help) on the field if you need more information.

Do not forget to click on **Save** to keep these settings!

20.3.5 Initialize the Work List

Finally you must initialize the work list, that is, the list of tables to be scanned. Choose **Scanner • Initialize • Worklist**. This starts a background job that will collect the tables and build the work list. This job normally has a short runtime of a few minutes at most.

Note

You can use the **Job Overview** button to monitor the SPUMG/SPUM4 jobs.

Click on **Monitor**. The status must be **Initialization Completed** (see Figure 20.15).

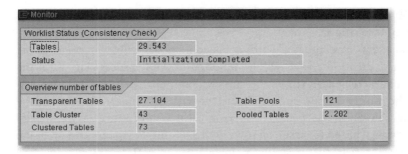

Figure 20.15 SPUM4 Monitor After Work List Initialization

Note

You cannot initialize the work list again. To regenerate it later, use **Scanner • Update Worklist**. The background job for the update normally has a longer runtime than the initial job.

You are now ready to start the first scan.

20.3.6 Table Scans

During the SPUMG/SPUM4 process, you will schedule a table scan no less than seven times, so let's start by explaining how to do this. The following screenshots are about the first scan (Consistency Check), but the procedure to schedule and follow up a scan is always the same, so you can use these instructions for all the other scans as well.

Work List for Scan

On the main transaction screen, you see seven tabs, each of which corresponds to a scan.

Open the tab for the scan you have to run next; in this example, you are at the very start of the process, so you have to schedule the **Consistency Check**.

When you open the tab for a new scan, you normally see the list of tables involved in this scan along with their current scanning status. A gray diamond means that the table has not yet been processed by the current scan.

By default, only 200 tables are listed. To change this and other selection criteria, click on **Selection**.

Scheduling Scan Jobs

The scan can be done by various jobs running in parallel. This is very useful; for the largest scans, like that of the tables without language information, it is even indispensable. To start the first scan job, click on **Schedule Worker Job** (see Figure 20.16).

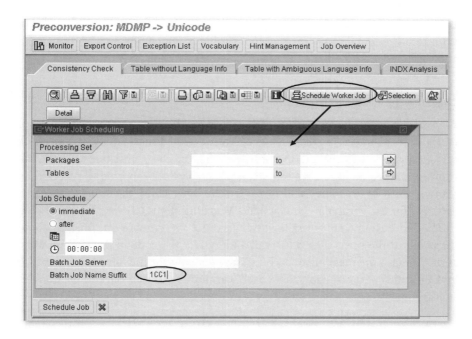

Figure 20.16 Schedule Worker Job in SPUM4/SPUMG

Here you enter the data for a single worker job. It is possible, but not necessary, to assign the job to specific packages (development classes) or even to specific tables.

Specify the start time (default is **Immediate**) and also give a suffix to the job name. A good convention is the following:

nSSq

- ▶ n = sequence number of the scan
- ▶ SS = type of scan (e.g. CC = consistency check)
- ▶ q = sequence number of the job

For example, the first worker job of the first run of the Consistency Check would then have the suffix "1CC1".

Note

Giving a different suffix to each worker job in the scan is essential for parallel processing. SPUMG/SPUM4 will not start a job with the same name as one that is already active.

Monitoring the Scan

You can use **Job Overview** to see the names and current state of the scan jobs. With **Monitor,** you can see the number of tables scanned, the number remaining to be scanned, and the table being processed by each job.

Checking the Result of the Scan

When a scan is finished, return to the tab strip for the scan, and refresh the list of tables. Tables showing a green light icon were scanned successfully; the meaning of "successful" depends on the scan process. In the Consistency Check, all scanned tables should receive this status; any tables not reported as successfully scanned must be examined and fixed. On the other hand, the scans that collect text data for the vocabulary will assign a **Warning** status to every table that contributed at least one entry to the vocabulary. To obtain more information about the result of the scan, click on **Detail** and look at the code in the column **Message**. You find the meaning of each message code by clicking on F4; you can also look up detailed information about each warning or error message in the Conversion Guide.

An effective way to list all tables with a status other than **Successful** after the scan is as follows:

1. Open the tab strip for the scan you want to check the results of.

2. Click on **Selection.**

3. Erase the value in the field **Number of lines**.

4. Click on the **Multiple selection** arrow on the far right of the **Status** field.

5. In the **Multiple Selection** window, go to the tab strip **Exclude Single Values,** and enter the status "K" (consistent = completely scanned and no warning/error returned). If the scan is still in process, also exclude status "I" (in process). See Figure 20.17 for an example.

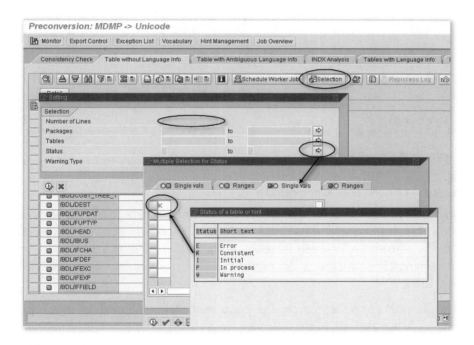

Figure 20.17 Selections for Scan Result

Overall Status

At any time, you can check the overall status of the entire preconversion process by choosing **Scanner • Status**. Figure 20.18 shows a status screen requested during the vocabulary processing stage. The two scans that follow the vocabulary maintenance (Reprocess and INDX Repair) have not yet been run.

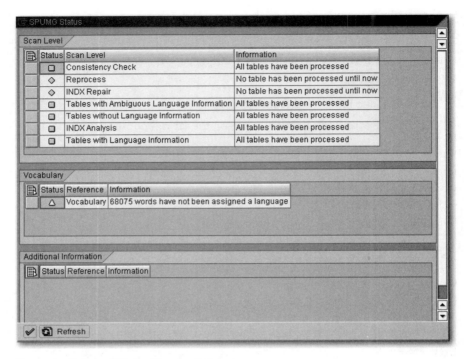

Figure 20.18 Overall Status (Scanner R Status)

20.3.7 Consistency Check (Scan 1)

The Consistency Check is mandatory, both for single codepage and MDMP systems. This scan looks at all tables in the work list and performs several checks, like the consistency between the table in the database and its definition in the dictionary. The scan process also performs a basic read test by selecting the first 100 rows.

The Consistency Check program distributes the tables in the work list over separate work lists for each of the following scans (tables without language information, tables with ambiguous language information, INDX type tables, and tables with language information).

As mentioned before, the result of the Consistency Check should be **Consistent** (green) for all tables. If you find tables with any other status at the end of the Consistency Check, then use the status code (**Details**, column **Message**) and the instructions in the Conversion Guide to take corrective action.

20.3.8 Tables Without Language Information (Scan 2)

The scan for tables without language information is mandatory for MDMP systems. All tables that do not contain a formal language field are scanned for words containing non-USASCII characters, and any such words are added to the vocabulary.

This is the longest and heaviest of all the scans because it has to process over three quarters of the tables in the database, including almost all the largest tables. Runtimes of several days for a single table are no exception, and the overall scan might easily take more than a week. Make sure that you schedule sufficient worker jobs in parallel, without overloading the server. In this case, it is also sensible to run dedicated worker jobs for some of the biggest tables (tables such as BSEG, BSIS, CDPOS, and CDCLS are often good candidates for this).

At the end of the scan, all tables that contain non-USASCII text data will be flagged with the status **Warning** (yellow triangle). Most of these tables will have the status code 5 ("Words added to the vocabulary"). You may also find some tables with code 9 ("Table is marked for reprocess"). Figure 20.19 shows the result screen of the scan.

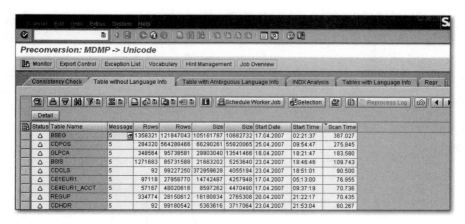

Figure 20.19 Result of "Table Without Language Info" Scan

20.3.9 Tables with Ambiguous Language Information (Scan 3)

If a table has a language field, but this field contains any of the language codes that were added to the Ambiguous Language List (see Section 20.3.3), then it is scanned in scan 3. For every row that has an ambiguous value in its language field, all words in the row are added to the vocabulary.

In MDMP systems, the Ambiguous Language List must always contain an entry "SPACE". This setting covers all records where the language field is empty; because in an MDMP system you cannot know the codepage of the data if the language indicator is blank, words in such records are placed in the vocabulary so that you can examine them and assign them to the proper language.

The duration of this scan is hard to predict because the number of tables may vary, but it will normally be significantly shorter than the scan of the tables without language information.

The outcome will be similar to that of scan 2, that is, several tables will receive a yellow status, mostly with code 5 (words added to vocabulary).

20.3.10 INDX Analysis (Scan 4)

INDX tables, sometimes confusingly called "INDX clusters[4]," are special tables used to save structured data (mostly ABAP internal tables) for later retrieval. They are named INDX tables because they derive their special structure from a SAP table named INDX. There are several hundred of these tables in the SAP database. Apart from INDX itself, a well-known example is the MONI table, which stores SAP workload (performance) information.

INDX tables contain a transparent and a raw binary part. The transparent part contains directly readable text and numeric fields; the binary part (a table field named CLUSTD) stores the structured program data, which will also partly consist of texts but must be decoded by the SAP database interface before it can be read. The transparent part of the INDX table is processed along with the other transparent tables, mostly in the scan of tables without language information. The binary part is handled by the INDX Analysis scan (scan 4 in the SPUMG/SPUM4 sequence).

Scheduling, monitoring, and evaluating the INDX Analysis scan is the same as for the other scans. The runtime is usually not too long — a few hours at most — and the outcome comparable to that of scans 2 and 3, that is, some tables will be reported with status code 5 (words added to the vocabulary).

20.3.11 Process Vocabulary

At the end of scan 4, the vocabulary is complete. It contains every word in the SAP database that contains codepage-dependent characters and whose language

---

4 The term "cluster" is misleading because in SAP dictionary terminology INDX tables are transparent tables (they exist as separate entities in the database) and not cluster tables (logical tables grouped into a physical cluster).

cannot be determined. The next step, and a big one at that, is to assign these words to a language and thus to a codepage.

Processing a vocabulary containing tens or even hundreds of thousands of words is a daunting task, so it's best to apply the principle of least effort when tackling it. Browsing through the vocabulary and assigning words manually is only the last step. Before you come to that, a many methods with varying degrees of automation and accuracy are at your disposal to help you assign as many vocabulary entries as possible.

Vocabulary Display

In SPUMG/SPUM4, click on **Vocabulary**. By default, the list shows the first 500 entries, without distinction of language, processing status, and so on. The following information is displayed:

▶ The word itself, displayed in the characters of the codepage of your current logon language. If the word contains characters that are not defined in this codepage, then the word will be partly or wholly unreadable.

▶ The language to which the word was assigned. For words that are still unassigned the value is blank.

▶ **Collision** indicator. A collision occurs when the scan of tables with language information (scan 5, described later in this chapter) finds the word in two different languages belonging to incompatible codepages. If, for example, the family name *Möller* was found in a table row with language indicator DE (German), but also in another row with language indicator CS (Czech), then the word would appear in the vocabulary with the **Collision** flag set to X. The person processing the vocabulary must the decide to which language/codepage the word is to be assigned.

▶ **Filled by** indicates whether and how the word was assigned to a language. This is a field you will frequently use for selecting entries to display. The following values indicate an unassigned entry:

  ▶ 2: Entry added by scan 2 (tables without language key).

  ▶ A: Entry added by scan 3 (tables with ambiguous language values).

  ▶ I: Entry added by scan 4 (INDX tables).

  Assigned entries can take on the following values:

  ▶ 3: Entry resolved in scan 5 (tables with language key).

  ▶ V: Entry resolved by importing an external vocabulary.

  ▶ H: Entry resolved through a hint.

  ▶ C and S: Entry resolved through technical/statistical methods.

▶ M: Entry assigned manually.

▶ Name, date, and time: For unassigned entries, this is the user name, date, and time of the scan job that added the entry. For assigned entries it refers to the user, date, and time of the assignment.

Selecting Entries

In many cases, the default display (the first 500 entries) is of little interest, and you want to make a selection. For this, click on the **Selection** button, and specify the criteria for the vocabulary entries you want to see. A selection you will often need is to see only unassigned entries. You do this by opening the **Multiple Selection** box for the **Filled by** field and entering the three unassigned status codes "2", "A", and "I" (see Figure 20.20).

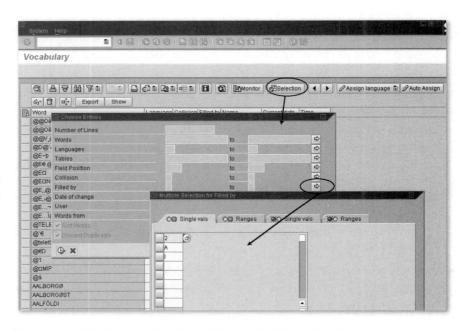

Figure 20.20 Selecting Unassigned Vocabulary Entries (Status 2, A, I)

Detailed Information

By marking an entry in the list (to mark an entry, click on the little square on the left-hand side of the data) and choosing **Detail**, you can see the table and field where the word was found, as well as the hexadecimal representation. You cannot see the actual table key here, but you can use the table browser (Transaction SE16) to try and locate the row or rows containing the word.

In Figure 20.21, an assigned vocabulary entry comes from table EKPO, field TXZ01. Via the table browser, two rows are found that contain the word. In both rows, the field WERKS (plant) provides a clue as to the language.

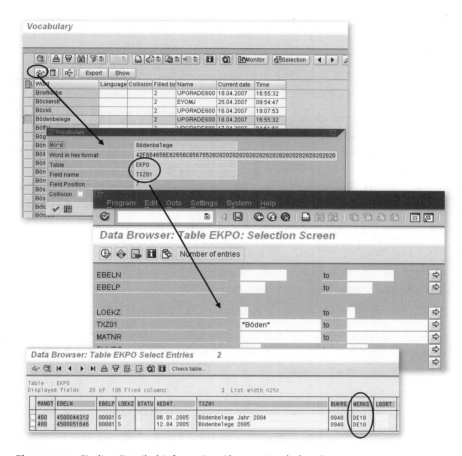

Figure 20.21 Finding Detailed Information About a Vocabulary Entry

Displaying Duplicates

If a word occurs in several tables, then the vocabulary contains a separate entry for each occurrence. The default display, however, only lists each word once. If you want to see all the occurrences, then click on **Selection** and uncheck the option **Discard Duplicates**. The vocabulary display now also shows the table name.

Vocabulary Statistics

To see statistics on the number of unassigned entries per table, run the report UMG_VOCABULARY_STATISTIC (for SPUMG) or UM4_VOCABULARY_STATISTIC (for SPUM4).

Importing Vocabularies

Now that you know how to display vocabulary entries, let's look at the different methods for resolving entries.

If you have already converted one or more SAP systems in the current landscape, then you will probably have exported the assigned vocabulary from the previous systems. Because the text data is usually very similar within a landscape, importing this vocabulary into the present system is likely to resolve most of the entries, leaving only a small number of words for processing by other methods or manual assignment. The vocabulary import should therefore be the first method you use.

In Transaction SPUMG (for Basis 6.20 and higher), there are two methods for transferring the vocabulary between systems:

▶ Download the vocabulary into vocabulary files (extension *.voc*) on the workstation, and upload these into the target system.

▶ Export and import the vocabulary via a transport request.

In 4.6C/4.6D with Transaction SPUM4, only the transport method is available. Detailed instructions on how to export and import the vocabulary are given in the Unicode Conversion Guides.

SAP also delivers vocabularies for many languages as attachments to Note 756535. These come in the form of VOC files for SPUMG and a transport request for SPUM4. Although obviously less effective than the tailor-made vocabulary export prepared in the same landscape, these generic vocabularies will still be helpful, and we recommend that you always use them.

Tables with Language Information (Scan 5)

This scan looks at all tables that have a language key. It is different from scans 1 to 4 in that those scans *add* entries to the vocabulary, whereas scan 5 is intended to *resolve* entries. All texts found in rows with a nonambiguous language setting are then used to try and resolve entries in the vocabulary. If a word is found under different and codepage-incompatible languages, then it is left unassigned in the vocabulary, and the **Collision** marker is set.

Note that tables that contain also ambiguous language values are processed twice, once in scan 2 (while building up the vocabulary) and now again in scan 5 (while resolving the vocabulary).

This scan is not mandatory, and it won't work miracles, but in our experience the scan of the language-dependent tables is able to typically solve between 20 % and 30 % of all the entries in the vocabulary.

The scan technique is the same as for the other scans. No warnings or errors should be returned.

Technical and Statistical Methods

SAP supplies predefined methods for identifying the codepage of a vocabulary based on technical or statistical analysis. These methods are only available for SPUMG (Basis 6.20 and higher), not for SPUM4.

For the methods based on character statistics, see SAP Note 756534. Currently the available methods are the following:

▶ CL_UMG_AL_NA_CHARSTAT for single-byte languages
▶ CL_UMG_AL_YA_CHARSTAT for double-byte (Asian) languages

These methods must be supplied with language-dependent files, which you find attached to Note 756534.

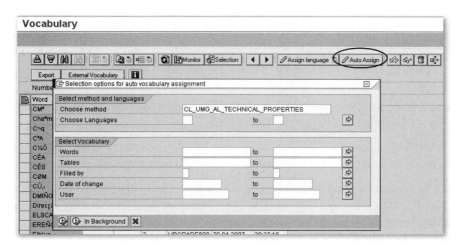

Figure 20.22 Assignment Using Technical/Statistical Method

In Transaction SPUMG, there is also the "technical" method CL_UMG_AL_ TECHNICAL_PROPERTIES. This method attempts to determine the language by looking at the byte representation of the entry. Some combinations of bytes are only valid in one specific codepage and illegal in all others. If such a combination is found, then the word can be assigned to a language of the codepage. This method is particularly effective for Japanese.

To call up a method, go to the **Vocabulary** list, and click on **Auto Assign**. Enter the name of the method, and choose between **Execute** and **Execute in background** (see Figure 20.22).

Vocabulary Hints

Hints are a very effective method for resolving vocabulary entries, but they are also labor-intensive. It is often the case that, even though a table does not contain a formal language key, other fields may be present that can provide clues as to the language. By defining a hint, you create and execute code that will assign vocabulary entries to a language based on the values found in these fields. Typical candidates are the company code (BUKRS), the country (LAND1), or the plant (WERKS). Other fields are also possible depending on how the business data has been defined; for example, if a company rigorously follows a convention of prefixing every customer number (KUNNR) with the two-letter country code, then that field can also convey reliable language information.

To create and execute hints, choose **Hint Management** from the main SPUMG/SPUM4 screen. A screen with two tab strips now opens: **Hints** and **Wordlist (Condition)**. A vocabulary hint is made up of three parts:

▶ The *condition* specifies a WHERE clause. The condition only refers to fields. It does not mention a table or view name, which means that you can use the same condition in the context of many tables/views, as long as the field names match.

▶ The *word list* determines the actual table or view to be scanned using the specified condition.

▶ The *hint* specifies a word list and a table whose vocabulary entries are to be processed based on the strings in the word list and a target language.

We better clarify this with some examples because the available SAP documentation describes hints only superficially, and examples are sorely lacking there. In order not to overload the text of this chapter, you find the instructions for creating and executing hints in Appendix A.

Patterns

SAP supplies files with typical text patterns for various languages (and you can freely add to these or create your own). For example, words ending in *-ción* or *-ería* are very probably Spanish, whereas words containing the sequence *-keit-* or *-ität-* are most often German.

Note 871541 contains as attachment a ZIP file with pattern files for several languages. This ZIP archive contains a set of TXT files with typical character patterns for the language in question.

Assignment based on patterns is *not* an automatic method. As we'll see later, you use the selections in pattern files to display all matching words in the vocabulary. You must then examine the words in the list and assign them manually (manual assignment is explained in the *Manual Assignment* section below).

Proceed as follows to apply a pattern file (also see Figure 20.23):

1. Log on in a language belonging to the same codepage as the language you want to process; otherwise, you will not be able to read the words in the vocabulary.

2. Call Transaction SPUMG or SPUM4, choose **Vocabulary,** and click on **Selection**.

3. Click on the arrow ("multiple selections") to the right of the field **Words**.

4. In the **Multiple Selection** window, click on **Import from text file**.

5. Select a pattern file. The patterns are loaded into the selection list.

6. To see only unassigned entries, also open the **Multiple selection** box for the **Filled by** field, and select the three status codes for unassigned entries (2, A, and I) (see Section 20.3.11, subsection *Vocabulary Display*).

7. Choose **Execute.** The matching words are displayed in the vocabulary list.

8. Review the words, and manually assign them to the selected language where this seems reasonable. Keep in mind that it is the codepage that counts and not the language. Assigning words to the "wrong" language is acceptable as long as those words belong to the same codepage. For example, it is acceptable to assign words selected with the German pattern list to language DE (or to any other Latin-1 language) even if they come from Dutch or from Scandinavian languages.

   However, pay attention to warnings in Note 871541 regarding words being selected from languages with a different codepage. For instance, the French and Spanish patterns sometimes return Latin-2 words. It is perfectly acceptable to assign a French word to language Spanish or vice versa, but you cannot mix French and Hungarian in the same vein because these languages are incompatible, and wrongly assigned words would get corrupted in the Unicode conversion process.

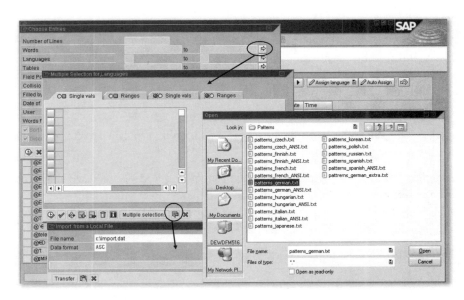

Figure 20.23 Loading Patterns from a Text File

Manual Assignment

At last, all methods for automatic or partially automatic assignment are exhausted, and you are left with a residue of words that must be inspected and assigned manually.

Go to the SPUMG/SPUM4 Vocabulary display, and again select the entries you want to display via the **Selection** button. Make whatever selection that suits you, for example, you can restrict the number of entries that you want to see, select only words that contain certain characters or pattern, and so on. To see only unassigned entries, restrict the **Filled by** status to value 2, A, and I only, as you have seen before.

You can look at detailed information (table, field, and hexadecimal display) to further analyze "difficult" entries. With the table and field information you can look up the original table record via the SE16 table browser.

In the example shown in Figure 20.24, we select up to 1,000 unassigned entries containing the e acute ("é") character.

To assign one or more entries, mark them by clicking on the square to the left (see Figure 20.24). You can select a block of entries by pressing ⟨⇧⟩ + left mouse button, and you can select multiple entries by pressing ⟨Ctrl⟩ + left mouse button. After marking the entries, click on **Assign Language,** and choose a language from the list. If you make a mistake, you can undo the assignment by clicking on the **Reset** button (in the top-right corner).

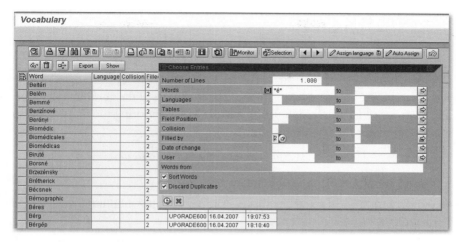

Figure 20.24 Advanced Selections in the Vocabulary

Vocabulary

Word	Language	Collision	Filled by	Name	Current date	Time
CHARTRESANNULé			2	UPGRADE600	16.04.2007	19:25:44
CHQretrourné			2	UPGRADE600	17.04.2007	02:21:37
CIPéterfalvi			2	EYOMJ	23.04.2007	18:46:46
COMMANDé			2	UPGRADE600	17.04.2007	02:21:37
CPéter			2	UPGRADE600	22.04.2007	01:28:27
CTé			2	UPGRADE600	19.04.2007	02:46:45
Campé			2	EYOMJ	25.04.2007	09:54:47
Camédia			2	UPGRADE600	18.04.2007	16:55:32
Caméras			2	UPGRADE600	18.04.2007	16:55:32
Canapés			2	UPGRADE600	18.04.2007	16:55:32
Cathédrale			2	EYOMJ	25.04.2007	09:54:47
Cathédrales			2	UPGRADE600	18.04.2007	16:55:32
Certifiée			2	UPGRADE600	17.04.2007	02:21:37
Chômé			2	UPGRADE600	20.04.2007	08:23:39
Clearée			2	UPGRADE600	16.04.2007	19:25:44
CompactEOSpériode			2	EYOMJ	25.04.2007	09:54:47
Consigné			2	UPGRADE600	22.04.2007	01:28:27
Coopératif			2	UPGRADE600	17.04.2007	02:21:37
Copiefaxée			2	EYOMJ	25.04.2007	09:54:47

CS (Czech)
DA (Danish)
DE (German)
EL (Greek)
EN (English)
ET (Estonian)
FI (Finnish)
FR (French)
HU (Hungarian)
IT (Italian)
JA (Japanese)
KO (Korean)
NL (Dutch)
NO (Norwegian)
PL (Polish)
RU (Russian)
SV (Swedish)
TR (Turkish)
ZF (Chinese trad.)
ZH (Chinese)

Figure 20.25 Manual Assignment in the Vocabulary

Unsolvable Vocabulary Entries

Chances are that even after long and concentrated manual assignment work, you will be left with hundreds or even thousand of words in the vocabulary that defy all analysis. This is not abnormal; not every text string in the database represents a term from a human language. There might be codes, encrypted strings, and even plain garbage. Aiming for a 100 % solution rate for the vocabulary is therefore unrealistic. You will get another chance of solving any remaining entries in the Reprocess stage (see Section 20.3.12) and even after the Unicode conversion in Transaction SUMG.

20.3.12 Reprocess Scan (Scan 6)

You carry out the reprocess scan after you have processed the vocabulary as thoroughly as possible. The technique for starting and monitoring the reprocess scan is the same as for the previous scans.

The process looks for records that contain any of the following:

▶ Words not assigned in the vocabulary

▶ Strings with special characters that are shorter than the minimum word length (default 3)

▶ Strings with special characters that are longer than the maximum word length (30)

▶ Records with words where a conversion collision occurred. These are records containing vocabulary entries that were assigned to conflicting codepages, for example, records with a mixture of Chinese and Japanese words.

If a table contains at least one such record, it is flagged with a yellow warning status in the scan result, and the status code is set to "C" (reprocess log created) or "D" (conversion collision detected, see Figure 20.26).

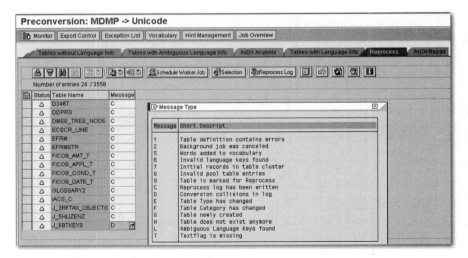

Figure 20.26 Result of Reprocess Scan

While the scan is still running, you can already work on the Reprocess log of these tables. Mark one table in the scan result, and choose **Reprocess Log**.

The interesting thing in the Reprocess log is that you now see the actual *primary key* of the table record. This can make it easier to identify the data. For instance, in Figure 20.27, a table appeared in the Reprocess log because it contained language-dependent entries for language Japanese, but no Japanese was installed in this system.

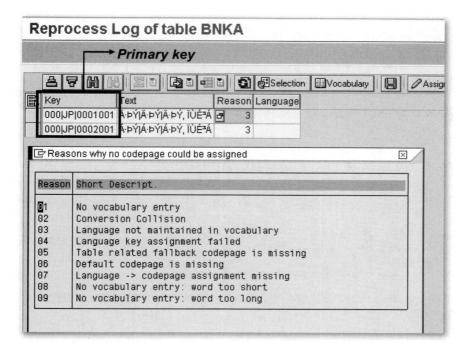

Figure 20.27 Reprocess Log

The assignments in the Reprocess log are not used during the Unicode conversion; instead, they serve as the basis for the automatic text repair process after the conversion (Transaction SUMG).

20.3.13 INDX Repair Scan (Scan 7)

This is the only scan that *changes* data in the database. The aim of the INDX repair scan is to correct where needed the indication of the codepage used in the binary part (CLUSTD field) of the INDX table records.

If manual checking and language assignment is needed, then the table receives a yellow warning status in the scan result. You must proceed in the same way as with the Reprocess log, that is, mark each table in turn and click on **INDX Log**.

The words with special characters are then listed along with the primary key, and you must assign a language manually (see Figure 20.28).

Figure 20.28 INDX Repair Log

20.4   Upgrade in the CU&UC Scenario

Why?	The release upgrade must be completely performed before the Unicode conversion.
When?	After completing the SPUM4/SPUMG preconversion analysis. SAPup checks for this and refuses to start if the analysis is not finished.
Where?	In the source release of the system to be upgraded.
How?	Using the standard upgrade tools. No "special" version of SAPup is required for CU&UC upgrades.

20.4.1   Preconversion Complete

When all the scans are finished, a flag is set in a status table to indicate that the preconversion process is complete. In Transaction SPUM4, this will be visible because the system displays the message Upgrade status is set to "Preparations on start release finished" (see Figure 20.29).

You can continue the upgrade only when SPUM4 is complete and you see this status. If you try to start the upgrade before that, an error will immediately occur in upgrade phase UCMIG_STATUS_CHK:

```
ERROR: The Unicode Conversion Preparations on the startrelease
(Transaction SPUMG/SPUM4) have not been finished yet. You cannot
proceed with the upgrade unless the preparation has been finished.
```

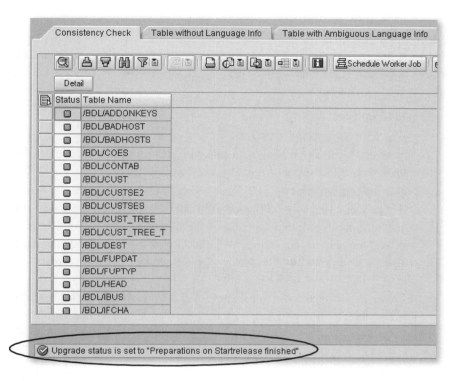

Figure 20.29 SPUM4 Completion Message

20.4.2 Process New Tables

It is possible that new tables have been imported into the system since the time when you ran SPUMG/SPUM4. You must repeat the analysis process for these new tables. Proceed as follows:

1. Start SPUMG/SPUM4, and choose **Scanner • Update Worklist**.

2. Wait until the job completes, and then check the table list under the **Consistency check** tab. Any new tables will appear with the status **Initial**.

3. For single-codepage systems, you only need to run the Consistency Check for these new tables.

4. For MDMP systems, you must also run the scans **Tables without Language Info** and **Tables with Ambiguous Language Info**. Then you must process the vocabulary entries for these added tables, including rerunning the **Tables with Language Information** scan, applying hints, and the using various other methods described earlier. Finally, you must run the **Reprocess** scan and clean up the Reprocess log.

20.4.3 Upgrade Activities

When the SPUM4/SPUMG conversion is truly finished, you may start SAPup in the usual manner. The upgrade process in the CU&UC scenario does not differ from a normal upgrade except that extra phases are executed to prepare the system for the Unicode conversion:

▶ **Phases in uptime:**

 ▷ **Phase JOB_UM4_COPY_RESULTS**
 The results of the preconversion analysis, including the vocabulary, are transferred to the tables of the target release.

 ▷ **Phase RUN_RADCUCNT_ALL**
 The Unicode nametabs are generated for the dictionary objects. The nametab is the "compiled" version of the dictionary definition. Although the upgrade during downtime will pick up and process any nametabs added or changed after this phase, it is recommended not to make any more changes to the dictionary after this phase.

 ▷ If errors occur during the generation of the Unicode nametabs, then follow the detailed instructions given in the Unicode Conversion Guide.

▶ **Phases in downtime:**

 ▷ **Phase JOB_UM4_FILL_RLOAD**
 This phase assigns a master language to ABAP source code objects (table REPOSRC).

 ▷ **Phase RUN_RADCUCNT_NEW**
 Unicode nametabs are generated for dictionary objects created or changed after the uptime phase RUN_RADCUCNT_ALL.

20.4.4 Actions Between End of Upgrade and Unicode Conversion

Between the end of the release upgrade and the database export/import for the Unicode conversion, some extra actions are required. You will again find up-to-date instructions in the CU&UC Conversion Guide. We list some of the key actions here.

> **Note**
>
> The time between the end of the upgrade and the Unicode conversion must be considered as *downtime*. No concurrent user activity must be allowed.

Report TWTOOLo1

Matchcodes are no longer supported in Unicode systems. All match codes must be converted to search help functions before the conversion. Report TWTOOL01 will find all active Matchcode Pool IDs. You must convert any matchcodes the program reports.

Run report TWTOOL01 until the message Check successful, no action necessary is shown.

Update Database Statistics

To avoid long runtimes during other activities, especially the table-specific preparation programs, you should schedule an update of the database statistics, at least for the tables mentioned in the CU&UC Guide.

Report UMG_ADD_PREP_STEP

Unless the Basis support package level of the upgraded system is 700/11 or higher (in which case, UMG_ADD_PREP_STEP is scheduled automatically in the next step), run the program now. Instructions are in Section 20.3.2, subsection *Preparation Report UMG_ADD_PREP_STEP*.

Report UM4_FINISH_PREPARATION

This utility program (called UMG_FINISH_PREPARATION for Start Release 6.20/6.40) is only used in a CU&UC upgrade, not in a standalone Unicode conversion (including the TU&UC scenario). It performs three final activities before the Unicode conversion:

▶ Update of the SPUMG work list

▶ Consistency Check for tables added during the upgrade

▶ Merge of the SPUMG control tables created before and after the upgrade

Before you run the report, check that the table UMGPOCNV is empty.

When you execute the program, a window opens with the three operations shown in the left pane (see Figure 20.30). Select each operation in turn, and click on **Execute**.

The program starts background jobs for the actual processing. You can use **Refresh** to get an up-to-date status (gray = not started; yellow = job active; green = process complete). Refer to the instructions in the CU&UC Guide if you get an error status (red).

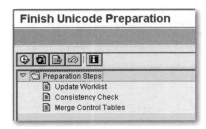

Figure 20.30 UM4_FINISH_PREPARATION Step Selection

After completing `UM4_FINISH_PREPARATION`, the table UMGPOCNV should contain at least an entry for table pool ATAB. If this entry does not exist, go to Transaction SE38, and run report `UMG_POOL_TABLE` manually.

Empty Critical Nametab Tables

Make sure that the following tables are empty. This is critical because, otherwise, the control files generated for the R3load export will be incorrect:

▶ DDXTF

▶ DDXTT

▶ DDXTF_CONV_UC

▶ DDXTT_CONV_UC

These tables contain entries for inactive nametabs and should normally be empty. If you find that the tables contain data, do not delete these records! If the number of entries is small, you can try activating the objects involved. If this does not work or there are too many entries to make manual activation an option, open a support message with SAP.

Table-Specific Actions

Various table-specific activities, for example, emptying the tables containing update requests, are also needed before the Unicode conversion. At the time of writing, no such actions were listed in the CU&UC Guide for 4.6C, but several were described for CU&UC with Start Release 6.20 and 6.40.

20.5 The Unicode Conversion

Why?	All data must be exported from the non-Unicode database and imported into a new Unicode database.
When?	In CU&UC: during the downtime for the update and Unicode conversion.

Where?	In the system that is being upgraded.
How?	With the R3load utility. The data is converted during the export step, based on the codepage assignment information of Transaction SPUMG/SPUM4.

20.5.1 Tools for System Copy, Migration, and Unicode Conversion

The default conversion method is to export the entire database using R3load, create a new Unicode database, and then import the database again. The procedure is, in principle, a homogeneous system copy extended with a conversion to Unicode. The conversion to Unicode is done during the database export. The installation of the new Unicode system is very similar to the installation of a new SAP system. Instead of using the standard export CDs delivered by SAP, the export dump files are used.

Description of the Tools

With the SAP installation tool, the SAP Landscape Implementation Manager (SAPINST), the database can be exported and imported using a format that is independent of the DBMS, the OS, and the codepage. The procedure creates a database export of all SAP objects that are defined in the SAP dictionary.

On the source (export) side, SAPINST call three utilities:

▶ R/3 Load Control utility (R3ldctl)

▶ R/3 Size Check utility (R3szchk)

▶ R/3 Data Unloader/Loader (R3load)

On the target (import) side, R3load is used to import the data after the database has been created. R3ldctl and R3szchk are not used in the import process.

The functionality of each component is explained here:

▶ R/3 Load Control (R3ldctl) reads the SAP data dictionary and creates a list of all tables and indexes to be migrated. Tables are grouped into packages, whereby all tables of the same "data class" belong to the same package. The data class of a table is specified in its technical settings in the SAP data dictionary. The data class of all SAP owned objects is defined by SAP. For example, all cluster tables have table class CLUST. Customers may create their own data classes for customer objects.

▶ R/3 Size Checker (R3szchk) estimates the size of each table in the database. These estimates are used by R3load to create the tables in the target database during the data import. The same calculations are also used to estimate the size of the target database.

459

▶ During the data export, R/3 Data Loader/Unloader (R3load) will unload all data from the packages created. An R3load process is started for each package. The number of R3load processes that run in parallel is controlled by SAPINST or the Migration Monitor (see Section 20.5.2). During the data import, R/3load creates the tables in the target database, loads the data, and builds the indexes.

Migration Files

The migration process (based on R3ldctl, R3szchk, and R3load) will create different types of files. One set of files contains the actual database data, another contains the metadata such as the structure definitions from the SAP dictionary, and yet another set controls and logs the progress of the export and import processes.

Each file type is identified by a three-character extension. Table 20.1 gives the extensions and the description of the corresponding files.

Extension	Description
.str	**Structure files** Define the structure of database objects (tables and indexes).
.ext	**Extent definition files** Define storage characteristics (extent sizes) for tables and indexes in the target database. EXT files exist only for database systems with explicit extent size allocation.
.tpl	**Database template** Contains database-specific structure and storage information. There is only one TPL file per DBMS.
.001, .002, ...	**Data files** Contain the actual database data in compressed form.
.toc	**Table of Contents files** List the contents of the data files for their export class (tables names, starting address of the data for each table in the data file).
.tsk	**Task files** Log the export status (source) or import status (target) of each database object.
.cmd	**Command files** Drive the export and import processes.
.log	**Logfiles** Log the export and import processes.

Table 20.1 Migration File Types

Extension	Description
.xml	**SAPINST control files** Control the source export, target installation, and target import process if SAPINST is used. For the Unicode conversion, R3load also creates logs in XML format on behalf of the postconversion processing with Transaction SUMG.

Table 20.1 Migration File Types (cont.)

Directory Structure

All the files in Table 20.1 reside in one of the following directories:

▶ The *installation* directory: This is the directory used by the installation utility (SAPINST).

▶ The *export* directory: All files containing data and metadata are placed here. The export directory is built up on the source side and must be transferred entirely to the target side for the import.

▶ The export directory is itself subdivided into two areas: the *DATA* subdirectory contains the data files along with the DBMS-independent metadata; the *DB* subdirectory contains DBMS-specific information.

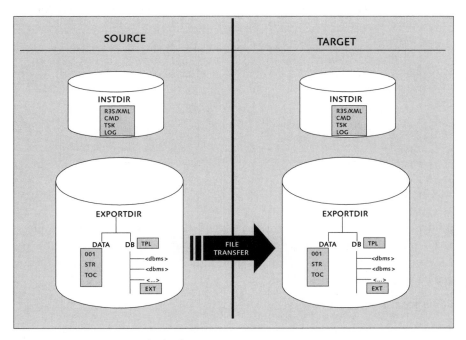

Figure 20.31 Directories and Files for Export/Import

461

The subdirectory *DB* in its turn contains one subdirectory per DBMS:

- *ADA*: SAP DB
- *DB2*: DB2 for z/OS (OS/390)
- *DB4*: DB2 for iSeries (AS/400)
- *DB6*: DB2 UDB for UNIX/Windows
- *INF*: Informix
- *MSS*: Microsoft SQL Server
- *ORA*: Oracle

Figure 20.31 shows a schema of the directory tree and the location of each file type.

Structure File (STR)

The structure file has extension *.STR*, and defines the database-independent structure of each table to be loaded. The STR file is created by the R3ldctl tool, which runs before the export process, and resides normally in the same directory as the data files (*<exportdir>/ABAP/DATA*). An extract from an actual file follows:

```
tab: FUNCT
att: SSEXC 3      T GX all    FUNCT~0                     SSEXC 3
fld: SPRAS        LANG    1      0    0 not_null  1
fld: FUNCNAME     CHAR    30     0    0 not_null  2
fld: PARAMETER    CHAR    30     0    0 not_null  3
fld: KIND         CHAR    1      0    0 not_null  4
fld: VERSION      NUMC    4      0    0 not_null  5
fld: STEXT        CHAR    79     0    0 not_null  0

ind: FUNCT~1
att: FUNCT                           SSEXC 3   not_unique
fld: FUNCNAME
fld: PARAMETER
fld: KIND
```

R3ldctl creates one STR file per data class (TABART). The name of the file is *SAP<art>.STR* where *<art>* denotes the class name; for example, for APPL1, the file name is *SAPAPPL1.STR*. The class splitter (described later) will create further classes, all with their own STR file.

Some special classes are used:

- Pools and cluster tables are assigned to a data class POOL and CLUST.
- All views are recorded in a separate class *SAPVIEW.STR*.

- Class *SAP0000.STR* contains the generated code tables (ABAP loads, screen loads, etc.). Because these loads are OS- and database-dependent, the contents of these tables must not be exported to the target side. The migration procedure will therefore only create the tables and indexes listed in the SAP0000 class but will not unload or load the data.

- Class SAPNTAB contains the non-Unicode and Unicode nametab tables.

Inside the STR file, tables normally appear in alphabetical order. If a table has secondary indexes, the index definitions follow the table definition.

Each line in the STR file is identified by a leading attribute, consisting of three lowercase characters:

- tab: Table name
- ind: Secondary index name
- att: Table (+ primary key) or index attributes
- fld: Table or index field
- vie: View name
- qry: View query

For a table, there is one tab: entry, one att: (attribute) entry, and as many fld: entries as there are fields in the table. The ind: entries identify secondary indexes.

The attribute line (att:) is the most interesting. For a table, the tokens on this line mean the following, starting from the left:

- Data class (TABART) of the table in the SAP dictionary
- Size category (TABKAT) of the table, taken from the Technical Settings in the SAP dictionary
- Table type flag (T = transparent, P = pool, C = cluster)
- Internal table type indicator, used for instance to identify SAP report or dictionary metadata ("nametab") tables
- Load flag (all = create + load data; data = load data only, structure must exist; struct = create structure, do not load data yet)
- Name of primary index
- Data class (TABART) of primary index; by default, the same as the table's
- Size category (TABKAT) of primary index; by default, the same as the table's

For an index, the att: line contains the following tokens:

- Name of the parent table
- Data class of the index (normally the same as that of the table)

▶ Size category of the index

▶ Uniqueness of the index

In a table definition section, the field descriptors (`fld:`) fully describe the field characteristics, such as the data type and length. In an index section, the field descriptors simply list the fields that are part of this specific index.

Extent File (EXT)

The extent file lists objects with their initial extent size. They exist only for target databases with explicit storage clauses for the initial extent size. These files are created by R3szchk before the data export. The EXT files reside in the directory *<exportdir>/ABAP/DB/<dbms>*. There is one extent file per data class.

The structure of the file is very simple: Each line contains the name of the object (table or index) followed by a space and the initial extent size in bytes. Example:

```
FUNCT     267632640
FUNCT~0   1884160
FUNCT~1   282337280
etc.
```

DBMS Template File (TPL)

There is one template file for each DBMS. The file contains all the information needed to generate the database-specific DDL (Data Definition Language) statements during the import process.

The name of these files is *DDLdbs.TPL*, where *dbs* is a suffix identifying the database system (e.g., *DDLORA.TPL, DDLINF.TPL*). The TPL files reside in the export area, in the directory *<exportdir>/ABAP/DB*.

The following example shows the template file for Oracle (*DDLORA.TPL*). Each relevant section of the list is followed by a description.

```
prikey: AFTER_LOAD ORDER_BY_PKEY
seckey: AFTER_LOAD
```

These lines define the action regarding the primary key (unique index) and secondary indexes. The keywords `AFTER_LOAD` or `BEFORE_LOAD` indicate that the index is to be created after or before loading the table. The `ORDER_BY_PKEY` argument is important when exporting. If specified, the query used to export from the source database includes an `ORDER BY` clause on all fields of the primary key. Without this keyword, the query is a full sequential scan. Exporting without primary key sort provides a significant performance gain, but the exported data cannot be used on the import side by all DBMS.

The data export can be done sorted or unsorted. The default setting is sorted. Exporting tables without the order by key and the performance improvement it brings might sound tempting, however, the following factors should be taken into account before doing so:

▶ Tables should only be exported unsorted if the target database does not need sorted data. This is not the case if the target database is Microsoft SQL Server or MaxDB. Unsorted data has a huge performance impact during the data load in these database systems.

▶ SAP dictionary tables must always be exported in sorted order. This goes for tables of type report (R), nametab (N), and dynpro (D). The table type is part of the STR file. It is the fifth column of the att: line of the corresponding table.

▶ If a codepage conversion is to be performed, which is the case during a Unicode conversion or migration from an AS/400 EBCDIC system to a UNIX or Windows system, the cluster tables must not be exported unsorted.

▶ If the goal of the exercise is to reorganize the database, the export should be done sorted.

Although there is one big advantage when you export the data unsorted, you have to consider the disadvantages as well. Tables should only be unloaded unsorted if the runtime of a sorted unload exceeds the downtime limits of the project. In general, unload as few tables as possible unsorted.

> **Note for Oracle**
>
> The *DDLORA_LRG.TPL* is a DBMS template configured to unload tables unsorted.

The three following SQL statements are taken from the template file for Oracle (*DDLORA.TPL*). They are used during the data load to create tables, primary key indexes and secondary indexes. The template files for the other databases supported by SAP contain comparable entries compatible to those databases (template *DDLDB2.TPL* for DB2 on OS390, *DDLDB4.TPL* for DB2 on OS400, *DDLDB6.TPL* for DB2 on Windows/Unix, *DDLMSS.TPL* for SQL-Server, *DDLINF.TPL* for Informix and *DDLADA.TPL* for MaxDB)

```
.cretab: CREATE TABLE &tab_name
        ( /{ &fld_name &fld_desc /-, /} )
        TABLESPACE &location
        STORAGE (INITIAL     &init
                 NEXT        &next
                 MINEXTENTS  &minext
```

```
                           MAXEXTENTS   &maxext
                           PCTINCREASE &pctinc )

crepky: CREATE UNIQUE INDEX &pri_key
        ON &tab_name
        ( &key_fld /-, )
        TABLESPACE &location
        STORAGE (INITIAL      &init
                 NEXT         &next
                 MINEXTENTS   &minext
                 MAXEXTENTS   &maxext
                 PCTINCREASE &pctinc )

creind: CREATE &unique INDEX &ind_name
        ON &tab_name
        ( /{ &fld_name /-, /} )
        TABLESPACE &location
        STORAGE (INITIAL      &init
                 NEXT         &next
                 MINEXTENTS   &minext
```

After the create statements, come the "negative" entries lists for tables, indexes, and views:

```
negtab: LICHECK MLICHECK
negind: LICHECK~0 MLICHECK~0 LICHECK^0 MLICHECK^0
negvie:
```

The objects appearing in these "negative" entries are tables, indexes, and views that are not migrated. After the data import, R3load checks whether all objects have been created (using the list of objects created by R3ldctl on the export side). Normally, a missing object would lead to an error. For the objects listed here, however, their absence from the database is acceptable.

The entries for the objects not to be migrated is followed by the data classes and their storage areas for the database tables:

```
# table storage parameters
loc: APPL0 PSAPSTABD                      0000
     APPL1 PSAPBTABD                      0000
     APPL2 PSAPPOOLD                      0000
     CLUST PSAPCLUD                       0000
     POOL  PSAPPOOLD                      0000
     SDIC  PSAPDDICD                      0000
     SDOCU PSAPDOCUD                      0000
     SLDEF PSAPEL40BD                     0000
```

```
SLEXC  PSAPEL40BD                    0000
SLOAD  PSAPLOADD                     0000
SPROT  PSAPPROTD                     0000
SSDEF  PSAPES40BD                    0000
SSEXC  PSAPES40BD                    0000
SSRC   PSAPSOURCED                   0000
TEMP   PSAPPROTD                     0000
USER   PSAPUSER1D                    0000
USER1  PSAPUSER1D                    0000
```

```
sto:  0   0000000016K 0000000040K 0001 0300
      1   0000000016K 0000000160K 0001 0300
      10  0000000016K 0001310720K 0001 0150
      11  0000000016K 0002621440K 0001 0150
      12  0000000016K 0005242880K 0001 0150
      13  0000000016K 0010485760K 0001 0150
      14  0000000016K 0020971520K 0001 0150
      2   0000000016K 0000000640K 0001 0300
      3   0000000016K 0000002560K 0001 0300
      4   0000000016K 0000010240K 0001 0300
      5   0000000016K 0000020480K 0001 0300
      6   0000000016K 0000040960K 0001 0300
      7   0000000016K 0000081920K 0001 0300
      8   0000000016K 0000163840K 0001 0300
```

This is an important section. The entries that follow `loc:` associate load processes (data classes) with storage areas (in the case of Oracle, these are tablespaces). If you create your own load processes, then you must enter information here, so that the import process knows where to place the tables. The third token is specific for Oracle and contains the `PCTINCREASE` value (always 0). For other database systems this, token is absent.

The part beginning with `sto:` lists the `STORAGE` parameters for each size category. Note that there are more size categories here than you can normally specify in the Technical Settings in the SAP dictionary. For Oracle, each line contains the size category, initial extent (only used by the import if there is no EXT file), next extent, minimum extent, and maximum extent.

Next, the storage section for the indexes:

```
# index storage parameters
loc: APPL0 PSAPSTABI                 0000
     APPL1 PSAPBTABI                 0000
     APPL2 PSAPPOOLI                 0000
     CLUST PSAPCLUI                  0000
     POOL  PSAPPOOLI                 0000
```

467

```
        SDIC   PSAPDDICI                      0000
        SDOCU  PSAPDOCUI                      0000
        SLDEF  PSAPEL40BI                     0000
        SLEXC  PSAPEL40BI                     0000
        SLOAD  PSAPLOADI                      0000
        SPROT  PSAPPROTI                      0000
        SSDEF  PSAPES40BI                     0000
        SSEXC  PSAPES40BI                     0000
        SSRC   PSAPSOURCEI                    0000
        TEMP   PSAPPROTI                      0000
        USER   PSAPUSER1I                     0000
        USER1  PSAPUSER1I                     0000

sto: 0   0000000016K 0000000040K 0001 0300
     1   0000000016K 0000000080K 0001 0300
     10  0000000016K 0000327680K 0001 0150
     11  0000000016K 0000655360K 0001 0150
     12  0000000016K 0001310720K 0001 0150
     13  0000000016K 0002621440K 0001 0150
     14  0000000016K 0005242880K 0001 0150
     2   0000000016K 0000000160K 0001 0300
     3   0000000016K 0000000640K 0001 0300
     4   0000000016K 0000002560K 0001 0300
     5   0000000016K 0000005120K 0001 0300
     6   0000000016K 0000010240K 0001 0300
     7   0000000016K 0000020480K 0001 0300
     8   0000000016K 0000040960K 0001 0300
     9   0000000016K 0000081920K 0001 0300
```

The format is the same as that for tables, except that it refers of course to the index tablespaces. Note that the size categories have the same number as those of the tables, but the NEXT extent sizes are different (smaller).

> **Note**
>
> The DB2/UDB template only lists the tablespaces. DB2 creates all tables and indexes using the same extent size. The template for Microsoft SQL Server and MaxDB does not list any tablespaces at all because neither DBMS uses the tablespace concept. All table and indexes are distributed over the available data files. Informix does not define separate storage characteristics for the indexes. The DBMS template for Informix does not contain a tablespace (dbspace) section.

Data Files (001, 002 ...)

The data files reside in the directory *<EXPORTDIR>\ABAP\DATA*. You can find the actual path in the `dat:` entry of the CMD file. The files are compressed binary files, internally organized in fixed-size blocks of data.

The export process limits the size of each data file to a value set in the CMD file (see the next section). Typical sizes are 640 MB (meant to fit on a CD), 1,000 MB, or 2,000 MB. This is done to avoid problems with maximum file sizes, which tend to differ between platforms. If one file is not sufficient to hold all the data of the class, then R3load automatically uses continuation files. The extension of the first data file is always 001. Continuation files, if they exist, have extensions 002, 003, and so on.

It is not documented which compression technique R3load uses, but in our experience, the compression rate is usually very high. We have never seen compression rates below 5:1 (except for cluster tables, whose data is already compressed in the source database). Take this fact into account when you look at the growth of the data files to monitor the progress of an export process; from the fact that the file size increases slowly, you might mistakenly conclude that the process is very slow.

Main Command File (CMD)

The CMD file contains directory paths and other file information that R3load needs to locate its input and output files. The installation tool SAPINST or the Migration Monitor (see Section 20.5.2) creates a command file for each data class.

CMD files reside in the SAPINST or Migration Monitor installation directory *<INSTDIR>*.

A typical CMD file may look as follows:

```
icf: /sapexport/DATA/SAPSSDEF.STR
dcf: /sapexport/DB/DDLORA.TPL
dat: /sapexport/DATA/ bs=1K fs=2000M
dir: /sapexport/DATA/SAPSSDEF.TOC
ext: /sapexport/DB/ORA/SAPSSDEF.EXT
```

As in the STR file, entries in the CMD file begin with a three-character identifier. The entries have the following meaning:

▶ `icf:` Path to the STR file.

▶ `dcf:` Path to the DBMS-specific TPL file.

- ▶ dat: The first token is the directory where the data files are to be created (export) or where the import process must look for them (import). The token bs= gives the block size of the data files. The token fs= gives the maximum size of one data file.
- ▶ dir: Path to the TOC file.
- ▶ ext: Path to the EXT file (for target DBMS using explicit initial extent sizing).

In the example, the dat: entry in the command file refers to a data file */sapexport/DATA/SAPSSDEF.001* with a size of up to 2,000MB. If the amount of data exceeds this space, then the R3load export creates continuation files with extension *.002, .003,* and so on. Each file can again be up to 2,000MB in size. The import process uses the entry to locate the first data file of the class. The information stating whether continuation files are present or not is contained in the TOC file.

The dat: entry may also contain the string NULL, which means that there is no data for this class, only structure information. This is the case for example for the report load tables (class SAP0000) in a heterogeneous migration. In that case, only the table definitions are imported into the target system but not the actual data. The command file for the views (*SAPVIEW.cmd*) also has a NULL here.

The ext: entry does not always appear. If it exists, it points to the EXT file, which lists the INITIAL extent size for all tables and indexes in the class. If the command file for an import process refers to a nonexistent EXT file, then the import will not fail; instead, R3load will use a default INITIAL extent size taken from the TPL file.

Task Files (TSK)

Starting with Basis Release 6.10, R3load uses a new file type with extension *.tsk* ("task files"). These files contain the list of objects to be processed along with their installation status. The TSK files are initially created for each class with all objects in state xeq (= to do). When R3load starts, it renames the TSK file of the data class it is about to process to <class>.TSK.bck. As R3load processes database objects, it builds up a new TSK file in which each object gets an entry with the status ok or err.

Example of a TSK files (for import):

```
T DBMAPS C ok
P DBMAPS~0 C ok
D DBMAPS I ok
T FINPL C ok
P FINPL~0 C ok
D FINPL I ok
```

```
I FINPL~Z01 C ok
T KTEST11 C ok
P KTEST11~0 C ok
D KTEST11 I ok
T M_ADMC C ok
P M_ADMC~0 C ok
D M_ADMC I ok
T M_ADRC C ok
P M_ADRC~0 C ok
```

Each line begins with the object type (T = table, P = primary key, D = data, I = secondary index, V = view), followed by the name of the object, the operation (C = create, I = import), and the status.

Creating the TSK file for the data class is the first step in the export or import process. You can see this in the *Logfile* (described later in this section), which in its first few lines will show a command-line image for R3load containing the argument -ctf (create task file).

The TSK files are essential to allow R3load to restart after an error. If for instance an R3load import encounters a database error (e.g., failure to create a table), then it will assign the status err to the erroneous object. Depending on the context, R3load may either stop immediately, leaving the remaining unprocessed objects in status xeq, or may continue processing the remaining objects until the end of the class. SAPINST will detect the failed R3load and will report an import error. When you then retry the import, the new R3load process for the failed class knows from the TSK file which objects remain to be processed (all objects not in status ok).

Because of their nature, you will understand that meddling with the TSK files should be avoided. As a rule, do not modify a TSK file unless you are absolutely certain of what you are doing, or SAP support instructs you to change a file. Improper changes to TSK files can lead to severe problems, such as missing data, which in the worst case could even force you to repeat the entire migration. Before changing TSK files, always consult SAP Note 455195, which explains the TSK file mechanism and provides up-to-date information about their usage.

One situation where you may have to alter the TSK files is when an active R3load terminates abnormally (e.g., Ctrl – C, kill, core dump), and then both the *TSK* and *TSK.bck* files remain in existence. When R3load restarts, it will immediately report an error: the fact that the two files are present at the same time is taken as an indication that another R3load is already processing this class. If you run into this situation, there are two ways of restarting R3load:

1. Run R3load again with the same arguments as normal (you find these in the *Logfile*) but adding the argument -merge_bck. This argument merges the two files together. In the log, you will see that R3load then tries to drop each table or index before creating it again. As a result, the log will contain numerous nonfatal error messages.

2. Merge the two files manually. Append the contents of the *TSK.bck* file to the TSK file, starting with the first object not mentioned in the TSK file. When this is done, you must delete or move the *TSK.bck* file.

Table of Contents File (TOC)

The TOC file for a data class acts as a directory for the data file (or files, if continuation files exist) of that class. The file resides in the same directory as the data files, that is, *<EXPORTDIR>/ABAP/DATA*. You can find the actual path in the dir: entry of the CMD file.

Classes without a data file (e.g., SAPVIEW, SAP0000 in heterogeneous migrations) do not have a TOC file. The dir: entry in the CMD file then contains NULL.

Example:

```
tab: AANK
eot: #20030904124547
tab: AANL
eot: #20030904124547
tab: ATAB
fil: SAPPOOL.001 1024 #20030904124547
1   14953 #983585 rows
eot: #20030904125319
tab: BPHIER
eot: #20030904125319
tab: CFIS
eot: #20030904125319
tab: DVPOOLTEXT
eot: #20030904125320
tab: FINPL
fil: SAPPOOL.001 1024 #20030904125320
14954   15625 #21563 rows
eot: #20030904125407

(...)

tab: YMUS
eot: #20030904133139
tab: ZEXT
```

```
fil: SAPPOOL.002 1024 #20030904133139
4132   4132 #3 rows
eot: #20030904133139

eof: #20030904133139

cnt: 15879803
```

For each table, the TOC file contains a set of lines beginning with the identifier `tab:` and ending with the identifier `eot:`. If no other lines appear in between, then the table was empty when it was exported. If the table contained data, then its TOC section contains a `fil:` entry giving the name of the data file holding the exported table data. This entry is followed by a line without a specific identifier, which gives the offset of the first and last block in the data file where the table data is located.

In the example, only the tables ATAB, FINPL, and ZEXT contain data. The other tables will be created empty during the import of the SAPPOOL class. The data for ATAB fills blocks 1 to 14,953 of the data file *SAPPOOL.001*. The data of FINPL follows this, occupying blocks 14,954 to 15,625. The last table in the class, ZEXT, contains only 3 rows, which are held in a single block (4132) of the file *SAP-POOL.002*. In this case, you can see that the data in the class did not fit into a single data file, so a continuation file was created during the export.

SAPINST Installation Files (XML)

SAPINST does not use the proprietary R3S format for its control files as R3SETUP did[5]; instead, it uses XML (Extensible Markup Language) files. The main XML files reside in the installation directory *<INSTDIR>*:

- *PACKAGES.XML*: List of needed CDs and their labels.
- *DIALOG.XML*: Layout of the screens generated by SAPINST.
- *CONTROL.XML*: Control flow for the installation.
- *KEYDB.XML*: The most important control file, which tracks all options chosen by the user and the progress of the installation.

SAPINST does not have separate files for every installation and migration scenario. All scenarios are defined in a single file, *PRODUCT.XML*, which resides on the Installation Master CD.

---

5 R3SETUP was used for SAP installations and migrations as of R/3 4.0B up to 4.6D.

Another important XML file during migrations is *DBSIZE.XML*. This file contains information about the size of the target database. *DBSIZE.XML* does not reside in the installation directory, but in *<EXPORTDIR>\ABAP\DB\<dbms>*.

With the exception of *DBSIZE.XML*, you are not supposed to modify the XML files of SAPINST directly; exceptions to this rule may occur, but these are then explicitly documented in SAP Notes. Rather than by changing the control files directly, you control the process flow through the use of command-line arguments (properties) that you pass to SAPINST.

20.5.2 The Migration Monitor

The Migration Monitor is a tool that may help speed up the data unload and load process. As of AS 6.40, it is integrated into the SAP installation tool (but its usage is optional). You can also use the monitor for copying older releases by installing and starting it manually.

The main advantage of the Migration Monitor is that it allows running the data export and import in parallel. With the normal migration procedure, the entire database will first be exported before the export files are transferred to the target server (e.g., with FTP); only then can the data import begin on the target side. The Migration Monitor will control the active data exports. As soon as the export process of a data class finishes, the export files are transferred to the target server, and the data import is started immediately. Synchronizing the data export and import can result in significant time gains, especially for very large databases.

Processing Steps

With the Migration Monitor, the system copy happens as follows:

1. The Export Monitor starts individual R3load files for the packages to be exported.
2. The R3load logfiles *.cmd and *.TSK are written to the installation directory of the Export Monitor.
3. When a package is successfully exported, the Export Monitor will transfer all files belonging to that package to the export directory on the target host.
4. When the package has successfully been transferred, the Export Monitor writes a signal file in the exchange directory on the target host.
5. The Import Monitor reads the signal file in the exhange directory and starts R3load to import the package.

Migration Monitor Properties

The Migration Monitor uses a property file on the export and import sides:

export_monitor_cmd.properties
import_monitor_cmd.properties

The settings in these files control the behavior of the Migration Monitors.

Export Properties

The properties listed in this section must be set on the export side in the property file *export_monitor_cmd.properties* (see Tables 20.2, 20.3, and 20.4).

Property	Description
installDir	The installation directory is the directory in which the Migration Monitor was installed and where the R3load TSK and logfiles are to be created.
exportDirs	The export directory. More then one directory can be specified if disk space is of concern. The separator for the list is ; on Windows and : on UNIX.
client / server	Client or server mode. In the client mode, the export is done by SAPINST, the Migration Monitor is only used to transfer the exported dump files to the target system. In server mode, the migration is entirely done by the Migration Monitor.
orderBy	File name that contains the table or package names to be exported before the others.
ddlFile	File name of the DDL control file. The default is *DDL<DBTYPE>.TPL*.
ddlMap	File that maps DDL control files to package names.
r3loadExe	Path to the R3load executable.
Tskfiles	Should be set to "no" for releases < 6.20 and to "yes" for higher releases.
dataCodepage	Codepage for data files. The possible values for Unicode conversions are 4102 or 4103. Codepage 4103 should be used for target systems running on Alpha, Intel X86 (and clones), X86_64, Itanium (Windows and Linux), and Solaris X86_64. Codepage 4102 should be used for target systems running on IBM 390, AS/400, PowerPC (AIX), Linux on zSeries (S/390), Linux on Power, Solaris SPARC, HP PA-RISC, and Itanium (HP-UX).
taskArgs	Additional R3load arguments for the TASK phase.
loadArgs	Additional R3load arguments for the LOAD phase.
jobNum	Number of parallel export jobs. A recommended value is two times the number of CPUs.

Table 20.2 Export Parameters

Property	Description
Net	This value sets the network operating mode. Exported dump files are on a shared file system and accessible by both the export and import host.
netExchangeDir	This directory is used for communication between the Export Monitor and Import Monitor. The Export Monitor will write a file *<PACKAGE>.SGN* to this directory to indicate to the Import Monitor that the export has finished successfully and the import can be started.

Table 20.3 Network Exchange Options

Property	Description
ftp	This value sets the FTP operating mode. Package files will be transferred automatically as soon as an export finishes successfully.
ftpHost	Hostname of the import server.
ftpUser	The FTP user should be the <sid>adm user to make sure that transferred files can be read by the Import Monitor, which is started as <sid>adm.
ftpPassword	Password of <sid>adm on the import server.
ftpExportDirs	Directory on the import server in which the dump files should be stored. More then one directory can be specified if disk space is a concern. The separator for the list is ; on Windows and : on UNIX.
ftptExchangeDir	This directory is used for communication between the Export Monitor and Import Monitor. The Export Monitor will write a file *<PACKAGE>.SGN* to this directory to indicate to the Import Monitor that the export has finished successfully and the import can be started.
ftpJobNum	Number of parallel FTP jobs (default is 1).

Table 20.4 FTP Exchange Options

Import Properties

These properties must be set on the import side (property file export_monitor_cmd.properties) as listed in Tables 20.5 and 20.6.

Property	Description
installDir	The installation directory is the directory in which the Migration Monitor was installed and where the R3load TSK and logfiles are to be created.
importDirs	The import directory. More then one directory can be specified if disk space is of concern. The separator for the list is ; on Windows and : on UNIX.
orderBy	File name that contains the table or package names to be imported before the others. This option is only valid when all export dump files exist on the import host before the Import Monitor is started or when the table splitter is used and the parallel data import in the same table is not supported in the target database.
ddlFile	File name of the DDL control file. The default is *DDL<DBTYPE>.TPL*.
ddlMap	File that maps DDL control files to package names.
r3loadExe	Path to the R3load executable.
Tskfiles	Should be set to "no" for releases < 6.20 and to "yes" for higher releases.
extFiles	Specify "yes" if the EXT files should be included.
dbCodepage	Codepage for the target database. The possible values for Unicode conversions are 4102 or 4103. Codepage 4103 should be used for target systems running on Alpha, Intel X86 (and clones), X86_64, Itanium (Windows and Linux), and Solaris X86_64. Codepage 4102 should be used for target systems running on IBM 390, AS/400, PowerPC (AIX), Linux on zSeries (S/390), Linux on Power, Solaris SPARC, HP PA-RISC, and Itanium (HP-UX).
Omit	R3load omit value -o D: Omit data; do not load data. -o T: Omit tables; do not create tables. -o I: Omit indexes; do not create indexes. -o P: Omit primary indexes; do not create primary indexes. -o V: Omit views; do not create views. Special omit values can be specified (for example, -o TI).
taskArgs	Additional R3load arguments for the TASK phase.
loadArgs	Additional R3load arguments for the LOAD phase.
jobNum	Number of parallel export jobs. A recommended value is two times the number of CPUs.

Table 20.5 Import Parameters

Property	Description
exchangeDir	This directory is used for communication between the Export Monitor and Import Monitor.
	The Export Monitor will write a file <PACKAGE>.SGN to this directory to indicate to the Import Monitor that the export has finished successfully and the import can be started. It this value is not set, the monitor runs in the standalone mode (export was already done at an earlier stage). All export files must be available in the directory specified with the parameter importDirs.

Table 20.6 Import Exchange Options

Properties Applicable to Export and Import

The properties in Tables 20.7, 20.8, and 20.9 can be set both in the export and import files.

Property	Description
monitorTimeout	During a timeout, the monitor sleeps for the indicated number of seconds and does not analyze any files written by R3load.

Table 20.7 Common Options

Property	Description
mailServer	SMTP server name.
mailFrom	Email address that is used as sender.
mailto	Email address or list of address that will be notified if errors occur. An address list must be separated by ; or spaces.

Table 20.8 E-mail Options (When Set, an E-Mail Is Sent in Case of Errors)

Property	Description
Trace level	Possible values All, off, 1 (error), 2 (warning), 3 (info), 4 (default), 5, 6, 7 (trace).

Table 20.9 Trace Level

Additional Features of the Migration Monitor

The Migration Monitor offers some additional features such as the possibility to use more then one DDL file (to export some tables in sorted order while exporting others unsorted), to influence the import order, and to handle databases that do not support parallel data import. All these are discussed in the next section.

Assigning DDL Files to Packages (the ddlMap File)

Several *DDL<DBTYPE>.TPL* files may be used during the export and import. This is required if several tables or table groups must be exported unsorted. The assignment of a specific DDL file to a single package is done within a simple text file, which then has to be specified via the ddlMap option in the Migration Monitor's properties file. Packages not listed in the *ddlMap* file use the default DDL control file.

For example, assume that tables BSIS, COEP, and MSEG are to be exported unsorted. The following entries are to be set in the *ddlMap* file:

```
[ UNSORTED UNLOAD ]
ddlFile = /tmp/MBM/DB/DDLORA_LRG.TPL
```

The Data Control File (ddlFile) is set to DBMS template file in which the order by clause has been removed (see Section 20.5.1, subsection *DBMS Template File* in this chapter). This is followed by the list of tables to be exported unsorted:# table names

```
BSIS
COEP
MSEG
```

Defining Package Order (the orderBy File)

The export order can be influenced via the *orderBy* file (option orderBy). It is a simple text file that contains the table or package names to be exported before the others. In our example, tables BSIS will be exported first, followed by EDI40-1, RFBLG-1, COEP, and CDCLS-1. Tables not mentioned in the list are exported in alphabetical order. Example:

```
BSIS
EDI40-1
RFBLG-1
CE1MB01
COEP
CDCLS-1
```

Processing Split Tables

If tables have been split during the export, you must ensure before the import starts that the table exists and that the primary key and the indexes are created (before or after the data load, depending on the database system). These tasks will be synchronized by the Migration Monitor automatically.

However, parallel data import is not supported on the following databases:

▶ IBM DB2 UDB for UNIX and Windows

▶ IBM DB2 UDB for z/OS

▶ Microsoft SQL Server

You must ensure that data is not loaded in parallel by defining package groups.

Example: Table BSIS and MSEG have been split into three and six packages. Add the following entries to the *orderBy* file. With these entries, you specify that only one package for table BSIS and MSEG can be imported at a time.

```
[ BSIS ]
jobNum=1
BSIS-1
BSIS-2
BSIS-3

[ MSEG ]
jobNum=1
MSEG-1
MSEG-2
MSEG-3
MSEG-4
MSEG-5
```

Output Files of the Migration Monitor

During the system copy, the Migration Monitor writes to the following files:

▶ On the export side:

export_monitor.log
export_state.properties
ExportMonitor.console.log

▶ On the import side:

import_monitor.log
import_state.properties
ImportMonitor.console.log

The export and import state files contain the state of the individual packages. The format of the lines is <PACKAGE>=<STATE> where the following are possible values for <STATE>:

0	Package export/import has not yet started.
?	Package export/import in progress.
-	Package finished with errors.
+	Package finished successfully.

Lines may contain a second state, if FTP or network exchange is used, which refers to the state of the data transfer. Possible values are the following:

0	Package export/import has not yet started.
?	Package export/import in progress.
-	Package finished with errors.
+0	Package finished successfully, transfer not yet started.
+?	Package finished successfully, transfer in progress.
++	Package finished successfully, transfer done.

Restarting or Skipping Packages

The state file may be used to manually restart R3load processes. For example, if a package failed and has state -, the state can be set to 0 to restart the package.

The following modifications are possible:

▶ To restart package processing, set the package state from — to 0.

▶ To skip package processing, set the package state from 0 or — to +. This might make sense if you ran the package manually after resolving the error.

▶ Packages with state ? (currently being processed) should not be changed. If the package is being processed, manual modifications to the state are ignored.

20.5.3 Database Export

The next sections deal with the export process. This process reads all the data from the source database, converts it to Unicode, and stores the data in compressed format in data export files. It also generates and calculates all the metadata (such as table and index definitions and storage requirements). All these will be used during the import to rebuild the system in Unicode.

Using and Controlling SAPINST

All SAP systems based on 6.20 and above use SAPINST for installations and migrations. SAPINST uses XML-based control files.

481

There are three phases in an SAP installation with SAPINST:

▶ The PREPARE phase in which the installation directory used during the installation is created and all necessary files are copied inside

▶ The ASK phase in which SAPINST asks the user for the installation options

▶ The DO phase, in which the SAP system is created and configured

SAPINST always uses a GUI. SAPINST is really two processes: the server process, which handles the actual installation, and the client (GUI) process, which is used for parameter input (in the ASK phase) and for monitoring the installation (in the DO phase). The two processes do not need to run on the same machine: you can start only the server process on the migration host, and start the SAPINST GUI on your local workstation. The SAPINST server and GUI communicate through TCP/IP ports (by default ports 21212 and 21213, but this can be changed via the command line).

Note

SAPINST uses the Java Development Kit 1.4.2 or above. Java versions for different OSs can be downloaded from *http://java.sun.com*. The installation is different for each OS and therefore out of the scope of this book. We assume, however, that it has been installed and correctly configured.

The XML control files are not meant to be modified manually, except for *DBSIZE.XML*. This file is not needed, however, as the target size of the database can be modified through the GUI.

To influence the behavior of SAPINST, you can assign specific values to its runtime properties. You do this by passing one or more property/value pairs on the SAPINST command line.

```
<path>/sapinst property=value property=value ...
```

To list all possible command-line arguments, use:

```
sapinst -h
sapinst --help
```

(Notice the double dash when you type the keyword in full.)

Similarly, to obtain a list of all SAPINST properties, use:

```
sapinst -p
sapinst --properties
```

Table 20.10 shows some useful SAPINST properties.

Property	Description
SAPINST_START_GUI=TRUE|FALSE	When FALSE, only the SAPINST server is started. Use this when you run the SAPINST GUI on a different host (typically your PC). Note: You can also use the command-line argument `--nogui` for this.
SAPINST_SKIP_ERRORSTEP=TRUE	With this property set to TRUE, SAPINST will skip over the first error it encounters. Use this with great caution!
SAPINST_DIALOG_PORT=nnnnn	Instructs the SAPINST server to listen for incoming SAPINST GUI connections on port nnnnn. The default port is 21212. Specifying a different port is useful if the default port is in use by another program, or if it is still blocked by a previous aborted run of SAPINST (it may take some time before the port is released at OS level).
SAPINST_USE_HOST-NAME=host	Tells SAPINST to use "host" as the local host name instead of the physical host name as returned by the hostname command. Using this property is mandatory when you use virtual rather than physical host names for the SAP instance and database installation, for instance, in a cluster (High Availability) configuration.
SAPINST_SET_STEP-STATE=TRUE	Enables the step editor, which will let you change the SAPINST process flow. You can use this for example to insert an "exit" point where you want SAPINST to stop.

Table 20.10 SAPINST Properties

Obviously, you may combine several properties in a single command, for example:

```
sapinst SAPINST_START_GUI=FALSE SAPINST_DIALOG_PORT=21214
```

To start SAPINST without the GUI (in this example, an HP UNIX system), proceed as follows:

```
# /<INSTMASTER>/SAPINST/UNIX/HP11_64/sapinst --nogui
```

Next, start the SAPINST GUI on your PC:

```
<DRIVE>:\<INSTMASTER>\SAPINST\NT\I386\startinstgui.bat
```

The SAP Installation GUI appears (see Figure 20.32). Enter the host name of the server and the port number of SAPINST (default 21212).

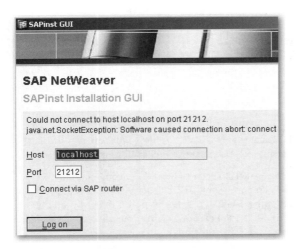

Figure 20.32 SAPINST GUI — Connect to SAPINST

You can use a command like the following to supply the hostname and port number of SAPINST right away:

```
<DRIVE>:\<INSTMASTER>\SAPINST\NT\I386\startinstgui.bat
-host <HOSTNAME> -port 21212
```

Preparation for Table Splitting

Instead of exporting and importing one table with one R3load process, it is now possible to export/import one table with, for example, five processes. Each R3load process takes care of a different part of the table (using a WHERE clause).

Following are the main advantages of splitting tables:

▶ Large tables are processed in smaller packages. If one fails, only the failed package needs to be redone and not the complete table.

▶ The export and import can be done in parallel by several R3load processes that work on the same table.

The Unicode conversion is done during the export and is very CPU intensive. More processes improve the overall conversion time. This is very important for cluster tables such as RFBLG, EDI40, and CDCLS because they need to be uncompressed, converted, and compressed in binary export files.

Prerequisites

When the table splitting feature is used, the export and import must be done with the Migration Monitor (see Section 20.5.2 for more information on the Migration Monitor).

Parallel data export of a table is supported by all database platforms but not parallel data import. When the target database platform does not support the parallel data import, the Migration Monitor has to be configured in the way that the data import processes the packages sequentially. At the time of writing, this was the case for SQL Server and IBM DB2.

Proceed as follows:

1. Log on to your host as user `root` (UNIX) or with local administrator rights (Windows).

2. The determination of the `WHERE` clauses is done with the tool R3ta. Update the R3ta tool and database library in the kernel directory. Download the latest R3ta tool and database library from the Software Distribution Center in the SAP Service Marketplace (*http://service.sap.com/swdc*)

> **Note**
>
> Apart from R3ta and the database library, R3ldctl, R3load and R3szchk are used for the data export and conversion to Unicode. It is highly recommended to download and install the latest versions from the Software Distribution Center in the SAP Service Marketplace (*http://service.sap.com/swdc*). All should be installed in the kernel directory.

3. Start SAPINST from the Installation Master DVD at *<DRIVE>:\<INSTMASTER>\ SAPINST\NT\IA64\sapinst.exe*.

4. After a few seconds, the Welcome Screen appears, which shows all possible installation scenarios organized as a hierarchical tree. It derives its information from the *PRODUCT.XML* file on the Installation Master CD.

5. Choose **SAP NetWeaver 2004s Support Release 2 • Additional Software Life-Cycle Tasks • System Copy • Oracle • Source System • Central System • Based on AS ABAP • Table Splitting Preparation**.

6. Next, SAPINST asks for the installation options (see Figure 20.33).

7. **Table Splitting Preparation**: Here, you specify the general parameters for table splitting:

   ▷ **SAP System ID**: Enter the SAP System ID.

   ▷ **File with tables to be split**: Create a text file with the table names and the number of packages in which each table should be exported. The file could

485

for instance look as follows:

```
CDCLS%10
EDI40 %6
KOCLU%6
RFBLG%6
```

▶ The %<NUMBER> instructs R3ta into how many processes the table should be divided for export. In this example, CDCLS will be exported by 10 R3load processes, and EDI40, KOCLU, and RFBLG each will be exported by 6.

▶ **Export Directory**: Select the export directory, keeping in mind that the size of the export files is normally between 15 % and 20 % of the used data size in the source database

▶ **Number of parallel R3ta runs**: Enter the number of concurrent R3ta runs. Because R3ta uses extensive SELECT statements on the table in question, to determine the best WHERE clause, it might have a serious impact on system performance.

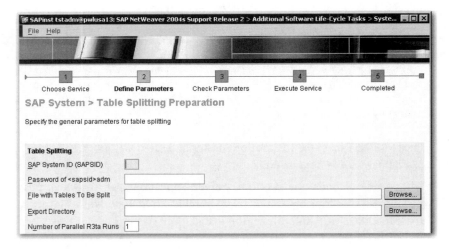

Figure 20.33 SAPINST — Table Splitting Preparation

8. After filling in the screen, click on **Next**.

9. The summary screen appears. Click on **Next** to continue.

SAPINST starts R3ta to construct the WHERE clauses to be used by R3load. Files with extension .whr will be created in the subdirectory DATA of the export directory. R3load will use these files automatically during the database export. At the end, SAPINST creates a text file that contains the tables to be exported in parallel (whr.txt file). This file is also copied to the data directory in the export directory and will be used by package splitter when preparing the export (see Section *Prepare the Export Using SAPINST* below).

Prepare the Export Using SAPINST

The Table Splitting tool has to be used together with the Migration Monitor. With the Migration Monitor, SAPINST is only used to prepare the export. As such, it creates the export directory and uses the R/3 Load Control tool (R3ldctl) and the R/3 Size Checker (R3szchk) to create the export templates. Next, SAPINST calls upon the package splitter to split the packages created by R/3 Load Control and R/3 Size Checker in smaller groups. Finally, SAPINST prompts you to start the Migration Monitor to unload the system.

1. Start SAPINST from the Installation Master DVD at *<DRIVE>:\<INSTMASTER>\ SAPINST\NT\IA64\sapinst.exe*.

2. After a few seconds, the Welcome Screen appears. This screen shows all possible installation scenarios organized as a hierarchical tree.

3. Choose **SAP NetWeaver 2004s Support Release 2 · Additional Software Life-Cycle Tasks · System Copy · Oracle · Source System · Central System · Based on AS ABAP · Database Export**

4. First you must choose between a typical or a custom export. With the default setting **Typical**, SAPINST runs with default settings. You only have to respond to a number of prompts. Default settings can still be modified in the parameter

summary screen. However, we very much prefer the **Custom** setting because it allows you to change settings right away. Choose **Custom**, and click **Next**.

5. Furthermore, you have to specify the profile directory of the SAP System ID and enter the password of the SAP System Administrator. Select the export directory, keeping in mind that the size of the export files is normally between 15 % and 20 % of the used data size in the source database. If you select **Stop running system**, and your system is still running at the time when the export is to be started, you will be prompted to manually stop the system.

6. Specify the common export parameters (see Figure 20.34):

   ▶ Choose the target database system from the **Target Database Type** drop-down list.

   ▶ Enable **Split STR files** to allow SAPINST to split the export classes.

   ▶ Enable **Start Migration Monitor manually**. The Migration Monitor is required if the Table Splitter is to be used. This should always be the case in Unicode migrations. Especially for cluster tables such as CDCLS, RFBLG, and EDI40 because they take a long time to be exported.

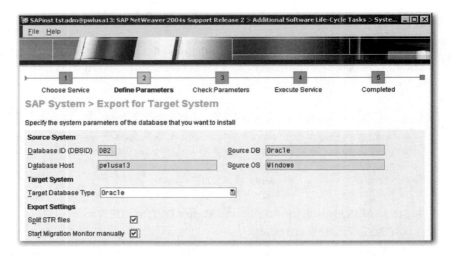

Figure 20.34 SAPINST — Specify Target System

7. Click **Next** to continue.

8. Specify the parameters for the Splitting Tool (see Figure 20.35). Choose between or combine the following options:

   ▶ Enable **Largest tables in separate packages** to create separate data classes for the largest tables. Specify the number of largest tables to be extracted (for example, 100 will isolate the 100 largest tables in individual packages).

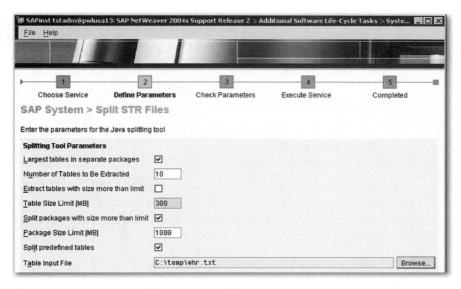

Figure 20.35 SAPINST — Splitting Export Packages

> ▶ Enable **Extract tables with size more than limit,** and specify a size limit. This will create a separate data class for each table of the size specified or more.

> ▶ Enable **Split packages with size more than limit,** and specify a package size. This combines tables into classes so that every data class is approximately the specified package size.

> ▶ Enable **Split predefined tables,** and supply the table input file created during **Preparing for Table Splitting** (see *Preparation for Table Splitting* earlier in this section).

9. Click on **Next** to continue.

10. Next, you can specify whether the database statistics should be updated before the export start.

11. Finally, the Parameter Summary screen appears. Parameters can still be modified by selecting a topic and choosing **'Revis'**. To start the export, click on **Start**.

12. SAPINST performs the different installation tasks up to the point that the data is to be loaded in the database. At this point, it prompts you to start the Migration Monitor (export) (see Figure 20.36). Click on **OK** when the export is finished. SAPINST continues with the postactivities and finalizes the data export.

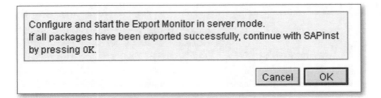

Figure 20.36 SAPINST — Start Migration Monitor

Data Export with the Migration Monitor

The functionality of the Migration Monitor was described in Section 20.5.2. SAP-INST extracted the Migration Monitor when it prepared the data export. Following are the instructions for how to configure the properties and start the Migration Monitor.

Set Export Properties

First configure the export properties file *export_monitor.cmd.properties*. See Section 20.5.2, subsection *Export Properties* for a list of export properties. Following is an example of an export properties file used for a Unicode migration. FTP is used to send the completed packages to the target system. The largest tables were exported before the others (see the contents of the *orderBy* file listed here). In addition, tables BSIS, COEP, and several others were exported unsorted (set in the *ddlMAP* file).

```
# Export Monitor options
#
# Server operating mode
server
#
# Exchange mode: ftp | net
ftp
#
# Common options
# List of export directories, separator on Windows ; on UNIX :
exportDirs=F:\export_PRD\ABAP
# Installation directory
installDir=F:\migmin_PRD
# Package order: name | file with package names
orderBy=orderBYlist
# DDL control file, default is DDL<DB_TYPE>.TPL
ddlFile=
# File with mapping between DDL files and package names
ddlMap=ddlMAP
```

```
# Monitor timeout in seconds
monitorTimeout=30

# R3load options
# Optional path of R3load executable
r3loadExe=
# Generation of task files: yes | no
tskFiles=yes
# Codepage for data files
dataCodepage=4103
# Additional R3load arguments for TASK phase
taskArgs=
# Additional R3load arguments for LOAD phase
loadArgs=
# Number of parallel export jobs
jobNum=10

#
# FTP options
# Remote FTP host
ftpHost=pwlusa14
# Name of remote FTP user
ftpUser=prdadm
# Password of remote FTP user
ftpPassword=test1234
# List of remote FTP directories for export dump, separator : or ;
ftpExportDirs=F:\export_PRD\ABAP
# Remote FTP exchange directory
ftpExchangeDir=F:\exchange_PRD
# Number of parallel FTP jobs
ftpJobNum=1
```

orderBy and ddlMAP files
Entries in the *orderBY* file:

```
BSIS
EDI40-1
RFBLG-1
CE1MB01
COEP
CDCLS-1
KOCLU-1
REPOSRC-1
MSEG
CDHDR
CDCLS-2
...
```

Entries in the *ddlMAP* file:

```
[ UNSORTED UNLOAD ]
ddlFile = F:\export_PRD\ABAP\DB\DDLORA_LRG.TPL

# table names
BSIS
COEP
MSEG
LIPS
VBRP
CMFP
```

Start the Export
On Windows:

Connect as <SID>adm.

```
# cd F:\migmin_PRD
# set JAVA_HOME=c:\java1.4_64bit
# set SAPSYSTEMNAME=PRD
# export_monitor.bat
```

On UNIX:

Connect as <SID>adm.

```
# cd /migmin_PRD
# export JAVA_HOME=/opt/java1.4
# export_monitor.sh
```

On iSeries:

Connect as <SID>OFR.

```
# cd '\usr\sap\SAPinst\NW04\COPY\EXPORT\ABAP\COPY\NUC\DBEXP'
# call R3PRD400/R3INLPGM
# call qp2term
# export JAVA_HOME=/QIBM/ProdData/Java400/jdk14
# export_monitor.sh
```

20.5.4 Uninstall the Non-Unicode System (In-Place Conversion)

With an in-place conversion, the source system equals the target system, which means that the database is unloaded, removed, and recreated in Unicode, and the data is reloaded. The non-Unicode system must be completely removed before the Unicode system can be built.

> **Note**
>
> Make a backup of the SAP directories before removing the non-Unicode installation. Move the existing SAP profiles aside because many SAP instance parameters will have to be compared and probably set after the installation of the Unicode system. Entries like the login client, installed languages, and the default login language should be taken.

Start SAPINST from the Installation Master DVD at *<DRIVE>:\<INSTMASTER>\ SAPINST\NT\IA64\sapinst.exe*.

After a few seconds, the Welcome Screen appears.

Choose **SAP NetWeaver 2004s Support Release 2 · Additional Software Life-Cycle Tasks · Uninstall · Uninstall System — Standalone Engine — Optional Standalone Unit**.

Perform the following steps:

1. Specify the SAP profile directory of the source system.
2. Select the SAP instance to uninstall. Enable **Remove all instances of the SAP system or standaline engine on this host**. Leave **Remove OS users of SAP system or standalone engine on this host** disabled. Click on **Next**.
3. Deselect **Uninstall Database (or parts of the database)**. There is no need to uninstall the RDBMS software or to remove the database. Removing the database will be done while installing and creating the Unicode system.
4. Click on **Start** to continue.

20.5.5 Central System Installation and Data Load

A Unicode system needs to be installed in case of an inplace migration or migration to another platform.

Installation Types

Whether you do an in-place conversion or you migrate to a new server, a new Unicode system always needs to be installed. The installation of a SAP system with SAPINST is always done in one or two independent steps depending on the installation type:

▶ **Central System**

Central System Installation creates the users, groups, services and directory structure for the SAP central instance (CI), installs the SAP kernel, installs the DBMS (or stops to let the user install the software), creates the database, imports the data, and starts the SAP system.

▶ **Distributed System**

Central Instance Installation creates the users, groups, services, and directory structure for the SAP CI, and installs the SAP kernel.

Database Instance Installation creates the directory structure for the database, installs the DBMS software (or stops to let the user install the software), creates the database, imports the data, and starts the SAP system.

For background information on SAPINST control files and runtime properties, see Section 20.5.3, subsection *Using and Controlling SAPINST*.

Note

After the initial installation, upgrade the SAP kernel to the latest version. The Kernel CD in the installation package is probably several months old, and the kernel it contains has in the meantime been superseded by a newer version. You can download the latest kernel version from the SAP Service Marketplace at *http://service.sap.com/PATCHES*.

Note

After the initial installation, it is wise to compare the SAP instance profiles between the source and target. Entries like the login client, installed languages, and the default login language should be taken over from the source system. On the other hand, the system architecture and the amount of memory is probably different on the target server, so profile parameters related to memory configuration should probably be left the way SAPINST created them.

SAPINST Interaction

Start SAPINST from the Installation Master DVD at *<DRIVE>:\<INSTMASTER>\ SAPINST\NT\IA64\sapinst.exe*.

After a few seconds, the Welcome Screen appears. This screen shows all possible installation scenarios organized as a hierarchical tree. It derives its information from the *PRODUCT.XML* file on the Installation Master CD.

1. Choose **SAP NetWeaver 2004s Support Release 2 · Additional Software Life-Cycle Tasks · System Copy · Oracle · Target System · Central System · Based on AS ABAP · Central System Installation**.

2. On the GUI the following interaction is required:

3. Choose between a typical and custom installation. **Custom** is usually the bext choice because it gives you much more control over the installation settings. Choose **Custom,** and click on **Next**.

4. **General Parameters**: Enter the SAP System ID (SAPSID) of the target system. Enable **Unicode System.** Click on **Next**.

5. **Master Password**: Enter the master password. The password will be used for all accounts created during the installation. Click on **Next**.

6. **Domain Information for the SAP System Accounts**: If the SAP system is to run on a single machine, you can perform a local installation. The SAP users and groups will only be created on the local machine. If the system is to be distributed across more then one machine (using different application servers), you should either create the SAP users and groups in the domain or run the installation as domain administrator to allow SAPINST to create them during the installation. Always create the users in the domain although SAP is installed on a single host because as the system grows, additional application servers may be needed. Make the necessary changes, and click on **Next**.

7. Enter the passwords of the OS users. Enter the passwords of the SAP System Administrator <sid>adm and SAP System Service User (SAPService<SID>). Click on **Next**.

8. **Select the installation method**: For Unicode Conversions, select **Standards System Copy/Migration (load-based)**. Enable **Start Migration Monitor manually**. This allows you to install the Unicode system and create the database while the source system is still being exported. Click on **Next**.

9. **Database Parameters**: Choose a Database ID. Click on **Next** to continue.

The Prerequisite Checker checks whether the target systems meet SAP system requirements. If a condition is not met, the pop-up shown in Figure 20.37 appears. Choose **OK** to repeat the Prerequisite Check or **Cancel** to ignore the reported error/warning conditions and continue SAPINST.

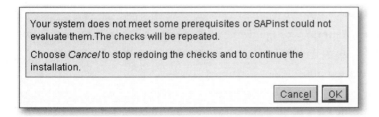

Figure 20.37 SAPINST — Prerequisites Not Met

Proceed as follows:

1. **Migration Directory Browser**: Enter the location of the dump directory, and click on **Next**.

2. **Oracle**: Enter the parameters of the database system.

   ▶ For an in-place Unicode Conversion, SAPINST detects the existing database and asks whether you want to drop and re-create it or install an MCOD (Multiple Components on One Database) system. Choose **Drop database and recreate**.

   ▶ Enter the new ABAP schema. As of AS 6.20, you can define a Schema ID (consisting of three alphanumeric characters) independent of the SAPSID and DBSID. This Schema ID is used instead of SAPSID as a unique code for the database schema and tablespace name (see Section 20.5.6, subsection *The Schema ID* for more information). Click on **Next** to continue.

3. **Oracle**: Enter the parameters of the database system and database layout.

   ▶ **Distribution of the Database Directories**: Map the SAP data directories to the drives available. Choose a location for the redo and mirrored logfiles, the archive directory (oraarch) and the SAP data home directory (saptrace, saparch, and sapreorg).

   ▶ Enable **Advanced DB Configuration**. In the **Advanced DB Configuration** section, you can change parameters for creating the database, creating tablespaces, and file system distribution. Click on **Next** to continue.

4. In the **Advanced Configuration** screen, you can select which aspects of the database configuration you want to configure. We advise you to select at least the following options:

   ▶ **SAP Directory Mapping**: To customize the location of the database data files.

   ▶ **Windows Drive Mapping**: To select the location of the individual sap data directories (saparch, sapbackup, sapreorg, sapcheck, and saptrace).

   ▶ **Create Tablespaces**: To configure the data files, their location, and size for each tablespace.

   ▶ **Autoextend**, **General Storage**, **Default Storage**, and **Extent Management**: To configure the database storage parameters in detail.

   ▶ Click on **Next** to continue.

5. **ABAP System, create Database Statistics**: Specify whether you want the database statistics to be created automatically after the import. You might skip the statistics creation until after all postprocessing actions are finished. Only remember to create database statistics before releasing the systems to end users.

6. **SAP System Central Instance Parameters**: Enter the CI number. SAPINST detects any other SAP system instances running on the same hosts. Make sure to enter a number that is not already used. Click on **Next** to continue.

7. **SAP System Central Instance Parameters**: Enter the CI parameters such as the ABAP Messaging Service Port, the Internal ABAP Messaging Service Port, and the Host with the Transport Directory.

8. **SAP System, DDIC User**: Enter the password for the user DDIC in client 000, and click on **Next**. SAPINST needs this information because near the end of the installation, it will start (via RFC) some background jobs in the newly created system.

9. **Media Browser, Software Package Request**: Enter the location of the Unicode Kernel and Oracle Client DVD.

10. **SAP System, Unpack archives**: SAPINST allows you to integrate newer versions of the kernel executables in the installation. As such, the SAP system is at the latest level after the installation. Newer archives for the kernel, Internet Graphics Server, Oracle Client, the SAP Crypto Library, and the Oracle BRTOOLS, can be provided. Enter the location of the archives downloaded from the SAP Service Marketplace in the column **Downloaded To** (see Figure 20.38). Click on **Next**.

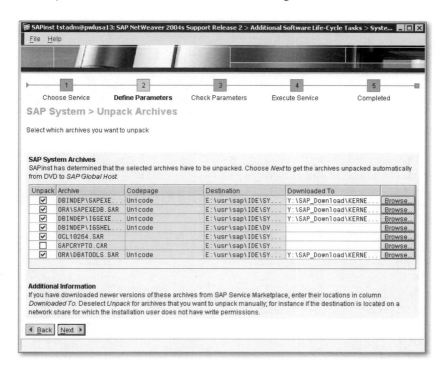

Figure 20.38 SAPINST — Unpack Archives

Finally, the **Parameter Summary** screen appears. Parameters can still be modified by selecting a topic and choosing **Revise**. To start the export, click on **Start**.

SAPINST performs the different installation tasks up to the point that the data is to be loaded in the database. At this point, it prompts you to start the **Migration Monitor (import)**. Click on **Continue** if the load is finished. SAPINST continues with the postactivities and finishes the installation.

Data Import with the Migration Monitor

SAPINST extracts the Migration Monitor while preparing the data import. The following sections provide instructions on how to configure the properties and start the Migration Monitor on the import side.

Set Import Properties

First configure the import properties file *import_monitor.cmd.properties*. See Table 20.4 earlier in this chapter for a list of export properties.

```
# Import Monitor options
#
# Common options
# List of import directories, separator on Windows ; on UNIX :
importDirs= F:\export_PRD\ABAP
# Installation directory
installDir=F:\migmon_PRD
# Package order: name | size | file with package names
orderBy=size
# DDL control file, default is DDL<DB_TYPE>.TPL
ddlFile=
# File with mapping between DDL files and package names
ddlMap=
# Monitor timeout in seconds
monitorTimeout=30

#
# R3load options
#
# Optional path of R3load executable
r3loadExe=
# Generation of task files: yes | no
tskFiles=yes
# Inclusion of extent files: yes | no
extFiles=yes
# DB code page for the target database
dbCodepage=4102
```

```
# Migration key
migrationKey=1WagfeM50T000UqtdaEu1Q9v
# R3load omit value, can contain only 'DTPIV' letters
omit=
# Additional R3load arguments for TASK phase
taskArgs=
# Additional R3load arguments for LOAD phase
loadArgs=
# Number of parallel import jobs
jobNum=10

#
# Exchange options
#
# Exchange directory
exchangeDir=F:\exchange_PRD
```

Start the Import
On Windows:

Connect as <SID>adm.

```
# cd F:\migmin_PRD
# set JAVA_HOME=c:\java1.4_64bit
# set SAPSYSTEMNAME=PRD
# import_monitor.bat
```

On UNIX:

Connect as <SID>adm.

```
# /migmin_PRD
# export JAVA_HOME=/opt/java1.4
# import_monitor.sh
```

On iSeries:

Connect as <SID>OFR.

```
# cd '\usr\sap\SAPinst\NW04\COPY\EXPORT\ABAP\COPY\NUC\DBEXP'
# call R3PRD400/R3INLPGM
# call qp2term
# export JAVA_HOME=/QIBM/ProdData/Java400/jdk14
# import_monitor.sh
```

20.5.6 Database-Specific Aspects — Oracle

Many SAP installations use Oracle. We therefore offer some recommendations for Oracle installations in SAP environments. In addition, we suggest some parameter settings to optimize the data unload and load during the Unicode conversion.

Database Layout as of SAP Basis 6.20

Data storage technology, as well as handling of data in the Oracle DBMS, makes continuous advances. The original database design SAP provided for Oracle databases distributed the data over more than 20 tables paces. Each tablespace contained either data (tables) or indexes, but not both. The underlying idea was to optimize data throughput by spreading the database over several physical disks and to keep tables apart from their indexes to avoid I/O hot spots. Today, with the advent of huge storage arrays, this subdivision no longer makes much sense. Therefore, starting with basis 6.20, SAP has introduced a greatly simplified tablespace layout.

In the new model, all SAP tables and indexes reside in just three tablespaces:

▶ PSAP<SID>: Default tablespace for all SAP objects.

▶ PSAP<SID>USR: Default tablespace for all customer objects.

▶ PSAP<SID><REL>: Default tablespace for release-dependent data (SAP repository).

Note that the tablespaces include the SAP system ID. This is done in view of MCOD support (multiple SAP systems in one database).

Some special tablespaces exist as separate units:

▶ SYSTEM: Tablespace for Oracle dictionary.

▶ PSAPTEMP: Temporary segments for sorting.

▶ PSAPUNDO: Undo segments.

All SAP solutions based on Basis 6.20 or higher are installed with this reduced tablespace set. Furthermore, the default name of the SAP schema owner becomes SAP<SID> instead of SAPR3 (again on behalf of MCOD). As explained next, you may also define a *Schema ID* independently of the SAP system ID and the database ID.

Another change is that the data tablespaces (and PSAPTEMP) are created by default as "locally managed" instead of "dictionary managed". A locally managed tablespace (LMTS) manages its space allocation itself rather than through the central data dictionary of the database. This reduces space management overhead because it is no longer necessary to update system tables and to generate rollback information. LMTS also introduces a more efficient technique of managing extents, making it easier to accommodate tables and indexes of greatly varying sizes and different growth phases in a single tablespace.

The Schema ID

For all products based on 6.20 and above, you can define a Schema ID (consisting of three alphanumeric characters) independent of the SAP SID and DB SID. This Schema ID is used instead of the SAP SID as a unique code for the database schema and tablespace name.

By default, SAPINST will use the same SAP SID, DB SID, and Schema ID. In the case of a system copy with Oracle backup/restore, you can continue to change the SAPSID and DBSID but not the Schema ID. As a result, after performing a refresh of the acceptance system using backup/restore, you might end up with an acceptance system that internally still bears the name of the production system. Although there is nothing wrong with this from a technical point of view, it might create confusion during system administration.

This issue can be avoided if the Schema ID (that is, the database schema or the tablespace name) does not explicitly refer to a SAP system or database SID (for example Schema ID SAPDAT).

If you select the Schema ID independent of the SAP SID (which is strongly recommended), then the resulting situation will resemble the old situation with the SAPR3 schema and the fixed tablespace names PSAPBTABD, PSAPDOCUD, and so on. For an example, see Table 20.11.

	Layout <= 4.6C	Layout > 6.20	Modified Layout
SAP SID	PRD	PRD	PRD
DB SID	PRD	PRD	DB1
Schema ID	SAPR3	SAPPRD	SAPDB1
Tablespace	PSAPSTABD	PSAPPRD	PSAPDB1
	PSAPSTABI	PSAPPRDUSR	PSAPDB1USR
	PSAPUSER1D		
	PSAPUSER1I		

Table 20.11 MCOD Schema IDs as of AS 6.20

Database Configuration for the Unicode Conversion

While the SAP system is in normal use, the database parameter settings are optimized for that system's typical operation, which can be either transactional (OLTP) as for R/3 or CRM, or decision-support oriented (OLAP) as for BW. However, the database activity during the import is highly untypical (massive insertions and index creations). It, therefore, makes good sense to adjust the database configuration to achieve the best possible export performance.

Here are a few recommendations:

▶ Data is sorted in the PSAPTEMP tablespace. To avoid a tablespace overflow, the size of the PSAPTEMP tablespace in source and target database should be at least 20 % of the used data.

▶ Database archiving should be disabled, which is done by SAPINST by default.

▶ Disable redo log mirroring during the database load. Use only one redo log member per redo group. This will reduce unnecessary disk I/O.

▶ Tune the database parameters shown in Table 20.12 during the database export/import.

Parameter	Database Export	Database Import
db_cache_size	50 %	20 %
db_writer_processes	20	20
disk_asynch_io[6]	true	True
filesystemio_options	setall	Setall
log_buffer	10MB	10MB
parallel_execution_message_ size	16384	16384
parallel_threads_per_cpu	1	1
parallel_max_servers	#CPU*#R3LOAD*2	#CPU*#R3LOAD*2
pga_aggregate_target	40 %	70 %
_pga_max_size	2GB	2GB
Processes	processes + parallel_max_ servers	processes + parallel_max_ servers

Table 20.12 Optimized Parameter Settings During the Data Export/Import

---

6   Check SAP note 834343 for more information on async_io and direct_io.

20.5.7 Database-Specific Aspects — SQL Server

With the availability of SQL Server 2005 64-bit, the number of installations using this DBMS has greatly increased. We therefore offer some general recommendations for the setup of SQL Server in SAP environments.

Transaction Log

The logfiles are written sequentially; therefore, a performance gain cannot be achieved by using multiple logfiles distributed on different partitions. The only reason to have more then one logfile could be the lack of space on one partition. The transaction log should be big enough. For high-end systems, the transaction log should have a size between 10 and 20GB.

Number and Size of Data Files

When a database is set up with multiple files, SQL Server collects these files in the so-called "default" file group when not specified differently in the CREATE statement. Inserting data into the database, SQL Server tries to fill these different data files in a proportional manner. From time to time, the proportional fill factor for each of the files gets recalculated based on the available free space in each data file. This means the data of every table in this file group gets distributed over all the data files of this file group. In the past, this was a great feature to avoid hot spots on specific files/disk partitions. There is only one little issue regarding this feature. As soon as one of the files of the file group grows full, the proportional fill gets out of balance, filling up all the other files and then only growing one of the files. This implies that situations where the automatic growth kicks in should be avoided by all means. The data files should be extended manually, ideally by the same portion.

> **Note**
>
> Huge data files should be avoided. Keep in mind that behind a productive system, an acceptance system needs to be set up and from time to time refreshed using a database backup of the production system. In such cases, it might be difficult to handle four 250GB data files instead of 8 files with 125GB each.

For performance reasons, one data file only does not make sense. On the other side, there is no performance penalty to having a dozen or more data files, although the administrative overhead does get out of balance compared to the benefit of a larger number of small files. In regards of performance, the number of data files could be one-half to one times the number of CPUs. The number of partitions available for data files should impact the decision for the number of the data files, too. If there is only one partition, the number of data files should be kept small. If there is a need to distribute the data file over two, three, or even more different partitions, the data files should be distributed evenly over the available partitions.

New data files should be added with caution because it might disturb the way SQL Server is proportionally filling up the data files. Reasons for adding more files might be driven by reconfigurations of hardware or increase of workload and hence more concurrency on the system. When going from three to six data files, for example, the best method would be to extend the old data files in a way that the free space in each of the three data files is around the same. Then another thee database files can be added. Their size should be around the same size of the free space that exists in the old three files. In this way, SQL Server will now distribute its new inserted data in an even manner between those six files. If some different ratios of inserting data should be achieved between the new and old database files, then this could be controlled by the ratio of the free space in the old and the new database files. Although over the years, old data gets archived, the most affected files usually are the "old" data files. To compensate for the data that got deallocated from the old data files, it might be necessary to extend the free space in the new data files to maintain an even distribution of new data over all the data files.

> **Note**
>
> Adding data files might disturb the way SQL Server fills up the data files. Keep this in mind when configuring your database. If you have four partitions, for example, then it might be wise to create eight data files (two on each partition). If new (ideally four) partitions are added, data files can be relocated without impacting the data distribution within SQL Server.

Database Configuration During the Data Import

Allow SQL Server to allocate all memory dynamically during the database load. SAP is not running during the data import, so all memory may be assigned to the database. Also set **Max degree of parallelism** to "0" to allow SQL Server to use all available CPUs on the database server.

20.6   CU&UC Postprocessing

This chapter covers the activities to be carried out in the target system after its conversion to Unicode. Some of these activities are specifically related to Unicode, whereas others are of a more general nature and occur in most new installations or system copies.

20.6.1 Actions on OS Level

Some activities are needed on the OS level before continuing. This includes upgrading the SAP kernel and adapting the profile parameters to the increased Unicode requirements (and to the new platform if the system was migrated to a new OS).

Kernel Upgrade

During the conversion to Unicode, SAPINST installed the SAP kernel delivered with the installation media. This version can be relatively old. After the database load, it is advisable to upgrade this kernel. You can download the latest kernel version from the SAP Service Marketplace at *http://service.sap.com/PATCHES*.

It is strongly recommended that the kernel version that you install matches the support package level of the system.

Adjust Profile Parameters

SAPINST installs a new system with new parameter profiles. After the installation, compare the SAP instance profiles between the original non-Unicode and the new Unicode system. Entries like the login client, installed languages, and the default login language should be taken over from the non-Unicode system. When setting the parameters, you must also take into account the increased Unicode resource requirements; these will most likely affect the memory management parameters and the SAP buffer sizes. Specific advice on setting profile parameters in Unicode systems is given in SAP Note 790099.

If the system was migrated to another OS or database, parameters should only be taken over with caution, as the architecture and the amount of memory might be totally different. Also, the source profiles may have contained database-specific parameter settings, which are no longer relevant — or could in the worst case even be harmful — in the new environment.

20.6.2 Actions on Database Level — Oracle

Some postprocessing actions are needed for Oracle, for example, adapting the memory parameters to the Unicode requirements and to productive operation, and updating the database statistics.

Truncate Tables

Most of the following tables are used for monitoring, or they contain configuration data that is only valid for the old source environment. The data is useless on the new platform. Truncate the tables using Oracle tools (SQLPLUS):

```
SQLPLUS> connect / as sysdba;
SQLPLUS> truncate table DBSTATHORA;
SQLPLUS> truncate table DBSTAIHORA;
SQLPLUS> truncate table DBSTATIORA;
SQLPLUS> truncate table DBSTATTORA;
SQLPLUS> truncate table DDLOG;
SQLPLUS> truncate table MONI;
SQLPLUS> truncate table PAHI;
SQLPLUS> truncate table OSMON;
SQLPLUS> truncate table DBSNP;
SQLPLUS> truncate table SDBAD;
SQLPLUS> truncate table SDBAH;
SQLPLUS> truncate table SDBAP;
SQLPLUS> truncate table SDBAR;
SQLPLUS> truncate table TPFET;
SQLPLUS> truncate table TPFHT;
SQLPLUS> truncate table ALCONSEG;
SQLPLUS> truncate table ALSYSTEMS;
SQLPLUS> truncate table CSMSEGM;
```

Archive Log Mode

Archive logging is automatically enabled at the end of the installation. Always verify that ARCHIVELOG is switched on before releasing the system for productive use.

```
SQLPLUS> connect / as sysdba;
SQLPLUS> archive log list
```

Archive logging must be enabled for productive operation. In the context of a CU&UC, however, you may still have some postprocessing work to do, for which it is better to leave archive logging disabled.

Oracle Parameters

If you changed Oracle parameters to optimize the data import, then set the parameters to the recommended values for normal system operation. You find the parameter recommendations in SAP Note 830576.

Update the Database Statistics

Schedule a full update of the database statistics as soon as possible. With Oracle 10g (the Oracle version used with all SAP NetWeaver 2004s-based products), all tables must have statistics. Use the following command:

```
brconnect -u / -c -o summary -f stats -t all -p <PARALLEL>
```

<PARALLEL> is the number of parallel threads to be used. Set this to the number of CPUs on the database server unless you have other work to do in parallel that might also need significant processor power.

20.6.3 Actions on Database Level — SQL Server

Some actions are needed for SQL Server before SAP can be used productively again. The most important one of these is probably setting the Instance parameters for productive operation.

Truncate Tables

Certain tables in the SAP database contain server-dependent or system-dependent information. You must empty these tables before you start SAP. Use the following instructions (in SQL Query Analyzer):

```
use <SAPSID>
go
setuser '<sid>'
go
truncate table DDLOG
truncate table MONI
truncate table PAHI
truncate table OSMON
truncate table DBSNP
truncate table SDBAD
truncate table SDBAH
truncate table SDBAP
truncate table SDBAR
truncate table TPFET
truncate table TPFHT
truncate table ALCONSEG
truncate table ALSYSTEMS
truncate table CSMSEGM
truncate table sap_perfhist
truncate table sap_perfsample
truncate table sap_perfinfo
```

Configure the SQL Server Instance

Check the database log mechanism; the installation sets it to FULL while SIMPLE is sufficient for most development and acceptance systems.

The automatic update statistics for database tables VBHDR, VBDATA, and VBMOD should be disabled for performance reasons. These tables are updated too often to make database statistics useful. Disable the statistics as follows:

```
use <SAPSID>
go
setuser '<sid>'
go
EXEC sp_autostats VBHDR, 'OFF'
EXEC sp_autostats VBDATA, 'OFF'
EXEC sp_autostats VBMOD, 'OFF'
```

In addition, disable page locking for database tables VBHDR, VBDATA, VBMOD, ARFCSDATA, ARFCRDATA, and TRFCQUEUE:

```
use <SAPSID>
go
setuser '<sid>'
go
EXEC sp_indexoption 'VBHDR', 'DisAllowPageLocks', TRUE
EXEC sp_indexoption 'VBDATA', 'DisAllowPageLocks', TRUE
EXEC sp_indexoption 'VBMOD', 'DisAllowPageLocks', TRUE
EXEC sp_indexoption 'ARFCSDATA', 'DisAllowPageLocks', TRUE
EXEC sp_indexoption 'ARFCRDATA', 'DisAllowPageLocks', TRUE
IF OBJECT_ID('TRFCQUEUE') IS NOT NULL
BEGIN
   EXEC sp_indexoption 'TRFCQUEUE', 'DisAllowPageLocks', TRUE
END
```

Also disable page locking for table D010TAB to avoid wait times during ABAP compilation:

```
EXEC sp_indexoption 'D010TAB','DisAllowPageLocks', TRUE
```

> **Note**
>
> Some configuration options are advanced options. You can only see and modify them if the configuration option **Show advanced options** is set. This is automatically done by SAPINST during the installation. Execute the following SQL script to set this manually:
> ```
> exec sp_configure 'show advanced options', 1 reconfigure with override
> ```

Set the following configuration options:

▶ Disable tracing options in SQL (switch off trace 1204, 3604); see OSS Note 32129 for more information:

```
DBCC TRACEOFF (1204)
DBCC TRACEOFF (3605)
```

▶ The configuration option **max degree of parallelism** defines how many processors SQL Server can use to execute a single SQL command in parallel. This may decrease the response time of a single, long-running SQL command, but this will also decrease the overall throughput of SQL Server. Therefore it only makes sense to use parallelism, if the number of CPUs used by SQL Server is greater than the number of all concurrently running SAP work processes. Because this is typically not the case, SAP strongly recommends turning off parallel query execution. You can do this by executing the following SQL script:

```
EXEC sp_configure 'max degree of parallelism', 1 reconfigure with
override
```

▶ The only common SAP scenario that benefits from parallel query execution is the aggregate building in a SAP BW system. You may set **max degree of parallelism** to 0 during aggregate building and set it to 1 during normal operation of SAP BW.

▶ Some SAP transactions, such as the database monitor ST04, need to execute the stored procedure xp_cmdshell. This fails unless you have set the configuration option xp_cmdshell to 1. You can do this by executing the following SQL script:

```
EXEC sp_configure 'xp_cmdshell', 1 reconfigure with override
```

Auto Update/Create Statistics

SAP strongly recommends setting the database options **auto create statistics** and **auto update statistics**. SQL Server 2005 introduced a new database option, which is also recommended: **auto update statistics async**. You can set all three database options for the <SID>-database by executing the following SQL script:

```
alter database <SID> set auto_create_statistics on
alter database <SID> set auto_update_statistics on
alter database <SID> set auto_update_statistics_async on
```

Page Verify

SQL Server 2005 can write a checksum to each database page written to disk. This allows you to detect disk errors and database corruptions as soon as the page is read from disk the next time. SAP recommends turning on this option by executing the following SQL command:

```
alter database <SID> set page_verify checksum
```

The overhead of the checksum will result in a few percent additional CPU usage on the database server. We think the value added justifies this overhead. Nevertheless, you may not have the same opinion. In this case, we strongly recommend turning on the less effective torn page detection, which does not result in any measurable overhead. You can do this with the following SQL command:

```
alter database <SID> set page_verify torn_page_detection
```

If you changed SQL Server parameters to optimize the data import, then set the parameters to the recommended values for the normal system operation. See SAP Note 879941 for SQL Server 2005 and Note 327494 for SQL Server 2000 for more information.

20.6.4 General Actions in SAP

Actions in the SAP system make up the bulk of the postprocessing activities. In the case of a CU&UC, a distinction must be made between general postprocessing activities for the system copy (described in this section) and activities related to Unicode, which are described in Section 20.6.5.

Test Stop/Start of the System

At the end of the installation, the database and SAP CI are running. Nevertheless, it is a good idea to perform a complete system and database stop and restart using the normal methods (`stopsap`/`startsap` commands on UNIX, Microsoft Management Console [MMC] on Windows) to make absolutely sure that the system will come up.

After a successful restart, log on to client 000 as a fully authorized user (e.g., SAP* or DDIC).

Installation Check (Transaction SICK)

Transaction SICK (SAP Initial Consistency Check) should display No errors reported. The SAP Consistency Check determines basic inconsistencies in the system installation. This function is also called automatically when you start the system on an application server. The installation check checks whether the following are true:

▶ The release number in the SAP kernel matches the release number stored in the database system.

▶ The character set specified in the SAP kernel matches the character set specified in the database system.

▶ The critical structure definitions in both the data dictionary and the SAP kernel are identical.

Errors reported by SICK must be investigated and fixed with the highest priority because they will make the system unusable.

Transport System

Initialize the transport system with Transaction SE06.

Configure the Transport Management System (Transaction STMS); this must be done in client 000, both in the new system and on the transport domain controller.

General Postprocessing Activities

For these activities, it is better to log on to the default production client and not to client 000. You must sill log on as a fully authorized user though.

▶ Request and install the license (Transaction SLICENSE).

▶ Import the parameter profiles (Transaction RZ10).

▶ Generate the instance configuration and configure operation modes and time-tables (Transaction RZ04).

▶ Test the operation mode switch (Transaction RZ03).

▶ Configure output devices (Transaction SPAD).

▶ Configure standard maintenance jobs (SM36).

▶ System log (SM21); simply confirm the initial pop-up saying that the instance was entered in TLSE4.

▶ Test the background processing system (Transaction SM65). Perform a complete check with **Goto · Additional tests**.

   ▶ In the section **System-wide tests**, mark all checkboxes except **Remove inconsistencies**.

   ▶ In the subscreen **Server-specific tests**, mark all four checkboxes

   ▶ Leave the other fields unchanged, and click on **Execute**.

   ▶ Check the result screen for errors or abnormalities. You may normally ignore the message

```
User SAPCPIC not defined in client XXX. External programs can not be
executed in this client!
```

▶ Configure database administration activities (Transaction DB13). Note that for DB13, you log on as a *permanent* user and not as a temporary user (e.g., the one you created for the upgrade). The periodic database administration jobs are scheduled with the logon user ID, so this user should exist permanently.

▶ Transaction ST06 (Operating System Monitor): Check the status of the local collector. Click on **OS Collector**, and then **Status**. The status entry on the line **Collector** should be **running**.

▶ Transaction SM59 (Display and maintain RFC destinations): Correct the RFC destinations that were affected by the system copy (e.g., external programs with an explicit host reference). Do not forget to alter the gateway options.

To avoid problems with outgoing R/3 connections after the Unicode conversion, you should check the connections before using the destinations. Select the RFC connection, and click on the **Change** button on the taskbar.

▶ When the destination is a Unicode system, you should set **Character Width** in **Target System** to **Unicode**.

▶ When the destination is a non-Unicode system, you should set **Character Width** in **Target System** to **non-Unicode**.

To avoid problems with internal TCP/IP connections after the Unicode conversion, you must also maintain those connections that refer to the Unicode system itself, before using the destinations (for example, SAPFTP, SAPFTPA, SAPHTTP, and SAPHTTPA connections with activation type Start on AS).

▶ Open the tree TCP/IP connection, choose a connection, and click on the **Change** button on the taskbar.

▶ Select the tab strip **Special Options**. In the **Character Width in Target System** dialog box, select the **Unicode** radio button. Save the settings.

Caution

Don't forget to set the **Character Width** to Unicode in RFC connections in satellite or in backend systems to the converted Unicode system.

Note

After the Unicode conversion, due to technical limitations TMS configurations must be deleted on the domain controller and afterwards created again.

20.6.5 Unicode Activities

This section describes postprocessing activities specifically related to the Unicode conversion.

Run Report UMG_HISTORY

This report is used to archive and display important data of the Transactions SPUMG and SUMG. These data were used and created during the preparation and the postprocessing of a Unicode conversion.

1. Run this report to save and display data from Transactions SPUMG and SUMG.
2. Call SE38, and enter report UMG_HISTORY.
3. Click on the **Save** button.

Run Report UMG_POOL_TABLE

UMG_POOL_TABLE is used to update the dictionary information of table pools in the SAP dictionary after a Unicode conversion or after the installation of Unicode systems. For a conversion, the report has to be executed twice: before the conversion in the non-Unicode system and after the conversion in the Unicode system. In the non-Unicode system, report UMG_POOL_TABLE is executed automatically during the initialization of the work list (Transaction SPUMG).

Proceed as follows:

1. Call SE38, and enter report UMG_POOL_TABLE.
2. Click on **Execute**.

A check is done to determine whether UMG_POOL_TABLE has been executed already and all actions that are necessary are executed afterwards. Note that no message is displayed after the successful execution of UMG_POOL_TABLE. If no short dump occurs, the report was executed successfully.

Run Report RUTTTYPACT

When you install a Unicode system or convert a system to Unicode, the entire nametab of the dictionary is also converted. This can cause various inconsistencies in the runtime objects. However, these inconsistencies are easily eliminated with the RUTTTYPACT program.

Proceed as follows:

1. Open Transaction SE38, and enter report RUTTTYPACT (see Figure 20.39).
2. Modify the log name in the entrance screen if desired.
3. Enable **Display Log Immediately**.
4. Execute the report in the background because the runtime can be relatively long.

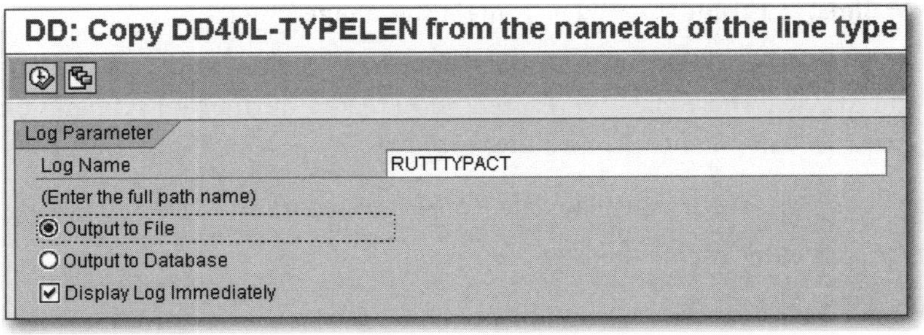

Figure 20.39 RUTTTYPACT Program

Run Report RSCPINST

RSCPINST is a setup and diagnostic tool for NLS (Native Language Support) configurations in R/3. The user can specify the set of languages needed, and the report automatically determines the settings required for a consistent NLS configuration. The report also automatically updates the necessary database tables. However, modifications to the application profile parameters must be carried out manually.

Proceed as follows:

1. Open SE38, and enter report RSCPINST.

2. Click on **Execute**.

3. Confirm the message **This is a Unicode system**.

4. Verify if all languages installed in the system are listed. Add missing language keys if needed.

5. Click on **Simulate** to verify the current NLS configuration. In this mode, RSCPINST checks the consistency of new configurations and generates a list of new setting information and problematic areas found through the check, such as inconsistent database table entries, missing locales, obsolete parameters, and so on. These problems need to be repaired before proceeding to activation. No database updates are carried out within this mode.

6. Click on **Activate** to correct any consistencies that might exist in the database tables. During activation, all neccessary database updates are done. A list of required profile parameter modifications is generated, and these have to be done manually. Missing OS locales must be installed on the host. After changing the parameters or installing missing locales, restart the system.

Special Handling of Table DBTABLOG (Single Codepage only)

After the conversion to Unicode, change logs can no longer be read. Log analysis report RSVTPROT can be used to run a codepage conversion via the logs. However, before this can happen, you need to know until what logging time this is necessary and what the former codepage was. This section describes how you can retrieve the required data.

> **Note**
>
> The log entries themselves remain unchanged during this process.

1. Start Transaction SM30 for the maintenance view V_P_LOG_CP, and select **Maintain**.
2. Select **New entries**.
3. Specify when the codepage migration occurred in a new entry:
   - In the **Used until: Date** column (see Figure 20.40), make a note of the latest date that logs could have been created in the old codepage (in other words, the time of system shutdown before the migration).
   - In the **Time** column, specify the relevant time.
   - In the **Code page** column, make a note of the codepage that was active before the migration. You can use the search help provided to help you in this case.
4. Save your input.

Table Logging: Codepages and Migration Times

Used Until: Date	Time	Code Pa	Name
26.03.2005	⊕:00:00	120	EBCDIC 0697/0500 Latin-1, Multilangual
05.02.2007	18:00:00	1100	SAP internal, like ISO 8859-1 (00697/00819)

Figure 20.40 Postprocessing for Table Logging (DBTABLOG)

Import the Proposal Pool for the Translation Workbench

This activity is only needed if you use the translation system (SE63). You must now import the Proposal Pools you exported earlier.

Run report RS_TRANSLATION_IMPORT_OLD_PP if translations have been done before the import of Basis 6.20 SP25. Run report RS_TRANSLATION_IMPORT_PP if translations were done after the import of Basis SP25. This is needed for every language combination

Proceed as follows:

1. Open Transaction SE38, and enter report `RS_TRANSLATION_IMPORT_OLD_PP` or `RS_TRANSLATION_IMPORT_PP`.

2. Click on **Execute**.

Run Report UMG_SCAN_STATISTICS

Report `UMG_SCAN_STATISTICS` collects and analyzes SPUMG statistics, database sizes, number of vocabulary entries, the duration of the export, and the reprocess logfile. `UMG_SCAN_STATISTICS` uses the log and XML files (only for MDMP systems) created by R3load during the export.

Proceed as follows:

1. Copy the log and XML files from the directory used by the Migration Monitor from the non-Unicode to the Unicode system.

2. Create *file_info.txt*. This file contains all names and complete paths to the XML files and logfiles created by R3load:

```
c:\temp\workdirectory\ACCTIT.log
c:\temp\workdirectory\ACCTIT001.xml
c:\temp\workdirectory\AGR_HIER.log
c:\temp\workdirectory\AGR_HIER001.xml
c:\temp\workdirectory\AGR_HIERT.log
c:\temp\workdirectory\AGR_HIERT001.xml
c:\temp\workdirectory\APQD.log
c:\temp\workdirectory\APQD001.xml
c:\temp\workdirectory\ATAB.log
c:\temp\workdirectory\ATAB001.xml
c:\temp\workdirectory\BKPF.log
...
```

3. Open Transaction SE38, and enter report `UMG_SCAN_STATISTICS`.

4. Click on **Execute**.

5. `UMG_SCAN_STATISTICS` has two operating modes: to calculate or to display previously calculated statistics.

6. Specify input *file_info.txt*. Choose **Calculate**.

Unicode Postconversion Tool: Transaction SUMG

SUMG is the companion transaction to SPUMG and SPUM4. Where SPUMG and SPUM4 were executed in the non-Unicode source system, SUMG is used only in the new Unicode system. It is only required in systems that had a multi-codepage (MDMP) configuration before being converted to Unicode. SUMG can be seen as a "clean-up" transaction whose main function is to handle unconverted or incorrectly converted data.

Purpose of SUMG

After the Unicode conversion, not all data might be correctly converted. That is, the data must be converted again, using the correct language information (codepage).

There are several reasons why data might have been converted wrongly:

▶ Entries in the vocabulary have not been assigned to a language.

▶ The codepage cannot be determined during the export.

▶ The language or codepage assignments are wrong.

Missing entries in the vocabulary and codepages that cannot be determined during the export are reported by R3load. R3load generates a logfile in XML format for each table whose codepage could not be determined. This file contains the name of the table, the category, key fields, and the used codepage. SUMG reads the generated R3load log and saves the data for further usage. Depending on the table type and source of the problem transaction, SUMG provides several methods for completing the conversion of corrupt data.

Mistakes in language or codepage assignments have to be maintained manually after being detected in the Unicode system because these are not reported by R3load. Data needs to be reconverted after the correct codepage has been assigned.

R3load Logs and Completion Types

Proceed as follows:

1. Call Transaction SUMG.

2. In the menu bar, go to **Edit • Load R3load log**. Enter the path and name of the file that contains the path of the R3load log. Transaction SUMG uses the same file as report UMG_SCAN_STATISTICS (*file_info.txt*).

3. In the menu bar, go to **Edit • Worklist • Initialize Worklist**.

4. The SUMG work list is displayed (see Figure 20.41).

Depending on the table type and source of the problem transaction, SUMG categorizes the tables in different groups (see Table 20.13), providing several methods for completing the conversion of corrupt data.

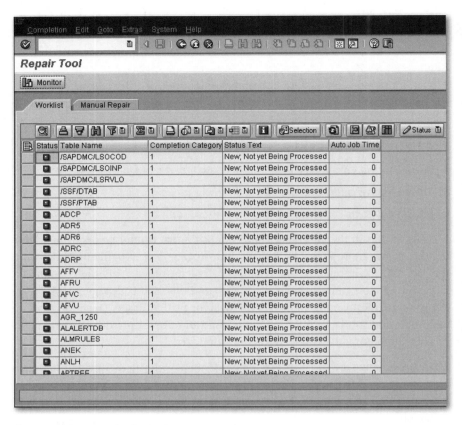

Figure 20.41 SUMG Work List

Category	Table	Method
1	Transparent, cluster, and pooled tables	Automatic completion
2	Dynpro sources	Display only
3	Report sources	Display only
4	INDX-type tables	Manual repair
5	Transparent, cluster, and pooled tables	Manual repair
6	INDX-type tables	Manual repair

Table 20.13 Categories in Transaction SUMG

Category 1 tables are transparent, cluster, and pooled tables that can be converted automatically using the Reprocess log created in Transaction SPUMG in the non-Unicode system. The Worker job will reprocess data according to the Reprocess log created in SPUMG in the non-Unicode system.

For categories 2 (Dynpro sources) and 3 (Report sources), the log entries exist because sources contain language-dependent comments without a language key. These cannot be repaired with SUMG. Instead, access the sources and verify whether they contain any errors. If they do, repair them directly in the source and afterwards delete the source from the SUMG work list.

A manual intervention is needed for categories 4, 5, and 6 (category 5 is for transparent, pool, and cluster tables in need of manual repair; categories 4 and 6 are for INDX-type tables).

▸ These tables cannot be completed automatically because they have not been maintained in the Reprocess log (for example, table entries have not been assigned a language). For those tables, you can create repair hints or maintain entries manually. Maintaining entries manually should be done by someone who speaks the language.

▸ For INDX-type tables that have not been maintained in the INDX Log (for example, because table entries exist that have not been assigned to a language yet), the affected table entries have to be maintained manually.

Automatic Completion

The process to schedule jobs is the same as in SPUM4 and SPUMG. Select **Schedule Worker Job**. Enter the tables that have been completely maintained in the Reprocess log (SPUMG), and schedule the job (to select all tables, leave the selection field empty or enter an asterisk as wildcard) as shown in Figure 20.42. You can run multiple jobs simultaneously, but you must add a suffix to the second and all subsequent jobs. The Worker job maintains all entries according to the Reprocess log created in the non-Unicode system. If errors remain, the table is marked for manual repair

---

Note

As with Transactions SPUMG/SPUM4, there is no need to enter a different table range when starting jobs in parallel. This system automatically divides the tables to be processed over the available jobs. Be careful, the system is still used productively. Running too many jobs in parallel might cause a performance bottleneck.

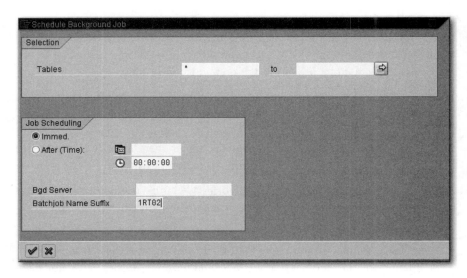

Figure 20.42 SUMG Job Scheduling

Manual Repair

Tables can be manually repaired by using repair hints or by manually setting the language used during the conversion (which is wrong) and the correct language into which the table entries must be converted. Technically, the table entries need to be converted back from Unicode to the codepage with which they have been converted during the export and converted again using the correct codepage. Select **Manual Repair** (see Figure 20.43), and all tables that could not be maintained automatically are displayed. You might add tables that you believe should be maintained again. Select **Hint Management** to use repair hints.

Proceed as follows for manual repair:

1. Select the tables, and lock them (choose **Lock**).

2. Mark the tables, and select **Table Entries**.

   ▷ **Tables with category 1**
   Choose **Convert to** to set the assumed correct language and converted the table entry.

   ▷ **Tables with category 5**
   Choose **Current lang.** to set the — wrong — language the entries have been converted with during the R3load procedure. Then choose **Convert to** to set the assumed correct language and convert the table entry. The changed table entries are displayed.

▶ **Tables with category 4 and 6**

Choose **Set to** to set the correct language. The codepage information is changed, but the table entries are not yet converted.

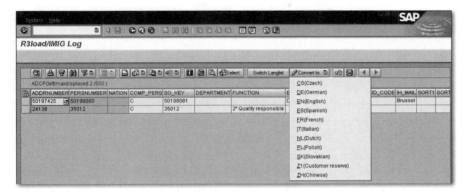

Figure 20.43 Manual Repair in Transaction SUMG

Note

The actual conversion of INDX-type table data does not take place during the data upload in the Unicode system but when the data is used in the Unicode system for the first time. In Transaction SUMG, only a codepage is set for the later conversion of the table entry.

Special Handling of TLOCK and Related Tables

After the conversion to Unicode, the enqueue key needs to be corrected for the lock tables TLOCK, TLOCKP, and TLOCKPC.

Call Transaction SE38, and execute the following reports (in TEST mode):

▶ Report RDDTLCKU for table TLOCK

▶ Report RDDTLCKPU for table TLOCKP

▶ Report RDDTLCKPCU for table TLOCKPC

If warning or error messages are issued, run the programs again, deactivating the test mode.

Actions for BI Migrations

Some additional actions are needed for BI migrations. Among those are the reconnecting to the backend systems and the running of ABAP report RS_BW_POST_MIGRATION to update the PSA tables:

1. Correct the RFC connections in the SAP BI system and all backend systems (Transaction SM59).

2. Log on to the productive client as a fully authorized user.

3. Verify the connection (Transaction RSA1, **Source systems** • **Right-click on <TRG_SID>** • **CHECK.**

After the successful import, you must call the RS_BW_POST_MIGRATION report. Before you start the RS_BW_POST_MIGRATION program, connect all source systems to the migrated BW system. This is necessary to update all PSA tables. You must ensure that all connected SAP systems are active while the RS_BW_POST_MIGRA-TION program is running. Depending on whether or not you have changed the database platform, you must call the RS_BW_POST_MIGRATION report with another variant in the background. You should call the program in the background so that the spool log is maintained. When you do so, DB2 is valid for zOS, DB4 is valid for AS400, and DB6 is valid for UNIX/NT as three different database platforms. Use the variant &POSTMGRDB if you have changed the DB platform, and use &POSTMGR if you have *not* changed the DB platform. The RS_BW_POST_MIGRATION program carries out necessary adjustments after the system copy. When it does so, database specific DDIC entries are adjusted (modified, deleted, and expanded), database-specific (generated) programs are invalidated, temporary objects from certain LRU buffers are deleted, new versions for the PSA tables are transferred, and the DBDIFF table is adjusted. The runtime of the program may take a few hours.

20.7 Twin Upgrade & Unicode Conversion (TU&UC)

SAP developed the Twin Upgrade a Unicode Conversion (TU&UC) technique primarily for upgrades of systems running releases between 3.1I and 4.6B and also for products with Basis Release 6.10 (no version of R/3 based on 6.10 exists). With these versions, it is not possible to use the SPUM4/SPUMG preconversion tools in the source system before the upgrade.

20.7.1 Information and Support

SAP supplies a TU&UC Conversion Guide that describes the entire process in detail. See Section 19.3.5, subsection *Twin Upgrade and Unicode Migration (TU&UC) Guide* for the download location for this guide. In contrast with the CU&UC documentation, a single TU&UC guide covers all supported source releases.

The key SAP Note for TU&UC is Note 959698.

TU&UC is supported for *all* source releases, not just for the ones that do not allow using CU&UC. For instance, it is perfectly legitimate to use a TU&UC scenario instead of CU&UC when upgrading from R/3 4.6C to SAP ERP 2005. With CU&UC, the Unicode preparation runs in the live system during uptime, which causes a certain overhead. If you want to avoid this, then doing the preparation in an isolated system — as you do with TU&UC — may be preferable. Without questioning the technical correctness of such an approach, we doubt whether it makes much practical sense. As we already remarked when discussing the choice between downtime-minimized and resource-minimized upgrades, if the server is unable to support the extra overhead (in this case of the SPUM4 scans), then it will certainly be unable to bear the extra load caused by the new release, not to mention the capacity requirements of Unicode. Nevertheless, TU&UC is a supported option, so the choice is yours.

The main drawback of the TU&UC method is that it requires a copy of the production system to be created. This does not seem like much of a problem; however, in most upgrade projects, the production system is copied to a test system for the release upgrade anyway, so this system might just as well be used to prepare and test the Unicode conversion as well.

With respect to the codepage configuration of the system, TU&UC is only relevant for systems with multiple codepages (MDMP) or with Ambiguous Blended Codepages. Single codepage systems can easily be upgraded first and converted to Unicode afterwards; there is no need to combine the two operations. At the time of writing (May 2007), TU&UC was generally released for MDMP systems but was still on Pilot Project status for Ambiguous Blended Codepages. Keep an eye on Note 959698 for the latest status.

20.7.2 TU&UC Phases

The key characteristic of the TU&UC process is the creation of a copy of the SAP production system. This copy, the *twin*, is then upgraded to the Unicode-compatible target release (such as SAP ERP 2005) and is used for the preconversion analysis using Transaction SPUMG. Optionally, the twin can also be used for the ABAP preparations (UCCHECK).

These are the major steps in a TU&UC process:

1. (Optional) Creation of an ABAP preparation system for UCCHECK. The twin can also be used for this purpose. Considerations regarding the ABAP preparation system are the same as for CU&UC (see Section 20.1).

2. Creation of the twin (copy of production) using the normal homogeneous system copy method.

3. Upgrade of the twin.

4. Preconversion analysis (SPUMG) in the twin.

5. Export of the SPUMG results for use in the production system.

6. (Optional) Unicode conversion and postprocessing of the twin. This is done only to test the actual conversion process; it is not actually a part of the TU&UC itself.

7. Upgrade of the production system.

8. Import of the twin's SPUMG results into the production system.

9. Unicode conversion and postprocessing in the production system.

20.7.3   The Twin Preparation Run

The process of setting up the twin system and carrying out the SPUMG preparation in this system is called the *Twin Preparation Run*. This process consists of the following steps (all documented in the TU&UC Guide):

1. If necessary, upgrade the kernel in the production system (not just in the twin system) to the level mentioned in the TU&UC Guide. This is necessary to prevent the creation of new INDX table entries with invalid codepage information.

2. Perform a homogeneous system copy from the production system to the twin system.

3. "Freeze" the dictionary in the production system. No imports that create or change dictionary objects should be allowed from this point. This obviously includes applying new support packages. Discrepancies between the dictionary of the production system and that of the twin could invalidate the results of the SPUMG analysis; therefore, the two systems must remain consistent in terms of their dictionary objects.

4. Release upgrade of the twin system. The upgrade happens in the normal manner, that is, without any of the extra actions that occur with a CU&UC upgrade.

5. Perform ABAP preparation in the twin or (if you have used another system for UCCHECK) import the ABAP correction transports.

6. Perform preparatory actions for SPUMG; these are described in the Unicode Conversion Guide (not the TU&UC Guide) for the target release (normally Basis 7.00).

7. Configure the scanner settings in SPUMG (see Section 20.3.4).

8. Activate Twin Mode by running the report UMG_ACTIVATE_TWIN_MODE. This report does nothing else than set the TWIN flag in the control table UMGSET-TINGS.

9. Carry out the complete SPUMG process (table scans, vocabulary processing) in the twin.

10. Save the SPUMG results by running report `UMG_TWIN_CREATE_TRANSPORT`. Despite the word "transport" in the name, this program does not create transport requests but downloads the SPUMG results of the twin to files on the user's workstation.

20.7.4 Production Run

Upgrading the production system and converting it to Unicode using the results from the Twin Preparation Run is known as the *Production Run*. These are the steps:

1. Release upgrade of the production system using the standard (not CU&UC) procedure.

2. Import the ABAP preparation (UCCHECK) transports after the upgrade.

3. Import the results of the SPUMG analysis carried out in the twin.

4. Process with SPUMG any dictionary changes (new or changed tables) made in production since the Twin Preparation Run.

5. Carry out the additional tasks (activities between the end of SPUMG and the Unicode conversion) as described in the section *Additional Preparation Steps* of the Unicode Conversion Guide for Basis 7.00. This includes generating the Unicode nametabs with report `RADCUCNT`.

6. Convert the production system to Unicode using the normal database export/import method.

7. Carry out the postconversion activities in the Unicode system (chapter *Unicode Conversion Completion Phase* in the Unicode Conversion Guide for Basis 7.00). The principal activity here is executing Transaction SUMG.

Many SAP objects are imported in your SAP system during the release upgrade. You may have modified some of them to adapt them to your needs. This is where Modification Adjustment comes in. Many people consider Modification Adjustment something magical. This chapter reveals a little of the magic by explaining Modification Adjustment in detail.

21 Modification Adjustment

Modification Adjustment is the process of reconciling changes made by SAP to standard SAP repository objects (as a result of an upgrade, support package import, or note correction) with customer changes to those same objects.

Modification Adjustment applies both to dictionary objects (tables, structures, data elements, and domains) and development objects (programs, function groups, screens, and menus). Because an upgrade changes SAP objects on a massive scale, Modification Adjustment is critical to ensuring the preservation of data and functionality.

For technical reasons, Modification Adjustment is divided into two parts. Each part uses its own transaction to carry out the adjustment:

► Modification of dictionary objects is done with Transaction SPDD.

► Modification of development objects is done with Transaction SPAU.

This distinction did not come about because of a developer's whim or a design flaw. There is an essential difference in the way the two types of objects are handled. Dictionary objects must be activated *during* the upgrade, and structure changes may lead to physical conversion in the database and also during the upgrade. This has two important implications:

► The Modification Adjustment of dictionary objects must take place before the activation, relatively early in the upgrade process.

► Omitting the Modification Adjustment, or doing it wrong, can cause loss of data.

Development objects are less dangerous in this respect. They are not used in the upgrade, so their adjustment can wait until afterwards. They do not store business data, so mistakes or omissions can cause dysfunctions (generation errors, short dumps, missing functionality) but not irretrievable data loss.

Note that our distinction between *dictionary* and *development* objects is not entirely accurate. In fact, Transaction SPAU also deals with certain types of dictionary objects, namely those that do not store data. Examples are type groups, table types, search helps, and lock objects. Dictionary objects are also development objects: Creating a new table can hardly be called anything but "development." Nonetheless, these terms are in fairly common usage, so we'll stick with them.

If you are one who will actually do the technical upgrade, then there is another very crucial difference between SPDD and SPAU. Because the SPDD has to be done during the upgrade, the person who will do it is *you*, providing you have at least an adequate knowledge of the SAP dictionary. If you are not comfortable with the dictionary, then you should delegate the task to someone who is.

After reading these paragraphs, it may seem to you that SPDD is a real challenge and that compared with it, SPAU is a real treat. Not quite: There is one thing that is definitely to the advantage of SPDD. In terms of the number of objects to adjust, the workload in SPDD is almost always far smaller than that of SPAU. A typical SPDD involves fewer than 100 objects, many of which only require routine handling. SPAU on the other hand can range from just a few to many thousands of objects (the highest tally we have seen to date is around 7,500). Fortunately (for you, that is), carrying out the SPAU is not a burden that will fall on your shoulders. SPAU adjustments are a task for the developers, and they can distribute the work among themselves.

In the following sections, we will illustrate the Modification Adjustment process by looking at Transaction SPDD, as this is the more important of the two transactions for the target audience of this book. Operations in SPAU are very similar, except that they will take you into the appropriate editor (ABAP code, screen painter, menu painter).

> **Note**
>
> The upgrade control program offers a preview mode of Transaction SPDD and SPAU that displays all modified objects that are currently in the system and will be imported by the upgrade. The preview mode is available during PREPARE after the verification module has run.

21.1   The Modification Browser SPDD

Transaction SPDD is used during the activation phase of the upgrade to solve conflicts between new versions of SAP objects and modifications to the same.

Transaction SPDD is started in the shadow instance during the first phase of the upgrade (i.e., still in uptime if you use the downtime-minimized strategy). SPAU runs after the upgrade. Both transactions initially bring up the same selection screen (see Figure 21.1).

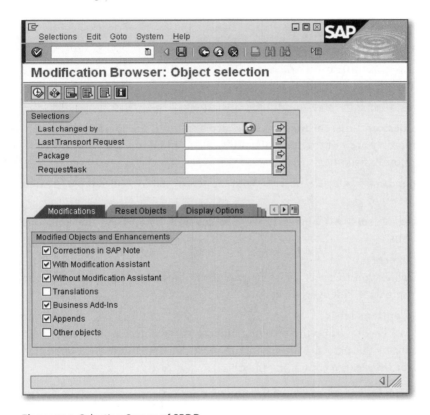

Figure 21.1 Selection Screen of SPDD

In the Object selection screen, you can narrow your search to the objects you need. With SPDD, you normally accept the selection screen as it initially appears.

▶ **Last changed by**
Lists modified objects based on the **last modified by** field.

▶ **Last transport request**
Lists modified objects that appear in a particular transport request.

▶ **Package**
Lists modified objects member of a particular development class.

▶ **Request/task**
Lists objects affected by a certain transport request/support package.

You can further narrow your selection by marking options in the different screen tabs:

▶ **Modifications** tab

  ▶ **Corrections in SAP Note**: Corrections delivered by SAP Notes (as of Basis 6.10 or when the Note Assistant is installed).

  ▶ **With Modification Assistant**: Objects modified as of release 4.5B.

  ▶ **Without Modification Assistant**: Objects modified before the SAP release 4.5B.

  ▶ **Translations**: Displays modified translations.

  ▶ **Business add-ins**: Business add-ins also appear in the **Modifications** tab. While they are not true modifications, they can be tracked with the Modification Assistant.

  ▶ **Appends**: To display objects with appends (tables, structures, search helps, etc.).

  ▶ **Other objects: All object types not covered by any of the previous options.**

▶ **Reset objects** tab
This enables you to select different groups of objects that have been reset to their original, SAP-delivered version.

▶ **Display options** tab
Provides a way to group the resulting objects list by object type, by user who last changed the object, by transport request that transported the modified object, or by package containing the object.

Click on **Execute**, and an information window pops up, informing you about the use of the Modification Assistant. You can simply confirm this. The main screen (object list) of SPDD appears.

21.2 SPDD Object List

The object list is presented as a hierarchical list structured as shown in Figure 21.2.

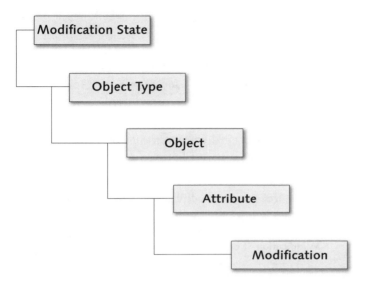

Figure 21.2 SPDD Hierarchy

▶ **Modification State**

▷ **Without Modification Assistant**: In this section of the list, a green traffic light indicates automatic adjustment mode. There is no overlap between the updates included in the new SAP-supplied object and your previously modified object. Clicking on the green traffic light automatically re-applies your modification. It does not mean that your modifications were retained during the upgrade, but rather that your modifications are compatible with the new standard version and can be easily reapplied.

▷ **With Modification Assistant**: Here a yellow traffic light indicates semiautomatic adjustment mode. There is some overlap between the updates included in the new SAP-supplied object and your previously modified object. Clicking on the yellow traffic light brings up a dialog box to correct the identified conflicts. In SPDD, this is the most critical group of objects because you will need to decide upon an action. See Section 21.3 later for details.

▷ **Deleted Objects**: The objects shown here are standard SAP objects that were modified locally but are deleted in the new release. If necessary, you have to recreate these objects manually.

531

▶ **Object Type**
At this level, objects are grouped together by their type, for example, tables, structures, domains, and data elements.

▶ **Object**
By clicking open an object type node, you see the list of objects.

▶ **Attribute**
This level in the hierarchy does not exist for all object types. If applicable, it indicates which subobject is affected by the change. For example, for the "Table" object in the list, a modification might concern one or more of the following subobjects: table fields, technical settings, or indexes.

▶ **Modification**
At the bottom of the hierarchy, displayed when you click open the modified attribute (or the object if it does not have attributes), you see the traffic light icon, the transport request, and the date and owner of this request.

Figure 21.3 shows the complete tree for one modification, in this case for a standard index deleted in the upgrade.

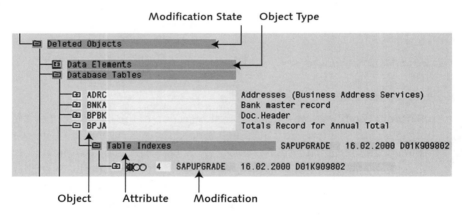

Figure 21.3 Example of SPDD Tree

21.3 Adjusting Objects

The objects that require your attention are those in the "yellow" section. Proceed as follows:

1. Open the nodes until you reach the modification detail with the traffic light icon in front.

2. Double-click on the traffic light.

3. Depending on the object type, three things can happen:

> ▶ For table fields and structure fields, the Modification Adjustment generates a proposal, which you can accept, edit, or reject. Rejection means that you return the object to the SAP standard. Handling proposals for table and structure fields is described in Section 21.4.

> ▶ For the technical settings of a table, SPDD also makes a proposal. See Section 21.4.2 for instructions.

> ▶ For other object types (indexes, data elements, domains), no proposal is generated. You must compare the custom version of the object with the new standard version and if necessary make the adjustment manually in the SAP dictionary with Transaction SE11.

21.4   Table and Structure Fields

Tables delivered as part of the SAP standard can be modified in various ways. This section describes the modification adjustment in SPDD for tables and structures to which fields were added, or for which the data type and length of fields were changed. SPDD adjustment for field changes is one of the most common but also one of the most delicate operations, especially for database tables. Mistakes may lead to data loss (for which SPDD will duly warn you) or to lengthy and unwanted table conversions (for which SPDD will not warn you at all).

21.4.1   New Fields Added in Standard

If you added your own fields to a standard SAP table or structure, and a new version of this table or structure (which probably also includes new fields) is delivered with the new release, then SPDD will propose to register your "customer" fields in a special dictionary object, known as an *append structure*.

For example, assume that a table TAB in the source release contained four standard fields (MANDT, SAPFLD1, SAPFLD2, SAPFLD3). Because there was a business need for additional information fields, two customer fields CUSTFLD1 and CUSTFLD2 were added to the table.

The new version of TAB that comes in with the repository of the target release contains two extra SAP fields, SAPFLD04 and SAPFLD05 (see Figure 21.4). Obviously, this standard version knows nothing of the two customer fields.

Modification Adjustment notices this conflict and creates a proposal to keep the two customer fields. Instead of adding the fields directly to the table object in the dictionary, the fields will be placed in an append structure linked to table TAB.

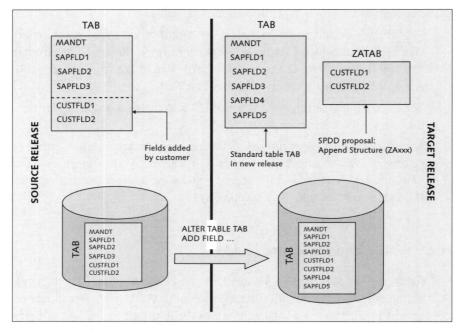

Figure 21.4 Customer Fields and Append Structures

By default, append structures are always named ZA<object> (the "Z" indicates that this is a customer object and not an SAP object).

During the conversion phase (PCON), the upgrade finds that TAB needs two extra fields (the two new fields of the SAP standard) and adds them at the end of the field list using the SQL statement ALTER TABLE. Adding fields at the end is not a costly operation because it does not require a conversion (unload/load) of the table data.

In this case, you proceed as follows:

1. When you double-click on the yellow traffic light, a proposal for an append structure appears, listing the customer fields. Normally, you want to keep these fields; in that case, choose **Accept proposal**. A pop-up opens proposing a name for the append structure. Press **Enter** to accept this. You are then prompted for a change request (see Figure 21.5).

2. SPDD now tells you that the proposal matches the current version and asks you whether to reset the table to the SAP standard (see Figure 21.6). This may seem a bit confusing because the object as a whole does *not* correspond to the new standard but rather contains your own fields. However, if you look at the Figure 21.5, you can see that the definition of the object TAB in the dictionary *is* identical to the standard; it contains just the six SAP fields. The reference to

the append structure is recorded separately, and future upgrades will not delete this reference. Therefore, you can safely answer **Yes**. The advantage of returning the object to SAP standard is that it will not reappear in the **SPDD** of a future upgrade. For the system, your modification is a closed chapter.

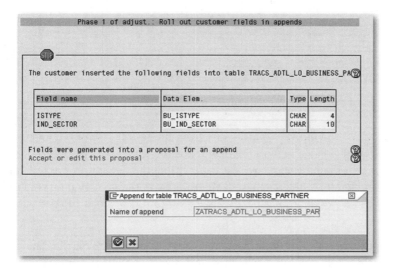

Figure 21.5 Creating an Append Structure

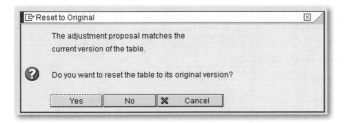

Figure 21.6 Confirm Resetting to SAP Standard

21.4.2 Proposals for Different Data Elements

Another type of modification occurs when you change the attributes of a standard field by assigning another data type (which may or may not have changed the field length). In this situation, the SPDD proposal will list the fields whose data type was changed. Look, for example, at Figure 21.7.

In the standard version, the field FIPOS of a given table or structure (whose name is not shown here) had the data type FIPOS, which is of type CHAR(acter) with a length of 14. Because of a business requirement, the customer changed the data type of the field to FIPEX, which is also of type CHAR but with a length of 24.

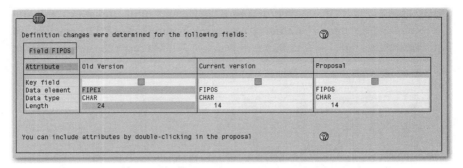

Figure 21.7 Field with Custom-Assigned Data Element

Figure 21.7 shows the old version (the one from the source release), the current version (the one that came in with the new repository), and the default proposal, which is to accept the new standard. Here, accepting the default proposal would reduce the field length in the database table from 24 to 14, which would result in loss of data and a possibly long table conversion (unload/reload of data necessary).

To keep the custom version with the longer field, double-click on the data element in the **Old Version** column. The **Proposal** column will now show your local version of the object (see Figure 21.8).

Field DMBE2			
Attribute	Old Version	Current version	Proposal
Key field			
Data element	Z_DMBE2_VZ_X	DMBE2_VZ	DMBE2_VZ
Data type	CURR	CURR	CURR
Length	15	13	13
Decimal places	2	2	2

Figure 21.8 Keeping the Custom Data Element

After you have adapted the proposal in this way, click on **Accept proposal,** and return to the SPDD object list.

21.5 Technical Settings for Tables

The technical settings of a table determine where and how that table is stored in the database and also control certain forms of special treatment for the table inside the SAP application layer (logging and buffering). If the technical settings for a SAP table were changed, for example, logging was enabled for auditing purposes, and the new standard differs from this local setting, then a pop-up will appear showing the old (custom) settings, the new (new standard) settings, and the proposal. The course of action is the same as for changes in the data type: Either accept the proposal or change it by double-clicking on the appropriate column. If the proposal corresponds to the new standard, then SPDD will suggest that you return the object to the SAP standard.

Changing the technical settings can never lead to data loss or table conversions, so it is basically free of risk (unless you upset the auditors by inadvertently switching off logging for a table with sensitive data). Mistakes can easily be corrected after the upgrade.

21.6 Other Objects

For data elements, domains, and indexes, SPDD does not generate a proposal. When you click on the traffic light, the version-comparison screen appears. This is the standard screen that you can call up in virtually all SAP development transactions via **Utilities • Versions • Version management • Compare**.

The best thing to do here is to click on **Delta display**. Rather than showing the two versions of the object in full, the versions are now compared, and their differences, if any, are displayed. Figure 21.9 shows an example.

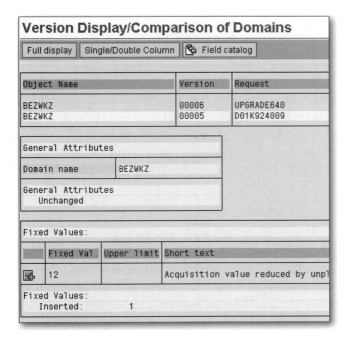

Figure 21.9 "Delta" Display in Version Management (1)

The screenshot shows the delta display for a domain. There is one difference: The new version adds a new fixed-value entry for the value "12." In this example, you would obviously want to keep this change. In practice, you would therefore return the object to original, that is, to the new SAP standard. If for some reason you decided not to keep the changes in the new SAP version, then you would have to edit the object manually in Transaction SE11.

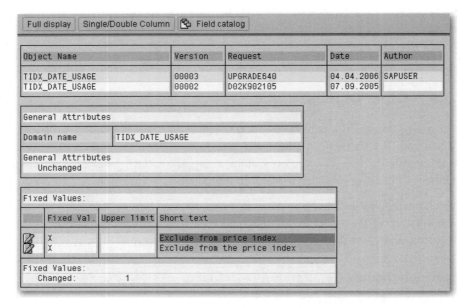

Figure 21.10 "Delta" Display in Version Management (2)

Figure 21.10 shows another situation. Here, the Modification Adjustment has found a difference in the short text between your local version (light background, version 00001) and the new SAP standard version (dark background, version 00002). The actual difference here is very small — just omitting the article "the" — so again you would probably accept the new standard and reset the object to original.

21.7   Returning an Object to the SAP Standard

If you see that the new standard object is identical to the current object in your system, then you can and should return the object to the SAP standard. You do this by selecting the object and clicking on the **Reset to original** icon (see Figure 21.11).

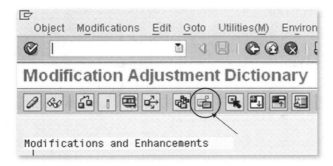

Figure 21.11 Reset Object to SAP Standard

21.8 Keep the Transport for the Upgrade of the Next System

Rather than repeating the SPDD in the upgrade of the next system, you can save the transport with your SPDD modifications in the current system and have the upgrade use this transport in the coming upgrades. In Chapter 9, we saw that PREPARE will look for such transports (their existence is recorded in a file in */usr/sap/trans/bin*) and ask you whether you want to use this method.

Although there is something to say for this method — objects modified in one system in the landscape are likely also to have been modified in the others — we are somewhat distrustful and never use this technique. If a long time passes between upgrades, or if objects were for some reason modified locally in individual systems without transporting these changes throughout the landscape, important differences in the SPDD lists could arise. A recent change could even conflict with one that is recorded in the SPDD transport. Rather than entrusting the resolution of these conflicts to the automatic import of a transport request, we prefer to keep control and repeat the SPDD each time. With proper documentation (see the next section), this becomes a routine job taking fairly little time, unless there are important differences with the previous upgrade.

If you do decide to use the transport technique, then do the following:

1. When you are finished with the adjustments, go to the Transport Organizer (Transaction SE09), and list your open requests. The change request that you opened for the SPDD will be listed. Click to open this request to show the tasks and/or repairs. Release the tasks and repairs. You cannot release the change request itself because this is not allowed at this point in the upgrade, and the system will refuse it.

2. Leave SE09 and return to the SPDD object list. Click on the **Select for transport** button (on the far right of the SPDD toolbar) when you are finished with the adjustments. A search screen appears. Locate and select the open SPDD request.

3. You may now leave SPDD. The upgrade process records the number of the transport request and will release the request later.

21.9   Documenting Your Modifications

Modification Adjustment is one of the most important upgrade tasks, and it is crucially important that you document your work. This will save you both time and headaches.

Your documentation must contain all the information that you need to correctly perform the SPDD in the next upgrades. In the first SPDD in your upgrade cycle, this will cost you extra time, but that investment will pay off later. How you organize the documentation is your own choice, but you should at least keep track of the following:

▶ Object type

▶ Object name

▶ Change request that contains the modification

▶ Owner of this request

▶ Which action to take (e.g., accept proposal, return to original)

▶ Wherever necessary, detailed instructions for processing the modification

Our method is to create a table of modified objects in the upgrade documentation with all this information plus a reference to a notes section with instructions. Table 21.1 shows an extract from such a table.

The first column contains the type (TABL = table fields, TECH = technical settings, INDX = index, STRU = structure, DOMA = domain, DTEL = data element). The Action column shows what was done for this modification: accept the proposal, reset the object to the SAP standard, or keep the local change (for object types where no proposal is generated). The Note column refers to a more elaborate note paragraph further on (described next). The Systems column shows in which system(s) the object showed up in SPDD.

Type	Object	Owner	Request	Action	Note	Systems
TABL	TBPCA	MARKM	DEVK913488	Accept	1	all
TECH	TBPCA	MARKM	DEVK913488	Reset	1	all
INDX	SWWWIHEAD-C	MARKM	DEVK915020	Accept	2	all
STRU	SVVCUST1	BERTV	DEVK914866	Reset		all
STRU	SVVCUST2	BERTV	DEVK914866	Reset		all
DOMA	ATNAM	DIRKM	QASK900030	Keep	3	QAS
DTEL	INVNR	DIRKM	DEVK912535	Reset		all

Table 21.1 Keeping Track of SPDD Actions

The Notes to which the table refers would give background information and detailed instructions on how to handle the objects. For example:

```
1. TBPCA: accept creation of append structure for customer fields MYFLD
1, MYFLD2. Technical settings correspond to standard R reset
2. Index C changed to improve performance—SAP note 684130
3. Local correction in QAS (add several fixed values) made Oct-
2004. Keep for now, later apply in DEV and transport to all systems.
```

21.10 Modification Adjustment with SPAU

The companion transaction of SPDD for development objects is SPAU. Both transactions are built upon the Modification Adjustment concept and support automatic and semi-automatic reconciliation of changes made to objects. Their user interface is also very similar.

Unlike SPDD, SPAU is executed after the upgrade. It is a safer transaction in the sense that mistakes cannot lead to loss of data. On the other hand, there are usually many more objects to process than in SPDD, and the decision whether to keep the modification or to accept the new standard is often less straightforward and requires analysis of the code and knowledge of the business functionality.

As mentioned earlier, as the technical person who performs the upgrade, you will normally not be involved with the SPAU. The developers are responsible for this. Sufficient time and personnel must be available for this task. In a simple scenario, changes to development objects were only made on the basis of SAP corrections without extending or altering the functionality. If this policy has been strictly followed, then the SPAU effort is minimal and could even amount to simply returning all objects to SAP standard. At the other extreme are two much more problematic scenarios:

▸ Extensive changes to standard functionality, resulting in a large number of modifications with code that must be manually re-entered

▸ Old — and often poorly documented — modifications made by developers who no longer work for the company, or by external consultants who are no longer available to assist

It is important that these challenging situations are recognized early in the development project. A test upgrade on a copy of the development system, run several weeks or longer before the first "live" upgrade, can be immensely helpful in this context.

In certain situations, you may be forced to abandon the PREPARE or upgrade processes and to start again from the beginning. With good planning and timing, and rigorous respect for the upgrade procedure, the chance of this actually happening is very remote indeed, but accidents can always happen.

22 Resetting the Upgrade

The following are some possible reasons for resetting PREPARE or the upgrade:

▶ A user mistake leading to irreversible problems in the upgrade.

▶ Errors in the Modification Adjustments leading to data loss:

▶ Severe bugs in the upgrade tools. This is of course *very* rare, and if it does occur, SAP will quickly correct the problem and issue a high-alert note.

▶ Errors in the PREPARE, for example, specifying an incorrect target level for support packages, or making a mistake in the add-on binding.

The procedure for cancelling the upgrade and returning the system to its pre-upgrade state depends on how far the upgrade has progressed. The general rule is that the more the upgrade advances, the more effort is required to undo it. The key point for the ABAP upgrade is phase MODPROF_TRANS. This phase marks the beginning of "absolute" downtime, that is, downtime regardless of the chosen upgrade strategy. This is also the point where the upgrade comes out of the shadows and starts changing the real system. Beyond this point, you can only return to the pre-upgrade situation by restoring a backup of the SAP database.

> **Note**
>
> The Java upgrade has no reset functionality. The upgrade can only be undone by restoring a backup of the SAP database.

There are three reset scenarios:

▶ Reset during PREPARE (applicable to SAPup and SAPjup)

▶ Reset during SAPup *before* reaching phase MODPROF_TRANS

▶ Reset during SAPup *after* reaching phase MODPROF_TRANS

For all three scenarios, the SAP Upgrade Guides contain precise instructions on how to reset the upgrade. We summarize these in the following sections.

22.1 Reset During PREPARE

The PREPARE of the ABAP upgrade can be reset at any time *except* between the phases TOOLIMPD1 and NPREPCRE0. In typical upgrades, these phases are 30 to 60 minutes apart. If PREPARE is not reset between these phases, then you reset it as follows:

1. In the UA GUI, exit from PREPARE.
2. Issue the command to reset PREPARE (log in as `<sid>adm` first):

   ```
   cd <PUTDIR>/bin
   ./SAPup reset prepare
   ```

3. Empty the upgrade directory *<PUTDIR>*.
4. Restart PREPARE from the very beginning, that is, perform the initial extraction (see Section 9.3) and copy the SAR (service application archive) file with the correction transports to *<PUTDIR>* (see Section 9.4.2).

To reset the PREPARE of the Java Upgrade, empty the upgrade directory and restart PREPARE from the DVD as described in the section "Starting PREPARE for the First Time" in the Upgrade Guide. As for the ABAP upgrade, don't forget to copy the corrections transports back into the *<PUTDIR>* directory.

22.2 Reset SAPup Before MODPROF_TRANS

These instructions are valid when the upgrade process has not yet reached the phase MODPROF_TRANS. After this phase starts, the upgrade process then changes the database and SAP system in ways that cannot be turned back without a physical restore.

1. In the UA GUI, terminate SAPup.
2. Stop the shadow instance if it is running (see Section 10.7.2).
3. If the SAP central instance is stopped (resource-minimized strategy from EU_IMPORT1 or REQSTOPPROD), then restart it (`startsap r3`).
4. Execute the report `RSUPGRES`, which deletes the shadow repository.
5. Empty the upgrade directory *<PUTDIR>*.

6. For your next attempt, restart PREPARE from the very beginning, that is, perform the initial extraction (see Section 9.4), and copy the SAR file with the correction transports to *<PUTDIR>* (see Section 9.4.2).

22.3   Reset SAPup After MODPROF_TRANS

As soon as the upgrade reaches MODPROF_TRANS, a lot of extra work becomes necessary to reset the upgrade:

1. Restore the database using the last backup made before entering downtime. The beginning of downtime is the point where you confirm the input window warning you that the central instance will be shut down. In downtime-minimized mode, the system was in normal use. If the last backup was not made just before entering downtime, then you must recover the business data by performing a point-in-time recovery up to the downtime point.

2. As soon as downtime begins, the upgrade process replaces the normal parameter profiles. Reinstate the normal profiles in directory */sapmnt/SID/profile*. The original profiles can be found in *<PUTDIR>/sapnames*. They are named *PROFX.BCK* (for the instance profile) and *DEFPROF.BCK* (for the default profile). The start profile is not changed and does not need to be restored.

3. If the upgrade had reached the phase KX_SWITCH, then the kernel has been replaced. You must then restore the kernel from a backup or copy it from a system that is still on the source release.

4. For UNIX, if the upgrade had reached the phase ENVCHK, then the start/stop scripts and the login scripts may have been replaced. Log in as <sid>adm and try restarting the central instance. If you experience problems, restore the start/stop scripts and the login scripts from the directory *<PUTDIR>/exe/INSTALL*. You find the list of scripts to restore in the Upgrade Guide under *Resetting the Upgrade, Detailed Description of the Individual Actions*.

5. Restart the central instance (startsap r3).

6. Restore the backup of the upgrade directory that you made when the upgrade reached the downtime point (see Section 10.17.5). In this case, you can later restart the upgrade, which will then resume at the downtime phase. If you *empty* the upgrade directory, then the system is out of sync (it already contains the shadow repository), and you can then only drop the shadow repository with RSUPGRES and restart from the very beginning.

A   Vocabulary Hints

In this Appendix, we describe in detail how to define a vocabulary hint in the Unicode preconversion analysis (Transactions SPUMG and SPUM4). Two examples are worked out here:

▶ A straightforward case where the language of texts in a table can be identified based on the value of a "hint" field in that same table

▶ A more complex case where the hint field is in another table than the text itself, and you must therefore joint the two tables using a database view

A.1   Example 1: Field in the Same Table

A.1.1   Case Study

The financial table BSIS does not have a language field; however, BSIS does possess a company code field BUKRS. Suppose that after applying vocabulary imports and other automatic methods, you still have more than 10,000 unassigned entries from BSIS. The company owning the SAP system uses 5 company codes:

▶ U001: Subsidiary 1 (United States)

▶ E101: Subsidiary 2 (Italy)

▶ E102: Subsidiary 3 (Slovakia)

▶ A050: Subsidiary 4 (China)

▶ A060: Subsidiary 5 (Thailand)

Based on the geographical regions handled by each of the subsidiaries, you find that company codes U001 and E101 only work with Latin-1 (Western) languages, E102 works with Latin-2 languages, A050 uses Simplified Chinese, and A060 uses Thai. This means that BUKRS is a reliable indicator of the language (or better, the codepage). This assumption is valid not just for the data in BSIS but for text data in *every* table that contains the company code.

Because you can use BUKRS to determine the codepage, and the number of vocabulary entries from BSIS is substantial, you decide to create a hint. Because many tables contain the company code, you will be able to reuse part of your work (namely the condition) to also process vocabulary entries coming from other tables with a BUKRS field.

A.1.2 Creating the Conditions

The first step is to define conditions. In the **Hint Management** in Transaction SPUMG/SPUM4, open the tab strip **Wordlist (Condition)**. This tab strip is subdivided into two panes: conditions on the right and wordlists on the left. In the right-hand pane, click on **Create**. A window opens where you can give a name to the condition and enter the text.

You start with the condition for Thailand, that is, company A060. Choose a name for the condition, for example, BUKRS_THAI (see Figure A.1). Enter the condition text in the format of the WHERE clause in a SELECT (without the WHERE keyword itself). Save the condition.

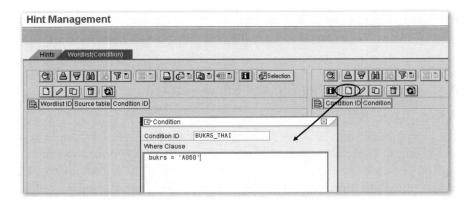

Figure A.1 Create a New Condition

You could now repeat the same steps to create the other conditions, but since these are similar to the first one, it is easier to copy the existing condition to a new one. Still in the Conditions pane, mark the condition you have just created (by clicking on the small square on the left), and choose **Copy condition**. The edit window opens with the name and text of the existing condition. Enter the new name, adapt the condition text, and save.

Repeat this process until you have defined all the conditions. Note that for the Latin-1 condition, two company codes are involved, so you have to use an OR operator. When you are done, the condition list looks like Figure A.2.

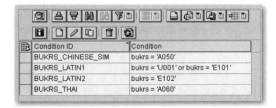

Figure A.2 Condition List

A.1.3   Creating the Wordlist

Although you will probably use the conditions in several tables, the one you are initially interested in is BSIS. For this table, you will now create the wordlists. In the left-hand pane, click on **Add Wordlist**. Choose a name for the wordlist, specify the table you want to apply the condition to, and specify the name of the condition (see Figure A.3). Save the wordlist.

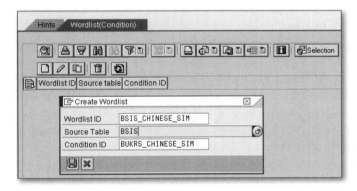

Figure A.3 Create a New Wordlist

Like you did with the conditions, use the **Copy** function to create the other wordlists (see Figure A.4).

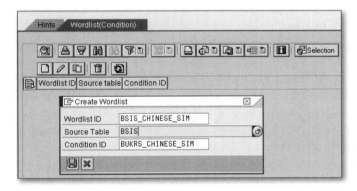

Figure A.4 Wordlists

A.1.4   Creating the Hints

Now open the **Hints** tab strip, and click on **Create**. Choose a name and a description for the hint.

In the **Table** field, specify the table whose vocabulary entries the hint must handle. At this point, you might be asking why you must specify the table again because you've already done that when creating the wordlist. The reason for that will be made clear soon. For now, just enter "BSIS".

Finally, enter the name of the wordlist you want the hint to use, and also enter the language to assign to the words in the vocabulary the hint will select.

Notice that in Figure A.5, we chose English (EN) as the target language for the Latin-1 data. Now remember that company code E101 is located in Italy, so presumably users there will work most of the time in Italian. If company code E101 works for the rest of Western Europe, there may also be French, German, Spanish, and so on. The same goes for the company in the United States, which might for instance use Spanish if they work for Latin America. However, the choice of target language is not problematic here. The only condition is that the *codepage* must be correct; whichever language in that codepage you choose as target language is immaterial. It would have been perfectly acceptable to assign the entries from the American and Italian company code to language Spanish; the conversion of the Latin-1 data would still be correct. This is of course no longer true if a company works for countries with incompatible codepages. What if, for example, the U.S. company also processes Japanese data? In that case, assigning the entries of the U.S company to language EN would be incorrect and would cause the Japanese data to become corrupted in the Unicode conversion.

To avoid this problem, it is essential that you test the hint before you actually apply it. As you'll see next, such a test function is available on the **Hint Management** screen.

You can again use the **Copy** function to create the remaining hints. In the case of Latin-2, you must choose one of the languages supported by this codepage as the common target language. For Simplified Chinese and Thai, there is no choice to make because the codepage is designed for just one language.

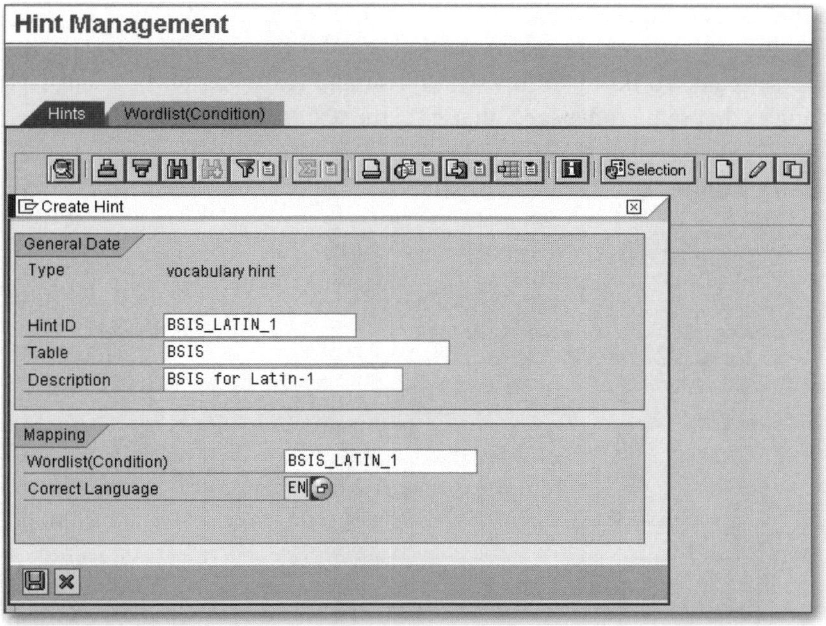

Hint Management

Figure A.5 Creating a Hint

A.1.5   Effect of the Hint

With the pieces joined together to form a vocabulary hint, what will happen when you execute this hint? Let's take BSIS_THAI as an example:

1. The generated code of the hint reads all the rows of BSIS (which you set in the wordlist) that have BUKRS='A060' (which is the condition you attached to the wordlist).

2. The hint extracts all non-ASCII words from these BSIS rows.

3. The hint then goes through all the vocabulary entries belonging to BSIS.

4. Every vocabulary entry that corresponds to a word found in the BSIS scan (step 2) is then assigned to language TH.

A.1.6   Testing the Hint

As we just said, before you execute the hint you must test it to make sure that only words matching the expected codepage are selected. To do this, select a hint (by clicking on the square on the left), and choose **Display Words**. This function runs in the foreground so the screen may block for quite some time if a large table has to be scanned.

When the test is complete, all words selected by the hint are displayed (see Figure A.6). Browse through the list to check that only texts of the expected codepage are selected. To do this properly, you should really log on in a language belonging to that same codepage; otherwise, the texts will appear as garbage.

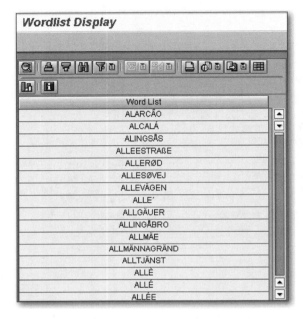

Figure A.6 Test Hint ("Display Words" Function)

A.1.7 Executing the Hint

If the result of testing the hint is satisfactory, mark the hint again, and choose **Execute hint**. This starts up a background job (hints always run in the background). The status icon on the left indicates whether the hint is still running (yellow), successfully finished (green), or failed with an error (red).

A.1.8 Executing Hints in Parallel

You can speed up the analysis by executing hints in parallel. The rule is that you can run hints in parallel if they have a different *target table*. This means that, for example, you can run a hint to process the vocabulary entries of KNA1 for a certain codepage and at the same time a hint to process the vocabulary entries of LFA1 for that same codepage. However, you cannot run two hints in parallel on vocabulary entries of LFA1, even for different codepages.

Trying to start a hint execution for a table that is already being processed by an active hint triggers the error message `Job already exists`.

A.1.9   Reusing the Hint

Let's now return to a question that was left unanswered. When you created the wordlist, you specified that you wanted to scan the text data of a set of rows in table BSIS. When you created the hint, you again specified table BSIS. Why specify the table twice?

For the answer, look at the brief description of the hint logic in the earlier Section A.1.5. The hint collects all text data from a first table (step 2) and then uses that data to resolve vocabulary entries coming from a second table (step 4). In this case, the two tables were one and the same, namely BSIS, but this does not always have to be so. You could also collect text strings from a table A and use those to resolve the vocabulary entries of table B. In fact, BSIS is an excellent case in point. BSIS is an "index table" built around the large financial document cluster table BSEG. BSIS is just one of a group of such index tables, which also includes BSID, BSIK, BSAD, BSAK, BSAS, and some others. Text fields that are present in one of these tables are often also present in the others, as well as in BSEG itself. Therefore, it would make perfect sense to use the strings collected from BSIS to also resolve vocabulary entries from BSEG, BSAS, and so on. To do this, you would only need to create new hints specifying the table whose vocabulary entries you want to process. The wordlist and the condition remain the same.

Figure A.7 shows this schematically. A single condition/wordlist combination based on table BSIS is used for two vocabulary hints, one for words from BSIS itself, and the other for entries from BSEG.

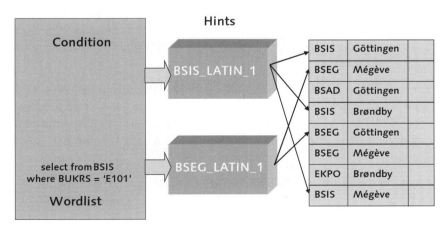

Figure A.7 Reuse the Same Wordlist for Different Hints

> **Note**
>
> In the hint definition, you can enter "*" for the table name, meaning that the date collected in the wordlist must be used to resolve matching vocabulary entries for *all* tables. This is a powerful feature, but you must pay attention to the performance; these hints can have very long runtimes.

A.2 Example 2: Fields from a Different Table

We stay with the BSIS-BUKRS example, but now we change the assumptions:

- There are many more than just five company codes.
- Because of the number of company codes, deriving the language directly from the company code ID becomes too tedious. You would have to write very large conditions with many OR clauses.

This is a much more difficult situation, but all is not lost. If you look at the master company code table T001, you will see that this table actually contains a language field SPRAS. This means that you can determine the "home" language and codepage of the company code in every BSIS row by retrieving its language setting from T001. Therefore, you must somehow connect the data in BSIS, including the text fields, with this language key in table T001. To achieve this, you must join the two tables by creating a *view*. In this case, the view connects together the relevant fields from BSIS with the relevant fields from T001 via the company code BUKRS.

A.2.1 Creating the View

To create a view in the SAP dictionary, call Transaction SE11, click on **Database View,** and enter a name for the view in the customer name range (starting with Y or Z). Here we take the name ZVUNI_BSIS_BUKRS. Choose **Create**. Enter a description for the view.

Open the tab strip **View fields,** and add the fields you need from the two tables. You must select at least the join field (BUKRS), the language SPRAS from the company code table, and the text fields from BSIS. The view shown in Figure A.8 contains more fields than that, for example, the country field LAND1, but that is not important.

Now open the **Table/join conditions** tab strip (see Figure A.9). Here you specify that the two tables are to be joined via the BUKRS field. Save and activate the view, and test it with the SE16 table browser.

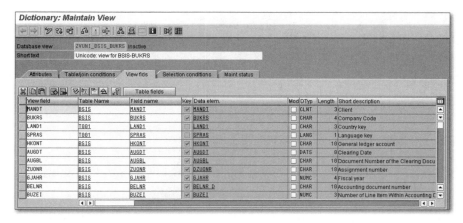

Figure A.8 View Fields

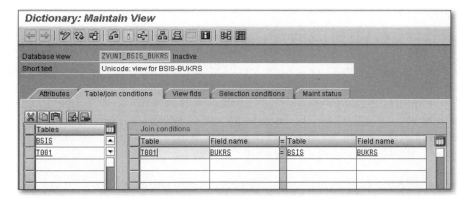

Figure A.9 Join Condition for the Hint View

A.2.2 Create Conditions, Wordlists, and Hints

Go to Transaction SPUMG or SPUM4, open the **Hint Management,** and create conditions for the field SPRAS (unless you already have conditions for a field named SPRAS; remember that a condition can be reused everywhere as long as the field name is the same). In Figure A.10, the condition is called SPRAS_LATIN1 and uses an IN clause to test for Latin-1 language codes.

> **Note**
>
> For conditions on language fields, you should specify the single-character language code (e.g., "D" for German) and not the two-character code ("DE"), which is more often used inside SAP. The reason is that the language is physically stored in the database table in the one-character format. The SAP screen shows the two-character form because the language code is implicitly converted before it is displayed.

Figure A.10 Condition on SPRAS Field

For the wordlists, you do not specify the base table BSIS; instead, you use the view (see Figure A.11).

Figure A.11 Wordlist Using the Hint View

The hint uses this wordlist, but the table in the hint is the one recorded in the vocabulary, that is, BSIS. Do not specify the view here because there are no vocabulary entries for this view. Choose any language compatible with the code-page as the target language (Figure A.12).

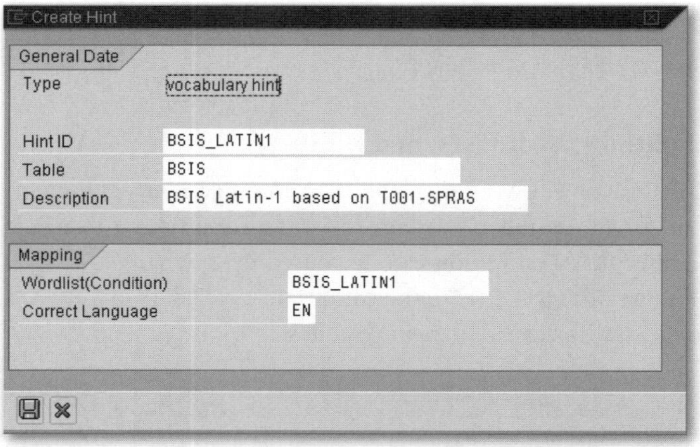

Figure A.12 Hint Definition

A.2.3   Test and Execute the Hint

Now test the hint as described for Example 1 earlier, and execute it if the result is satisfactory. Make sure you monitor the performance because there may be a problem with the join condition; this is explained in the next section.

A.2.4   Extra Index for Hint Performance

Both T001 and BSIS are client-dependent tables, that is, the client (MANDT) is the first field of the primary key. In both tables, BUKRS is the second field of the primary key. You must take this into account when you create views on behalf of vocabulary hints because these hints select data in a client-independent manner. In the preceding example, the generated code for the hint executes

```
select * from ZVUNI_BSIS_BUKRS where SPRAS = <language>
```

and *not*

```
select * from ZVUNI_BSIS_BUKRS where SPRAS = <language>
and mandt = <client>
```

Without the MANDT, the database system might not be able to use an efficient index to join BUKRS with T001, which could lead to full table scans (and BSIS is huge!) and thus to unacceptable runtimes.

When you test or execute a hint on a view that you created, always use the SQL Trace (ST05) to examine whether the execution path of the SELECT statement is efficient. If you see that there is a problem, you must create a secondary index on BUKRS alone. This is normally not needed for T001, which is very small, but it is certainly true for BSIS. Creating a secondary index on a very large table takes time and usually locks the table for the duration of the index build. This is not acceptable in a production system, therefore, you must prepare and test your hints, views and related indexes well in advance.

B   SAP Releases and Upgrade Paths

This appendix provides information about the release history of the principal SAP components. Table B.1 provides release data at the end of this appendix and also shows which previous releases can be upgraded directly to the current release; these "upgradable" releases are shown in **bold**.

Before you look at the tables, some background information might be useful.

B.1   SAP NetWeaver and Basis Releases

The leftmost column of the tables shows the release of SAP NetWeaver. SAP NetWeaver is not a "product"; it is the application and integration platform that is used across all SAP solutions and selected SAP partner solutions. Until the present, SAP has released two versions of the NetWeaver platform: SAP NetWeaver 2004 and 2004s. This numbering scheme consisting first of a calendar year and then of a year-with-suffix has fortunately been abandoned previously: today, SAP NetWeaver 2004s is simply called SAP NetWeaver 7.0.

The technological basis for SAP NetWeaver, that is, the infrastructure to develop, deploy, and run applications, is the SAP NetWeaver Application Server (SAP NetWeaver AS). From the beginning, SAP has always referred to the technological layer that underlies its business applications as the Basis or Basis Component (BC). In the now somewhat distant past, the Basis was simply part of SAP R/3, and consequently, there was no need to assign separate version numbers to the Basis. For example, in an R/3 system with Release 3.1I, the Basis version would also be 3.1I. There was simply no reason and no need to make a distinction.

With the advent of Release 4.0, the picture changed, and SAP extended its product offering in the client-server market. A range of new solutions was developed, for which SAP originally coined the term "New Dimension." Under the New Dimension umbrella were software products for production planning (Advanced Planning and Optimization [APO]), data warehousing (SAP Business Information Warehouse [BW]), managing customers and prospective customers (Customer Relationship Management [CRM]), and so on. Technically, a New Dimension installation contained the SAP Basis Component, which was identical to the one found in every R/3 system, but without the business applications of R/3 such as

FI, MM, HR, and the like. The new products also had their own version-numbering scheme; for example, the APO release called 2.0A would run on top of a SAP Basis with Release 4.5B. This evolution made it increasingly obvious that the common Basis component needed a version track separate from its R/3 origin. The first time this actually happened was in version 4.6D. SAP released a Basis 4.6D and used it to support several products, for example, BW 2.1C; however, there never was an R/3 version 4.6D.

With SAP Basis version 6 (there never was a version 5), SAP introduced two extremely important innovations. The first version, 6.10, brought native support for Web-based applications and interfaces to the ABAP environment, which turned the old SAP Basis into the *SAP Web Application Server ABAP*. Release 6.10 was only used as the basis for a limited number of products, for instance, the first release of SAP Solution Manager. SAP did not implement a version of R/3 on top of 6.10, so the highest available version remained R/3 4.6C.

In the next release, 6.20, SAP introduced for the first time a technological platform based not on ABAP but on Java. This new platform, the *SAP Web Application Server Java*, adhered to the J2EE (Java 2 Enterprise Edition) standard, and opened up the SAP world to the rapidly growing avalanche of business applications written in Java (and developers skilled in building these applications). The SAP Web Application Server 6.20 became the technological foundation for an extensive range of SAP solutions; R/3 — now renamed to "R/3 Enterprise" — was just one of those solutions and no longer the "core" product from which everything else somehow derived.

Following its introduction in Basis 6.20, the Web AS Java underwent a major revision, which among other things brought its architecture and operation more in line with the Web AS ABAP. This new architecture was first delivered with Basis 6.30, a release that only existed on the Java side.

The next Basis version to be used throughout the SAP product line was the Web AS 6.40, which became the technological platform for SAP NetWeaver 2004. From now on, the Basis was no longer called *SAP Web Application Server* but *SAP NetWeaver Application Server* (*SAP NetWeaver AS*, or simply *AS*). On the 6.40 platform, SAP also released a new version of R/3, which underwent another name change and became SAP ERP[1] (more information on ERP versions is given later in this appendix).

---

1 Formerly called mySAP ERP. As mentioned in the introduction to this book, the "my" prefix was dropped in early 2007.

The successor to SAP NetWeaver 2004, and the most recent platform in use, is the somewhat curiously named SAP NetWeaver 2004s[2], which is built upon Basis version 7.00. AS 7.00 again supports a wide range of solutions, including the newest and latest release of SAP ERP. All the upgrade scenarios described in this book concern components running on the AS 7.00 platform, for example, SAP ERP 2005 or SAP SCM 5.0.

B.2   R/3 Releases

As just mentioned, the name R/3 remained in use until version 4.6C. The next release, running on the Basis 6.20 layer, was named R/3 Enterprise. This was the first release where a distinction was made between the "core" applications, which evolved from the previous releases, and "extensions," which provided new and in some cases sector-oriented functionality. The core applications were named the *R/3 Enterprise Core* and received the version number 4.70. The extensions were collectively called the *Extension Set*. This Extension Set had its own version track: the first release was 1.10, and the second was 2.00. As a result, there are two versions of R/3 Enterprise: Core 4.70 with Extension Set 1.10 (470x110 in shorthand notation) and the same Core 4.70 with Extension Set 2.00 (470x200).

In the next major release, the name changed to *SAP ERP* (originally mySAP ERP). For this release, SAP adopted a naming convention that included the calendar year, and the full name became SAP ERP 2004. The concept of a core and an extension set was maintained, but the two no longer had separate version numbers. The R/3 Enterprise Core of the previous version now became the Enterprise Core Component (ECC), with a version number 5.0. Thus, you could refer to this release in full as SAP ERP 2004 (ECC 5.0).

The naming was kept in the next — and current — release, which was called SAP ERP 2005 with an ECC 6.0, so in full SAP ERP 2005 (ECC 6.0). As with SAP NetWeaver, SAP decided to drop the year numbering scheme for the SAP ERP product in early 2007. The current version name is simply SAP ERP 6.0.

---

2 Now renamed to SAP NetWeaver 7.0; however, the previous name continues to be widely used and therefore still appears in this book.

SAP NetWeaver	SAP Basis	SAP R/3 – SAP ERP	APO/SCM	CRM	BBP/EBP/SRM	BW/BI	Java	XI/PI	Portal	Mobile	SAP Solution Manager
<= 3.1H	<= 3.1H	<= 3.1H	–	–	–	–	–	–	–	–	–
3.1I	3.1I	**3.1I**	–	–	–	–	–	–	–	–	–
4.0A	4.0A	4.0A	–	–	–	–	–	–	–	–	–
4.0B	4.0B	**4.0B**	–	–	–	1.2A	–	–	–	–	–
4.5A	4.5A	4.5A	1.1	–	–	1.2B	–	–	–	–	–
4.5B	4.5B	**4.5B**	2.0A	1.1	BBP 1.0B	–	–	–	–	–	–
4.6A	4.6A	4.6A	–	1.2 2.0A	BBP 2.0A	2.0A	–	–	–	–	–
4.6B	4.6B	**4.6B**	–	–	–	–	–	–	–	–	–
4.6C	4.6C	**4.6C**	3.0A	2.0B	**BBP 2.0B** (EBP 1.0)	2.0B	–	–	–	–	–
	4.6D	–	3.1	2.0C	**BBP 2.0C** (EBP 2.0)	2.1C	–	–	–	–	–
	6.10	–	–	3.0	EBP 3.0	3.0A	–	–	–	–	2.0
	6.20	**R/3 Enterprise (4.7) Extension Set 1.10 Extension Set 2.00**	4.0	3.1 4.0	**SRM 2.0** (EBP 3.5) **SRM 3.0** (EBP 4.0)	3.0B 3.1C	Web AS Java 6.20	1.0 2.0	5.0 6.0	2.1	**3.1 3.2**
	6.30	–	–	–	–	–	Web AS Java 6.30	–	–	–	–
2004	6.40	**SAP ERP 2004 (ECC 5.0)**	4.1	–	**SRM 4.0**	3.50	AS Java 6.40[3]	3.0[3]	6.0[3]	2.5[3]	–
2004s	7.00	SAP ERP 2005 (ECC 6.0)	5.0	5.0	SRM 5.0	BI 7.00	AS Java 7.00	PI 7.00	7.00	7.00	4.0

Table B.1 SAP Release and Upgrade Matrix

---

3   Support package level must be at least 6.40 SP 09.

C   Database Transaction Log Modes

The actual terms denoting the archiving and nonarchiving modes of transaction logging are different for each database system. Table C.1 shows the parameter or configuration setting to enable either mode.

DBMS	Archiving	Nonarchiving
DB2 UDB for UNIX/Windows	LOGRETAIN = ON USEREXIT = ON	LOGRETAIN = OFF USEREXIT = OFF
DB2 UDB for iSeries	CHGJRN JRN(QSQJRN) DLTRCV(*NO) (automatic deletion of journal receivers)	CHGJRN JRN(QSQJRN) DLTRCV(*YES)
DB2 for z-OS (OS/390)	Not applicable: The entire upgrade runs with log archiving enabled.	
Informix	LTAPEDEV = <device>	LTAPEDEV = <null>
MaxDB/SAP DB	Overwrite OFF	Overwrite ON
Microsoft SQL Server	Recovery model = Full	Recovery model = Simple
Oracle	ARCHIVELOG	NOARCHIVELOG

Table C.1 Database Transaction Logs

Instructions on when and how to set the transaction log mode are in the Component Upgrade Guide, more specifically in the section *Database-Specific Aspects* of the *Component Upgrade* chapter.

D   Codepages

SAP supports multiple languages without any restrictions as long as the characters required are in the same code page. The languages and language combinations in Table D.1 are supported on SAP systems with a single system codepage.

Codepage	Supported Languages
ISO8859-1	Danish, Dutch, English, Finnish, French, German, Italian, Icelandic, Norwegian, Portuguese, Spanish, Swedish
ISO8859-2	Croatian, Czech, English, German, Hungarian, Polish, Rumanian, Slovakian, Slovene
ISO8859-5	English, Russian
ISO8859-7	English, Greek
ISO8859-8	English, Hebrew
ISO8859-9	Danish, Dutch, English, Finnish, French, German, Italian, Norwegian, Portuguese, Spanish, Swedish, Turkish
ISO8859-11	English, Thai
Shift JIS	English, Japanese
GB2312-80	English, Chinese
Big 5	English, Taiwanese
KSC5601	English, Korean
TIS620	English, Thai
EBCDIC 0697/0500	Danish, Dutch, English, Finnish, French, German, Italian, Icelandic, Norwegian, Portuguese, Spanish, Swedish
EBCDIC 0959/0870	Croatian, Czech, English, German, Hungarian, Polish, Rumanian, Slovakian, Slovene
EBCDIC 1150/1025	English, Russian
EBCDIC 0925/0875	English, Greek
EBCDIC 0941/0424	English, Hebrew
EBCDIC Thai	English, Thai

Table D.1 Standard Codepages and Languages

E   SAP Notes

This appendix lists important notes for the main subject areas covered in this book:

▶ Upgrades to SAP NetWeaver 2004s Service Release 2 (SR2) and SAP Business Suite products based on SAP NetWeaver 2004s SR2

▶ Unicode conversions, including Combined Upgrade & Unicode Conversion (CU&UC) and Twin Upgrade & Unicode Conversion (TU&UC)

▶ Migration tools (used for Unicode conversion)

Only the main notes are listed here, that is, those that you will definitely need for upgrades and Unicode conversions. In the SAP guides for the upgrade or Unicode conversions, you find an extensive list of notes covering detailed aspects of the operation.

E.1   Upgrade Notes

Although we hope that you find this information useful, keep in mind that this part of the book may have a close sell-by date. The set of upgrade notes changes not just with a new version but also with every new service release. The final authority on which upgrade notes you need is always the SAP Upgrade Guide for the applicable component, version, service release, and platform.

General Notes for Components

960783	SAP NetWeaver 2004s SR2 ABAP
970039	SAP NetWeaver 2004s SR2 Java
961410	SAP ECC 6.0 (ERP 2005) SR2 ABAP
995762	SAP ECC 6.0 (ERP 2005) SR2 Java
961511	SAP CRM 5.0 SR2 ABAP
995764	SAP CRM 5.0 SR2 Java
947991	SAP CRM 5.1
961512	SAP SCM 5.0 SR2 ABAP

995761	SAP SCM 5.0 SR2 Java
1010762	SAP SCM 5.1 ABAP
961513	SAP SRM Server 5.5 SR2
995763	SAP SRM LAC 5.0 SR2 Java

Platform-Specific: ABAP

817463	SAP NetWeaver 2004s ABAP — MaxDB
815202	SAP NetWeaver 2004s ABAP — DB2 z/OS (OS/390)
822296	SAP NetWeaver 2004s ABAP — iSeries
833876	SAP SRM 5.5 Server — iSeries
819876	SAP NetWeaver 2004s ABAP — DB2 UDB (UNIX/Windows)
825146	SAP NetWeaver 2004s ABAP — SR1/SR2 — SQL Server
819655	SAP NetWeaver 2004s ABAP — Oracle

Platform-Specific: Java

879691	SAP NetWeaver 2004s Java — iSeries
851229	SAP NetWeaver 2004s Java — MaxDB
885167	SAP NetWeaver 2004s Java — Oracle

Support Packages, Fix Buffers and SAPup Patches

822379	Known Problems for support packages in SAP NetWeaver 2004s
813658	Repairs (fix buffers) for products based on SAP NetWeaver 2004s
821032	SAPup 7.00 corrections

E.2   Unicode Conversions

Unicode and Language Support

079991	Multilanguage and Unicode support of SAP solutions
073606	Supported languages and codepages

Unicode Conversion Process

| 548016 | Unicode conversion
(release status and possible restrictions for all products) |
| 551344 | Unicode conversion
(contains conversion guides and other documentation as attachments) |

Upgrade and Unicode Conversion Strategies

928729	Combined Upgrade & Unicode Conversion (CU&UC)
959698	Twin Upgrade & Unicode Conversion (TU&UC)
867193	ABAP and kernel patches for CU&UC in 4.6C
959892	Patches for TU&UC tools
857081	Unicode conversion: downtime estimates

Help for SPUMG/SPUM4 Analysis

| 756535 | Predefined vocabularies for SPUMG/SPUM4 analysis |
| 871541 | Predefined lists of language-specific text patterns |

E.3 System Copies and Migrations

System Copy Procedure (General)

| 970518 | System Copy SAP NetWeaver 2004s SR2 |
| 888210 | System Copy SAP NetWeaver 2004s Supplementary Note |

System Copy Procedure (Platform-Specific)

936441	Settings for R3load-based system copy: Oracle
941635	System copy with MaxDB 7.6
986907	Settings for R3load-based system copy: SQL Server
744735	iSeries: Migrating storage parameters to DB2/400

Performance Optimization

855772	Distribution Monitor (documentation is in note attachment)
925214	Using the table splitting feature
954268	Optimization of export: unsorted unloading

F   References

SAP Service Marketplace

The Upgrade Portal on the SAP Service Marketplace (*http://service.sap.com/upgrade* and *http://service.sap.com/upgrade-erp*) is the first location to look for more information on the subject. The Upgrade Portal contains many brochures, presentations, and dos and don'ts. It has a very interesting upgrade questions and answers section that explains the terms and procedures used during the upgrade. The General Modification Adjustment FAQ can be found at *http://service.sap.com/spau*. For information on CU&UC, go to *http://service.sap.com/unicode@sap* and *http://service.sap.com/unicode*.

SAP Installations and Documentation Manuals

All SAP component Upgrade Guides and installation manuals can be consulted and downloaded from *http://service.sap.com/instguides* and *http://service.sap.com/instguidesNW70*. Use the following paths:

▶ **For SAP ERP (and also CRM, SCM, and SRM)**
   SAP Business Suite Applications • (select product) • Upgrade.

▶ **For SAP NetWeaver**
   SAP NetWeaver 7.0 (2004s) • Upgrade.

▶ **For SAP Business Intelligence (BI)**
   Same path as for SAP NetWeaver.

▶ **For System Copy Guides**
   SAP NetWeaver 7.0 (2004s) • Installation. In the list at the end of the window, open node "Installation – SAP NetWeaver Systems."

In this publication, we referenced the following guides:

▶ SAP NetWeaver 2004s: Upgrade Master Guide

▶ SAP ERP 2005: Upgrade Master Guide

▶ SAP ERP Central Component 6.0 SR2 ABAP: Upgrade Guide (one guide per OS/database combination)

▶ SAP NetWeaver 2004s SR2 Business Intelligence ABAP: Upgrade Guide (one guide per OS/database combination)

▸ SAP NetWeaver 2004s SR2 Java: Upgrade Guide (one guide per OS)

▸ System Copy for SAP Systems Based on NW 7.0 SR2 (separate guide for ABAP-only, Java-only, and ABAP+Java systems)

The Unicode conversion manuals are available at *http://service.sap.com/unicode@sap*. In this publication, we referenced the following Unicode conversion manuals:

▸ Combined Upgrade & Unicode Conversion SAP R/3 4.6C non-Unicode to ECC 6.0 Unicode

▸ Combined Upgrade & Unicode Conversion SAP R/3 Enterprise 4.7 non-Unicode to ECC 6.0 Unicode

▸ Combined Upgrade & Unicode Conversion SAP R/3 ECC 5.0 non-Unicode to ECC 6.0 Unicode

▸ System Copy Optimization for Unicode Conversions

▸ Unicode Conversion Troubleshooting Guide

How-to Guides

The How-to Guides for BW can be found at *http://service.sap.com/bi*:

▸ SAP BW 3.5 Upgrade Preparation and Post-Upgrade Checklist

▸ SAP Net Weaver 7.0 BI Upgrade Specifics by Roland Kramer

Articles and Other Publications

▸ Baseler, Doreen, *How SAP Solution Manager Can Smooth Your Next Upgrade Project*; published by *SAP Insider*, January-March 2005.

▸ Vanstechelman, Bert, and Mergaerts, Mark, *The SAP OS/DB Migration Guide. SAP PRESS Essentials 5;* SAP PRESS 2005.

G   The Authors

Bert Vanstechelman works as an independent SAP Basis Consultant and has approximately 12 years of SAP experience. His most recent long-term assignments have been in SAP Basis consulting roles running all kinds of SAP versions in combination with all possible databases and operating systems supported by SAP. Bert specializes in SAP administration, upgrades, installations, operating system and database migrations, and Unicode conversions. Bert is the author of the SAP Essentials the *SAP OS/DB Migration Project Guide* and the *mySAP ERP Upgrade Project Guide*, both published by SAP PRESS. He is a frequent contributor to the *SAP Professional Journal* and panel expert for SAP Release Upgrades and OS/DB migrations on *SearchSAP.com*'s Ask the Expert feature. *SearchSAP.com* has a panel of 20 SAP experts who answer questions for the 140,000 active members. Bert can be reached at *bert@logosconsulting.be*.

Mark Mergaerts is Principal Technology Consultant at SAP Belgium and has more than 12 years experience with SAP Basis. His consulting activities, mainly with large SAP accounts, concentrate on the key areas of system administration, database management, upgrades and installations, performance and workload analysis, and OS/DB and Unicode migrations. He also teaches advanced database administration, upgrade, and SAP performance classes to an international audience.

After seven years of R/2, Dirk Matthys started with in R/3 back in 1997. Dirk is a Senior ABAP developer working for one of the biggest Belgian Metal Transformation companies. In the past few years, his main activities have diverted to the twilight zone between the SAP technical and application world. He is responsible for the coordination of SAP Basis application change projects, as upgrade, migration, mergers, and splits, installation of support packages.

Index

U

Background knowledge and indepth administration advice

Planning, adnministration, development

Includes extra chapters on Java, BW, Adaptive Computing, and more

approx. 800 pp., 89,95 Euro / US$ 89,95
ISBN 978-1-59229-120-5, Oct 2007

SAP Database Administration with Oracle

www.sap-press.com

Michael Höding, André Faustmann, Gunnar Klein, Ronny Zimmermann

SAP Database Administration with Oracle

Oracle is one of the most significant, but also one of the most complex, DB platforms available for SAP systems—so why hasn't someone written a book on how to configure the interaction? Well, here it is: With this in-depth reference book, administrators get much needed background knowledge, as well as complete details on architectural and software/logistics issues, in addition to step-by-step instructions for all of the most important administration tasks. Every aspect of system landscape planning and maintenance is covered, helping administrators hone their problem solving skills. Bonus chapters deal with Java, BW, Adaptive Computing and the highly complex issues of Backup, Recovery, and Restoration.

Input and output processing basics, validation, BDoc modelling, groupware integration, data exchange, and more

Optimization measures for queues, mass data processing, distribution model, and Replication & Realignment

approx. 360 pp., 69,95 Euro / US$ 69,95
ISBN 978-1-59229-121-2, Aug 2007

SAP CRM Middleware Optimization Guide

www.sap-press.com

Juliane Bode, Stephan Golze, Thomas Schröder

SAP CRM Middleware Optimization Guide

This book, based on the experience of SAP Active Global Support, helps you proactively avoid problems with CRM Middleware — whether they be performance losses or even complete system freezes. You'll learn the basics of data processing in the Middleware (input processing — validation — output processing) and get concrete administration advice for troubleshooting. Plus, uncover a vast array of optimization options for all critical parts of the Middleware, as well as practical instruction on how to avoid system freezes and on how to handle those freezes once they've occurred.

Teaches how to implement and successfully run SAP on Windows

Provides best practice methods and detailed descriptions of technologies, tools, and requirements for fail-safe operations

approx. 570 pp., 69,95 Euro / US$ 69,95
ISBN 978-1-59229-157-1, Aug 2007

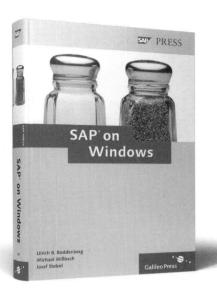

SAP on Windows

www.sap-press.com

Josef Stelzel, Uwe M. Hoffmann,
Ulrich B. Boddenberg, Michael Mißbach

SAP on Windows

No SAP system can exist without an operating system: This book provides consultants, administrators, and project managers with proven methods and solutions for the successful implementation and operation of SAP applications on the Windows platforms.

Each chapter features highly detailed information on topics such as application requirements, data center technologies, and IT operations. You'll get a firsthand look at common issues related to operating a Windows data center, as well as proven best practices for the consistent administration of systems, different virtualization and automation technologies, as well as monitoring and deployment solutions.

Learn the Basic Principles of Administration and Development

Master the ins and outs of Knowledge Management, Collaboration, Unification, Application Management, and Transport System

approx. 400 pp., 69,95 Euro / US$ 69,95
ISBN 978-1-59229-145-8, Dec 2007

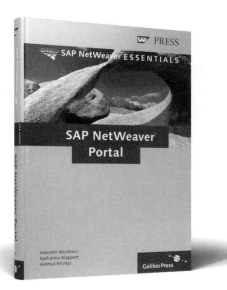

SAP NetWeaver Portal

www.sap-press.com

Valentin Nicolescu, Katharina Klappert, Helmut Krcmar

SAP NetWeaver Portal

This book introduces IT managers, portal administrators and consultants to the structure and application areas of SAP NetWeaver Portal Release 7.0 (2004s). A main focus is to describe key portal functions and the underlying architecture – all from the technical viewpoint. Topics covered include role management, authentication mechanisms, knowledge and content management, developing and administrating applications, application and system integration, as well as many more. Readers gain a solid technical grounding in all the relevant aspects of the SAP NetWeaver Portal, and the skills needed to effectively implement them in practice.

Expert insights on local SAP scheduling facilities such as CCMS, BI and Mass Activities

Techniques to maximize the full capabilities of SAP central job scheduling by Redwood

312 pp., 2006, 69,95 Euro / US$ 69.95
ISBN 1-59229-093-0

Job Scheduling for SAP

www.sap-press.com

K. Verruijt, A. Roebers, A. de Heus

Job Scheduling for SAP

With this book, you'll learn the ins and outs of job scheduling with "SAP Central Job Scheduling by Redwood" and "Redwood Cronacle." Uncover critical details on the architecture, plus exclusive technical insights that cannot be found elsewhere. The authors cover both decentralized and centralized SAP job scheduling and provide you with practical advice to drastically bolster standard installation and configuration guides. Special attention is paid to both individual CCMS and SAP BI jobs as well as to integration methods for these enterprise-level job chains. Best Practices from real-world case studies ensure that this book leaves no stone unturned.

**Revised new edition,
completely up-to-date
for SAP ERP 6.0**

**New functions and
technologies: Archive Routing,
Transaction TAANA, XML-based
archiving, and many more**

405 pp., 2. edition 2007, 69,95 Euro / US$ 69,95
ISBN 978-1-59229-116-8

Archiving Your SAP Data

www.sap-press.com

Helmut Stefani

Archiving Your SAP Data

This much anticipated, completely revised edition of our
bestseller is up-to-date for SAP ERP 6.0, and provides you
with valuable knowledge to master data archiving with SAP.
Fully updated, this new edition includes two all-new
chapters on XML-based data archiving and archiving in SAP
ERP HCM and contains detailed descriptions of all the new
functions and technologies such as Archive Routing and the
TAANA transaction. Readers uncover all the underlying
technologies and quickly familiarize themselves with all
activities of data archiving—archivability checks, the
archiving process, storage of archive files, and display of
archived data. The book focuses on the requirements of
system and database administrators as well as project
collaborators who are responsible for implementing data
archiving in an SAP customer project.

Detailed methodology for developing and implementing functional and load tests

Functionality and implementation of eCATT, SAP Solution Manager, SAP Test Data Migration Server, and more

367 pp., 2007, 69,95 Euro / US$ 69,95
ISBN 978-1-59229-127-4

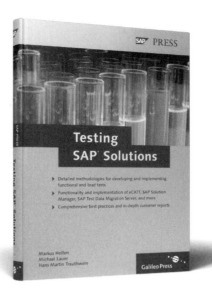

Testing SAP Solutions

www.sap-press.com

Markus Helfen, Michael Lauer,
Hans Martin Trauthwein

Testing SAP Solutions

This book provides you with comprehensive coverage of all testing requirements and techniques necessary for implementing, upgrading or operating SAP solutions. Readers get an overview of all existing tools, their functionalities, and best practices for utilization. The authors focus mainly on SAP Solution Manager, Test Workbench and eCATT, and their use in functional and load tests is highlighted in detail.

>> www.sap-press.de/1408

Interested in reading more?

Please visit our Web site for all
new book releases from SAP PRESS.

www.sap-press.com